To Henrietta Larson
A pioneer not only in business
history but also in the history
of oil. This effort is in
imitation of her high standards
of scholarship and my only
hope is that it will come
at least half way up to
hers.

Arthur M. Johnson
January 11, 1968

HARVARD STUDIES IN BUSINESS HISTORY
XXIV

Edited by Ralph W. Hidy
Isidor Straus Professor of Business History
Graduate School of Business Administration
George F. Baker Foundation
Harvard University

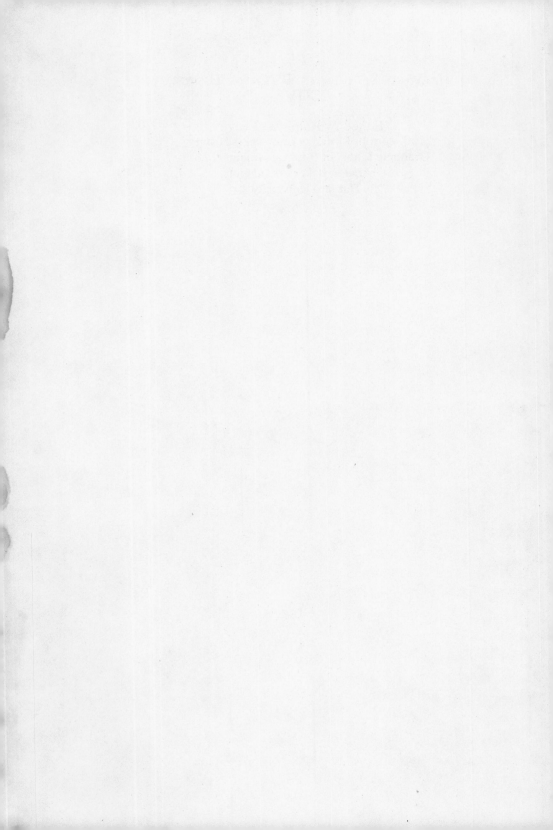

Petroleum Pipelines and Public Policy, 1906-1959

ARTHUR M. JOHNSON

HARVARD UNIVERSITY PRESS
Cambridge, Massachusetts
1967

FOREWORD

By the mid-1950's research and thought in business history displayed a wider range of interest than that demonstrated by most publications in the Harvard Studies in Business History. Almost all the books in the series dealt with histories of firms, neither an unreasonable nor illogical emphasis during the early years of the new discipline. Stalson's *Marketing Life Insurance* concentrated on an approach by function, and Larson's *Guide to Business History* demonstrated the inclusive view of the field by one of the earliest workers in the vineyard. Nevertheless, these two exceptions tended to dramatize the fact that most of the Studies were expositions of policies and practices of individuals or families or firms.

Accordingly, in recognition of the "state of the art" of business history, via a series of conferences in 1957-58, the undersigned suggested a changed course of action to the Dean of the Harvard Business School. Among the proposals was the desirability of demonstrating, through publication in the Studies, the possible range of research in the history of business. Not all possibilities could be explored, but over a period of years several could be probed. One suggested topic for investigation — the policies of Boston investors in the development of the Trans-Allegheny West — resulted in an analysis of regional investment decisions entitled *Boston Capitalists and Western Railroads,* number 23 in this series. I decided that out of possible studies of business in relation to its environment the most feasible and desirable to encourage at the moment was the interaction between business and government. This decision led to engaging a scholar already displaying a preoccupation with such research, the author of this book.

On first glance at the title of this study readers may think that Arthur Johnson has merely written a sequel to *The Development of American Petroleum Pipelines,* his first book on the subject. Such assumption, however, would be far from accurate. The focus of analysis in the first monograph was the formation of public policy to 1906. In the second, Professor Johnson centers his attention on alterations in the policies of a group of pipeline corporations in response to changes in the political and regulatory climate, in technology, and in the economics of producing, transporting, and marketing petroleum products within an industry characterized by a high degree of vertical integration. Some of the new environmental conditions appear with almost subtle indirectness and gradualness, others appear with the unanticipated suddenness of a thunderclap. That the author has probed deeply into published sources as well as numerous corporate records is substantiated by the note citations. That he has analyzed his data effectively and presented his findings clearly is attested by a score of readers of the manuscript. Both the Harvard University Press and I are happy to publish it in the Harvard Studies in Business History.

Cambridge, Massachusetts
March 1967

RALPH W. HIDY
Editor, Harvard Studies
in Business History

PREFACE

This book is an attempt to trace and evaluate the development of petroleum pipelines since the turn of the century in the context of a changing oil industry and to consider the public policy constraints with which it had to deal. In many respects this volume is a supplement to my work of a decade ago devoted to the genesis of petroleum pipelines and the origins of public policy concerning them.[1] The object in that book was to discover what role oil pipelines played in the early history of the American oil industry and Standard Oil's dominant position therein as they affected the development of public policy. It was demonstrated there that public policy on both state and federal levels was largely the product of intraindustry conflict, with independent producers and refiners seeking to employ governmental authority as a source of countervailing power against Standard Oil. Chronologically, this study starts where the other one ended, and its focus is on the implementation and consequences for pipeline management in this century of public policy measures rooted in the preceding one.

The American oil industry changed rapidly after new oil discoveries at the turn of the century and in response to a market shifting from illuminants to motor fuels. If anything, these developments increased the importance of petroleum transportation by pipeline, but Standard Oil was increasingly forced to share ownership of this strategic sector of the oil business with others. The dissolution of the Standard Oil combination in 1911 as the result of antitrust action further contributed to this trend. As a result, public policy constraints became a concern of managers of new pipeline companies and companies split off from the pioneering combination, as well as of those who remained in its service.

This study approaches the various problems they faced and the strategy and tactics evolved to cope with them in terms of managerial decision-making. There has been an extended effort to investigate the widest possible range of sources, including company records, for insights on the way in which several generations of pipeline managers perceived the challenge of a changing environment and the opportunities for adjusting to or anticipating changes in it. To put their decisions in the most meaningful perspective it has also been necessary to devote considerable attention to the development of the oil industry itself in this century, to review historically the alternatives open to public policy in dealing with its pipeline sector, and to examine the elements that apparently conditioned the adoption and effectiveness of one alternative as opposed to another in specific situations. The continuing interaction between public and private administrators, then, provides the main theme of this work.

The central issue of the continuing interaction process was the appropriate role of pipelines in the oil industry. Viewed historically, the issue became one of whether pipelines built with private capital to serve the needs of integrated oil companies could be forced to serve others as common carriers on terms that significantly diminished the advantages of pipeline ownership. Just what these advantages to an integrated concern were, other than low-cost transportation per se, and their effects on competitiveness at various levels of the industry were matters of continuing controversy, as was the appropriateness of the public policy measures advocated or adopted for dealing with them.

The uses and abuses of pipeline power led to state and federal regulation of pipelines and to persistent but unsuccessful efforts to prohibit their ownership by companies engaged in more than one stage of the oil business. This study is therefore focused primarily on the historical place of pipelines in completely or partially integrated oil operations and the factors that have strengthened or weakened attachment to this form of organization and control. In an effort to shed light on a limited but significant area of government-business relations, it also attempts to present and evaluate the positions of those who defended integrated pipeline operations and those who attacked them. Over-all, the present volume might be characterized as an extended case-study of a subindustry, undertaken with the hope that it will contribute to knowledge of the strengths and weaknesses of both public policy and private enterprise in serving the public interest in an area vital to the nation.

The origins of this study owe much to the encouragement and support of the late Mr. Robert Andress, former executive vice-president of Service Pipe Line Company, Tulsa, Oklahoma. Mr. Andress read my first pipeline book and felt that it merited a sequel. Largely through his initiative, a number of pipeline companies were persuaded to open their records to me and to underwrite the cost of research by a grant to the Harvard Graduate School of Business Administration. Under the terms of the grant, the companies agreed in advance to give me freedom of access to their records, freedom of interpretation in dealing with them, and the right to publish the results. Control of the project was in the hands of the School, under the general supervision of Professor Bertrand Fox, Director of Research, and Professor Ralph W. Hidy, Isidor Straus Professor of Business History. Neither the sponsoring companies nor these gentlemen determined what I would write nor how I would write it. On the contrary, they encouraged me to follow whatever approach I deemed appropriate and to present the results as I saw them. In reviewing the product of this research they made numerous factual suggestions and editorial comments, but in no instance did they ask me to alter my approach or change my interpretations or conclusions.

This undertaking was a research study of some magnitude, involving a number of people over a period of five years. Accordingly the list of people to whom I am indebted is too long to include in full. However, in addition to those already named, I should mention the following: Professor Richard Meriam, who read the entire manuscript and made many helpful suggestions; Professors John McArthur, J. F. Bateman, and George Harmon, who as doctoral candidates did extended field research for this study; and Miss Catherine Ellsworth and Mrs. Nell Strachan, who provided invaluable background studies and editorial comments.

Messrs. Jack Horner, D. F. Sears, W. J. Williamson, and George Wolbert of Shell Pipe Line Corporation were generous hosts during an extended field research visit in Houston. Mr. J. L. Burke and Mr. Harris Squire of Service Pipe Line, Mr. Phelan Hunter and Mr. Charles Shaver of Humble Pipe Line Company, Mr. Earl Unruh and Mr. Dudley Phillips of Sinclair Pipe Line, Mr. Jack Rice of Marathon Oil Company, Mr. R. L. Lockwood of National Transit Company, and Mr. George Patterson of Buckeye Pipe Line all aided me in numerous ways with "no strings attached." To them and to many other helpful pipeliners I owe a large debt of gratitude. Finally, the dedicated services of many typists must be acknowledged. Miss Ruth Cohen, Miss Janet McMahon, Mrs. Joan Parker, and Miss Susan Foley all participated extensively in the preparation of the manuscript. Although I could not have gotten along without the contributions of all these people, I am solely responsible for the content and interpretations that follow.

Cambridge, Massachusetts   A. M. J.
March 1967

CONTENTS

PART I Pipelining and Public Policy in Transition, 1900-1917

CHAPTER 1	Crude-Oil Pipelines in an Expanding Industry	3
CHAPTER 2	The Pipeline Amendment to the Hepburn Act	20
CHAPTER 3	New Fields, New Companies, and Old Pipeline Practices	34
CHAPTER 4	Antitrust Policy and Standard Oil Pipelines	54
CHAPTER 5	Managerial Response to the Hepburn Act	69
CHAPTER 6	The Impact of Public Policy on Standard Pipelines	82
CHAPTER 7	State Regulation in the Southwest	99

PART II Integration, Investigation, and Regulation, 1915-1931

CHAPTER 8	The Role of Pipelines in Integrated Oil Operations	119
CHAPTER 9	Adaptation to Dissolution: Three Former Standard Pipeline Companies	145
CHAPTER 10	Federal Investigations	173
CHAPTER 11	State and Federal Regulation	188

PART III The Challenge of Accelerating Change, 1931-1941

CHAPTER 12	The Changing Environment of Managerial Decision-Making	209
CHAPTER 13	Managerial Adaptation to Change: Crude-Oil Pipelines	236
CHAPTER 14	Innovation and Its Repercussions: Gasoline Pipelines	251
CHAPTER 15	The Revival of Antitrust Interest in Integrated Oil Operations	268
CHAPTER 16	Antitrust Conflict and Compromise	286

PART IV The Wartime Experience, 1941-1946

CHAPTER 17	Pipelines in the War Effort	307
CHAPTER 18	Pipeline Management Problems	328

PART V The Transformation of Pipelining, 1946-1959

CHAPTER 19	Postwar Pipeline Expansion: The First Round	351
CHAPTER 20	Postwar Pipeline Expansion: The Second Round	372

PART VI   The Public Policy Parameter, 1941-1959

CHAPTER 21   The ICC and Petroleum Pipelines   391
CHAPTER 22   The Public Policy Process and Pipeline Management:
             Key Issues   408
CHAPTER 23   The Continuing Attack on Integrated Operations . .   421
CHAPTER 24   From Congressional Investigation to Judicial Decision   440

PART VII   Conclusions

CHAPTER 25   Pipelining in Perspective   461

APPENDIX A   Principal large-diameter crude-oil pipelines constructed
             in the United States, 1946-1958.   481

APPENDIX B   Principal products pipelines constructed in the United
             States, 1946-1958.   486

BIBLIOGRAPHY   495

NOTES   505

INDEX   545

TABLES

1. Deliveries of crude and refined oil to the Atlantic Seaboard by Standard, Tide Water, and United States pipelines, 1900-1906.   8

2. Location and length of minor independent pipelines, Appalachian field, 1906.   10

3. Comparison of pipeline runs of the Standard Oil group with total reported pipeline runs, Appalachian field, 1894-1905.   11

4. Comparison of runs of the Buckeye and Indiana pipelines with total crude-oil production, Lima-Indiana field, 1894-1905.   13

5. Companies operating pipelines controlled by Standard Oil Company (New Jersey), 1906.   25

6. Standard Oil pipeline routes and rates, November 1, 1905, to August 28, 1906.   44

7. Rate and minimum tender data, Buckeye Pipe Line Company, 1906-1907.   60

8. Deliveries of crude oil by pipelines of Prairie Oil & Gas Company, 1910-1912.   91

9. Cost of pipe and pipeline construction, Prairie Pipe Line Company, 1916-1920.   146

10. Estimated cost per mile of pipeline based on average cost of pipelines in Kansas, Oklahoma, and Texas, 1919.   148

11. Pipeline and tanker movements of domestic crude oil to New York, 1924, 1926.   149

12. Pure Oil Pipe Line Company of Texas. Barrels of oil delivered by destination, 1926-1927.   152

13. Prairie Pipe Line Company. Barrels of oil delivered by destination, 1923-1927.   154

14. Prairie Pipe Line Company revenues derived from principal consignees, December 31, 1929 — December 31, 1931.   157

15. Oil movements and operating income of disaffiliated and integrated pipelines, 1920, 1921, 1924.   169

16. Sinclair and Prairie pipeline rates for crude oil shipped to Whiting, Indiana, 1919-1922.   183

17. Key physical characteristics, Big Inch and Little Big Inch pipe lines.   325

18. Crude and product pipeline mileage by sizes, 1936, 1941, 1950.   352
19. Innovations or improvements in construction and operation of
    pipelines, 1950.   354
20. Total domestic demand for all petroleum products, 1944-1953.   355
21. Productivity of pipeline employees, 1946-1953.   380

CHARTS

1. Gasoline prices in six Pennsylvania cities served by gasoline pipeline compared to fifty other cities, 1927-1939.   259
2. Gasoline prices in eight cities near Great Lakes Pipe Line compared to fifty other cities, 1927-1939.   260
3. Pipeline diameters and operating costs per barrel, 1943.   323
4. Deliveries of petroleum into PAW District No. 1 (East Coast),
   1941-1945.   327

MAPS

Major oil fields and their pipeline connections, 1906. 6
Principal trunk pipelines from the oil fields of Southeastern Texas,
    1906. 16
The Glenn Pool-Baton Rouge trunk pipeline, 1910. 42
Major trunk pipeline routes, 1910. 84
Pipeline route from Healdton, Oklahoma, to Texas, 1914. 105
Trunk pipelines of Shell Pipe Line Corporation, December 31, 1931. 126
Sinclair-Standard trunk pipeline route from Texas to East Chicago,
    1921. 132
Stanolind Pipe Line System, December 1931. 134
Major trunk pipeline systems, 1930. 144
Southern Group of pipelines and National Transit Company, Decem-
    ber 31, 1931. 165
Buckeye Pipe Line as part of through route from Indiana to New
    York state, 1931. 167
Pioneer gasoline pipelines, 1931. 257
Eastward petroleum movements: pipeline flow map, June 1941. . . . 313
Emergency pipeline projects for delivery of petroleum to the East
    Coast, 1943. 321
Crude oil flow diagram, 1952. 359
Petroleum transportation patterns in the United States, crude-oil
    pipelines, 1958. 376
Petroleum transportation patterns in the United States, products
    pipelines, 1958. 385

ILLUSTRATIONS

TWENTIETH-CENTURY PIPELINE CONSTRUCTION
(following page 206)

1. Mule teams hauling pipe to the site of pipeline construction on the Glenn Pool-Baton Rouge trunk line in Oklahoma, 1910.
   Courtesy Sinclair Pipe Line Co. and Bob Hawks, Inc., Tulsa, Oklahoma.

2. Preparation of a ditch by hand to receive pipe at De Queen, Arkansas, on the Glenn Pool-Baton Rouge trunk line, 1910.
   Courtesy Sinclair Pipe Line Co. and Bob Hawks, Inc., Tulsa, Oklahoma.

3. Machine ditcher, ca. 1916.
   Courtesy Shell Pipe Line Corporation.

4. Machine ditcher of the 1950's.
   Courtesy Sinclair Pipe Line Company.

5. Hand tong gang screwing pipe together by hand, ca. 1910.
   Courtesy Sinclair Pipe Line Co. and Bob Hawks, Inc., Tulsa, Oklahoma.

6. Pipe screwing machine, ca. 1916.
   Courtesy Shell Pipe Line Corporation.

7. Water crossing, Buffalo Creek, Oklahoma, ca. 1910.
   Courtesy Paul Hendricks and Buckeye Pipe Line Company.

8. Water crossing, 1950's.
   Courtesy Buckeye Pipe Line Company.

9. Coating an early pipeline by hand to prevent corrosion.
   Courtesy Buckeye Pipe Line Company.

10. Cleaning and priming machine in use during 1950's.
    Courtesy Service Pipe Line Company.

11. Pipe is machine-wrapped with protective covering before being lowered into the ditch.
    Courtesy Sinclair Pipe Line Company.

12. After the pipe is laid in the ground, the trench is filled.
    Courtesy Sinclair Pipe Line Company.

GAUGING AND PUMPING OIL
(following page 388)

1. Gauging a lease tank, early 1920's.
   Courtesy Sinclair Pipe Line Company.

2. Lease Automatic Custody Transfer (LACT) unit, 1950's.
   Courtesy Service Pipe Line Company.

3. Steam pumping station, 1920's.
   Courtesy Sinclair Pipe Line Company.

4. Steam-powered pump at a pipeline station, Fort Madison, Iowa, 1920's.
   Courtesy Sinclair Pipe Line Company.

5. Diesel-powered pump station, 1948.
   Courtesy Humble Pipe Line Company.

6. Diesel engine used to power pipeline pumps, Martinsville, Illinois, 1947.
   Courtesy Marathon Pipe Line Company.

7. Electrically powered centrifugal pumps, early 1950's.
   Courtesy Sinclair Pipe Line Company.

8. Evolution of pump stations.
   Courtesy Sinclair Pipe Line Company.

9. Evolution of pump stations.
   Courtesy Service Pipe Line Company.

10. Control panels for electric pumping station, Martinsville, Illinois, 1958.
    Courtesy Marathon Pipe Line Company.

11. Modern dispatching and control center.
    Courtesy Buckeye Pipe Line Company.

12. Modern dispatching and control center.
    Courtesy Marathon Pipe Line Company.

ABBREVIATIONS

API   American Petroleum Institute
ICC   Interstate Commerce Commission
LACT   lease automatic custody transfer
LPG   Liquid petroleum gas
MEEC   Middle East Emergency Committee
MER   maximum efficient recovery
NIRA   National Industrial Recovery Act
NRA   National Recovery Administration
ODM   Office of Defense Mobilization
OPA   Office of Price Administration
OPC   Office of Petroleum Co-ordinator
PAD   Petroleum Administration for Defense
PAW   Petroleum Administration for War
PIWC   Petroleum Industry War Council
RFC   Reconstruction Finance Corporation
SPA   Surplus Property Administration
TNEC   Temporary National Economic Committee
WAA   War Assets Administration
WEP   War Emergency Pipelines, Inc.
WPB   War Production Board

Pipelining and Public Policy in Transition, 1900-1917

CHAPTER 1

CRUDE-OIL PIPELINES IN AN EXPANDING INDUSTRY

In 1900 there were some 6,800 miles of interstate crude-oil pipelines,[1] and about 90 per cent of the investment in them had been made by the Standard Oil Company (New Jersey) group of companies.[2] Standard's trunk pipelines therefore transported nearly all the oil produced in the major oil fields of that era,[3] helping to give the Standard combination its predominant place in the oil industry. Pipelines were of major importance to Standard Oil and the American petroleum industry, but to the general public the presence of these vital underground arteries of oil transportation was for the most part unknown.

Pipelines were used to gather oil in the field and also to transport it for long distances. The wrought-iron pipe used to collect oil from the wells and move it to storage tanks or to a trunk-line connection was typically not over 2 inches in diameter at the turn of the century. Sections of pipe were laid on the ground, the ends screwed together by manual labor, after which the pipe was sometimes buried a few inches under the ground. The trunk pipelines, generally no more than 5 or 6 inches in diameter, that carried the oil over longer distances were laid a few feet deep in ditches dug by work gangs with few mechanical aids. Once the ditch has been backfilled, there was scarcely more than the right-of-way clearing through forested areas to signify to the observer that oil was moving below his feet. In other areas, where farmers planted their crops over the pipeline's route, even this visual evidence was lacking. An occasional pump station with buildings for its crew was the most obvious manifestation of a pipeline's presence.

The lack of physical evidence of pipelines above the ground should not obscure their significance as petroleum transporters. The meaningful measure of this significance was not the line's diameter or length alone, or in combination, but the number of barrel-miles of oil it moved in a day. A trunk line of 8-inch diameter, operating at capacity, might move 20,000 barrel-miles of oil a day, but its capacity could be still further increased by the addition of more pumping units, typically double-acting pumps powered by steam engines, or by "looping" or paralleling strategic sections of the line with additional pipe of the same or greater diameter.* Since friction was the main

*The size of the pipe employed assumes obvious importance because, with a full load and other factors being equal, capacity rises more than proportionately to a given increase in diameter, while investment per mile per unit of capacity decreases, as do operating costs per barrel.

obstacle to be overcome in moving oil through a pipeline, such variables as gradients encountered and the viscosity of the crude affected the amount of power that had to be applied to move a particular column of oil. Generally the most efficient level of operation, and therefore the one giving the lowest barrel-mile operating expense, was at or near a line's designed capacity. Under these conditions, there was no cheaper form of overland oil transportation.

A trunk pipeline required a large initial capital investment, the recovery of which depended on adequate supplies of crude oil to keep the line full and a market demand sufficient to insure a constant flow through the line. Accordingly, it was natural for pipelines providing large, assured movements of crude oil to be under common ownership with refineries. Standard Oil in the 1870's and 1880's, for example, had found it both desirable and profitable to build and operate pipelines to serve its various refineries.

That pipeline ownership should have become so concentrated in the hands of the combination as it was by 1900 was as much the result of Standard's pipeline strategy as it was of pipeline economics. This strategy had been based on the fact that production in the East was relatively concentrated and pipelines could be used to control access to markets. After the turn of the century, however, the discovery of new fields in the Southwest offered opportunities for new companies and their pipelines to enter the oil industry. With this development, the structure of the American oil industry began to undergo significant changes. Just as pipelines had helped to shape the original structure, they played an important role in bringing about a new one.

THE APPALACHIAN FIELD

By 1905 the Appalachian field, where the American petroleum industry had been born in 1859, was in decline. This field, roughly parallel to the Appalachian mountain range, extended from Wellsville, New York, through western Pennsylvania, into western West Virginia, eastern Ohio, and eastern Kentucky and Tennessee. Pennsylvania and New York were the principal, and up to 1885 the only, significant producing states in the country. Except for one spurt in 1891, production in Pennsylvania and New York reached its peak in 1882. In the meantime, production of Appalachian oil had commenced in eastern Ohio. For the Appalachian field as a whole, the peak was reached in 1900 when 36,300,000 barrels were produced.[4] Thereafter, production declined; in 1905 it amounted to 29,400,000 barrels.

The Appalachian field was noted for the production of so-called "Pennsylvania crude." Although its characteristics varied somewhat from pool to pool, this crude was generally regarded as a light oil (high specific gravity on the Baumé scale). The absence of sulphur and other impurities made it relatively easy to refine, and it was especially well adapted to refining into kerosine, the oil industry's major product at the turn of the century. Pennsylvania crude, especially that from the Franklin, Pennsylvania, area, also made a superior lubricating oil.

The geographical location of early oil discoveries in the Appalachian field gave transportation economies great importance in the oil business from the very beginning. This was so because the major demand for illuminating oil was at the seaboard and at inland population centers far from the scene of oil production. The obvious importance of transportation under these conditions provided the cornerstone of the strategy adopted by the leading refining firm in Cleveland.

The Appalachian Field and the Rise of Standard Oil

Starting in Cleveland, Ohio, in 1863, John D. Rockefeller and an expanding group of associates steadily built up their refining business until their Standard Oil group of companies owned or leased some 90 per cent of domestic refining capacity in the late 1870's.[5] This dominance was attained by canny business decisions, efficient management, and a keen appreciation of the important role of transportation in the oil business.[6]

Standard Oil refineries were located primarily in centers of oil consumption served by both rail and water, such as Cleveland, New York, Philadelphia, and Baltimore. Standard Oil managers were able to offer the railroads serving these centers from the oil producing regions large volume shipments of oil in return for favorable rail rates. This practice, together with adroit alliances with the railroads and occasional pressure tactics, resulted in Standard Oil's gaining significant transportation advantages over its competitors.

Pipelines early became a weapon in the competition. By innovating in trunk pipeline transportation, various independent producers and refiners (i.e. relatively small operators typically engaged in only one stage of the oil business) hoped to bypass the Standard Oil-railroad control of long-distance oil transportation. Once the competing method of underground oil transportation had proved successful, Standard Oil adopted and improved on it, beginning with long-distance trunk pipelines laid from the Oil Regions to the seaboard in the early 1880's.

By using these lines for carrying crude oil and by retaining the railroads' favor through the continued rail shipment of products, Standard Oil was able to enjoy the economies of pipelines and to prevent producers and competing refiners from gaining access to the same forms of transportation at comparable costs. The move into trunk pipelining, inaugurated as a defensive measure, tied refining and production more closely together, lowered transportation costs to the Standard Oil group, and provided a powerful weapon that could be used to prevent or repel challenges to its dominance.

Standard Oil did not, however, gain complete control over trunk pipeline transportation of crude oil. The great production of the Bradford field in western Pennsylvania during the late 1870's had been more than Standard's collecting, storing, and transporting facilities could accommodate. This first "flush" field in the United States created new competitors in a pattern

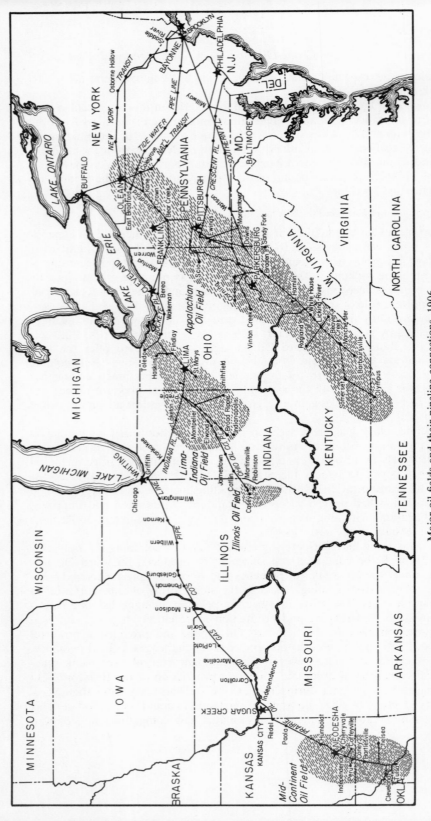

Major oil fields and their pipeline connections, 1906.

Source: United States of America, Petitioner, v. Standard Oil Company of New Jersey et al., Defendants, Petitioner's Exhibits, VII, facing p. 150.

that was to become familiar after 1900. In that instance the Tide Water Pipe Line, taking advantage of the situation, had pioneered construction of the first trunk pipeline over the Alleghenies and thereby set an example for Standard Oil. Despite Standard's intricate efforts to acquire financial control over Tide Water Pipe Line, it succeeded in obtaining only a limited ownership in this aggressive competitor company.[7]

In the 1890's another group of Pennsylvania producers and refiners organized the Pure Oil Trust, whose subsidiaries also constructed and operated crude-oil trunk lines. It was the objective of this group to combat the dominance of Standard Oil. They successfully defied purchase or penetration by Standard,[8] and again pipeline innovation was involved. By 1904 the Pure Oil group had completed a products line to carry kerosine from Oil City and Titusville, Pennsylvania, to tidewater at Marcus Hook, Pennsylvania.* Like Standard, the Tide Water and Pure Oil companies were fully integrated concerns by the turn of the century, engaging in all four major operations of the oil industry: producing, transporting, refining, and marketing.

Although Standard Oil's relative position in the Appalachian field was eroded between 1880 and 1899, its predominance was still substantial in the latter year. According to estimates made by the industry's most recent historians, Standard's share of Appalachian crude-oil production (measured by pipeline runs) had only slipped from 92 to 88 per cent. The decline in its share of refining capacity and of products markets was more pronounced. According to Harold Williamson and Ralph Andreano, Standard Oil's control over refinery capacity declined from about 95 to 82 per cent between 1880 and 1899. Kerosine was the major refined product, and the percentage of this product sold by Standard Oil dropped from 90–95 per cent in 1880 to 85 per cent in 1899. Its share of lubes and waxes fell much more precipitously.[9] But Standard Oil was still the outstanding American oil firm.

Changing conditions demanded changes in strategy with respect to Standard's oil operations. Up to 1888 Standard Oil confined its activities mainly to refining and transporting crude oil purchased from independent producers. In that year, according to Rockefeller's own testimony, Standard Oil companies were producing only about 200 barrels of crude oil a day; yet the national daily average production was 75,649 barrels.[10]

In 1888 Standard Oil officials decided to increase production of crude oil substantially. The need for an assured supply of crude was an important factor leading to this decision. In the late 1880's an increasing number of dry holes and lower average yields per well characterized Appalachian production,[11] which was not staying even with, let alone surpassing, current consumption. These facts especially worried Charles Pratt, an influential member of Standard Oil's Executive Committee. As a refiner, he had once argued that Standard Oil, while maintaining a liberal reserve of crude, should not become involved in oil purchases beyond its day-to-day needs.[12]

---

*This 5-inch line, 350 miles long, remained in service until 1919 when it was taken up and the pipe shipped to the Mid-Continent field. *Oildom* (March 1919), 34.

Table 1. Deliveries of crude and refined oil to the Atlantic Seaboard by
Standard, Tide Water, and United States pipelines, 1900–1906.
(barrels of 42 gallons)

Year	Standard pipelines	Tide Water Pipe Co.	Total Standard and Tide Water	United States Pipe Line[a]	Grand total[b]	Percentage of total delivered by Standard and Tide Water
1900	29,881,848	2,721,003	32,602,851	963,826	33,566,677	97.1
1901	32,467,861	2,739,699	35,207,560	906,990	36,114,550	97.5
1902	31,741,479	3,183,721	34,925,200	1,225,313	36,150,513	96.6
1903	28,537,478	2,982,112	31,519,590	1,317,493	32,837,083	96.0
1904	27,793,328	2,736,884	30,530,212	1,372,462	31,902,674	95.7
1905	30,258,951	2,775,713	33,034,664	1,566,323	34,600,987	95.5
1906	31,256,262	2,750,906	34,007,168	1,760,633	35,767,801	95.1

Source: United States of America, Petitioner, v. Standard Oil Company of New Jersey et al., Defendants, Petitioner's Exhibits,
VIII, 904.

[a]Includes crude and refined.
[b]Includes crude received from Lima-Indiana as well as Appalachian field.

By September 1888, however, Pratt was writing to John D. Rockefeller, who up to that time had shown no great interest in entering production, *"What we want is a safe position* and we want a large, very large production." [13]

This refiner's view was strengthened in Standard's management councils by representatives of its pipelines. Daniel O'Day, the chief pipeline official, and other top executives also favored integration into production. They pointed out that a growing number of independent oilmen were having success with pipelines of their own. As a purchaser rather than producer of crude, Standard Oil was hurt by any development of this kind that reduced its access to independents' production on favorable terms. Furthermore, Standard's pipeline managers were eager to obtain and maintain capacity loads and thus reduce their unit operating costs.[14] One way to do it was for Standard Oil to control its own production. Other executives favoring integration into producing operations felt that in order to be accurately informed about the costs of producing oil, it was necessary for the company to produce oil itself.[15]

Once resolved to enter production, Standard Oil managers moved quickly and vigorously. Drawing on the National Transit Company, the group's major pipeline affiliate, they had invested more than $22,000,000 in the producing end of the business by the end of 1891.[16] Producing properties in the Appalachian field were vested in the North Penn Oil Company and the South Penn Oil Company, whose activities made Standard Oil the largest producer in that field. However, in 1890 this production still represented less than 10 per cent of the field's total output.[17]

Pipelines built or extended by Standard Oil to serve the needs of its new producing affiliates met competition from other firms seeking to gain and retain independent production.[18] In fact, by 1903 declining Appalachian production and mounting competition made the job of keeping Standard's pipelines full a major undertaking. Under these conditions, a new importance was attached to securing access to crude as one principal function of pipelines, and new emphasis was placed on economies of operation. A top Standard Oil executive in May 1903 stated that a branch of the Cumberland Pipe Line in a new district should be built "not as a paying investment but as a means of securing oil and stimulating operations." [19] Of the effort to maintain the pipeline business, Daniel O'Day reported, "We are enlisting the services of every one of our people, whether they are producers, pipeline people, gas people, or refiners, to aid us in this direction." [20] Meanwhile, Standard's National Transit Company sought to reduce expenses in every possible way, including substitution of natural-gas for steam engines at pump stations and introduction of economical fly-wheel pumps.[21]

In seeking to keep its pipelines filled with Pennsylvania-grade crude in the period of declining production and annoying, though minor, competition, Standard Oil alternated between stick and carrot in dealing with independent producers and refiners. For example, National Transit had been delivering crude to refiners in western Pennsylvania, who in 1902 organized

Table 2. Location and length of minor independent pipelines
Appalachian field, 1906.

| Pipeline | Location | Length of pipe (miles) | | | |
		Total	3-inch	2-inch	1½-inch
Allegany Pipe Line Company	Allegany County, N.Y.	17.0	—	15.8	1.2
Columbia Pipe Line Company	Allegany County, N.Y.	80.0	5.0	65.0	10.0
Union Pipe Line Co.	Allegany County, N.Y.	165.5	20.0	84.0	61.5
Emery Pipe Line	Bradford field, Pa.	480.0	60.0[a]	420.0[b]	—
Penn Pipe Line	Bradford field, Pa.	small	—	—	—
Glade Oil Works	vicinity of Warren, Pa.	small	—	—	—
Cornplanter Refining Company	vicinity of Warren, Pa.	70.0	—	70.0	—
Continental Refining Company	vicinity of Oil City, Pa.	small	—	—	—
W. H. Daugherty & Sons Refining Co.	vicinity of Petrolia, Pa.	8.0	—	8.0	—
Wilburine Pipe Line	Tiona field and southwest Pa. field	c	—	—	—
National Pipe Line Company	Scio field and Marietta field, O.	110.0	35.0	75.0	—

Source: U. S. Bureau of Corporations, *Report . . . on the Petroleum Industry*, I, 135.
[a]Includes some 4-inch and some 2-inch pipe.
[b]Includes some 1½-inch pipe.
[c]The main 4-inch pipe from Shannopin, Pa., to Warren, Pa., was about 125 miles long. The length of the collecting pipes is not known.

the National Petroleum Association with a view to co-operative action in the face of declining crude-oil production and price-cutting. Apparently fearing that this action presaged a competitive threat, National Transit in October 1903 reduced its deliveries of crude to such refiners. Agreement to deliver 150,000 barrels a month to members of the association was reached only after the refiners had agreed to sell to Standard Oil all the refined oil that they produced for export.[22]

Table 3. Comparison of pipeline runs of the Standard Oil group
with total reported pipeline runs
Appalachian field, 1894–1905.
(barrels of 42 gallons)

Year	Total reported pipeline runs	Runs of Standard Oil lines[a]	Standard Oil proportion of total reported runs (per cent)
1894	30,117,096	25,813,062	85.7
1895	30,351,414	26,237,160	86.4
1896	33,505,197	31,506,601	94.0
1897	34,773,565	32,911,214	94.6
1898	31,156,449	29,390,708	94.3
1899	32,260,689	30,468,989	94.4
1900	35,540,964	33,681,373	94.8
1901	33,091,120	31,306,478	94.6
1902	31,404,187	29,029,795	92.4
1903	30,693,947	28,213,972	91.9
1904	30,358,671	27,823,504	91.6
1905	28,080,834	25,696,308	91.5

Source: U.S. Bureau of Corporations, *Report . . . on the Petroleum Industry,* I, 139, which attributes figures to reports of Geological Survey on Petroleum, 1904 and 1905.

[a]Includes National Transit, South-West Pennsylvania, Eureka, Buckeye (Macksburg division), Cumberland, Tide Water, Franklin, Western and Atlantic (1894 only), and Octave (1894 only) pipelines.

Statistics shed some light on the important role of Standard's pipelines in the declining Appalachian field after the turn of the century. In 1904 total pipeline runs from the field were over 30,000,000 barrels, of which pipelines directly controlled by the combination moved nearly 26,000,000 barrels. When the runs of two other pipelines in which Standard Oil had a part interest were added, the latter figure became almost 28,000,000.[23] But affiliates of Standard Oil in that year produced only a little over 9,000,000 barrels in the field.[24] In short, the combination was still dependent on non-affiliated producers for most of the Pennsylvania-grade crude that it transported.

This oil was bought at posted prices set by Standard's Seep Purchasing Agency. Prior to 1895, Standard Oil had purchased Appalachian crude by acquiring pipeline certificates traded on oil exchanges, but in that year it switched to the use of posted prices. On January 23, 1895, Joseph Seep, Standard Oil's purchasing agent in the Oil Regions, announced that the posted price was to be "as high as the markets of the world will justify."[25] Under the new procedure, a producer ran his oil into a Standard pipeline, receiving a run ticket to represent his credit balance. This crude was purchased then or later by Standard Oil at the price announced for that grade of oil on the day of sale. No charge was imposed for the first thirty days storage so that the producer in effect had his choice of prices offered during the month after his oil was run. This practice, which had earlier been tried in the Lima-Indiana field, was later carried to new fields in the Southwest.

THE LIMA-INDIANA FIELD

Exploration for gas in Ohio had given way to excitement over oil discoveries in late 1885 at Lima in Allen County and Findlay in Hancock County. Although the heavy, black oil with a high sulphur content did not seem well adapted to use as an illuminant, it had possibilities as fuel oil. Standard Oil moved into the area in March 1886 when National Transit supplied capital and personnel to organize the Buckeye Pipe Line Company. The Seep Purchasing Agency followed. It bought all the oil run by the pipeline, and Standard began construction of a refinery at Lima, assigning it to the Solar Refining Company.[26]

Standard Oil again attempted to exercise control over a new field by means of its power over transportation. Benjamin Brewster, writing to Rockefeller in June 1886, summarized the combination's position on Lima crude in these words: "We can not afford to allow anyone else to handle it, neither can we afford to load ourselves with it, at a price above its value — The question is — How to utilize it & where?"[27] Provision of storage tanks and construction of gathering pipelines, which were soon connected by trunk line with a new gathering system in northeastern Indiana, were temporary expedients to win time pending a solution of the problem that Brewster posed.

To maintain Standard's position in the field, the Seep Agency purchased, and the Buckeye Pipe Line stored, more than 85 per cent of the total production in the years 1886–1892.[28] Buckeye Pipe Line also built a 50-mile, 6-inch trunk line from the Cygnet, North Baltimore, and Findlay fields to the new Solar refinery at Lima, which skimmed naphtha and gasoline from the crude before it was shipped by tank car to fuel oil markets.[29] These markets grew to the extent that Buckeye extended a pipeline from Lima to Chicago in 1888. Right of way was acquired from the Chicago & Atlantic Railroad, which in return received a guarantee of one-third of Standard Oil's western shipments of refined products.[30]

Acquisition of the Ohio Oil Company in 1889, two years after its organi-

zation, gave Standard Oil an important producing interest in the new Lima-Indiana field. Shortly, Ohio Oil was producing more than 50 per cent of the field's output.[31]

Meantime, a systematic attack on the problem of rendering the Lima crude usable for refining a quality illuminant had produced a notable triumph. The Frasch process, developed between 1888 and 1890, successfully eliminated the objectionable sulphur content of Lima crude and produced acceptable refined products. To refine the Lima crude, Standard Oil constructed the largest refinery in the world up to that time. Located at Whiting, Indiana, it was within the Chicago railroad switching district and also had access to water transportation on Lake Michigan. To operate this refinery, Standard Oil Company (Indiana) was organized in 1889.

These developments implemented the basic decision that it was cheaper to transport crude in volume by pipeline to the Whiting refinery than to ship refined products in small lots by rail from Lima to midwestern markets. Accordingly, the first Buckeye 8-inch line to Chicago was supplemented by a 6-inch line, completed in June 1890. The Indiana Pipe Line Company, organized in 1891, took over the Chicago fuel-oil line and the new line to Whiting. The link between the two systems was furnished by the Connecting Pipe Line Company, organized in 1888.

Pipelines also moved Lima crude eastward. Connections from Buckeye's terminal at Cygnet, Ohio, eastward to Mantua and Cleveland were provided

Table 4. Comparison of runs of the Buckeye and Indiana pipelines with total crude-oil production, Lima-Indiana field, 1894–1905.
(barrels of 42 gallons)

Year	Total production	Pipeline runs	Difference	Proportion of runs to production (per cent)
1894	17,296,510	16,074,350	1,222,160	92.93
1895	20,236,741	18,415,630	1,821,111	91.00
1896	25,255,870	22,210,011	3,045,859	87.94
1897	22,805,033	19,670,514	3,134,519	86.26
1898	20,321,323	17,128,897	3,192,426	84.29
1899	20,225,356	17,183,804	3,041,552	84.96
1900	21,758,750	18,230,579	3,528,171	83.78
1901	21,933,379	18,570,770	3,362,609	84.67
1902	23,358,626	19,984,366	3,374,260	85.55
1903	24,080,264	20,489,023	3,591,241	85.09
1904	24,689,184	21,341,058	3,348,126	86.44
1905	22,294,171	18,944,547	3,349,624	84.97

Source: U.S. Bureau of Corporations, *Report . . . on the Petroleum Industry,* I, 145.

by the Cygnet Pipe Line Company. To differentiate the elements of the old National Transit system carrying the "sweet" Appalachian crude from those carrying the new "sour" western crude, the Northern Pipe Line Company was organized in 1889 and given the trunk lines running between the Ohio and New York borders through Kane and Colegrove, Pennsylvania.[32]

The proliferation of these pipelines made it possible to refine Lima crude at a variety of locations. In 1890 Buckeye was delivering Lima crude to Standard refineries in Cleveland; in 1893, Standard's plants at Olean, New York, also were refining this stock;[33] and two years later Lima crude was moving in volume through Standard's pipelines to its refineries at Philadelphia and at Bayonne, New Jersey.[34] Indeed, it is not too much to claim, as historians of the industry have done, that "based on Lima crude, the American petroleum industry measured by processing and transport facilities and the volume of products manufactured and distributed, had emerged as one of the world's major industries." [35]

Standard Oil was able to exert very considerable influence in the new Lima-Indiana field largely because it could afford to purchase production, make the crude merchantable, and provide pipeline services and storage even in advance of market demand. This strategy was to prove vulnerable, however, to widespread flush production in new areas where water transportation was a feasible alternative to rail or pipeline shipments, as in the case of the Gulf field.

THE GULF FIELD

Except for limited production and refining at Corsicana, Texas, in the late 1890's, Texas had played no role in the oil industry prior to 1900. The age of Texas crude began with the spectacular strike at Spindletop, near Beaumont, Texas, in January 1901. The Lucas gusher came in with a roar, flowing at the rate of 75,000 to 100,000 barrels daily.[36] This outpouring of oil attracted capital and wildcatters from all over the country. Wild speculation followed, and soon the coastal plain of Texas and Louisiana blossomed with oil rigs, giving birth to the Gulf field and a new era in oil industry development.

The series of oil discoveries along the Gulf Coast gave rise to a host of new companies, some of which survived to challenge Standard Oil on its own terms. The location of the Gulf field gave it great significance for potential entrants into the oil business. The railroad and pipeline transportation bottleneck that Standard Oil had exploited successfully in the Appalachian field was relatively unimportant in this new area. With oil production located only a few miles from the Gulf of Mexico, water transport offered cheap, easy access to the seaboard refining centers of the East Coast and to the markets of the world.

Added to the geographical factors favoring the emergence of new firms in the Gulf field was the reluctance of Standard Oil to enter this new area directly on a large scale. There were several reasons for Standard's lack of eagerness. First, Gulf crude was not thought to produce the same high percentages of gasoline and kerosine as crude from the Mid-Continent field, where Standard Oil already had major investments. Second, sustained production from the flowing wells along the Gulf seemed unlikely. In fact, despite the spectacular performance of individual wells, total Texas production was exceeded by that of California in 1905, and Texas output declined sharply thereafter.[37] This unfavorable production showing, together with political hostility in Texas and legal attacks against Standard-backed companies in that state, discouraged major commitments there under the Standard Oil name.[38]

The Standard Oil group, however, was indirectly represented in Texas by two companies, the Corsicana Refining Company (later Navarro Refining Company) and the Security Oil Company. The Corsicana Refining Company was organized by J. S. Cullinan, a Pennsylvanian who obtained support from H. C. Folger, Jr., and Calvin N. Payne, top figures in Standard Oil's management. Substantial funds were also supplied by the National Transit Company. The Corsicana Company, which engaged in production, pipeline, and refining operations, sold its products to the Waters-Pierce Company, a Standard Oil marketing affiliate[39] that distributed Standard oil products on a wide scale in the middle and southwestern areas of the United States. The Security Oil Company, financed by a London corporation which in turn obtained the funds from New York Standard, established a refinery near Beaumont in 1903.[40] This concern built pipelines from the new Gulf Coast fields — Humble, Dayton, Batson, and Sour Lake — to its refinery and to Sabine, an ocean shipping point.[41]

Waters-Pierce and the two refining companies fell afoul of the Texas antitrust laws. The former was fined and banned from the state while the latter two were forced to liquidate in 1909;[42] the Navarro and Security Oil properties were later absorbed into the Magnolia Petroleum Company, a producing affiliate of Standard Oil Company of New York.

The flood of oil from the salt domes of the Gulf Coast field and the absence of the dominant firm in the industry encouraged the entry of new companies. Reportedly, "over 400 companies with a total capitalization of approximately $200,000,000 were organized within less than one year" after the Spindletop discovery.[43] Among the more important of them were the Guffey Oil Company and the Texas Fuel Company. Both the Guffey and Texas companies constructed refineries at Port Arthur and gained access to the Gulf of Mexico by a short ship channel to Sabine Pass.

Initially pipelines of the new companies ran from producing areas toward the Gulf and water transportation, for their primary function was to collect and transport crude oil to affiliated seaboard refineries, or directly to ocean-going tankers which moved the crude to eastern refineries or fuel-oil markets. By 1902 there were two pipelines from Spindletop to Port Arthur, a distance of 19 miles, and one to Sabine, a distance of 24 miles.[44] One of the Port Arthur lines was the property of the National Oil and Pipe Line Com-

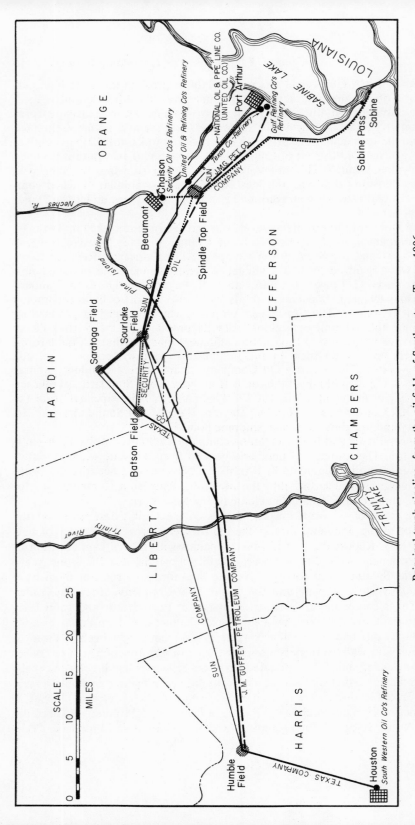

Principal trunk pipelines from the oil fields of Southeastern Texas, 1906.

Source: U.S. Bureau of Corporations, *Report of the Commissioner of Corporations in the Petroleum Industry*, Part 1 (Washington, 1907), facing p. 148.

pany; the other was constructed by the Texas Company. The Sabine line was part of Security Oil's 66 miles of 8-inch pipe.[45]

An increasing number of pipelines soon crisscrossed the coastal plain. Between 1902 and 1907 gathering lines were constructed in the Beaumont-Sour Lake district by the J. M. Burt refinery (later part of Magnolia). The J. M. Guffey Petroleum Company also had pipelines serving these fields, bringing their output to its new refinery at Port Arthur.[46] The Sun Pipe Line Company entered the area, collecting crude from the Humble and Sour Lake fields for transport by tanker to Sun's refinery at Marcus Hook, Pennsylvania. When the Humble field in Harris County, north of Houston, came in during 1904–05, the Guffey and Texas company pipelines were extended to it, and the latter concern pushed a pipeline south to Houston, where it served the South Western Oil Company's refinery. The pipelines of these concerns acted "to some extent as common carriers of oil for others." [47] During 1904 additional pipeline facilities were constructed in southeast Texas, and at the end of the year they totaled 513.5 miles.[48] In the same year, runs of the Security, Texas, Guffey, Sun, and United pipelines reportedly totalled 18,600,000 barrels of oil.[49]

THE MID-CONTINENT FIELD

Developments along the Gulf Coast had their counterparts in Kansas and Indian Territory, which the oil industry knew as the Mid-Continent field. There, however, Standard Oil was a far more important factor than in Texas.

In 1895, as Lima-Indiana oil flowed to the seaboard through Standard pipelines, Standard Oil's managers had turned their attention to a new producing area in southeast Kansas. W. M. Mills, a Pennsylvanian, had discovered oil near Neodesha, Kansas, in 1892. Since local capital was inadequate to develop the area, he sold his leases to a pair of Pennsylvania wildcatters, James M. Guffey and John H. Galey, who had also been drilling in Kansas. They developed some producing oil wells near Neodesha, Kansas, and then moved on into Indian Territory.

Although they laid some short pipelines from their early wells, Guffey and Galey found no major market close at hand, and the level of rail rates ruled out transportation to Kansas City and Omaha markets. With 150,000 barrels of oil in storage and a daily output of 1,800 barrels adding to their stock in 1895, the wildcatters approached Henry M. Flagler and John D. Archbold of Standard Oil with their problem. As a consequence, in October 1895 the Forest Oil Company, a Standard Oil producing affiliate, purchased Guffey and Galey's leases and properties for $225,000.[50]

Under the direction of John H. Fertig, another transplanted Pennsylvanian, Forest Oil expanded its activities rapidly. The Guffey and Galey pipeline was extended; exploration, leasing, and production proceeded apace. Meantime, a 500 barrel-per-day refinery was erected at Neodesha. The first revenue was received from the sale of the plant's products at Chicago in March 1897.[51]

The entry of Standard Oil into the new field awakened• enthusiastic response from Kansans, and the oil fever spread rapidly. A federal report in 1901 listed oil and gas fields at Paola, Osawatomie, Fort Scott, Wyandotte, Rosedale, Greeley, Iola, La Harpe, Chanute, Peru, Cherryvale, Coffeyville, Humboldt, and Neodesha.[52]

Neither the charter of Forest Oil nor that of Standard Oil Company (Kansas), which operated the Neodesha refinery, seemed adequate to meet the needs of anticipated expansion. Therefore Standard Oil in 1900 organized a new corporation in Kansas to produce, buy, store, and transport petroleum. The Kansas properties of the Forest Oil Company were transferred to this new concern, which in 1901 changed its name to The Prairie Oil & Gas Company.[53]

Until 1905, Prairie Oil was the chief purchaser of Kansas oil and engaged in only limited production for its own account.[54] With the striking of the first flowing well near Bartlesville in Indian Territory in 1903 and the opening of the Cleveland pool in 1904, Oklahoma's annual production increased from 139,000 barrels to 1,367,000. After Congress authorized construction of pipelines across Indian Territory, Prairie extended the lines acquired from its predecessor and laid 6- and 8-inch pipe from Red Fork to its storage farm at Humboldt, Kansas. During 1905 and 1906 lines from the fabulous Glenn Pool and neighboring districts in Indian Territory joined this one. Although the capacity of the refinery at Neodesha was increased to 2,500 barrels per day, it still fell far short of providing adequate facilities to refine all the outpouring of Mid-Continent oil offered for sale.[55]

Despite its best efforts to provide storage and to buy and transport Mid-Continent production, Prairie Oil could not meet the many demands on its resources. Although the company provided tankage at an average daily rate of 10,000 to 18,000 barrels and even hit 35,000 barrels a day for a time during the summer of 1905, these facilities lagged behind production.[56]

A market was desperately needed for this flood of oil. To aid in providing one, Prairie Oil laid pipes as rapidly as possible and Standard Oil Company (Indiana) constructed a refinery at Sugar Creek, close to Kansas City. Prairie Oil extended a trunk line from Humboldt, Kansas, to Sugar Creek, and oil was flowing into the refinery through this line by October 20, 1904.[57] The original 8-inch line proved inadequate, and it was soon paralleled by an 8–12-inch line, with 8-inch loops to increase its capacity further.[58]

These moves were geared to a decision reached at 26 Broadway, New York, the nerve-center of the far-flung Standard Oil empire, to extend the Prairie line from the Mid-Continent into the Whiting refinery. In June 1905 the 460-mile, 8-inch line was completed from Humboldt, Kansas, to Griffith, Indiana, located a few miles south of Whiting at a junction point with Standard Oil's trunk pipelines running eastward to the seaboard. The completion of this $16,000,000 transportation artery from the Mid-Continent eventually relieved Whiting of its dependence on sulphur-laden Lima crude (leading to changes in the refining process since Kansas crude was sweet instead of sour),[59] and made it possible to send Mid-Continent crude to the centers of eastern refining and consumption. In this way a widespread market was established for Mid-Continent petroleum. The rapid expansion of demand for the pipeline's services was evidenced by the building of a second trunk line from Humboldt, Kansas, to Griffith, Indiana, during 1906, employing a sizable segment of 12-inch pipe.[60]

CALIFORNIA

California also had important oil production by the turn of the century. While Standard Oil was active there beginning in 1900, pipelines did not quickly assume importance. In 1906 most long-distance oil transportation in and from that state was by rail or water.[61] Since California was to be geographically isolated and insulated from the rest of the oil industry for many years, pipeline development there and public policy with respect to it is only an incidental concern of this study, which focuses primarily on the area east of the Rockies.[62]

In the years between 1900 and 1906, the structure of the oil industry was beginning to undergo important changes because of the discovery of new fields, construction of new pipelines, and the organization of many companies. While Standard Oil dominated the older fields and established itself firmly in the new Mid-Continent field, newcomers both large and small were active in the Gulf and Mid-Continent areas. To a significant degree the survival and growth of these new firms was based on pipeline ownership which reduced their transportation costs and gave them access to markets on a competitive basis. Although Prairie Oil & Gas was by far the largest pipeline operator in the Mid-Continent in 1906 both in the mileage of its pipelines and quantity of oil transported, its position was potentially vulnerable to pipelines built into the area from the Gulf, where new companies were becoming established. It was against this background that the perennial conflict between independent producers and Standard Oil flared anew, this time leading to federal pipeline regulation.

CHAPTER 2

THE PIPELINE AMENDMENT TO
THE HEPBURN ACT

In response to the demands of producers in the Appalachian field seeking better prices for their crude and escape from the grip that the railroads and Standard pipelines held over crude-oil traffic, statutory public policy in the early oil-producing states had from the 1870's sought to impose restraints on, as well as to open new opportunities for, oil transportation. None of these measures sufficed to still the recurring conflicts between producers and purchasers of oil. As the public generally became more concerned with the growing concentration of private economic power in the economy, the stage was set for national legislation to curb big business generally, and, more particularly, the railroads and Standard Oil. A presidential effort in 1906 to increase federal regulatory authority over railroads emphasized their past relations with Standard Oil and opened an opportunity for dissatisfied elements in the oil industry to demand the assertion of comparable authority over interstate oil pipelines. The result, incorporated in the Hepburn Amendment to the Interstate Commerce Act, had long-run consequences for American petroleum pipelines.

OIL PIPELINES AND STATE LEGISLATION

The early history of public policy with respect to oil pipelines can largely be told in terms of efforts by Appalachian producers and refiners to countervail the power of Standard Oil with the power of the states in which that combination operated. This strategy in turn was based on the belief that Standard's advantages in oil transportation could be offset by granting the right of eminent domain to pipelines and by enforced use of Standard pipelines as common carriers. The attempts to reach these objectives supplemented other attacks on Standard Oil, including endeavors to outlaw various discriminations in oil transportation by rail as well as by pipeline.

Obtaining the right of eminent domain for pipelines was early regarded by Pennsylvania producers as one step toward solution of their problems in oil transportation. They hoped that invocation of public authority for the taking of private property could overcome some of the difficulties encountered in obtaining pipeline rights of way. The oil-carrying railroads, on their own behalf and then in alliance with Standard Oil, sought to bar this right to promoters of oil pipelines. Railroad managers naturally fought the threat to their business posed by the pipeline innovation in oil transportation. Standard Oil benefited by and built on this reaction, which fitted nicely with Standard's basic strategy of keeping competitors dependent on the railroads. Despite repeated efforts to get a "free pipe line law" through the Pennsylvania legislature, this goal of Pennsylvania oilmen was not achieved until 1883. In New York similar legislative action was taken in 1878. Other states followed these examples, and by 1906 ten of them had conferred the right of eminent domain on pipelines.[1]

Governmental aid to a private facility is generally accompanied by a legal obligation to serve the public. A common corollary of exercising the right of eminent domain to construct a pipeline, therefore, was acceptance of common-carrier status. States might also impose the same legal obligation to transport for hire where there was a voluntary devotion of pipeline facilities to public use. The specific application of any such statutory requirement, however, was a matter for court determination.[2]

In 1906 most of the older oil-producing states had some kind of common-carrier requirement for oil pipelines. The Pennsylvania courts had held pipelines to be common carriers.[3] New York had required pipelines to be common carriers under its law for incorporation of pipeline companies,[4] and West Virginia also imposed this requirement.[5] Kansas, in the heat of anger over Standard Oil's practices in that state, enacted a common-carrier pipeline law in 1905.[6] Ohio also had a common-carrier pipeline law prior to 1906.[7]

These state requirements were, however, more formal than effective. In the declining Appalachian field, Standard Oil pipelines accepted oil for storage, but this practice was not a prelude to transportation for outsiders. Instead, it was intended to give sellers the opportunity to pick for themselves the specific time when they wished to sell their oil to Standard.[8] The Tide Water Pipe Company followed a similar storage practice.[9] Ohio Oil, on the other hand, took title to all oil that entered its pipelines, as soon as it entered.[10] In the Mid-Continent field, Prairie Oil & Gas Company imposed a similar requirement.[11] It can thus be said with some assurance that state common-carrier requirements up to 1906 had had little impact on use of Standard-affiliated pipelines by outside shippers.

The fact that crude oil pipelines were unseen carriers of a commodity of no use to the consumer in its unrefined state, made employment of these lines a matter of little concern beyond the borders of oil-producing states. Even in those states, public interest in oil pipelines tended to rise and fall with economic conditions, and conflicting objectives of groups adversely affected by Standard Oil's control of these underground carriers helped to prevent effective remedial legislative or legal action.

Although there was little public interest in or understanding of the pipeline's economic or competitive functions, the role of railroad discriminations in the oil traffic was widely known. Writers, politicians, and members of the oil industry in the late nineteenth century made Standard Oil a symbol of corporate power based on railroad discriminations, as well as an example of an increasing concentration of economic power in private hands. Therefore, when public indignation at railroad practices and the trust movement made them political issues of national significance around the turn of the century, Standard Oil and, as a result, its pipelines found themselves in the center of the maelstrom.

TROUBLE IN KANSAS

Standard Oil policies and practices in Kansas brought public wrath and state legislation in their wake and led directly to federal action. When Kansas oil production soared between 1903 and 1904, Prairie Oil & Gas, the principal purchaser, was unable to keep up with the flow. Accordingly the price of oil dropped from $1.38 a barrel in late 1903 to 80 cents and less in 1904.[12] Thereupon producers, many of them newcomers to the business and overextended in the oil frenzy that Prairie Oil's initially high offering price had precipitated, concluded that they had been duped into exploration and production to save the combination that expense.[13]

The reduction of Prairie Oil's offering price for Kansas crude apparently reflected hedging by Standard Oil managers against the mounting production of higher quality oil in Oklahoma, as well as the disparity between the great supply and limited demand for Kansas crude oil.[14] Prairie Oil's decision in November 1904 to base Kansas prices on the gravity of the oil reduced the income of many producers, and from their vantage point the action seemed both arbitrary and discriminatory. Daniel O'Day, Standard's veteran pipeliner, had anticipated this reaction but had not been able to overcome the Standard Oil refiners' arguments in favor of the pricing change.[15] The fact that the price of refined products in Kansas was not also lowered gave the angry producers a broad base of consumer sympathy from which to work their revenge.

Standard Oil's response to the growing hostility of Kansans created more antagonism. From a managerial standpoint, the possibilities of governmental interference apparently created some uncertainty about the future of Standard's operations in Kansas. In any event, in the winter of 1905, Prairie Oil temporarily suspended construction of pipeline and storage facilities.[16] This move was interpreted by producers as a naked powerplay and further fanned the flames of their indignation and resentment, as well as adding unemployed construction workers to the ranks of the disgruntled.

Though some producers were sobered by Prairie Oil's move, Standard Oil managers could scarcely have done more to encourage the very legislation that they apparently had hoped their action would discourage. Producers and politicians exploited the mistake, and the Kansas legislature quickly passed bills authorizing construction of a state-owned refinery, declaring oil pipelines to be common carriers, establishing regulation of railroad and pipeline rates, and banning price discrimination in the marketing of petroleum products in the state.[17]

State legislation, however, proved to be of only limited value. The major market for Kansas crude oil and refined products lay beyond the borders of the state. The legislation of 1905 encouraged the construction of some independent refineries in Kansas, but their owners soon found that access to a larger market was barred to them. In 1906 they wrote to federal Commissioner of Corporations James A. Garfield complaining: "We are hemmed in on all sides. Like prison guards, the railroads and the Standard Oil Company lurk on the borders of the State, gun in hand, ready to call a halt on any man who has the temerity to try to ship his oil, either crude or refined, outside the borders of the State.[18] Despite the inaccuracy of the analogy employed, the message of these Kansans was clear and their testimony was welcome to Garfield, who had been assigned the task of determining the extent and nature of Standard Oil's power over oil transportation and the oil industry.

FEDERAL INVESTIGATION OF THE OIL INDUSTRY, 1905

The Garfield investigation grew directly out of the Kansas uproar. Congressman Philip P. Campbell of Kansas in February 1905 asked for a federal investigation of the low price of crude oil and of the wide disparity between crude oil prices and the price of refined products in Kansas, a determination whether a combination or conspiracy in restraint of trade was involved, and such other information as might be helpful in dealing with these problems.[19] His resolution was accepted by the House on February 5, 1905, and responsibility for conducting the inquiry was assigned to the newly created Bureau of Corporations, forerunner of the present Federal Trade Commission, which broadened the investigation to cover the entire oil industry.[20]

This congressional action happened to coincide with mounting interest by the Executive Branch in strengthening the powers of the Interstate Commerce Commission. Since passage of the Act to Regulate Interstate Commerce in 1887, there had been some additions to and changes in the statute. In 1903, for example, the same Congress that had authorized the establishment of the Bureau of Corporations also passed the Elkins Act, aimed against rebating and making the recipient as well as the grantor of rebates an offender under the law. What concerned President Theodore Roosevelt, however, was the inability of the ICC to exercise effective jurisdication over railroad rates. Though the Commission had been in existence for nearly two decades, the courts had blunted its effectiveness where it did not already lack power to deal with the railroads.[21] During 1905 Roosevelt put increasing emphasis on the need for remedial legislation, and with his backing, Representative William P. Hepburn introduced a bill on January 4, 1906, to confer additional power on the ICC.

THE HEPBURN BILL

The Hepburn bill stirred violent reactions in the railroad industry and heated debate in Congress, where the conflict centered on the amount and kind of judicial review to which ICC actions should be subjected.[22] A victory for the administration seemed in doubt until the question of Standard Oil's relation to railroad rate discriminations was injected into the proceedings.

In the meantime, proposals to subject oil pipelines to federal regulation had also been placed before Congress. One bill was introduced by Representative Joseph L. Rhinock of Kentucky on February 22, 1906.[23] In supporting legislation similar to what he advocated on this occasion, the Kentuckian subsequently declared:

> The pipelines ought to be brought under the control of the Interstate Commerce Commission. Its enormous traffic — the largest in the world — makes it peculiarly appropriate that it should be brought under this control. It has the right of eminent domain and exercises it; it occupies the place of a public market; it has been declared a common carrier by the legislatures of several States; and the [Standard Oil] company itself, through one of its counsel, has admitted that it is a common carrier in all the territory of the United States east of the Mississippi River; it deals in an article most essential to public use, and by all means it should be regulated and controlled.[24]

Rhinock recognized the claim that pipelines were not built to do a general business for the public, but he dismissed it on the grounds that Standard Oil pipeline companies bought oil, measuring and grading it in their own way, and therefore occupied the position of a public market subject to public control.[25] He found support for his position in the Supreme Court's verdict upholding a Minnesota statute that regulated private grain elevators on this basis.[26] Although Rhinock asked for general pipeline legislation, he left no doubt that Standard Oil was the primary target of his proposed legislation.

The Kentuckian obtained much of his ammunition from Senator Henry Cabot Lodge of Massachusetts who, on April 16, 1906, proposed his own amendment to the Hepburn bill, also advocating that oil pipelines be made common carriers subject to ICC regulation. His proposal replaced the Rhinock measure as the basis for congressional debate.

The genesis of the Lodge amendment is not clear except that it appears to have been geared to presidential strategy in winning approval of the railroad rate bill.[27] The nature of this strategy was revealed on May 4, 1906, when Roosevelt sent a message to Congress summarizing the first findings of the Garfield investigation, which linked Standard Oil with railroad discriminations of a type that the pending legislation would presumably help to control. The gist of the Garfield report was that Standard Oil had profited from secret railroad rates and that this advantage over competitors was re-enforced by the use of pipelines. Garfield charged that a combination of high pipeline and railroad rates denied independent oilmen access to oil transportation on terms that would allow them to compete with Standard

Table 5. Companies operating pipelines controlled by Standard
Oil Company (New Jersey), 1906.

Pipeline companies	Capital stock authorized	When incorporated	Where incorporated
Appalachian field:			
National Transit Co.	$25,455,200	1881	Pennsylvania
New York Transit Co.	5,000,000	1892	New York
Crescent Pipe Line Co.	3,000,000	1891	Pennsylvania
Cumberland Pipe Line Co.	1,000,000	1901	Kentucky
Eureka Pipe Line Co.	2,000,000	1890	West Virginia
Northern Pipe Line Co.	4,000,000	1889	Pennsylvania
Southern Pipe Line Co.	10,000,000	1890	Pennsylvania
South-West Pennsylvania Pipe Lines	3,500,000	1885	Pennsylvania
Lima-Indiana field:			
Buckeye Pipe Line Co.	10,000,000	1886	Ohio
Indiana Pipe Line Co.	1,000,000	1889	Indiana
Manhattan Oil Co.	150,000	1890	Ohio
Illinois field:			
Ohio Oil Co.	2,000,000	1887	Ohio
Mid-Continent field:			
Prairie Oil & Gas Co.	10,000,000	1900	Kansas
California:			
Standard Oil Co. of California	25,000,000	1906	California

Source: U.S. Bureau of Corporations, *Report . . . on the Petroleum Industry,*
I, 85–86.

Oil. Furthermore, he stated, "The development of the pipe-line system by
the Standard Oil Company was the result of special agreements with railroad companies." [28]

Whether the juxtaposition of railroads and pipelines had any particular
importance in the President's eyes is doubtful. He did not mention pipelines
specifically in his message of May 4. However, the findings of Commissioner
Garfield connecting Standard Oil, the object of widespread public suspicion, with railroad rate discriminations, the object of the administration's
attack, were propitious. "The report," Roosevelt told Congress, "is of capital importance in view of the effort now being made to secure such enlargement of the powers of the Interstate Commerce Commission as will confer
upon the Commission power in some measure adequately to meet the clearly
demonstrated needs of the situation." [29]

While public reaction to Roosevelt's message was favorable, only minor
attention was given to its implications regarding pipeline legislation. Ida
Tarbell, whose recently published history of Standard Oil had done much

to shape public opinion against the oil combination, declared that pipelines were at the heart of the oil transportation problem.[30] Lewis Emery, Jr., a successful Pennsylvania oilman and long-standing opponent of Standard Oil who had been in close touch with the oil investigation, expressed confidence to a reporter that both the rate bill and the Lodge amendment would be passed.[31] Except for members of the oil industry like Emery, or observers of the industry like Miss Tarbell, the pipeline aspect of the pending legislation was largely ignored, even in Congress. The railroad's role in oil transportation dominated the interest of both the public and government officials. Only a few days after Roosevelt's message, for example, the ICC launched a new inquiry into railroad discriminations in the transportation of coal and oil.

The fact that the Roosevelt message meshed with Senate debate on the Lodge amendment may have been a coincidence, but, if so, it was a happy one for the Massachusetts Senator. The message — drawing on the Garfield report — seemingly substantiated charges against New England railroads whose practices in the oil trade allegedly favored Standard Oil.[32] This undoubtedly prompted, at least in part, Lodge's interest in the railroad rate and pipeline legislation. The Chief Executive's endorsement of Garfield's charges against Standard Oil also created a favorable environment for congressional acceptance of legislation directed to regulation of pipelines. As the *Boston Evening Transcript* observed, "It is not so easy to ignore the chief magistrate of the United States when he brings against this business an indictment so sharp and direct as that contained in this message." [33]

Against this favorable political background, the Lodge amendment passed the Senate with little difficulty. Senator Joseph B. Foraker of Ohio suggested that regulation of interstate pipelines should be limited to those "operated for the public," but this proposal, which would have deprived the legislation of most of its meaning in view of existing pipeline use, was dropped.[34] Lodge reported that he had numerous complaints from producers against both Standard Oil and Pure Oil pipeline practices, but he made it clear that he was not proposing a reduction in rates.[35] Rather, he wanted to establish a jurisdiction for hearing rate complaints. When Senators concerned about the possible inclusion of pipelines devoted to carrying natural gas or irrigation water made their objections known, Lodge quickly quieted them and the language of his amendment was clarified. "All I want to get at is the transportation of oil," he said.[36] With the way so smoothly cleared, the Lodge pipeline amendment rolled through the Senate by a 75–0 vote.[37]

MANAGERIAL REACTION TO THE LODGE AMENDMENT

When the Lodge amendment was introduced, Standard Oil was quick to give its reaction. Within twenty-four hours a representative of the combination was in Lodge's office arguing that the measure was both useless and unjust.[38] Roosevelt's message to the Senate on May 4 and the subsequent adoption of the Lodge amendment by that body provoked a public response from two of the combination's top executives, Henry H. Rogers and John D. Archbold.

In a statement issued on the same day as the Senate's action, Rogers and Archbold attempted to answer Garfield's charges of improper and illegal relations with the railroads and predatory use of pipelines. They denied the allegations, raised questions as to their meaning, and, among other things, appealed for a rational appraisal of the benefits conferred by pipeline ownership. Responding to the charge that ownership of pipelines enabled Standard Oil to obtain low intrastate rail rates, they declared: "To say that a man in Ohio who never expended a dollar for a pipe line to Whiting should be able to transport his oil to an inland town in Illinois over an all-rail line at the same rates that we enjoyed by reason of our pipelines must appear absurd to any one." [39] Whatever the equities or absurdities involved, however, neither the public nor Congress was in a mood to weigh them. The editor of *The Outlook,* for example, saw the very fact of the reply as proof of "the seriousness with which Mr. Garfield's charges are to be taken," as well as evidence of a new awareness by Standard Oil of the importance of public opinion.[40]

Managerial reactions were further revealed in a statement to Standard Oil stockholders issued on May 16, 1906, by Charles Pratt, Jersey Standard's secretary. He again denied the charges of monopolizing through illegal and unfair practices, and pointed out that Standard's production was "a very moderate" percentage of total crude output, that there were 125 independent refineries, and that a major portion of the combination's refined products went abroad. Pratt emphasized that Garfield had not pinpointed a single clear-cut case involving rebates prohibited by law. While he admitted that clarification of some points might be required, he reassured stockholders that Standard Oil was free from legal guilt or reprehensible behavior.[41] But, almost literally, Standard Oil executives were talking to themselves. On the next day Commissioner Garfield replied to Pratt by reiterating several statements of his report, which was submitted to Congress in full on the same date.[42]

THE COMMODITIES CLAUSE OF THE HEPBURN BILL

While the Lodge amendment was still pending, oil pipelines also accidentally became involved in a legislative effort to separate the production and transportation of coal from common ownership. In the West Virginia and Pennsylvania coal fields, major railroads had employed much the same strategy that Standard Oil had applied in the Pennsylvania oil fields. They had become involved in the ownership of coal mines and production of coal and used their transportation facilities to benefit this ownership to the detriment of independent coal operators. Up to 1906, however, there had been little effective political pressure to forbid the ownership of coal production by coal-carrying railroads.

In response to complaints from independent coal operators against alleged railroad discriminations, the Senate in March 1906 authorized a sweeping ICC investigation of the whole coal problem. In the House, the resolution was extended to cover oil and oil properties.[43] It was this investigation, deferred at the request of Theodore Roosevelt to prevent conflict with the Garfield report, that the ICC initiated two days after the President's message to Congress on Standard Oil and the railroads.

As in the oil industry, the intercorporate relationships that had developed in coal production and transportation were complicated. Again, as in the oil industry, they were the result of decades of development. For these reasons, it might have been deemed proper to defer legislation concerning them, pending the results of the ICC investigation. However, an impatient minority in the Senate, sensing the public mood of distrust and suspicion of corporate bigness, proposed adding a commodities clause to the pending Hepburn bill. On May 7, 1906, Senator Stephen B. Elkins of West Virginia offered such an amendment directed against conditions in coal-mining states. "I want to confine the railroads to the legitimate business for which they are incorporated — the transportation of freight and passengers," he said.[44] But, a reading of the debate on his proposal indicates that the Senate was less concerned with the transportation question than with the possibility of breaking the railroads' power in the coalfields.[45]

Pipelines became involved in this question quite inadvertently. The Lodge amendment proposed to make them common carriers, and the Elkins amendment, as originally worded, applied to common carriers. Thus, as the Hepburn bill first went to conference committee, it transformed pipelines into common carriers and then forbade their having an interest in the oil they transported. A direct attack on the integrated operations of the oil industry had thus seemingly been initiated by the discontinuity of the legislative process.

Although some note was made of the consequences for Standard Oil of this casual conjunction of circumstances, the conference committee was at first unconcerned. Senator Shelby Cullom reported that the mood of the conferees was such that the Elkins amendment as applied to pipelines "was not discussed except to agree generally that whatever would curb the Standard Oil Company we ought to be for." [46] As a result, the first conference committee report left pipelines under the commodities clause.

Senators from oil-producing states were soon reminded, however, that an effort to smite Standard Oil could also have adverse repercussions on the whole oil industry. Senator Elkins now found that producers in his state of West Virginia feared the consequences if the commodities clause was applied to pipelines. As a result, he made it clear that he considered that such a provision would hurt independent producers while Standard Oil could be expected to find means of circumventing it.[47] Senator Cullom of Illinois, where oil production was just beginning to come into prominence, did not want to give the impression of knuckling under to the oil combination; yet he did not want to penalize the producers of his state, where Standard's Ohio Oil Company was a major producer and purchaser. Accordingly, he too opposed, though somewhat reluctantly, applying the commodities clause to pipelines.[48]

Senator Chester I. Long of Kansas, the state where producers' discontent had sparked the current controversy over oil transportation, found common cause with his colleagues from West Virginia and Illinois. In his view, pipelines were "not in fact common carriers." "Pipe lines," Long declared, "are not constructed for the purpose of carrying oil for hire, but for the purpose of reaching the field, getting the product, and transporting it to the refinery."[49] Kansas, he pointed out, had made pipelines common carriers but recognized that prohibition of their ownership of the oil they transported would destroy the oil industry.[50] He also predicted that the imposition of such a federal requirement would wreck the pending effort to connect the Mid-Continent field with the Gulf of Mexico.[51]

"Pitchfork Ben" Tillman, the picturesque Senator from South Carolina, by a quirk of circumstance had been placed in charge of the Hepburn bill and was also a bitter critic of both the coal-carrying railroads and Standard Oil. He refused to take serious account of oil producers' objections to the commodities clause. Tillman pictured their interest as being served by pipelines free from refiners' or producers' control, carrying for all who sought their services. Any retreat from the position taken in the first conference committee was, in his view, a concession to the power of the Oil Octopus. For this reason he declined to sign the second conference committee report which substituted "railroad" for "common carrier" in the wording of the commodities clause, thus relieving pipelines from its application.[52]

Senator Joseph W. Bailey of Texas, where Standard Oil was far from welcome, gave some appearance of support to the South Carolinian. On the other hand, he did not interpret the Lodge amendment, and therefore the Elkins amendment, as applying to *all* interstate oil pipelines. Despite Lodge's declaration that this was his intent, Bailey held that congressional action could not convert pipelines into common carriers unless they had carried for hire or had exercised the right of eminent domain.[53] By taking this position he appeared to be supporting the attack on integration of oil operations, but at the same time he left the integration path open to his constituents in the oil business.

The commodities clause as applied to pipelines raised basic questions of economics and public policy: Were oil pipelines basically transportation facilities properly subject to the same kind of regulatory treatment as railroads, or were they so specialized in their economic relation to other levels of the oil industry as to constitute an integral part of that industry and therefore a different kind of public policy problem? If the former was the case, then it was as logical to apply the commodities clause to pipelines as to railroads. If the latter was the case, it was even questionable whether pipelines should be declared common carriers.

Lodge and Rhinock, who had proposed the common-carrier legislation but had not initially coupled it with prohibition on engaging in producing or refining, took the next step when the latter issue was thrust on them. After the conference committee's decision to eliminate pipelines from the commodities clause, Lodge declared: "I can see no possible reason why the men controlling these great trunk lines of pipes should not make a carrying business and be content to carry oil for all producers at a reasonable rate. We make the railroads do it, and I do not see the slightest reason for this change." [54]

Rhinock also accepted the logical corollary of his original proposal. He told his House colleagues: "I want to say that I hope the conferees will insist upon the Senate amendment which also denies to all monopolies the right to transport and produce products of any kind. If they are in the transportation business, let them engage in that alone, and not use their transportation lines to monopolize oil, coal, or any other necessity." [55] He found some support in the House for his position. Congressman Gillespie of Texas, for example, favored applying the commodities clause to pipelines. "We should make no such exception, in my opinion," he declared. "The large oil concern which can pipe its product to distant markets will always enjoy a monopoly, because it can fix the price so low as to destroy a competitor." [56]

In the Senate, Foraker and Long took a different stand. Foraker, who had been employed as counsel for Standard Oil at various times,[57] argued that application of the commodities clause to pipelines on the basis of an analogy with railroads was ill-founded. He declared that railroads were built to carry for hire and their prospects were constantly improving as the country developed. Pipelines, on the other hand, were built to connect oil wells with a market, were limited to the transport of a single commodity, and ran the risk that the wells might run dry in a few years.[58] Senator Long, as already indicated, took much the same position. He cited an editorial from the *Kansas City Star* which questioned the railroad analogy and stated: "In a good many instances it might be desirable for producers of oil to build and operate pipe lines primarily for the transportation of their own products." In the *Star*'s view, regulation of such lines by the ICC would provide adequate protection against the abuses charged to Standard Oil.[59]

A flaw in this type of reasoning was spotted by Senator Knute Nelson of Minnesota. He pointed out to the Senate: "Whether the Standard Oil Company or the pipe lines which it owns is a common carrier or not, unless you divorce production from transportation, the amendment is of no practical value. They are immune from regulation because they are transporting their own goods, and if not so immune, what is the use of attempting to regulate the charges which they shall make for transporting their own products?" [60]

Nelson had hit on a key point, and one that was to create continuing controversy. His own position was clear: Business structure determined business behavior; unless oil production and transportation were separated, the regulation of transportation rates and practices would, for practical purposes, be meaningless. Regulation of one element of an integrated structure, in his view, could not be expected to counteract the advantages conferred by that total structure in any competitive situation.

Nelson, like others, was analyzing the problem primarily in terms of getting at Standard Oil; yet Congress was legislating for the entire oil industry, where the changing centers and conditions of oil production had created new concerns in the structural image of the dominant one. This fact added significance to the decision to be made regarding the commodities clause. Already it was difficult to strike at Standard Oil without hurting other important interests in the oil industry. The decision not to take drastic legislative action, therefore, would further strengthen the same pattern of integration as that of Standard Oil and one that newcomers to the industry were also adopting. As a result, any subsequent attempt to reverse the decision would become increasingly difficult.

There is little evidence that in 1906 Congress considered such long-range consequences or alternatives. It was acting in the heat of a situation partially contrived by the President, partially engendered by popular writers on the evils of big business, and given specific shape by an accidental combination of circumstances. There had been no hearings on the pipeline question, and the governmental investigation of the oil industry, aside from the Garfield report which was limited to railroad transportation of oil, was in its early stages.

Under these conditions a legislative decision had to be made pragmatically, and the oil industry itself determined the outcome. Adoption of the Lodge amendment was a foregone conclusion; memorials in favor of it from the oil industry and the absence of countervailing pressures were reflected in the 75–0 Senate vote. But the situation was reversed in the case of the commodities clause. Protests flowed in from all oil-producing areas. Congressmen who accepted the protests as genuine credited producers with knowing what was in their best interests, even if it had the appearance of favoring Standard Oil. Die-hard opponents of Standard Oil claimed that the protests were inspired by the combination and were only further evidence of the bondage to which producers were subjected by Standard's pipeline power.[61] Most legislators, however, were seemingly indifferent to pipelines as such. Since the weight of oil industry opinion seemed to be against applying the commodities clause to pipelines, this fact determined the action taken.

In subjecting oil pipelines to federal regulation, Congress satisfied the political requirement of hitting directly at Standard Oil; in refusing to apply the commodities clause to them, it kept open the opportunity for development of other fully integrated oil concerns. These decisions, made almost casually, had far-reaching repercussions in terms of the oil industry's further growth and the application of public policy to it.

THE HEPBURN ACT

With the signature of the President on June 29, 1906, the Hepburn bill became law, to go into effect in sixty days. It marked a substantial step toward increased scope and depth of administrative relationships between government and business. The new law extended the ICC's jurisdiction to express companies and sleeping-car companies, as well as to oil pipelines, and it defined "railroad" and "transportation" in ways that brought switches, spurs, tracks, and terminal facilities, as well as private-car lines, under the Commission's authority. More important, however, was the authorization, provided stipulated procedures were followed, for the ICC to review protested railroad rates and to prescribe maximum rates. The commodities clause, applied to all but logging railroads, was to become effective in 1908. Private passes were prohibited. The Commission was expanded from five to seven members and empowered to establish a uniform system of accounting. By comparison with these provisions affecting primarily the railroad industry, the Lodge pipeline amendment seemed insignificant.

All the expanded powers of the ICC, however, potentially applied to oil pipelines just as they did to railroads. As it related to pipelines, the new statute read:

> That the provisions of this Act shall apply to any corporation or any person or persons engaged in the transportation of oil or other commodity, except water and except natural or artificial gas, by means of pipe lines, or partly by pipe lines and partly by railroad, or partly by pipe lines and partly by water, who shall be considered and held to be common carriers within the meaning of this Act . . . from one State or Territory of the United States, or the District of Columbia, to any other State or Territory of the United States, or the District of Columbia, or from one place in a Territory to another place in the same Territory.[62]

Presumably, then, interstate oil pipelines were obliged under the law to maintain reasonable rates, avoid discrimination, file tariffs of rates and charges with the ICC, submit to regulation of rates as defined in the Hepburn amendment, and otherwise to conduct their business in the manner of a federally regulated common carrier.

THE PIPELINE AMENDMENT AND BUSINESS INTEREST IN PUBLIC POLICY

As we have seen, much of the legislation affecting pipelines up to and including the Lodge amendment was basically a product of intra-industry conflict. In large measure this legislation resulted from the unity which independent producers and refiners found in their opposition to Standard Oil. But this unity even at the height of the Trust's power was a precarious one. By 1906, because of changing conditions in the oil industry, it was even more sporadic and fragile.

The initiative for public policy actions may come from outside the business community entirely, reflecting and building on some generally-felt but ill-defined public feeling that the economy or an important sector of it is not performing as it should. The way that this feeling is brought to a specific focus on a firm or industry may be entirely accidental, as it was in the case of the Elkins amendment applied to pipelines. In such cases, from a managerial standpoint, the results are generally unpredictable except in one respect. Business managers typically find greater unity with their fellows when they are opposing a governmental action, such as adoption of a restrictive public policy, than when they are attempting to promote a positive one. And, the more widely the impact of a negative action is likely to be felt, the more unity of opposition it will create. A further hypothesis might be added: The chances of successful opposition are enhanced in proportion to the complexity of the issue involved. For example, although the commodities clause applied to pipelines might have been expected to benefit some members of the oil industry, the preponderant weight of industry opinion was clearly against it. In such a complex situation, involving the internal structure and workings of an industry, most legislators had neither the time, interest, nor means to challenge this opposition. In the absence of countervailing political pressures, therefore, it was easier to bow to the industry's opposition than to override it.

CHAPTER 3

NEW FIELDS, NEW COMPANIES,
AND OLD PIPELINE PRACTICES

The spectacular discovery of new flush fields, construction of new trunk pipelines, and establishment of new integrated oil companies in the Southwest during the period 1906–1911 constituted a far greater challenge to Standard's industry position than the adoption of the pipeline amendment to the Interstate Commerce Act. While Standard was able to dominate production and transportation of crude oil in the new Illinois field through its affiliate, the Ohio Oil Company, the dramatic development of vast new sources of oil along the Gulf Coast and in the Mid-Continent region brought forth many new concerns engaged in producing and/or refining of crude oil. In addition to such newcomers, older firms from the North sought new sources of oil in the Southwest. The managements of the new entrants into this area were quick to recognize the need for pipelines and the advantages of their ownership. Consequently, numerous short pipelines were laid between producing areas and small refineries on a combined-interest basis. This marked the beginning of integrated-company oil operations on a small scale in the Southwest. In addition, two new fully-integrated, large-scale oil companies developed in the Gulf Coast area during the period 1906–1911. These were the Gulf Oil Corporation and the Texas Company, each of which constructed a trunk pipeline from the Gulf to the new Mid-Continent field.

The owners of new pipelines in the Mid-Continent and Gulf Coast regions soon found that operation of their lines was most efficient and economical when carried on in a manner similar to that employed by Standard Oil. Hence, the new pipeline owners as well as Standard became concerned with implementation of the new federal pipeline law. A brief review of the early development of the more important new companies and their pipelines, as well as Standard Oil's operations in the oil fields that came into prominence at this time, is therefore a necessary prelude to an examination of the evolution of public policy with respect to interstate oil pipelines during this era.

34

THE ILLINOIS FIELD

Although oil had been known in Illinois since 1889, it first attracted major attention in 1904 as the result of discoveries at Casey in Clark County. By 1907 an oil boom was under way, resulting in intensive and successful drilling in most of southeastern Illinois. From 1907 to 1914, Illinois ranked third among the oil-producing states.

Standard Oil companies moved quickly into this field. The Buckeye Pipe Line Company entered it in 1904 and constructed a small gathering system that delivered oil to tank cars for shipment to Whiting. After a few months, however, Buckeye discovered that its charter did not cover operations in Illinois, and it therefore sold its properties in that state to Indiana Standard.[1]

Meanwhile, J. C. Donnell, vice-president and general manager of the Ohio Oil Company, Standard's producing affiliate in Ohio and Indiana, had become convinced that the potential of the newly discovered Illinois field was large.[2] After discussing the matter at Standard Oil headquarters in New York, Donnell sent agents into the field to purchase leases and producing wells. With respect to pipelines, a personal investigation by Donnell led to his decision that Ohio Oil would have to develop its own gathering system even though the company had had no previous experience in this phase of the oil business and large amounts of money would be needed for construction of pipelines and storage facilities. There was no hesitation, however, in carrying out this new undertaking.

Donnell's first step in establishing a pipeline system was to purchase the few existing gathering facilities in the field.[3] Subsequently, in May 1906, Ohio Oil laid an 8-inch pipeline, with a 12-inch segment for about five miles, from Martinsville, Illinois, to Montpelier and Bluffton, Indiana, where connections were made with the Indiana Pipe Line Company.[4] Other 8-inch and 12-inch lines were constructed in 1906 and 1907 from Stoy, Casey, and Bridgeport, Illinois, to the Martinsville pumping station, and a 191-mile, 8-inch pipeline completed the connection with the Indiana Pipe Line Company at Preble, Indiana.[5] A tank farm consisting of 237 tanks was constructed at Martinsville to store the oil produced in the Illinois field.

The basic problem in the new area of Illinois production, as it had been in the Lima field, was to build a market for the crude. The strategists of 26 Broadway decided that a refinery in the St. Louis area would meet this need. It could be located in a concentrated industrialized area, close to sources of cheap coal and adjacent to water transportation, on the threshold of a great agricultural market for refined products. Also, transportation savings could be realized by shipping refined products to expanding midwestern markets from St. Louis instead of Whiting.[6] These factors played a role in the decision of 1906 for Indiana Standard to establish a refinery at Wood River, Illinois, near Alton on the Mississippi River. Construction commenced in April 1907 and was completed early in 1908.

To serve the new refinery, Ohio Oil built an 8-inch line to Wood River. In addition, the company laid two 8-inch lines from Bluffton, Indiana, to Negley, Ohio, at the Pennsylvania state line. At this point they tied into the A. C. Bedford (later Tuscarora) pipeline which was being built across Pennsylvania as part of a new through route to the Jersey Standard refinery at Bayonne and the newly constructed plant at Bayway, New Jersey.[7] Thus, by 1908, Ohio Oil moved crude both east and west from Martinsville, and its trunkline system formed part of a continuous line from the Mississippi River to the seaboard.

Like Prairie Oil & Gas in the Mid-Continent, Ohio Oil became Standard Oil's principal purchaser and pipeline transporter of oil from the new Illinois field. Even in 1907, the company was said to control from two-fifths to two-thirds of the acreage and to produce from one-sixth to two-fifths of the entire output of the Illinois field. To move this oil, Ohio Oil employed 182 miles of double 8-inch and some 12-inch pipe.[8]

THE GULF AND MID-CONTINENT FIELDS

Standard Oil's position was different in the Gulf and new Mid-Continent fields. There, pipelines other than those controlled by the combination were beginning to become important factors in oil transportation. Among them were pipelines of the Gulf Oil Corporation, the Texas Company, Sun Oil Company, and the National Refining Company. The last two companies had been active in Pennsylvania and Ohio while the Gulf and Texas companies were newly formed. A number of new, smaller firms had also entered the refining business, especially along the Gulf Coast, and found it financially feasible, in view of the terrain and location of production, to lay pipelines for themselves.[9]

During the years since Spindletop's discovery in 1901, the Mellons of Pittsburgh had financed the interests and operations of the J. M. Guffey Petroleum Company in that area to a large extent. When the flow of oil from Spindletop and other important oil pools along the Gulf Coast began to decline, the Mellons had a $5,000,000 investment in Texas.[10] By late 1906, the drop in output of the Gulf field and the relatively high price and low quality of its production threatened the survival of the Mellon-backed companies.

Meantime, however, the great Glenn Pool near Tulsa, in Indian Territory, had suddenly been brought in, flowing at an even greater rate than Spindletop and yielding a much higher quality of crude. This Indian Territory petroleum was similar to Pennsylvania oil in content and easy to refine. It was potentially rich in gasoline for which a significant market was already developing in 1905 with more than 75,000 registered motor vehicles in the United States.[11] By the following year, the high quality crude from Glenn Pool with a gravity of 32° or better was selling for only 39 cents a barrel while Texas oil with a gravity averaging about 22° was selling at 65 cents a barrel.[12] Moreover, the output of Glenn Pool was so enormous that even the expanding pipeline system of the Prairie Oil & Gas Company was inadequate to draw it off.

The Mellons were quick to recognize the opportunity to obtain high quality, low-cost crude oil from the new Glenn Pool. The decision to act was made easier by the fact that their refinery at Port Arthur had been built by Guffey to refine Pennsylvania-grade crude, not the heavy asphalt base, sulphurous Texas oil. Although the capital cost would be considerable, the Mellons decided to take over active management of their interest in the J. M. Guffey Petroleum Company, seek crude oil production of their own at Glenn Pool, and build a trunk pipeline to transport the oil to Port Arthur.[13]

Prior to the construction of this pipeline, the Gulf Pipe Line Company of Texas was incorporated under Texas law on November 10, 1906. This carrier, controlled by the Gulf Refining Company, was empowered to store, transport, buy, and sell oil and gas, salt brine, and other mineral solutions. In January 1907 the Gulf Oil Corporation, a New Jersey holding company, was formed to own a majority stock interest in the pipeline company, the Gulf Refining Company of Texas, and the J. M. Guffey Petroleum Company. On September 1, 1907, the Gulf Pipe Line Company acquired the pipeline properties of the J. M. Guffey Petroleum Company for $2,239,857.82, which was represented by a short-term note.[14]

Representatives of the new integrated concern scouted Glenn Pool and a possible right of way for a pipeline from there to Sour Lake, the northernmost Texas point of the Gulf Pipe Line Company's existing network. While over 100 miles of gathering line were being laid at Glenn Pool, construction began from both ends of the 6-inch trunk line in February of 1907. This job was completed late that year. It was then possible for Gulf Oil to gather and run its own production from Glenn Pool to its Port Arthur refinery through its own pipelines. Built at a cost of approximately $5,000,000, the 480-mile line from Oklahoma to Port Arthur had a capacity of 13,500 barrels daily* — enough to run Gulf's refinery entirely on Oklahoma crude.[15]

When the Oklahoma legislature passed its Strain-Yeager law in March 1909, requiring domestic pipeline companies to be common carriers, Gulf Oil found it expedient to organize a separate pipeline company in the Sooner State. The Gulf Pipe Line Company of Oklahoma was therefore incorporated on September 21, 1909, and authorized to buy and sell petroleum and to transport it by pipeline for itself and for others for hire.[16] Apparently the Oklahoma company took over operation of the trunk line from Perryman, Oklahoma, to the Oklahoma-Texas border, while in Texas, where there was then no common-carrier law, operations were handled by Gulf's pipeline company incorporated in that state.[17]

The Texas Company faced substantially the same problem as the Mellons

---

*This line had the first large-scale installation of internal combustion engines for pumping purposes. Four diesel engines of 85 horsepower each were installed in each pump station. *Diesel Progress,* Historical issue (May 1948), 43.

when Gulf Coast production began to decline. Although the Texas Company was well established in the fuel-oil business, the managers of this company were anxious to expand in as many ways and places as possible. They therefore decided to extend their 8-inch pipeline from the Humble pool, near Houston, to the new Oklahoma field. In the early part of 1907, the company began construction of its 8-inch trunk line from Humble to Tulsa, Oklahoma. This 470-mile line also connected the Oklahoma oil fields with the company's refineries in Corsicana and West Dallas. When completed in January 1908, it could deliver 17,000 barrels of crude per day and its construction cost was estimated at close to $6,000,000.[18]

The Texas Company's alert managers soon discovered that with Oklahoma crude they could refine twice as much kerosine as with Texas oil and five times as much gasoline.[19] The company therefore commenced selling its gasoline to an ever-expanding market, and in 1909, with superior Oklahoma crude at its disposal, the company's West Dallas refinery was devoted entirely to the manufacture of No. 4 motor gasoline. Despite the fact that these facilities were built to serve the parent company's needs, the Texas Company's pipelines — like those of Gulf Oil — filed tariffs of rates and charges with the ICC in accordance with the provisions of the Hepburn Act.[20]

The Sun Oil Company,* which was active in Pennsylvania and Ohio, also became a major operator in Texas as a result of the Gulf Coast oil boom. Like the Mellons of Gulf Oil, members of the Pew family, chief promoters of Sun Oil, were attracted to Texas at the time of Spindletop. J. Edgar Pew bought land near Smith's Bluff, Texas, on the Neches River. There storage and transportation facilities were constructed so that oil could be shipped by rail or water. Pew then commenced buying Texas crude, relying at first on pipelines of other companies to deliver the oil to tidewater for further movement to Sun's refinery near Philadelphia. With the acquisition of the bankrupt Lone Star and Crescent Oil Company's property in the late spring of 1904, however, Sun Oil itself went into the pipeline business in Texas.[21] The Sun Pipe Line Company (Texas) was organized under laws of that state on July 1, 1904, and commenced operation of a 6-inch pipeline extending 27 miles from Gladys City to the Sabine Pass docks. Since their pipeline operations were intrastate, Sun Oil's management did not feel it necessary after the passage of the Hepburn Act to file tariffs with the ICC.[22]

The importance of the new fields to firms that had experienced difficulties with Standard Oil in the older areas was exemplified by the National Refining Company. This concern was incorporated in Ohio in July 1906 as the successor to a company of the same name organized in 1884. Its pipeline affiliate, the National Pipe Line Company, had been in existence since 1899, but apparently entered into trunkline operations only after Standard Oil in the latter part of 1903 refused further pipeline service to National's refinery at Marietta, Ohio.[23] By paying a premium for crude oil, the pipeline had

*The Sun Oil Company was incorporated as a holding company in New Jersey in 1901 under the name Sun Company. The name changed in 1922.

been able to supply its parent's refinery needs, and it was also successful in resisting pressure on the part of Standard Oil to sell out. The latter tactics reportedly included lightly veiled threats to independent producers that Standard Oil, or more specifically its Buckeye Pipe Line, might not take their oil when National voluntarily, or otherwise, withdrew from the field.[24]

National Refining subsequently moved into the Mid-Continent field, where the National Refining Company of Oklahoma was incorporated in 1910. Its pipelines also served National's refinery at Coffeyville, Kansas. The National Pipe Line Company, however, declined to file schedules of rates with the ICC.[25]

The many new, relatively short pipelines constructed in the Mid-Continent region between 1906 and 1911,[26] and their integrated relation with producers or refiners or both, indicate that Standard Oil's operation of pipelines as part of a vertically integrated structure was not unique. Also, as will be shown later in this chapter, there were significant similarities between Standard's pipeline practices and those of the newer concerns. In part these practices reflected the way in which the industry was organized and the economics of pipeline transportation. In part they also reflected the need of new competitors of Standard Oil to protect themselves against the combination in the producing and transporting phases of the oil business.

STANDARD OIL IN A NEW ENVIRONMENT

The completion of the Gulf Oil Corporation and Texas Company trunk pipelines from the Texas Gulf to Glenn Pool brought these companies face-to-face with Standard's Prairie Oil & Gas Company, which had obtained leases in Indian Territory even before Glenn Pool was developed. Prairie was the first major firm to connect the field, in August 1906, providing a route northward for the crude at the rate of 20,000 barrels a day.[27] The Associated Producers Company, an affiliate of the Pennsylvania-based Tide Water Company in which Jersey Standard had an interest, also entered the pool, purchasing leases and storing large amounts of oil in addition to selling to Prairie.[28]

But, despite the rapid construction of the Prairie, Gulf, and Texas companies' pipelines and storage facilities, Mid-Continent production swamped transportation arteries and tremendous backlogs of stored petroleum were built up. Prairie Oil alone had 43,000,000 barrels of Oklahoma crude in storage in 1909.[29] With production hitting a daily rate of 150,000 barrels, prices plummeted.

The competitive position of Prairie Oil & Gas in relation to newcomers to the integrated oil business had been reversed in a few short years as the result of pipeline construction. To maintain its leading position, Prairie had been paying 41 cents per barrel for crude of 32° gravity or above, while the Gulf and Texas companies had made contracts with producers for similar crude at 25–35 cents a barrel. By 1909, the newcomers were paying 33–35 cents a barrel respectively, and were planning expansion of both their runs and their pipelines.[30] For the first time, and under unfavorable circumstances, Prairie faced major competition. Prairie Oil's vice-president and general manager, James E. O'Neil, was not comforted by the thought that his competitors enjoyed not only a lower cost of crude but a lower cost of transportation to eastern refineries by a combined pipe-and-water route which challenged Standard Oil's all-pipe overland route. One short-run response was to cut Prairie's offering price for Mid-Continent crude, an action taken in July 1909.

To meet the problems posed by the flush Mid-Continent production and aggressive new competitors,[31] Jersey Standard executives had already decided to create a market closer to the Mid-Continent area than that of any of their existing refineries. Texas' successful efforts to expel companies indirectly affiliated with Standard Oil re-enforced Jersey's earlier decision not to enter that state, but the adjoining state of Louisiana was hospitable and well located with respect to both production and transportation. Accordingly, the Standard Oil Company of Louisiana was organized in April 1909 to produce, transport, manufacture, and market petroleum and its products.

The Jersey company planners selected a desirable refinery site at Baton Rouge, which was accessible to ocean-going tankers from the Gulf as well as to barges plying the Mississippi River. They proposed to supply this facility with crude transported by pipeline from the Caddo field near Shreveport in northwestern Louisiana and from the bountiful new Oklahoma fields.

The feasibility of the Oklahoma pipeline project depended on obtaining a right of way across Indian lands under the control of the federal government. Discretion in this matter was a responsibility of the Secretary of the Interior. In December 1906, Secretary E. A. Hitchcock had issued an order that only common-carrier pipelines could be granted a right of way through tribal lands and violations of departmental regulations would result in the cancellation of the right-of-way privilege. No pipeline company was willing to accept such conditions at that time. Standard Oil representatives objected to both the common-carrier requirement and the discretionary role assigned to the Secretary in canceling right-of-way permits.[32]

In 1908 the Roosevelt administration had rejected a Standard Oil application for a permit, but in March 1909, when R. A. Ballinger took over the Interior post under President William H. Taft, the restrictions at which Standard Oil officials had balked were removed. This action was in response to Standard's request for changes in departmental regulations, re-enforced by pressure from Oklahoma oil producers anxious for new markets for their crude. Since the Gulf Pipe Line Company had accepted the government's restrictions in building its line from the Gulf to the Mid-Continent field, Gulf Oil's management protested Ballinger's decision. But the protest was in vain.[33]

Obtaining the federal permit, which was issued to Prairie Oil & Gas, was only the first hurdle that had to be overcome by Standard Oil lawyers. The proposed pipeline also had to cross Oklahoma state territory, and Oklahoma's Attorney General, Charles J. West, interpreted the state constitution and the newly-adopted Strain-Yeager Pipe Line Law as forbidding foreign corporations to cross state highways and as requiring newly formed domestic pipeline companies to be common carriers. This interpretation ruled out operation of the proposed pipeline by Prairie Oil & Gas if that company was to retain its status as a private carrier. But Oklahomans wanted the new pipeline outlet and Jersey Standard wanted their goodwill. Therefore, at the suggestion of West himself, Jersey organized a new corporation, the Oklahoma Pipe Line Company, under Oklahoma law, to act as a common carrier in that state. Prairie Oil's vice-president, James E. O'Neil, became president, and some of Prairie's most experienced pipeliners joined the new concern. Two members of the Jersey board sat on the Oklahoma Company's board of directors, and Jersey Standard held all but the qualifying shares of stock.[34]

Some delay was encountered in getting Prairie Oil's federal right-of-way permit transferred to the new Oklahoma company. Prairie's reduction in its offering price for Mid-Continent crude added fuel to the fire.[35] The price reduction, in fact, had come only a week after the Interior Department had conferred the right-of-way permission which the Roosevelt administration had denied. The First Assistant Secretary of the Interior, who apparently still had hopes that Prairie Oil & Gas could be forced to accept common-carrier status in Oklahoma, was quick to seize on the price cut as a breach of faith. Only after O'Neil and other Standard Oil representatives had demonstrated that Prairie's price was still higher than its competitors and that the pipeline would provide new markets did the Assistant Secretary finally consent, though reluctantly, to the transfer of rights across Indian lands from Prairie Oil & Gas Company to the Oklahoma Pipe Line Company.[36]

Prairie Oil & Gas remained a producer and purchaser of crude oil in Oklahoma, and it also built and operated across Arkansas, where there was no common-carrier requirement, the connecting segment of the new trunk line between Oklahoma and Louisiana. To avoid any claims of state jurisdiction over the pipeline because of highway crossings, Prairie obtained licenses from property owners abutting highways at pipeline crossings. The theory, according to Prairie's attorney, was that these owners had given the highway only an easement — not title — to the land they occupied.[37] Since Prairie was not qualified to do business in Louisiana, the final segment of the pipeline to the Baton Rouge refinery was constructed by the Standard Oil Company of Louisiana, which assigned operation of the facility to its Crude Oil Department.

With an eye on the new federal pipeline law, Standard Oil managers tried to avoid giving the appearance of engaging in common-carrier pipeline operations in interstate commerce between Glenn Pool, Oklahoma, and Baton Rouge, Louisiana. The separate direct ownership of the three major segments of the new pipeline was well adapted to this strategy. Moreover, at McCurtain on the Oklahoma-Arkansas border and at Ida on the Arkansas-

Louisiana state line, ownership of the oil in the pipeline was transferred from one Standard-owned company to another. While such a transfer was legal fiction, Standard Oil lawyers apparently hoped that it would bolster their claims that this new pipeline was properly exempt from federal regulation.[38] This was only one of the ways in which the leading owners of American pipelines attempted to carry on business within the letter, if not always the spirit, of the new federal pipeline law.

The Glenn Pool-Baton Rouge trunk pipeline, 1910.
Source: John L. Loos, *Oil on Stream!* (Baton Rouge, La., 1959), p. 5.

STANDARD OIL PIPELINE RATES AND PRACTICES, 1906

Filing of Tariffs to Transport for Others

The first requirement of oil pipelines imposed by the ICC after the Hepburn Act became effective was the filing of a tariff of rates and charges with respect to interstate transportation of crude oil. To file such tariffs, of course, represented acknowledgment by pipeline managements that the act applied to their lines. Pipelines owned by Standard Oil did not respond uniformly to this requirement.

As previously noted, Prairie Oil & Gas Company had taken every precaution since its beginning not to be classed as a common carrier. It had not used the right of eminent domain. It had never held itself out to be a common carrier and only accepted oil that it had purchased. The enactment of the Kansas common-carrier statute in 1905 had not changed Prairie's practice,[39] and the company made no move to comply with the tariff-filing requirement of the new federal statute, though its pipelines crossed state lines, gathering crude oil in Kansas and Oklahoma and transporting it to points in Kansas, Missouri, and Indiana. Prairie Oil stood on its claim to be a private carrier when it rebuffed attempts in late 1906 by two different refining concerns, one in Pennsylvania and the other in Kansas, to obtain shipments over its lines.[40]

The Ohio Oil Company took a similar position. At the time of the Hepburn Amendment, it was engaged in its first pipeline ventures in the new Illinois field. Although the new trunk line connecting the Illinois field with the Indiana Pipe Line crossed state borders, no tariffs were filed with the ICC.[41] Ohio Oil, like Prairie, continued to insist on the sale of oil as a condition of carriage.[42] Apparently referring to the new line that was to connect with the A. C. Bedford line at Negley, Ohio, the Bureau of Corporations reported that the Ohio company was planning to build a line to the seaboard to avoid connecting with Standard lines that had issued tariffs of rates from the Lima-Indiana field.[43]

New York Transit, whose interstate operations had been terminated in 1905 as the result of the transfer of its New Jersey lines to Jersey Standard, naturally did not file rates for shipments originating on its own lines.[44] However, where its pipes were being used in connection with interstate through routes, concurrence in these tariffs was filed with the ICC.

Tariffs were filed for certain Standard pipelines in the Appalachian and Lima-Indiana fields, such as Buckeye and Indiana Pipe Line, but in such a manner as to render them of little help to potential outside shippers. For example, of seven destinations listed in the tariffs from the Appalachian field, two were only storage or pumping-station points near state lines. New York Harbor and Baltimore, major Standard Oil refining centers, were not included, for the connecting lines to these points had been transformed into private carriers by the moves made in 1905. Ten destinations were named for shipments from the Lima-Indiana field, but again New York and Baltimore were not among them. Three destinations were pumping stations at state lines, and one was Cygnet, Ohio, a junction point of two divisions of Standard's pipeline system.[45] Table 6 gives sample routes and rates.

Since Standard's pipeline system had been designed to serve the needs of affiliated companies rather than outside shippers, it is not surprising that the destinations listed in these tariffs reflected this fact. And, while complying with federal requirements where necessary, Standard Oil did not seek to ease the task of outsiders who might wish to use its lines.

Table 6. Standard Oil pipeline routes and rates, November 1, 1905,
to August 28, 1906.
(barrels of 50 gallons each)

From	*To*	*Via*	*Rate (in cents)*
Lima, O.	Philadelphia, Pa.	Buckeye Pipe Line Co. Northern Pipe Line Co. National Transit Co.	65.6
Lima, O.	Unionville, N.Y.	Buckeye Pipe Line Co. Northern Pipe Line Co. New York Transit Co.	50.4
Lima, O.	Olean, N.Y.	Buckeye Pipe Line Co. Northern Pipe Line Co.	41.6
Lima, O.	Whiting, Ind.	Buckeye Pipe Line Co. Indiana Pipe Line Co.	38.4
Lima, O.	Marcus Hook, Pa.	Buckeye Pipe Line Co. Northern Pipe Line Co. Crescent Pipe Line Co.	65.6
Lima, O.	Cleveland, O.	Buckeye Pipe Line Co.	28.8
Somerset, Ky.	Pittsburgh, Pa.	Cumberland Pipe Line Co. Eureka Pipe Line Co. South-West Pennsylvania Pipe Lines National Transit Co.	50.0
Somerset, Ky.	Philadelphia, Pa.	Cumberland Pipe Line Co., Inc. Eureka Pipe Line Co. Southern Pipe Line Co.	70.4
Morgantown, W. Va.	Centerbridge, Pa.	Eureka Pipe Line Co. Southern Pipe Line Co. National Transit Co.	36.0
Morgantown, W. Va.	Fawn Grove, Pa.	Eureka Pipe Line Co. Southern Pipe Line Co. National Transit Co.	31.2
Morgantown, W. Va.	Philadelphia, Pa.	Eureka Pipe Line Co. Southern Pipe Line Co.	51.2
Griffith, Ind.	Philadelphia, Pa.	Indiana Pipe Line Co. Buckeye Pipe Line Co. Northern Pipe Line Co. National Transit Co.	84.8

Table 6—continued.

From	To	Via	Rate (in cents)
Griffith, Ind.	Fawn Grove, Pa.	Indiana Pipe Line Co. Buckeye Pipe Line Co. Northern Pipe Line Co. National Transit Co.	64.8
Griffith, Ind.	Unionville, N.Y.	Indiana Pipe Line Co. Buckeye Pipe Line Co. Northern Pipe Line Co. New York Transit Co.	69.6
Griffith, Ind.	Buffalo, N.Y.	Indiana Pipe Line Co. Buckeye Pipe Line Co. Northern Pipe Line Co. New York Transit Co.	62.4
Olean, N.Y.	New York, N.Y.	New York Transit Co.	52.8
Olean, N.Y.	Buffalo, N.Y.	New York Transit Co.	27.2
Greggs, Pa.	Marcus Hook, Pa.	Crescent Pipe Line Co.	51.2
Bear Creek, Pa.	Olean, N.Y.	National Transit Co.	50.0

Source: United States of America, Petitioner, v. Standard Oil Company of New Jersey et al., Defendants, Petitioner's Exhibits, VIII, 903.

Rate Provisions

Aside from the question of destination, the tariffs filed by Standard Oil pipelines were also of little help to potential outside shippers because the rates specified were based on those charged by the railroads. The United States Bureau of Corporations found that when both modes of transportation were available, the pipeline rate and the rail rate were, with few exceptions, substantially identical.[46] Thus, the economies of pipeline transportation were not reflected in tariffs filed by Standard lines accepting ICC jurisdiction. But this was nothing new.

Internal company records uncovered in connection with this project support the conclusions about the identity of rail and pipeline rates from the Lima-Indiana and Appalachian fields to tidewater. A schedule of rates, for example, discovered in 1962 in the attic of a Buckeye Pipe Line pump station was significantly entitled "Schedule of PIPE LINE TRANSPORTATION RATES ON 'LIMA OIL' Taking Effect January 1, 1900, to Agree with Railroad Rates."

This schedule, and others pertaining to Standard Oil pipelines between 1900 and 1906, reveal several interesting facts about rate practices before and immediately after adoption of the Hepburn Amendment. For example, gathering charges remained 20 cents on a barrel of 42 gallons, a measure and a charge that dated back to the early days of pipelines. However, the transportation barrel had been changed to 50 gallons instead of 45 gallons, effective December 1, 1894. As a result, pipeline rates were figured on the 50-gallon barrel converted into weight at 320 pounds a barrel. Using this figure and the railroad rate, based on 100 pounds between points specified in the tariff, the trunk pipeline rate for the same haul was established.

A comparison of schedules shows that rates on Lima oil shipped over Standard pipelines to New York Harbor were the same in January 1900 and August 1906. New York Transit apparently collected the entire transportation charge and then divided it with the various Standard Oil pipelines which had participated in the carriage. Based on a railroad rate of 22 cents for 100 pounds, the 50-gallon barrel (320 pounds) pipeline rate from Lima to New York was therefore 70.4 cents. It was divided in the following manner in January 1900 and August 1906:

January 1900

New York Transit Co., N. Y. Division	52.80
The Buckeye Pipe Line Co., Cygnet Division	13.20
Northern Pipe Line Co.	4.40
Total	70.40

August 28, 1906

New York Transit Co.	20.62
The Buckeye Pipe Line Co., Cygnet Division	13.75
The Buckeye Pipe Line Co., Lima Division	6.87
The Northern Pipe Line Co.	9.16
Terminal charges	20.00
Total	70.40

This oil moved 657.78 miles through 24 pumping stations at an average rate of .00107 cents per barrel-mile.

In November 1905, based on a rail rate from Chicago to New York of 28 cents per 100 pounds, Standard's pipelines had a tariff for Kansas and Indian Territory crude of 89.6 cents per 50-gallon barrel between Griffith Station, near Chicago, and New York Harbor, a distance of 799.44 miles. The fact that these rates were identical with rail rates for comparable quantities indicates that the cost of pipeline transportation was not a factor in the determination of rates. For internal purposes they represented a transfer price; for external purposes they were barriers to pipeline use by outside shippers.

Minimum Tender Requirements

Standard Oil placed a further barrier in the way of potential outside pipeline shippers by requiring that very substantial volumes of oil be offered for shipment. With a few exceptions, Standard's pipeline tariffs filed in 1906 for the Appalachian field required a minimum tender of 75,000 barrels. While this total amount might be made up by several shippers, it had to be consigned to the same destination. Most independent refiners using Appalachian crude oil could not handle this volume at one time, nor could they afford to provide the storage necessary to receive it and keep it on hand.[47]

That pipeline operational considerations were not the only basic factors in setting tender requirements was suggested to the Bureau of Corporations by the fact that the size of tenders showed some correlation with the amount of competitive use that might be expected for the pipelines in question. For example, tenders as low as 1,000 barrels were specified for some lines whose destination was a collecting point for Standard Oil seaboard shipments. At that point, the tender requirement rose sharply to 75,000 barrels. Other data, however, weaken the bureau's explanation of such phenomena. For example, the minimum tender from three Pennsylvania points to Olean, New York, where only Standard Oil had a refinery, was 20,000 barrels; yet from Bearcreek, Pennsylvania, to Franklin, Pennsylvania, where the same situation existed, the tender was 75,000 barrels.[48] Such differing requirements can best be explained by the need to keep pipelines full, with the anticompetitive effect an incidental but undoubtedly welcome result.

The defensive role of minimum tenders as published in Standard Oil's early pipeline tariffs was further confirmed for the Bureau of Corporations by the differences between those specified for Lima and Appalachian crude oil. Independent refineries using the former crude needed more of it on the average than their counterparts working on the Appalachian product. However, tariffs of the Indiana and Buckeye Pipe Lines, which gathered and transported oil from the Lima field, specified a minimum tender of 300,000 barrels, or four times the requirement in the Appalachian field. This amount, according to the Bureau, was almost the equivalent of a total year's supply for the largest independent refinery using Lima crude.[49] But again there were operational as well as competitive considerations involved in setting minimum tenders, and Standard Oil's defense of these practices is covered in the next chapter.

PIPELINE PRACTICES REPORTED AT ICC HEARINGS, 1911

Standard Oil's pipeline practices were well known and fully documented by 1911, but in that year the ICC sought further information as a basis for gaining a better understanding of pipelines and how they should be regulated. Testimony taken by ICC representatives at Houston, Texas, and Tulsa, Oklahoma, in late September and early October provided public evidence for the first time on the construction and operation of major new pipelines outside the Standard Oil complex. Representatives of the Gulf Oil and Texas companies, especially, reported on their pipeline activities, while independent producers and officers of Standard-owned companies in the Mid-Continent area also testified.

Testimony of Pipeline Management

F. A. Leovy, vice-president of Gulf Pipe Line, stated that his company had extended its trunk line to Oklahoma to obtain crude oil in the face of the declining Gulf Coast supply. At Glenn Pool, however, he claimed that Gulf representatives had encountered stiff competition from Prairie Oil &

Gas Company, whose paternalism toward producers made them reluctant to sell to a newcomer. As a result, Leovy stated, Gulf Oil developed production of its own, and its pipeline affiliate to the Texas Gulf Coast was soon running 55 per cent oil produced by the company and 45 per cent purchased oil.[50] The latter oil, he said, became the property of the pipeline when it left the producer's field tankage. The price paid was the Mid-Continent posted price for crude, with Prairie Oil acting as the price leader. The price to the refinery was the posted field price plus the transportation charge.[51]

Testimony showed that tariff schedules of the new companies were comparable to those of Standard Oil pipeline companies in the sense that pipeline rates approximated railroad rates and only a sizable volume of oil was accepted for shipment. Leovy defended Gulf Pipe Line's 25,000-barrel minimum tender requirement as necessary to make it worthwhile to connect with a shipper's tankage and to avoid trivial shipments. The only requests for service by outside shippers, he reported, had involved tenders of 100,000 barrels, or four times the company's minimum requirement.[52]

Leovy produced Gulf's Tariff #10 submitted to the ICC. It showed a transportation charge of 40 cents per barrel from Oklahoma points to the Gulf Coast at Port Arthur and Lucas, Texas. There was an additional charge of 12 1/2 cents for gathering and 2 1/2 cents for loading aboard vessels or railroad cars.[53]

The Texas Company had a comparable charge of 50 cents a barrel to Port Arthur; the rail rate, which did not include the various handling charges, was 46 1/2 cents. J. S. Cullinan of the Texas Company made no secret of the fact that his company had an eye on the rail rate in setting the pipeline rate, but he qualified this statement to make the criteria embrace a range of other factors.[54]

Cullinan estimated the cost of moving Oklahoma crude to Texas by pipeline at about 18 cents a barrel, a figure very close to the estimate made by an attorney for the ICC. Much of Cullinan's cost figure, of course, depended on the methods used in determining depreciation and other charges. He testified that the Texas Company had extended its pipeline to Glenn Pool in the expectation of recovering its investment in 10 years. However, for bookkeeping purposes, depreciation had been charged at the rate of 18 per cent a year, largely on the basis of guesswork.[55]

On the question of depreciation accounting there was some difference of opinion between Leovy, vice-president of the Gulf Pipe Line, and George S. Davison, its president. The former declared that his company charged off depreciation solely on the physical aspects of pipeline operations and not its hazards.[56] The latter questioned this statement, and it appeared that the Gulf Pipe Line was still experimenting to determine what was the best method.[57]

Representatives of the new pipeline companies defended their high rate practices as a necessary defensive tactic, at least in part. For example, according to F. C. Proctor, attorney for the Gulf Pipe Line Company, a reduction in pipeline rates by his company could only benefit Magnolia Petroleum Company, which had taken over the Security refinery and that of Navarro Refining Company at Corsicana. While questioning Dave F. Connolly, an experienced oil man, Proctor elaborated on this point:

> Mr. Proctor: Mr. Connolly, in your judgment, are not the refinery and pipe line usually of equal capacity?
> Mr. Connolly: About the same.
> Mr. Proctor: Then a refinery would need all its line capacity to conduct its business in the most satisfactory manner.
> Mr. Connolly: I think it would.
> Mr. Proctor: Then if, as a common carrier, the pipe line should be required to transport a large quantity of another's oil, and this condition was persisted in for some time, the refinery would be compelled to draw on its stocks and when they were exhausted would practically be forced to shut down?
> Mr. Connolly: I think that is about right.
> Mr. Proctor: Your honor, I am endeavoring to show you a condition which exists in the Gulf Coast country. At the Houston hearing, charges were made that the Magnolia Petroleum Company, which operates a refinery in Beaumont, is a Standard Oil Company concern and this feeling generally exists in that part of the country. With the pipe line as a common carrier with a reduced tariff, we believe that this refinery, with a large daily capacity and no pipe line of its own, could step in and use our line to such an extent as to make our operating a refinery impossible.[58]

Thus, Proctor invoked the name of Standard Oil as a defense for adopting substantially the same practices that the combination followed.

Testimony offered at the hearings also showed that pipeline investment by major new companies was beginning to approach the levels to which Standard Oil was accustomed. Although early pipeline development in the Gulf fields had not required large outlays, construction of trunk lines from there to the Mid-Continent involved major commitments that would bar small operators. The total actual plant expenditure by Gulf Oil's pipeline companies in Texas and Oklahoma, for example, was about $9,300,000. And, despite the magnitude of these "sunk" costs, the Gulf pipeline companies had thus far paid no dividends.[59]

Representatives of both the Gulf and Texas pipeline companies agreed, however, that rates and profits in pipeline operations had to be considered in the context of a company's total operations from well to consumer. That is, the rewards of pipeline ownership did not rest primarily in transportation for others. Cullinan, who had long experience in the oil business, declared that he knew of no instance where a pipeline was operated as "a commercial proposition for the tariffs."[60] Witnesses also offered considerable testimony to the effect that pipelines were only built when their owners could realize substantial transportation savings after discounting the uncertainty of production in specific fields and the financial risks associated with a "sunk investment."

The testimony also showed that a variety of transportation arrangements characterized new fields. For example, Gulf Oil operated in the new, rich Caddo field of northwestern Louisiana,* which had attracted other companies like Louisiana Standard. A Gulf pipeline extended from that field to Nacogdoches, Texas, where the oil was transferred to tank cars for the remainder of its journey to the Gulf. Considering the uncertain life of the Caddo field and the special rate that the railroad gave on these volume shipments, the pipe-rail route was held to be preferable to investment in a pipeline to run all the way to the Gulf.[61]

In another instance the Gulf and Texas companies were both selling their production to Prairie Oil & Gas in Pawnee County, Oklahoma, rather than running their own pipelines into the field. This arrangement, the *Oil and Gas Journal* pointed out, was based on the facts that a new pipeline into the field might have cost a quarter of a million dollars, production was uncertain, and Prairie Oil was already there with adequate capacity and good relations with producers. Thus both competitive and economic considerations indicated that a new pipeline investment might not be recovered.[62]

James E. O'Neil of Prairie Oil & Gas Company had his chance to testify for the benefit of the ICC investigators. Like so many of his predecessors in Standard Oil when under public scrutiny, O'Neil proved a disappointing witness. Because Standard Oil management had always denied that Prairie Oil & Gas was a common carrier, O'Neil testified only after he had made this point explicit for the record. For that record at least, this experienced pipeliner maintained that he knew nothing about the 1905 Kansas common-carrier law and also claimed to lack knowledge of Standard Oil pipelines running eastward from Griffith, Indiana, where Prairie's north-south trunk line ended. He did, however, provide some information about Prairie's relations with the Oklahoma Pipe Line Company and Louisiana Standard. The Prairie executive acknowledged that the pipeline from Glenn Pool to Baton Rouge had been organized in separate companies on advice of counsel. And he also cautiously admitted that his company had a "hand" in making the price of Oklahoma oil.[63]

When D. C. Stewart, general superintendent of the allied Oklahoma Pipe Line Company was called as a witness, a Prairie Oil attorney objected to Stewart's giving figures on the business as the company was an intrastate carrier. ICC Commissioner Franklin Lane overruled this objection on the grounds that the company was a common carrier under Oklahoma law and

---

*The opening of the Caddo field in 1906 was without fanfare. In 1907 there were new discoveries of both oil and gas from various pay sands. By 1908, output was 499,937 barrels, and in 1909 more than 1,000,000 barrels. The yield spurted to more than 5,000,000 barrels in 1910 with the discovery of a new pay zone and drilling of gushers producing up to 12,000 barrels per day. By 1910 Caddo had become the largest oil field in Louisiana (Rister, *Oil!*, 96–100). About 6/7 of the yield from the western half of the field was of Pennsylvania-grade crude oil. U.S. Geological Survey, *Mineral Resources of the United States*, (1911), Part II, 418.

engaged in a through route of interstate commerce. On the basis of the figures provided after this ruling, an ICC attorney estimated that the pipeline's cost for the haul across Oklahoma, including depreciation and interest, was 11 cents a barrel against a tariff of 20 cents.[64]

Pipeline executives developed several significant points in their testimony for the benefit of the ICC. The most basic point, perhaps, was their insistence that pipelines were built to realize transportation savings for those willing to accept the financial risks of recovering their investment in the face of uncertain and unpredictable oil production. Transportation for others and the revenue derived from such service was an incidental concern, if it was a concern of pipeline managers at all. Pipelines were the refiner's life line to shifting centers of crude oil production, and a pipeline's cost had to be recovered as quickly as possible. Rates quoted to outside shippers reflected this fact. Minimum tender requirements were presented as necessary to insure efficient and economical pipeline operation.

Producers' Testimony on Pipelines

Producers' complaints about pipeline practices were solicited by ICC investigators in both Tulsa and Houston during the fall of 1911, but with indifferent results. The producers appeared to be interested in pipelines only to the extent that changes in pipeline practices could increase their market and improve the prices for their crude oil.

The testimony of Walter B. Sharp, president of the Producers' Oil Company, the producing affiliate of the Texas Company,[65] was fairly typical of the producer's position. When asked what could be done to help him, he replied: "Anything, common carrier, common purchaser, common consumers or common something to give us relief." He charged that Standard Oil had manipulated the price of crude oil in the Caddo field to break small refiners and that Prairie Oil refused to run his production. While he said that Standard pipelines should be made common carriers, he did not pursue the point with vigor. When asked again whether the ICC could do anything for him, he replied: "I don't know of anything." [66]

C. L. Wallis of the Higgins Oil and Fuel Company was not much more helpful, but his testimony tended to confirm what pipeline managers told the investigators were basic considerations of pipeline investment. His firm specialized in fuel oil. Prior to the 1907 Panic, Wallis stated, he had considered laying a pipeline to Oklahoma. He had been unable to raise the capital but figured that if the project had gone through, it would have had to return its cost in two or three years. To protect against the instabiliy of production, therefore, he said that he would have set the initial pipeline rate at 40 cents a barrel (approximately that of the Gulf and Texas companies) and gradually have reduced it as the fields to which the line was connected proved themselves. Wallis testified that he had to pay premiums to get crude and that neither the Gulf nor Texas companies' pipelines had been of much help to him. What he wanted was common-carrier transportation at reasonable rates, but he found it difficult to specify what they should be.[67]

Other producers stressed the importance of pipelines in helping them reach national or world markets, especially markets for fuel oil. But, under pointed questioning from pipeline attorneys, they revealed that they had not given much serious thought to developing these possibilities.

Attorney W. S. Fitzpatrick of Prairie Oil & Gas and F. C. Proctor of Gulf Pipe Line each pursued a line of questioning designed to show that producers were primarily interested in selling their producing property to pipeline companies. The pipeline representatives had little difficulty in demonstrating directly or indirectly that this was a position typical of many producers. Fitzpatrick was also able to obtain from one producer a warm testimonial to Prairie's fair treatment during the flush days of Glenn Pool production.[68]

In the absence of vigorous expressions of producer interest in pipelines, Commissioner Lane sought to elicit some reactions by his questioning at the Houston hearings. Speaking to Joseph S. Cullinan of the Texas Company, Lane asked if the producer was not completely at the mercy of the pipeline in the absence of a local refinery or market. Cullinan agreed that this was the case, though there might be more than one pipeline in a field. Lane then went on: "Is there any remedy for that situation, so far as the independent oil producer is concerned, except that all pipe lines shall be held as common carriers, or that this independent producer with others should start a pipe line, or that the government should build a line?" Cullinan replied: "I don't see anything except your three propositions. My judgment is that all pipe lines should be common carriers and carry oil for everybody on equal terms." [69]

There was nothing in the experience of either the Gulf or Texas companies, however, to warrant much optimism about the possibilities of expanding the use of their own pipelines as common carriers. Although both concerns formally held their lines to be in this category, apparently only the Gulf Company had actually done any outside business, and that was limited to 325,000 barrels of crude oil delivered to the Standard-affiliated Security refinery at Beaumont.[70]

The 1911 ICC pipelines hearings in the Southwest produced a good picture of contemporary pipeline practices, but there were as many views on what should constitute public policy with respect to pipelines as there were different interests represented. The *Oil and Gas Journal* noted that "The thing most noticeable was the total lack of organization [of the producers] and the apparent variance in the things wanted."[71] Producers generally favored separating pipeline ownership from that of production, believing that this would increase the price of crude. As an alternative, some favored common-carrier status for pipelines to enable producers to reach markets outside the oil field, but such sentiments were weakly expressed. Refiners owning pipelines did not want them opened to outside use, and to protect their investments, they did not want to be deprived of the right to engage in production. On the other hand, refiners without pipelines favored common-carrier requirements and were not unwilling to see production separated from pipelining.

The whole proceedings in Texas and Oklahoma lacked the aura of excitement and indignation of comparable episodes in Pennsylvania during the halcyon days of Standard Oil's domination. In fact, attorneys for the new Gulf and Texas companies were frequently anxious to make the same points as Prairie Oil's representative, though they also took advantage of every occasion to stress their willingness to act as common carriers and cited fear of Standard Oil as the justification for some of their pipeline practices.

A major development of the period 1906–1911, then, was a continuing and growing challenge to Standard Oil based on aggressive exploitation of new discoveries in Oklahoma and Kansas by both large and small, old and new firms. Many of them owned pipelines, primarily to assure a supply of crude through a low-cost transportation medium over which they themselves could exercise control. Since the discovery and output of flush fields was unpredictable, the construction and investment in trunk pipelines was feasible only when a quick "payout" seemed reasonably certain. No more than Standard Oil did the new concerns want outsiders to pre-empt or benefit from lines built to serve their own integrated operations. Even where state or federal law required pipelines to be operated as common carriers, high rates and minimum tender requirements provided obstacles to use of the lines by outside shippers.

The chief complaints about these practices came from producers seeking outlets for their oil and higher prices through access to more purchasers. For the most part, however, even the producers did not appear particularly interested in forcing common-carrier status in fact, as well as in form, on existing carriers. As yet the federal pipeline statute had not been tested.

CHAPTER 4

ANTITRUST POLICY AND
STANDARD OIL PIPELINES

Direct public regulation of certain types of business enterprise — banking, insurance, and railroads — was a well-established public policy by 1906, but indirect regulation of business through the medium of antitrust policy was comparatively new. It was not until the *Northern Securities* case of 1904 [1] that the Sherman Antitrust Act became a potentially useful weapon against the holding company, a corporate device that had facilitated the concentration of private economic power. While President Theodore Roosevelt, building on this court decision, established a reputation as a "trust-buster," he did not make a frontal assault against big business. Rather, he drew distinctions between "good" and "bad" business combinations on the basis of relatively subjective criteria. There was no question, however, that Roosevelt considered the Standard Oil Company (New Jersey), which had been organized as a New Jersey holding company in 1899, as a "bad" combination.[2] This view was strengthened by reports of federal agencies on the oil industry.

The investigation and subsequent report of the United States Bureau of Corporations on the *Transportation of Petroleum,* issued in May 1906, had aided passage of the Hepburn Act and was followed by further reports*concerning the practices of Standard Oil as the dominant company in the American oil industry. On the basis of these findings, the Roosevelt administration instituted antitrust proceedings against the Standard Oil group of companies which resulted in the corporate separation or divorcement of numerous affiliates, including pipeline companies, from their parent holding company in 1911. The outcome of this type of public policy enforcement conditioned much of the subsequent history of the pipeline sector of the oil industry.

INTERSTATE COMMERCE COMMISSION FINDINGS, 1907

New strictures on Standard Oil's pipeline practices came from the Interstate Commerce Commission early in 1907 as a result of its investigation of

*U.S. Bureau of Corporations, *Report of the Commissioner of Corporations on the Petroleum Industry,* Part I: *Position of the Standard Oil Company in the Petroleum Industry.* Part II: *Prices and Profits* (Washington, 1907).

54

discriminations and monopolies in coal and oil authorized by Congress prior to passage of the Hepburn Act. The ICC submitted its findings on January 28, 1907, a few months before publication of the first installment of the Commissioner of Corporations' report on the petroleum industry, which dealt at length with pipeline questions. The conclusions of both governmental agencies were similar regarding pipeline practices by Standard Oil, but the agencies differed in their attitudes toward remedial action.

The ICC did not use guarded language in appraising Standard Oil's pipeline power. For example, its report contained such sweeping statements as the following:

> At the basis of the monopoly of the Standard Oil Company in the production and distribution of petroleum products rests the pipe line.
>
> The possession of these pipe lines enables the Standard to absolutely control the price of crude petroleum and to determine, therefore, the price which its competitor in a given locality shall pay.
>
> There is nothing recondite or unusual in the construction and operation of a pipe line. Any person with sufficient capital — and the expense is not great — and with the requisite opportunity can construct and operate those lines.[3]

Each of these statements had important elements of truth, but each was also subject to important qualifications. The cost of constructing the trunk lines from Oklahoma to the Gulf Coast, for example, ranged from a low of $5,733 to a high of $6,970 a mile.[4] Thus the ICC's verdict that the expense of pipeline construction was "not great" depended on the magnitude of the measure — and the length of the line. The Commission's conclusion about pipeline construction costs could best be applied to gathering lines of short length in the producing field. But such lines offered no answer to producers' problems of gaining wider markets.

Precisely because the cost of constructing a trunk pipeline was large, companies that undertook such building generally did so only when they had the means to justify, protect, and recover their investment. And usually this position resulted from prior investments in other sectors of the oil industry. The officials of the Bureau of Corporations, whose information was based on private inquiries in the industry, acknowledged the importance of such integrated relations, but did not feel that they precluded the possibility of common-carrier pipeline operations.

Given the existing structure of the oil industry, the ICC seemed to discount the potential importance of the federal regulatory statute which it was charged with enforcing. The Commission's report to Congress concluded: "It will probably be found necessary to disassociate in the case of oil, as in that of other commodities, the function of transportation from that of production and distribution." [5] In this statement the Commission had put its finger squarely on a public policy issue that was to become a

perennial one: Was divorcement of pipelines from integrated oil operations a necessary condition of common-carrier usage, or could such usage
be achieved by regulation of pipelines within an integrated structure? The
same question had been raised by Senator Nelson — and action avoided —
in congressional debate on the commodities clause in 1906.

BUREAU OF CORPORATIONS' REPORT ON THE PETROLEUM INDUSTRY, 1907

The May 1907 report of the Bureau of Corporations on the petroleum
industry and Standard Oil's position in it disclosed a vast amount of information relative to pipelines and the public policy issue. As the factual
basis for making a statutory public policy decision, however, this report
came a year too late. In any case, the conclusions that it embodied were
applicable to either side of the congressional pipeline debate that had
taken place in 1906.

In this report the Bureau especially stressed the strategy and tactics
employed by Standard pipeline officials in the Appalachian field to keep
others from enjoying transportation costs or services comparable to those
available to members of the Standard group. The resort to harassing litigation, pre-emption of rights of way of potential competing pipelines,
connivance with the railroads in the matter of rates, and payment of discriminatory premiums for crude oil to win producers away from competing pipelines, were among the tactics attributed to Standard Oil by
Commissioner of Corporations Herbert K. Smith.[6] He emphasized the importance of Standard's extensive pipeline network, protected by such devices from active competition, in reaching refineries advantageously located near the largest distributing and exporting centers of the country.
Building on this point in Part II of his report on the petroleum industry,
bearing the subtitle "Prices and Profits" and issued in August 1907, Commissioner Smith declared: "The great advantage which the Standard en-
joys from its pipe-line system is in the transportation of crude oil to points
distant from the oil field." [7] Thus, Smith re-emphasized the fact that one of
Standard Oil's most decisive advantages over its competitors in the oil
industry lay in its long-distance trunk pipelines.

But, like the congressmen who had grappled earlier with the pipeline
problem, Commissioner Smith and the Bureau's investigators found it
easier to pinpoint specific past abuses of pipeline power than to develop
an optimal model of future pipeline ownership and use. While condemning Standard Oil's use of pipeline power against producers, refiners, and
competing lines, the authors of the August 1907 report were forced to concede: "In fact, it may be admitted that, taking the pipe-line business as a
whole, including the local collection of oil, its trunkline transportation,
and the storage of temporarily superfluous production, the Standard with
its approximate monopoly, doubtless possesses considerably more efficiency than could possibly be secured under competition, even if the com-

peting concerns were large." [8] Size and efficiency in pipeline operations, then, were admittedly related. The objection in the case of Standard Oil was, in the words of the Bureau's final report, that the oil combination had "neither legal nor moral claim to pocket all or the preponderant part of the gains due to its superior efficiency in the pipe-line business." [9]

But, this proposition begged the basic policy question: Could federal regulation of pipelines as common carriers be reasonably expected to force Standard pipelines to share transportation savings with competitors and ultimately with the public? The Bureau's authors qualified their statements on this issue. They admitted that a pipeline was not like a railroad in that it could not transport in two directions, nor could it carry a variety of items. While a railroad could keep an infinitude of items separate, the pipeline was conceded to have a problem in merely keeping different grades of oil separate. Furthermore, a trunk pipeline could not reasonably be expected to take any amount of oil offered and deliver it to a particular place where a shipper wanted to use it if he lacked storage facilities at the receiving point or wanted delivery at a place off the trunk line. With crude-oil production an uncertain matter in terms of occurrence, amount, and geographical location, the Bureau of Corporations granted that it would also be unreasonable to expect a pipeline company to connect with any well upon request and provide the facilities needed to handle the oil tendered by all shippers. In short, while showing little sympathy for Standard Oil, the Bureau admitted that oil pipelines because of their specialized function posed difficult problems when considered as common carriers.[10]

It was the view of the Bureau, supported by much credible data, that Standard Oil had deliberately denied outside shippers access to pipeline transportation on reasonable terms, if on any terms at all. Regrettably, from the standpoint of the common-carrier argument, the Bureau also had to report that pipelines of the Pure Oil group showed a similar unwillingness to perform in this capacity.[11] The government agency still did not conclude, however, that it was impractical to achieve pipeline common carriage. Rather, it held that even within the integrated structure of the industry, pipelines could be utilized to meet the needs of outside shippers as well as the pipelines' owners. The members of the Bureau insisted that "the difficulties in the performance of the common-carrier service by pipe line can beyond question be met by proper regulations." [12]

In its emphasis on past practices of Standard Oil, the Bureau tended to ignore the fact that the oil industry was undergoing significant changes in areas beyond the combination's control. New firms entering the oil business were threatening Standard Oil's power, but they were reiterating the same economic arguments as Standard for building and operating pipelines as part of an integrated corporate structure.

This new challenge from the Gulf and Mid-Continent fields could exercise a salutary competitive influence on the oil industry by promoting competition between different refining centers. Pipelines from Glenn Pool to the Gulf Coast, for example, could be regarded as competing with Standard Oil pipelines from the Mid-Continent to Whiting and the East Coast. Such indirect pipeline competition conceivably could exercise a direct restraint on Standard's pipeline rates. Moreover, new competition in retail markets previously dominated by Standard Oil was already evident. Standard managers were keenly aware of these facts, even if the government investigators were not.

STANDARD OIL ANTITRUST CASE

Notwithstanding differing views of government agencies regarding future public policy concerning pipelines, their investigatons helped to document an antitrust case against the leading oil firm. Roosevelt was convinced that the oil combination had achieved its pre-eminence by illegal as well as unfair means. Accordingly, he personally endorsed the initiation of antitrust proceedings.

On November 15, 1906, federal attorneys filed a bill in equity charging violation of the Sherman Antitrust Act by Standard Oil Company (New Jersey), John D. Rockefeller, six other directors, and the constituent elements of the holding company. The government attorneys proposed to prove that the defendants constituted a monopoly and a conspiracy in restraint of trade, and they asked for dissolution of the combination, including separation of ten of Standard's pipeline affiliates from the parent concern.

As both sides squared away for combat, the various governmental reports just discussed came before the public. Whether by design or otherwise, their timing was helpful with respect to influencing the public's attitude toward the antitrust case. In January 1907 came the ICC report on monopoly and discriminations in coal and oil. In May the Commissioner of Corporation's report on the "Position of the Standard Oil Company in the Petroleum Industry" was delivered. In August came a crushing fine by Judge Kenesaw M. Landis against Indiana Standard for violation of the Elkins Act, and the Bureau of Corporations' critical report on "Prices and Profits." Against a background of public opinion shaped in this way, hearings on the federal antitrust suit began on September, 17 1907, and lasted for more than 15 months.[13]

Pipelines figured in the testimony introduced by both sides in the antitrust case, but competitive marketing practices took the spotlight and constituted over half the space in the record. Most of the charges, as well as the witnesses, were familiar to those who had followed the history of the oil industry. The whole record of Standard Oil was subjected to scrutiny as the proceedings moved slowly along.

In the pipeline testimony, the government attempted to sustain the various findings of the Bureau of Corporations and of the ICC. Thus attention was focused on producer's complaints that crude-oil prices were arbitrarily set at 26 Broadway, New York City, that Standard pipelines did not perform as common carriers, and that when they did profess to do so their rates and minimum tenders were such as to exclude outside shippers. Independent refiners testified that they could not obtain deliveries from Standard pipelines.

Standard Oil denied that it had monopolized the purchase and transportation of crude oil through its control of pipelines. Defense lawyers argued that pipelines of Prairie Oil, Ohio Oil, Jersey Standard, and California Standard were not common carriers, and stated their position that "no private pipe line can be arbitrarily compelled by Congress to assume the duties of a common carrier, unless it holds itself out to carry oil for others than its owners." [14]

On the other hand, Standard Oil lawyers stressed that some of the defendant pipeline companies were common carriers by law and reported that all in this category, such as Buckeye Pipe Line, had filed tariffs with the ICC to the extent that they were engaged in interstate commerce.* The defense argued that the rates named in these tariffs had been in existence prior to passage of the Hepburn Act and that there had been no proof that either independent shippers or the ICC had raised any question as to their reasonableness, and, in fact, no one had done so.[15]

Among its charges the government had included the finding of both the ICC and Bureau of Corporations that Standard pipelines did not file tariffs between points of importance to independent refiners. The defense claimed that Standard Oil had done all that could be expected of it in those cases where tariffs had been filed. For example, among the points of destination named in Standard pipeline tariffs were Philadelphia and Marcus Hook, Pennsylvania, where — excluding Pure Oil — there were at least six independent refineries. At Pittsburgh, also named in Standard pipeline tariffs, there were at least nine competing refineries, and at Cleveland there was the refinery of the National Refining Company. Standard's pipelines engaged solely in intrastate transportation did not file tariffs with the ICC, but the defense stated that in addition to the tariff points stated above, the intrastate lines made deliveries to numerous independent refineries in Pennsylvania and Ohio, including those at such points as Titusville and Bradford, Pennsylvania, and Toledo Ohio.[16]

The government contended, however, that if high rates and service to unimportant destinations were not enough to bar outside shippers from use of Standard's pipelines, the large minimum tenders imposed certainly did achieve this result. The defense therefore went to some lengths to demonstrate that minimum tenders were dictated by technical, not competitive, considerations. For this purpose defense attorneys introduced

*These companies were Buckeye Pipe Line Company, Eureka Pipe Line Company, Indiana Pipe Line Company, National Transit Company, Cumberland Pipe Line Company, South-West Pennsylvania Pipe Lines, Northern Pipe Line Company, Crescent Pipe Line Company, New York Transit Company, and Southern Pipe Line Company. The latter four originated no interstate shipments but where such shipments passed through their lines, tariffs had been filed with the ICC. Supreme Court of the United States, October Term, 1909, *Standard Oil Company of New Jersey et al., Appellants, against United States of America, Appellee, Brief for Appellants*, II, 118–119.

Table 7. Rate and minimum tender data, Buckeye Pipe Line Company, 1906–1907.

Connecting lines named in ICC tariff	From	To	Rate per bbl. of 42 gals. (in cents)	Additional charge for gathering, per bbl. (in cents)	Minimum no. bbls. will accept for shipment	Date effective
Northern Pipe Line Co. National Transit Co. New York Transit Co.	Lima, O.	Unionville, N.Y.	52	20	300,000	Aug. 28, 1906
New York Transit Co.	Lima, O.	Olean, N.Y.	35	20	300,000	Aug. 28, 1906
New York Transit Co.	Cygnet, O.	Unionville, N.Y.	52	20	300,000	Aug. 28, 1906
New York Transit Co.	Cygnet, O.	Olean, N.Y.	35	20	300,000	Aug. 28, 1906
South-West Pa. Pipe Lines Eureka Pipe Line Co. Southern Pipe Line Co. National Transit Co.	Lima, O.	Centerbridge, Pa.	52	none	300,000	Dec. 1, 1906
Northern Pipe Line Co. National Transit Co. South-West Pa. Pipe Lines Crescent Pipe Line Co.	Lima, O.	Marcus Hook, Pa.	53¾	20	300,000	Mar. 20, 1907
Northern Pipe Line Co. National Transit Co. Southern Pipe Line Co.	Lima, O.	Philadelphia, Pa.	53¾	20	300,000	Mar. 20, 1907

South-West Pa. Pipe Lines Eureka Pipe Line Co. Southern Pipe Line Co.	Lima, O.	Philadelphia, Pa.	53¾	none	300,000	Mar. 20, 1907
Northern Pipe Line Co. National Transit Co. Southern Pipe Line Co.	Cygnet, O.	Philadelphia, Pa.	53¾	20	300,000	Mar. 20, 1907
Northern Pipe Line Co. National Transit Co. South-West Pa. Pipe Lines Crescent Pipe Line Co.	Cygnet, O.	Marcus Hook, Pa.	53¾	20	300,000	Mar. 20, 1907

Source: United States of America, Petitioner, v. Standard Oil Company of New Jersey et al., Defendants, Petitioner's Exhibits, VII, 124.

the testimony of Forrest M. Towl, a Cornell graduate in civil engineering, who had served Standard Oil as a pipeline engineer for more than two decades.

Towl explained that the characteristics of pipeline construction and operation dictated the minimum tender requirement. Pipes of varying diameters were laid parallel to one another to accommodate varying demands. At junction points the head of a column of oil in a large pipe would normally be far ahead of the column in a smaller pipe. Since many grades of crude oil (the higher the gravity the lighter and more valuable the oil) were run through a pipeline system, and since lower grades generally followed and preceded higher grades, mixture of the two inevitably occurred. The longer the transit involved, other things being equal, the greater was such mixture.[17]

According to defense testimony, the mixing of various grades of crude oil resulted in considerable economic loss.* A higher grade oil mixed with one of a lower gravity would bring only the latter's price. On the basis of experiments conducted between Morgantown, West Virginia, and Millway, Pennsylvania, Standard's engineers had proved to their own satisfaction that there was an average loss of 15,000 barrels of high-grade oil when batches of 80,000 to 155,000 barrels were sent through the line, followed and preceded by lower grade oil. The defense estimated the monetary value of the oil loss at $12,450 and pointed out that the minimum tender on the Southern Pipe Line, the one of question, was set at 75,000 barrels — or less than the minimum batch employed in the tests.[18] The imposition of the 300,000-barrel minimum tender on Lima-Indiana crude oil shipped to the seaboard was dictated by the greater distance and therefore the probability of increased mixing, defense claimed.

This testimony was given the ring of validity by the statement that minimum tenders had been in effect for shippers in the Standard Oil family of companies "for some years prior to the filing of the tariffs."[19] During that time these shippers had "rarely" failed to conform to such requirements and since the Hepburn Act the tenders had been "rigidly observed." In addition, the defense argued that independents' pipelines, also built to serve the interests of their owners in the oil business, required batches of a size not less than Standard Oil's when sizes of pipe and conditions of transport were relatively the same.[20]

Finally, with respect to the minimum tender, the defense lawyers made a startling claim. They maintained that an outside shipper could get around the minimum tender requirement by bringing forward a small amount of crude oil and combining it with that of a Standard Oil shipper, "the two together making up the minimum shipment and thus conforming to the tariff requirement."[21] But, if such a practice was actually condoned, which

*Tariff regulations of Standard lines handling Appalachian crude specified that delivered oil was subject to mixing for which the pipeline could not be held responsible. *Pet. Ind.* I, 190.

does not seem to have been the case, the outside shipper still had to consider the destination and rates quoted in the tariff.

An argument basic to the defense of Standard Oil's pipeline ownership was the claim that its pipelines were part of an organic whole. This question went to the heart of the pipeline matter, as evidenced by the tesimony taken later by the ICC in which representatives of fully or partly integrated concerns outside the Standard group maintained that pipeline investment for common-carrier purposes alone was unwarranted. It is not surprising, therefore, that Standard Oil explained its interest in pipelines in terms of its own refining requirements. The fact that separate pipeline companies were organized (and the extent to which they were common carriers) was a requirement imposed by state laws, not by the nature of the business. Standard pipelines were not built to compete for common-carrier business and never had so competed. Or, in the words of defense attorneys, "Collectively they form a single unified means for transportation of the raw material to the Defendants' refineries." [22]

With the exception of the Crescent Pipe Line Company's trunk and gathering lines, purchased from the Mellons in the 1890's, Standard Oil had built its pipelines with its own funds. According to a statement of defense attorneys, this fact lay at the basis of the combination's commanding position in pipeline ownership: "Throughout this case, Counsel for the Government have inveighed against what they call the Standard's monopolistic 'control' of the pipe lines, as if these were navigable rivers or public highways. This charge is unreasonable. The Standard Oil 'controls' its common carrier pipe lines, *because it paid for the rights of way, built the lines with its own money, and has ever since owned them.*"[23]

Counsel for the defense also pointed out that Standard's gathering lines acted as common carriers and served many independent refiners located near oil fields, but the trunk lines were not and never had been operated as common carriers.[24] On this point, Calvin N. Payne, a Standard Oil pipeline executive, testified: "I never knew a pipe line to be built that was not built to take care of the owner's own production, or to convey oil to the refinery that the investor in the pipe line owned . . . or sometimes both." [25]

This kind of relationship had an important effect on the way one should look at the rates and profits of Standard Oil pipelines, defense counsel argued. Standard's lawyers pointed out that a gathering charge of 20 cents a barrel was reasonable and even fixed by law in West Virginia. In fact, it was "an almost universal charge." [26] Whether trunk line rates were unreasonable or pipeline profits high, however, was actually a matter of little consequence, the lawyers claimed, since payments for pipeline transportation involved merely a transfer price within the Standard Oil organization. In any case, pipeline profits were merged with those of the entire Standard organization, and over-all they had been shown to be reasonable. Defense counsel ignored, when they did not deny, the government's contention that high rates, whatever their significance within the combination, also served to keep outside shippers from using Standard pipelines.

Finally, there was the question of the relation of pipelines to the price of crude oil. Defense counsel argued that Standard Oil did not control the price of crude oil. Supply and demand, both domestic and foreign, yields of particular types of crude oil, and cost of production were factors that entered into price.[27] No producers had been brought forward by the government, defense counsel emphasized, to testify that Standard Oil prices were arbitrary or abusive. The charge that Standard pipelines paid premiums to obtain crude oil and thus excluded its competitors from purchasing at reasonable prices was true in only a few instances and, according to defense lawyers, such occurrences had been satisfactorily explained.[28]

In short, the defense attorneys argued that the behavior of pipeline management within the total Standard Oil structure had reasonable explanations based in economics and not in predatory competitive practices. And, taken piece by piece, this argument was sustained.

But the government was looking at the whole, and the total impact of Standard Oil operations was greater than its pipeline parts. Therefore, what might have been an inoffensive practice if followed by a pipeline of a smaller concern became an instrument of coercion when employed by the dominant one. That awareness of this fact was shown by management in some instances where power was exercised with self-restraint, did not change the fact that this power existed and could and had been used in other instances without restraint. Presumably, a major purpose of the antitrust law was to correct situations of this kind.

DISSOLUTION OF STANDARD OIL

On November 20, 1909, the judges of the United States District Court at St. Louis found unanimously for the government in the Standard Oil antitrust case. Their decision was based on broad grounds. Transfer of stock of subsidiary defendant companies (33 companies initially charged were excluded from the verdict) had given absolute control of them to Standard Oil Company (New Jersey) in 1899. Since these companies were held to be potentially competitive, the court found that the unification of ownership and direction accomplished by this transfer had substantially restricted interstate commerce in petroleum and its products. Therefore, creation of the holding company in 1899 had produced an unlawful monopoly and the resulting power had been unlawfully exercised since that time. Accordingly, the court ordered that Jersey Standard and those in its service be perpetually enjoined from voting the stock of 38 affiliated companies or attempting to influence these companies through Jersey's ownership of their stock. The severed affiliates were to pay no dividends to Jersey Standard and were prohibited from allowing that company to vote any of their stock. Thirty days were allowed to take appropriate action or to file an appeal.[29]

This decision was appealed to the United States Supreme Court. Four companies involved in the decree, including Security Oil Company and

Corsicana Refining Company, which had been sold at public auction since initiation of the federal antitrust suit, were not included in the appeal. Another defendant, Standard Oil of Iowa, had been liquidated.[30] Arguments with respect to the remaining companies and seven individuals were heard before the Supreme Court on May 14–16, 1910, but before a decision was reached, one of the justices died. Therefore, the case was reargued on January 12, 13, 16, and 17, 1911. The decision was handed down May 15, 1911.

Again the decision was unanimously against the company, though Justice Harlan differed with his colleagues on interpretation of the Sherman Act. Chief Justice White presented the decision of the court. Noting that the record ran to 23 volumes and 12,000 printed pages of testimony and exhibits, White declared: "Both as to the law and as to the facts the opposing contentions pressed in the argument are numerous and in all their aspects are so irreconcilable that it is difficult to reduce them to some fundamental generalization, which by being disposed of would decide them all." [31] Actually, a large part of the decision was devoted to a construction of the Sherman Act itself, and the finding that there was room in it to draw distinctions between reasonable and unreasonable restraints of trade.

The resulting "Rule of Reason" was of primary importance in permitting interpretation of the antitrust law to allow employment of large aggregations of capital without violating the law, and it was particularly on this point that Justice Harlan entered his dissent. However, he had no difficulty in joining the remainder of the court in finding Standard Oil, even under a relaxed interpretation of the Sherman Act, guilty as charged. The dissolution decree of the District Court was upheld, though it was modified in some details and six months instead of 30 days were allowed to carry it out.

One of the modifications to the decree involved the prohibition placed by the District Court on any future combination between the separated elements of Jersey Standard. Chief Justice White used pipelines to illustrate the inequity of this provision. Under the decree as originally cast, he pointed out, Standard pipeline companies could be guilty of violating the decree without violating the antitrust law. For example, he suggested that former affiliates of Jersey Standard might, as independent entities, find it in the public interest to form a continuous line of pipe involving agreements or joint ownership among the companies. Such a development did not challenge the law but it would flout the decree as originally drawn. He therefore ordered modification of section 6 of the decree which contained this prohibition. Again Justice Harlan objected, but only for the record.

Ten common-carrier pipeline companies and three partially or wholly integrated oil companies owning pipelines were separated from Standard Oil Company (New Jersey) as a result of the decree.* Although ties of

---

*The pipeline companies were Buckeye, Crescent, Cumberland, Eureka, Indiana, National Transit, New York Transit, Northern, Southern, and South-West Pennsylvania Pipe Lines. The wholly or partially integrated companies owning pipelines were Standard Oil Company (California), Ohio Oil Company, and Prairie Oil & Gas Company. Gibb and Knowlton, *Resurgent Years,* 8.

personal stock ownership and business relationships built up during the preceding decades were not dissolved by this action, the seeds of significant change had been planted. Succeeding chapters will cover the adjustments that had to be made by Jersey Standard's managements as well as by the managements of its former pipeline subsidiaries whose dependence on their former parent for business could not be changed simply by judicial pronouncement.

PUBLIC REACTION TO THE STANDARD OIL DISSOLUTION

Like the testimony in the Standard Oil case itself, public reaction to the Supreme Court's decision was varied and therefore is difficult to appraise in general terms. However, it is important to note major reactions because this case provoked discussion of alternatives of public policy that became closely intertwined with the subsequent history of the American oil industry and especially its pipeline sector.

There was widespread popular approval of the fact that Standard Oil had been found guilty of transgressing the law,[32] but there was also anticipation among lawyers and scholars that the dissolution would prove meaningless where it was not harmful to the public interest. An editorial in the legal periodical *Bench and Bar*, for example, declared: "That we shall ever achieve any useful result by rending the fabric of business into fragments, large or small — we do not believe." [33] *The Green Bag* observed, "The law cannot itself create freedom of competition, which is an economic and not a legal status, without resorting to more drastic artifices than any yet employed." [34] Jeremiah Jenks, an economic expert who had been employed by the Industrial Commission at the turn of the century in connection — among other things — with its probe of Standard Oil, was convinced that dissolution would prove ineffectual. With the benefit of nearly a year's perspective, he reported in the *Journal of Political Economy*: "It has been the judgment of many persons — lawyers, economists, business men — that these decisions [referring to the remedy for evils of combinations applied by the Supreme Court in both the Standard Oil decision and a comparable one involving the American Tobacco Company] cannot be enforced as a matter of fact. It has been thought that, although there might be a reorganization in form, they would still remain combinations in fact." [35] *The Law Journal* of England was more blunt: "The special genius of American legal advisers known as corporation lawyers will surely find some means for reconstituting the combination . . . in some way that will at once evade the law, satisfy the judgment, and protect the shareholders." [36] Another English law journal, *The Law Times*, took a similar view.[37] Many other journals and newspapers, American and foreign, concurred.

Announcement of the "Rule of Reason" was accepted with a sigh of relief by many businessmen because, in their view, it eliminated certainty that "*every* combination or conspiracy" would be held a *per se* restraint of trade under the law. For example, Andrew Carnegie, the retired steelmaster, hailed the rule with enthusiasm because, he said, it was "founded on common sense and the spirit of the law rather than on the letter of the law." [38] *The New York Times* declared of the decision: "It leaves malefactors, actual and intending, where they were, in peril of the law. It frees honest businessmen from their doubts, from their dread, from their want of confidence almost akin to despair." [39] To James M. Beck, a former Assistant Attorney General of the United States, however, it seemed that the decision had added to the businessmen's perils because it created uncertainty about what was reasonable and unreasonable behavior. "If the Supreme Court, after twenty-one years, can not tell the businessmen of the country what is 'reasonable' and what is 'unreasonable' in the combination of energy and resources, it is clearly oppressive to require laymen to do so," he said.[40]

According to Andrew A. Bruce, writing in the *Central Law Journal*, the Standard Oil decision was "utterly disregardful of the fact that we must have oil and that the closing of the factories and the refineries and the digging up of the pipe lines can hardly be of economic value[41] . . . Our mistake . . . has been that we have relied too much on the assumed and questionable right of destruction and too little on the unquestionable right of regulation." [42] While he exaggerated the impact of dissolution on Standard Oil, Bruce identified a troublesome problem: Was dissolution of large aggregations of capital necessary to curb their abuses, or was their regulation feasible and more in the interest of the economy, society, and the businessman? Bruce left no question on where he stood, but the nation as a whole, both admiring and fearful of power, took an ambivalent position.

The issue of dealing with big business came up for popular review in connection with the presidential election of 1912. Eugene V. Debs, the Socialist candidate, would have eliminated the problem by government ownership. Running as a candidate of the Progressive party, Theodore Roosevelt asked for regulation of business. The Democratic candidate, Woodrow Wilson, asked for the regulation of competition, while the Republican, William Howard Taft, advocated judicial application of the Sherman Act. But distinctions between these approaches were easily blurred. As *Harper's Weekly* observed: "The question as yet perplexes the experts, and is too hard for most of the voters. They want something done; precisely what, they don't know yet." [43]

In a more specific vein, it will be recalled that producers in the Southwest had expressed similar sentiments the year before when questioned by the ICC about pipeline regulation. And, in significant respects, the public policy problem of dealing with pipelines in terms of behavior or structure exemplified the larger national issues of coping with the consequences of industrialization. In fact, the oil industry had done much to crystallize these issues.

A Democratic victory in 1912 brought in its wake a more explicit statutory definition of some antitrust offenses in the form of the Clayton Act, plus creation of a Federal Trade Commission to police certain competitive practices and to furnish data on the conduct of American business. These steps, like the introduction of the rule of reason, represented a pragmatic solution to the problem of reconciling the economies of large-scale production with protection of the public and competitors against the abuse of private economic power. The nation chose no single path to accomplish its objectives, and the Standard Oil decision of 1911 was one major landmark in the search for new points of departure.

From the standpoint of the pipeline sector of the oil industry, the repercussions of 1911 were major ones, though their full impact was not felt for more than a decade. Meantime, pipeline owners and managers had to face the first efforts of the ICC to give meaning to the federal pipeline legislation of 1906.

CHAPTER 5

MANAGERIAL RESPONSE TO THE HEPBURN ACT

What restrictive legislation means in practice hinges on the vigor, speed, and consistency with which it is implemented and applied. Furthermore, the reactions of those subject to the legislation affect significantly the results that it produces. The power-dividing structure of American government that invites exploitation, the complexity of legal, constitutional, and economic issues involved in implementing a new statute, the release that pent-up public emotions and political pressures find in the mere fact of new legislation, all help to insure that the impact of a restrictive statute will not be fully felt immediately. Where the legislation affects adversely an established business enterprise, managerial adaptation to, and legal exploitation of, these aspects of the public policy process can be expected. So it was in the response of Standard Oil and other companies to the Hepburn Act of 1906 as it affected oil pipelines.

MANAGERIAL ALTERNATIVES FOR ADJUSTING TO FEDERAL PIPELINE REGULATION

As the major owner of oil pipelines in the United States in 1906, Standard Oil was confronted with the problem of how to adjust to the pipeline provisions of the Hepburn Act. Several alternative courses of action were available to Standard management in seeking to avoid or minimize the intended effect of the new law. First, since the statute was based on the interstate commerce power, one alternative was to rearrange pipeline operations so that they did not involve interstate commerce. Second, application of the law could be avoided by withdrawing from the pipeline business. Third, formal application of the law might be accepted but compliance structured in ways that negated the statute's practical impact. Fourth, it might be possible to initiate a successful attack on the statute in the courts, or to modify it through inspired congressional action. Fifth, the law could be accepted and complied with fully in terms of its obvious intent. Finally, management could ignore the statute completely and leave the next move up to the government.

The choice between action or inaction with respect to each alternative was partially governed by the historical situation. For example, a refusal to acknowledge that the new law applied to Standard pipelines that had neither exercised the right of eminent domain nor acted as common carriers would presumably provide a sound legal basis on which to build a case in court should the issue be litigated. Where the precedent was less favorable, as in the case of lines that were common carriers under state law, one of the other modes of adaptation enumerated above could perhaps be employed to advantage.

Passive acceptance by Standard's management of a restrictive law and full compliance with it intent, which, as stated in congressional debate, was to open Standard pipelines to outside shippers for common carriage, was unthinkable. Such action would have involved sacrifice of long-held beliefs about the sanctity of private property rights. Also, from a business standpoint it would have constituted voluntary surrender of an important and profitable strategic asset. Therefore, before accepting a statutory declaration that Standard's private lines operate for others as common carriers, Standard's management resolved to exhaust every business and legal stratagem. On the other hand, these executives had sufficient respect for the government's power not to ignore the new statute completely. Accordingly, several varied approaches characterized their initial adaptation to federal regulation of pipelines.

ANTICIPATORY MOVES BY STANDARD OIL

In at least one respect Standard Oil had anticipated the possible legislative consequences of the Garfield report on oil transportation and had taken positive action prior to introduction of the Hepburn Amendment. On November 1, 1905, Standard Oil Company (New Jersey) purchased all segments of New York Transit Company's pipeline system in the state of New Jersey and also National Transit's pipeline properties in New Jersey and Maryland. Both New York Transit and National Transit were affiliates of Jersey Standard and common carriers by law in the states of their incorporation. After the transfer, their former pipelines in New Jersey and Maryland were operated as the private property of Jersey Standard.[1]

As the result of Standard's purchase, the New York Transit Company's line terminated on the New York-New Jersey state line at Unionville, New York; the National Transit Company's pipelines ended at Centerbridge, Pennsylvania, on the New Jersey state line, and at Fawn Grove, Pennsylvania, on the Maryland state line.

The legal concept behind the property transfers appears to have been related to the fact that while New York and Pennsylvania had pipeline common-carrier requirements, New Jersey and Maryland had none. By acquiring the lines in the last two states and operating them as private carriers, Jersey could meet its own transportation needs without opening these lines to competitors. And, in the event interstate oil pipelines should be declared common carriers by federal statute, Jersey's pipelines in New Jersey and

Maryland would presumably be unaffected because of their intrastate nature.[2]

New tariff schedules were adopted for internal use and made effective simultaneously with the transfer of the New Jersey and Maryland pipelines to Jersey Standard. They showed that the Cygnet Division of Standard's Buckeye Pipe Line moved Lima oil through Ohio to the Pennsylvania state line where movement continued via Standard's Northern Pipe Line Company to Olean, New York. From that point New York Transit Company was the carrier to the New Jersey state line. There the oil entered Jersey Standard's newly acquired pipes. Division of rates was on the basis of mileage and the number of stations involved in each segment of the through route.

The National Transit pipeline network carrying Appalachian crude was also affected by the 1905 rearrangement of pipeline ownership. As noted in Chapter 3, such points as Centerbridge, Pennsylvania, on the New Jersey line and Fawn Grove, Pennsylvania, on the Maryland line were listed as destinations in tariffs filed with the ICC,[3] but were useless to outside shippers desiring to move crude oil to the eastern seaboard.

REACTION OF TIDE WATER AND PURE OIL

Standard Oil pipeline officials were not, however, alone in their endeavor to avoid regulation as interstate common carriers of crude oil. The Tide Water Pipe Line Company (Limited), an early pipeline pioneer and competitor of Standard Oil but one in which the combination had acquired an interest,[4] took a somewhat different tactical approach. This company's lines also crossed both the Pennsylvania-New Jersey border and the New York-Pennsylvania border. Until August of 1906, the Tide Water Company had received oil for storage without simultaneously acquiring ownership. Effective August 21, 1906, shortly before the Hepburn Act became operative, the management announced that thereafter the company would receive only oil purchased outright. In other words, it would store and transport only oil that it owned. To the Bureau of Corporations this action appeared "an open defiance of the new act." [5]

The Pure Oil Company, which had been founded and developed by oil-men seeking to counteract Standard's monopolizing methods, particularly through the use of pipelines, also challenged federal pipeline regulation. In the 1890's, Pure Oil had successfully resisted penetration by the dominant concern and had even adopted its Trust form of organization. Subsequently, it had been reorganized in the holding company pattern adopted by Standard Oil. In 1906 Pure Oil had two major pipeline subsidiaries. One was the United States Pipe Line Company, which operated a crude-oil trunk line and a refined oil pipeline from western Pennsylvania to Marcus Hook, near Philadelphia. The other subsidiary was the Producers' and Refiners' Oil Company, which operated a pipeline gathering system in western Pennsylvania, West Virginia, and southeastern Ohio, delivering oil to refineries in the former state and to the United States Pipe Line.[6] The latter company, incorporated in Pennsylvania and employing the right of eminent domain, was admittedly a common carrier prior to 1906. Nevertheless, its officers resisted federal regulation as did those of the Producers' and Refiners' Company, which in building its pipelines had not exercised the right of eminent domain in Pennsylvania nor operated them as common carriers. The Producers' and Refiners' pipeline also insisted on the sale to it of all oil that it received.* [7]

Like Standard's management, the officers of these companies did not propose to change the status of their lines voluntarily. They explained that operation as a private carrier was necessary, at least in part, to avoid any Standard Oil attempt to tie up their lines.[8] However, testimony presented to the Bureau of Corporations by one outside shipper suggested that Pure Oil's methods of pipeline operation were even more arbitrary than those of Standard Oil.[9]

In January 1907 the Pure Oil Pipe Line Company was incorporated under Pennsylvania law. In the succeeding three years it constructed a 243-mile pipeline from the West Virginia oil fields to the tank farm of its parent concern at Marcus Hook, Pennsylvania. Although seemingly subject to pipeline regulation as a common carrier in interstate commerce, this concern apparently joined the other pipeline affiliates of Pure Oil in declining to file tariffs with the ICC.[10]

REACTION TO REGULATION IN THE SOUTHWEST

In the Southwest there was a greater willingness among new, integrated companies to comply with formal ICC requirements for filing tariffs. As noted earlier, both Gulf Oil and the Texas Company filed tariffs for their trunk lines from the Mid-Continent to the Gulf Coast.

Conspicuous exceptions were the National Pipe Line Company, discussed in Chapter 3, and the Uncle Sam Oil Company, a corporation organized in 1905 under the laws of the Territory of Arizona. The latter company owned and operated a pipeline solely for the purpose of carrying crude oil produced from its wells in Oklahoma to its refinery across the state line in Cherryvale, Kansas.[11] In the subsequent controversy over Uncle Sam's refusal to file tariffs with the ICC, this kind of interstate pipeline operation assumed major significance as an exception to the requirements of the federal pipeline statute.

ICC IMPLEMENTATION OF PIPELINE REGULATION

While pipeline managers moved in various ways to avoid the impact of the Hepburn Act on their activities, the Interstate Commerce Commission, the agency charged with implementing the statute, was relatively passive

---

*National Transit owned a minor interest in both the United States and Producers' & Refiners' pipelines. Hidy and Hidy, *Pioneering,* 608.

with respect to its new responsibility. The first and most obvious reason for its lack of initiative was that the pipeline form of transportation was new to the Commission, whose activities since its formation had been concerned with railroads. Before attempting to implement the law with respect to pipelines, therefore, the ICC needed time to familiarize itself with their operations. But time for such inquiries was in short supply because of the dramatic increase in the number of railroad cases demanding attention after passage of the Hepburn Act, as well as the enlarged sphere of jurisdiction and increased responsibilities assigned to the Commission by that legislation.

The basic duties of the Commission had been to act upon complaints from those who considered themselves injured by a carrier's rates, methods, services, or practices. In 1905 a total of only 65 such complaints had been filed, involving preparation of some 2,500 letters and notices. In 1907, however, 415 formal cases and investigations were instituted relating directly to the rates and practices of 2,236 rail carriers. Paperwork connected with them amounted to more than 15,000 letters and notices. Approximately 2,500 answers and other pleadings also had to be filed, docketed, and acknowledged. In addition, 276 hearings were held during 1907 at which more than 35,000 pages of testimony were taken. The Commission estimated that the number of hearings increased by 350 per cent as compared with the years 1905 and 1906, while informal complaints received increased more than 400 per cent compared with the preceding year.[12] And this was only the beginning of an upward trend in the Commission's workload.

As a result of this increase in the Commission's railroad activity, with which an expanded organization and added employees failed to keep pace, pipeline matters were given a low priority. In 1908, for example, when a uniform system of accounts went into effect for rail carriers under the jurisdiction of the ICC, pipelines were not included. Operating accounts for express companies and electric railways received attention before they were required of pipelines. For the underground carriers, this requirement was to take effect January 1, 1911, and, in anticipation of it, a special report form was distributed to elicit information about this unfamiliar kind of transportation.

Meantime, the Mann-Elkins Act of 1910 had further increased the Commission's powers. Among the provisions of this act was one that carriers subject to the law could be required to designate a representative in Washington on whom the Commission would serve notices and processes. This called for designation of pipeline representatives in the Capital. In addition, the Commission was authorized to undertake, on its own initiative, investigations to determine whether rates of regulated carriers were unreasonable or discriminatory or otherwise in violation of the law. The Commission was empowered to suspend proposed advances in rates and to prescribe a maximum rate if it was not satisfied by presentation at open hearings.

Under this new authority, the ICC on June 8, 1911, on its own initiative undertook an investigation of oil pipeline ownership, location, practices, and rates. Companies using pipelines for the interstate transportation of oil were made respondent parties to the order authorizing the inquiry.*

The Commission scheduled hearings in major oil centers. In connection with this inquiry the Houston and Tulsa hearings discussed in Chapter 3 were held in the fall of 1911. Testimony was also taken in Los Angeles and additional hearings were held in New York, January 24–27, 1912.

At this time a jurisdictional question arose. The Commission had ordered some 60 interstate oil pipeline companies to file tariffs, but thirteen of them had declined to comply.† In New York on January 26, 1912, ICC Commissioner Franklin Lane indicated that a question of law was involved and that he proposed to frame a set of questions to put to the full Commission with respect to the carriers who were ignoring the order to file tariffs. The Commission's decision with respect to these questions would determine whether it would assert jurisdiction in these instances. A hearing for this purpose was held in Washington on May 10, 1912.

A number of companies submitted briefs for this occasion. Attorney F. C. Proctor of Gulf Pipe Line in his brief argued that common-carrier status could properly apply only to small, independent lines. Such a finding, of course, would have made a farce of congressional intent in adopting the Hepburn Act. Therefore, Proctor asked that the ICC leave the pipeline situation as it was, or go to Congress for a law more appropriate to proper control of pipelines.[13] The Tide Water Pipe Line brief stressed that the pipeline was an adjunct of the refinery. According to Tide Water's attorneys, to open their line to outsiders would overload it and ruin Tide Water's refinery investment because acquisition of a new right of way through urban territory would be prohibitively expensive.[14] Attorney W. S. Fitzpatrick of Prairie Oil & Gas and attorneys for Jersey Standard and Louisiana Standard repeated now-familiar arguments. Basically, they maintained that private carriers could not be converted into common carriers by statute.[15]

J. J. Hemphill, representing the National Oil and Development Company, and C. E. Chamberlain, representing Pennsylvania Oil Regions pipelines and refineries, argued that the intent of Congress was clear. The statute, they asserted, meant exactly what the statute said: Oil pipelines were to be devoted to public use. As to the devices employed by the various Standard pipelines to prevent such use, Chamberlain declared: "It must appear clear that the result, as shown by the facts in evidence, is the monopolization of the transportation of crude oil by pipe line by the dominant respondents before the Commission, all of whom are inter-related in trans-

*A representative of Prairie Oil & Gas Company later charged that the inquiry was instigated by the National Refining Company. *Oil and Gas Journal* (October 12, 1911), 12.

†The companies were Oklahoma Pipe Line Company, Prairie Oil & Gas Company, Standard Oil Company of Louisiana, Ohio Oil Company, Standard Oil Company of New Jersey, Tidewater Pipe Company, Limited, Producers and Refiners Oil Company, Limited, United States Pipe Line Company, Pure Oil Company, National Pipe Line Company, Uncle Sam Oil Company, and Uncle Sam Oil Company of Kansas.

actions connected with such transportation, if not actually owned by substantially the same stockholders." [16]

The specific question before the Commission, however, was whether 13 pipeline companies should be specifically ordered to file tariffs. Before reaching this decision, the Commission formulated seven questions on the basis of information gained from the country-wide hearings. The questions were all centered around one main point: Did the Commission have jurisdiction over the rates, rules, and practices of the offending pipelines as common carriers?

The first of these questions was whether the Hepburn Act applied to carriers built on privately acquired rights of way and transporting only oil that they owned. In other words, did Congress intend to make common carriers of pipelines that had not sought to be nor acted as common carriers? Looking at the legislative record, the Commission had no trouble in concluding that "Congress intended to convert the interstate oil pipe lines of the country into common carriers." [17] As an administrative body charged with implementing the law, the ICC did not presume to question the constitutionality of what Congress had done. That question was properly one left to the courts to decide.

The next question was whether the segmentation of pipeline ownership into a different corporation in each state through which oil was transported and the transferring of title to that oil to each corporation divested such traffic of its interstate character. This procedure characterized the pipelines owned by Standard Oil interests which extended from Glenn Pool, Oklahoma, to Baton Rouge, Louisiana. Pointing to the fact that transfer of ownership of oil at state lines was a matter of convenience and not part of a *bona fide* transaction, the Commission concluded that these arrangements met neither the provisions of Section 7 of the Act to Regulate Interstate Commerce nor the test applied by the Supreme Court in the *Social Circle* case to determine what constituted intrastate traffic. Therefore, the Commission concluded "that the traffic referred to is not divested of its interstate character by the devices shown in the record." [18]

The third question referred specifically to Prairie Oil & Gas Company operations in Kansas. Did that state's common-carrier pipeline act of 1905 apply to Prairie, which had been incorporated in the state before 1905 and had built its lines on privately acquired property? That is, did the requirements of state law refute Prairie's claim to be a private carrier and provide a basis for federal regulation? The ICC found that this question was irrelevant; federal jurisdiction depended on federal acts. [19]

The next question was whether construction of a pipeline along a common-carrier railroad right of way impressed the same common-carrier requirement on the pipeline. This question applied to Prairie Oil & Gas, to Ohio Oil, and to Jersey Standard lines in New Jersey. The answer, the ICC decided, was again in the negative. "The mere fact that [pipelines] are so built does not impress them with common-carrier obligations . . . Whether a facility is a public facility does not depend on whether it exercises the right of eminent domain. Furthermore, in this question of federal regulation the nature of the title to right of way is not controlling," the Commission said.[20]

Fifth, did pipeline use of a highway acquired for or devoted to public use impress upon the line the obligations of a common carrier? Once more, the question — which had particular relevance to Tide Water Pipe Company and also Prairie Oil — was answered by the ICC in the negative. The ICC found that the usual policy of pipelines was "to deal with the owner of the abutting property in acquiring such highway rights" and "that such abutting owners own also the fee in the highway, and that the public right therein is a mere easement of passage." [21] Hence, in the opinion of the ICC, a pipeline was not imbued with the obligations of a common carrier merely because it had used a public highway for right-of-way purposes.

Next, the Commission raised the question of whether the operations of New York Transit in New Jersey and National Transit in New Jersey and Maryland before 1905 made the pipelines of these concerns common carriers in these two states which had no common-carrier laws. Since the companies in question had been incorporated in states with common-carrier requirements, and prior to November 1905 had carried through shipments to Standard Oil refineries at tidewater, the ICC held that the carriage in New Jersey and in Maryland had been a common-carrier operation. The fact that these pipelines had delivered only to Standard Oil did not change the fact that they had accepted all oil that was offered for transportation and had carried it on a for-hire basis.[22]

The ICC then posed the final question: Did Jersey Standard's acquisition of New York Transit's lines in New Jersey and National Transit's pipelines in New Jersey and Maryland relieve them of common-carrier status as just defined. Again, the answer of the Commission was in the negative. "The facts in this case," the decision read, "show rather an arrangement whereby a common carrier divested itself of its terminals and turned them over to its principal patron for that patron's sole use." [23] Thus, the precautions taken by Jersey pipeline lawyers and managers in anticipation of federal regulation were declared ineffectual by the ICC.

On the basis of these findings, the ICC on June 3, 1912, ordered the 13 recalcitrant pipeline companies to file schedules of rates and charges by the first of the following September. However, this order was still far from fully binding. Recourse to the courts was still available to pipeline lawyers challenging the constitutionality of the pipeline statute and the ICC's interpretation of it.

THE UNITED STATES COMMERCE COURT

The Mann-Elkins Act of 1910 had created a United States Commerce Court to which appeals from the ICC could be directed and their disposition supposedly expedited. This device, favored by President Taft, was intended to remove a heavy load of specialized cases from lower federal courts that were not equipped to handle them. Direct appeals from the new Commerce Court to the Supreme Court were also authorized. But the Commerce Court's handling of such cases, particularly its tendency to retry questions of fact already established by the ICC, led to increasing criticism of its usefulness. As a result of such attacks, the Commerce Court did not remain long in existence after the Democrats took office in 1913. It was to this body, however, that the pipeline companies objecting to the ICC's decision appealed in 1912.

Before the Commerce Court, pipeline lawyers repeated their objections to the pipeline provisions of the Hepburn Act as construed by the ICC. If applied to all interstate oil pipelines, regardless of how built or operated, the law took private property for public use without compensation, the lawyers argued. In their view it was clearly unconstitutional to convert a private carrier which had never offered to carry for shippers other than its owners into one which had to carry for all who requested its services.[24]

Assistant Attorney General Winfred T. Denison, who was in charge of the government's case, did not base his argument on a question of property rights. Rather, he took the position that the regulatory statute was aimed at monopoly. In his words: "The present act is designed to go *beyond* the Sherman Act. The Sherman Act cuts down the full-grown plant. The pipeline amendment pulls up the roots from which it grew. It does not prohibit the private operation of these pipelines because they *are* monopolies, but because such private ownership has proved itself to be the source of monopolies, because it contains an *inevitable tendency* toward monopoly."[25] This was the same line of attack followed in the government's landmark case against the Northern Securities Company in 1904, and in that instance it had resulted in the first great victory in enforcement of the antitrust law against "close" combinations.

The Commerce Court, however, refused to entertain the idea that regulatory methods could be justified as a means to achieve antitrust ends. Presiding Justice Martin Knapp, formerly of the ICC, pointed out that the government had recently won its antitrust case against Standard Oil employing the appropriate means as set forth in law. In his view, regulation was a matter quite separate from antitrust, and attempts to achieve the objectives of the latter through the former were ill-advised. Certainly, Knapp felt, such objectives could not be seriously entertained in construing the meaning and constitutionality of the ICC's action.[26]

The Commerce Court agreed with the ICC's construction of the statute: Congress had intended that it cover all interstate oil pipelines regardless of their previous status. But, where the ICC had been content to ignore the constitutional issue, the Commerce Court seized on it. In Knapp's words, "It seems to us too plain for argument that these private pipe lines cannot be legislated into public facilities, and that the amendment necessarily deprives the owners of such lines of their property rights without just compensation."[27] While Justice Mack concurred in the construction of the statute, he did not concur in its lack of constitutionality. In view of the majority's finding, the court issued an injunction against enforcement of the Commission's order, and the ICC promptly appealed to the Supreme Court.

THE UNITED STATES SUPREME COURT

In the highest court, Solicitor-General John William Davis of the United States presented a brief for the government. He repeated the government's contention made before the Commerce Court that the pipeline amendment was designed to protect producers and independent refiners from duress by pipeline owners and that private operation of interstate pipelines tended to create monopoly. Charles W. Needham for the ICC continued this line of reasoning. He maintained that Congress in legislating with respect to oil pipelines had exercised the police power in a proper and appropriate manner and that "taking" of property contrary to the Fifth Amendment was not involved. Rather, destruction of monopoly was the only "property" at issue.[28]

All the appellees, except for the Uncle Sam Oil Company and, perhaps, technically, Tide Water Pipe, were members of the former Standard Oil combination and still had a close community of interest. John G. Milburn and others representing Ohio Oil, Jersey Standard, and Louisiana Standard objected to the taking of private property; for Jersey Standard Milburn argued that the 1905 acquisition of the New Jersey and Maryland lines had deprived them of whatever common-carrier attributes they might previously have had. As for Louisiana Standard, it was not engaged in interstate pipeline operations.[29]

W. S. Fitzpatrick, counsel for Prairie Oil & Gas, stressed anew the claim that the pipeline law was unconstitutional. He urged that the intent of the statute be determined from its wording — not by reference to the circumstances that had accompanied its adoption. He maintained that any expenditure of capital required to meet provisions of the law but otherwise not required in Prairie's business would be a taking of property in violation of the Fifth Amendment to the Constitution. Attorneys for Tide Water Pipe employed much the same reasoning.[30]

Albert L. Wilson, on behalf of the Uncle Sam Oil Company, presented the most impassioned brief. He maintained that Uncle Sam was involved in moving only its own oil from its own wells to its own refinery. Since it had never offered to carry for others, it was not, Wilson claimed, a common carrier in the common-law sense of the term. Then he declared: "The public highways are for the use of the public. The Uncle Sam Oil Company is a part of the public, and it has as much right to use the public highway to transport its oil in a pipe line as it would have to transport its oil in a wagon drawn by oxen." [31] This type of analogy, whatever its strength or weakness, apparently caught Justice Holmes's attention, for in dealing with the Uncle Sam case he adopted a similar one.

Speaking for a majority of the court in upholding the ICC and reversing the Commerce Court, Holmes was brief. The government's monopoly argument had struck home with him, and it was on this basis that he sustained much of his finding. Thus he declared: "Availing itself of its monopoly of the means of transportation the Standard Oil Company refused through its subordinates to carry any oil unless the same was sold to it or to them and through them to it on terms more or less dictated by itself. In this way it made itself master of the fields without the necessity of owning them and carried across half the continent a great subject of international commerce coming from many owners but, by the duress of which the Standard Oil Company was master, carrying it all as its own." [32] Holmes did not find it difficult to identify the purpose of the act. It was "to bring within its scope pipe lines that although not technically common carriers yet were carrying all oil offered, if only the offerers would sell at their price." [33]

Holmes, however, made an exception for the Uncle Sam Oil Company. He likened its pipeline activities to those of a man drawing water from a well for household use. This was not "transportation" as Holmes saw it. Since Uncle Sam used its pipeline to carry only oil that it had produced itself, transportation was only incidental to the use of the oil made at the end of the carriage. Therefore Uncle Sam was not properly subject to federal regulation.

The constitutional argument was dismissed. There was no question of the taking of property as far as future pipelines were concerned. As for those already in existence and challenging the law, all that was demanded of them was to give up requiring the sale of oil as a condition of carrying it. This, Holmes ruled, was no taking of property in violation of the Fifth Amendment.

Chief Justice White concurred in the majority finding, but based his verdict as to the Uncle Sam case on different grounds. Transportation was involved, he said, and it was interstate in character considering the use of the end-product. But to him the key point was the fact that in serving only is own wells and refinery, the Uncle Sam Oil Company was conducting a genuinely "private business." Therefore, to force compliance with the pipeline amendment would be a clear-cut violation of the Fifth Amendment.[34]

To the lone dissenter, Justice McKenna, these arguments seemed to lack cogency. The *principle* of the majority's decision was objectionable to him. In effect, the majority had adopted the view that pipelines were public markets for oil in the same sense that grain elevators were for that commodity. Thus, they were conveniently clothed with a public interest that justified the application of regulation to them. McKenna objected to the validity of the analogy, claiming that grain elevators, where the principle had been developed, were voluntarily devoted to public use as evidenced by their actions, but the same was not true of oil pipelines.[35]

McKenna concurred in essence with the argument of W. S. Fitzpatrick of Prairie Oil that reliance on the motivation for the pipeline amendment was an inadequate basis for deciding its application. As to the charge that Standard Oil pipelines constituted a monopoly, "The facts of the case do not sustain it except as they exhibit the advantages of the possession of property which others do not possess," McKenna said. "Must it be shared by those others for that reason?" he asked. In his view protection afforded by the Fifth Amendment was clearly violated by such reasoning.[36]

The Uncle Sam case posed a difficult question for McKenna. Again, he felt that the principle underlying the majority's position was weak. Seemingly it was based on the fact that Uncle Sam did not purchase its oil but produced it. Adopting this principle as the basis for determining the applicability of federal regulation, McKenna argued, was a contradiction of the declared intent of the legislation — to create markets for independent producers.[37] Thus, for example, the majority's argument by extension implied that large companies, whose pipelines would presumably be of the most use to producers, could like Uncle Sam secure exemption from common-carrier status by the simple expedient of transporting only the oil that they produced. Such a development would make a mockery of the statute as a buttress to the independent producers' position. Nevertheless, McKenna went along with the majority in exempting Uncle Sam from the operation of the statute.

EVALUATION OF THE PIPE LINE CASES

That the Supreme Court in its decision in The Pipe Line Cases was looking through form to substance was noted both in the majority decision and, with varying degrees of approval, in legal commentary on the case. The *Central Law Journal* in an editorial pointed out: "Though the dissenting justice may pound out his logic, he forgets that the court, when it finds a situation that needs correction for the smooth flow of commerce between the states, will correct it and by some brief 'antithesis of words' like those employed by Mr. Justice Holmes in the majority opinion." [38] The *Harvard Law Review* commented that both in this decision and in a current one on insurance rates, "The right to regulate prices is restored to its place as a branch of the police power of state and nation." Furthermore, "it must be clear that abstract principles of liberty and antiquated economic theories can no longer be invoked to justify the abuse of economic advantage, however honestly it may have been acquired." [39]

In these and other commentaries, lawyers made the point that the Supreme Court, while reacting to public opinion and changing conceptions of property rights, had found it essential to base regulation on the concept of a "public calling." This requirement was met by finding pipelines to be common carriers even though they might not be so in form and possibly not even in fact. While the decision was generally approved, there was also considerable sympathy for McKenna's position that the majority had employed a legal fiction and therefore had entered dangerous ground.[40]

It seems clear that the majority of the Supreme Court justices were looking at the federal pipeline statute in terms of Standard Oil just as the legislators of 1906 had done. Almost all legal commentators made the point that the court was striking at monopoly in its findings in The Pipe Line

Cases. McKenna, however, had raised the question of whether this monopoly in fact existed, and the Commerce Court had based its verdict in part on a finding that regulatory means were not permissible to achieve antitrust ends.

Actually, much had taken place in the oil industry since 1906 that challenged the validity of what the Supreme Court had to say with respect to the pipelines' role in creating and maintaining monopoly. Newcomers had entered and consolidated their position, in many cases integrating pipelines into their operations. Standard Oil had been made the object of successful antitrust actions on both state and federal levels. But, typically, the public policy process lagged behind these developments.

The Commerce Court rendered its decision on March 11, 1913; the Supreme Court handed down its verdict June 22, 1914. A combination of managerial strategy, administrative passivity, and the complications of the legal process had thus allowed eight years to pass between the time the statute applying federal regulation to oil pipelines had been adopted and the time when it received a judicial interpretation from the highest court.

Some points still remained moot. The exception of the Uncle Sam Company from the decision was unanimous. Though Justices McKenna and White arrived at this conclusion by routes somewhat different from their colleagues, it was clear that the Supreme Court would not in all cases support a literal interpretation of the statute's provision that it should apply to "any corporation or any person or persons engaged in the transportation of oil." Relative degrees of corporate power, as well as conditions antecedent to and following the transportation of oil, appear to have been relevant to the adoption of this view, which had its antitrust counterpart in the "Rule of Reason." As a result, the court left considerable room for further interpretation and adaptation by pipeline managers considering the applicability of the federal regulatory statute to their activities.

CHAPTER 6

THE IMPACT OF PUBLIC POLICY
ON STANDARD PIPELINES

The Standard Oil dissolution decree of 1911 and the Supreme Court's decision in The Pipe Line Cases three years later hit directly at the American oil industry's major firm. The antitrust action culminating in 1911 had aimed at restructuring that industry in a more competitive mold; the pipeline section of the 1906 Hepburn Act, upheld by the Supreme Court in 1914, had aimed at making oil pipelines in general — and Standard's in particular — available to nonowners. Inevitably, adjustments had to be made by the managements of these companies to the new circumstances created by public policy at the federal level. This chapter reviews the situation and analyzes the changes made up to early 1915 to meet these requirements.

PIPELINE COMPANIES SEPARATED FROM JERSEY STANDARD IN 1911

The ten individual pipeline companies separated from Jersey Standard in 1911 were National Transit, New York Transit, Buckeye, Indiana, Northern, Crescent, Cumberland, Southern, Eureka, and South-West Pennsylvania pipelines. All were admittedly common carriers. The two oil companies owning extensive interstate pipeline systems that were also divorced from Jersey Standard in 1911 were the Prairie Oil & Gas Company and the Ohio Oil Company. Both of these concerns maintained that their lines were private carriers.

The judicially decreed separation of pipeline and other companies from Jersey Standard did not quickly alter relations that had existed before the antitrust decree. Functionally the concerns were still related to one another much as they had been within the old Standard Oil integrated framework.

This economic relation was re-enforced by ownership. As many observers had predicted, the chief change that took place as the immediate result of the antitrust decision was that stockholders in Jersey Standard now individually held the stock of its disaffiliated elements. A single share of Jersey Standard, for example, entitled its owner to 509,033/983,383 of a share in National Transit, the numerator representing that company's shares and the denominator the total number of Jersey Company shares outstanding. Put another way and using Eureka Pipe Line Company as an example, the 6,078 Jersey shareholders were entitled to .054 shares of Eureka stock for each share of the holding company that they owned. Or, to cite still another example, John D. Rockefeller, as an individual, now held 25 per cent of the stock of the Ohio Oil Company, instead of exercising ownership through the holding company.

Nevertheless, the dissolution also began the gradual process of dispersing ownership of Standard companies among an expanding group of investors. For example, by 1915 John D. Rockefeller had reportedly turned over to the Rockefeller Foundation nearly all his stock in the ten disaffiliated common-carrier pipeline companies.[1]

It had been decided that fractional shares would not be entitled to a vote in any Standard Oil company, so small stockholders in many instances cashed in on a rising market, finding eager buyers among several large brokerage concerns. Securities analysts either through contact with Standard Oil executives or through extensive perusal of the evidence revealed in the trial record, knew that Standard Oil stock had not been increased in proportion to additions of real property.* Standard Oil Company (Indiana), for example, had been capitalized at a mere $1,000,000, but after dissolution this amount was increased to $30,000,000 in keeping with the size of its assets. Thus stockholders in that company received 29 additional shares for each one they had previously held.[2]

Shareholders in the pipeline companies shared to some extent in this windfall. The amount bid per share on March 12, 1912, compared with December 18, 1911, showed a 100 per cent increase for Buckeye Pipe Line Company. Prairie Oil had advanced 45 points, and New York Transit 80. On the other hand, Northern Pipe had declined 35 points, National Transit 70, and Cumberland Pipe 5.[3] Obviously the market was now evaluating the relative worth and prospects of these companies in their new context of operations.

National Transit

National Transit was the oldest of Standard's pipeline companies, having been organized in Pennsylvania in 1881 to take over all the pipelines in the Standard Oil combine at that time. The map of National Transit's pipelines in 1885 shows that Standard Oil, even at that early date, owned an extensive network of pipelines connecting the Oil Regions of the Appalachian field with refineries in Cleveland to the west, Buffalo to the north, the Atlantic Coast on the east, and Baltimore to the south.

This network expanded in succeeding years, and National Transit was

*F. S. Smithers & Co., New York City, told their customers in a letter in September 1913: "We doubt if so vast a corporation has ever existed about which so little was known, and about which so many stockholders were seeking information." Obviously, these analysts had overlooked the extensive government literature on the combination, dating back to the 1880's.

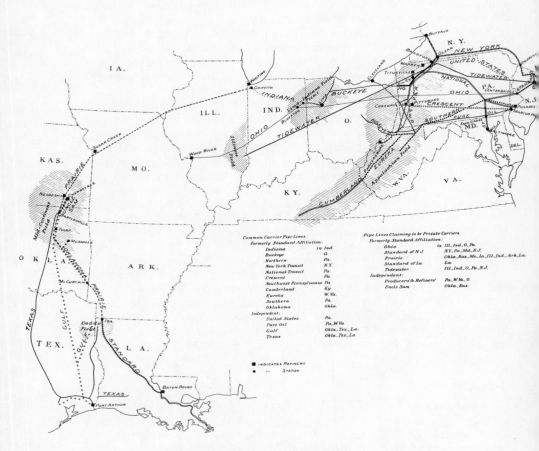

Major trunk pipeline routes, 1910.
Source: The Pipe Line Cases, 234 U.S. 548 (1913), Cases and Points, vol. 34,
facing p. 56.

the nucleus from which many other Standard Oil pipelines grew. Between 1886 and 1890, for example, three new Standard pipeline companies were organized as Pennsylvania corporations under the guidance and with the financial help of National Transit. These were the South-West Pennsylvania Pipe Lines incorporated in 1886, the Northern Pipe Line Company formed in 1889, and the Southern Pipe Line Company organized in 1890. Buckeye and others of the Standard group of pipelines also owed much to National Transit.

As of June 1911, just prior to the dissolution decree, the Standard Oil Company (New Jersey) held 99.9 per cent of the stock of the National Transit Company. The latter's ownership of subsidiaries at that time was as follows:[4]

	Capital stock (in thousands of dollars)	Percentage of stock held by N.T.
Cumberland Pipe Line Co., Inc.	$1,000.0	99.9
Franklin Pipe Co., Ltd.	50.0	39.0
New Domain Oil & Gas Co.	1,000.0	99.9
Prairie Oil & Gas Co.	18,000.0	99.9
Producers' and Refiners' Oil Co., Ltd.	250.0	12.0
United States Pipe Line Co.	1,193.9	3.4

Upon dissolution, stocks of these companies were turned over to the Standard Oil Company (New Jersey) and distributed to the latter's stockholders on a pro rata basis, along with those of National Transit.

National Transit itself was left in a most disadvantageous position as the result of the dissolution. It was confined to the state of Pennsylvania, an area of declining production. The lines of the newly formed Northern Group of pipelines, now under separate management, ran right through its backyard, so to speak; and the vital link between Kane and Colegrove, Pennsylvania, had not been left to it.

Pipeline veterans at Oil City in November 1962 advanced several explanations for this situation. One explanation revolved about the personalities of the two leading families of Standard Oil pipeliners — the Bushnells and the Towls. According to one story, in implementing the dissolution decree National Transit was interposed between the two systems to keep these rival managers apart. Another explanation rests on the fact that National Transit retained the Oil City Pump and Machine Works, which manufactured machinery for all Standard Oil units. Possession of this additional source of revenue, this version of the story goes, was regarded as sufficient justification for leaving National Transit an essentially local, truncated pipeline carrier.

Although National Transit operated an extensive gathering system and provided oil-storage facilities in the western part of Pennsylvania, the bulk of its business came from long-haul traffic. It participated in the movements that supplied Jersey Standard's refineries at Bayonne and Baltimore; Atlantic Refining's plants at Pittsburgh, Franklin, and Point

Breeze, Pennsylvania; and other refineries at Warren and Oil City, Pennsylvania. The story of this business from 1911 to 1915 was one of adjustment and readjustment to the realities of declining Pennsylvania crude-oil production and changing demands for pipeline transportation of Mid-Continent crude to eastern refineries. Revenue from the Pump and Machine Works, which was incorporated as a separate company after the Supreme Court's decision in The Pipe Line Cases, helped cushion the financial impact of such changes.

The Northern and Southern Groups

In handing down its Standard Oil decision in 1911, the Supreme Court had indicated that it would not be contrary to the decree if some of the connecting pipelines separated from the Standard organization were operated as a continuous system. Accordingly, two groups of pipeline companies were formed and became known respectively as "the Northern Group" and "the Southern Group," each of which was united under a single management.

The Northern Group consisted of the New York Transit Company, the Northern Pipe Line Company, the Buckeye Pipe Line Company, and the Indiana Pipe Line Company. Each of the four pipelines in the Northern Group composed a connecting link for the transportation of crude oil across Indiana, Ohio, Pennsylvania, and New York to a connection with Jersey Standard's own pipelines in New Jersey. They also served intermediate points. Through connections with National Transit's lines, oil carried by the Northern Group could also be moved to refineries in Pennsylvania, Maryland, and West Virginia.

The Southern Group was composed of the Eureka, Southern, Cumberland, and South-West Pennsylvania pipelines. These lines connected with each other and with National Transit's system at various Pennsylvania points and with carriers from other states at the Pennsylvania state border.

The selection of Forrest M. Towl,* a long-time Standard pipeliner, as head of the Southern Group of pipelines, chairman of the board and a director of the Eureka Pipe Line Company, and president and a director of the Southern Pipe Line Company, South-West Pennsylvania Pipe Lines, and Cumberland Pipe Line Company was evidence of the group's close link with Jersey. At the same time, Forrest's brother, Allan T. Towl,† was made president and a director of the Eureka Pipe Line Company and vice-president of the South-West Pennsylvania Pipe Lines.

D. S. Bushnell, who had also for many years been engaged in Standard Oil pipeline operations, became president and a director of each of the companies making up the Northern Group of pipelines. The other officers

---

*Forrest Towl was the son of Theodore M. Towl, manager of Jersey Standard's Real Estate and Tax Department.

†Allan T. Towl was a former superintendent of the Northern Division of Prairie Oil & Gas.

of each of the four companies in this group also served in the same official capacity in each company. Bushnell's office continued to be on the same floor at 26 Broadway as it had been before the court had handed down its decision in 1911. To many persons already distrustful of Standard Oil, this was evidence of the ineffectiveness of the dissolution decree.[5] But, of course, pipelines of the Northern and Southern Groups had been built to serve Jersey's needs, and no judicial decree could overnight change their physical orientation or their dependence for business on their former parent.

The most important member of the Northern Group was Buckeye Pipe Line. Following an Ohio state antitrust action against Standard Oil in 1892, Buckeye had acquired three subsidiary companies: the Connecting Pipe Line Company, the Cygnet Pipe Line Company, and the Macksburg Pipe Line Company. Buckeye's capitalization of $10,000,000 [6] at the time of the dissolution dated from this earlier era and was at least double that of any other member of the Northern Group.

The Buckeye trunk-line system consisted of the following elements just after dissolution. A trunk line connected Toledo and Haskins, Ohio, with Lima, Ohio. From there the line went west to a connection with the Indiana Pipe Line at the Ohio-Indiana state line and east through Findlay and Cygnet to Mantua, Ohio. From Mantua a branch supplied Cleveland while the main trunk line divided — one element running east to a connection with the Northern Pipe Line at the Pennsylvania state border and the other southeast to a juncture with the South-West Pennsylvania Pipe Lines, also at the state line. At Lima, Buckeye had steel tankage of 3,500,-000 barrels capacity and at Mantua, 1,500,000 barrels.[7]

Buckeye's gathering operations were performed by two major divisions. The Lima Division covered northwestern Ohio and collected substantially all the oil produced there; the Macksburg Division operated in the eastern, central, southern, and southeastern part of the state. The Cygnet Division was concerned primarily with trunkline operations.*

The preservation of monthly accounts for this era permits us to reconstruct the nature of Buckeye's operations immediately after dissolution. The following information is drawn from one such statement apparently prepared for use at 26 Broadway and relating to the month of January 1912.†

---

*In 1913, Jersey's Canadian affiliate, Imperial Oil Company, Limited, constructed a pipeline from Cygnet to the international boundary near its Sarnia refinery, which thus gained access to crudes from the major American oil fields.

†Like James Donnell of Ohio Oil and other former Standard Oil executives accustomed to secrecy, Buckeye's president, D. S. Bushnell, apparently disliked the idea of publicly accounting for his stewardship, despite the meticulous and detailed manner in which company records were kept. Thus the results of annual operations were announced on small squares of paper which could easily be lost in the pages of a single detailed report of monthly operations, prepared for 26 Broadway. Copies of both monthly statements and annual reports to stockholders were found in the attic of the Adgate Pumping Station, Buckeye Pipe Line Company, Lima, Ohio, in April, 1962.

Buckeye's major revenue came from through pipage accounts with the Ohio Oil Company, National Transit, New York Transit, and Southern Pipe Lines. The total of these accounts for the month stood at $809,631.99. Another $25,000 came from gathering, storage, and miscellaneous activities.

A breakdown of the Lima Division's operations in that month shows that Buckeye was supplying National Transit, as the connecting carrier, with Kansas oil destined for Unionville and Buffalo, New York, and Illinois crude oil consigned to Philadelphia and Centerbridge, Pennsylvania. Southern Pipe Line was also taking Illinois crude from Buckeye for delivery at Philadelphia. Buckeye itself was delivering Illinois crude oil to Lima, while New York Transit was receiving Lima oil for Unionville, New York. In other words, these lines were continuing to serve Jersey's varied refinery needs.

Net Buckeye income for 1912 was $6,000,422.41, or 60 per cent on the $10,000,000 capital stock. Dividends amounting to 40 per cent of the par value of the stock were paid, and the surplus account still stood at $9,775,-302.53, or nearly the amount of the total capital stock. But, like many Standard Oil companies, Buckeye had been undercapitalized. For bookkeeping purposes, plant investment stood at 50 per cent more than authorized capital stock, and the Tax Commission of Ohio placed a value of $35,000,000 on the pipeline's properties in that state during 1912.[8]

In the years following 1912, Buckeye did not approach the financial performance of that year. Although it paid the same dividend in 1913, net income did not cover the distribution. Even the war years failed to push revenues to the earlier level. During the years 1914 and 1915 net profits declined steadily and dividends of 28 per cent in 1914 and 16 per cent in 1915 were partially paid from surplus.[9]

The Cumberland and Crescent Pipelines

As a result of the antitrust decision of 1911, the Cumberland Pipe Line became a junior partner in the Southern Group operating in the Kentucky fields and extending into West Virginia. This concern was regarded as one of the less valuable of the former Standard Oil group, since its lines constituted strictly a gathering system in a large territory that had not up to that time fulfilled its earlier promise as an oil producing area.[10] Oil gathered by the Cumberland Pipe Line Company was carried to Standard Oil refineries via the Eureka and connecting trunk lines. The Crescent Pipe Line Company operating a 250-mile trunk line from Greggs, near Pittsburgh, to Marcus Hook, Pennsylvania, at tidewater functioned as a separate company following the dissolution.

COMMON-CARRIER STATUS OF DISAFFILIATED COMPANIES

All of the pipeline companies just discussed were common carriers under state law and admitted jurisdiction of the ICC. The Buckeye, Eureka,

Indiana, National Transit, Cumberland, and South-West Pennsylvania pipelines had duly filed all tariffs required by the Interstate Commerce law in the month of August, 1906. Although no interstate shipments originated with the Northern, Crescent, New York Transit, and Southern pipeline companies, these four concerns had "respectively filed with the ICC concurrences in the various schedules of rates filed by the companies upon whose lines interstate shipments originated." [11]

The situation was different with Prairie Oil & Gas and Ohio Oil, both of which were also separated from Jersey in 1911. As shown in the preceding chapter, these companies, which engaged in the production, purchase, and storage of crude oil as well as the transportation of it, had resisted federal pipeline regulation until they were left with no alternative by the decision in The Pipe Line Cases.

Prairie Oil & Gas Company

Although incorporated in Kansas, the Prairie Oil & Gas Company had qualified to do business in Missouri, Illinois, Indiana, Oklahoma, and Arkansas. By 1911 it owned and operated the largest pipeline system in the Mid-Continent,[12] with trunk lines extending from the Oklahoma oil fields to Griffith, Indiana, near Chicago.

As was the case with other disaffiliated companies, Prairie stock was distributed on a pro rata basis to individual Jersey stockholders. Total Prairie assets at the time of dissolution were over $65,000,000, and surplus amounted to more than half that amount.[13] As a result, the company was able to pay a $25 per share annual dividend in 1912. However, for reasons to be discussed shortly, the dividend dropped to $6 per share in 1913, and no dividends were paid in 1914 and 1915.[14] During this period $14,000,000 of debt was retired, leaving $4,000,000 of 50-year debentures on the books in 1915.[15]

The president of Prairie Oil & Gas Company, with headquarters in Independence, Kansas, was James E. O'Neil, who had begun his career in the oil business with the Ohio Oil Company in 1890 and joined Prairie in 1905. Other prominent Prairie officials were W. S. Fitzpatrick, a former president of the Kansas State Senate, and T. J. Flannelly, a former district judge in Independence. The public service experience of these executives was not without significance in view of Prairie's past difficulties in the state.

Formally, though not actually, disassociated from the Standard Oil companies, Prairie Oil & Gas made their business its chief concern. Prairie's trunk and gathering facilities exceeded the combined capacity of all other interstate pipelines carrying oil from the Oklahoma fields,[16] and expansion continued. In 1913 an 8-inch trunk-line extension was built a distance of 194.07 miles from Prairie's main line at Carrollton, Missouri, to serve Indiana Standard's refinery at Wood River (E. St. Louis), Illinois. There it also connected with Ohio Oil's Illinois Pipe Line, built in 1907 to serve the Wood River refinery from the eastern part of the state. Together the two lines provided a new route for moving Mid-Continent crude to the Northeast. When Prairie's Wood River branch was opened in 1913 it had a capacity of about 21,000 barrels a day, and, indicative of the mounting flow of Mid-Continent oil northward, this capacity was doubled in the next two years.[17]

The rapid expansion of Prairie's facilities was expensive and accounted for the reduction and then temporary suspension of dividends. During 1913, for example, Prairie Oil & Gas Company expended more than $9,-000,000 as follows: $5,000,000 in pipeline extension; $1,500,000 in acquiring production; $1,000,000 in drilling new wells; $600,000 in rentals and new leases; and $1,080,000 in dividends. With enlarged facilities, the company's pipeline runs showed a gain of 7,850,000 barrels over the previous year, 1912; shipments increased by 1,500,000 barrels, and stocks of oil rose from 38,900,000 barrels at the end of 1912 to 42,900,000 million barrels at the end of 1913.[18]

Besides serving Indiana Standard's Neodesha and Sugar Creek refineries and — for the last two months of the year — the Wood River refinery, Prairie pipelines in 1913 delivered more than 24,000,000 barrels of crude to the Indiana Pipe Line Company at Griffith, Indiana.[19] From there the oil was routed to Indiana Standard's Whiting refinery or eastward via the various routes described in connection with the Northern and Southern Groups of pipelines. The strategic importance of these lines is suggested by the fact that from 1911 through 1914, Mid-Continent crude-oil production marketed east of the Mississippi River rose from about 30 per cent to almost 60 per cent of eastern production.[20]

During this period, Prairie's management fought and lost the battle to avoid federal regulation of its pipelines. Prairie executives therefore decided in the aftermath of The Pipe Line Cases to separate transportation operations from crude-oil production, purchasing, and sales. Accordingly, the Prairie Pipe Line Company was organized on January 14, 1915, to hold and operate all Prairie pipelines and storage facilities. The new company was capitalized at $27,000,000, which was the value of the pipeline properties shown on the books, and stock was distributed pro rata among stockholders of Prairie Oil & Gas Co.* [21] As in other cases of company separation, this procedure initially changed only the form in which stockholders in Prairie Oil & Gas Company held ownership in Prairie's pipelines.[22]

The Ohio Oil Company

The Ohio Oil Company was one of Jersey Standard's oldest producing affiliates, and it too was divorced from its parent by terms of the 1911 antitrust decision. On December 9, 1911, John D. Archbold of Jersey Standard resigned as president of the Ohio Company and was succeeded by James Donnell. Under Donnell and his sons, Ohio Oil was eventually to be trans-

---

*Establishment of a subsidiary company was reportedly blocked by a Kansas law against holding companies. *National Petroleum News* (December 18, 1929), 27.

Table 8. Deliveries of crude oil by pipelines of
Prairie Oil & Gas Company, 1910–1912.

Deliveries to	1910 Barrels	1910 Per cent	1911 Barrels	1911 Per cent	1912 Barrels	1912 Per cent
Standard Oil Co. of Kansas, Neodesha, Kan.	3,996,460.17	12.12	4,033,847.37	12.67	3,145,434.98	8.76
Standard Oil Co. of Indiana, Sugar Creek, Mo.	6,426,036.46	19.49	7,027,930.19	22.08	6,661,946.12	18.54
Standard Oil Co. of Indiana, Whiting, Ind.	10,531,934.12	31.95	10,098,602.10	31.74	11,931,035.45	33.21
Standard Oil Co. of New York, Buffalo, N.Y.	1,137,935.59	3.45	1,120,942.42	3.52	1,157,455.53	3.22
Standard Oil Co. (New Jersey), Unionville Invoiced to P.S. Trainor	2,170,806.45	6.59	694,477.40	2.19	6,154,455.40	17.13
Standard Oil Co. (New Jersey), Centerbridge, Pa. Invoiced to P.S. Trainor	—	—	3,164,252.93	9.94	300,000.00	.84
Standard Oil Co. of Louisiana, Baton Rouge, La. (cars)	2,961,256.65	8.98	414,399.88	1.30	—	—
Standard Oil Co. of Louisiana, Ida, La.	302,049.61	.92	2,298,068.44	7.22	1,703,568.91	4.74
Atlantic Refining Co., Philadelphia, Pa.	2,151,749.43	6.52	2,579,212.99	8.11	2,620,915.72	7.30
Atlantic Refining Co., Marcus Hook, Pa.	2,892,435.50	8.77	—	—	295,995.79	.82
Saddle River Oil Co., Unionville, N.Y.	—	—	1,285.91	.01	1,564,859.70	4.36
Northern Pipe Line Co. (fuel)	—	—	1,896.40	.01	1,256.36	—
National Transit Co. (fuel)	—	—	—	—	—	—
Oklahoma Pipe Line Co. (fuel)	17,976.01	.05	16,622.42	.05	24,085.15	.07
Prairie Oil & Gas Co. (fuel)	313,521.17	.95	330,118.33	1.03	362,393.61	1.01
George Robinson (fuel), Independence, Kan.	—	—	396.28	—	332.76	—
White & Mason (fuel), Independence, Kan.	—	—	—	—	194.51	—
A.B. Reese (fuel), Tulsa, Okla.	—	—	—	—	—	—

(continued on next page)

Table 8—continued.

Deliveries to	1910		1911		1912	
	Barrels	*Per cent*	*Barrels*	*Per cent*	*Barrels*	*Per cent*
Great Western Portland Cement Co., Mildred, Kan.[a]	6,537.88	.02	—	—	—	—
United States Portland Cement Co., Yocemento, Kan.[a]	241.12	—	10,639.16	.03	—	—
Concordia Ice & Cold Storage Co., Hays City, Kan.[a]	—	—	966.40	.01	—	—
Buffalo Brick Co.[a]	725.52	—	4,724.16	.02	—	—
Hays City Milling & Elevator Co., Concordia, Kan.[a]	—	—	723.98	—	—	—
The Topeka Edison Co.[a]	—	—	963.15	.01	—	—
Iola Portland Cement Co., Iola, Kan.[a]	3,443.06	.01	—	—	—	—
New Era Milling Co.[a]	—	—	483.64	—	240.90	—
Goodland Ice & Cold Storage Co., Goodland, Kan.[a]	—	—	723.52	—	—	—
Fire loss	54,618.87	.18	20,445.46	.06	844.30	—
Other losses	—	—	—	—	100.00	—
Total	32,967,727.61	100.00	31,821,722.53	100.00	35,925,115.19	100.00

Source: In Re Conditions Affecting the Production, Transportation, and Marketing of Crude Petroleum, 36 ICC 429 (1915), 482–483.

[a]These shipments moved in tank cars and were invoiced to Standard Oil Company (Indiana).

formed from a domestic producing and pipeline company into a fully integrated international oil concern.

Donnell had come to Ohio after many years in the Pennsylvania oil fields. According to one historian of the company, Donnell "possessed a capacity for a quick assimilation of facts, a keen memory for detail, and a most perceptive mind." He was "an accurate judge of men," and "as an executive, no detail was too minute for his inspection." [23] By this account, "the dissolution had no effect whatsoever on the policies of the Company, for the policies of the past had largely been those of J. C. Donnell." [24]

In 1911, Ohio Oil was the largest corporation operating in the Ohio, Indiana, and Illinois oil fields, where it owned large areas of oil lands. In addition, it had a profitable pipeline system, extending some 900 miles from Casey, Illinois, to Centerbridge on the border between Pennsylvania and New Jersey. All of Ohio Oil's runs were from its own gathering lines, and it had a long trunk-line haul as well. The company's assets were in considerable excess of its capitalization and its current earnings in excess of 100 per cent of capital stock per year.[25]

After the dissolution of 1911, Ohio Oil maintained its reputation as a profitable enterprise. According to the company's report for the year 1913, the profits available for dividends, after allowance of more than $1,000,000 for depreciation on pipeline properties, were equal to 152 per cent on the $15,000,000 capital stock. While the company paid dividends in 1913 amounting to three times those disbursed in 1912, it had earned the 1913 dividends almost three times.

Ohio Oil's management worked hard to secure new production. In 1912–1913 the Ohio Company entered Wyoming, where it had partial success, and Michigan, where up to May 1914 it had found no success.[26] Meantime, the connection of its Wood River line with that of the Prairie Oil & Gas Company from the Mid-Continent gave Ohio Oil a new role in through movements of Mid-Continent crude.

In the wake of The Pipe Line Cases decision, Ohio Oil's management faced the possibility that federal authorities with their newly confirmed power over pipelines might gain access to the company itself. Also, it appeared that if the pipelines remained in the company, it would be subject to an Ohio common-carrier tax with a higher rate than other corporation taxes. Therefore, the management, like Prairie Oil & Gas Company's, decided to segregate pipeline activities in a separate company. On January 1, 1915, they assigned over 1,800 miles of trunk line, plus gathering and storage facilities in three states, to the newly organized Illinois Pipe Line Company, whose stock was then distributed to Ohio Oil's owners on the basis of one share of pipeline stock for each three shares of oil company stock held. Although Illinois Pipe was thenceforth a separate entity, in fact it continued to serve Ohio Oil's needs exclusively.[27]

JERSEY STANDARD PIPELINES AFTER DISSOLUTION

Despite the dissolution decree, Jersey Standard remained a very large company — second in size only to the United States Steel Corporation — and Jersey also continued in the pipeline business. As a result, Jersey Standard's net pipeline earnings in 1912 were over $1,000,000, and in following years they continued to increase.[28] Nevertheless, Jersey was still heavily dependent on its former pipeline affiliates for crude-oil transportation, just as they relied on it for patronage.

Jersey Standard's great network of crude-oil pipelines had grown by 1908 to 9,389 miles of trunk and 45,228 miles of gathering lines, and substantial additions had been made to both by 1911.[29] This carefully integrated system of pipes connected nearly all the major producing fields of the United States with Jersey's large refineries in the Northeast. As pointed out in the foregoing section, many of Jersey's disaffiliated pipelines had played an important role in the movement of crude oil from West to East, and from the southern Appalachian region to Pennsylvania and New York. But while centralized corporate ownership and control by Jersey Standard over its disaffiliated pipelines was forbidden according to the dissolution decree, the continued functioning of these lines as separate corporate entities, and their business dealings with each other and with the pipelines retained by Jersey Standard, was permissible. Hence, within a relatively short period of time, new contracts were drawn up between Jersey Standard and its disaffiliated pipelines and the flow of oil from fields to refineries continued in much the same way as it had before 1911.[30]

Under the 1911 decree, Jersey Standard was permitted to retain a significant number of pipelines. These included the pipelines serving Jersey's various refineries in the state of New Jersey plus those of the Oklahoma Pipe Line Company, the Tuscarora Oil Company, Ltd., and Louisiana Standard, plus a share of ownership in the Tide Water Pipe Company, Ltd.

The Oklahoma Pipe Line Company, as explained in an earlier chapter, was organized by Jersey Standard in 1909 to carry crude oil from Glenn Pool and surrounding oil fields in Oklahoma to the refinery of Louisiana Standard at Baton Rouge. This was accomplished via a connecting line across Arkansas owned by the Prairie Oil & Gas Company and by lines of the Louisiana Company in that state. Following The Pipe Line Cases decision, to which all three companies were parties, tariffs were filed with the ICC on this traffic.[31]

The Tuscarora Oil Company, Ltd., had been formed in Pennsylvania in 1910 as a limited partnership to take over the A. C. Bedford Pipe Line, then under lease to the Ohio Oil Company. The Bedford line had been built in 1907 to supply Jersey's large new refinery at Bayway with crude oil, and it extended from a connection with Ohio Oil's trunk line at Negley, Ohio, 309 miles to Centerbridge, Pennsylvania.

At Centerbridge and at Saddle River, near the New York-New Jersey boundary, Jersey Standard had access to a vast network of pipes transporting crude oil from oil fields in Oklahoma, Kansas, Illinois, Indiana, and Ohio. From Saddle River, Jersey had three pipelines of its own carrying crude oil to Bayonne. The company also owned and operated three lines with 48,500 barrels-per-day capacity stretching from Centerbridge across New Jersey to the Bayway refinery. One of the latter continued to Bayonne and the Eagle Works at Jersey City. The Jersey Company also owned and operated eight inter-refinery pipelines between Bayonne and Bayway, as well as two lines between Bayonne and the Eagle Works.[32]

Louisiana Standard, also retained by Jersey after the dissolution, was a fully integrated operation. This meant that Jersey retained control of an important and expanding company with a significant pipeline investment. Louisiana Standard had been a party to The Pipe Line Cases and had concurred in a tariff filed by Oklahoma Pipe Line Company with the ICC in 1914 on movements from Oklahoma to Baton Rouge,[33] but the Louisiana Company itself filed neither pipeline tariffs nor reports with the federal body prior to 1921.[34] Although some thought was given to making the Pipe Line Department of the company a separate concern, it would have involved amending Louisiana Standard's charter under a new incorporation law which might be interpreted adversely to the parent company. Therefore, Louisiana's pipeline activities were left in the integrated company during this period.[35]

Following the 1914 decision on The Pipe Line Cases, Jersey divested itself of all crude-oil pipelines that it had held directly. In July 1915, it sold the Centerbridge-Bayonne line to its affiliate Tuscarora and the Unionville-Bayonne line to New York Transit, a member of the Northern Group. The line from Fawn Grove, Pennsylvania, to Baltimore was sold to National Transit, which assigned this property to the Maryland Pipe Line Company, a subsidiary organized for this purpose.[36]

Since 1905 when Jersey had taken over these lines in anticipation of federal regulation of pipelines, it had operated them as private carriers; in The Pipe Line Cases the United States Supreme Court, upholding the ICC, had ruled that they were common carriers. Therefore Jersey took itself formally, though not actually, out of the crude-oil pipeline business. Following these moves of mid-1915, the company's Legal Department informed the Federal Trade Commission that Jersey had severed itself "completely from the business of transporting crude petroleum by pipe line in which, indeed, it had never voluntarily engaged." [37] In fact, through its subsidiaries, Jersey was still very much engaged in pipeline transportation. As historians of the company have pointed out, "Far from having severed itself from the pipeline business, Jersey management had worked out a system of central planning which actually was superior, in point of effective control, to that which characterized producing operations of the day." [38]

During this era Jersey's transportation picture was slowly but surely changing not only in response to public policy decisions but also in the light of new economic considerations. Although Jersey Standard had been a pioneer in supplying East Coast refineries with Mid-Continent crude via pipeline, companies like Gulf, Sun, and Texas had from the first adopted pipeline transportation to the Gulf and water carriage from there to the Philadelphia-New York area. By 1914 Jersey was taking a fresh look at this approach. The dissolution of 1911 had not only separated from Jersey key pipeline companies providing a through route from the Mid-Continent but had also deprived it of an American-flag tanker fleet, which had been controlled by New York Standard. The outbreak of war in Europe in August 1914 led Jersey to transfer to the American flag tankers previously belonging to its German affiliate, and this decision opened the way for their use in intercoastal trade from the Gulf. Also, to meet its expanding requirements, Jersey was building new tankers in American yards.[39] These developments, supplemented by the ICC's newly confirmed authority over interstate pipeline rates, put pressure on the disaffiliated Standard pipelines forming the through route from the Mid-Continent to Jersey's East Coast refineries to re-examine their tariffs on this traffic.

The impact of the new situation was felt most by National Transit, since a major part of its revenue came from participation in through movements of Mid-Continent oil. As a result, it announced reductions on such movements, reportedly amounting to as much as 50 per cent of existing rates, effective August 15, 1914.[40] Although, as the company later reported, competition with water transportation may have been the principal cause for the reduction of rates, the fact that they were not filed until after The Pipe Line Cases were decided is also probably not without significance. If the move was made necessary by increased competition, it was equally desirable from the standpoint of discouraging active ICC interest in pipeline rates.

Although Prairie was not as dependent as National Transit on through traffic to the East Coast, it participated in the rate reduction on this traffic. Under the tariff filed by Prairie after The Pipe Line Cases, the charge for moving a barrel of crude the entire distance from Bartlesville, Oklahoma, to Bayonne, Bayway, Brooklyn, and other eastern seaboard refineries was a flat 70 cents. This contrasted with a 1913 tariff in which the charge for moving a barrel of crude just from Griffith, Indiana, the end of Prairie's Mid-Continent line, to the New Jersey border, had been 67 cents. In other words, the new tariff added about 700 miles of transportation at an additional cost to the shipper of only 3 cents. Since Prairie's gathering charge was 12 cents a barrel, Oklahoma oil worth 75 cents at the well could now be laid down on the East Coast via pipeline for a total of $1.57 a barrel.[41] Even at the reduced rate, however, the transportation charge obviously bulked large.

Because of its strategic location and possession of the Arkansas link in the pipeline route from Oklahoma to Baton Rouge, Prairie was in a position to share in the proceeds of increased crude-oil shipments from the Mid-Continent destined for water transportation to the East Coast. Although earlier the Oklahoma and Arkansas portion of this line had not been used to capacity,[42] Prairie Pipe was reported early in 1915 as co-operating to increase capacity by about 10,000 barrels per day.[43] The tariff on Oklahoma shipments to the Gulf by this route was 37.5 cents a barrel, with an additional 2.5 cents for loading at the destination. This charge, plus water transportation to the East Coast, came to about 70 cents a barrel,[44] or the same as the all-pipe charge. But the significant fact was that tanker rates were now beginning to set the pace in the competition for Jersey's business between the two forms of transportation.

Railroad tank car shipments of crude were sometimes used by refiners for special purposes, but, unlike water carriers, they posed no threat to trunk pipelines. The rail rate from the Cushing, Oklahoma, field to Bayonne, New Jersey, in 1915, for example, was double that of the pipelines.[45]

The repercussions of competition from water transportation were apparently reflected in the reduction of a number of pipeline rates. In 1914 Oklahoma Pipe Line cut its rate on shipments to Prairie for northward movement from 20 cents to 12 cents a barrel.[46] Since crude from the Southwest met that from other areas on the eastern seaboard, pipelines serving these territories were also forced to reduce rates. Eureka Pipe Line cut its rate on through shipments from West Virginia to Baltimore, Philadelphia, and New York, and Buckeye did the same on movements from Lima to the seaboard.[47] A desire to avoid ICC scrutiny may have contributed to these rate reductions, but it seems more likely that increased competition between different crude-producing areas and forms of transportation caused pipelines seeking Jersey's continued patronage to initiate or imitate the moves just described.

By mid-1915 the first phase of adaptation to the federal pipeline regulatory statute had been completed by the managements of Jersey Standard's pipelines and those of disaffiliated companies. Although ties of common ownership and functional interdependence continued to exist between Jersey and its disaffiliated pipeline companies, they were not so strong as they had been prior to 1911. Jersey was therefore more free to consider new ways of moving Mid-Continent crude to the East Coast. By the latter half of 1914 the mere existence of this possibility began to exert a downward pressure on pipeline rates of disaffiliated pipeline companies. Presumably, though this cannot be documented, the newly confirmed authority of the ICC to regulate these rates provided an additional incentive to lower them. This still did not mean that rates were unremunerative or that patronage of independent operators was solicited, but the changes were indicative of more to come in the future.

The most immediate impact of The Pipe Line Cases was a further reorganization of pipeline activities by companies in the Standard group (or tied to it) which also engaged in other phases of the oil business. Ohio Oil and Prairie, fearing that the 1914 Supreme Court decision on pipelines presaged further governmental intervention in their business, segregated their pipelines in newly incorporated companies. National Transit incorporated its Pump and Machine Works as a separate entity. Jersey rid itself of all crude lines under its direct ownership. Thus, although the evolution of federal public policy with respect to pipelines between 1906 and 1915 had been slow, both directly and indirectly it had contributed to, where it had not required, changes which significantly lessened Jersey's direct control of the bulk of the nation's pipeline mileage. The exercise of federal authority was now clearly a consideration in the organization and management of these pipelines. However, the managements of these companies appear to have initially exaggerated the threat that it posed.

CHAPTER 7

STATE REGULATION IN THE SOUTHWEST

Federal pipeline legislation, triggered by developments in Kansas in 1905, had been largely the product of intra-industry conflict there and in the Appalachian field, with Standard Oil as a prime target of complaints. The pattern of governmental action established in these oil-producing areas was repeated and elaborated in the Southwest, but this time it also involved new companies expanding to challenge Standard Oil. Again producer discontent and state legislation were involved, and again the reverberations were heard in Washington, where federal jurisdiction over pipelines was then being reviewed. Out of these encounters came important new state statutes affecting pipeline ownership and operation.

THE EXPANDING MID-CONTINENT OIL FIELD

In November 1912, W. S. Fitzpatrick of Prairie Oil & Gas Company had a long talk with President William Howard Taft. In arguing that his company should not properly be considered a common carrier, Fitzpatrick pointed to the rapid growth of competition in the Mid-Continent field. As he recalled the conversation, he had said: "The best evidence in the world that our business was not creating a monopoly in the Mid-Continent field was that the other two pipe lines [Texas and Gulf] had built into the field since we came, and that more than twenty-five independent refineries were operating in or near to the field, all of which had been built since our pipe lines were established and put in operation; that they were getting all the oil they needed and all claimed to be prosperous; that most of them showed prosperity by continued enlargement of their plants in the field of their activities." [1]

Underlying this proliferation of new oil companies and pipelines in the Mid-Continent area was the finding of new oil fields. In fact, these discoveries led to repeated changes in the official designation of the Mid-Continent field by the United States government. In 1906, the United States Geological Survey had described it as embracing western Missouri, the state of Kansas, and Oklahoma and Indian Territories. [2] In the following year, Missouri was dropped and the field was designated as southeastern Kansas, the newly incorporated state of Oklahoma, and northern Texas. [3] The development of the Caddo field in Louisiana resulted in the addition of the northern part of that state by 1911, and by 1915 the Mid-Continent field was described as embracing Kansas, Oklahoma, the northern and central parts of Texas, and northern Louisiana.[4]

Discovery and rapid exploitation of a number of outstanding fields characterized this era. In northern Texas, for example, the Electra field began production in 1911, and in 1959 it had an all-time rank of fifty-fifth among the 120 greatest American oil fields.[5] Burkburnett, another, even larger, flush field came in north of Electra in 1913. It ranked fifty-second in the 1959 review of all-time great American oil fields.[6] Beginning in 1914, the Cushing field, 40 miles from Tulsa, Oklahoma, in unpromising farm territory which the government had allotted to Creek Indians, provided a high-quality crude in great volume. Still another great field of the period was located at Healdton in southern Oklahoma, where easy, low-cost drilling gave Healdton its reputation as "the poor man's pool."

As a result of these discoveries, the Mid-Continent field provided nearly 37 per cent of the total marketed crude-oil production in the United States in 1914.[7] The new fields also gave birth or brought maturity to wholly or partially integrated oil concerns. New conflicts with producers followed in the wake of these developments.

PRODUCERS' COMPLAINTS AND PROPOSED REMEDIES

In an era of uncontrolled production, the competitive rush to find and develop new sources of crude oil resulted in periodic gluts that sent the price of oil skidding downwards. Inability to stay drills or to maintain a united front against crude-oil purchasers led producers to turn to government, state and federal, as a source of countervailing power. It had been this way in the Appalachian field, and it was so in the new fields of the Southwest.

At the heart of the producer-purchaser controversies was the desire of each side to make the best bargain possible. Crude-oil purchasing in the Mid-Continent and Texas fields was done on the basis of a posted price and long- or short-term contracts. The movement of the posted price seemed to many producers to be determined by the power of key purchasing companies rather than by the value of the producer's oil or the operation of market forces. Depending on the relation of contract to posted prices over time, therefore, contract sales might prove the more advantageous to the producer. If not, the producer who chose this path to profit added to his stock of grievances against large crude-oil purchasers, who were typically involved in the pipeline business directly or indirectly.

The prices offered in the field by integrated companies were frequently associated by dissatisfied operators with the pipeline power of these concerns. Pipelines carried away the producer's oil, but — according to the dissatisfied producer — on terms dictated by the pipelines' owners. Despite the dissolution of 1911, the Standard group of companies was widely believed to be still following a coordinated policy of crude-oil purchasing that exploited the producer, and new integrated companies were accused of following this example.

The rebuttal to such charges by the leading crude-oil purchasers presented the other side of the coin. By extending pipelines to new production, the integrated company brought a market to the producer at no cost to him. Since the rapid exhaustion of any given field was always a real possibility, the pipeline company in extending its facilites was assuming a financial risk that the producer neither wanted nor could afford to assume. Furthermore, the state of mutual dependence established by a pipeline connection was a protection to the producer if production declined. In this explanation, prices were based on supply, demand, and competition — not on arbitrary decisions and collaboration or conspiracy among purchasers. Crudes of any given field had to compete with one another and with others from different locations on the basis of quality and distance from the refineries that gave crude oil its real value. Mere access to a trunk pipeline was, in this view, no solution to the producer's problem since he had to have a customer at the other end. If he could find such customers, there was nothing to prevent him from building his own pipelines.

Producers who rejected such arguments sought three avenues of relief through governmental action. First, they advocated the desirability of forcing pipelines to behave as true common carriers by separating the business of transportation from that of production. Failing that, producers wanted pipeline rates and regulations revised to the extent that outside shippers could utilize the pipelines of integrated concerns at or near the cost to those companies. Finally, they demanded that pipeline companies and their purchasing affiliates be required to purchase and move oil on an equitable basis — that is, producers wanted to prevent integrated concerns from favoring their own production.

In the new oil-producing states of the Southwest, oil producers had sufficient political power in the first two decades of this century to achieve some statutory or constitutional recognition of their various claims. When distress in the oil fields became sufficiently acute, and the national mood seemed propitious, producers also made an effort to move these issues into the congressional arena. Events in Oklahoma and Texas contemporaneous with the evolution of federal policy respecting oil pipelines illustrate the development of a second, and in many respects a more immediate, level of governmental restraint on the freedom of decision-making by pipeline owners and managers.

OKLAHOMA COMMON-CARRIER AND COMMON-PURCHASER LAWS

Since Oklahoma was an oil-producing area before it became a state in 1907, the new Oklahoma constitution made specific reference to oil pipelines. Article 9 of the constitution authorized "reasonable control and regulation" of oil pipelines by the state's Corporation Commission.

In 1909 the legislature, acting in response to producers' charges of discrimination by pipeline companies in running crude from Glenn Pool, supplemented the constitutional provisions with new legislation. The first of these measures defined a pipeline common carrier as one engaged in the business of carrying petroleum or crude oil for hire, or otherwise.[8] The right of eminent domain accompanied common-carrier status. Such a carrier was also designated a common purchaser by another statute adopted at the same time[9] — that is, the individuals or corporations involved were required to purchase and transport all petroleum offered in their vicinity and, if this was impossible, to purchase and to allocate space ratably (in proportion to daily production) without favoring their own production in the process. This requirement meant that connecting a field by pipeline to serve the owner's own production automatically required him to purchase oil produced by others. Discrimination as to purchase, carriage, transportation, storage, or delivery was expressly forbidden. There was also a specific provision in the statute that upon proper showing that they were not devoted to public purposes, persons, firms, associations, and corporations could obtain an exemption from public regulation.[10]

Some troublesome questions arose in connection with these laws. Although pipeline companies organized as such in Oklahoma were required to be common carriers, it was not clear whether this requirement applied to a situation where the ownership of pipelines was an adjunct to refining and not a business in itself. For example, if a refining company operating pipelines accommodated an adjoining refiner by transporting crude oil in pipeline space that would otherwise have been empty, did it thereby incur common-carrier obligations?

The proposition that it was possible to own a pipeline and carry for others without thereby becoming a common carrier under Oklahoma law received a judicial test when the Pierce Oil Corporation in March 1918 notified the Phoenix Refining Company that it would no longer carry the latter's oil. The Pierce Company, a Virginia corporation, had entered Oklahoma in 1913 and had obtained a certificate from the Corporation Commission exempting it from regulation in connection with a 33-mile pipeline that Pierce constructed between the prolific Cushing field and the Pierce refinery at Sand Springs, Oklahoma. Apparently having excess capacity in this line, Pierce carried under contract for Phoenix, which also had a refinery at Sand Springs. This arrangement, begun in 1915, was the one terminated in 1918. Meantime, Pierce had seemingly also carried for other parties.

The Phoenix company appealed to the Corporation Commission for relief, and the Commission found that Pierce was a common carrier within the meaning of Oklahoma law. Pierce, which maintained that its pipeline had carried for others only as an accommodation, was ordered to resume service to Phoenix. This order was appealed to the Oklahoma Supreme Court, which sustained the Commission, and then to the United States Supreme Court. The latter tribunal upheld the Oklahoma decision and pointed out that Pierce, as a foreign corporation, had accepted Oklahoma's constitution and laws when commencing operations in the Sooner State. Its exemption from regulation had been based on an ex parte showing, which did not stand in the way of the Commission's order. The defendant's claim that the order violated the Fifth and Fourteenth Amendments to the United States Constitution was dismissed as invalid.[11]

Seemingly this was a victory for the Oklahoma statute impressing common-carrier status on oil pipelines in that state, but whether the decision had any practical impact is not so clear. For example, the Corporation Commission's order to Pierce did not specify any rate at which the Phoenix business had to be done. Managers of many other pipelines had found that rates and regulations could be used to keep unwanted business off their lines while they still complied with the letter of the law. Acceptance, or imposition, of common-carrier status on a pipeline, whether by state or federal authority, did not necessarily open it to outside use.

OKLAHOMA PRODUCERS, PIPELINES, AND PUBLIC POLICY

Inevitably pipelines became involved in the problems arising from flush production in Oklahoma fields and resulting efforts to deal with them by state action. As the nation's leading oil-producing state, Oklahoma witnessed one clash after another between crude-oil producers and purchasers in the years just preceding and following the outbreak of the European War in 1914. The Healdton field in Carter County, not far from Ardmore in southern Oklahoma, provides a particularly good example of the resulting interaction between producers, pipeline management, and public officials.

At Healdton, wells producing as much as 4,000 barrels a day could be drilled for as little as $4,000,[12] but the field lacked outlets for the resulting flood of oil, which overflowed even hastily erected earthen reservoirs. Railroad connections with Ardmore provided limited relief, but there was a pressing need for the large-volume, continuous-flow capabilities of pipeline transportation.

One of the concerns most interested in the royalty and lease trading at Healdton was the Magnolia Petroleum Company. Magnolia embraced properties formerly belonging to the Corsicana Refining Company and Security Oil Company and was tied to Standard Oil, though indirectly. As a result of Texas antitrust action, this arrangement was terminated in 1913 and the controlling shares placed into the hands of a nonvoting trustee appointed by the state.*

At the time the Magnolia Petroleum Company was organized in 1911, it owned gathering lines in north Texas but transported crude oil from that area to its Corsicana and Beaumont refineries by railroad tank car. During 1911 and 1912, however, gathering lines and storage facilities

---

*Henry C. Folger and John D. Archbold, Standard Oil executives, held 88 per cent of Magnolia's stock in 1913. It was this stock that was put in trust. In 1917, New York Standard purchased the shares. Williamson, Andreano, et al., *Age of Energy*, 103.

were constructed in the Electra and Burkburnett pools of Texas, and in the latter year an 8-inch trunk line was begun from Electra to Beaumont via Corsicana and Fort Worth.[13]

If Magnolia could purchase Healdton oil on a basis that made it competitive with the output of other fields, the proximity of the new Electra-Beaumont trunk line some 40 airline miles away made it feasible to pipe Healdton crude southward. Accordingly, while representatives of the affiliated Corsicana Petroleum Company sought to buy producing property, D. C. Stewart, manager of Magnolia's pipeline department and a former Prairie Oil and Oklahoma Pipe Line pipeliner, stated that his company would take all high-grade Healdton oil offered at $1.03 a barrel, the prevailing Mid-Continent price. Pending completion of a branch line from the Healdton field to a connection with Magnolia's Electra-Beaumont trunk line Stewart furnished producers with steel tankage.[14]

The Magnolia Pipe Line Company, incorporated in Oklahoma in December 1913, was formed by the stockholders of the Magnolia Petroleum Company, a Texas joint-stock association, to enable the latter company to tap the Healdton field. Under Oklahoma law, of course, the new concern was a common carrier and subject to the common-purchaser requirement. The pipeline company first constructed a gathering system, working tanks, and a pump station at Healdton. It then built a 6–8-inch trunk line southward from Healdton to Mud Creek, Waurika, and the Red River. Meanwhile, the Magnolia Petroleum Company pushed a 41-mile, 8-inch trunk line from Alvord, Texas north to the Red River, where it was to connect with the Oklahoma line.[15]

Magnolia Pipe Line began to take crude oil from Healdton producers in January 1914, and the trunk line to Fort Worth was opened in March. In accordance with an agreement between the two Magnolia concerns, if the refineries of the Magnolia Petroleum Company could not realize a satisfactory profit on crude handled at the current price, there was to be a settlement with Magnolia Pipe Line on mutually satisfactory terms. More important, for the time being, Magnolia had a virtual monopoly of both crude-oil gathering in, and trunk pipeline transportation from, the Healdton, Oklahoma, field.[16]

The conflict that soon developed with producers was reminiscent of the days when Prairie Oil had dominated the early Kansas oil fields. On a quick and early judgment that Healdton oil would be of comparable quality to that from Cushing and other high-grade fields, Magnolia had made its offer to pay $1.03 a barrel. By the time the trunk line was in operation, however, it was apparent to Magnolia's management that the gravity of much of the Healdton oil was of a quality below 32° Baumé. Accordingly, Magnolia Pipe Line announced on March 2, 1914, that thenceforth it would pay only 70 cents a barrel for Healdton crude under 32° Baumé but it would match the prevailing Mid-Continent price for crude of higher test by paying $1.05 a barrel.[17]

To Healdton producers this announcement seemed to represent a clear

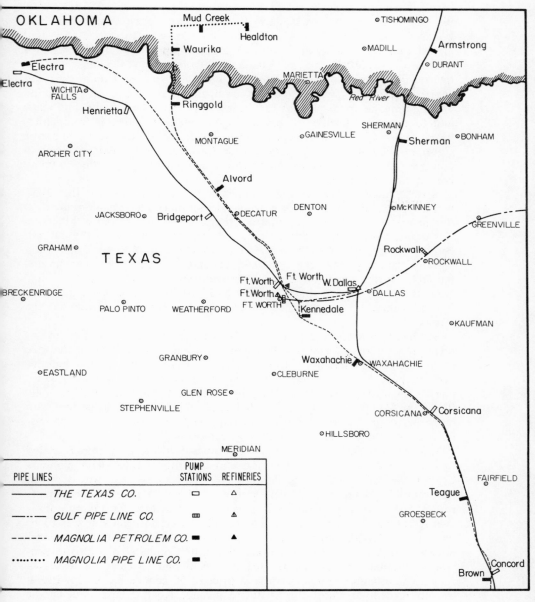

Pipeline route from Healdton, Oklahoma, to Texas, 1914.
Source: Federal Trade Commission, *Report on Pipe-line Transportation* (Washington, 1916), inside back cover.

revocation of Magnolia's earlier offer to buy all oil offered at $1.03 a barrel. The change was a particularly hard blow to producers who had paid bonuses of as much as $1,000 an acre for their leases in the expectation that "the flat basis of buying oil would continuously obtain." [18] Therefore, they organized, protested to the Oklahoma Corporation Commission, requested an investigation by the federal Department of Commerce, and shortly petitioned Congress to forbid pipelines to engage in production and refining, to force an end to alleged discriminations in pipeline runs, and to exercise effective supervision over interstate pipeline companies. These actions, it so happened, coincided with the United States Supreme Court's deliberations on The Pipe Line Cases and presumably helped to create a public sympathy for producers in comparison to pipelines fighting common-carrier status.

Several inconclusive hearings were held by an inspector for the Oklahoma Corporation Commission while Healdton production continued to mount and Magnolia cut its offering price. By April 20, 1914, Magnolia was offering producers a flat 50 cents a barrel for their oil. In the interim, company representatives had explained to the Corporation Commission and to producers that they planned to make special arrangements for refining, storing, and increasing the transportation of Healdton oil.[19] Nevertheless, it seemed that Magnolia had initially miscalculated the quality and volume of Healdton crude and did not intend to compound the mistake.

Producers next turned to the state's Attorney General for aid, just as their predecessors in Pennsylvania and Ohio had done earlier in the face of Standard Oil pressure. Attorney General Charles West, who had his eye on the Governor's chair, had already launched the so-called "sandbag" cases against the Texas Company,* Prairie Oil & Gas, and Magnolia Pipe Line Company for alleged violation of Oklahoma's antitrust law.[20] In response to producers' demands, he requested the Corporation Commission to take action against purchasing companies.[21]

Since the common-purchaser law had not solved the problem associated with overproduction in the Cushing and Healdton fields, the Oklahoma Corporation Commission put its authority behind new measures of relief. Its order 814, dated May 7, 1914, required Magnolia Pipe Line Company to take the following action: Before May 12 it was to begin taking a daily average of 8,000 barrels of Healdton crude a day; this amount was to be increased to 12,000 barrels on or before July 1, 1914, and was to be continued until April 1, 1915. Magnolia Pipe Line Company was also to provide additional tankage in the Healdton field and to clear all leases of accumulated, merchantable crude at a price of 50 cents a barrel. Finally, it was to provide facilities for loading Chicago, Rock Island and Pacific Railroad tank cars at or near Addington (subsequently changed to the

*Oklahoma law forbade a company to own another in the same line of business. Such a relationship, West claimed, existed between the Texas Company and the Producers' Oil Company. *Oildom* (July 1914), 32.

Waurika pump station) and to provide reasonable rates to producers offering oil for transportation in carload lots.[22] A less comprehensive order of the same date governed the Cushing field,[23] where similar producer unrest existed. For the first time in the history of pipelining, governmental authority had sought to regulate directly the conditions of doing business on a day-to-day basis.

Meantime, the whole matter of Oklahoma crude oil prices and pipelines had been thrown into the congressional arena, where there was evidence of growing discontent with the oil industry in general and pipelines in particular. For example, a year earlier in June 1913, the legislature of Minnesota had petitioned Congress to enact a law providing for government ownership and control of "oil-producing industries sufficient to control prices." [24] On May 13, 1914, Senator Robert L. Owen of Oklahoma, who a year before had asked for a federal investigation of the price of Oklahoma oil,[25] introduced a bill calling for government ownership and operation of trunk pipelines, pumping stations, and terminal facilities.[26] Two days later he asked President Woodrow Wilson to include pipelines in the antitrust legislation then pending.[27] Oklahoma's other Senator, Thomas P. Gore, introduced a bill to regulate transportation of oil by pipeline,[28] and a companion measure was offered to the House of Representatives on May 15, 1914, by Representative James S. Davenport of Oklahoma.[29]

Prominent among the producers behind this flurry of pipeline bills in Congress was Wirt Franklin, an Oklahoma producer who was a key figure in the newly organized Ardmore Producers' Association. Franklin had helped to work out the compromise represented by the Oklahoma Corporation Commission's order of May 7, and he was appointed a field umpire to supervise its implementation.[30]

As president of the producers' association, which was then only two months old, Franklin appeared before the House Committee on Interstate and Foreign Commerce in support of the Davenport bill. Repeating the story outlined above, he charged Magnolia Pipe Line Company with unwarranted discrimination in its offering price for Healdton crude and declared that refusal to pay the market price was "prima facie evidence of the conspiracy by the Standard Oil interests against the operators in this field." [31]

Oklahoma Attorney-General West also testified. He maintained that given the early lead and restrictive practices of Standard pipelines, "the notion that pipe line companies practically can be made to become common carriers is probably a long way off." [32] After pointing out that common-carrier pipeline transportation of petroleum was of no advantage to independent operators unless there was storage and a use for crude oil on the delivering end of the line, he concluded that "divorcement"* of pipelines from production was essential. In his words: "That divorce, I think, can not be brought about by requiring directly that the pipe lines engaged in inter-

*This term, now a part of pipeliners' vocabulary when speaking of antitrust action against integrated companies, appears to have originated with West.

state commerce shall not be engaged in production. I think you will have to take the other horn of the dilemma and provide that no pipe line engaged in interstate commerce shall transport oil as to which it is interested in the production." [33] Although his point was not clearly made, West apparently believed that the second device would hit directly at integrated operations whereas the former would only call for organizational adaptation in order to continue pipeline operations as before.

The independents took some pains to explain to congressional investigators their helplessness in dealing with integrated concerns. They maintained that control of pipelines gave these companies power over the price of crude oil and that this power was exercised to encourage wildcat drilling after which the price would be reduced to permit the integrated firms to benefit from the new production at the expense of the independent producer. Alternatively, or simultaneously, they charged, the large companies would drill a few wells in the vicinity of independent leases, requiring the independent operator to drill offset wells to protect his interests. With no outlet to market except by the pipelines of the integrated companies, and saddled with a drilling investment allegedly forced on him by the integrated concerns' strategy, the producer had no alternative but to sell his oil or his property at prices determined by these companies.[34] Other complaints were specific and familiar ones: The price of Oklahoma crude was not on a par with Pennsylvania crude, a fact which producers attributed to arbitrary decisions rather than genuine differences in quality; pipeline rates were fixed at railroad rate levels; and pipeline companies favored producing affiliates in violation of the law that required Oklahoma pipelines to take ratably from all producers.[35]

Charles J. Wrightsman of Tulsa summed up the Healdton producers' complaints. He pointed out that Magnolia Pipe Line Company and Magnolia Petroleum Company had common ownership. The pipeline company had admitted an ability to transport 12,000 barrels a day but was, he claimed, taking only a third of that amount on the excuse that Magnolia Petroleum was unwilling to accept more because of its commitment in Electra, Texas, crude.[36]

Figures subsequently compiled by the Federal Trade Commission shed some light on this charge. They show that the daily pumping capacity of the Electra station was 16,000 barrels in April 1914 and that of the Alvord station was 20,000 barrels.[37] Since Healdton crude entered the main trunk line at Alvord, the 4,000 barrel daily limit, if actually imposed by Magnolia on movement of Healdton crude,* appears to have had some justification in terms of existing pipeline capacity. And, of course, the quality of the respective crudes was a factor in Magnolia Petroleum's decision as to how

---

*Apparently, Magnolia during this period actually ran a minimum of 6,000 barrels a day, the amount necessary to fulfill its contract with the Pierce-Fordyce Oil Association. *Oil and Gas Journal* (October 29, 1914), 3.

much of each it would take.* On the other hand, as Magnolia's concurrence in increased Healdton shipments under pressure from the Oklahoma Corporation Commission showed, it was also possible, though not necessarily desirable nor remunerative from a business standpoint, to increase pipeline throughout.

Wrightsman was seemingly not interested in such details of business decision-making by oil company management; he was more intent on capitalizing on congressional sympathy for the consumer and the independent producer. Thus he emphasized that the price of gasoline in Oklahoma was higher than in other parts of the country — a result of "great and unjustifiable discrimination" for which the public paid the bill. And, he went on to declare: "The merciless control of transportation wreaks vengeance on the common public. It aids in arbitrary market control. It manipulates the machinery of various discriminations and monopolies in the oil business." [38]

The Oklahoma producer was asked what he would expect to be the result of the impending Supreme Court decision if it upheld the federal regulation of all interstate oil lines. He replied: "It will be a very beneficial result, provided that these pipe line companies are divested of producing properties. They are monopolizing the oil industry by buying producing properties, and if they can take the full capacity of their lines with their own production to the exclusion of the public, your common carrier phase of the case is a nullity." [39] When asked whether pipelines still purchased all the oil that they transported, the producer answered: "The pipe lines, which are incorporated as common carriers, put up such an impossible tariff and embarrassments that all the oil they transport is oil they buy. There is not a barrel of it goes otherwise in Oklahoma that we know of." [40]

Wrightsman also charged that Gulf, Texas, and Prairie pipelines acted in a manner, including similarity in the prices they offered for crude, that suggested "a very benevolent arrangement between these suspiciously disinterested business concerns." [41] Testifying on the Gore bill, however, representatives of the Gulf, Magnolia, and Texas companies made the rejoinder that competition and overproduction, not pipeline rates or purchasing practices, were at the heart of the producers' problems. [42]

It was evident from such proceedings that independent Mid-Continent producers felt that possession of pipelines gave integrated companies arbitrary power over the price of crude, that ownership of production by integrated concerns was achieved at the expense of independents, and that existing public policy measures did not offer adequate relief. Seeking to win the widest popular support, they couched their attack in terms of the price of refined products as well as of their own specific difficulties. To make the point easier to comprehend they continued to talk in terms of a monopoly of the old Standard Oil type. Where they acknowledged the

*Magnolia also insisted that the Corporation Commission allow a consistent differential between the price of Cushing crude and that of Healdton. *Ibid.*

existence of other pipelines, they charged or implied collusion at the expense of the producer. Their strategy was the time-honored one of seeking support from government to offset private economic power that they could not challenge successfully with their own resources.

That dissatisfied producers were basically attacking the pattern of integration characterizing the larger companies is clear from the remedies they proposed. Divorcement of pipeline transportation from oil production was the most common solution advanced by the producers. However, some were willing to go farther yet and advocate government ownership of pipelines.

A declaration supporting Senator Owen's bill for government ownership of pipelines was submitted to Congress by C. D. Chamberlin,[43] general counsel of the National Petroleum Association, which traced its origin to independent refiners' efforts to combat Standard Oil in Pennsylvania shortly after the turn of the century. Chamberlin had aided the ICC investigation of discriminations in coal and oil, and the Bureau of Corporations' investigation of the oil industry, as well as participating in the pipeline investigation that led to The Pipe Line Cases.[44] Now he suggested that government ownership of interstate oil pipelines would be to the public's advantage and would promote conservation, end discrimination, help the Navy to obtain fuel oil, and bring welcome revenue to the public treasury.[45]

Testifying on the proposal to build a government-owned pipeline to the Gulf of Mexico from the Oklahoma fields, James E. O'Neil of Prairie Oil & Gas declared that there would be no objection from him. "My only regret," he said, "is that the Government is not here now with such a line, to help us care for the oil we are unable to handle and thus help out the producer." [46] Meanwhile a representative of the Oklahoma Corporation Commission was in Washington with a delegation of producers who hoped to induce the War Department to provide tankage for 10,000 barrels of oil in the Cushing and Healdton fields.[47] Whether the independent oil operator or the president of Prairie Oil & Gas really favored any form of government ownership in a key sector of the oil industry seems doubtful, but clearly the former believed that strong steps should be taken to deal with private pipeline power while the latter apparently saw little danger in endorsing a government pipeline in the name of patriotism.

In the absence of a widespread popular outcry against the oil industry or big business in general, such as had characterized the Roosevelt era, no congressional action resulted from any of these proposals. Eventually the Commissioner of Corporations, as one of his last acts before the new Federal Trade Commission took over the Bureau's duties, submitted a report on *Conditions in the Healdton Oil Field* (March 15, 1915). By that time, however, there was little disposition to renew the combat of a year earlier between producers and the purchasers of Oklahoma crude oil. Meanwhile, new steps had been initiated to effect some control over Oklahoma production.

PIPELINES AND OIL CONSERVATION IN OKLAHOMA

Failure to reduce Oklahoma production by voluntary agreement among producers* was followed by efforts at mandatory control. With the encouragement of the Independent Oil Producers' Association and the concurrence of the pipeline companies, the Oklahoma Corporation Commission on July 1, 1914, issued an order requiring its approval before pipeline connections with new wells could be made in certain prolific fields.[48] But the Commission was buffeted by pressures from conflicting interests. Crude-oil prices continued to decline. As the deadline approached for Prairie Oil & Gas to submit pipeline tariffs to the ICC in accordance with the Supreme Court's decision in The Pipe Line Cases, rumors spread that it would discontinue taking oil as a common purchaser and rely on its own stocks of oil for an indeterminant period.[49] The Milliken Refining Company, which owned a pipeline extending from a shallow sand oil field to its refinery at Vinita, Oklahoma, reportedly refused to comply with the Commission's orders to prorate its pipeline runs among producers in that district.[50] In short, nothing that producers or state authorities had been able to do significantly reduced the chaos in Oklahoma crude oil markets under the pressure of flush production. The outbreak of war in Europe further confused the situation because it led to a brief shutdown of eastern refineries supplying the export trade.

The Attorney General asked that crude prices be fixed. The first effort of the Corporation Commission, pegging the price of crude at 75 cents a barrel, was ignored. In desperation, the Commission held a public hearing on the situation and followed it with a new order on September 22, 1914. Under its provisions an attempt was made to limit Oklahoma oil production temporarily to the amount that could be sold for 65 cents a barrel.[51]

By this time the major pipeline companies had cut their pipeline runs 40 to 50 per cent,[52] and they were being excoriated for discriminatory practices, which the Commission described as a "species of extortion." [53] As H. G. James had earlier commented in *Oildom*, "All shafts have been directed toward the big pipe line companies, with the idea that something will be accomplished by crippling and humiliating them. The general result is hurtful to the entire industry." [54] The same commentator noted: "The corporation commission has shown a disposition to tackle the control of anything from hell to the aurora borealis." [55] However, an effort to fix gasoline prices in the state had failed, and the prospects for stabilizing the crude-oil market by decree seemed equally poor.

---

*Cushing producers had agreed with the pipeline companies that for the month of May 1914 the companies should run all oil produced by two earlier-developed sands and prorate production from the deeper Bartlesville sand "according to the potential capacity of the various producing properties." This appears to have been the origin of the term "pipeline proration," used decades later inappropriately to attack pipelines. In this case, no limit was placed on production and the device failed to remedy overproduction. W. P. Z. German, "Legal History of Conservation of Oil and Gas in Oklahoma," in *Legal History of Oil and Gas* (Chicago, 1938), 118–119.

The attempts to control pipeline connections and to fix crude-oil prices in the face of flush production met major resistance. With the issuance of the September 22 order, Prairie Oil & Gas, which was most active in the Cushing field, ceased purchasing Oklahoma crude. It had fulfilled its promise, made early in the turmoil, to purchase at the 75-cent price; yet large amounts of oil had since then changed hands among other parties for as little as 55 or 50 cents a barrel.[56] Rather than accept the 65-cent price stipulated by the Commission, therefore, Prairie suspended purchasing and running oil of independent producers in Oklahoma from September 23 to September 30, 1914.[57] On September 24, Magnolia Pipe Line announced that it would pay only 40 cents a barrel for Healdton crude on and after September 30, and the Commission, which in the interim had come down from 65 cents a barrel to 50, forbade Healdton producers to sell oil at less than the latter price.[58]

The impasse at Cushing was broken in October when Prairie resumed purchasing at 55 cents a barrel,[59] but the Healdton controversy persisted. Therefore, a new hearing was held at Ardmore on October 22–23, 1914. At that time representatives of Magnolia, which had not yet put its announced price reduction into effect, presented testimony on the costs of operating at Healdton and the relative inferiority of that crude oil compared to Cushing's. With the promise of Magnolia's management that it would take as much Healdton crude as it could use — some 5,000 to 8,000 barrels a day at 50 cents a barrel, the producer–purchaser conflict in that field was finally resolved. To clear accumulated oil which hung over the market, the Commission's Order 878, dated November 25, 1914, authorized the sale of all Healdton oil stored in earthen reservoirs with 3.33 barrels sold at 30 cents a barrel treated as the equivalent of two barrels of fresh crude worth 50 cents a barrel.[60]

The great outpouring of oil from the Healdton and Cushing fields had led to experimentation in Oklahoma with state-enforced methods of controlling production and sustaining prices. Despite the failure of these efforts, the concept of linking production to market demand had emerged, and the inadequacy of the common-purchaser law in dealing with the conditions of overproduction had been demonstrated. The resulting emergency measures, in which pipelines as representatives of leading crude-oil purchasers had been subjected to heavy criticism, were followed by an Oklahoma conservation statute, signed into law by Governor Robert L. Williams on February 11, 1915. Among other things, it proposed to limit crude-oil production that was in excess of transportation and marketing facilities, or market demand.[61]

Out of the producers' distress had come a pioneering oil conservation law to which other states later turned. Out of Oklahoma's travail also came new constraints on the freedom of pipeline managers. Meantime, somewhat comparable developments had been taking place in the neighboring state of Texas.

TEXAS, 1905–1917

Texas lagged behind Oklahoma in imposing a pipeline common-carrier requirement, but its incorporation laws complicated the organization of fully integrated oil companies. These two statutory areas became connected in the sporadic conflicts between Texas producers and newly integrating oil companies in the state from 1905 until 1917. The legislative compromise spanning their respective interests in the latter year affected the organization of all pipeline companies subsequently incorporated in Texas, as well as the conditions under which both domestic and foreign (i.e., out-of-state) corporations conducted pipeline activities there.

The law governing incorporation of companies in Texas was quite specific and detailed as to the functions that could be performed by a private corporation. Thus, when oil was discovered at Spindletop in 1901, there was no authority in Texas law to incorporate a company that could engage in oil production, transportation, and refining under a single charter. Oil transporting companies, or pipelines, for example, could be organized under a statute adopted in 1899, which granted them the right of eminent domain and forbade discrimination in charges or services.[62] Refining operations, on the other hand, were not specifically recognized in the incorporation law until the 1899 statute was amended in 1915.[63] Meantime, refining companies might be organized under a section of the law pertaining to manufacturing or mining companies.[64] When a question arose as to whether this section permitted a corporation to engage in two different lines of business under the same charter, the Texas Supreme Court in 1902 ruled that it did not.[65] Therefore, the provisions of Texas law, as interpreted by the state's highest court, stood in the way of efforts to organize integrated oil companies in that state.

Since the Texas and Gulf companies were anxious to integrate their operations, each sponsored bills in the 1905 session of the Texas legislature to permit oil companies to perform all functions under the authority of a single charter.[66] These proposals stirred the wrath of independent Texas producers. Fearful of big business in any case, they were afraid that passage of either bill would strengthen the large companies and result in oil-purchasing and pipeline practices that would hurt the small operator. After conferring in Beaumont, the producers adopted a policy of offense as the best defense. Accordingly, they sponsored bills to regulate oil pipelines, to declare them common carriers, to restrict them to transportation functions alone, and to make their rates subject to the Texas Railroad Commission.[67] Although a compromise proposal, giving something to each side in this controversy, was also introduced at Austin, none of these bills was adopted. Instead, the legislature requested that the Attorney General take action against oil companies acting illegally under existing laws.[68]The matter rested there for another ten years until the Texas Company, which meantime had acquired increasingly closer control of the Producers' Oil Company,* sought to validate such *de facto* integration by sponsoring another bill in the legislature.

Independent producers met at Houston in January 1915, to denounce the new Texas Company bill. To fight it, they organized the Texas Oil Producers and Landowners Association and elected a leading independent, R. S. Sterling, president. The association hoped not only to defeat the bill but also to impose state regulation on oil pipelines. Lack of unity in the producers' ranks prevented successful action, and the legislature amended the corporation law to allow a single company to perform all functions but production.[69] This action legalized the refining activities of companies organized under the 1899 law governing pipeline corporations, but it still kept transportation formally separated from production in the eyes of law.

W.S. Farish, later a principal promoter of Humble Oil & Refining Company and a leader in Jersey Standard, was among the Texas producers who had not been in complete sympathy with the objectives of the Sterling-led organization. Because of his own experience, however, he favored state regulation of pipelines. On one occasion Sun Pipe Line had refused to run his oil from Sour Lake to shipside at the Gulf, standing on its rights as a private carrier and plant facility. On another occasion Gulf Pipe Line had held the firm of Blaffer & Farish to a long-term contract sale which did not allow for a subsequent rise in market prices in which Farish felt entitled to share. His indignation at such treatment was reflected in an address to the Texas Oil Producers and Landowners Association late in 1915 in which he declared that refiners made the market for crude, bought flush production at a discount, and exploited the small producer. In his words, "Whether it be right or wrong, lawful or unlawful, they have, through allied companies, come almost wholly in control of the production, handling, piping, and refining of oil in the State of Texas." Farish therefore urged opposition to the Texas Company bill, advocated an end to the contract method of selling crude, and supported the movement to obtain state regulation of pipelines. More affirmatively, he argued that the way to increase the price of crude was for Texas producers to publicize the attractive refining qualities of Texas crude, thereby enlarging their market. Out of these proposals came a new association, the Gulf Coast Oil Producers Association, formed in January 1916 and more broadly based than its predecessor.[70]

When the Texas Company in early 1917 sponsored new legislation to authorize completely integrated operations by a single company, the new Producers Association countered with a bill to declare pipelines common carriers, to forbid their discrimination against individuals or corporations, and to give the Texas Railroad Commission jurisdiction over pipelines. At the same time, Farish, in the name of the association, requested that the ICC hold hearings on rates charged by the Sun, Gulf, and Texas Company pipelines.[71]

---

*See above, p. 106, for Oklahoma's attempt to condemn the relationship that existed between these two companies.

The final result of the Texas agitation was passage of a statute authorizing a company owning oil pipelines in the state to engage also in oil and gas production, provided the pipeline activities were organized and conducted by a separate company. Furthermore, no oil company could own the stock of more than one producing company or one pipeline company.[72] The next day, the common-carrier bill was also adopted.[73] Both measures were signed into law on February 20, 1917. To administer the law, a new bureau was created in the Railroad Commission and placed under the direction of W. B. Wortham, former state treasurer.

The 1917 Texas laws traded off the right to do an integrated business in the state against regulation of oil pipelines by the state. With reference to this regulation, *Oildom* reported hopefully: "It is expected that this law will be a great boon to the small oil producer as he will be able to market his product in a competitive market." [74]

AN ERA IN PERSPECTIVE

During 1905–1917, and especially in the latter part of that period, public policy affecting oil pipelines in Oklahoma and Texas evolved in much the same way as it had earlier in Kansas and in eastern oil-producing states before the turn of the century. The discovery of new fields, and resulting problems of overproduction and falling prices, the emergence of partially or wholly integrated oil companies, and the complaints of distressed independent producers set the stage for enactment of state pipeline regulatory statutes. In addition, some tentative beginnings were made toward the state control of oil production.

These developments and those in other states, coupled with the congressional assertion and judicial confirmation of federal jurisdiction over interstate oil pipelines, imposed a number of new, moderately restrictive requirements on the owners and managers of pipelines. Neither singly nor in combination, did these measures seriously challenge the right of an individual or corporation to conduct a pipeline business as part of integrated operations. Even the break-up of the Standard Oil combination by antitrust action did not immediately affect the use to which former pipeline elements of that group were put. However, it did create a number of common-carrier pipeline companies whose claims on Jersey Standard had to be justified by economical performance of transportation services in an increasingly competitive market.

The chief change that had been brought about in the pipeline sector of the oil industry as the result of public policy since 1906 was an increasing segregation into corporate entities of pipeline activities conducted by integrated and semi-integrated companies. Although formally subject to either or both state and federal regulation as common carriers, these pipeline companies in practice continued to serve the needs of their owners.

PART

*Integration, Investigation,
and Regulation,
1915-1931*

CHAPTER 8

THE ROLE OF PIPELINES IN
INTEGRATED OIL OPERATIONS

In the years between 1915 and 1931, the American oil industry took on many of its present-day characteristics in terms of organization and structure. The dominance of a single firm, which even by 1911 had been severely shaken, disappeared beyond recall as former affiliates began to grow in their own right, new firms based in the flush production of the Mid-Continent field consolidated their hold, and older companies of the pre-1914 period expanded their operations. Behind these developments lay discoveries of vast new crude-oil supplies; a decline in the importance of kerosine as a major refined product compared to fuel oil and motor gasoline to power the new industrial, automobile age; and an upward surge in the demands for these and other petroleum products generated first by World War I and then the Prosperity Decade of the 1920's. Neither supply nor demand curves for the industry moved smoothly or continuously upward, but their general thrust in this direction nurtured and confirmed the importance of petroleum to the nation's changing economy. They also confirmed the pattern of integration toward which Standard Oil had pointed the way before 1900.

Assured, smooth flows of crude into refineries at competitive laid-down costs became virtually a condition for successful invasion of major products markets and retention and expansion of a company's hold there. For this reason, ownership of crude-oil pipelines by refiners continued to characterize the industry. Disaffiliated Standard refining and marketing companies left by the dissolution decree of 1911 without such transportation facilities increasingly felt a need for them. As time passed, they integrated backward to their own sources of crude.

Important newcomers to the industry began with semi- or completely integrated operations, and the construction of pipelines by them and by integrated companies organized before 1915 kept pace with their over-all growth. As a result, total petroleum pipeline mileage in the United States almost tripled between 1915 and 1931, and the great majority of the resulting network belonged to integrated companies.

NEW MAJOR INTEGRATED COMPANIES: SHELL AND SINCLAIR

The interrelationship of pipeline transportation with the other phases of the domestic oil business in the era between World War I and the Great Depression is exemplified by the growth of the Shell and Sinclair companies. Each got its start in the Mid-Continent area as the demand for gasoline boomed with the rapid growth of automobile transportation, reinforced by wartime demands for petroleum products. Each company sought to challenge Standard Oil companies, and each turned to the pattern of integration that had underpinned the power of that leading oil combination prior to 1911. The Royal Dutch-Shell affiliate, Roxana Petroleum, entered the American oil business as a well-financed subsidiary of an international oil company while the Sinclair Company was uniquely the product of a single individual's ambition, ingenuity, and aggressiveness. The dissimilarities of origins, however, only qualified basically similar strategies and tactics of growth — including, in each instance, pipeline ownership and operation.

Shell Oil

The Royal Dutch–Shell Group of companies resulted from an alliance of Dutch and English oil interests that found common cause during the first decade of the twentieth century. Guided by H. W. A. Deterding, Royal Dutch subsidiaries became active in the United States during 1911–12, providing a West Coast outlet for Sumatra-produced gasoline and a challenge to Standard Oil companies in the United States as well as abroad. From these beginnings, Shell Oil Company of California soon developed integrated operations in that state.[1] Simultaneously, the Roxana Petroleum Company, another Royal Dutch–Shell subsidiary, prepared for producing operations in the booming Mid-Continent field. The hopes of Roxana's backers were symbolized in its name, which in Persian meant "Dawn of a New Day." Roxana initially proposed to purchase the Gulf Oil Company's properties in order to enter the industry with established facilities and markets, but when this proposal was rejected by Gulf, Roxana settled down briefly to producing and selling oil. The big interstate pipeline companies and small independent refiners were among its customers, National Refining being one of the best.[2]

In May 1915 Roxana began the long process of developing its own integrated operations by purchasing in the Cushing field the Yarhola leases (named for two Creek Indian girls), which produced abut 8,500 barrels a day. Included in this purchase was the Yarhola Pipe Line Company, incorporated June 27, 1914, under the laws of Oklahoma and possessing 25 miles of 4-inch pipe which connected the tank farm at the producing property with a loading rack on the Santa Fe Railroad.[3] From this beginning, Roxana Petroleum quickly moved into the new Healdton field, with the result that the company's production rose from 500,000 barrels in 1914 to 2,600,000 barrels in 1915. But to obtain this rapid increase in production,

Roxana had invested $6,000,000 in six months,[4] and steps had to be taken to protect and recover this large outlay.

Roxana's acquisition of producing property in the Mid-Continent area had been predicated in part on plans to construct a trunk pipeline to the Gulf Coast, where the Mid-Continent crude could be refined and loaded aboard tankers. In June 1915, therefore, Roxana Petroleum entered into a partnership agreement with Patrick White and Harry Sinclair, Cushing producers, to build a pipeline to the Gulf, erect a refinery there, and establish marketing operations along the East Coast.[5] Except in the partnership arrangement, this strategy, of course, closely resembled that adopted a decade earlier by such companies as Gulf Oil, Sun Oil, and the Texas Company.

Roxana needed to make an investment in production pay more than could be gained from merely selling oil in the field. It had not commenced operations in the Mid-Continent to supply Prairie Oil & Gas with crude for Standard Oil refineries, but rather, in order to challenge these companies. Harry Sinclair and his associates had comparable ambitions. Thus, a cooperative pipeline, spreading the risk and the financial burden between the two groups, promised to be mutually beneficial. Had the 1915 pipeline proposal gone through, it would have set a significant precedent — joint ownership of a major trunk pipeline.

Ironically, the Shell—Sinclair plan to establish integrated operations in competition with Standard Oil companies was upset by the charge that it was all a ruse to cover the grant of new privileges to the Standard Oil group. "Standard Oil" still provided a rallying cry for those who opposed any development in the oil industry that threatened their interests and who wanted to broaden their support. In this instance, a cry went up that Harry Sinclair was being used as a tool of Standard Oil.[6] Perhaps the resulting furor was caused in part by the crude-oil purchasing companies which stood to lose if such large-scale producers as Sinclair and Roxana moved successfully into integrated operations.

Sinclair's plan to finance his half-interest in the pipeline hinged on a governmental decision. He had hoped to organize a company of Cushing producers with crude supplies large enough to warrant borrowing the requisite capital. However, since Cushing production was located largely on territory subject to Department of the Interior regulations, it was necessary for Sinclair in implementing his plan to secure an exception to a federal law prohibiting an individual from owning an interest in more than 4,800 acres of oil and gas leases on Indian lands. As interpreted by the Department of the Interior, this requirement meant that a stockholder in a corporation with leases of this size automatically disqualified any other corporaton in which he might also be interested from owning any Indian leases.[7] Because the law had been passed to get at Standard Oil,[8] Sinclair's request that he be exempted from it was interpreted as a surreptitious move on the part of Standard Oil interests in their own behalf.

Protests flowed into the Interior Department against granting any exemptions to Sinclair. His denial that he was acting for Standard Oil and his demand that the facts be verified by contacting Sir Marcus Samuel of the Royal Dutch–Shell Group were met with ill-disguised contempt. The Secretary of the Interior reportedly declared that even if Sir Marcus verified Sinclair's claim, it would still not be proof that Standard Oil money was not backing the pipeline.[9] Rebuffed in this way, Sinclair could not carry out his plan as originally conceived,[10] and Roxana temporarily abandoned the idea of a pipeline to the Gulf.

A new strategy then emerged, this time imitating in large measure what Jersey Standard had done in the preceding decade. Roxana Petroleum built a temporary refinery at Cushing, located a refinery site on the Mississippi River above New Orleans where ocean-going tankers could be loaded, and farther up the river above St. Louis selected another refinery site at Wood River, Illinois. The Louisiana property, called Sellers, was initially served by tank car from the Mid-Continent field, and products were assembled there for shipment abroad by water. The Cushing refinery was designed primarily for producing fuel oil. The Wood River refinery was not completed and in operation until the latter part of 1918 when it began to turn out fuel oil, gasoline and distillate made from Healdton crude.[11]

To serve these refineries, a new network of pipelines emerged. The decision to build a pipeline from Healdton, where Roxana Petroleum had acquired significant production, to Cushing was made early in January 1916. The engineering firm of Sanderson & Porter, which had earlier built a pipeline for Shell in California, made a quick estimate of $1,714,000, exclusive of right of way, for a line with a 12,000-barrel daily capacity. More detailed estimates, based on pipeline capacities ranging from 5,000 to 20,000 barrels daily, were provided in February 1916.[12] The final decision was to build a 6-inch line, with one pumping station, capable of delivering 5,500 barrels of oil a day from Healdton to Cushing.[13] The Sanderson & Porter firm was engaged to do the work, which got underway in the summer of 1916.

The Healdton-Cushing line was but the first step in the ultimate plan to supply the Wood River refinery with Mid-Continent crude. In the summer of 1916 Sanderson & Porter provided cost estimates for the proposed 450-mile artery from Cushing to Wood River, and the oil company decided on a 10-inch line with five pumping stations, for daily delivery of 24,000 barrels.[14]

Construction of this line took place in 1917–18. Teams with eight or more animals, drawing two wagons in tandem, delivered pipe to the site where ditching operations, done mostly by machine, had prepared the route. Pipe was bent (to fit the contours of the trench) and the sections of pipe were screwed together, by machine. On the Healdton-Cushing line, the best 9-hour day performance was the laying of 11,740 feet of pipe, which involved making 28 bends, by a crew of 26 men. On the Wood River line, however, the best comparable performance was 8,200 feet, including 24 bends, by a crew of 36 men.[15] While the Wood River line was still under construction, the Healdton-Cushing line's capacity was increased to 8,000 barrels per day by addition of a second pumping station.[16]

The new refinery was not yet ready when the Wood River line was completed in 1918, so Yarhola Pipe Line contracted to move crude oil for Indiana Standard on a common-carrier basis. Even after the Wood River refinery went "on stream," the pipeline continued some common carriage, handling more than 2,000,000 barrels annually for outside parties in 1919–20.[17]

Although the 10-inch Cushing–Wood River Line was something of an innovation in an era when trunk lines were typically 8 inches in diameter, expansion of the Yarhola pipeline system was generally on a more conservative basis. The growth of refining capacity dictated the amount of additional pipeline capacity needed. Looping, the addition of parallel lines along the same right of way, or installation of more pump stations were satisfactory methods of increasing pipeline capacity with a comparatively small incremental investment. The Cushing–Wood River 10-inch line, for example, had a daily rated capacity of 24,000 barrels when it was opened in August 1918, but with looping and the addition of other facilities this capacity was raised to 67,000 barrels a day within a decade.[18]

In October 1919* the Yarhola pipeline property was transferred to a new Maryland corporation, Ozark Pipe Line Corporation. This concern had a capitalization of $10,400,000, the bulk of which was represented by preferred stock mostly issued to Roxana Petroleum. Roxana in turn transferred it to Shell of California, as that company had been the source of the funds used in pipeline construction and expansion. The common stock, except for the directors' qualifying shares, was held by Royal Dutch Petroleum Company (The Hague), Shell Transport and Trading Company (London), and Dundee Petroleum Company (New York). In October 1920 an $18,000,000 stock dividend, made possible by a revaluation of pipeline investment, was distributed.[19]

During these years, Roxana Petroleum sought new production on its own to avoid the high cost of purchasing proved production,[20] but it also worked in fruitful cooperation with Ernest Marland, an independent operator who needed funds to develop his important oil discovery at Tonkawa in north central Oklahoma. A joint Roxana–Marland enterprise, the Comar Oil Company, was organized in 1921 and controlled about 50 per cent of the field's production in 1925. To serve these wells, Ozark Pipe Line Company built a 6-inch line from Tonkawa to Cushing in 1922. The initial rated capacity of 8,000 barrels daily was tripled within a year by addition of a duplicate line and additional pumping facilities.[21]

The high gravity of Tonkawa crude made it especially suitable for gasoline manufacture, and the field quickly attracted many companies and pipelines. According to Carl Rister, by May 1, 1923, fifteen pipelines served the field and eleven more were under construction.[22] Storage was also available

*The structure of the entire Royal Dutch–Shell Group as of April 28, 1919, is in *Oildom* (June 1921), 36–38.

in adequate quantity.[23] These were unusual situations in flush fields, and they helped to maintain the price of Tonkawa crude.

The strategy of Roxana and of Shell of California was based on integrated operations. Therefore they constantly sought to expand their base in production. As part of this strategy, the two companies were among those joined in 1922 with the Union Oil Company of Delaware, which was producing about 16,000 barrels of crude oil daily in the Mid-Continent.[24] Although the possibility of including Marland in this combination had been considered, he placed too high a price on his properties.[25] The new Shell Union Oil Corporation, organized under the laws of Delaware, acquired the producing properties in the Mid-Continent owned or otherwise bound to Union Oil. The Ozark Pipe Line system was then extended to serve them where, as in the Burbank field near Tonkawa, it seemed feasible and profitable. To refine Tonkawa crude and serve states east of the Rockies, Roxana Petroleum erected a refinery at Arkansas City, Kansas, in 1923. A pipeline with 24,000 barrels-per-day capacity supplied this refinery from Tonkawa, 38 miles distant.[26]

To compete with the growing Indiana Standard and Sinclair companies, which had refineries in the Chicago area. Roxana Petroleum acquired a site that straddled the line between East Chicago, Illinois, and Hammond, Indiana, and constructed a 25,000 barrel-per-day refinery there. To supply this facility, an 8-inch pipeline was extended from Wood River and went into operation in March 1927. Initially capable of delivering about 15,000 barrels of crude oil per day, the capacity of this line was soon expanded to 27,000 barrels daily by looping and by the addition of three additional intermediate stations.[27] This move made the map of Shell's major pipeline routes and refinery locations in mid-America a fair facsimile of those developed in the same area by Jersey Standard before 1911.

The major expansion of Shell refining facilities called for new sources of crude oil and new pipelines. West Texas provided the crude. The McCamey field was brought in during September 1925, followed in July 1926, by the Hendrick field and in September of that year by the Yates field, 25 miles southeast of McCamey. In each of these new fields, Roxana Petroleum acquired significant acreage.

To service the west Texas production, the Shell pipeline system expanded rapidly. In 1927 a 6-inch line was laid from Hendrick through Monahans to McCamey. Initially, railroad tank cars were loaded at the latter two points to complete the delivery to other Shell facilities. However, this was a temporary arrangement pending completion of a pipeline connection between McCamey and the mid-Continent trunk line at Cushing. A 10-inch line with a daily capacity of 42,000 barrels was laid over this stretch of 482 miles and completed in 1928.[28]

Shell, which now was also marketing on the East Coast, needed a refinery to supply that market and an additional outlet for its west Texas production.* Accordingly, a refinery was built on the banks of the Houston Ship Channel during 1928–29, and a 446-mile, 10-inch pipeline was extended from McCamey to Houston. From there, barges moved crude to the Norco, Louisiana, refinery, which served local markets. When major east Texas production came in during 1930–31, a 10-inch line was laid from Kilgore to Houston with an initial capacity of 32,000 barrels daily.[29] These pipelines constituted the main axes of Shell pipeline movements and provided an outlet for Shell-produced crude, transportation savings, and a means of assuring a constant flow of crude into Shell refineries.

Pipeline expansion was expensive, and in 1927 it brought about changes both in the financing and the name of Shell Union's pipeline subsidiary. Instead of lending to the pipeline company, as in the past, Shell Union's management decided that its pipeline subsidiary should borrow new construction funds from the public. This was a major departure from typical pipeline financing techniques of the time.

A $30,000,000† issue of sinking fund gold debentures, to run 25 years with both principal and 5 per cent interest guaranteed by the parent company, was floated on November 1, 1927, through Lee, Higginson & Company. A total of $28,500,000 cash was realized from this issue.[30] The resulting debt was refinanced twice to take advantage of lower interest rates. To make the debentures more acceptable to the public, top management decided that the pipeline company should be more closely identified with the Shell name. Therefore, Ozark Pipe Line Corporation was renamed Shell Pipe Line Corporation in October 1927.

In connection with these financial operations, the book value of Shell Pipe Line's capital stock was reduced. The predecessor company's preferred and common stock had earlier been replaced by a total of 300,000 shares of no-par common, carried at a book value of $8,916,100. In 1927 this book value was reduced to $6,649,977.50, the amount actually realized on com-

---

*Pipeline capacity (barrels per day) out of west Texas was reported to be as follows in August 1929 (*Pipeline News* [August 1929], 22):

Humble	150,000
Texas Co.	60,000
Illinois Pipe Line (Ohio Oil)	50,000 (delivered to Humble at Lytle)
Shell	40,000
Atlantic	40,000
Magnolia	33,000
Gulf	28,000
Pasotex	17,000

†At the time the loan was under consideration, construction expenditures of $16,783,600 were foreseen. The size of the issue was determined by the favorable state of the money market and the desire to acquire additional funds for long-term expansion.

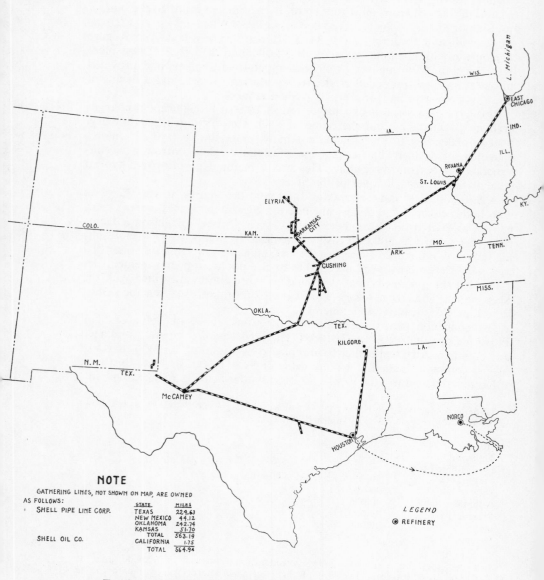

NOTE

GATHERING LINES, NOT SHOWN ON MAP, ARE OWNED
AS FOLLOWS:

SHELL PIPE LINE CORP.	STATE	MILES
	TEXAS	224.63
	NEW MEXICO	44.12
	OKLAHOMA	242.74
	KANSAS	51.70
	TOTAL	563.19
SHELL OIL CO.	CALIFORNIA	1.75
	TOTAL	564.94

Trunk pipelines of Shell Pipe Line Corporation, December 31, 1931.
Source: 72 Cong., 2 Sess., House Report No. 2192, Part I, facing p. 152.

mon and preferred stock in 1919.* All but the directors' qualifying shares were held by Shell Union Oil Corporation.[31] Except for its public borrowing, Shell Pipe was organized and operated like most pipeline subsidiaries of contemporary integrated oil companies.

In reply to a questionnaire prepared in connection with a congressional investigation of pipelines in the early 1930's, Shell Union declared that Shell Pipe acted "as a pipe line department for the producing company [Shell Petroleum Corporation]† and derives practically all of its income from the business of carrying our own oil from our fields to our refineries." Pointing out that it owned 100 per cent of the stock of both companies, Shell Union stated that "the profits of the two companies should be considered together." [32] This statement made it quite clear that the "profitability" of integrated pipeline operations was largely a function of intracorporate transfer pricing. Thus, while Shell Pipe, drawing down accumulated surplus, paid Shell Union dividends amounting to $27,200,000 in 1931, the parent company closed the year with a net loss almost equal to this figure.

The apparent profitability of pipeline operations measured by the size of dividends could be misleading. Since only 1.43 per cent of the pipeline company's income from 1929 through 1933 represented income from transportation for shippers having no interest in the lines,[33] outside patronage was not the source of pipeline profits. Rather, the dividends paid to Shell Union in 1931 represented chiefly a refund of transportation revenues accumulated by Shell Pipe in the course of serving Shell companies. It was, for example, the customary practice for Shell Union to assume Shell Petroleum's indebtedness to Shell Pipe for transportation services. This indebtedness of the parent was partially offset by dividends declared by the pipeline subsidiary. Shell Union, therefore, ended up, as one might expect, by obtaining crude-oil transportation at actual cost. Again, this was typical procedure for most integrated companies. Understandably, however, the magnitude of the dividends in relation to outstanding stock of the pipeline company invited misunderstanding and attracted congressional interest, as will be discussed later.

The level of rates that made such dividends possible helps to explain why outside patronage of Shell lines was unimportant in generating revenue during this era. Shell, like other integrated companies, built pipelines for transportation savings and to protect and service its investments in production and refining — not to move oil for others who were or might become competitors. Shell Pipe had to comply with the federal common-carrier pipeline law, but, in following the pattern of pipeline usage established by Standard Oil before 1906, it had little business from shippers

---

*Ozark Pipe Line had sold $400,000 par value common stock for $50,000 and preferred stock with a par value of $8,516,100 for cash amounting to $6,599,977.50. The sum of these cash values was taken as the book value in 1927. Alexander Wylie, Bureau of Accounts, ICC, to Shell Pipe Line Corporation, April 27, 1928.

†Roxana Petroleum changed its name to Shell Petroleum in 1928.

outside the Shell group. This high-rate policy was within its legal rights and, as will appear later, the same form of managerial adaptation to public policy requirements was typical of integrated companies.

Sinclair Oil and Refining Corporation

Harry F. Sinclair, whom Shell had considered as a pipeline partner in 1915, had operated aggressively in Kansas and Oklahoma oil fields and with profitable results. From an office in Tulsa, whence he moved from Independence, Kansas, in 1912, he and his associates guided wildcatting and production activities throughout the Southwest. Harry, his brother Earl, and the two White brothers, Pat and Tom,[34] were the principal stockholders in various producing companies, which sold many of their leases to Prairie Oil & Gas.[35]

With the advent of the European war and its great stimulus to the oil business, Sinclair began to think seriously of creating an integrated oil company. Out of his initial steps in this direction came the proposed pipeline alliance with Shell, and later a parting of the ways with the White brothers. In the course of dissolving this partnership, jointly-owned producing properties worth many millions were sold to a subsidiary of Tide Water Oil.[36] But in breaking ties with the past, Sinclair also opened the path to future integrated operations.

While starting to drill on the undeveloped properties left from the old partnership,[37] Sinclair also began to acquire new producing leases and some small refineries and pipelines. Included in these acquisitions were the Cudahy, Milliken, and Chanute refining companies, and about 500 miles of gathering and trunk-line mileage, the latter extending from the vicinity of Cushing, Oklahoma, to Coffeyville, Kansas.

To control these properties, Sinclair organized the $50,000,000 Sinclair Oil and Refining Corporation in April 1916,* and he turned to New York investment bankers for capital. According to H. P. Wright of Kansas City, who took part in the New York operation: "It was the largest deal ever put over in Wall Street by Kansas City men." With pride Wright declared: "Mr. Sinclair certainly made their eyes bulge with his audacity and fearlessness." For a time, he reported, there was some healthy Wall Street skepticism about the operation, "But after the brokers, of whom [Theodore] Roosevelt, junior, was one, saw that Sinclair had appraised properties to back up his ideas and that the Standard Oil Company would not fight the new company, they came through in fine style." In Wright's view, the willingness of Kansas City capitalists to put up cash was a key factor in the success of the entire financial scheme.[38]

*A syndicate contracted to sell $16,000,000 first-lien, 10-year sinking fund, gold bonds. It was reported that the new company's producing properties should show net earnings of $7,000,000 in the next year, while its refining and pipeline activities were expected to show earnings in excess of $3,000,000. Members of the syndicate were: Kissell, Kinnicutt & Co.; White, Weld & Co.; Montgomery, Clothier & Tyler; J. & W. Seligman & Co.; Spencer Trask & Co.

The constituent parts of Sinclair Oil and Refining Corporation were the Cudahy Refining Company, the Exchange Oil Company, the Sinclair-Cudahy Pipe Line Company, and the Sinclair Oil and Gas Company.[39] Together they represented producing, transporting, refining, and marketing facilities under a single control. A completely integrated company had been established virtually at a single stroke by the deft combination of going concerns.

The Sinclair-Cudahy Pipe Line Company was incorporated under the laws of Maine on April 25, 1916.[40] J. M. Cudahy became its president, and John R. Manion, formerly of Prairie Pipe Line, was named general manager. The company had an authorized capital stock of $2,000,000 which, together with $1,000,000 (par value) First Lien Mortgage 7 per cent bonds, was issued to Sinclair Oil and Refining. On May 1, 1916, Sinclair-Cudahy acquired the pipeline properties of Milliken Pipe Line Company, Chanute Refining Company, and Cudahy Refining Company.[41] The value of the carrier property was reported as $1,877,175.41. As of December 31, 1916, the system consisted of 487 miles of gathering and trunk pipelines, centered on the Cushing field but also serving other points.[42]

Within a year, the Sinclair companies had shown that they were a force to be reckoned with in the oil industry. In December 1916, for example, Sinclair Oil and Gas took the lead in upping the posted price of Kansas and Oklahoma crude by 10 cents a barrel. This was a direct challenge to Standard Oil-oriented companies like Prairie which had long set the posted price in the Mid-Continent.[43] Furthermore, Sinclair had an aggressive program of expansion well underway. New refineries were planned and put under construction at Kansas City; Fort Madison, Iowa; and East Chicago.

To link the new refineries with the Mid-Continent oil fields, Sinclair's management had decided in September 1916 to build a 6- and 8-inch trunk line from Drumright, Oklahoma (in the Cushing field) to Chicago.[44] Fortuitously the pipe was acquired before wartime conditions sent its price skyrocketing. By February 1, 1917, construction gangs had completed the line to Chanute, Kansas, some 50 miles north of the Oklahoma border, saving Sinclair's refinery there an estimated $30,000 a month in transportation charges.* [45] By November 1917 the line had been completed beyond Fort Madison, Iowa, and six gangs were at work to finish the remaining 175 miles into East Chicago.[46] Despite difficulties in obtaining right of way across Illinois, which prompted some of the established companies to predict that Sinclair would never reach Chicago,[47] the line was finished by March 1918, a few months ahead of Shell's comparable one to Wood River. In the words of an observer who visited the work in late 1917: "The important feature of this pipe line system is that it enables the Sinclair Company not only to distribute its own production, but also to render

---

*The cost of rail transportation from the Cushing field to Coffeyville, Kansas, was 31 cents a barrel compared to 10 cents a barrel for pipeline transportation.

facilities for independent production to reach destination at the great refining centres on the Great Lakes and elsewhere." [48]

During and following World War I, the Sinclair organization continued
its vigorous pipeline expansion program. In 1918 the Sinclair Gulf Pipe
Line connected Healdton to the Drumright terminus of the Chicago trunk
line and added another line from Healdton the following year. The War
Pipe Line Company, incorporated in July 1918 and affiliated with Sinclair,
extended the Healdton-Drumright line 151 miles to Freeman, Missouri,
during the last year of the war. This extension was laid parallel to the
Drumright-Freeman portion of the line built by Sinclair-Cudahy to Chicago in 1916–17. Sinclair Gulf also entered the prolific Ranger, Texas,
field and connected it with Healdton during 1919. Thenceforth Ranger
crude could be moved to Chicago via the Sinclair-Cudahy line.

Sinclair-Cudahy Pipe Line Company acquired the properties of Sinclair
Gulf and the War Pipe Line Company on December 31, 1919.[49] The following month its name was changed to the Sinclair Pipe Line Company.[50]

One New York financial analyst in September 1919 reported enthusias-
tically on the expansion of Sinclair's integrated operations. "There is
profit in transporting oil just as there is a profit in producing it, in refining
it and in wholesaling and retailing it. But when the producer has to go to
the company that pipes and refines, he passes to that company some of the
profits in the oil business. Sinclair is a large purchaser and transporter of
crude oil not produced in its own properties." [51] However, two years later
a Boston brokerage house noted that the bold expansion program might
prove the rock upon which Sinclair would founder, and it cited the pipeline expenditure of some $30,000,000 as one example.[52]

INDIANA STANDARD AND SINCLAIR

Fortunately for Harry Sinclair there was an oil company that needed
access to crude-oil supplies and transportation savings as sorely as he was
beginning to need cash. Standard Oil Company (Indiana) had been left by
the 1911 dissolution decree as a refining and marketing operation dependent on others for crude oil and its transportation. Until World War I dis-
rupted the relationship, Prairie Oil & Gas and Prairie Pipe Line served
Indiana's needs adequately. With the country's full involvement in hostilities, however, the demands for crude oil at seaboard refineries left inland
refiners, and Indiana Standard especially, short of oil. Under this pressure,
as well as a nationwide shortage of crude, the company began to acquire
its own producing property and to increase its purchases from Sinclair Oil
& Gas, taking delivery through Sinclair's trunk line to Chicago.[53] At that
time, however, the capacity of the line was only 20,000 barrels a day, and
the Whiting refinery could use all this space plus what Prairie Pipe Line
could deliver.[54]

Indiana management was forced to reappraise its use of common-carrier
pipelines when pipeline rates from the Mid-Continent to Chicago were

advanced in September 1920. Based on the increased cost of pipeline construction and maintenance and the desire to approach rail rates more closely, Sinclair had taken the lead in raising pipeline rates.[55] Between Mid-Continent points and East Chicago, the rate jumped from 42 to 74 cents per barrel. The Kansas City rate rose from 28 to 46 cents, while gathering charges climbed from 12 to 15 cents per barrel.[56] At the same time, Prairie Pipe Line raised its trunk-line rates 25 per cent.[57] As a result, pipeline rates from Oklahoma points to Indiana Standard's territory rose above average rail rates for the same haul.[58] Reacting to these developments, Indiana Standard management began to consider seriously the construction of its own trunk line to the Mid-Continent area.[59] However, there emerged an alternative possibility: purchase of a half-interest in the Sinclair line.

Sinclair Consolidated Oil Corporation, as the Sinclair holding company was renamed in 1919, had expanded rapidly and was in need of cash; Indiana Standard had cash but needed a pipeline and its own sources of crude. Indiana Standard's construction of a new pipeline from Chicago to the Mid-Continent, however, would have cost many times the amount needed to expand Sinclair's existing line to accommodate Indiana's traffic. The Sinclair trunk line was not then running at capacity,[60] but the rapid growth of Sinclair refining facilities made the need for future pipeline expansion appear likely. Therefore, the basis for a mutually beneficial arrangement appeared to exist.

Colonel Robert Stewart, president of Indiana Standard, found Harry Sinclair receptive to the idea of the Indiana Company's purchasing a half-interest in the Sinclair pipeline system. On February 9, 1921, the sale was executed, with Standard paying $16,390,000 in cash for 142,500 shares of Sinclair Pipe Line Company. On the same day the Sinclair Crude Oil Purchasing Company was organized to buy, store, and sell crude for the two parent companies, which also shared equally in its ownership.[61]

In initiating the 1920 rate advance, Sinclair Pipe Line had indirectly helped to increase the transportation costs of its nonintegrated competitors because Prairie Pipe quickly followed the Sinclair example. Prairie next seized the initiative by reducing its rates in mid-1922 to meet tankship competition. Since Sinclair Pipe Line served only Sinclair and Indiana Standard inland refineries,[62] the rates it charged these parent companies were largely intracorporate transfers. Presumably, then, its 1922 rate reductions to match Prairie were made to keep transportation costs in line with those of competitors and to provide a check on the profitability (in terms of transportation savings) of ownership of the pipeline system.

Expansion of the Sinclair pipeline system continued during the 1920's. Soon after Indiana Standard acquired its interest in the Sinclair Pipe Line Company, the capacity of the Oklahoma–Chicago line was increased through looping and the addition of pumping stations.[63] To handle crude from the Ranger and Mexia fields in north and east-central Texas, Sinclair Pipe Line in 1923 built an extension, capable of handling 20,000 barrels

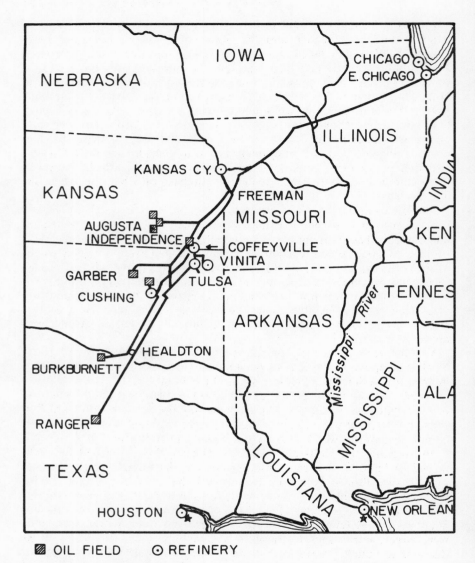

☒ OIL FIELD   ⊙ REFINERY

Sinclair-Standard trunk pipeline route from Texas to East Chicago, 1921.
Source: National Petroleum News (February 16, 1921), p. 24.

per day, from its Ranger-Healdton line south through Mexia to Sinclair's new Houston refinery.[64]

Another major addition to the Sinclair system came in 1923–24 with the construction of an 8- and 10-inch line from Wyoming to a connection with the Oklahoma–Chicago trunk line at Freeman, Missouri. The Wyoming line was intended primarily to run oil from the Teapot Dome lease under contractual arrangements with Harry Sinclair's ill-fated Mammoth Oil Company; but Sinclair Crude Oil Purchasing and the Sinclair Pipe Line Company were also to take government royalty oil from the Salt Creek, Wyoming, field.[65]

The Wyoming trunk line was completed in 1924, but the furor that developed over Mammoth Oil's access to the government's Teapot Dome oil reserve ended that venture and the major anticipated source of traffic for the pipeline. The line therefore remained idle from 1928 to 1931.* [66] Meantime, on September 22, 1930, Indiana Standard had acquired 100 per cent ownership of Sinclair Pipe Line Company. The following year the Indiana Company leased the Wyoming line for transportation of natural gas. The section from Freeman, Missouri, to Cormick Junction, Nebraska, went to the Kansas Pipe Line and Gas Company and the remainder of the line (to Welch, Wyoming) to the North Central Gas Company.[67] It was not until 1936 that the line was called back into crude-oil service, moving Wyoming oil eastward for Indiana Standard.[68]

Indiana Standard's purchase in 1930 of full ownership of Sinclair Pipe Line was a significant move toward full integration. The decision was probably made in reaction to Prairie Pipe Line's refusal to lower rates to the Indiana Company unless it was guaranteed volume shipments. However, the company's published history is silent on this point.[69] In any case, a larger strategy to confirm and strengthen the integration moves of the preceding decade is discernible, since Indiana Standard also purchased full ownership of Sinclair Crude Oil Purchasing Company. The pipeline purchase gave Indiana Standard a total investment of $58,889,913.70 in the capital stock of Sinclair Pipe Line, but offsets reduced the net cost to $53,311,941.01†[70] Acquisition of the remaining 50 per cent interest in Sinclair Crude Oil Purchasing cost Indiana $30,000,000 cash; Indiana also assumed full liability for the Purchasing Company's bonded indebtedness, amounting to $53,000,000.[71]

On January 1, 1931, the changed status of these properties was recognized in the revision of their corporate names. Sinclair Crude Oil Purchasing Company was renamed Stanolind Crude Oil Purchasing Company, and the Sinclair Pipe Line Company became the Stanolind Pipe Line Company. At the same time the various exploration and producing companies in the Southwest purchased in the course of Indiana's search for crude were merged into a new company, Stanolind Oil and Gas Company, headed by Frank O. Prior.[72]

*The line had never been operated at more than 50 per cent capacity and was operating at about 15 per cent when closed down. *Pipeline News* (December 1928), 20.

†For its pipeline investment, the Indiana Company received nearly 7,000 miles of pipeline with a carrying capacity of about 135,000 barrels a day. The Mid-Continent trunkline into Whiting alone was capable of delivering 75,000 barrels a day, and shortly this was stepped up to 90,000. Giddens, *Standard Oil Company (Indiana)*, 445.

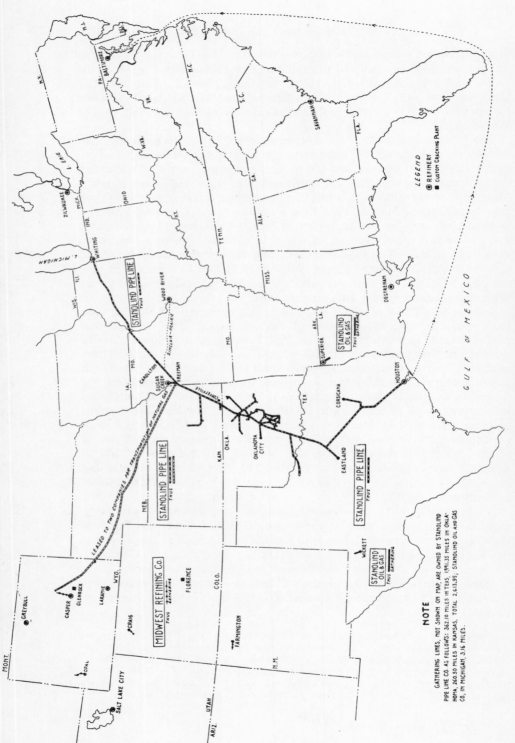

Stanolind Pipe Line System, December 1931.

Source: 72 Cong. 2 Sess. House Report No. 2192, Part I facing p. 100.

The various Stanolind companies, like their counterparts in other integrated oil companies, worked closely together to obtain crude oil and to move it from the well to the refinery. To cite one specific example, Stanolind Oil and Gas produced and ran oil from its own lease in Seminole County, Oklahoma, to lease tanks. Stanolind Crude Oil Purchasing bought this oil and gave Stanolind Pipe Line a connection order. The latter then extended a gathering line to the lease and took the oil into its system. (Alternatively, the oil might have been stored in tanks maintained by the Crude Oil Purchasing affiliate.) Stanolind trunk lines then moved the crude to one of Indiana Standard's three major refineries: Sugar Creek, near Kansas City; Wood River, near St. Louis; or Whiting, near Chicago. The Crude Oil Purchasing Company was the shipper, selling the oil to Standard Oil Company (Indiana) f.o.b. refineries. The minimum tender governing the shipment was 100,000 barrels.[73]

Stanolind Crude Oil Purchasing might also have purchased the oil from independent producers, the only difference being that in order to obtain a pipeline connection to the lease tanks, signature of the lease owners would have had to be appended to the division order.[74] In both instances, the pipeline company acted strictly as a common carrier. Unlike the early practice exemplified by Magnolia Pipe Line in the Healdton field, crude-oil purchasing was performed by a separate company. In fact, of course, both the purchasing and pipeline companies were acting in the interest of their parent concern.

The Indiana Company's purchase of 100 per cent control of Sinclair Pipe Line Company would probably not have been possible had not Harry Sinclair had an eye on the Prairie companies. Negotiations between Sinclair and Prairie had been going on for several years before the remaining 50 per cent of Sinclair Pipe was sold to Indiana. Sinclair's interest in Prairie was motivated by the lack of balance in the Sinclair expansion program during the 1920's. The ratio of Sinclair crude-oil production to Sinclair refinery runs in 1922 had been 90.7 per cent; by 1931 it had dropped to 41.4 per cent.[75] To compensate, Sinclair had to buy increasingly more crude oil from others to feed its refineries, thus losing some of the benefits of integration. From the Sinclair standpoint, purchase of the Prairie Oil & Gas Company, a major producing company, would help to remove some of this imbalance, while the Prairie Pipe Line Company operated lines that virtually paralleled the former Sinclair (now Stanolind) route from the Gulf and Mid-Continent to Chicago. For reasons to be discussed in the next chapter, the Prairie companies eventually agreed to sell out, and the transfer of their properties to Sinclair in 1932 replaced those Sinclair had sold to Indiana Standard.

The story of both Shell's and Sinclair's pipeline systems from the start of the gasoline age to 1931 illustrates the crucial role of the underground carrier in knitting producing properties to refineries under common control. In an integrated framework, pipelines provided an outlet for owned production, access to purchased production, and a means of reducing transportation costs to the refinery. While both companies' pipelines were common carriers, they performed transportation services primarily for their parent companies' purchasing and producing subsidiaries. While each did some common-carrier business, it was primarily for other large companies in times when the parent company did not need the lines' full capacity. Both Shell and Sinclair pipelines carried for Indiana Standard at times. When the cost of such service became too great, Indiana Standard found it cheaper to buy into the Sinclair lines than to duplicate them. A combination of circumstances later made it possible to acquire full ownership of these lines while Sinclair replaced them with a system that came on the market as a result of the Prairie companies' difficulties in a new era of integrated concerns.

Shell and Sinclair both developed virtually all areas of integrated operations simultaneously, but they differed in their relative emphasis on self-sufficiency in crude oil. Shell put heavy emphasis on this aspect of the business, and this strategy automatically governed the area and extent of its pipeline operations. Sinclair, on the other hand, put relatively more emphasis on purchasing crude, which meant that Sinclair Crude Oil Purchasing — and therefore Sinclair Pipe Line Company — became active in more areas than Shell Petroleum. This fact was reflected in a comparison of gathering-line mileage for the two companies. Shell had only 564.95 miles as of December 31, 1931;[76] Sinclair (judging by what was transferred to Stanolind) had over 2,600 miles.[77] Sinclair's acquisition of Prairie Pipe Line in 1932 gave it a total of nearly 8,000 miles of gathering lines.[78]

With both Shell and Sinclair, the pipeline investment was primarily justified on the basis of cost savings in delivering crude to refineries of the integrated group. Indiana Standard's backward integration into pipeline ownership was an acknowledgment that these savings were so substantial that no available alternative could completely offset them.

JERSEY STANDARD OIL PRODUCING COMPANIES

The dissolution decree of 1911 had broken up Jersey Standard's carefully devised integration pattern, and during the next two decades much effort and capital were expended to repair the damage. This adjustment necessarily emphasized the importance of pipelines.

As a result of the dissolution, the Jersey Standard Group was left very short on ownership of its own production. In 1912 it had supplied only 8 per cent of its domestic refinery requirements. Although the figure had risen to 17 per cent by 1917, the Jersey Company lagged behind such competitors as Gulf Oil, Texas Company, and Shell; yet it had refining capacity larger than any of them.[79] To help meet its crude-oil needs from Mid-continent sources, the Jersey Company had moved the headquarters of Carter Oil from West Virginia to Tulsa in 1915. The parent company also increased its reliance on Louisiana Standard for some of its requirements.

The Oklahoma Pipe Line Company, wholly owned by Jersey Standard, became the pipeline partner of Carter Oil's production activities. The benefits of such a relationship were illustrated in the case of the Hewitt pool in southern Oklahoma not far from Healdton. Carter and Humble Oil & Refining, another Jersey affiliate, both had leases at Hewitt. The oil could have been run through Prairie Pipe Line to Cushing and there delivered to Oklahoma Pipe Line for transportation to Baton Rouge. But the route was indirect, and Prairie Pipe's rates were high. During 1922–23 consultation among the various Jersey affiliates produced the decision that Oklahoma Pipe Line should build a 165-mile line direct from Hewitt to DeQueen, Arkansas, on the main Oklahoma-Louisiana pipeline route. Estimating a saving of 31 cents a barrel compared to Prairie Pipe's charges, Jersey managers believed that the cost of this new construction would be recovered within a few years. The decision to make the investment with this expectation was based on the fact that Jersey's producing affiliates could guarantee the throughput.[80]

As a corporate entity, Jersey Standard had steered clear of the Lone Star State since Spindletop, but this policy changed under the pressure to obtain additional crude-oil supplies. By 1918, Jersey was actively canvassing ways in which it could enter Texas. The alternatives were to obtain a permit for Carter Oil to operate in the state, to establish a new company under Texas law, or to purchase an interest in a going Texas producing company. The first possibility was ruled out in September 1918 when the Texas attorney-general indicated his opposition to granting a permit to Carter Oil, a West Virginia corporation, to do business in Texas.[81] Further consideration of alternatives was made unnecessary because a newly incorporated Texas concern, Humble Oil & Refining Company, was seeking just such an alliance as Jersey Standard had to offer.

The Humble Oil & Refining Company, the fifth largest crude-oil producing company in Texas in 1917,[82] was the fruit of the work and ambition of a small group of men, including William S. Farish and R. S. Sterling. The Humble Company was in part the outgrowth of their dissatisfaction with the treatment of Texas producers by the large integrated oil companies and affiliated pipelines. Both Farish and Sterling, for example, had been leaders in the effort to obtain pipeline common-carrier legislation in Texas, and Farish had advocated that producers ally themselves with refiners on the East Coast.

Until early 1917 Humble Oil & Refining's predecessor concern, Humble Oil Company, organized in 1911, had been dependent on the pipelines of integrated companies for crude-oil purchasing and for transportation.[83] In January 1917, however, Humble itself entered pipelining on a small scale by acquiring the Southern Pipe Line Company, a small operation organized in 1913 to connect the Goose Creek field near Houston with Baytown. This property was merged into Humble Oil & Refining Company when that concern was formally incorporated on June 21, 1917. Basically a production company, Humble in 1919 also had some refining facilities in addition to the Southern pipeline and the beginnings of a marketing division.[84]

For some years Farish had been advocating that a solution to Texas producers' problems lay in their making alliances with eastern refiners. Humble's need for capital and for an outlet for crude matched Jersey Standard's desire "to build up a large producing business in the State of Texas, and to accumulate storage reserves of crude oil." [85] On this basis the latter concern in 1919 acquired a 50 per cent interest in the Houston-based Humble Company.[86]

Part of the plan for bringing Humble into the Jersey picture involved tapping the new Ranger field in north-central Texas and moving the crude to tidewater on Galveston Bay. Implementation called for a major pipeline project. Therefore, under the amended charter of the Southern Pipe Line Company, Humble Oil & Refining organized the Humble Pipe Line Company, with R. S. Sterling as its president and eight of the nine directors from the parent company. For a few months, the pipeline company purchased crude, but apparently because of problems anticipated in connection with the new jurisdiction of the Texas Railroad Commission over pipelines, the purchasing function was assumed by the parent in July 1919.[87] From that time on, Humble Pipe Line served as a transporter and gatherer of petroleum, expanding its lines as Humble Oil sought new sources of production.[88]

President Farish of the Texas-based company and President Walter Teagle of the Jersey company differed in their views about pipeline rates. Several times during the 1920's, Teagle raised the question of reducing Humble's pipeline rates.[89] Jersey did not completely own Humble, so there was ample room for controversy between the two over pipeline charges. Concerned by the fickle nature of unregulated crude-oil production, Farish favored high rates to insure a quick pay-back of Humble's pipeline investment.[90] As a result of this policy, the pipeline company for a time provided nearly 90 per cent of Humble Oil & Refining's consolidated earnings.[91] Thus, while Jersey Standard did not get the rate reductions it would have liked, it presumably recovered part of its pipeline transportation charges through Humble Oil & Refining dividends. More important, Jersey gained access to the crude that it needed on terms that allowed it to remain competitive with newly integrated companies.

The final member of Jersey Standard's producing and pipeline group in the Mid-Continent-Gulf area was Louisiana Standard. For some years this company had controlled a comparatively small part of total production in the Caddo, De Soto, and River fields of Louisiana. In 1920 it also controlled about 20 per cent of the production in the new Homer, Louisiana, field. Gathered by the Pipe Line Department of Louisiana Standard, the Homer oil was initially shipped by tank car to Moore station near Shreveport, Louisiana, on the Oklahoma-Louisiana trunk line.[92] In a typical succession of transportation modes, an 8-inch line was laid from Moore station to the Homer field as production mounted. Plans to expand pipeline and tankage facilities were revised as the field went into decline in 1920, but new production appeared, first at Haynesville, just below the Arkansas border, and then at El Dorado, Arkansas.* As Louisiana Standard moved into these fields, its pipelines followed and those already laid were looped and doubled.[93]

The greatest strike of this period came at Smackover, Arkansas, in 1922. The resulting flood of oil threatened to overwhelm Louisiana's pipeline system with heavy, viscous crude. To take this load off the main line, a 95-mile branch was extended in 1925 from Smackover to Grand Lake on the Mississippi River, where the Smackover oil was transferred to barges for movement to Baton Rouge. This extension completed the geographical expansion of Louisiana Standard's pipelines, which after 1923 were operated by the newly incorporated Standard Pipe Line Company.[94]

Jersey Standard had the choice of moving its Mid-Continent production northward and eastward over Prairie pipelines and their connections, or routing it to the Gulf and thence to the Atlantic seaboard in tankers that it owned. Wherever possible, Jersey managers preferred to pocket transportation savings by avoiding the use of Prairie Pipe and its connecting carriers. During the early 1920's, therefore, Jersey increased its use of affiliated pipelines and tanker shipments of crude from the Gulf Coast — and briefly from California — to its Atlantic seaboard refineries. With the great upsurge of production in Oklahoma and Texas late in the decade, however, managers of several Jersey-owned companies began to consider construction of a new trunk line northward from the Mid-Continent. The novelty of this proposal lay in their idea that the line might be a joint undertaking with nonaffiliated companies.

THE TEXAS-EMPIRE PIPELINE

The idea of a continuing association of large companies in a common pipeline enterprise to serve each of them was a significant, though not unique, departure from contemporary practice. The cost savings from construction of a larger — and therefore more efficient in terms of cost per barrel — line than one company might build for itself presumably could more than offset any drawbacks of a pipeline partnership arrangement. A major precedent for a so-called "corporate form joint-venture" pipeline already existed. The Texas-Empire Pipe Line, incorporated as a common carrier under Delaware law in 1928, was owned equally by The Texas Corporation and the Empire Gas and Fuel Company, a subsidiary of the Cities Service Company. The line was to serve the refineries of affiliated companies at Lawrenceville, Lockport, and East Chicago, Illinois, with crude oil from the Mid-Continent.

Cities Service had done its refining in Texas and Oklahoma, shipping

---

*An independent pipeline — The Shreveport–El Dorado Pipe Line Company capitalized at $2,500,000 — was organized to move crude from these fields to Shreveport refiners. *Oildom* (June 1921), 66.

refined products northward by railroad tank cars.[95] As rail rates rose, the operating economies of pipelining crude took on great appeal. With a new pipeline moving crude into a new refinery at East Chicago, Cities Service hoped to place itself in a position to compete more effectively in Midwest markets. Likewise, The Texas Corporation planned to increase the output of gasoline from its Lockport refinery, which had been dependent on the Prairie Pipe Line.

During 1929 the Texas-Empire Pipe Line Company (Delaware) built a 12-inch line from Cushing, Oklahoma, to the Missouri–Illinois boundary. There it connected with the trunk line of a subsidiary, Texas-Empire Pipe Line Company (Illinois), which completed the route into the various refineries. On the southern end of the line, the property of the Empire Pipe Line Company was acquired by purchase in 1929, giving access to the flush production of the new Seminole field.[96] The cost of this whole undertaking was large, involving in excess of $17,000,000.[97] Therefore, division of the financial load between the two parent companies had obvious attractions. Indiana Standard and Sinclair had, of course, earlier adopted substantially the same approach, though in their case it had involved Sinclair's sale of a half-interest in an existing system.

THE AJAX PIPE LINE

In the line that it proposed to build from the Mid-Continent to the Midwest, Jersey Standard was joined by the Pure Oil Company and by the Standard Oil Company (Ohio). Although they had a pattern of operations quite different from the other companies discussed earlier in this chapter, Pure and Ohio Standard were equally anxious to obtain crude and reduce their transportation costs. Jersey's plan seemed to offer this possibility.

As a Pennsylvania-based operation before the turn of the century, Pure Oil had been active in pipelining, and by 1906 it had established itself as a significant, integrated competitor of Standard Oil. Control of the company was acquired by the Dawes interests of Chicago in 1917, and in the succeeding decade Pure Oil became an active producer in Texas, Michigan, and other states.[98] Pure Oil refineries at Muskogee and Ardmore, Oklahoma, Smith's Bluff, Texas, and Cabin Creek, West Virginia, were served by short, local pipelines. Refineries at Heath and Toledo, Ohio, received their crude by common-carrier pipeline.[99] Presumably, it was the desire to supply the latter refineries at a lower cost that led Pure Oil to become interested in Jersey's proposal for the new trunk line from the Mid-Continent.

Standard Oil Company (Ohio) was in a much more difficult situation than Pure Oil at this time. Left as a refining and marketing company by the 1911 dissolution decree, Ohio Standard had lacked the capital, and perhaps the ambition, to become a fully integrated concern.[100] During the days of the Standard Oil combination, this company had depended on

Prairie Oil & Gas for its main source of crude, and on Prairie Pipe Line, Illinois Pipe Line, and Buckeye Pipe Line for transportation. In the 1920's, however, the transportation charges paid by Ohio Standard had risen some 15 per cent, and the ratio of transportation charges to the total delivered cost of crude reached 41 per cent in 1928.[101] Unlike the integrated companies with pipelines, Ohio Standard could not recover a part of its transportation costs in the form of dividends from a pipeline subsidiary. Instead, its business was adding to the profits of pipeline common carriers, which prior to the 1911 antitrust decision had been allied with it under Jersey Standard's auspices.

As the result of pricing its products on the basis of manufacturing and transportation costs, Ohio Standard during the 1920's found itself being squeezed out of its market by aggressive newcomers.[102] Its position had slid so far by 1928 that a new president and new board of directors took over the direction of the company.[103] An important part of their strategy was to begin cautious integration backward toward sorely needed crude-oil supplies.

Against this background the Ajax Pipe Line Corporation, a holding company, and Ajax Pipe Line Company, an operating company, were organized in 1930. The operating company proposed to build twin 10-inch lines from the Oklahoma Pipe Line station at Glenn Pool, near Tulsa, to the Wood River station of Illinois Pipe Line Company, providing a daily carrying capacity of 65,000 barrels. Unlike the Texas-Empire, whose capital was supplied by the parents' purchase of stock, Ajax Pipe Line Company had only $20,000 of no-par common stock. Ownership was divided as follows: Jersey Standard, 53 per cent; Pure Oil, 24 per cent; and Sohio, 23 per cent.[104] Jersey advanced the money for construction, and this loan was to be repaid by the Ajax Pipe Line Company borrowing from Ajax Corporation, the holding company.[105]

To guarantee a throughput and repayment of the loan, the participating companies, which in the case of Jersey Standard were Imperial Oil and Standard Oil of New Jersey (Delaware), agreed to purchase specified amounts of crude oil on a five-year contract from Carter Oil, Jersey's Mid-Continent producing affiliate.[106] From Jersey's standpoint, this opportunity to secure a market for crude was presumably one of the major reasons for promoting the pipeline partnership.

Ohio Standard's management, however, was soon complaining that it was not appreciably better off than it had been when dealing with the Prairie companies for crude-oil supplies and their transportation. Carter Oil levied a marketing or brokerage charge of 10 cents a barrel that by 1933 represented about 23 per cent of the value of the crude.[107] Furthermore, Ajax Pipe Line charges were maintained at a high level. Ohio Standard officials estimated that the pipeline company's profit, before federal income tax, averaged over 22 cents a barrel in 1931 and 1932.[108] As Ohio's throughput amounted to nearly half the total but the company owned less than a quarter share in the line, it was not reaping the transportation savings that it had anticipated. Half the profits from the transportation revenues that it was contributing to the "common pot" were going to the other participants in proportion to their stock ownership. In the words of Ohio Standard's management: "If this company obtained the same share of this profit as it contributes thereto, there could be no objection to the high rates as such (except possibly that they tend increasingly to become the target of special tax levies and the like). The truth is, however, that this company contributes considerably more than twice as much of the profit revenue of Ajax as it can ever hope to obtain . . . under the present schedule of . . . stock participation." [109] This was clearly a hazard of the joint-venture pipeline in corporate form. If rates were appreciably above costs and one owner's throughput was greater than his share of ownership, he sacrificed part of his transportation savings to his partners — in effect, reducing their transportation costs.

On the other hand, by virtue of the joint ownership, Ohio Standard's pipeline investment in Ajax was small compared to what would have been required for a completely owned line. Because its share of ownership in Ajax was less than its share of shipments, the Ohio Company was paying a price to its pipeline partners. Still, it was conserving capital for alternative uses and was receiving cheaper transportation than if comparable volumes of oil had been shipped via Prairie Pipe Line, on whose dividends Ohio Standard had no claims at all.

The advantage of only a limited commitment to Ajax accrued when new oil fields were discovered in Illinois and other areas of the Midwest during the latter part of the 1930's. Moving into these areas as a producer and creating its own pipeline system, Ohio Standard reduced its consumption of Mid-Continent crude from 88 per cent of its refinery throughput in 1936 to 2.4 per cent in 1939.[110] As a result, the average distance traveled by crude oil moving through pipelines to the company's refineries dropped from 1,025 miles in 1935 to 465 miles in 1939.[111]

Ohio Standard's experience was one more example of the cost of a refiner's dependence on others for crude oil and transportation, and its escape from this situation was made possible by the discovery of new production closer to its refineries and by changed management attitudes toward integration. In the interim, participation in the Ajax line had provided an intermediate step toward, and at least some of the benefits of, backward integration.

PIPELINES AND THE INTEGRATION MOVEMENT IN REVIEW

The outpouring of oil in the Southwest had created the need and the opportunity for the Ajax line, and it led a number of oil companies to initiate or expand pipeline operations. For example, the whole west Texas producing area, which was first tapped by Humble Pipe Line in 1925, was soon crisscrossed by the underground carriers of other companies.

The flood of oil from Oklahoma and Texas in the late 1920's was so great that trunk lines built earlier to serve Healdton and the fields of east-central Texas, could not handle it. Thus, the Sinclair and Prairie pipelines expanded their carrying capacity to Chicago; and the Gulf Oil, Texas, and Humble companies doubled their main trunk lines to the Gulf. The Texas Company, as already noted, joined with the Empire Gas and Fuel Company to build a pipeline into Illinois.

Roughly paralleling the Ajax route, Gulf Oil in 1930 constructed its own line from Tulsa to Cincinnati and Spencerville, Ohio.[112] As in the Ajax case, the rationale was simple. In the words of Gulf's president, the new pipeline was "the most convenient and economical means to enable Gulf Oil to utilize fully the large production of its subsidiaries in the Mid-Continent . . . and Texas fields . . . In view of existing freight rates, this should mean a very substantial saving over the Gulf Corporation's present method of shipping refined products by rail from its refineries into the territory east of the Mississippi River It also will enable the company to economically reach territory which it does not now serve." [113]

The upswing in pipeline construction by companies that were already fully integrated, or striving to become so, resulted from the need to realize economies at every level of operation. The intense competitive situation in gasoline marketing and the influx of newcomers in this segment of the oil business emphasized the importance of crude-oil self-sufficiency and transportation savings. As a result, acquisition and expansion of pipeline systems by companies engaged in refining and marketing at a distance from the oil fields became virtually a condition of survival.

The quantitative aspects of the resulting spread of pipelines, much of which occurred in the 1920's, were impressive. In the interim between 1915 and 1931, total pipeline mileage in the united States nearly tripled, amounting in the latter year to 115,710 miles.[114] Gathering lines more than doubled, totaling 53,640 miles in 1931; trunk-line mileage tripled, increasing to 58,571 miles. Refined products lines, an innovation which will be discussed in a subsequent chapter, showed a tremendous increase in mileage in their first year — from 534 miles in 1930 to 3,499 miles in 1931.[115]

By 1931 there were 18 important crude-oil trunk pipeline systems traversing parts of the Mid-Continent and Gulf Coast regions, some of them extending eastward beyond the Mississippi River. Sixteen of these pipelines were owned by large integrated oil companies.* The other two belonged respectively to the Illinois Pipe Line Company of Texas, an Ohio Oil affiliate that entered the Yates field in 1927, and the omnipresent Prairie Pipe Line Company, whose ownership in 1931 was about to pass to Sinclair. In short, the expansion of pipeline capacity in the largest producing area of the country between 1915 and 1931 was a reflection and a confirmation of the hold that integration had gained in the oil industry.

*Ajax, Shell, Humble, Gulf, Texas, Texas-Empire, Stanolind, Magnolia, Oklahoma, Empire, Tide Water, Standard of Louisiana, Atlantic, Sun-Yount Lee, Pure-Van, and Sinclair-Texas.

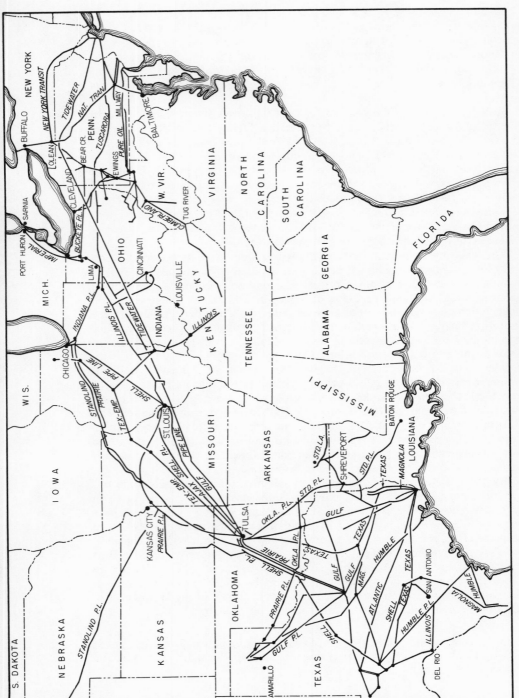

Major trunk pipeline systems, 1930.

Source: National Petroleum News (November 5, 1930), p. 23.

CHAPTER 9

ADAPTATION TO DISSOLUTION: THREE FORMER STANDARD PIPELINE COMPANIES

The integration movement of the years 1915–1931 had serious repercussions on the pipeline systems separated from Jersey Standard as a result of the 1911 dissolution decree. As common-carrier transportation companies, these concerns, whose business had previously been virtually guaranteed by their membership in the Standard family, increasingly had to make their own way on a competitive basis. The initial adjustment was cushioned by the continued dependence of Standard refining companies on the pipelines created by the old Standard integration pattern. In the short run, the dissolution decree, if anything, increased this dependence. Over the longer run, however, as shown in the previous chapter, the backward integration of Standard refining and marketing companies, the creation of new integrated companies, shifting centers of oil production, and competition from water transportation undermined the initially favorable position of Standard's disaffiliated common-carrier pipelines.

This chapter examines three such companies: Prairie Pipe Line, National Transit, and Buckeye Pipe Line. In comparing them, we are looking primarily at their experience as it sheds light on the relationship of common-carrier pipelines to the integration movement in the oil industry during this period. The comparison therefore involves consideration of the situation in which the dissolution decree left each pipeline concern, the flexibility and aggressiveness of managers in dealing with their problems, and external factors that influenced the results of their decisions.

THE PRAIRIE PIPE LINE COMPANY

Prairie Oil & Gas Company had been Standard Oil's oil purchasing, producing, and transporting affiliate in and from the Mid-Continent field. Its pipelines had not acted as common carriers until ordered to do so as a result of The Pipe Line Cases decision in 1914. Although the company had been separated from the Standard combination by the 1911 antitrust decision, Prairie was the largest buyer of crude in the Mid-Continent, and it maintained the largest reserves of crude oil in the United States. The size of its transportation activities may be judged by the fact that during 1914 its pipelines moved over 39,000,000 barrels of crude.[1]

In 1915, in reaction to The Pipe Line Cases, Prairie's pipeline properties were assigned to a new corporation, Prairie Pipe Line Company. This concern, which was legally a common carrier in Kansas, Oklahoma, Arkansas, Missouri, and Illinois, owned over 5,000 miles of trunk and gathering lines,[2] and was the largest pipeline system in the country. Its gathering lines connected with 4,000 producing leases and 16,000 producing wells in Kansas and Oklahoma and represented capacity of 170,000 barrels a day. They fed trunk lines capable of moving 125,000 barrels daily.[3] Despite its new status as a corporate entity, Prairie Pipe Line existed solely to provide transportation services for Prairie Oil & Gas and its customers.

Between 1915 and 1920, Prairie Pipe Line's management pursued an aggressive expansion program. It reinvested 71 per cent of the company's earnings,[4] increasing both gathering and trunk-line facilities. In 1916 the company opened an 8-inch pipe from the Augusta and Eldorado pools in Kansas to Neodesha and an 80-mile, 8-inch line from the Blackwell pool in Oklahoma to the trunk line at Jonesburg station in Kansas.[5] After looping the main line from Cushing, Oklahoma, to Carrolltown, Missouri, and doubling the trunk line from there to Wood River,[6] Prairie was moving 135,000 barrels a day to Indiana and Illinois points by September 1917.[7] Its total daily deliveries at this time were in the vicinity of 175,000 barrels.[8]

Table 9. Cost of pipe and pipeline construction,
Prairie Pipe Line Company, 1916–1920.
(per cent increase over 1915)

Year	2-inch	3-inch	4-inch	6-inch	8-inch	10-inch	12-inch
1916	2.0	7.5	7.4	7.2	9.5	7.0	2.2
1917	54.7	68.3	67.6	68.5	72.3	65.8	58.2
1918	94.5	111.5	108.0	110.0	115.0	105.8	94.8
1919	113.3	122.0	123.2	124.6	131.4	125.0	106.0
1920	148.0	155.7	160.0	160.5	160.5	143.7	129.7

Source: Prairie Pipe Line Company files.

After the Armistice, Prairie Pipe continued to add to its system. A wartime project to connect the prolific Ranger field in north-central Texas with tidewater at Galveston on the Gulf was liquidated and the properties involved were subsequently sold to Humble.[9] In January 1919, however, Prairie opened a 276-mile trunk-line extension connecting the Ranger field with its main line at Cushing. At the same time, pending completion of additional lines of its own, Prairie leased an 8-inch line from the Magnolia Petroleum Company, connecting Bowie, Texas, with its Manuel station at Cushing, giving an additional 20,000 barrels daily capacity out of the Ranger field.[10]

In addition to moving into Texas, Prairie Pipe Line took an early interest in Wyoming production. During the war, it began construction of a line in the Lost Soldier field but sold it to Ohio Oil's Illinois Pipe Line Company in January 1919. As explained later by Prairie president William F. Gates, Prairie had taken on "extra business in Texas which gave us about all the business we cared to look after at that time." [11]

Prairie's investment in pipelines and associated properties increased from $28,000,000 in 1915 to $68,500,000 in 1920.[12] Of this increase, proportionally more was spent on gathering lines than on trunk lines. Investment represented by the former rose from $4,340,000 in 1915 to over $14,000,000 in 1920,[13] while the trunk-line investment climbed from $20,000,000 to $37,-000,000.[14] With these facilities, Prairie Pipe delivered well over 53,000,000 barrels of oil during 1920.[15] The financial results were equally impressive. Despite the costs of the expansion program, the company declared cash dividends totaling $34,290,000 for 1915–1920 inclusive.*

Instead of keeping the company undercapitalized, a typical predissolution practice, the Prairie Pipe Line directors kept it fully capitalized. Although dividends in 1921 dropped to less than half the amount of the first years,[16] surplus had grown steadily and net assets were well in excess of the authorized capitalization of $27,000,000. As a result, in December 1922 the directors voted to increase the capitalization of Prairie Pipe Line to $81,000,000 and to declare a 200 per cent stock dividend, distributed pro rata among existing stockholders.[17]

Prairie Pipe Line's excellent earnings record reflected both the company's initial advantage of a pipeline monopoly in transporting Mid-Continent crude northward and eastward as well as the special relation that existed between Prairie Oil & Gas as a producer and purchaser of crude oil and Standard refineries depending on this source of supply. As long as Prairie customers did not integrate backward to their own production and lacked alternative sources of supply and means of transportation, Prairie Pipe's position was apparently secure.

With the confidence bred by this situation, Prairie Pipe Line's management made few concessions in rates or other requirements. In September 1920 it raised rates by 25 per cent.[18] Adopting a similar attitude, Prairie Oil & Gas in 1921 refused to tie the price of crude to the price of finished products even to satisfy such an important figure as President Walter Teagle of Jersey Standard.[19] This approach encouraged Prairie customers like Indiana Standard to look for other sources of crude and transportation and encouraged Jersey Standard to increase its emphasis on owned production and controlled pipelines.

---

*The dividends (as a per cent of total capitalization of $27,000,000) were as follows (Dividend report filed with the FTC, 1927, Company records):

1915	$ 1,350,000	5 per cent
1916	10,800,000	40 per cent
1917	9,450,000	35 per cent
1918	6,210,000	23 per cent
1919	3,240,000	12 per cent
1920	3,240,000	12 per cent

Table 10. Estimated cost per mile of pipeline based on average cost of pipelines in Kansas, Oklahoma, and Texas, 1919.

Construction items:	*Pipe size*						
	2-inch	*3-inch*	*4-inch*	*6-inch*	*8-inch*	*10-inch*	*12-inch*
Survey	$10	$20	$40	$40	$40	$40	$40
Damage	10	25	50	100	100	100	100
Clear right of way	50	75	100	150	150	150	150
Ditching	200	300	600	750	900	1,050	1,200
Painting	—	—	25	35	45	55	65
Laying	100	150	200	250	425	600	850
Stringing	75	100	125	275	450	675	900
Testing	—	—	20	30	40	50	60
Camp	—	—	—	340	460	580	700
TOTAL CONSTRUCTION	445	670	1,160	1,970	2,610	3,300	4,065
Right of way	20	40	80	130	130	130	130
Fittings	20	30	40	50	60	70	80
TOTAL	485	740	1,280	2,150	2,800	3,500	4,275
10 per cent overhead	48	74	128	215	280	350	426
Cost of pipe	1,080	2,120	3,030	5,343	8,480	12,111	14,832
TOTAL COST	$1,613	$2,934	$4,438	$7,708	$11,560	$15,961	$19,533

Cost of Laying Pipe Across Rivers

Items	*2-inch*	*3-inch*	*4-inch*	*6-inch*	*8-inch*	*10-inch*	*12-inch*
Cost of pipe (ex. heavy)	—	—	—	$ 7,920	$10,930	$15,629	$18,480
Construction	—	—	—	3,000	3,900	4,900	6,100
Cost of clamps	—	—	—	5,288	7,594	8,438	11,813
TOTAL COST	—	—	—	$16,208	$22,424	$28,967	$36,393

Source: Prairie Oil & Gas Company files.

Resuming a practice that had caused Prairie management to reduce rates in 1915, Jersey management began to increase the use of tankers for movements of crude oil from the Gulf Coast to Atlantic seaboard refineries. Between January 1, 1920, and the end of June 1922, for example, Jersey Standard moved twice as much crude to the Atlantic Coast by tanker as it did by pipeline.[20] Furthermore, availability of low-cost California crude oil made it possible to transport it profitably by water to Atlantic Coast refineries in competition with Mid-Continent crude. As a result, the decline of pipeline shipments from the Mid-Continent eastward between 1922 and 1923 was precipitous. The reason was not hard to find. Teagle was informed early in 1922 that a net saving of $0.8438 per barrel would accrue from using Jersey pipelines and tankers rather than the Prairie Pipe Line and its connections to the seaboard.[21]

Table 11.   Pipeline and tanker movements of domestic
crude oil to New York, 1924, 1926.

	Approximate comparative movement (barrels)	
	January–March 1924	*January–March 1926*
Panama Canal tanker route (California to Atlantic seaboard)	12,500,000	3,500,000
Gulf of Mexico tanker route (Gulf to Atlantic seaboard)	10,000,000	16,000,000
Overland pipeline route (Mid-Continent to Atlantic seaboard)	4,250,000	3,750,000

Source: U.S. Department of Commerce, Bureau of Mines, Information Circular 6011, "The Movement of Oil Through the Panama Canal" (July 1926), 3.

Wherever Jersey managers had the choice of using Prairie's or their own pipelines, they naturally favored the latter. One manifestation of this policy was the purchase by Louisiana Standard in 1922 of Prairie Pipe Line's Arkansas Division, originally organized in connection with the problems of securing a right of way for a line from the Mid-Continent fields to Baton Rouge. Acquisition of ownership in this line was part of the expansion program that had pushed a Louisiana Standard pipeline into the El Dorado, Arkansas, field and later added a connection to the Smackover field. Putting the best face possible on these developments, Prairie Pipe Line's president, W. F. Gates, declared that he was not unhappy to be rid of the Arkansas line which was geared to Louisiana Standard's needs and, according to him, had never been very profitable to his company.[22]

Meantime, Prairie Pipe Line had been forced to institute a series of rate cuts to meet the renewed threat from tankers and new potential pipeline competition. In July 1922 the management rescinded half of its 1920 rate increase, and, to meet the competition from tankers moving oil from the Pacific Coast, slashed southern tariff rates by 30 per cent in October 1923.[23]

Jersey Standard's increased use of its own transportation facilities also hurt Prairie's connecting carriers, who participated in the movement of Mid-Continent crude to the Atlantic seaboard.* At Wood River, Prairie delivered to the Illinois Pipe Line (Ohio Oil) which carried the oil to the Pennsylvania border. There the shipments were split between New York Transit, one of the Northern Group of pipelines resulting from the dissoluton decree, and Tuscarora, a subsidiary of Jersey Standard.[24] As the number and size of Jersey Standard shipments declined in the early 1920's, that company stopped using New York Transit in order to give its own affiliate, Tuscarora, as much business as possible. However, the decline in overland Mid-Continent shipments was such that by August 1926 Jersey's Teagle reported that even Tuscarora was virtually out of business.[25]

In that year Jersey managers faced the question of whether or not to reduce rates on their own lines to make the price of their crude, which they wished to sell in some quantity to nonaffiliated companies, more competitive. Jersey marketers and refiners, hoping for a more equitable allocation of profits among integrated operations, favored the reduction. In November 1926 their view prevailed. Jersey-affiliated pipelines dropped their commissions from 10 cents to 5 cents a barrel and gathering charges from 20 cents to 12.5 cents.†[26]

Prairie managers were angered by this decision because it undermined their hope of restoring old gathering charges and commissions. Reportedly, they threatened to encourage ICC action directed toward the separation of pipeline subsidiaries from integrated companies, but Jersey's management refused to budge.[27]

On the route northward from the Mid-Continent field, Prairie Pipe Line also had to face increasing pipeline competition from new integrated com-

*The following figures from *Oil and Gas Journal* (November 8, 1923) indicate the extent of the decline:

| | Barrels (42 gals.) moved | |
Pipeline	1922	1923
Eureka Pipe Line Co.	913,609	418,615
Buckeye Pipe Line	2,437,013	1,060,834
National Transit	1,169,002	654,514
South West Penn. Pipe Lines	1,268,753	632,910
Indiana Pipe Line	2,367,807	1,688,293
Cumberland Pipe Line	160	162
Southern Pipe Line	771,116	188,653
Crescent Pipe Line	158,343	78,753
Northern Pipe Line	857,100	131,797
New York Transit Co.	652,227	25,219
Illinois Pipe Line	289,199	89,976

†Louisiana Standard's difficulties with the Louisiana Public Service Commission also contributed to this reduction. The laid-down price of crude had consisted of average Mid-Continent price for the calendar month during which delivery was made plus a marketing commission of 10 cents a barrel plus gathering and trunk-line charges.

panies. During 1917–18, Sinclair-Cudahy built its line from Drumright, Oklahoma, in the Cushing field to Whiting, Indiana, where Sinclair was building a refinery alongside the great Indiana Standard facility.[28] In 1920, it will be recalled, Indiana Standard, one of the Prairie companies' best customers, acquired a 50 per cent interest in the Sinclair pipelines, including this one. According to Vice-President Clark Kountz of Prairie Pipe Line, the existence of the Sinclair line contributed to Prairie's 1922 decision to reduce rates. This was so, he said, because the new line almost paralleled Prairie's route to Kansas City and was competitive with respect to Sugar Creek and East Chicago.[29] Still another competitive threat was posed by Shell's pipeline system from Cushing to Wood River, which handled common-carrier shipments.

In response to such adverse developments, officials of the Prairie companies became more sales conscious. For example, in an effort to stimulate activity for both Prairie Oil & Gas and Prairie Pipe Line, W. S. Fitzpatrick, now chairman of Prairie Oil & Gas Company's board, was soliciting the business of the Paragon Refining Company of Toledo in February 1924. Such approaches were successful and apparently mutually advantageous.*

In 1926 Prairie Pipe Line strengthened its position as a common carrier by obtaining access to the Gulf of Mexico. As noted earlier, Prairie had made some moves during World War I to build a line from the Ranger, Texas, field south to Galveston, but that plan was abandoned. The next opportunity for a line to the Gulf Coast came when Prairie Oil & Gas acquired an interest in the Mexia field of east-central Texas.

Colonel A. E. Humphreys, a successful wildcatter, brought in major production at Mexia in November 1920. Indiana Standard was short of the very kind of crude that the Mexia field produced. Henry M. Blackmer, president of the Midwest Refining Company, a Wyoming concern in which Indiana Standard owned a substantial interest, determined to obtain this production. Whether he was acting for himself or others is not clear. In any event, he agreed to purchase 30,000,000 barrels of oil from Humphreys and then proceeded to find customers with the pipeline resources to move it. Pure Oil had already agreed to take 50 per cent of the production, up to a maximum of 40,000 barrels a day, and in November 1921, after some complicated negotiations, the remainder was allocated to Prairie Oil & Gas and Sinclair Crude Oil Purchasing.[30]

In connection with this agreement, Pure Oil Built a pipeline from Mexia to Smith's Bluff, Texas.† The line served Pure's new refinery at the Gulf

---

*According to the Federal Trade Commission in 1928, the use of pipelines to obtain Mid-Continent crude gave an Ohio refiner a 1.5 cent per gallon advantage over an Oklahoma refinery shipping gasoline into the same territory by rail. FTC, *Prices, Profits and Competition,* 42. As noted in the preceding chapter, the Texas, Cities Service, and Gulf companies were among those who chose in the late 1920's to maximize such savings by building their own pipelines, individually or in partnership, from the Mid-Continent to their Midwest refineries.

†Construction of this 8-inch line was by the Humphreys Pure Oil Company, which also acquired the gathering lines of the Humphreys Mexia Company.

and also loaded tankers that moved the Texas crude to the Pure Oil refinery at Marcus Hook, Pennsylvania. Under agreements made later in 1925 and early in 1926, Prairie Pipe Line acquired the Pure Oil Pipe Line Company of Texas for $7,564,000 cash and agreed to transport Pure's crude, as a common carrier, up to a maximum of 18,000 barrels per day.[31] Meantime, Prairie had also connected the Mexia field to its main trunk line.[32]

By acquisition of the Pure Oil line,* Prairie Pipe placed itself in a position to compete for crude-oil traffic moving to the Gulf as well as northward. Thus in April 1926 T. J. Flannelly, acting for the pipeline company's vice-president, told the Atlantic Refining Company: "We will be very glad to move any oil tendered to us for shipment to Smith's Bluff, under our regular published tariff applying to the movement. The tariff, of course, calls for a ten cent gathering rate and the carrying company is not in a position to discriminate.[33]

Table 12.   Pure Oil Pipe Line Company of Texas. Barrels of oil
delivered by destination, 1926–1927.

Destination	1926	1927
Smith's Bluff — Pure Oil Company	2,349,810.32	1,392,246.35
Smith's Bluff — Prairie Oil & Gas Company (Pure Oil Co.)	2,465,363.48	3,727,515.74
Humble — Prairie Oil & Gas Company (American Pet. Co.)	366,555.58	301,694.42
Humble — American Petroleum Company	448,696.19	101,406.25
Smith's Bluff — for boat loading	1,142,209.33	420,264.41
Smith's Bluff — Prairie Oil & Gas Company (Vacuum Oil Co.)	—	726,915.64
Total	6,772,634.90	6,670,042.81

Source: Statement prepared by Prairie Pipe Line Company for New York Stock Exchange, 1928.

In summary, despite mounting threats to its supremacy, Prairie Pipe Line during the 1920's maintained its position as the largest pipeline system in the country. It had extended its trunk and gathering systems into the Ranger field of Texas in 1919, into the Mexia field in 1922, and followed Prairie Oil & Gas into the Panhandle of Texas in 1926–27.† The principal

*The officers of the newly acquired Pure Oil Pipe Line Company of Texas were the same as those of Prairie Pipe Line, though the roles of Clark Kountz, vice-president of the parent, and W. F. Gates, president of Prairie Pipe, were reversed in the subsidiary. The principal office of the Texas company was in Independence, Kansas, but its operating headquarters were in Dallas.

†Prairie Oil & Gas laid a gathering system in the Panhandle field in July 1926. Prairie Pipe began a trunk line from the field in the same month and completed it in April 1927. Meantime, Prairie Oil & Gas had provided storage facilities. Letter, T. J. Flannelly to The Plains Pipe Line Company, Panhandle, Texas, February 2, 1928, Prairie files.

shipper using the Prairie pipelines was Prairie Oil & Gas, which originated about 95 per cent of the business.[34]

In mid-1928 the Prairie Pipe Line directors decided that the time had come again to adjust the amount of stock to actual assets and to reduce the price of shares. Earnings had recovered from the slump of 1923–24, there was no funded debt, and the company's surplus account stood at well over $42,000,000, without including the balances of the Pure Oil Pipe Line Company of Texas.[35] The purchase of a substantial number of Rockefeller shares in the company by the investment firm of Blair & Company may also have influenced the decision on a stock dividend. In any event, at a special meeting in Independence, Kansas, November 28, 1928, the directors agreed to reduce the par value of the stock from $100 to $25 and to increase the number of shares to 4,050,000, which included 810,000 shares to be distributed as a stock dividend. Upon approval of stockholders and public authorities, $20,250,000 was to be transferred from surplus to the capital stock account, bringing the capitalization of the company to $101,250,000.*[36]

These moves suggested that Prairie Pipe Line was going "public" in preparation for further expansion. At the directors' meeting, President W. F. Gates said as much. Gates indicated that he had suggested reduction in the par value of shares and an increase in their number because shares were currently selling greatly in excess of par and it was desirable to bring them within reach of a larger number of investors. To the same end, he proposed that the shares be listed on the New York Stock Exchange.[37] The favorable response of the directors to these suggestions was ratified at a stockholders' meeting on January 4, 1929.

The increased capitalization and attempts to interest more small investors were geared to plans already under way to make the Prairie companies the cornerstone of a completely integrated company.[38] The acquisition of a controlling interest in the Producers' and Refiners' Corporation in 1923 had been a first step in this direction. Incorporated in Wyoming in 1917, the P. and R. company by 1927 was an active producer of oil and gas in that state, in Texas, the Mid-Continent, and Canada. It operated refineries at Parco, Wyoming, and Tulsa and Blackwell, Oklahoma. The company also owned or controlled retail service stations in eight states.[39]

The new Prairie integration strategy was intertwined with the hopes, ambitions, and strategies of the Sinclair and Indiana Standard companies in obtaining crude oil. When these three companies had entered the Mexia field, it was under conditions that led to trouble for some of their top management. One of the arrangements affecting the relationship of the various parties was the provision that Mexia oil be bought for $1.50 a barrel and sold to Prairie Oil & Gas and to Sinclair Crude Oil Purchasing Company for $1.75 through an intermediary, the Continental Trading Company. This concern, which had a brief existence on paper, was appar-

*The company's properties included 12,500 miles of trunk and gathering lines, 3,000 miles of telephone and telegraph line, 44 main-line pumping stations, and 84 field pumping stations. Listing statement, A-8388, New York Stock Exchange, January 1929.

Table 13. Prairie Pipe Line Company. Barrels of oil delivered by destination, 1923–1927.

Destination	1923	1924	1925	1926	1927
Neodesha[a]	2,443,582.00	2,958,264.15	3,379,417.73	3,087,189.26	2,280,960.07
Sugar Creek[b]	3,164,103.66	1,751,962.27	1,211,311.94	1,908,778.96	1,921,693.83
Wood River[c]	5,090,470.53	5,480,455.03	7,319,453.49	7,303,385.18	7,288,722.07
Wood River[d]	18,158.02	655,350.92	654,832.41	906,638.18	1,445,328.07
Wood River[e]	—	—	—	—	944,259.71
Wood River[f]	13,916,993.45	9,499,059.46	12,799,819.40	9,959,137.56	16,215,548.25
Griffith[g]	24,329,642.35	21,080,812.82	25,218,742.17	25,206,640.28	26,972,093.02
Drumright[h]	686,312.65	112,050.23	—	—	223,919.27
Lockport[i]	—	1,117,189.53	1,808,895.20	2,043,229.40	2,131,467.97
Hewitt[j]	—	—	—	273,582.18	924,025.51
Bluitt[k]	—	—	—	—	4,177,886.75
Total	49,649,262.66	42,655,144.41	52,392,472.34	50,688,581.00	64,525,904.52

Source: Statement Prepared by Prairie Pipe Line Company for New York Stock Exchange, 1928.

a. Refinery, Standard Oil Company (Kansas) Neodesha, Kan..
b. Refinery, Standard Oil Company (Indiana), Sugar Creek, Mo.
c. Refinery, Standard Oil Company (Indiana), Wood River, Ill.
d. Refinery, White Star Refining Company, Wood River, Ill.
e. Refinery, Lubrite Refining Company, Wood River, Ill.
f. Illinois Pipe Line Company, Wood River, Ill.
g. Indiana Pipe Line Company, Griffith, Ind.
h. Oklahoma Pipe Line Company, Drumright, Okla.
i. Refinery, The Texas Company, Lockport, Ill.
j. Oklahoma Pipe Line Company, Hewitt, Okla.
k. Pure Oil Pipe Line Company of Texas, Bluitt, Tex.

ently introduced into the arrangements only to collect the 25-cent commission. Even after paying this commission, the purchasers were still acquiring crude oil at a price appreciably below the going Mid-Continent price of $2.00 a barrel. On the other hand, representatives of the companies involved, including James E. O'Neil of Prairie Oil & Gas, personally received a share of these savings via the short-lived Continental Trading Company.[40]

O'Neil, whose career in the oil industry stretched back to 1886*, resigned as Prairie Oil & Gas president in September 1923 for reasons of health and left for France early in 1924. Seriously ill, he returned to Montreal, Canada, in 1925 and there revealed some of the details of the Mexia agreements to W. S. Fitzpatrick, chairman of Prairie Oil & Gas, Clark Kountz, vice-president of Prairie Pipe Line, and Judge T. J. Flannelly, the Prairie companies' general counsel. O'Neil had not touched the proceeds of his share in the Mexia adventure, and, at his direction, the Prairie officials recovered $800,000 in 3.5 per cent Liberty bonds from O'Neil's son and kept them at their Independence headquarters.[41]

Similar Liberty bonds, acquired from the Continental Trading Company were also involved in the Teapot Dome affair, which seriously implicated Harry Sinclair and his Mammoth Oil Company and Colonel Robert Stewart of Indiana Standard. When legal proceedings and congressional investigations growing out of these complicated affairs came to a head in 1928, Fitzpatrick publicly revealed possession of the O'Neil bonds by Prairie Oil & Gas.[42]

With Harry Sinclair in the courts and in serious trouble, the Prairie companies and Bancamerica-Blair, an investment house, saw a possible opportunity to acquire the properties of Sinclair Oil.[43] Dependent on production, purchase, sale, and transportation of only crude oil, the Prairie companies were in a vulnerable position in an industry increasingly characterized by complete integration of operations.[44] The possible opportunity to acquire the Sinclair refineries, as well as Sinclair producing, purchasing, and pipe-line properties, therefore had a significant appeal for Prairie's expansion-minded management.

According to internal records of the Prairie companies, at least as early as the first half of 1927 Prairie officials had discussed among themselves the possibility "of consolidating the properties of their respective companies with another company, primarily Sinclair, so that their properties would form a part of an integrated company."[45] Clark Kountz reportedly broached this possibility informally with Harry Sinclair on a train en route to Chicago sometime in September 1927. Apparently this approach was not rebuffed, and two months later, Fitzpatrick requested that L. R. Crawford, an experienced refiner and gasoline marketer who was president of the Prairie-affiliated Producers' and Refiners' Corporation, make a survey of

*A brief summary of O'Neil's career is in *Oildom* (October 1923), 18. O'Neil died in 1932 in France. He left an affidavit denying that he had committed any offense against his government. M.R. Werner and John Starr, *Teapot Dome* (New York, 1959), 292.

Sinclair properties. At a meeting at the Plaza Hotel in New York City in January 1928, representatives of the three companies agreed to such a survey. Crawford subsequently visited Sinclair refineries and their most important marketing outlets, submitting his findings in May 1928. Reportedly, investigation of the possibilities of a consolidation had the personal approval of John D. Rockefeller, Sr.[46]

At this point it seemed that the Prairie companies were definitely stronger than Sinclair and would dominate any merger. Accordingly, in October 1928 Prairie management discussions were proceeding on the basis of exchanging nine shares of Sinclair for five of Prairie Oil and two shares of Sinclair for one of Prairie Pipe.[47] However, the Sinclair and Prairie companies remained far apart on their respective evaluations of the terms for a merger. In August 1929 both parties decided that outside appraisers should be employed. For this purpose Coates & Burchard were retained to appraise producing properties, tankage, and other facilities of both companies used in production. Ford, Bacon & Davis were asked to appraise the refining, distribution, and gas interests.[48] By the end of the year the appraisals had been completed.

Although 1929 was a banner year for Prairie Pipe Line, a flurry of new pipeline construction by integrated companies soon began to threaten the Prairie position. The Texas-Empire Pipe Line was constructed during 1929 from Cushing, Oklahoma, to the Missouri–Illinois state line, and by construction and purchase soon provided a trunk system from the Gulf to Chicago. In July 1930 the Gulf Pipe Line Company of Pennsylvania commenced construction of a 10-inch line from a point near Tulsa to Ohio. To these lines competing directly with Prairie Pipe, the joint-venture Ajax Pipe Line added another. This trunk line from Glenn Pool, Oklahoma, to Wood River, Illinois, commenced operations in late 1930. Meantime, Indiana Standard, which had been one of Prairie's best customers, signed an agreement with Sinclair to acquire complete ownership of that concern's pipeline and crude-oil purchasing facilities.

The list of Prairie reverses during 1930 lengthened steadily as one customer after another canceled its purchases from Prairie Oil & Gas and its shipments over Prairie pipelines. On March 10, Standard Oil Company of New York gave notice of discontinuance. In August, Pure Oil Company completed the Pure-Van Pipe Line from Van Zandt County in central Texas to Beaumont, in a move which Prairie Pipe officials thought completely violated the spirit and intent of the arrangements with which their company had acquired the Pure Oil Pipe Line Company of Texas in 1926. In the same month Gulf Oil purchased the Paragon Refining Company, a Prairie customer, and commenced a pipeline to supply its new affiliate. In September, Imperial Oil of Canada, a Jersey Standard affiliate, gave its notice, relying upon arrangements already concluded for service by Ajax. As that line neared completion, Jersey Standard and Ohio Standard joined the growing roster of companies who had withdrawn their patronage from Prairie; meanwhile Vacuum Oil had acquired the Lubrite and White Star

Table 14. Prairie Pipe Line Company revenues derived
from principal consignees, December 31, 1929 — December 31, 1931.

Consignee	1929	1931
Atlantic Refining Co.	$1,371,174	$449,960
Imperial Oil Refineries (Ltd.)	1,074,746	none
Lubrite Refining Co.	619,238	330,941
Paragon Refining Co.	1,356,460	none
Pure Oil Co.	553,546	none
South Penn Oil Co.	564,379	142,731
Standard Oil Co. (Indiana)	15,086,120	1,558,780
Standard Oil Co. (Kansas)	730,907	none
Standard Oil Co. (Louisiana)	1,034,010	15,483
Standard Oil Co. (New York)	800,675	none
Standard Oil Co. (New Jersey)	763,626	none
Standard Oil Co. (Ohio)	4,137,031	18,329
Sun Oil Co.	2,390,171	928,768
The Texas Co.	986,744	none
White Star Refining Co.	1,726,388	1,168,209

Source: 72 Cong., 2 Sess., House Report No. 2192, Part II, 148.

refining companies, which previously had depended on the Prairie companies.[49]

As a result of these defections, plus the great flood of oil from the newly-discovered east Texas field, Prairie Oil & Gas discontinued the general purchase of Mid-Continent oil as of January 1, 1931. Announcement of this move caused consternation among small producers in Kansas and Oklahoma, leading directly to a new demand that federal action be taken to separate oil pipeline and production activities from common ownership.[50]

A meeting of pipeline and crude-oil purchasing company representatives was held at Tulsa late in December 1930 to discuss the plight of the small well owner. A. W. Peake, vice-president of Indiana Standard, denied that his company had aggravated their situation by its purchase of 100 per cent interest in the Sinclair Pipe Line. Indiana, he said, still drew its crude from the same sources as before the transaction. Prairie, he charged, continued to run oil from its own properties while leaving other companies the responsibility for buying the production from small stripper wells. In fact, Peake claimed, Indiana, to help out, was currently taking 18,000 barrels a day from Prairie Oil & Gas and transporting it over Prairie Pipe Line even though Indiana's Stanolind pipeline system was running at less than capacity.* To Peake's attack, W. S. Fitzpatrick, of Prairie Oil & Gas, simply re-

*Stanolind Pipe Line Company made strenuous efforts to care for the stripper production abandoned by Prairie Pipe Line, and in January 1931, under pressure from newly elected Kansas Governor Harry H. Woodring, Indiana Standard paid Prairie a premium to collect and run 300,000 barrels of "distress" Kansas crude. Giddens, *Standard Oil Company (Indiana)*, 459–460.

plied: "I came here not to engage in a publicity contest with anybody." [51] Meantime, despite the decline in business, Prairie Pipe Line declared an extra dividend of 50 cents a share in addition to the regular quarterly dividend of 75 cents. On news of this decision, a previously worried Richmond, Virginia, owner of 500 shares wrote C. H. Kountz: "I congratulate you and your associates upon your splendid achievement." [52]

While the impact of changes in the Prairie companies' business was worrisome during 1930, it appeared catastrophic by the end of 1931. Pipeline operating revenue dropped from over $38,000,000 in 1929 to a little less than $10,000,000 in 1931.[53] As worried Prairie officials saw it, the backward integration of refining and distributing companies into crude-oil production and purchasing in the field, plus their construction of their own pipelines, had ended Prairie's chances of surviving without also becoming part of an integrated structure. In their words:

> The recent construction of the Ajax pipe line and Gulf pipe line to the East, the Texas-Empire line to Chicago, the Pure-Van line from central Texas to the Gulf, the line of the Standard of Kansas to the El Dorado field, and of other lines by local refiners, the construction of gasoline pipe lines, and the acquisition by the Standard of Indiana of the Sinclair's half interest in the Sinclair pipe line, have enabled these companies and refiners to transport their crude oil requirements over their own pipe line facilities, naturally causing a further decline of shipments over the lines of this Company. Moreover, as a result of the construction of such other facilities, a large portion of the Prairie Oil & Gas Company's current production is necessarily sold to purchasers either owning or holding an interest in such facilities, and such oil is being transported by such purchasers over their own lines.[54]

These developments had eroded Prairie's bargaining position vis-à-vis Sinclair to the point where their original roles — at least as contemplated by Prairie officials — had been reversed. At the annual meeting of the American Petroleum Institute in Chicago early in November 1930, Fitzpatrick and Sinclair had announced that no consolidation could be arranged. Apparently hoping that successful overtures to other companies might bring Sinclair around, Prairie officers began to sound out the National Refining Company and Tide Water, while also toying with the idea of purchasing the Keaton Oil Company and the Long Oil Company. In March 1931 the Prairie Pipe Line board was enlarged to seven members, and bankers representing Bancamerica-Blair — which was active in all the negotiations — were added to that body. The same procedure was followed at the Prairie Oil & Gas annual meeting in April.

By May, negotiations with Sinclair were in progress again, this time with ratios of stock exchange vastly altered from those proposed by Prairie management two years before. Now, the bargaining proceeded on the basis of one share of Sinclair for one share of Prairie Oil & Gas and 1.2 or 1.4 shares of Sinclair for each one of Prairie Pipe. By the end of June, the Rockefellers' attorney had agreed to a consolidation of the Prairie companies with Sinclair, provided that other companies, including Tide Water, were included.[55] In September, however, Tide Water was definitely dropped from the proposal.

After additional negotiations at the annual API meeting and at 26 Broadway, the consolidation of the Prairie companies with Sinclair was finally arranged. Consolidation was on the basis of an exchange of stock in the ratios discussed the preceding spring, with 1.4 shares of Sinclair being exchanged for each share of Prairie Pipe. In January 1932 Prairie stockholders were notified of the arrangement, to which concurrence of 80 per cent of them was necessary. Although there were many stockholder complaints, the consolidation was approved at a special meeting on March 1, 1932.

Arguments in behalf of the move were offered to stockholders by W. S. Fitzpatrick, chairman of the board of Prairie Oil & Gas. The Prairie companies, he said, had been divorced from the integrated oil industry by court order and could no longer count on old ties of common ownership to preserve a market for their crude oil and services. One alternative would have been to add refining and marketing to existing activities, but this course would have been costly, and competitive conditions and overcapacity in the industry did not favor it. The other alternative, and the one finally embraced, was to consolidate with a company already firmly established in those areas of the industry where the Prairie companies lacked facilities. In writing to the stockholders, Fitzpatrick pointed out:

> A consolidation of the properties of your Company with those of the Sinclair Company and The Prairie Pipe Line Company is a most logical one from your standpoint. The operations of the Sinclair Company are already well diversified. It has refineries with a rated capacity of more than 130,000 barrels a day. It markets more than a billion gallons of gasoline a year and is one of the largest manufacturers of lubricants. Its products are distributed through more than 33,000 retail outlets in 45 states of the United States, and in Mexico, Cuba, and European countries. It is also a large producer of crude oil.

Fitzpatrick concluded that:

> Combining the Prairie and Sinclair lines will result in no substantial duplication of lines and will create the largest oil pipe line system in the world, with facilities not only adequate for the pipe line transportation requirements of Consolidated's [the combined] business, but also of sufficient capacity to continue the general transportation of oil for others as heretofore.[56]

While concurring in the logic and prospects of the consolidation, at least one reputable investment advisory service felt that Prairie Pipe stockholders were getting the worst of the deal. This commentary declared: "It is our thought that stockholders in Prairie Pipe Line are not obtaining as liberal terms as they might have expected . . . We see little incentive to exchanging a share of Prairie Pipe Line for stock now selling . . . [at] around 7 7/8, when at last report the former had an equity . . . of about $14 a share." [57] The advance of $18,500,000 by the pipeline company to Prairie Oil & Gas in January 1932 to help liquidate the latter's indebtedness to

New York banks and to provide working capital[58] lends some credence to this judgment.

The Prairie purchase was part of a major shift in the organization of Sinclair activites. As of December 31, 1931, a holding company, the Sinclair Consolidated Oil Corporation, held 100 per cent interest in 13 subsidiaries engaged in all aspects of the oil business. Control of four pipeline companies was exercised through the Sinclair Refining Company. Three of them — the Union, Fords Brook, and Allegany — operated gathering facilities only and served the Wellsville, New York, refinery of Sinclair Refining. The Sinclair-Texas Pipe Line Company, incorporated in 1920, operated short trunk lines to Kansas refineries.[59] By acquisition of the Pierce Petroleum Corporation in 1930, Sinclair Consolidated had gained two additional pipeline companies — the Pierce Pipe Line Company operating in Oklahoma and Texas and the Consolidated Pipe Line Company operating only in Oklahoma but participating in interstate movements.[60] But these lines were insignificant compared to those that came from consolidation with the Prairie companies.

On March 31, 1932, the corporate changes and integration of Prairie properties with those of Sinclair took place. On that date Sinclair Consolidated Oil Corporation became Consolidated Oil Corporation. The Pierce, Consolidated, and Pure Oil Pipe Line of Texas, now renamed the Sinclair Prairie Pipe Line Company (of Texas), were placed under the holding company. Sinclair Refining continued its ownership of the gathering systems in the Appalachian field, and the Sinclair-Texas Pipe Line was reorganized to embrace the major trunk-line properties of Prairie Pipe Line.[61] These properties represented some 15,000 miles of pipe, almost evenly divided between gathering and trunk lines, and a net investment of nearly $71,000,000.[62]

Reviewing the experience of the Prairie companies after their formal separation from the Standard Oil group, it is hard to escape the conclusion that managerial attitudes and practices contributed to the ultimate necessity of consolidation with an integrated concern. The early monopoly that the Prairie Pipe Line Company exercised over pipeline movements northward and eastward from the Mid-Continent gave it a particularly advantageous position as a common carrier. Ironically, this early advantage, which management exploited to the fullest, appears to have been a major factor in the ultimate deterioration of Prairie's position. The refusal of the Prairie companies to do business except on their own terms alienated their customers, even within the previously closely allied Standard Oil group.

Factors beyond management's control, however, also contributed to the decline of the Prairie companies. The feasibility and cheapness of water transportation from the Gulf, the availability of cheap California crude, and the need increasingly felt by refining and marketing companies to control their own sources of crude and the means of transporting it worked against maintenance of Prairie's predominant position in the Mid-Continent. Flush production in new areas provided an opportunity for new entrants into both producing and transporting. Even the joint-venture device for splitting the costs of expensive pipeline construction can also be said to have contributed to the downfall of the Prairie companies, since it facilitated construction of facilities that otherwise might not have duplicated those offered by the independent carrier. But after all is said and done, the tendency of Prairie management to delay action until they were forced into it — whether in rate reductions or in moves toward integration — must be regarded as a crucial factor in the companies' eventual demise. Prairie Pipe Line's experience certainly suggests that a pipeline system existing simply as a common-carrier conduit between producing and refining properties under separate control could not survive a major movement to integrate all three of these phases of the oil business.

NATIONAL TRANSIT COMPANY

Located in an area of declining production and virtually at the end of the long network of pipe that moved Prairie's production from the Mid-Continent to the East Coast, the National Transit Company was potentially even more vulnerable to forces beyond its control than was the Prairie system. But, as it turned out, this concern managed to survive.

Once the cornerstone of Jersey's pipeline empire, National Transit was left by the dissolution of 1911 as a gatherer of local production and a participating carrier in through movements of crude from other areas to Jersey's seaboard refineries. Its operations were confined to the state of Pennsylvania, and this fact was the governing one in the company's adaptation as a common carrier to changing conditions between 1915 and 1931.

In some respects, National Transit's pump and machinery department, which manufactured steam pumps, oil and gas engines, pipe fittings, and other field and pipeline equipment, was one of the company's most valuable assets. Inherited from the days when National Transit was Jersey's pipeline construction agent, it specialized in "tailor-made" equipment for buyers from all over the world.[63] In 1915 the department was transferred to the newly incorporated National Transit Pump and Machine Company. This move avoided complications in accounting procedures for transportation and manufacturing activities (a point of some significance in view of the ICC's jurisdiction over the former), provided a basis for more effective advertising, and, most important, put the manufacturing subsidiary in a position to benefit from the tax exemption conferred on such enterprises by the state.[64]

In the same year, 1915, National Transit also acquired the 33-mile pipeline that ran from a connection with its lines at the Pennsylvania-Maryland border to Jersey's Baltimore (Canton) refinery. This property became available as a result of the New Jersey company's decision to end its direct ownership of crude-oil pipelines. The Maryland Pipe Line Company, a wholly-owned subsidiary incorporated June 15, 1915, was organized by National Transit to own and operate these facilities.[65]

As National Transit's capitalization was considerably in excess of its current and anticipated future needs, capital stock was reduced by 50 per cent in 1916 and a cash dividend of $12.50 per share was declared. Even so, the company still had a surplus of over $3,000,000 and no significant debt.[66]

The war years and 1922–23 were comparatively good ones for National Transit, but trunk-line revenues sagged ominously in 1924 and collapsed in 1925. In the latter year there was a net loss of more than $73,000 on trunk-line operations.[67] This reverse reflected the decline in through shipments of crude oil from the Mid-Continent and other points to the eastern seaboard. Tankers began to supply the needs of the Baltimore refinery and National Transit's subsidiary, Maryland Pipe Line Company, was operated only occasionally after 1924.[68] The poor showing of trunk pipeline operations was, however, at least partially offset by the good earnings of the manufacturing subsidiary which had expanded into the industrial field,* revenue from gathering operations, and income from a reserve fund of about $6,000,000 held primarily in the form of United States Government obligations. As a result, despite the slump in trunk-line revenue, dividends paid to National Transit stockholders in 1925 amounted to 10 per cent on the outstanding capital stock.[69]

While the reduction of through shipments was a source of concern, by 1927 the decline in Pennsylvania production had reached a point where it could no longer support competing pipeline systems, a fact which actually helped to ease National Transit's problem. Early in 1927 Pure Oil, which was reorganizing its operations on the basis of crude supplied from the Southwest, reached the decision to dismantle its Cornplanter Refinery in western Pennsylvania and to sell various parts of its pipeline system in that state, West Virginia, and Ohio. News of the decision to sell Pure's eastern pipeline system led to inquiries from several local refiners and oil brokers,[70] but South-West Pennsylvania Pipe Lines and National Transit in Pennsylvania, Eureka in West Virginia, and Buckeye in Ohio became the major interested parties. Pure Oil and National Transit agreed in August 1927 to the latter's purchase of the so-called "Blue Jay" lines stretching north from the southern boundary of Butler County to Titusville and Warren. However, the sale, involving $660,000, could not be consummated until it had the approval of the Pennsylvania Public Service Commission. Two groups appeared before this body to oppose the transaction. The resulting controversy revealed the basic strategy of National Transit's management.

The first of the protesting groups consisted of minority stockholders representing some 16,000 (out of a total of 509,000) shares. It was apparently led by Benjamin Graham, a New York investor in oil companies. These protestants questioned the adequacy of the data on the transaction filed with the commission and challenged the wisdom of the purchase by

---

*The Transit Company supplied all kinds and sizes of pumps and allied machinery and tools for varied uses. Among its customers were municipal waterworks and the U.S. Shipping Board. Standard Corporation Reports, April 7, 1932.

National Transit. In their petition, they asserted that the company's pipe-line operations had been conducted at a loss during 1926, that the trunk-line business was at the mercy of shippers who were free to transfer their business to tankers, and that acquisition of additional unprofitable pipe-lines was not in the best interest of the company or its stockholders.[71]

The other group opposing National Transit's acquisition of the Pure Oil pipelines was composed of local refiners: The Independent Refining Company, Continental Refining Company, Empire Oil Works, American Oil Works, Titusville Oil Works, and Crystal Oil Works. As manufacturers of lubricants from Pennsylvania-grade crude oil, they pointed out that unsatisfactory segregation of that crude by the Southern Group of pipelines and National Transit had led in 1925 to Pure's taking over the delivery to them of crude oil gathered by Eureka Pipe Line in West Virginia. The refiners not only had this specific grievance against National Transit, but also they had not forgotten the genesis of the Pure Oil pipelines as an answer to Standard Oil's power in the early days to the Pennsylvania oil industry. Therefore they declared "that the necessity for the independent operation of said pipe line system exists today and will continue to exist the same as existed in the past as set forth in this protest and that the approval of said sale will . . . work serious hardship on Protestants and again threaten with the destruction the business of said Protestants." [72]

President F. D. Williams of National Transit, a veteran of over half a century of pipelining, testified before the State Public Service Commission, October 27, 1927, in support of the proposed purchase. He declared that he had been considering the matter for two years or so and was convinced that the elimination of existing duplication between National Transit and Pure Oil pipelines would serve all interests. Producers would have access to a broader market than they had enjoyed previously; the purchase eliminated the possibility that stripper production might be left without pipeline connections for lack of its profitability to any new pipeline venture; National Transit could transport the increased amount of oil profitably, and the public would thereby benefit through postponement or avoidance of any request for a rate increase. Although he admitted the poor results from pipelining in the recent past, Williams expressed confidence that net income from the Pure Oil lines would pay the cost of their acquisition within five years. Norton H. Weber, vice-president of Pure Oil, made substantially the same points.[73]

By the time this hearing was held, the controversy had been narrowed down to one between National Transit's management and the group of minority stockholders, for the refiners had been pacified by a written agreement with National Transit and connecting carriers. Under its terms, the pipelines agreed not to discriminate, to keep Pennsylvania-grade crudes separate from lower quality oils as much as possible, and to allow a representative of shippers and consignees to inspect the procedures followed to maintain this purity.[74]

The Public Service Commission found no compelling reason to forbid the sale, and by mid-December 1927 the transfer of ownership and operation was complete. The additional capacity increased daily runs from customers' tanks by about 700 barrels and allowed better utilization of the entire National Transit system, which was delivering to 20 refineries in western Pennsylvania and numbered the Eclipse Works of Atlantic Refining Company at Franklin and the Pennzoil Company at Rouseville among its largest customers.[75]

At this same time, the outlook for the trunk-line business took a turn for the better. Crude oil delivered to Philadelphia by tanker was to be moved inland by pipeline. According to National Transit's 1927 report, "This is a radical departure from the practice since the beginning of the Transcontinental Pipe Lines, and the first time that oil will have been pumped west instead of eastward. Some changes in the line construction and pumping stations will be necessary to accomplish this plan. The prospect of the new westward traffic, together with increased interior deliveries, indicates in our opinion, that the pipe line business has a brighter outlook than it has had for some time." [76] These expectations were realized in 1928, when 3,000,00 more barrels than in 1927 were delivered out of the trunk-line system.[77] Perhaps to mollify the minority stockholders, and in any case to eliminate excess working capital from the business, the directors voted a special dividend amounting to $7.00 a share, payable in mid-June 1928. The losses of 1926–27 on pipeline operations were followed by a rise which brought operating income to 90 cents a share in 1929 and then a leveling off at about 50 cents a share.[78]

In 1931 National Transit was conducting a moderately successful common-carrier operation. Its lines carried for no parties having an interest in its securities, the Rockefeller Foundation with nearly 25 per cent of the stock being the largest holder. About 2,500 miles of gathering lines served 5,794 parties, either producers or purchasers of crude oil, and the 1,313 miles of trunk line handled shipments for 20 different parties. Tariffs were filed with both the Public Service Commission of Pennsylvania and the ICC. A little more than 75 per cent of the oil moved came under interstate tariffs and produced 71.4 per cent of the year's pipeline revenue.[79] Six new pipeline pump stations, five of them with electrically operated pumps, had been added to accommodate the westward traffic to Pittsburgh and Franklin.

National Transit Pump and Machine Company, which supplied this equipment, was substantially overhauled during the year. The outlay of approximately $1,000,000 was justified on the grounds of the low cost of labor and materials. On the other hand, the volume of manufacturing business was so low that National Transit's annual report concluded with a reminder that stockholders could help the parent company by referring business to the manufacturing subsidiary.[80] Maryland Pipe Line Company, the other subsidiary, was inactive.

Like the Prairie companies, National Transit depended on its affiliations with former members of the Standard Oil combination for the bulk of its pipeline revenues. However, gathering operations and transportation for independent refiners in western Pennsylvania were an important part of the business and helped to take up the slack created by a decline in through movements. Unlike Prairie Pipe Line, National Transit was in a position to recoup at least a part of the latter losses by reversing the flow in its lines to the seaboard. Finally, the Pump and Machine Company, which had no direct connection with National Transit's pipeline activities, had helped to absorb the impact of adjusting to changing conditions in the oil industry.

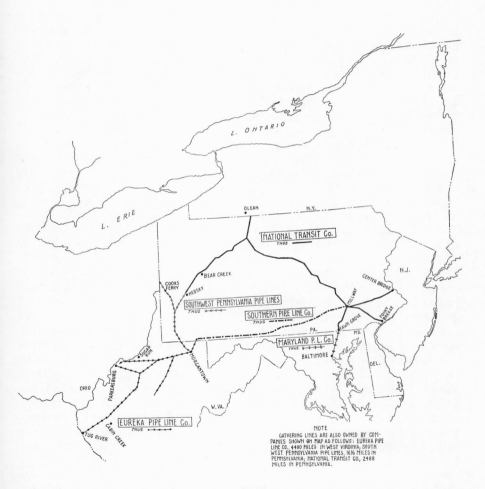

Southern Group of pipelines and National Transit Company, December 31, 1931. *Source:* 72 Cong., 2 Sess., House Report No. 2192, Part I, facing p. 408.

BUCKEYE PIPE LINE COMPANY

Buckeye Pipe Line was the dominant element in the Northern Group of pipelines that stretched from Chicago to New York State. These lines operated under a common management, which continued to be headed by D. S. Bushnell throughout this period. Unlike Prairie Pipe Line, Buckeye had no producing affiliate, and unlike National Transit, it had no subsidiary engaged in nontransportation activities. The key to Buckeye's survival as a common carrier lay in its strategic position with respect to the through route from the Mid-Continent to refining centers along the Great Lakes and the seaboard.

Like the other companies discussed in this chapter, Buckeye as an independent common carrier continued to serve substantially the same refineries as before the 1911 dissolution. At the Ohio-Indiana line, the Lima trunkline division received Mid-Continent crude from Indiana Pipe Line. Two 8-inch lines stretched to Lima, Ohio, where Buckeye supplied the Solar refinery. From Lima a lateral moved crude to Toledo. The main stem continued easterly to a connection with the Northern Pipe Line at the Pennsylvania border. A branch from Mantua, Ohio, supplied Ohio Standard's Cleveland refinery. In the southeastern part of the state, the Macksburg Division gathered crude oil for local deliveries. By 1918 Buckeye was operating about 5,000 miles of pipeline, much of it gathering mileage, and had storage facilities for about 5,000,000 barrels of oil.[81]

The financial results of Buckeye's operations became increasingly less impressive as time passed. From a high of over $6,000,000 in the year of dissolution, pipeline operating income declined rather steadily until it stabilized at a little over $1,000,000 in 1917–18. After rising to almost $1,600,000 in 1922, it dropped sharply in the following year as Buckeye, like National Transit and Prairie, felt the impact of tanker competition. For the remainder of the decade there was little improvement, and in 1931 operating income had fallen to $790,000.[82] Nevertheless, throughout the period the company managed to pay 8 per cent dividends, or better, on the 200,000 shares ($50 par value) of capital stock.

Buckeye's trunk pipelines clearly occupied a strategic location. With respect to shipments from the Mid-Continent, however, the locational advantage was fortuitous since the company had been organized by Standard Oil to handle local production. When it came to through movements, Prairie Pipe Line called the tune. One example involved a joint tariff in which the Northern Group lines had given Prairie Pipe managers the right to make certain changes in tariff provisions affecting both parties without obtaining prior consent. Apparently at Independence, Kansas, this concurrence was interpreted to mean that specific approval was not required from Buckeye's president, D. S. Bushnell, for changes in routing, rates, or regulations. In March 1921, following a conversation on the matter in Chicago, Bushnell formally complained about this practice in a letter to Clark Kountz. In a brisk reply, the Prairie Pipe Line vice-president agreed to

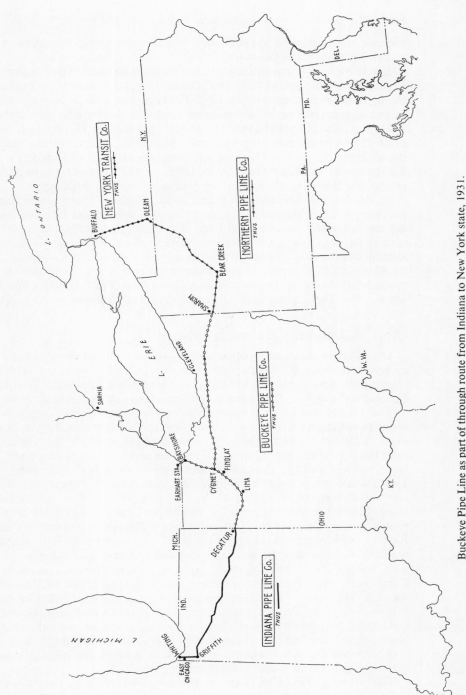

Buckeye Pipe Line as part of through route from Indiana to New York state, 1931.
Source: 72 Cong., 2 Sess., House Report No. 2192, Part I, facing p. 389.

exercise more restraint in the future, "without discussing the merits of our respective positions in the matter." [83]

If retention of independence is any criterion, Buckeye fared better than Prairie Pipe Line in the long run. Bushnell and his associates pursued a steady, conservative course. In 1931 Buckeye was still an intermediate or terminating carrier for Mid-Continent crude oil destined for the seaboard or Ohio points, as well as a gatherer of local production. During 1927 Buckeye had purchased gathering lines from Sun Pipe Line in western Ohio. In the southeastern part of the state it also acquired some of Pure Oil's pipeline gathering system.[84] Two years later, in 1929, Buckeye extended its lateral line from Toledo to Earhart Station (Detroit), Michigan.

In the interim between 1918 and 1931, Buckeye's new investment in gathering lines increased more than twice as much as that in trunk lines,[85] but the latter still provided the bulk of operating revenues.[86] Over 99 per cent of the trunk-line traffic was interstate in character,[87] and the common management and coordinated operation of the Northern Group of pipelines continued. Evidence of the changing pattern of oil transportation was exemplified, however, by the sale in 1928 of New York Transit's line from Olean, New York, to the seaboard and its removal from petroleum service.[88]

OTHER DISAFFILIATED STANDARD PIPELINES

Disaffiliated Standard pipeline carriers other than the three already discussed also suffered or collapsed as the result of declining oil fields, the integration movement, and the impact of tankship competition. The Cumberland and Crescent Pipe Lines provide particularly illuminating examples.

The Cumberland was a member of the Southern Group and gathered crude in eastern Kentucky for local use and further movement by associated lines. Although the future had not seemed bright in 1915, new oil discoveries the following year led to a 100 per cent increase in Cumberland's runs from wells. Profitable operations continued, with a few exceptions, until 1924, which marked the beginning of a decline that by the end of the decade was causing heavy deficits.[89] At that time the pipeline was collecting most of the oil in eastern Kentucky, and 75 per cent of it was being delivered to two refineries owned by the small Ashland Refining Company.[90] Paul G. Blazer, president of Ashland, recognized the economies that might be realized by acquiring the old Standard line. After a year of negotiations with Forrest Towl, head of the Southern Group, Ashland acquired the Cumberland properties— representing a total investment of $3,600,000 — for only $420,000.[91] The down payment was less than the value of the oil held in storage by the pipeline as the result of authorized deductions from producers' runs to compensate for possible evaporation and other natural losses. As a result of the integration of Cumberland's facilities into Ashland's operations, transportation savings soon paid for the pipeline's acquisition.[92] Again it was a case of integrate or perish.

The Crescent Pipe Line was one that perished. Built by the Mellons in

Table 15.   Oil movements and operating income of disaffiliated
and integrated pipelines, 1920, 1921, 1924.

Pipeline company	Barrels moved	Operating income
Disaffiliated from Standard Oil:		
Buckeye Pipe Line Co.		
1924	26,085,004	$ 822,905
1921	32,883,744	1,205,021
1920	32,040,834	1,065,321
Crescent Pipe Line Co.		
1924	128,638	133,971[a]
1921	2,781,362	59,625
1920	1,846,636	32,078
Cumberland Pipe Line Co.		
1924	4,364,566	300,892
1921	6,175,576	218,231
1920	7,527,693	323,386
Eureka Pipe Line Co.		
1924	12,625,210	98,605[a]
1921	17,840,216	349,946
1920	22,950,981	496,833
Illinois Pipe Line Co.		
1924	33,570,657	2,221,037
1921	15,664,649	3,916,810
1920	14,362,166	4,676,199
Indiana Pipe Line Co.		
1924	21,431,015	410,919
1921	29,894,192	870,368
1920	33,029,533	717,567
National Transit Co.		
1924	16,166,598	153,919
1921	23,014,925	468,276
1920	25,478,008	146,492
New York Transit Co.		
1924	6,388,361	146,201
1921	11,616,903	247,437
1920	12,626,975	154,539
Prairie Pipe Line Co.		
1924	91,853,664	10,914,042
1921	124,096,679	16,393,728
1920	111,486,503	9,264,005
South-West Pa. Pipe Lines		
1924	6,857,465	146,266
1921	10,140,428	87,874
1920	13,648,095	276,247

(continued on next page)

Table 15—continued.

Pipeline company	Barrels moved	Operating income
Integrated:		
Empire Pipe Line Co.		
1924	20,008,996	1,110,545
1921	8,535,781	161,577
1920	7,735,453	382,358
Gulf Pipe Line Co.		
1924	32,037,163	2,535,770
1921	16,622,811	3,266,820
1920	23,089,916	1,705,699
Humble Pipe Line Co.		
1924	68,408,595	6,784,266
1921	55,306,548	—
Magnolia Petroleum Co.		
1924	80,095,590	2,762,190
1921	58,157,164	812,554
1920	58,184,501	466,391[a]
Ozark Pipe Line Corp.		
1924	25,205,515	3,708,170
1921	7,279,392	695,151
1920	9,077,619	624,023
Sinclair Pipe Line Co.		
1924	44,516,900	3,347,641
1921	29,931,659	3,833,466
1920	26,869,997	2,298,145
Texas Pipe Line Co., of Texas		
1924	38,984,595	6,374,518
1921	33,132,689	3,504,501
1920	35,585,585	2,520,700
Tide Water Pipe Line Co., Ltd.		
1924	6,375,847	546,158
1921	5,437,473	1,171,978[a]
1920	7,375,613	486,467[a]

Source: *National Petroleum News* (October 21, 1925), 29–30.
[a]Deficit.

1891 to move crude for export from the vicinity of Pittsburgh to Marcus Hook, the line was acquired by National Transit in 1895. At the time of dissolution in 1911, it became a separate company outside both the Northern and Southern Groups. Since it operated only a trunk line, Crescent was dependent on other lines and on nonaffiliated refineries for its business. From a high of $426,000 the year after the dissolution, net income dropped with only occasional interruptions until it was less than $45,000 in 1923.[93] In 1924 there was a net loss of $1.04 on each barrel of oil transported.[94] Like the Prairie and other lines dependent on outside shippers and on movements to the East Coast, Crescent was a victim of shifting transportation and integration patterns and new sources of crude oil. Accordingly the company was liquidated in 1925 and its pipe was taken up in that year and the following one. It was a classic case of a pipeline facility that had outlived its usefulness under the impact of a changing environment.

ADAPTATION TO A CHANGING ENVIRONMENT

Both National Transit and Buckeye profited from the development of refining capacity in their respective territories. Although the Pennsylvania company — like Crescent — was tied to a declining area of production, reversal of its trunk lines to carry crude to inland refineries instead of to the seaboard cushioned the impact of change. Buckeye had the good fortune to have a strategic location with respect to through routes between the Southwest, the new center of production, and major refining points in the Midwest and the East. Although eastward through movements declined after the early 1920's, integrated companies increased their Midwest refining facilities. The new trunk lines constructed to supply them spelled an end to Prairie Pipe Line's dominance, but the owners of these new lines apparently found it less expensive to have Buckeye continue to furnish the connections with their refineries than to do so themselves. As a result, Buckeye in 1931 moved over 30,000,000 barrels of oil for 63 parties having no ownership interest in the pipeline company.

Prairie Pipe Line had a far different experience. Initially it occupied the most favorable position of the three companies, for its lines ran between a major, and increasingly important, center of oil production and the northern territory where this oil was refined. Moreover, for a time these lines were without competition. Confidently relying on these advantages, Prairie management seemingly decided to charge all the traffic would bear and to place primary reliance on a limited number of customers with whom it had had ties before the dissolution of the Standard Oil combination. Although this policy paid large dividends for a time, it ignored the fact that while the Prairie companies needed these customers, the customers did not necessarily need Prairie once other alternatives became available. Eventually, cheap water transportation and backward integration by refining and marketing companies to new sources of flush production spelled an end to Prairie's independence.

As "showpieces" for the merits or drawback of divorcement of pipelines from integrated operations, none of these companies provides a satisfactory example. If anything, their experience between 1915 and 1931 suggests that the changing requirements of the oil industry, based on changing centers of oil production and refining, were more important than either managerial or public policies in determining the fate of each concern. But public policy, of course, had created the situation with which the respective managements had to deal on a nonintegrated basis.

Finally, the story of these three pipeline companies over two decades suggests that their survival as unaffiliated common carriers depended on finding a niche that it would not pay large oil firms to invade. Relative isolation from the main currents of change in industry development helped to provide this niche for National Transit. A strategic location, conservatively exploited, provided it for Buckeye. But Prairie Pipe operated in an area of growing interest to large companies, and there was no safe haven except possibly through integration, a policy over which its management seemingly dallied too long.

CHAPTER 10

FEDERAL INVESTIGATIONS

Between 1915 and 1931, oil pipelines were, directly or indirectly, the subject of repeated investigations by agencies of the federal government. Various avenues were open to complainants who provided the initiative for these investigations. In the case of pipeline practices, they could complain directly to the Interstate Commerce Commission. But, though numerous complaints were made, only one became the subject of formal ICC action. An easier route for the dissatisfied was to ask a Congressman or Senator to request an investigation by a federal body such as the ICC or the Federal Trade Commission. In Congress, approval of such requests was almost automatic. Alternatively, or as a supplement, a congressional committee could itself conduct an investigation, presumably as a prelude to some corrective legislative action. All of these devices were employed in the years following The Pipe Line Cases.

Three major questions kept reappearing in these investigations. First, how was the power of integrated companies related to the price of crude oil and gasoline? Second, and as a corollary, had the dissolution of the Standard Oil combination been effective? Third, could anything be done about the failure of pipeline subsidiaries of large, integrated companies to perform more than nominally as common carriers? While these are convenient categories into which the results of federal investigations of the era may be classified *ex post*, both questioning and testimony were frequently *ad hominem*, confused, and confusing.

THE FEDERAL TRADE COMMISSION

The Federal Trade Commission, the successor body to Theodore Roosevelt's Bureau of Corporations, was established by congressional action in 1914 to provide a body with the expertise and flexibility to deal with business problems on a continuing basis. Although its major mandate was to deal with "unfair competition," it was also charged with enforcing — in conjunction with the Justice Department — certain sections of the Clayton Antitrust Act, as well as aiding other branches of the government in determining the effectiveness of antitrust actions. In addition, it inherited the job earlier assigned to the Bureau of Corporations of investigating business and industrial conditions that had a bearing on these other functions.

It was chiefly in this latter role that the FTC scrutinized the oil industry

173

and its pipeline sector in the period under consideration. Only one of these investigations focused directly on pipelines as such.* The remainder dealt primarily with the price of gasoline and other petroleum products,† or the structure and behavior of oil companies in specific regions such as Wyoming, Montana, and California.** Nevertheless, pipelines inevitably received some consideration in the latter studies.

The disturbed conditions that brought legislative action in oil-producing states with respect to pipelines just prior to World War I also had repercussions in Washington. Senator Robert Owen of Oklahoma introduced a resolution in June 1913 calling on the Secretary of Commerce to investigate the price of oil in Oklahoma and to determine whether it was being artificially fixed at a level below that of the general United States market, quality and transportation considered.[1] This investigation, commenced by the Bureau of Corporations, was concluded by the Federal Trade Commission, which issued its report on February 28, 1916.

The *Report on Pipe-Line Transportation of Petroleum* was confined to conditions in the Mid-Continent field and to the leading pipeline systems there. The FTC's conclusions about the practices and role of pipelines were similar to those drawn by the Bureau of Corporations in its investigation of the oil industry and Standard Oil nine years earlier. In essence the FTC found that: the margin between pipeline transportation costs and pipeline rates was unnecessarily great, minimum tender requirements were unnecessarily large, the costs of transportation represented a large part of the cost of crude delivered to the refinery, pipeline construction followed in the wake of proven crude-oil production and was therefore not especially risky, the Mid-Continent pipelines were not typically performing as common carriers, and for small concerns seeking to compete in a broad market there were no satisfactory alternatives to using these interstate carriers.†† [2]

Report on Pipe-Line Transportation of Petroleum (February 28, 1916).

†*Investigation of the Price of Gasoline* (April 10, 1916); *Report on the Price of Gasoline in 1915* (April 11, 1917); *The Advance in Price of Petroleum Products* (April 5 – June 1, 1920); *Petroleum Industry: Prices, Profits, and Competition* (December 12, 1927).

**Petroleum Industry of Wyoming* (January 3, 1921); *Pacific Coast Petroleum Industry,* Part I (April 7, 1921), Part II (November 28, 1921); *Petroleum Trade in Wyoming and Montana* (July 13, 1922). During this same period the FTC also reported on *Foreign Ownership in the Petroleum Industry* (February 12, 1923).

††The investigation of Mid-Continent pipelines brought out the fact that pipeline rates from the Cushing field to major destinations were now appreciably less than rail rates for the same haul. FTC, *Report on Pipe-line Transportation of Petroleum, 1916,* p. 445.

	Railroad rate per bbl.	Pipeline rate per bbl.
Cushing pool to Neodesha	.311	.200
Kansas City	.373	.280
Wood River	.544	.340
Whiting	.622	.420
Philadelphia	1.348	.700
Bayonne	1.403	.700
Port Arthur	.466	.400

These findings applied not only to the pipeline systems developed by or for Standard Oil but also to those of important integrated newcomers like the Texas and Gulf Oil companies.

The FTC report left no doubt that the federal agency thought that the cost and control of pipelines effectively insulated crude-oil markets from the beneficial effects of competition. First, the expense of building a pipe-line from the Mid-Continent to major distributing or refining points was found to be prohibitive for a small concern. For example, the report put the cost of an 8-inch line from Cushing to the Gulf at $4,500,000; from Cushing to Chicago, at over $6,000,000; and from Cushing to the seaboard in the vicinity of New York City, at about $13,500,000.[3] Second, taking in consideration the flood of complaints that Mid-Continent producers lodged against Mid-Continent crude prices compared to Appalachian, the FTC placed itself on record as believing that "Reasonable and equitable condi-tions of shipment by pipe line would tend to a greater equality in the prices of Mid-Continent and Appalachian crude oil and in the prices of refined products in different markets."[4] From this report it was quite clear that, although the key pipeline systems in the Mid-Continent field were for-mally complying with ICC requirements, they were not in fact acting as common carriers for unaffilated companies. Tariffs were filed, but their terms were such that outside shippers had no incentive to use the lines.

At least one company's management feared that these findings might lead to an investigation by the ICC of the reasonableness of pipeline rates. Reportedly, it was for this reason that representatives of Magnolia˙ Pipe Line Company journeyed to Washington in April 1916 to make a presenta-tion before the Trade Commission.[5] But, despite the emphatic nature of the FTC's recommendations, no action was taken by Congress or the ICC.

The *New York Times*, like Congress, looked on the FTC pipeline report as a contribution to knowledge — not as a call for action. Commenting editorially, the *Times* said of the report: "It is a considerable contribution to the fund of knowledge on a subject but little known and of great indus-trial importance." However, while approving the investigation, the news-paper questioned the desirability of increased regulation as an answer to the problems revealed. "Public control of their [pipelines'] rates and prof-its is substituted for reliance upon excessive profits to bring competitors into the business," the editorial observed. "That is easier for the small producers than self-reliance and combination of resources. Perhaps it is the better way. There is an obvious loss of initiative and efficiency to the extent that Government help is substituted for self-help."[6]

As long as general conditions in the oil industry favored new entrants, this application of the theory of perfect competition had some underpin-ning. As we have seen, flush production had led to the creation of new companies. However, newcomers who became large during this period typically adopted the same integrated structure and pipeline practices as those the FTC condemned. Therefore, the theory of perfect competition as a rationale for public policy with respect to pipelines had dubious utility for the long run.

Whether improved competitive results in the petroleum industry could be obtained by more effective pipeline regulation, or only by pipeline divorcement plus regulation, was an issue on which the FTC took a firm stand. It made its position clear in 1917 when reporting to Congress on the price of gasoline. Although it had found no evidence of outright collusion by Standard Oil companies in violation of the 1911 dissolution decree,[7] the FTC condemned arrangements whereby these companies, formally divorced from one another, still had common ownership. The report seemed to be challenging the desirability or inevitability of integration in the oil business.[8] Given the existence of this pattern, the 1917 report expressed doubt about the feasibility of public regulation as a way of opening pipelines to genuine common-carrier usage. It recommended "that no controlling portion of the stock of any pipe-line company engaged in interstate commerce should be owned by any individual, company, or corporation, or by any group of individuals, companies, or corprations, that are also interested as owners in any oil producing or refining properties; and vice versa." [9] The FTC reiterated this recommendation in its annual report for 1917 and renewed its charges that Standard Oil companies, despite the dissolution, still effectively dominated the oil industry.[10]

Jersey Standard officials, understandably sensitive to any attack by a federal agency, felt that the FTC report was unfair. Jersey, with a significant amount of oil in storage, had profited from a major crude-oil price rise in 1915 and, during the same period, had led gasoline prices upward, reaping still more profits.[11] As always, these rising prices harmed some elements of the industry and benefited others. To Jersey management the FTC seemed to consider only the former group.

That the FTC should treat the Standard Oil companies as though there had never been any dissolution was particularly galling to A. C. Bedford, who handled Jersey's relations with government. He was therefore moved to write a memorandum of protest in which he complained, "It is discouraging and disheartening to be met with an attitude of distrust and suspicion on the part of the Federal Trade Commission." [12] But, apparently upon more mature reflection, this memorandum was never sent. Instead, a more restrained public statement declared: "The fact is that Standard of New Jersey had scrupulously obeyed the decree in the dissolution decree as affirmed by the Supreme Court . . . The Federal Trade Commission, in its report of an exhaustive inquiry into our business, does not intimate that any practice or policy of this company is at variance either with the law or that decree." [13]

The FTC's hostility toward Standard Oil companies continued into the 1920's. In its 1922 report on the *Petroleum Trade in Wyoming and Montana*, for example, the FTC charged that Standard Oil interests in the latter state acted with common purpose and concern. And again it renewed its recommendation that Congress abolish by legislation common-stock ownership in combinations dissolved in Sherman Act proceedings.[14]

By 1927, however, there had been a significant change in the personnel of the FTC, which was now cooperating with many business groups, and an important change in its attitude toward Standard Oil companies. There seemed to be a greater willingness to acknowledge that major changes had taken place in the oil industry since 1911. Reporting to the Senate in a document entitled *The Petroleum Industry — Prices, Profits, and Competition*, the vice-chairman of the FTC, Abram F. Myers, declared of the Standard companies: "There is no longer unity of control of these companies through community of interest. Among different companies this community of interest varies widely, and is largest among the pipe-line companies." [15] The Commissioner took the position that long-run crude-oil prices were determined by supply and demand but that in the short run, the decisions of the large purchasing companies were very important.[16] Finally, he reported increased competition in the oil industry, although the "profits" of interstate pipeline companies for the years 1921–1926 were found to exceed those of other parts of the industry.[17]

Despite the mild tone of the letter of submittal to the Senate, the body of the FTC report still suggested the possible need for divorcement of certain pipelines from other sectors of the oil business. Arguing that common-carrier use of pipelines from the Mid-Continent would aid both independent eastern refiners and the public, the report declared: "Unless the Standard lines running eastward from the mid-continent oil fields voluntarily accept common carrier shipments on terms that enable both Standard and independent companies to use them freely, there should be absolute dissociation of pipe line ownership from interests engaged in producing and refining crude petroleum in order to establish free and fair competition in this branch of the petroleum industry." [18] In comparison with the FTC's unequivocal endorsement of divorcement in 1917, however, this was a relatively restrained statement of position.

The FTC's investigations had certainly contributed to public knowledge about developments in the integrated oil industry, but the efforts of its staff to affect the structure of the industry directly proved unavailing. For example, attempts to invoke the antimerger provisions of the Clayton Act against New York Standard's acquisition of capital stock in Magnolia Petroleum and against Jersey Standard's ownership in Humble Oil & Refining were dismissed by the FTC in 1920 and 1926 respectively.[19] In short, administrative initiative to promote divorcement of pipelines and to prevent mergers by large companies made little headway between 1915 and 1931. The public interest that had provided a background for more successful action by the predecessor Bureau of Corporations in an earlier era was lacking in this one.

THE LA FOLLETTE INVESTIGATION

An equally barren record of achievement in this area was compiled in Congress. Although Congressmen repeatedly called for investigations of gasoline prices and the petroleum industry almost as a matter of course, pipelines were not singled out and only one investigation of the industry as a whole was made. In that instance, pipeline ownership and practices previously attacked by the FTC were subjected to public scrutiny in connection with a retrospective congressional investigation of the rise in gasoline prices during 1920–1922.

By 1920 the expanding gasoline market had given a new importance to a refiner's possessing a large marketing system, high volume, and efficient cracking methods that would improve the percentage of gasoline recovered from each barrel of crude oil. Many small refiners lacked these assets, and they had to compensate for less efficient methods of recovering gasoline by advancing its price. Indiana Standard, which possessed the patent rights to the efficient Burton process for producing gasoline by cracking, had apparently extended its protective mantle over such minor competitors and led the upward price movement.[20]

Inevitably, this development attracted congressional interest. In June 1922 the Committee on Manufactures of the United State Senate entrusted the gasoline investigation to a subcommittee headed by Senator Robert M. La Follette of Wisconsin.

La Follette, a hero of the Progressive Era, had fallen from public favor during 1917, when he bitterly opposed President Wilson's policies and entry into the war by the United States. The tide of public opinion had been strong against La Follette and his opinions. Theodore Roosevelt, on a speaking tour at the time, even suggested that La Follette be expelled from the Senate, and Senator Frank B. Kellogg of Minnesota introduced a petition to this effect a short time later. Although the charges were eventually dropped, the public hostility aroused against La Follette did not entirely disappear. Faced with a campaign for re-election in the fall of 1922, his sponsorship of an investigation into the Teapot Dome leases and the high cost of gasoline was probably undertaken at least in part to create an acceptable public image.[21] In any event, the La Follette subcommittee held hearings in August and from mid-December 1922 to the end of February 1923. A parade of witnesses from every sector of the oil business filled the subcommittee's records with over 1,700 pages of testimony and documents.

The hearings provided an open invitation for anyone aggrieved by any oil industry practice to say his piece. In the opinion of some industry observers, the attempt of politicians and legislators to comprehend the industry in this fashion would have been almost laughable if it were not for the consequences that might ensue. Thus Warren C. Platt, for example, wrote: "In this investigation the whole oil industry is quite liable to get the worst of it just because of its tremendous size, multitude of important detail and the entirely pardonable business ignorance of the committee and the rest of the senate too, for that matter." [22] But, whether they liked it or not, major figures in the oil business had to account for their past decisions and actions.

The complaints against pipelines presented to the La Follette subcommittee were familiar ones in the oil industry, and the hearings served chiefly to bring them up to date. Some of the important charges revolved around the decrease in the price of Mid-Continent crude oil following 1920. The pattern, as W. H. Gray, president of the National Association of Independent Oil Producers, saw it, was the age-old one of high prices attracting "sucker" money into oil producing, followed by a steep decline in prices that wiped out the unwary. This development in the Mid-Continent he suggested, was also the product of a deflationary policy adopted by the Federal Reserve, the efforts of the ICC under the Transportation Act of 1920 to improve railroad earnings through increased railroad rates on refined products, and the competition from imports of Mexican crude oil.[23]

Against this comparatively sophisticated analysis of environmental factors, Gray fitted pipelines into the picture. He emphasized their failure to provide independent producers with access to markets or to stimulate competition in the field purchase of crude oil. He pointed, for example, to the high minimum tender requirements of Prairie Pipe Line which had been recently challenged before the ICC, with Gray himself taking some part. On this point the following exchange was representative:

> Chairman: Do you mean that the minimum tender is so large that it amounts to a denial of the use of the lines of these common carriers, the pipe lines, to a great many independent producers; is that what you mean?

> Gray: Yes, sir.

> Chairman: I wish you would state these matters as fully as you can in response to questions.

> Gray: The present rule of the 100,000-barrel minimum tender is, in the first place, very difficult to interpret. As an illustration, take the Prairie Pipe Line Co. They gather the oil for the Prairie Oil and Gas Co. They do not gather that oil in 100,000-barrel lots. They gather it from the field tankage of the various producers usually. Some of these tanks are 100-barrel tanks and some are 500-barrel tanks, some are 250-barrel tanks and some are 1,600-barrel tanks. The rule should be as open to the independent producer as it is to the Prairie Oil & Gas Co., as each of those claim to be separate institutions, each standing upon its own bottom. Therefore, the acceptance of 100 barrels of oil for the account of the Prairie Oil & Gas Co. and the refusal to accept the same amount from any individual producer or independent refiner is equivalent to a discrimination. There are no rules and regulations, however, by the Interstate Commerce Commission which provide for any discrimination by a pipe line.[24]

What Gray wanted was competition for producers' oil. High pipeline rates and high minimum tenders, as he saw it, barred potential northern purchasers from competing for Mid-Continent crude. Field refineries in the declining Appalachian and Illinois fields "must perish and pass away unless they can obtain their crude supply from the prolific areas upon the same basis as their competitors," Gray said.[25]

But the northern crude-oil market was not the only object of Gray's concern. He charged that the increase in rail freight rates authorized by the ICC under the Transportation Act of 1920 deprived the Mid-Continent field refiner of marketing territory in the North and East that integrated concerns could reach more cheaply by pipeline or water transportation.[26] Such developments hurt the producer because they diminished the number of competitors for his crude oil. The same was true, Gray stated, when large companies like Indiana Standard and Sinclair combined their purchasing activities under a single concern. He elaborated his point in these words: "You will of course appreciate the fact that you would rather have a thousand buyers in the market for your product than just one or two or three, and the more factors that we have in the purchase of crude the better our market will be. That is why our association lends as much assistance as it can to the mid-continent refiner and helps him in every way to get oil and to get it, as far as we can, upon a basis with the balance of the purchasers, in order to strengthen him and give us competition." [27]

Although virtually invited by subcommittee counsel Gilbert E. Roe, a long-time associate of La Follette in law practice, to make as angry a statement as he cared to, Gray pursued a middle course. Unlike many of his predecessors in comparable situations, he avoided bitter denunciations while making it clear that existing transportation arrangements hurt the interests that he represented.

Several independent refiners of the type described by Gray also testified before the La Follette subcommittee. One of them was B. V. Stoll of the Stoll Oil Refining Company, Louisville, Kentucky. Although his refinery was using crude oil from eastern Kentucky transported by tank car and barge, he thought Mid-Continent crude would cost him less.[28] Accordingly, Stoll testified, he had addressed letters to the Tide Water, Illinois, and Prairie pipeline companies inquiring about the possibilities of pipeline deliveries of Illinois and Mid-Continent crude. Stoll thought that his company might establish storage facilities near Louisville at a common-carrier trunk-line pumping station. Ingenuously, Stoll's letter to Tide Water suggested: "In case we locate such a tank it would be possible that we would figure with the Standard Oil Co., who have a refinery here at Louisville, and possibly handle oil for them, as well as for ourselves." [29] Tide Water, whose parent company was 41 per cent owned by Jersey,[30] replied formally and politely that Stoll would have to contact originating carriers. Their position was concisely stated by Illinois Pipe which replied: "This sort of plan would be impracticable with us from an operating standpoint, and, being an intermediate line, we do not care to take this up with the other lines." [31] Admitting that existing pipelines would deliver to independents at existing terminal points, Stoll maintained that that was no answer to his problem. What he would have liked was a connection at a pump station closer to his refinery or to have a large company, as he put it, "lay a little line down to our plant." [32]

The economics of the pipeline operation that Stoll proposed did not concern him. In his view, "The pipe lines are the big guns of the Standard

Oil Co. We can compete with them in any other department, but we can not compete with them on their pipe lines." [33] Since these lines were legally common carriers, he felt that steps should be taken to make them perform as such.

Like Stoll, independent refiners who were typically not located close to pipeline terminals used by integrated companies made it clear that they wanted multiple delivery points along pipeline routes. Benjamin F. Brundred, a member of the firm that had brought the first case before the ICC under the federal pipe-line law, made the same recommendation. [34] Stephen Schwartz, of the Indiana Refining Company, Columbus, Indiana, testified that he had inquired of Tide Water Pipe in November 1922 about the possibility of receiving deliveries at its Brooklyn, Indiana, station in lots of 10,000 barrels three times a month. He also mentioned another possible delivery point, about 25 miles away from the first. [35] Tide Water's president, A. W. Golden, had replied curtly that neither of these locations was a delivery point: "Consequently, we are not in position to serve your needs." [36] Schwartz thereupon applied to the ICC for a definition of "delivery point" in the vain hope that pipelines might be required to file tariffs to pumping station points.

Charles J. Wrightsman, the Tulsa producer who had shown no sympathy for pipeline companies in his testimony before another congressional committee at the time of the 1914 Healdton controversy, questioned the financial feasibility of providing the steel storage facilities necessary to make each pump station a delivery point. [37] Wrightsman, who had not forgotten his difficulties with Magnolia and ventilated his feelings on that score for the benefit of the committee, suggested that a Cabinet-level petroleum commissioner should have power over pipeline rates and regulations. [38]

Clark Kountz, vice-president of Prairie Pipe Line, testified at length about the practices of his company. Much of the questioning directed to him related to the company's minimum tender requirement of 100,000 barrels. Kountz defended the requirement on numerous grounds: first, it was of no importance in any case to the producer who, he claimed, only wanted to sell his oil in the field; second, it was a protection to the pipeline company that could only afford to lay its lines where it knew the investment could be recovered; third, practical operating problems such as contamination dictated shipment of large batches. These arguments did not differ substantially from those advanced in the course of the Standard Oil antitrust case some fifteen years earlier.

The following exchange between Kountz and subcommittee counsel Roe clarified the former's operational argument:

Mr. Roe: Is there any other objection, from your point of view, simply as a common carrier of crude oil, to the reduction of the minimum tender below 100,000 barrels, or even below 10,000 barrels, except the one [contamination] you have mentioned?

Mr. Kountz: Yes, sir.

Mr. Roe: What is it — the inconvenience of requiring you to extend your lines, possibly, into a different field for the purpose of securing a shipment?

Mr. Kountz: The practicability of receiving 10,000 barrels, as that is a very small amount to receive. Of course, these shipments come in from tanks, and it takes two or three days before we know what the exact amount is that we have got. They are in numerous small tanks, from 100 barrels capacity up to 1,600. A gauger goes out, and we have no communication with him, and he would turn on those tanks, and we would not know how much oil we had gotten into our line for three days. We have been tendered, we will say, only 10,000 barrels, or some small amount. The amount would be in our lines, and the tender would be overrun before we could give him a shut-off on the tank. That is the practical field part of it.[39]

Kountz's basic position was that 100,000 barrels was not much oil for anyone engaging seriously in the business, although he reluctantly admitted that much of the oil in the country was produced by men to whom that figure would represent a large amount. But this concession did not change his argument that the producer only wanted a market for his oil at the wellhead. "He is usually after the money," Kountz declared. "I do not blame them. That is not a facetious remark." [40]

That Prairie Pipe Line was also "after the money" was brought out in questioning about its rates and earnings. Kountz testified that trunk-line rates had been advanced 25 per cent on September 20, 1920, and decreased 12.5 per cent on July 26, 1922. Gathering rates were advanced from 12 cents to 20 cents on the former date and were maintained at that level.[41] He explained the increases as a response to increased costs and the reduction as a way of meeting tanker competition. Denying that either trunk line or gathering charges were too high, he argued that a rate of return of 30 per cent on invested capital or 41 per cent on capital stock was not too high for a pipeline company. This was so, he maintained, "on account of the money that you must reinvest in the business, or put back, in order to maintain your business and keep your line from becoming a junk proposition." As he put it, "A field comes in, and we have to go. At the same time, your production in other parts is falling off, and you have to keep putting money into the business all the time in order to maintain your business." [42]

Testimony by President Amos L. Beaty of the Texas Company was carefully directed by the subcommittee's counsel to cast doubt on the validity of Kountz's arguments about minimum tenders. Under questioning, Beaty declared that Texas Company pipelines specified no minimum tender in tariffs filed with the ICC, and in Texas a tender was specified only to comply with Railroad Commission regulations. He also declared that his company's pipelines had found it practicable to accept smaller tenders than 100,000 barrels and had done so a number of times.[43]

Table 16.   Sinclair and Prairie pipeline rates for crude oil
shipped to Whiting, Indiana, 1919–1922.

	Sinclair	
Date	*From Oklahoma and Kansas points (cents per bbl.)*	*From Texas and south Okla. points (cents per bbl.)*
Sept. 10, 1920:		
Rate	74.00	107.00
Gathering	15.00	15.00
Marketing	10.00	10.00
Tax	7.12	9.76
Total	106.12	141.76
Jan. 1, 1922:		
Rate	74.00	107.00
Gathering	15.00	15.00
Marketing	10.00	10.00
Total	99.00	132.00
Apr. 10, 1922:		
Rate	52.50	90.00
Gathering	20.00	20.00
Marketing	10.00	10.00
Total	82.50	120.00
Aug. 17, 1922:		
Rate	46.00	78.75
Gathering	20.00	20.00
Marketing	10.00	10.00
Total	76.00	108.75

	Prairie	
Date	*From northern Oklahoma and Kansas points (cents per bbl.)*	*From Texas and south Okla. points (cents per bbl.)*
Apr. 1, 1919:		
Rate	42.00	72.00
Gathering	12.00	12.00
Marketing	10.00	10.00
Tax	4.32	6.72
Total	68.32	100.72
Sept. 20, 1920:		
Rate	52.50	90.00
Gathering	20.00	20.00
Marketing	10.00	10.00
Tax	5.80	8.80
Total	88.30	128.80
Jan. 1, 1922:		
Rate	52.50	90.00
Gathering	20.00	20.00
Marketing	10.00	10.00
Total	82.50	120.00

(continued on next page)

Table 16—continued.

| | Prairie | |
	From northern Oklahoma and Kansas points (cents per bbl.)	From Texas and south Okla. points (cents per bbl.)
July 26, 1922:		
Rate	46.00	78.75
Gathering	20.00	20.00
Marketing	10.00	10.00
Total	76.00	108.75

Source: 67 Cong., 2 and 4 Sess., Senate Subcommittee of the Committee on Manufactures, "High Cost of Gasoline and Other Petroleum Products," *Hearings* (Washington, 1923), 782–785.

Beaty presented a favorable picture of his own company's pipeline operations. He testified that they did an active common-carrier business and that rates had been challenged only once. In that case, which involved a small shipper in Texas, a satisfactory adjustment had been made without formal action.[44] Questioned about the common-purchaser law in Oklahoma, he indicated that his company had been involved in a few cases but that for the most part he regarded the statute as a "negligible quantity." [45]

Harry F. Sinclair testified about the Sinclair Pipe Line. He reported that it had been a profitable enterprise and that it was operated as a common carrier. When subcommittee counsel Roe probed behind this statement, Sinclair admitted that the last common-carrier shipment, excluding Sinclair's or Indiana Standard's, had been on December 4, 1919. From the time the Sinclair pipeline was organized in 1916 until that date, however, it had carried a total of 1,450,000 barrels for outside shippers.[46]

Colonel Robert Stewart, president of Indiana Standard was subjected to extended questioning, which involved, among other matters, Indiana Standard's 1920 purchase of a half-interest in Sinclair Pipe Line. Despite the best efforts of subcommittee counsel Roe to get Stewart to admit that he had some specific knowledge of the economic benefits conferred by ownership of pipelines, the Indiana Company's president offered only the most obvious replies. In response to one such question, he declared: "I do not believe anybody on earth can tell what the cost of transporting a barrel of crude from Oklahoma to Chicago by pipe line would be, but I can tell you how much we have paid those people [Prairie]." [47]

Stewart persisted in maintaining that he took barrels transported and tariffs paid as a means of determining pipeline "costs." By using the published rates of his half-owned pipeline subsidiary and those of Prairie Pipe for comparative purposes,[48] he underplayed the rationale behind Indiana's reducing its dependence on Prairie. Although by mid-1922 the rates of Sinclair Pipe Line and Prairie for the same haul were substantially identical, ownership in the former brought a reduction in net transportation costs compared to the latter. In explaining Indiana Standard's acquisition of a half-interest in Sinclair Pipe Line, however, Stewart placed primary emphasis on its relation to Sinclair Crude Oil Purchasing. He regarded acquisition of the Pipe Line Company as complementary to that of the Purchasing Company in Indiana's efforts to gain access to crude-oil supplies.[49]

On broad issues of public policy, Stewart advocated more industry self-discipline and self-regulation. "I am not in favor of Government regulation of an industry until that industry has shown that it can not govern itself," he said. "I do not believe that the oil industry has yet demonstrated the fact that it can not govern itself. I think that the oil industry should go on and work out its own salvation." [50]

To the small independent refiner, on the other hand, government was not an opponent but a desirable ally. For example, Harry H. Willock, secretary and treasurer of the Waverly Oil Works, Pittsburgh, advocated government ownership of pipeline and crude-oil storage facilities when he appeared before the subcommittee.[51] Each witness, in short, seemed to approach the question of governmental authority in terms of his own interest as he conceived it.

The report of the congressional subcommittee put the integrated oil industry under a cloud which did not begin to lift until the FTC made its 1927 report on the industry. Like the FTC, the La Follette subcommittee focused primarily on the Standard companies. Without qualification, its report stated: "The dominating fact in the oil industry to-day is its complete control by the Standard companies." [52] Furthermore, this control in large measure rested on pipeline power. "Through the Standard control of the pipe lines connecting the producing centers of the West with the consuming centers of the East and Middle West," the report stated, "not only is the price fixed according to the will of the Standard group which any other interest must pay for the transportation of petroleum but members of the group really determine whether any concern outside their group shall have petroleum transported at any price." [53] This verdict not only overlooked such developments within the so-called Standard group as the conflicts between Prairie, Jersey Standard, and Indiana Standard, but it completely ignored the existence of the Texas Company, Gulf Oil, and Shell pipelines, to mention only some of their competitors. The contemporary impact of tanker competition on pipeline rates was likewise ignored.

Convinced that there had been a deliberate and successful design "to keep a complete monopoly of transcontinental pipe-line service in the hands of a few large companies," [54] the subcommittee saw a need for action. It was not clear as to what the remedies should be. On the one hand, the report suggested that Congress could, with advantage, follow the examples set by Oklahoma and Texas in regulating pipeline service to make it available to independent shippers.[55] On the other hand, it also declared that "The first step toward making pipe lines real common carriers is to divorce the ownership of the pipe lines from the ownership of the oil transported." [56] Apparently as an intermediate step, the report advocated the establishment of delivery points on pipeline routes where a reasonable demand for them could be shown to exist, plus more effective enforcement of existing law with respect to service and rates.[57]

While it is apparent that the La Follette subcommittee took the independents' complaints about pipelines at face value, it is equally apparent from the record of the hearings that pipeline management had generally used little discretion in handling such problems. Nor were the defenders of existing pipeline practices effective witnesses before the committee.

Like other investigations of pipelines during this period, the La Follette inquiry produced no changes in public policy. In the remarks prefacing its suggested remedies, in fact, the subcommittee admitted that it had no expectations in this regard. "It would be useless," the report said, "in the closing days of this session to present a bill — which there is no time to consider, much less to pass — attempting to regulate the oil industry in any comprehensive manner." [58] The *National Petroleum News* reflected the integrated oil industry's feeling that the whole affair had been engineered by La Follette to gain personal publicity.[59] If so, the public rebuttals of the report by officials of Standard companies, even though they questioned the Senator's veracity, could be regarded as contributing to his objective.* On the other hand, only 3 out of 20 leading newspapers surveyed by the same trade journal, commented editorially on the subcommittee's report. Of these, the *Cleveland Plain Dealer* rendered the most balanced appraisal, refusing to dismiss La Follette's charges completely yet also noting that an investigation of this kind opened up the way to "muckraking." [60]

It is difficult to appraise the indirect effects of the La Follette investigation, but a meeting of state attorney generals, representing 20 states, adopted a resolution in the fall of 1923 advocating divorcement of pipelines from other branches of the oil business and endorsing efforts to make them common carriers in intrastate as well as interstate commerce.[61] But, generally, outside the oil industry there still were few who knew or cared about pipeline operations per se.

The lack of congressional action on pipelines in the wake of the La Fol-

---

*Noting that the subcommittee's findings and report received considerably more attention from the press than the companies' rebuttals, a *New York Times* editorial of March 6, 1923, commented: "All these assertions [by the La Follette report against Standard Oil of New Jersey] are capable of disproof, if they are false or wildly exaggerated. It will doubtless be a difficult process to attempt to overtake the La Follette report, which has got so good a start in the newspapers which have freely published it, and to correct its errors one by one." President W. C. Teagle of Jersey replied in a letter to the *Times,* agreeing that it would indeed be a difficult task, but saying "The directors of this company realized that, because of its unfairness and inadequacy, the La Follette report must be answered in full. It is their purpose to meet the conclusions of the subcommittee at every point and to give the public the truth as to this company's management, policies, earnings and public relations — information which was tendered the subcommittee and refused." Quoted in *Commercial & Financial Chronicle,* March 10, 1923, p. 1012.

lette investigation could be interpreted to mean that this sector of the oil industry had little interest for the general public. The effort by small operators and the Senate subcommittee to connect the price of gasoline, a matter of general concern, with control of pipelines was apparently too complicated to sink into the public consciousness. Even the simplifying device of linking these problems with "Standard Oil" failed to awaken the popular response that it had in 1906. Nevertheless, the investigation had added one more piece of evidence to the accumulation that would eventually threaten ownership of pipelines by integrated oil companies. For the rest of the Prosperity Decade, however, Congress was quiescent on the subject of oil pipelines.

The investigations of pipelines by the FTC and the La Follette subcommittee might have led to antitrust or legislative action against the integrated oil industry; the fact that this did not take place underlines the importance of the time element in the public policy process. A long period of gestation typically precedes major moves to restrict or control business. For example, although Congress had apparently acted precipitantly in 1906 to bring pipelines under federal regulation, the event was actually the logical culmination of a long period of controversy and investigation at both state and federal levels. Moreover, that legislation was adopted in the heat of a situation carefully contrived by President Theodore Roosevelt, who built skillfully on general public concern about the excesses of big business.

The pipeline investigations of 1915–1931, on the other hand, did not proceed from widespread alarm about the structure or performance of the oil industry. Neither Congress nor the Executive Branch was disposed to challenge business leadership in the economy generally, or its energy sector in particular. In fact, the contemporary Teapot Dome scandal reflected the unduly close ties that had developed between key government officials and certain elements in the oil industry. Even public reaction to these revelations, however, was insufficient to create an environment favorable to drastic federal actions, either legislative or legal, that might have affected the place of pipelines in the integrated oil industry. Furthermore, intra-industry developments during this period did not lead to strenuous demands from within the industry for enforced changes in pipeline ownership.

The very passage of time had helped to alter — if not to eliminate — some of the points of friction that had in the past led to governmental intervention to restructure the industry. The consequences of public policy developments prior to 1914 therefore were given time to work themselves out, the dissolution of 1911 took on real meaning, and new companies took their place in the industry. Meantime, the regulatory mechanisms at both state and federal levels provided a means for adjusting the relatively infrequent, and usually localized, conflicts arising from day-to-day pipeline operations.

CHAPTER 11

STATE AND FEDERAL REGULATION

Although the potentialities of pipeline regulation were suggested in the isolated instances where it was fully implemented, regulatory requirements posed few problems for pipeline management during the period between World War I and the Great Depression. The Interstate Commerce Commission was preoccupied with railroad problems, particularly as they related to implementation of the Valuation Act of 1913 and then the Transportation Act of 1920. Therefore, aside from prescribing routine administrative requirements for pipeline companies subject to its jurisdiction, the ICC showed no disposition to initiate any substantive actions with respect to these carriers. Proceeding on the "fair return" principle, for example, the ICC assumed pipeline rates to be reasonable unless challenged by an interested party. Accordingly, tariffs filed by pipeline companies were automatically accepted. Only once during this period was a tariff challenged in a manner that led to a major ICC decision on it.

Presumably the lack of complaints to the ICC was related to the fact that those most likely to protest pipeline rates or practices were either satisfied with the situation as it was, or were more hopeful of obtaining redress of grievances at the state level, where the most direct contact took place between pipeline companies and those who had need for their services. In the oil-producing states whose laws imposed common-carrier status and prescribed rate and service regulations the impact of public authority was certainly most felt by pipeline companies. Like the ICC, however, state officials generally assumed that pipeline rates were reasonable unless challenged. On the other hand, where the federal law, except when it concerned public lands, imposed no requirements on where or how an oil pipeline should be built, the states's power to confer the right of eminent domain and to prescribe the conditions for intrastate pipeline operations placed state regulatory commissions in a potentially strategic position to affect managerial decisions.

STATE REGULATION OF PIPELINES

The Scope of State Regulation

Regulation could, of course, deal with both the conditions of competition and its results. Excessive common-carrier pipeline construction, for example, could lead to surplus capacity and unremunerative operations.

Regulatory authorities could soften the impact of such a development by authorizing rates high enough to support uneconomic operations, though they thereby increased the costs of transportation. On the other hand, regulation could allow the operation of competitive forces to eliminate the problem.

Such a competitive situation arose in the Cat Creek pool of Montana, connected to a rail shipping point at Winnett by two pipelines — one the property of a partially integrated company and the other owned by an independent carrier. Although the first of these lines had to accept common-carrier status under Montana law, it did not solicit common-carrier business. The other line depended on it. Since the pool was not large enough to support both lines, a problem of equity confronted the Montana Railroad Commissioners in the early 1920's. When they set rates high enough to give the weaker of the two lines a 7 per cent return on its investment, the other line could earn 76.28 per cent. Given the conditions as they existed, it was impossible by administrative action to insure both carriers a fair return. A review of the attempt to do so in 1922 led, therefore, to a reduction of the rate, in effect sounding the death knell of the weaker line.[1]

One way to eliminate such unpleasant choices was to limit entry into a regulated business by requiring a certificate of public convenience and necessity for a new entrant. This approach, applied to railroads in the Transportation Act of 1920, characterized federal regulation of motor and air carriers, among others, but was not applied in federal nor, as a rule, in state regulation of oil pipelines. However, there were exceptions. For example, under statutory authority, the Colorado Public Utilities Commission in 1927 required such a certificate for a common-carrier pipeline to transport natural gasoline and oil.[2]

The most common form of state regulation was legislation empowering a state authority to prescribe the conditions under which a common-carrier pipeline business could be done, including rate and service requirements. In some instances, such authority included the power to order pipeline expansion or extension to meet a need that impressed a state commission but not necessarily a pipeline owner. Texas, a major oil-producing state, conferred all these powers on its Railroad Commission. But, as in the case of the federal pipeline statute, it was the implementation of the law that gave it practical meaning.

State Law and Common-Carrier Status of Oil Pipelines

As of 1931, a total of 21 states had laws relating to common-carrier responsibilities of crude-oil or products pipelines, or both.* [3] As 66 per

---

*Most pipelines subject to federal jurisdiction were subject to state authority as well. Important exceptions were places where there was no state pipeline law, as in Indiana, or where a pipeline did only an interstate business, as was the case with Arkansas Transit Company which operated in Louisiana and Arkansas but accepted oil only for immediate shipment in interstate commerce. Beard, *Regulation of Pipe Lines as Common Carriers,* 48.

cent of all crude oil produced in the country in 1930 came from the Mid-Continent, and another 25 per cent from California, the states in these oil-producing areas were the most active in regulating oil pipelines. Judicial decisions on the California and Oklahoma laws helped to amplify and clarify the pipeline common-carrier concept during 1915–1931, while the Louisiana and Texas railroad commissions were among those showing the greatest administrative initiative in implementing comparatively wide-ranging regulatory statutes. Accordingly these four states will be taken as representative of regulatory developments at the state level in this period.

A 1913 California statute declared that common-carrier status should be imposed on all persons transporting oil through a pipeline "to or for the public for hire." A problem of interpreting this law arose in connection with the operations of the Associated Pipe Line Company, which was not chartered as a common carrier. It had built a line shared by its parent, Associated Oil Company, and the Kern Oil & Trading Company, an affiliate of the Southern Pacific Company. Purchased oil and oil produced by Associated moved through this line and two others owned solely by that company. In 1917 the California Supreme Court decided that, because there had been no use of the right of eminent domain* in this case and no showing of voluntary dedication to public use, these lines did not fall under the state's common-carrier law. In taking this position, the court stressed the lack of monopoly power associated with the operations in question, thus distinguishing them from the situation involved in The Pipe Line Cases.[4]

In 1920 the United States Supreme Court also had occasion to pass on the same California statute. The Producers' Transportation Company had built a pipeline, employing the right of eminent domain, to transport oil to the seaboard for particular producers under private contracts. The company maintained that it was exempt from the jurisdiction of the California Railroad Commission because it had not devoted its facilities "to public use." However, the highest federal court ruled otherwise, noting not only the use of the right of eminent domain but also the fact that the company was chartered to do a general transportation business and that the agency working with the pipeline readily admitted new producers seeking transportation.[5] In other words, the actual use of the pipeline, as well as its reliance on public authority for condemning land for a right of way, conferred common-carrier status.

In Oklahoma, which had a pipeline law dating from 1909, a situation involving somewhat similar transportation arrangements led to a similar result. The Champlin Refining Company operated pipelines to gather and transport crude oil in connection with its refining operation near Enid,

---

*A survey of pipeline companies in 1932 for the use of Congress showed that relatively few companies had invoked the right of eminent domain in building their lines. Stanolind Pipe Line, for example, with over 2,600 miles of gathering line and nearly 4,500 miles of trunk line had condemned land in only two cases. See Beard, *Regulation of Pipe Lines as Common Carriers,* 39, n. 36.

Oklahoma. Some of these movements were under private contracts that gave the Champlin Company the right to purchase the oil involved. When Oklahoma attempted to tax the company as a common carrier, Champlin objected on the grounds that it had not employed the right of eminent domain, that it was not a public service corporation, and that it was entitled to exemption from common-carrier status because there was no public need for use of its pipelines in this capacity. On appeal the Oklahoma Supreme Court in 1927 rejected this contention. In its words, referring to the private contracts, "The moment complainant engaged in the transportation of crude oil for hire, if it was not prior thereto in law a public service corporation, it was then and there by the law of the State declared to be a common-carrier." [6] Again, actual use of the pipeline seemed to be the governing consideration in determining its common-carrier status.

In Louisiana a running battle between the regulatory commission and large, integrated oil companies, especially Louisiana Standard, led to strengthened pipeline laws and aggressive action to enforce them. Producer discontent, politically ambitious public administrators, and managerial reluctance to accept pipeline regulation all played a role in these developments.

A 1906 Louisiana statute had declared that pipelines carrying oil in intrastate business for a consideration were subject to regulation as common carriers by the Railroad Commission.[7] A companion statute conferred the right of eminent domain on pipelines, conditional on the familiar requirement of their performing as common carriers.[8] In connection with the investigation of Mid-Continent pipelines ordered by Congress, the federal Bureau of Corporations, which was about to be merged into the newly-authorized Federal Trade Commission, in early 1915 checked pipeline tariffs filed with the Louisiana Railroad Commission. The fact that Louisiana Standard, Jersey's producing affiliate, had filed none was called to the attention of the Louisiana Commission, which shortly ordered the company to comply with the 1906 statute. Falling back on its claim that it was not an intrastate common carrier, Louisiana Standard, which had not employed the right of eminent domain, refused to comply. The Railroad Commission took no further steps at that time.[9]

In that same year, however, Louisiana producers followed the lead of their Oklahoma and Texas counterparts in an effort to obtain more effective state regulation of oil pipelines, which they claimed offered high prices to encourage drilling and then dropped the price to get these properties into their own hands.[10] In response to such complaints, Governor Luther E. Hall called a special session of the legislature to consider a pipeline bill closely modeled on the one that the Texas Producers' and Landowners' Association was advocating at Austin. Introduced by Representative Frank Powell of Beauregard Parish, the bill called for making all oil pipelines in the state common carriers, requiring them to provide tankage for shippers at their terminals, and subjecting them to the Railroad Commission, which was to have power to set rates and exercise control over pipeline transportation down to and including gathering operations.[11]

As in Texas, however, there was disagreement among the producers themselves as to the desirability of the proposed Louisiana legislation. While producers from the southern part of the state favored it, those from northern Louisiana felt that an effective common-carrier statute might hurt them more than it would hurt the pipelines.[12] In any event, a revised statute did not emerge until 1920. At that time the 1906 law was re-enacted, but the definition of those subject to it was broadened to include pipelines that appeared from the manner or nature of their business to be common carriers.[13] The so-called Tanner antidiscrimination bill was adopted as a companion measure, forbidding discrimination by pipelines, requiring ratable purchasing during flush production, and making warehouse receipts for oil negotiable instruments.[14]

This legislation was in part a response to producer discontent with large, integrated companies operating in the Pine Island Extension of the Caddo Field. Trouble had started when the Louisiana Standard, Texas, and Gulf companies cut back or canceled their purchases there.

During World War I there had been a brisk demand for Pine Island crude oil, but with the coming of peace the major companies readjusted their purchasing. Independent Pine Island producers quickly felt the effects, and it proved impossible to convince Huey P. Long, a young Louisiana politician who was elected to the state's Railroad Commission in 1918 and quickly came to dominate it, that the big companies were not trying to freeze small producers out of the field. For example, the commission compared Pine Island oil selling at less than 60 cents a barrel with oil of lower quality purchased and sold in California for $1.85 a barrel. Attributing this situation to the purchasing policies of the Standard, Texas, and Gulf companies, the commission declared: "No justification could be or was ever attempted for such a glaring disparity in price." [15]

After hearings in early 1919, the commission concluded that the pipeline companies had deliberately imposed an embargo on Pine Island crude and were causing wastage of oil in that field. Therefore, the commission recommended legislation to give it effective regulatory powers over pipelines, and during that summer Long called for the separation of production, transportation, and refining functions in the state.[16] Out of this agitation came the common-carrier and antidiscrimination legislation of 1920.

Louisiana Standard's rapid pipeline expansion programs at this time made that company vulnerable to attacks from both state and federal regulatory agencies. During 1921, as mentioned previously, the Pipe Line Department had run lines across the Louisiana state line into the El Dorado, Arkansas, field and the following year had extended operations to Smackover, Arkansas, as well as acquiring Prairie Pipe's Arkansas Division. As a result, Louisiana Standard was engaged in interstate pipeline operations yet its officers had filed no tariffs with the ICC nor had they made annual reports to that body.[17] The Pipe Line Department did not hold itself any more accountable to state regulatory authorities than to the ICC, but a hostile Huey Long had now appeared as chairman of the Louisiana Public Service Commission, which had replaced the Railroad Commission. Jersey managers became concerned that if either Long or the ICC decided to press the pipeline issue, all Louisiana Standard's records might be opened to public view.

On December 15, 1922, the Public Service Commission issued an order to Louisiana Standard asking the company to show cause why its pipelines should not be adjudged common carriers, forbidden to engage in oil production, and made subject to prescribed rates and other regulations.[18] Spurred by these developments, and upon advice from Jersey's Legal Department, Louisiana Standard turned its pipeline properties over to a newly organized subsidiary, Standard Pipe Line Company, in January 1923. Meantime, rates and tariffs were duly filed with the ICC.

Standard Pipe Line, legally a common carrier though serving only its parent concern, filed its Tariff No. 1 with the Louisiana Public Service Commission on February 3, 1923, and thus commenced a new era of controversy with that body. Acceptance of the tariff was revoked at Chairman Long's insistence, and the Public Service Commission began to investigate the factors that should govern rates and regulations for pipelines. Meanwhile, Standard Pipe Line continued its rates in effect pending further developments.

By April a fierce battle was raging between the Standard companies and the Public Service Commission, which was now demanding that the Baton Rouge refinery be declared a public utility subject to the regulatory body. The commission asked in vain that Louisiana Standard open its books relating to pipeline activities prior to the organization of the Standard Pipe Line Company.[19] Barred by injunction (subsequently modified by order of the state supreme court) from getting at these records, the commission rejected the value of nearly $21,000,000 placed by Louisiana Standard on the pipelines and tankage transferred to Standard Pipe Line. Claiming that monopolistic practices had resulted in earnings that had already paid for these facilities several times over, the commission proceeded to arrive at its own valuation for the property involved in intrastate transportation. This figure came out to only $4,143,750.[20] Next, the commission specified that the total rate for all pipeline movements within Louisiana, except from the De Soto field, which was nearly exhausted, should not involve a charge of more than 25 cents a barrel; from the De Soto field, 45 cents was permitted, but no gathering charge (which was included in the aforementioned tariffs) was to be more than 7.5 cents a barrel. In addition, the minimum tender was set at 1,000 barrels, and the pipeline was to store petroleum for as long as six months at a monthly charge of 3 cents a barrel.

The Standard companies challenged the Public Service Commission in the courts; Long did not press his case; and Standard Pipe Line continued its rates as originally published in February 1923. Still, no outside shippers used the lines.[21]

This long-standing controversy came formally to an end after Long ceased to be chairman of the Public Service Commission and one of his key supporters there was defeated for re-election. The new chairman was favorably disposed toward compromise. Standard representatives therefore offered to reduce gathering charges from 20 cents a barrel to 12.5 cents and to lower the trunk-line rate 5 cents a barrel for every point named in Tariff No. 1. On this basis the whole matter was settled by Order No. 433 issued by the Public Service Commission on December 16, 1926.

Implementation of the Texas pipeline law, adopted in 1917, did not take place until 1919. On July 8 of that year a public meeting was held to discuss the problem, and on July 26, 1919, the Texas Railroad Commission's Oil and Gas Circular No. 10 specifying pipeline rules and regulations went into effect. In preparation for this move the commission had its own engineers examine the books of pipeline companies, and the Gulf Coast and North Texas Producers' Associations agreed to each rule and regulation.[22]

The resulting regulations had several features advantageous to producers and shippers. The minimum tender requirement was set at 500 barrels and pipelines were required to provide shippers with five days free storage at or near the destination of their movements. Where tenders were in excess of facilities, pipelines were required to allocate transportation among shippers in proportion to the amounts offered by each.

On the other hand, the regulations also made some concessions to the carriers. To allow for evaporation, pipelines were authorized to use tank tables (i.e., to determine the amount of oil run from storage to pipelines) showing 2 per cent less than full capacity, except for the coastal fields, where the figure was to be 1 per cent. Pipelines were also allowed to make full deductions for basic sediment, water, and other impurities, plus an additional 1 per cent for evaporation and loss during transportation.[23]

Seeking to learn the extent to which this work might overlap that of the ICC, the chief supervisor of the Railroad Commission's Oil & Gas Department in December 1919 wrote to the federal body for information on its activities with respect to pipelines. Since it appeared that the ICC had only taken steps to classify financial data for pipelines and to control destruction of their records, the federal body had not pre-empted a very large area of regulation. The Texas Commission therefore announced that it intended to exercise the power of regulation over all pipelines in the state, including those engaged in interstate commerce.[24]

Aside from establishing its jurisdiction, however, the commission was chiefly concerned with routine administration of its pipeline responsibilities until a flood of oil from Texas fields in the late 1920's created new problems. The resulting difficulties were related to a more general crisis for the oil industry and its pipeline sector, and discussion of them will therefore be deferred to the next chapter.

With but a few significant exceptions, then, state regulation of oil pipelines from 1915 to 1931 was largely *pro forma*. Although in several states there was statutory authority to intervene directly in managerial decisions, it was little used — a fact largely attributable to the absence of shipper or producer complaints.[25]

THE INTERSTATE COMMERCE COMMISSION AND REGULATION OF PIPELINES

The record of federal pipeline regulations in this era was equally devoid of major controversy. If anything, the implementation of the federal law proved that management's early fear of its restrictive consequences had been exaggerated. With respect to oil pipelines, the Interstate Commerce Commission had been assigned a task by Congress for which it was not equipped in terms of its expertise. Also, its primary responsibilities in connection with railroads had been significantly increased since 1906. The task of preparing valuations for the nation's railroads, as required by the Valuation Act of 1913, was proceeding in this period and it was a staggering job. In addition, the Transportation Act of 1920, which sought to rescue the nation's railroads from their financial difficulties, imposed new burdens on the ICC. With limited resources, and apparently interest, the ICC's strategy with respect to pipelines was to let them go their way in the absence of violent, sustained complaints.

Administrative Requirements, 1915–1919

For the most part, state commissions had followed the federal body in prescribing pipeline accounting procedures. By 1920 the ICC had prescribed some minimum reporting requirements. In addition to the requirement for filing tariffs, which had started the controversy resulting in The Pipe Line Cases, the ICC prescribed the classification of investments in pipelines, operating revenues, and operating expenses, by an order effective January 1, 1915. This order was followed six months later by regulations governing the destruction of records by pipeline companies.[26] In June 1919 the ICC ordered all pipeline companies subject to its jurisdiction to submit a report for 1918 and for each year thereafter. This so-called "Form P" report was designed to reveal information about the ownership, management, and operation of oil pipelines. These moves constituted the sum total of positive, self-generated ICC actions with respect to pipelines between 1915 and 1919. However, some complaints about these carriers were being received at the ICC's Washington headquarters.

Complaints about Pipeline Practices, Docket 4199

As a resting place for complaints against pipelines, the ICC continued Docket No. 4199, its original pipeline proceeding, until 1919. A fairly typical example of the docket's contents was a letter from George F. Getty of the Minnehoma Oil Company of Los Angeles early in 1915. In this letter Getty declared:

It is now over eight years since the Common Carrier Pipe Line Law was enacted by Congress, and during all these years the pipelines have fought the law in various ways. A decision in favor of the law was only reached last July, by the Supreme Court of the United States. Since then the pipeline companies have by unreasonable conditions and exorbitant charges prevented the proper application of this law to the purposes for which it was intended. Some of these conditions are a minimum shipment of 100,000 barrels, rates of, say, 72 cents from Oklahoma to the Atlantic and 52 cents per barrel to the Gulf, and requiring the producers to furnish their own tankage both at the commencement and the ending of the shipment.

*   *   *

If the pipeline Companies were today regulated as the railroad companies are, strong independent refineries would be springing up all over the country at terminal points and a real competition in the refinery business would soon be established. Let that day speedily be brought about.[27]

Like other complainants, Getty charged that the delay in actively implementing the law was adding to the profits of Standard Oil companies, which remained the favorite targets of dissatisfied producers.

To complaints of this type, the ICC replied in bland and vague terms, indicating that inquiries were proceeding and positive action would be taken at an appropriate time. To W. D. Humphrey of the Oklahoma Corporation Commission, for example, the ICC's secretary wrote in June 1915: "Preliminary work is being done and in due course a hearing will be held." [28]

Avoidance of involvement in pipeline matters, however, seemed to be a basic ICC policy. In early 1917, for example, while the Gulf Coast Producers Association was promoting Texas pipeline legislation, its president, W. S. Farish, attempted to get the ICC to investigate the rates of the Texas, Gulf, and Sun pipelines on the grounds that their intrastate deliveries to shipping points on the Gulf of Mexico were part of interstate commerce movements. In two letters to the ICC on this subject, Farish indicated that as a representative of producers he was concerned about the reasonableness of these rates and about insuring that the pipelines would "handle this f.o.b. ship business." [29] The ICC's reply was that the rates in question applied wholly within the state of Texas and were therefore beyond its jurisdiction.* [30] As usual, the correspondence was docketed under No. 4199. Finally, on March 21, 1919, this docket with its accumulation of complaints was closed without any explanation or further action.

Rail Rates on Petroleum

While the ICC had not taken any initiative to force pipeline rates down or generally to affect pipeline practices, it indirectly, and to a limited degree, influenced decisions on building and using pipelines. In three separate decisions between 1915 and 1920, the ICC revealed a policy of not forcing

*The ICC Bureau of Statistics did not consider the movement of oil between points within a state, even though the shipment was destined for export, as subject to the federal regulatory authority. C. R. Lodge, Assistant Treasurer, Pure Oil Pipe Line Company of Texas to M. O. Lorenz, Director, Bureau of Statistics, ICC, February 24, 1928; Lorenz to Lodge, March 2, 1928, both in Prairie files.

a reduction in rail rates on petroleum to enable shippers of oil by rail to compete with others using pipelines.[31] Subsequent testimony before the La Follette subcommittee showed that ICC endorsement of increased rail rates on refined products limited the radius of field refiners' markets and indirectly strengthened the position of existing crude-oil pipelines by making producers more dependent on the pipelines' purchasing affiliates. As shown in Chapters 8 and 9, the upward trend in railroad rates also encouraged large Mid-Continent refiners to shift their operations northward, supplying them with crude via pipeline.

The impact of ICC rail-rate decisions on pipeline expansion was exemplified in the case of the Homer, Louisiana, field. The Commission approved a 10 cent per hundredweight rail rate from Homer to Port Arthur and other East Texas ports, reportedly slowing pipeline development in that field.[32] Nevertheless, this kind of situation was atypical, and the ICC evidenced no concern about pipeline rates per se except to see that they were properly filed.

ICC–Pipeline Company Cooperation

The ICC found a need to obtain cooperation from pipeline companies to implement the statutory requirements of the Transportation Act of 1920. To develop depreciation accounting rules for the pipeline business, as required by paragraph (5), Section 20, of the act, the ICC turned for assistance to the oil industry and its leading trade association, the American Petroleum Institute. Following a request for assistance by the chief of the Depreciation Section, ICC,* the Petroleum Institute in January 1921 called together representatives of all pipelines subject to the Commission. At this meeting a Pipe Line Depreciation Committee was organized. Consisting of seven members, it was headed by Clark H. Kountz of Prairie Pipe Line Company. Fayette B. Dow, a former ICC official who was connected with many oil industry groups, served as counsel and intermediary with the ICC.

Since the Depreciation Section of the ICC wanted to base its recommendations to the Commissioners on first-hand knowledge of existing pipeline depreciation practices, a long period of information-gathering ensued. After the Depreciation Section recommended that the ICC follow the example set in its decision on depreciation accounting principles and practices for steam railroads and telephone companies,[33] representatives of pipeline companies had to educate the Commissioners in the differences between pipelines and railroads. This approach was adopted at a hearing held on April 12, 1927, before ICC examiner A. M. Bunten.

Ralph G. Hare, treasurer of Prairie Pipe Line, made the formal statement

---

*This communication asked specifically for a statement or brief "With respect to the classes of depreciable property (by groups, if practicable), the method of ascertaining the service life and salvage value, the bases upon which depreciation charges should be accrued, the necessity of accruals, the relation of maintenance charges to depreciation, and the manner in which the percentages of depreciation applicable to the several classes of property should be determined."

for the API Pipe Line Depreciation Committee. After pointing out that the ratemaking and recapture provisions of the Transportation Act of 1920 were designed to alleviate the railroads' financial problems and affected depreciation rules with respect to railroads, he proceeded to differentiate pipelines from railroads.

> It may be stated that no important pipe line system has ever been constructed nor, in the [Depreciation] committee's belief, will ever be constructed for common carrier purposes. A pipe line normally carries one commodity in one direction and the amount of its traffic can never be predicted to a reasonable degree of accuracy. Unlike a railroad which develops and increases the traffic of the territory which it serves, and whose business normally increases as the life of the railroad lengthens, a pipe line exhausts the commodity upon which it is dependent and will carry less oil in its later than in its earlier years. The important pipe line systems have been built to carry the oil from new pools as they were discovered to refineries with which the pipe lines were associated in interest. The whole history of pipe line construction, both before and after the amendment to the act making interstate pipe lines common carriers, show that the hazards involved in a business venture confined to the transportation of oil are so great to make it impossible for such a venture to secure the large amount of capital which would be required. [34]

Basically, the Depreciation Committee wanted the ICC to continue the same unit (as opposed to group) method of depreciation recognized by the Bureau of Internal Revenue for tax purposes. Also, it wanted recognition of the fact that the useful value of a pipeline depended on the length of life of the oil pool to which it was connected. The physical life of a line, for example, might be far longer than its economic life.*

Aside from technical accounting questions, the spokesmen for the pipeline companies also emphasized strongly the need for uniformity in reporting to governmental agencies. H. A. Gidney, comptroller of the Gulf Company's pipelines, testified that reports to the Federal Trade Commission, ICC, and the Bureau of Mines required different statements based on the same set of facts in order to satisfy individual agency requirements and thus involved considerable expense.[35] Forrest Towl of Cumberland Pipe Line added that the variance between reporting requirements gave ammunition to critics of pipelines. "I do not know how the rest are, but our pipe lines are bothered by a certain group of men that come to Washington and go to the State Commissions and get out the reports there and then they come and want to know what is the reason for the difference between this and that and something they read in the Oil City Derrick, and things like that. That is principally due to the conflict in the different kinds of reports

---

*The Cumberland Pipe Line Company had found that the Bureau of Internal Revenue was willing to accept a decline in production as the basis for accelerated depreciation. In one such instance, where the flow of oil fell off precipitously after the first year, the Bureau permitted a write-off in five or six years to cover the loss in value of the pipeline. Hearing before the Interstate Commerce Commission, "Depreciation Charges of Carriers by Pipe Lines, Docket 19200," April 12, 1927, pp. 18, 22. (mimeo)

that we have to make." [36] In short, in seeking ICC approval of the method of depreciation accounting favored by pipeline companies, company representatives stressed the differences in function between railroads and pipelines and the need for greater uniformity in reports to government agencies.

The ICC had granted an extension in the railroad depreciation matter, so the pipeliners asked for and received comparable treatment. Years passed and the depreciation question was not settled. It was November 1934 when the ICC finally issued its order establishing rules, effective January 1, 1936, for pipeline depreciation accounting. Nearly 14 years had passed since the issue was first formally raised by the ICC. In another area of major importance, valuation of pipeline properties, ICC had just begun its work.

The Brundred Brothers Case

Coincidentally, fourteen years also elapsed between adoption of the federal pipeline law and the first effort to test its efficacy in rendering relief to potential oil pipeline shippers. Although the ICC had received some complaints about pipeline rates and practices, none prior to 1920 had led to adversary action of interested parties on whom the ICC made implementation of the statute primarily dependent. To the Brundred brothers, oil brokers of Oil City, Pennsylvania, however, the expense of this type of action seemingly presented no obstacle, and they undertook to challenge Prairie Pipe Line, the leading company in the business, before the federal regulatory body.

The Brundreds, Benjamin and William, had begun in 1916 to purchase credit balances of oil in the Pennsylvania fields to supply local, independent refiners. The difficulty of obtaining crude oil in that area of declining production led the Brundreds to propose that they act as agents for these refiners and supply them with Mid-Continent crude. As William J. Brundred later put it: "We knew that the pipe line companies were common carriers, and we saw no reason why the mid-continent crude could not be delivered to these refiners in order to supply that shortage." [37] As a first step, the Brundreds contacted Prairie Pipe Line Company regarding common-carrier service.

In a routine manner, Prairie Pipe Line had issued a joint tariff with the Northern Group of pipelines and National Transit in December 1916 covering the transportation of crude oil from points in Kansas and Oklahoma to Lacy Station (Warren), Pennsylvania. The through rate, via Griffith, Indiana, was 63.25 cents, to which a gathering charge of 12 cents a barrel was added for oil accessible to Prairie's gathering facilities. Among the regulations specified was the standard 100,000-barrel minimum tender. In the words of the regulation:

> Orders for the shipment of any specified kind of such crude petroleum shall only become effective when orders from the shipper, in connection with orders from other shippers, for the same kind and quality of crude petroleum shall amount in the aggregate to one hundred thousand (100,000) barrels,

or more, consigned to the same point of delivery; and subject to this requirement, orders for shipment shall become operative in the order in which they shall have been received.[38]

This requirement, as many federal investigators and independent oilmen had testified over the years, was a barrier to use of Prairie's lines by small shippers.

The 1916 tariff was reissued as ICC 114 in July 1919, the chief changes being the addition of two shipping points in Kansas and a change in the regulations affecting responsibility for loss or damage. Prairie Pipe Line tariffs ICC 112 and 142, which, along with 114, became effective August 8, 1919, specified rates and regulations for shipments between Kansas and Oklahoma points and Franklin, Pennsylvania.

On September 23, 1919, W. J. Brundred asked for copies of Prairie tariffs 112 and 114. In October there was further correspondence with Prairie Pipe's vice-president, C. H. Kountz, and in February 1920 the Brundred brothers discussed tariff 114 with W. F. Gates, Prairie Pipe Line's president.[39] They found that Prairie Pipe Line construed the minimum tender requirement to mean that "the shipper must have at least the minimum of 100,000 barrels in tankage above ground acceptable for shipment and available to the gathering lines of this Company to guarantee to this Company that the full amount of such Tender of Shipment can be secured by us." [40]

Believing this requirement was indefensible and that it discriminated against the small shipper, the Brundreds on June 2, 1920, filed a formal complaint with the ICC. For this purpose they employed the law firm of Carmalt, Hagerty and Wheeler, presumably because Camalt and Hagerty were former employees of the ICC and therefore familiar with its procedures and personnel. Carmalt, in fact, had been chief examiner for the Commission.[41] The Brundreds' complaint was directed primarily against Prairie's minimum tender requirement. They attacked it as favoring large companies, as having no basis in "practical transportation reasons," and as being, as a consequence, unreasonable and in violation of Section 1 of the Interstate Commerce Act. Rates apparently entered the case only because they were Carmalt's specialty.[42] The complaint did not attack the trunk-line rates as such, but maintained that Prairie's 12-cent gathering charge was unreasonable in view of the service afforded. The Brundreds suggested 2,000 barrels as the maximum amount that should be considered just and reasonable under the tender requirement of the tariffs in question.

A copy of this complaint was served on James K. Jones, a Washington lawyer who served as Prairie Pipe Line's resident agent in the capital. He forwarded the complaint to the company's headquarters in Independence, Kansas. Application was made and accepted for an extension of time in which to answer it. Meanwhile, Prairie Pipe Line officials examined their own position and in letters and conferences discussed the problem with connecting carriers.

One disconcerting fact emerged from this analysis: There was strong opinion both in the company and among officials of connecting carriers that the minimum tender requirement as interpreted by Prairie Pipe's top management could not successfully withstand attack. The company's own general counsel, T. J. Flannelly, expressed this view in a letter to Vice-president Kountz on June 21, 1920. With respect to the 100,000-barrel requirement Flannelly wrote, "I feel satisfied that under existing conditions, especially with reference to the price of oil and tankage, we cannot hope to sustain it as a reasonable requirement, and the Commission will undoubtedly modify it." He also was unable to offer any reason to hope that although the Brundreds had not actually made a tender to the Pipe Line Company, this fact would disqualify them as complainants before the ICC. In general, Flannelly took the position that some arrangement should be made with the Brundreds to induce them to drop their action.[43]

Following a pipeline conference in New York and another meeting with William J. Brundred, Clark Kountz wrote to other pipeline officers for their interpretation of minimum tender requirements, reaffirming Prairie's stand that it would consider no single tender smaller than 100,000 barrels offered at any given time.[44] The response of Forrest M. Towl of the Southern Group and D. S. Bushnell of the Northern Group contained small comfort for Kountz. Bushnell's view was that it did not matter how the aggregate tender of 100,000 barrels was made up. One hundred shippers offering 1,000 barrels each, as long as they shared the same destination, should be as acceptable as one shipper offering the whole amount himself. Of course, under this interpretation the pipeline company would have to be able to accommodate the individual shipper's tender at the initial point of shipment[45] — a situation that did not exist on the Prairie system because that company did not conduct a credit balance type of operation as the eastern lines did.

Towl was concerned that Prairie Pipe Line's persistence in its minimum tender interpretation would mean trouble for the other pipeline companies. He believed that Prairie's position was indefensible, and he said so in virtually the same terms as those later used by W. H. Gray of the National Association of Oil Producers in testifying before the La Follette subcommittee. In a letter to Kountz, the veteran Standard Oil pipeliner declared:

> I further do not believe that you can sustain your position that each shipment must be 100,000 bbls. or more, when you are moving, practically continuously, the same kind and quality of oil thru your lines. I do not consider that you are moving oil thru your system, nor is it moving over the lines of connecting carriers, in accordance with your regulation as interpreted by you; in fact, the three companies over which some of this oil passes and of which I am President, have always interpreted the handling of the oil in a different manner, and it is impossible for us to handle the business in a different manner, when you consider the way it is turned over to us by other carriers.[46]

It is evident from the tone of Towl's letter that he disapproved of Prairie's refusal to relax its interpretation of minimum tenders; yet Towl himself had been an effective advocate of the minimum tender requirement when testifying in connection with the Standard Oil antitrust case.

A hearing on the Brundreds' case took place at Kansas City during the last week in September 1920, only a few days after Prairie had raised its general level of rates. William J. Brundred was the sole witness for the complainants. He gave no testimony on rates but repeated his charges that high minimum tenders kept producers dependent on selling to large purchasing companies at low prices, a situation that the availability of pipeline transportation to the East on reasonable terms could surely improve. Cross-examination brought out the fact that he hoped to buy crude oil in the Mid-Continent area and sell it in the East on a brokerage basis but that he had no contracts to buy or sell oil at that time.

Judge Flannelly and Frank Lyon of Washington, representing Prairie Pipe Line, had a full panoply of witnesses on hand to support the company's position. Several producers testified that there was already adequate competition in the Mid-Continent area and reduction of Prairie's minimum tender requirement would flood the field with brokers and produce disastrous results. An independent shipper and a refiner were called to substantiate the wisdom and necessity of the 100,000-barrel requirement. None of these witnesses felt that a minimum tender requirement as low as 2,000 barrels, which Brundred had suggested, would afford a pipeline adequate incentive to extend into new areas.

On September 28, Kountz took the witness chair and defended his company's position. His remarks centered chiefly on the pipeline's need for an assured supply of oil and the requirement of a capacity load for efficient operation. When asked whether a money deposit in lieu of the 100,000 barrels would not do as well, he replied that a pipeline depended on oil, not money, to keep it going efficiently.[47]

At the conclusion of these hearings, Judge Flannelly felt that Prairie Pipe had made out about as well as could be expected. The witnesses for Prairie, who apparently had been carefully selected and included representatives of Tide Water and Sinclair, had performed well. Brundred was reported to have been discomforted by the adverse reaction of the producers, whose cause he had thought that he was promoting.[48] Exceptions to the examiner's report were made by both complaintant and defendants; argument on them was heard before Division 2 of the Interstate Commerce Commission; and a decision was finally announced on April 15, 1922. Commissioner John J. Esch presented the decision, which was the same as the examiner's.

After reviewing the circumstances surrounding the case, the Commissioner rejected each of the arguments for imposing 100,000 barrels as the minimum tender. On the other hand, he acknowledged that "pipe lines can not be successfully operated on a driblet basis, and there is a reasonable minimum below which they should not be required to accept oil for transportation."[49]

The validity of the testimony given by the various witnesses presented by

Judge Flannelly was specifically questioned in terms of their obvious self-interest. For example, producers who had supported the Pipe Line Company were also dependent on Prairie Oil & Gas as a customer. Refiners from Pennsylvania supporting Prairie's position apparently feared contamination of the pipelines carrying their high-grade oil if Mid-Continent crude was shipped into Lacy Station (Warren), Pennsylvania.[50]

That some minimum tender requirement should be properly required for pipeline shipments was widely accepted; that excessively large ones were stipulated to restrict the use of pipelines to large shippers was widely recognized. In July 1920, for example, the Texas Railroad Commission, which had set a 500-barrel minimum, communicated to the ICC its belief that the 100,000-barrel requirement was evidence of the "unreasonableness and evasion of the law in the attempt of the interstate pipeline companies to fix the minimum by their own regulations." [51] In its 1916 report on pipelines, the Federal Trade Commission had raised the question of whether even 25,000 barrels might not be an excessive minimum tender requirement.[52] During the course of the Brundred proceedings, the Okmulgee (Oklahoma) District Oil & Gas Association and the National Association of Independent Oil Producers intervened, after an initial rebuff by the ICC,[53] in support of the complaint against the Prairie minimum tender.[54]

Taking such evidence into consideration, the ICC finally concluded that a 10,000-barrel minimum tender should afford shippers adequate opportunity to use the pipelines and at the same time meet the operating requirements of the lines themselves. But the decision carefully noted that his figure was subject to verification through experience.

The question of rates had not been foremost in the case, but it was present. The complainants had charged that pipeline rates, which had been increased on September 20, 1920, were too high, but their charge relied primarily on evidence of the pipeline companies' past profitability. The ICC, pointing out that only individual rates were at issue, rejected the complainants' argument. Since the ICC lacked any yardsticks of its own by which to judge whether pipeline rates were reasonable, it accepted Prairie's comparisons of its rates with those of other lines and its explanations of the need for an increase in terms of rising price levels. "We find that defendants have shown that the increased rates in issue are just and reasonable, but this finding is without prejudice to any conclusion which may be reached upon a broader record as to the reasonableness of defendants' rates generally," the decision read.[55]

The ICC thereupon ordered the 10,000-barrel minimum tender into effect for Mid-Continent crude shipped to Franklin and Lacy Stations, Pennsylvania, on or before July 16, 1922. Despite the general terms in which the minimum tender requirement was discussed, these were the only points specifically affected by the decision. Through ignorance, the complainants had not recognized that they were challenging a pipeline practice of widespread and long-standing significance. Otherwise, William J. Brundred later said, the complaint would have been much broader in scope.[56]

Brundred wrote to the ICC in June 1922 and asked if anything could be done to extend the impact of the decision. When he was informed that this was not possible except on a voluntary basis, the Oil City man asked that the ICC attempt to get a voluntary reduction on the minimum tender for Baltimore. This matter was discussed with Clark Kountz of Prairie Pipe Line who replied to the inquiry that only one company at Baltimore, Interocean Oil Company, could conceivably benefit from such a reduction. This company was not a refiner, and used oil only in the manufacture of roofing and building materials; it appeared to have adequate stocks on hand, was importing crude from Mexico, and had not requested the lowering of minimum tender requirements. Prairie management, therefore, would make no change. However, Kountz apparently agreed to experiment with a 10,000-barrel minimum tender for Oil City.[57]

Managerial Reaction to the Brundred Decision

The reaction to the Brundred decision by Prairie Pipe Line and its counsel provides some indication of their evaluation of its practical meaning. Except in demonstrating the potential power of the ICC over oil pipelines, the conclusion of this case did not change anything of significance. Frank Lyon, the Washington lawyer who had been on the case with Judge Flannelly, made this point in writing to his colleague. "It looks to me," Lyon wrote, "as though the Commission wanted to pretend to do something for the complainant and yet was not able to find any way to do it practically. From what I learned during the course of the case, it seems to me that 10,000 barrels minimum will not be of any more practical use than 100,000 to Mr. Brundred and his class of people." In fact, Lyon wondered where the 10,000-barrel minimum had come from "as that amount was never suggested by anyone." [58]

Lyon's real concern had been that the ICC might take some action with respect to rates which would mean a "direct loss to the Pipe Line Company with no means of setting it off." But, of course, the ICC had taken no action on this point and, if anything, had expressed positive approval of Prairie's rates. Therefore, Lyon expected that the pipeline company would comply with the Commission's order and not seek to challenge it in the courts.[59]

Prairie management, however, was not accustomed to having public restraints placed on its freedom of decision-making. As late as May 24, 1922, Judge Flannelly in a telegram to D. S. Bushnell of the Northern Group indicated that application for a rehearing or an appeal to the courts was still under consideration.[60]

The occasion for this telegram was an expression of concern by Bushnell that the 10,000-barrel requirement might lead to contamination of crude passing through the Northern Group's pipelines. In a letter addressed to Vice-President Kountz of Prairie Pipe Line, Bushnell had written:

It occurred to us that it would be desirable in filing these tariffs [required by the ICC order] to specify a junction point, such as Griffith, Preble, or Lima, at which the 10,000 barrel shipments, originating on your line, would be assembled with other crude petroleum of the same kind and quality moving to the same destination or points east thereof. The purpose of this would of course be to avoid as far as possible complications on our lines in the East incident to the handling of different crudes, which complications might arise if the 10,000 barrel minimum is carried clear through to destination.[61]

This letter, written only for pipeliners' eyes, suggests that there was some genuine concern, among members of the Northern Group, at least, that independent shippers might take advantage of the ICC's decision and that contamination of shipments might result from accepting the minimum tender specified. On the other hand, Bushnell did not think that arrangements to prevent such an occurrence would require much adaptation, and Kountz did not believe that it would even require any alteration in the regulations governing shipment.[62] This, in fact, proved to be the case.

Effect of the Brundred Decision

Although the ICC on June 1, 1922, amended its order to permit August 15 instead of July 26 to become the effective date of compliance, Prairie Pipe Line issued a new joint tariff to take effect on the date originally specified. In addition to the reduced minimum tender, as required by the ICC, the published tariffs showed reductions in trunk-line rates reflecting the system-wide effort to combat the tanker competition about which Kountz was soon to testify before the La Follette subcommittee.

In the case of Lacy Station (Warren), Pennsylvania, the rate from Kansas and Oklahoma points was stated to be 69.25 cents plus a gathering charge of 20 cents a barrel. The latter figure represented the advance made on September 20, 1920, which was maintained. The trunk-line charge had been increased from 63.25 cents, as specified in the original 1916 tariff, to 79 cents in February 1921, while the Brundred case was still in process. Thus, the new rate, though a reduction from the 1921 level, still represented a substantial advance over the one in force at the start of the case.[63]

From the standpoint of management, the irony of the whole thing was that up to 1920, at least, and presumably thereafter, no shipments had actually been made under the challenged tariff. In fact, National Transit had been trying to revoke it for this very reason at the time the Brundreds took their case to the ICC.* [64] From the standpoint of the small shipper, however, the Brundred case had demonstrated the possibility of challenging the largest pipeline company in the country before a public body and obtaining at least token satisfaction. Seemingly this was the primary pur-

---

*In December 1920, the ICC ruled that the schedule of rates to Lacy Station should not be withdrawn. *Crude Petroleum oil from Kansas and Oklahoma to Lacy Station, Pennsylvania*, 59 ICC 483 (1920).

pose of the Brundred brothers, since neither they nor any other small shipper took advantage of the revised tariffs in question.* [65]

Between July 26, 1922, when the revised tariffs went into effect, and the end of 1931, the Prairie Pipe Line Company received only twenty tenders of under 100,000 barrels for the points involved in the decision. Only six of these tenders were for 10,000 barrels. Five tenders destined for Lacy Station and eight tenders for Oil City (to which the 10,000-barrel minimum was voluntarily extended) came from the Prairie Oil & Gas Company and were destined for the South Penn Oil Company. Seven tenders came from the Atlantic Oil Producing Company and were destined for the large Atlantic refinery at Franklin, Pennsylvania.[66] Thus all the companies involved were former members of the Standard Oil group, but, according to William J. Brundred's testimony before the La Follette subcommittee, some of the shipments to South Penn may have been destined for independent refiners.[67] Out of nearly 13,500,000 barrels moved during this period to Lacy Station and Franklin, only 474,974 were included in the twenty small tenders mentioned.[68]

THE IMPACT OF REGULATION, 1915–1931

As far as rates and practices of interstate oil pipeline companies were concerned, the impact of federal regulation between 1914 and 1931 was minimal. Even the Brundred case worked no significant changes in minimum tender requirements. For practical purposes, federal regulation remained largely a formality, and the pipeline companies found the ICC willing, and even anxious, to consult with them on how the formalities should be handled. As representatives of the companies frankly said, pipelines were not built as common carriers. Because no one appeared before the ICC and demanded active measures to make them so, the Commission was satisfied merely to go through routine procedures of regulation thus reconciling the requirements of statutory public policy with the realities of existing pipeline structure and practice. Although there was more regulatory activity at the state level, its impact — with but few exceptions — does not appear to have been substantially different from what it was on the national level.

The most distinctive characteristics of pipeline regulation in this era appear to be the lack of complaints to activate it and the consequent long period of time involved in establishing regulatory mechanisms and acquiring information on which to base decisions in the field. Under the impact of overproduction of oil and the onslaught of a national depression however, the character of regulation was soon to undergo rapid and significant changes.

*According to one story still prevalent in Oil City, Brundred Brothers did make a shipment which remained in National Transit tanks so long for want of a buyer that the crude oil solidified, creating a problem in its removal. According to this story, the problem was solved by cutting a hole in the side of the tank and carting away the contents in wheelbarrows!

1. Mule teams hauling pipe to the site of pipeline construction on the Glenn Pool-Baton Rouge trunk line in Oklahoma, 1910.

2. Preparation of a ditch by hand to receive pipe at De Queen, Arkansas, on the Glenn Pool-Baton Rouge trunk line, 1910.

3. Machine ditcher, ca. 1916. Pipe has already been jointed and is ready to be placed in the ditch.

4. Machine ditcher of the 1950's.

5. Hand tong gang screwing pipe together by hand, ca. 1910.

6. Pipe screwing machine, ca. 1916. The machine travels on the jointed pipe, which is suspended above the ditch.

7. Water crossing, Buffalo Creek, Oklahoma, ca. 1910. Note complete absence of powered machinery for pipeline construction.

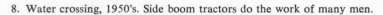

8. Water crossing, 1950's. Side boom tractors do the work of many men.

9. Coating an early pipeline by hand to prevent corrosion.

10. Cleaning and priming machine in use during 1950's. Rotating scrapers first clean the pipe, then the machine applies a protective, tar-like primer. The pipe is suspended by a side boom equipped tractor.

11. Pipe is machine-wrapped with protective covering before being lowered into the ditch.

12. After the pipe is laid in the ground, the trench is filled. In this picture, a side boom tractor is finishing the job of restoring the right of way to the condition in which the construction crew found it.

PART

The Challenge of
Accelerating Change,
1931-1941

CHAPTER 12

THE CHANGING ENVIRONMENT OF
MANAGERIAL DECISION-MAKING

Between 1931 and 1941 more restraints were placed on managerial decision-making in the pipeline business than during the whole history of oil pipelining up to that time. The first half of this decade was one of deep crisis for a rich nation stricken with the most severe depression in its history. The whole system of business enterprise and industrial self-regulation that had been applauded a scant few years earlier now came under mounting suspicion and attack. For a time even leaders of the business system lost confidence in their ability to arrest and then turn back the destructive forces with which they found themselves confronted. Drastic measures had to be taken; government was called upon to point the way and support new departures in many economic and business relationships. When the crisis was passed, some fundamental changes had been made. The business sytem had been saved but it had been severely tested and modified. Many probems still remained.

For the petroleum industry these were years of danger and change. Since its founding, it had always contained large elements of uncertainty and chance associated with the very character of the mineral on which it was built. Stability achieved by business combination had proved vulnerable both to public policy and flush production. Nevertheless, the basic hourglass characteristics of the industry structure remained, with a relatively small number of large or medium-sized integrated concerns controlling the flow of oil from thousands of producers to thousands of distributors. Much of the oil that flowed through these channels was also produced by integrated concerns and this fact, plus their control of pipelines, made it possible for them to exercise a stabilizing influence on the producing end of the oil business.

Stability and profits achieved in this manner, however, were still highly susceptible to the disrupting effects of flush production. Carefully developed controls that in periods of rising demand benefited both the producer and the purchaser of crude oil could not withstand a prolonged and substantial oversupply of oil in relation to demand for it. And once the price structure began to collapse, those most harmed by it inevitably sought the aid of government, state and federal, to redress a condition that seemed inexorably and malevolently directed toward their destruction. This pattern was virtually as old as the oil industry, but never before the 1930's had the adverse effects of flush production and a paralyzing national depression coincided. With the entire business system under hostile fire, the times favored drastic solutions to long-standing problems that were given a look of newness and urgency by the plight of the whole economy.

Out of this situation could have come a drastic reorganization of the petroleum industry, including the separation of the ownership of pipelines from that of other branches of the industry. Instead, there emerged during the early 1930's a pattern of government-enforced prorationing that reduced in significant measure the traditional uncertainties in the producing end of the business. But the threat of divorcement by congressional action still hung over the integrated companies, new taxes penalized old pipeline practices, and the environment of managerial decision-making was significantly altered.

THE BACKGROUND OF CONSERVATION LAWS

Instability, feast or famine, glut or shortage, were characteristic of the oil industry's experience with crude-oil production since its earliest days. Standard Oil had attempted to bring a measure of stability but at a price that neither the industry nor the nation was willing to pay. During the 1920's the question of imposing some order on oil production received increasing attention in the industry, especially since the national administration seemed anxious to promote cooperation with the self-regulation forces in business.

Henry L. Doherty, a top figure in the Cities Service group of companies, was an industry leader in the movement for conservation. Although a director of the American Petroleum Institute, the industry's leading trade association, Doherty found little inclination among his fellow-directors to listen to either his condemnation of wasteful industry practice or his proposed remedies. Accordingly he presented his case directly to President Calvin Coolidge. In a letter dated August 11, 1924, Doherty emphasized the need for conservation measures and suggested that if the oil-producing states were unwilling to act, the federal government should.[1] Apparently taking his lead from Doherty, Coolidge in December 1924 created a Federal Oil Conservation Board, composed of the Secretaries of War, Navy, Interior, and Commerce The board accomplished little of a remedial nature, but it helped to define some of the problems that had to be faced, such as the antitrust implications of adjusting petroleum supply and demand, the question of whether the states or the federal government should be the primary regulatory agency, and determination of the best method for administering any oil conservation program.

While the board was still engaged in consideration of these problems, the oil industry provided another spectacular example of flush production and its consequences. The Greater Seminole field of Oklahoma consisted of a number of fields — Seminole City, Searight, Earlsboro, Bowlegs, and Little River — centered in Pottawatomie and Seminole counties. Production in this area commenced in 1923, and by 1926 it had hit a pace that led operators to begin discussing voluntary methods to keep production under control. In late February 1927 Seminole City reached its peak production of 265,000 barrels a day. The Bowlegs field had just been discovered, and the Little River field was to follow in July. Attempts to curtail pipeline runs voluntarily and with the aid of the Oklahoma Corporation Commission did little to stem the tidal wave of oil. On July 30, 1927, Greater Seminole's ten major fields reached their peak production of 527,400 barrels daily. During that year Jersey Standard's producing affiliate, Carter Oil, alone produced more than 17,000,000 barrels of oil in these fields, approximately equaling the combined output of Humble and Louisiana Standard.[2] Also active in the Greater Seminole area were Sinclair, Barnsdall, Prairie Oil & Gas, Magnolia, Gulf, and many more companies.

Prairie Oil & Gas had a significant amount of high-priced crude in storage and offered to do its part toward maintaining price if other companies would do their share. The others, however, were not interested, and, led by Carter Oil, they dropped the posted price of crude oil. It was not expected by Jersey officials that this move would reduce production, and they were proved correct. However, the slash in Seminole prices was mirrored in other fields throughout the country and even abroad.

In Texas, Humble Oil & Refining also cut price and took the lead in a voluntary prorationing program that was a landmark of its kind. The Yates field in west Texas had been discovered late in 1926; by the following September the field was potentially capable of producing 192,000 barrels daily but as yet lacked an outlet to market. President W. S. Farish of Humble, which had the only pipeline in the area, offered to buy 30,000 barrels daily and to provide pipeline facilities if Yates operators would agree to share their runs to the pipeline on the basis of the proportion that the potential production of each operator bore to the estimated output of the entire field. The alternative, Farish pointed out, would be to construct expensive storage facilities and still, through unrestrained production, irretrievably lose much of the oil that could otherwise be recovered. Humble's offer was accepted, but it did not curtail production satisfactorily because no limit was placed on the number of wells that could be drilled to establish an operator's potential production.[3]

By 1930 flush production of over a billion barrels a year had led to the industry's accumulation of huge stocks of stored crude oil and imports had continued to increase. Drastic remedial measures were indicated. In June 1930 the Oklahoma Corporation Commission launched a state-wide program to curtail production, and Texas quickly followed this example.

Texas Conservation Measures

Texas conservation statutes dated back to 1899, and an amendment to the constitution in 1917 had declared that conservation and development of natural resources was a public right and duty. The Texas Railroad Commission, entrusted with the implementation of this provision, had backed the Humble program in the Yates field and in 1928 had attempted field-wide production control in the Hendricks field in Winkler County.[4]

The next step taken to attack the problem of overproduction in Texas was to enact a common-purchaser law in imitation of what Oklahoma had done in 1909. Adoption of this legislation was facilitated by the resentment created as a result of Humble's drastic cut in crude prices in January 1930. The provisions of the statute required a purchaser of crude, whether a common carrier or affiliated with one, to purchase ratably and without discrimination.[5] That is, a purchaser was to take oil, without discrimination among producers, in the ratable proportion that such production bore to the total production offered for sale in a given field.

This approach to overproduction raised many questions about the role of pipelines. For example: Could a pipeline chartered only to transport oil be converted by legislative fiat into a purchaser of oil?[*][6] Could a purchasing company that had a separate corporate existence but was controlled by the same interests as a pipeline company be forced to observe this statute?[7] Could an oil company incorporated before the passage of the law and acquiring an interest in a pipeline before passage of the law be made to observe its provisions? What if the acquisition came after the passage of the law? Some of the best legal talent in Texas believed that the law could not be sustained against such challenges, but the Railroad Commission showed no disposition to force a showdown.

Proration of production and pipeline prorationing became entangled with one another. The former, implemented by regulatory authority as will be shown shortly, allocated production in accordance with varying formulas and within an over-all amount of permissible production. Common-purchaser laws required pipelines or affiliated purchasing companies to buy crude without discrimination. This apparently meant that a subsidiary of an integrated concern was required to purchase ratably from independent producers in fields where it was taking oil from the wells of the parent company. However, a frequent charge, and one that was later made before the Temporary National Economic Committee by the Independent Petroleum Association of America, was that pipelines ignored such requirements and simply refused to purchase oil on a ratable basis. This was the meaning attached by producers to the term "pipeline prorationing."[8] In essence they charged that the owners of pipelines, rather than state regulatory authorities, determined whose oil would be purchased and in what amounts.[†]

The integrated industry's position was that this conception was incorrect. Pipelines were common carriers and by law were required to run whatever

---

*This question was eventually answered in the negative by the highest court of at least one state, Oklahoma. See *Gulf Oil Corporation v. State of Oklahoma* (Okla. Sup. Ct. 1961), 360 Pac. 2d 933.

†The recurring, sporadic character of "pipeline prorationing" charges was reflected in the complaints of Texas producers in 1957–58, discussed in Chap. 23.

oil was offered to them. The only time when they could be said to be prorating was when production exceeded pipeline capacity and, in order to treat all shippers alike, it was necessary to take a pro rata share of each tender.

The 1930 Texas common-purchaser law failed to solve the problem of overproduction that confronted the state because the statute dealt with the results rather than the causes of the situation. By this time there were over 147,000,000 barrels of oil in storage in Texas alone. In the Panhandle, which had an estimated producing capacity of 140,000 barrels a day against a market demand for about 40,000 barrels, 18,000,000 barrels were already in storage.[9] Faced with this condition, some of the large companies and their pipeline affiliates declined to connect with independent leases.[10] These producers were left without a market outlet; they lacked the means to provide storage; and, following the law of capture, if one producer drilled, his neighbor had to do so to prevent oil from being drained from one property to another.

The next step, then, was to try to curb the excesses of production. Accordingly, the Railroad Commission in August 1930 issued an order to curtail state-wide production to 750,000 barrels a day, or about 50,000 barrels a day less than average daily production during 1929. Inevitably, this order was challenged. The Danciger Oil and Refining Company asked for an injunction against it. This action was the first of a series that challenged, on the grounds of illegal price manipulation, efforts to adjust oil production to market demand.

Meantime, the oversupply problem had been further aggravated by the discovery of a vast quantity of high-grade oil in east Texas. Although the discovery well was brought in by C. M. "Dad" Joiner in October 1930, several months passed before the prolific nature of the field was widely recognized. Once this took place, however, a frenzy of activity in the tradition of all oil booms occurred. Voluntary restraint proved hopeless; yet for several months the Railroad Commission, beset with many problems, failed to act.

In April 1931, the commission tardily attempted to limit east Texas production, but operators either sought injunctions or simply ignored the order. In July a federal district court invalidated the order on the grounds that it was directed against the loss of market price and was based on engineering concepts that were unsound.[11] Both prices and proration efforts collapsed; Humble, the largest purchaser, had ceased to post a price for east Texas crude and the deterioration of prices there spread to other areas.

A special session of the Texas legislature was called to consider new conservation measures, most specifically a limitation of production to market demand. However, as the federal court decision had outlawed this device, Governor Ross Sterling announced that he would veto any effort to incorporate it in the law. As a result, the legislature adopted a statute that, on the one hand, prohibited all types of physical waste but, on the other, specifically forbade the limitation of production to market demand.[12] This action seemed an invitation to ignore all prorationing, and a new orgy of production took place.

After some initial hesitation, pipelines in the east Texas field had proliferated at a rapid pace. By August 1931, trunk lines out of east Texas totaled 1,600 miles, with an additional 355 miles in gathering lines.[13] Humble Pipe Line with 135,000 barrels daily capacity and Magnolia with 145,-000 led the way, and Gulf followed with 82,000 barrels a day. Shell Pipe Line was constructing a 200-mile, 10-inch line from Gregg County to Houston, and Sun Pipe Line and Yount Lee Pipe Line were jointly building a 200-mile, 10-inch line to tidewater near Beaumont.[14] While the lines of large companies transported oil out of east Texas to refineries or water shipping terminals, others served small field refineries which could exist only as long as cheap oil was available. This element, of course, opposed efforts to curtail production.

In Oklahoma, Governor William H. Murray finally closed in the fields, and on August 17, 1931, as a last resort in coping with the flood of oil, Governor Sterling ordered all east Texas wells shut in and called out the National Guard to enforce the order. This military control was challenged in the courts, and in February 1932 a federal court ordered an end to it.

A month later the Austin Court of Civil Appeals upheld the Danciger decision, which had sustained the Texas Railroad Commission's August 1930 production curtailment order.* Thus there was a conflict between the position of the Texas state courts, which seemingly upheld prorationing to market demand, and the Texas statute that had outlawed such measures in the wake of the federal court's decision on the question.

The final rounds in the legal battle over prorationing were soon at an end. A new Railroad Commission order that limited east Texas production to 325,000 barrels daily, allocated on a flat per-well allowable, was taken into the federal court. As in 1931, the court's decision went against the commission. In the interim, however, the United States Supreme Court had upheld the Oklahoma market demand law on the grounds that it was reasonably related to the prevention of physical waste and that any effects on price were incidental.† This development gave the Texas legislature an opportunity and an incentive to repeal its anti-market demand law of 1931. The appropriate action was taken by a special session of the legislature in November 1932, which defined "waste" to include "production of . . . oil in excess of transportation or marketing facilities at reasonable market demand."

Further legal actions followed, but they centered chiefly on the mechanics of setting top field allowables. The 1932 conservation statute was upheld

---

Danciger Oil and Refining Company v. Railroad Commission of Texas et al., 49 SW 2d 837 (1932).

†*Champlin Refining Co. v. Corporation Commission of Oklahoma et al.,* 286 U.S. 210 (1932).

and, finally, in February 1934 a federal court approved commission orders limiting production in east Texas to market demand. A significant shift had taken place in the conditions affecting oil production in Texas — ineffective voluntary self-restraint had been supplanted by governmental controls.

Pipelines and the Texas Railroad Commission

Against this interplay of political, economic, legal, and administrative pressures and decisions, significant steps were also taken with respect to pipeline rates and practices in Texas. Since the issuance of Oil and Gas Circular No. 10, July 26, 1919, the Texas Railroad Commission had exercised chiefly *pro forma* regulation of oil pipelines, but the same crisis that brought conservation legislation also renewed interest in statutory regulation of pipeline rates and practices.

As noted, the 1930 common-purchaser law affected pipelines.* Section 4 directed the Railroad Commission to establish and enforce rules and regulations relating to rates, charges, and requirements governing storage of crude petroleum. Section 7 authorized the commission, upon complaint or its own initiative, to require extension of common-carrier pipelines or enlargement of storage facilities if it found such action reasonable and required in the public interest. In signing this bill, sponsored by the Texas Independent Petroleum Association, Governor Dan Moody declared: "I cannot foretell the results of this bill. It was intended to prevent a monopoly and to improve present distressing conditions. It was so represented to the legislature and it has been so represented to me . . . Hoping that the bill will be a help to our State and citizenship generally, I have determined to let it become a law." [15]

Texas pipeline rates had become a significant issue. In April 1931 the Independent Petroleum Association petitioned the Railroad Commission for a reduction in trunk pipeline rates.[16] A bill requiring that the rates of common carriers be fixed to return 10 per cent of their investment was at this time on the House calendar, but was later withdrawn by its author, Representative Dewey Young. Instead, pipeline rates were made the subject of a bill re-enacting the common-purchaser law and extending it to gas as well as oil pipelines.

The new statute placed Texas pipeline companies in the same public utility category as electric, gas, and water companies. It required the Railroad Commission to fix maximum rates and charges for transportation, storage, and loading crude oil so as to yield a "fair return" upon the aggregate value of the property, giving due allowance for depreciation, reasonable operating expenses, and so on. Like federal procedure, specific rates put into effect by a carrier were subject to challenge before the Railroad Commission. In addition, general re-evaluation of rates by the commission

*Under this law, on December 13, 1930, the Railroad Commission ordered common-carrier pipelines to refuse to accept tenders of crude oil for transportation in excess of the allowable production of crude oil allotted to each lease and/or property.

was to be made annually, and no pipeline was to disconnect its lines without the permission of the commission or of the owner of the lease.[17] This law became effective August 14, 1931, in the midst of the great excitement over the east Texas field.

Despite its potential for creating major changes in pipeline regulation, implementation of the statute was slow. In September 1931 the Railroad Commission scheduled a hearing to determine what action should be taken prior to execution of its newly authorized responsibilities.[18] However, the North Texas Oil & Gas Association protested that premature action with respect to rates might hurt shippers, and the hearing was postponed indefinitely.[19] Meanwhile, nine pipeline companies contributed to a fund with which to hire a rate lawyer and valuation engineer to support their case.

Reports to the Railroad Commission continued to show a high rate of return on pipeline investment. For 1931 they indicated an average return of 29.67 per cent on investment, whereas Ernest O. Thompson of the Railroad Commission declared the intent of the law was to allow only 8 per cent.[20] Nevertheless, a proposal to levy a one-cent tax on each barrel of oil moved by pipeline in the state was defeated in the Texas senate despite its author's emphasis on the profitability of pipeline companies.[21]

After hearings and with the concurrence of pipeline representatives, the commission finally ordered pipeline rate reductions to specific points in February 1933. An incidental source of pipeline revenue was also reduced when the commission ordered a 25 per cent cut in the amount of oil that was authorized to be deducted from pipeline runs for natural losses that often did not occur. In the hearing on this order, pipeline attorneys estimated that voluntary rate reductions in the state since January 1931 had already saved shippers over $7,500,000.[22]

A further hearing was held in August 1933, and on the last day of that month the commission issued an order on common-carrier pipeline rates and charges for the entire state of Texas. This order, specifying maximum rates between major pipeline points in the state, was to become effective December 1, 1933.[23] Another order issued the same day further reduced authorized pipeline deductions for unmerchantable oil by requiring that pipeline runs be based on tank tables at 99 per cent of capacity rather than 98 per cent as allowed in Rule 9 of the 1919 Circular No. 10.[24] In this order, Texas was following the example of the federal government which several years earlier had ordered similar reductions for pipeline runs of government oil.[25]

These were steps of major importance. Although they applied only to intrastate shipments, they inevitably affected interstate rates. The decreased allowance for potential loss of oil due to natural causes also reduced a source of income to the pipeline companies, because they gained title to the oil that was not in fact lost yet was within the shrinkage allowance. Managerial adaptation to these new constraints is a major concern of Chapter 13.

FEDERAL PIPELINE INVESTIGATIONS

The Hoch Bill

Distress in the oil industry as a result of overproduction and federal investigations of pipelines in connection with proposed remedial legislation bore a high correlation to one another. While Texas was seeking ways of curbing flush production and making pipelines more accessible to small shippers, new interest in both problems was displayed at the national political level, where the benevolence of the 1920's toward business was being replaced by growing hostility.

As far as pipeliners were concerned, Prairie Oil & Gas, staggering under the impact of the integration movement and plummeting oil prices, appears to have triggered the first response in this new environment. It did so by announcing formally on December 31, 1930, that, effective with the new year, it would withdraw from the general purchase of crude oil on the market.[26] This decision had been known at least a week previously, and Prairie Pipe Line had announced to its superintendents and district foremen that it was soliciting business as a common carrier.[27] While producers were now invited to use Prairie pipelines, the invitation was of little value so long as they lacked purchasers for their crude. Reportedly, out of 37,695 wells connected by Prairie Pipe, only about 4,800 were owned by Prairie Oil & Gas;[28] therefore the cessation of the latter's purchasing activity created a major problem for small, stripper well operators. Their plight led state, federal, and industry officials to seek both explanations for and relief from the consequences of this decision.[29]

As noted elsewhere, the decrease in Prairie business as one major customer after another sought its own sources of crude oil and transportation was behind the suspension of market purchases. However, the fact that Prairie Oil & Gas continued to produce its own leases at the full allowable rate was proof enough for independent producers that they were being made to bear the brunt of Prairie's misfortunes.

This industry development was at least one of the factors contributing to the proposal made by Congressman Homer Hoch of Kansas that the commodities clause of the 1906 Hepburn Act be applied to pipelines.* His bill, H.R. 16695, introduced on January 29, 1931, was the first of a number of such proposals that, stretching throughout that decade and the next, sought to separate pipeline transportation from other phases of the oil business.

Another element besides oil industry distress contributing to the introduction of the Hoch bill was the growing desperation of the railroads. Hard hit by the depression, they feared that their petroleum traffic —

---

*On the initial day of hearings on his measure, Hoch declared that fear of the consequences of pipeline ownership by major producing oil companies had led to his bill and the hearings. *Hearings* on H.R. 16695, 71 Cong. 3 Sess., February 17–18, 1931. Representative T. B. Parks of Arkansas charged the Hoch bill was inspired by the the railroads. *Oil and Gas Journal* (February 26, 1931). 22, 54, 55.

especially in refined products — would be lost to pipelines. Vice-President Charles C. Paulding of the New York Central, speaking for the Association of Railway Executives which represented every Class I railroad in the country, had launched the attack on pipelines in November 1930. In an interview with the *New York Times* he declared that the railroads had been hurt by the growth of new and unregulated competitors, including motor, water, and pipeline carriers. Therefore his group proposed to undertake a legislative program to subject these carriers to the same restraints as those imposed on railroads. In the case of both crude oil and the new gasoline pipelines, this meant application of the commodities clause.[30]

E. B. Reeser, president of the American Petroleum Institute, struck back by denying any similarity between railroads and pipelines, suggesting that the proposed legislation would add to the customer's burdens, and claiming that railroad tonnage and revenues from petroleum and its products had risen between 1924 and 1930.*[31] The API was sufficiently concerned about this new threat, however, to appoint a 12-man committee headed by Henry M. Dawes of Pure Oil to fight any commodities clause proposals affecting pipelines.[32] Meantime, Senator Gerald Nye had added urgency to such defensive moves by proposing a sweeping investigation of the oil industry.

Testimony on the Hoch bill before the House Committee on Interstate and Foreign Commerce covered familiar ground. Charles E. Bowles, statistician for the Independent Petroleum Association, maintained that it was not overproduction but concentrated economic power that worried him.[33] He introduced, apparently for the first time before a federal body, the concept of 20 companies exercising control in the industry through their ownership of pipelines.[34] But, on a more familiar note, it was also clear that he hoped legislation could create more competition — and higher prices — for oil.[35]

Neither Bowles nor A. S. Ritchie, an independent refiner from Wichita, Kansas, who also testified, could tell the House committee specifically how divorcement of pipelines from other parts of the industry would improve the picture, and some members of the committee seemed more interested in defending integration than attacking it. Ritchie was personally most concerned about the recent development of gasoline pipelines and their threat to his market.[36]

Prior to hearing testimony on the Hoch bill, the committee had sought an expression of opinion from the ICC. In a letter replying to committee chairman James S. Parker, Joseph B. Eastman of the ICC cited the major cases involving pipelines with which the ICC had been concerned since 1906. While Eastman pointed out that these proceedings had shown a community of interest between pipeline companies and oil-producing and oil-refining companies, he also said that: "Upon present information we feel unable

*For a discussion of this claim, see Chap. 14.

either to oppose or approve what is sought to be accomplished by H.R. 16695." [37]

In fact, nothing beyond the airing of familiar charges was accomplished by discussion of this bill. Although Hoch introduced a similar one the following December,[38] again nothing came of it, and his congressional career came to an end when he failed to win re-election in 1932.

The Splawn Investigation and Report

Instead of inviting shotgun blasts at pipelines, Congressman Sam Rayburn of Texas in December 1931 proposed a detailed exploration of the existing situation. His resolution, adopted by the House on January 19, 1932, called for an investigation of common carriers other than railroads, their ownership and control, and the effect of the same on interstate and foreign commerce. The inquiry into oil and gasoline pipelines was to be only the first part of a trilogy that was to include electric power and gas companies and communications companies. The task was made a responsibility of the House Committee on Interstate and Foreign Commerce, which had earlier heard the testimony on the Hoch bill and of which Rayburn was now chairman. He appointed Walter M. W. Splawn, a former professor of economics and president of the University of Texas, to take direct charge of the investigation. Splawn already had some experience of this kind because he had conducted an investigation of railroad holding companies for the same committee during the preceding Congress.

Splawn's basic procedure was to send detailed questionnaires to pipeline companies and their corporate owners, supplementing the replies with material from the ICC, interviews, and other sources. When the job was done, Chairman Rayburn estimated that 95 per cent of the nation's pipelines had been covered, including a number of companies that were not common carriers and did not report to the ICC. The results were presented in two volumes with a total length of well over 1,000 pages. Inevitably the product of these efforts became known as "The Splawn Report," and it was the most extensive report on pipelines ever prepared up to that time. Therefore the conclusions drawn from it by Splawn in early 1933 were of major significance in the consideration of subsequent legislation affecting this sector of the oil industry.

The fact that oil pipelining should be regarded as a sector of the petroleum industry rather than an industry in itself was one of Splawn's principal points, and one which oilmen quoted with approval for years thereafter. The report stated: "Oil pipe lines are found as a result of this investigation to be plant facilities in an integrated industry." With obvious reference to measures such as the Hoch bill, Splawn added: "It appears very difficult to apply the 'commodities clause' to oil pipe lines. If the oil companies were forced to sell the pipe-line companies, who would buy them and who would build to newly discovered oil fields?" [39] For defenders of the *status quo*, this rhetorical question understandably had great appeal.

No previous federal investigation of pipelines had got as far as such an obvious question

The Splawn survey showed that ownership of crude-oil pipelines in large measure, and of the new gasoline lines wholly, rested with large or medium-sized integrated units. Although out of some 111,000 miles of pipeline, both trunk and gathering, pipeline companies as such owned over 99,000 miles,[40] this form of ownership reflected the oil industry's practice of assigning a single function to each of the companies making up an integrated group. [41] Legal and regulatory, as well as operating and financial considerations, were also found to underlie this pattern as it applied to pipelines.[42] With just minor exceptions, all pipeline companies reporting to the ICC engaged only in the pipeline business,[43] a development which was attributed to the desire of integrated companies to keep government regulatory authorities out of other aspects of their activities.[44]

Ownership of pipeline companies was found to fall into three groupings; subsidiaries owned directly by the parent company, as in the case of Sun Oil; subsidiaries clustered around intermediate subsidiaries, as in the case of Sinclair Consolidated Oil where ownership of Sinclair-Texas Pipe Line Company was vested in Sinclair Refining Company, one of several intermediate companies; or subsidiaries substantially owned by a single sub-parent of a holding company, as in the case of Atlantic Refining.[45] The Splawn report also showed that control of pipeline companies was exercised, with very few exceptions, through equity investment by their owners. Only five companies had securities other than a single class of common stock.[46] Of these, only Shell Pipe and Stanolind had debt owned by the general public.[47]

Not surprisingly, concentration of pipeline ownership was found to be accompanied by concentration of use. Over 60 per cent of the pipeline subsidiaries of large or medium-sized integrated companies reported that they carried no "outside" oil in their gathering lines, and about 50 per cent of them reported the same for their trunk lines. The investigation indicated that in the latter case outside shippers were typically members of other large, integrated units.[48]

The report also commented on pipeline costs and rates. While exact figures on pipeline costs were not obtained, a comparison of rail and pipeline rates showed that the latter were generally materially lower than the former.[49] Even so, the earnings of pipeline companies were found to be "high at the rates charged." [50] But high earnings did not mean high profits except where the business was provided by outside shippers, which was more the exception than the rule, or where it could be shown that an unreasonably high pipeline rate was used to justify paying a lower price to the producer for his oil. On this latter point, Splawn expressed considerable skepticism.[51]

In respect to minimum tenders, the Splawn inquiry showed that little change had taken place since 1914. The most common requirement for interstate shipments was found to be 100,000 barrels, with 25,000 barrels the next most common.[52] The new Texas-Empire line offered the most prominent example of the latter figure. Only a minority of pipeline companies — of which Shell, Illinois, Continental, Texas, Atlantic, and Producers were the best known — themselves owned storage facilities for holding oil until it was ready for movement, for sale, or for refining.[53]

The rate of return on pipeline investment was still another area of inquiry. Using ICC statistics, the Splawn report showed that the average return on investment for the decade 1921–1931 was 14.49 per cent and on net investment, 1923–1931, 25.43 per cent.[54] However, these figures had to be used with caution, Splawn pointed out, because investment included large amounts applied from charges against operating expenses for depreciation and depletion as well as reinvested earnings. He also properly noted that use of earnings or dividends per share as a guide to profitability was misleading since pipeline companies were typically undercapitalized.[55] Most of these significant qualifications to pipeline financial data were overlooked by both critics and defenders of pipeline operations later in the decade.

The conclusion that pipelines were essentially plant facilities was clearly supported by the evidence, but this finding related to the past; with respect to the future, Splawn recommended that the ICC give consideration to use of its existing powers to determine what, if any, relief, it could afford to small operators without transportation or storage facilities. However, his first conclusion was that "any regulation directed toward an operation or function performed by a particular corporation would have to reach the owning or controlling corporations." [56] This the Interstate Commerce Act plainly did not do, and the Splawn report showed that federal pipeline regulation had been nominal.

Splawn's conclusions also touched on conservation. In this area he found that it was desirable to rely on the states for police action, but he suggested that it might be necessary for the states to form compacts to enforce conservation measures. Even though he appeared to approve of the actions being taken by Texas and Oklahoma, Splawn did not rule out cooperation by the federal government or the ultimate possibility that it might have to take over the conservation job.[57]

THE NATIONAL INDUSTRIAL RECOVERY ACT

By the time the Splawn report appeared, a new administration had come to Washington, and between March and June 1933 it demanded and received congressional approval for wide-ranging measures designed to combat the stifling national depression. Some of them had important effects on the oil industry, including its pipeline sector.

A number of American industries had tried and failed to regulate their affairs on a basis of self-restraint. Some of these agreements, administered through trade associations, had proved vulnerable to antitrust action. As the economy sank deep into depression, there was a widespread demand from businessmen that the federal government give its sanction to such arrangements, suspending the antitrust law governing their operation. The incoming Roosevelt administration responded favorably to these proposals, and a novel experiment in government-business relations was soon initiated.

In March 1933 the domestic petroleum industry was overwhelmed with crude oil. Prices had dropped steadily since the preceding fall; flush production continued despite state efforts to curb it. The situation was such that Secretary of the Interior Harold L. Ickes called a conference of oil industry representatives and representatives of the governors of oil-producing states to meet in Washington shortly after the Roosevelt administration took office. Symbolically perhaps, the state representatives were asked to hold their sessions on the sixth floor of the Interior building while industry representatives met in the first-floor auditorium. In recognition of the diversity of interests within the industry group, it was subdivided into representatives of major companies and representatives of independents.[58]

The basic question confronting the conference was the nature and extent of measures to be taken to curtail the flood of oil that was undermining the industry's price structure. After three days of discussion, a committee of 15 members, headed by Governor Alfred M. Landon of Kansas and including W. J. Brundred of Oil City, formulated a list of recommendations for combined industry, state, and federal action. The majority's report was innocuous on the subject of pipelines. But the comfortable assurance that there was a common ground for government-industry cooperation was shattered by a minority report advocating divorcement of interstate pipelines from other branches of the oil industry.

This proposal was advanced by a group styling itself the "Independent Petroleum Association Opposed to Monopoly." Headed by John B. Elliott, it represented California producers who opposed any curtailment of production and attributed the ills of the oil industry to the large, integrated companies. In the words of this minority report: "The petroleum industry of the United States is in a more healthy condition than industry generally. It suffers, however, from certain ills, chief among which are monopolistic control, agreements in restraint of trade, price-fixing agreements, unfair practices, burdensome taxation, false propaganda and excessive governmental regulation." [59] Their remedy, therefore, was to divorce pipelines from the integrated structure that made these alleged practices possible.

Franklin D. Roosevelt, confronted with many pressing and difficult problems, relied heavily on Ickes in matters concerning the oil industry. The Secretary, who himself was no expert in oil matters, was asked to draft a letter for the President to send to governors of oil-producing states reporting the results of the conference.[60] Included in the letter sent on April 3, 1933, was an expression of the President's approval of pipeline divorcement as a "reasonable request" and his recommendation that it should be made the subject of early legislative action.[61] Presumably, Ickes had accepted the arguments of the Elliott group in favor of divorcement and Roosevelt had endorsed the proposed remedy in routine fashion.

Whether the Chief Executive was aware of the significance of his endorsement is questionable, but it certainly provided high-level support for those who were seeking to change the structure of the oil industry. Congressman Wesley E. Disney of Oklahoma took advantage of the opportunity to reintroduce a divorcement bill that he had first submitted, without result, in December 1931. Other Congressmen and Senators quickly followed suit until there were five such proposals before Congress.[62]

The integrated oil industry was stunned by the ease with which opponents of integration had found support in the White House. The immediate industry tactic, therefore, was to point out that pipelines were already regulated by the ICC and that a very recent government-sponsored investigation had found them to be plant facilities. President R. C. Holmes of the Texas Company adopted the latter approach, suggesting that probably neither the President of the United States nor his staff assistants had had time to acquaint themselves with the Splawn report.[63]

Events were moving fast in Washington during the spring of 1933, and the question of pipeline divorcement was a minor matter compared to the banking, agricultural, relief, and other emergency measures that concerned the administration. One major piece of legislation, however, provided a convenient dumping ground for diverse proposals affecting many different areas of the economy. Within the elastic contours of the National Industrial Recovery Act (NIRA) were to be included provisions dealing with subjects as diverse as emergency relief, labor-management relations, and industrial self-regulation. On May 20, 1933, Roosevelt urged congressional action on the oil industry, and his request was met in Section 9 of the NIRA which became law in June of that year.

From the standpoint of the oil industry, the opportunity had at last presented itself in the NIRA to win the federal government's support of a program to curtail production and increase the price of petroleum and its products. But such assistance was not offered without a *quid pro quo*. Section 9 (c) of Title I of the statute gave the President the power to prohibit transportation in interstate or foreign commerce of oil produced or withdrawn from storage in conflict with the orders of state regulatory authorities. This provision gave teeth to the faltering state conservation programs without inserting the federal government directly into them. From the standpoint of the pipeline sector of the oil industry, however, Sections 9 (a) and (b) of Title I were more important. The former authorized the President to initiate proceedings before the ICC to obtain regulations to control pipelines and to require reasonable, compensatory rates. The latter section authorized the President to initiate proceedings to separate a pipeline from a holding company where the pipeline company by unfair practices or exorbitant rates tended to create a monopoly. Thus the NIRA gave a basis both for requiring more effective pipeline regulation and for starting divorcement proceedings if this device failed.

Administration of the statute was made a joint government-industry endeavor. Secretary of the Interior Ickes was named Petroleum Administrator to represent the government. The industry was represented by the Planning and Coordination Committee, initially headed by Wirt Franklin who in 1915 had led the demand of independent producers for pipeline divorcement. To represent the transportation interest of the oil industry, a subcommittee of eight members, headed by J. Howard Pew of Sun Oil, was appointed.[64]

The basic program adopted under the NIRA concerning oil production was federal government support for state regulatory measures. Under Section 9 (c), the channels of interstate commerce were to be closed to shippers of "hot oil" (i.e., oil produced in violation of state law). The effectiveness of this ban however, depended on the machinery for enforcing it. Initially, federal control called for affidavits by producers, refiners, shippers, and carriers on the oil they were handling. Although this regulation was strengthened in the summer of 1934, it still did not prevent shipments of hot oil. Therefore a Federal Tender Board was established. Its function was to issue certificates of clearance to interstate shippers who supplied proof of the legality of the oil they were handling. The new system proved so effective that between 60 and 80 of the east Texas refineries working on illegally produced oil were closed down in the space of a few months.[65] Under both state and federal law, pipelines became involved in the mechanics of enforcing the ban on running hot oil. For example, tenders for oil to be run had to be submitted to both the Texas Railroad Commission and the Federal Tender Board.

At the same time, the constitutionality of Section 9 (c) had been challenged. In the Panama Refining Company case early in 1935 the section was struck down by the United States Supreme Court on the grounds that it involved an invalid delegation of legislative power.[66] Because the way in which the section had been drafted seemed to be at the heart of the problem, a new bill was written and passed in February 1935.* The resulting Connally Act was initially adopted on a temporary basis but became a permanent statute in 1937. The Tender Board was succeeded by the Federal Petroleum Board in 1942, and in 1946 administration of the Connally Act was transferred to the new Oil and Gas Division of the Department of the Interior.

In 1935 the whole NIRA experiment collapsed, but a comprehensive system for stabilizing, protecting, and regulating domestic oil production had emerged. An Interstate Compact to Conserve Oil and Gas, bringing together oil-producing states for cooperative endeavors to prevent waste, received congressional approval in August 1935. Monthly forecasts of market demand, first employed in the days of the Federal Oil Conservation Board, were prepared from 1933 to 1935 under the NIRA with the help of the Bureau of Mines. Since that time, with the exception of the war period, the bureau has continued to provide this service.

*Act of February 22, 1935, U.S. Code, Title 15, Section 715 *et seq.*

Pipelines Under the NIRA

A code to govern the oil industry, prepared by the industry, was signed by President Roosevelt on August 19 and became effective on September 2, 1933. Among its severest critics was Ernest W. Marland, an Oklahoma oilman and freshman Congressman who was shortly to begin a successful campaign to win the governorship of his state. Marland had been forced out of Marland Oil Company which was merged by the Morgan interests into Continental Oil. Accordingly, he had little sympathy for investment bankers or for large, integrated oil companies. He made no secret of his belief that the large oil companies had written the oil industry code for their own benefit and that pipeline profits were the key to their power. Marland therefore offered bills to forbid transportation of oil produced in violation of state laws, to prohibit pipeline companies from filing consolidated income tax returns, and to levy an income tax directly on pipeline companies that would bear heavily on earnings in excess of 10 per cent on unamortized investment.[67]

Reportedly, Marland also urged Roosevelt in the fall of 1933 to take action against pipelines under Section 9 (a) of the NIRA. In this way, he was reported to have argued, the ICC could cut down illegal production by controlling pipeline purchases of crude oil. It was the situation in east Texas rather than in his home state that the Oklahoma Congressman was said to have had in mind.[68] In any event, on November 27, 1933, Petroleum Administrator Ickes announced that the Petroleum Administrative Board would conduct an investigation of pipelines with a view of giving effect to Section 9 (a).[69]

Under Article VI of the Code of Fair Competition for the Petroleum Industry, investigation of transportation practices and rates was a responsibility of the Transportation Sub-Committee of the industry's Planning and Coordination Committee. On April 10, 1934, Ickes wrote to Amos. L. Beaty former president of the Texas Company and now chairman of the P. and C. Committee, calling his attention to the fact that the committee had not taken action. As Ickes put it:

> The Code has been in effect for almost eight months and no recommendations have been made under this Article. It is reasonable to suppose that current criticisms of pipe line practices and rates are not entirely unfounded and that an investigation made by your transportation sub-committee might lead to important recommendations for the general good of the petroleum industry. With this thought in mind, I would suggest for your consideration the desirability of making an investigation, and would appreciate receiving recommendations from the Planning and Coordination Committee relative to transportation practices and rates.[70]

Apparently to meet this request, the Transportation Sub-Committee rushed to completion a "Report Upon Pipe Line Practices, Rates and Related Subjects," which appeared in mineographed form in June 1934. The report was a down-the-line defense of pipelines as they were then operating. Starting from the plant facility concept, the report stressed that the ICC had adequate regulatory power, pipeline rates and earnings were reasonable, minimum tender requirements were necessary but might be reduced, and application of the commodities clause or divorcement was unnecessary and unwarranted. Common carriage was related to the plant facility argument in these words: "Because of the extensive development of pipe lines as plant facilities of integrated companies, the pipe line companies are in a position to conduct an effective common carrier service that otherwise would be impossible." [71] Finding no evidence of monopoly, discrimination, or other abuses, the committee declared that the attacks on integrated companies arose "principally from economic distress resulting from over-production, depression and unfavorable competitive position in a highly competitive industry." [72] On the other hand, the ICC's regulatory powers were being "capably and effectively administered." [73] Over-all, the report concluded that "with the exception of lowering the minimum tender requirement, there is no need for fundamental changes in either pipe line practices or rates when the industry is considered broadly." [74]

It seems doubtful that this report was ever circulated outside the industry. The August 9, 1934, issue of the *Oil and Gas Journal* stated that a report was to be made in September containing points of the type summarized above. In October, however, the Transportation Sub-Committee asked to be relieved of the necessity to comply with Ickes' letter of April 10. In the interim since the June report, the Interstate Commerce Commission had begun an investigation of pipeline rates and gathering charges and had finally initiated proceedings for the valuation of pipelines. On these grounds, plus the existence of the Splawn report, the Transportation Sub-Committee, now headed by A. E. Watts, saw no need for making a further report to Ickes. The Petroleum Administrator concurred on October 18, 1934.

Although the NIRA itself was declared unconstitutional in 1935, this brief interlude of close government-business cooperation had contributed to significant changes in the oil industry and policies of major pipeline companies. Most important, the federal government had become committed to supporting state measures for conservation of oil and gas resources, thus changing the conditions under which pipelines were built and operated. The risks of building into flush fields and then seeing them collapse with the consequent loss in pipeline investment had perhaps been exaggerated by pipeline management in testimony for the public record, but the risks had existed and provided a rationale for high pipeline rates in order to recover the investment as quickly as possible. With federally supported prorationing, these risks were appreciably diminished, though of course no human actions could eliminate them completely.

President W. S. Farish of Jersey Standard, testifying before the Temporary National Economic Committee in 1939, willingly conceded that prorationing had reduced pipeline construction risk. As he put it, "Like many other parts of the oil business, pipelines have been in a period of transition.

For one thing the risk element in their construction has been reduced through the effects of proration in lengthening the useful life of oil fields." [75] Elsewhere in his testimony, he declared that "under our system of conservation that is prevailing in the oil fields today, you know you are going to have a reasonable life for that pipeline, you know you are going to have production to keep it at maximum capacity for a definite length of time." [76]

But the major impact of the NIRA experience as far as pipelines were concerned came from the expression in statutory form of the administration's intention to force ICC action and, if that were not satisfactory, to press for divorcement. This combination of threats made it clear that unless pipeline managements took the initiative in revising rates and practices, they might be forced to do so under adverse circumstances and with unpredictable consequences. The changing tax picture also added weight to the other pressures for such voluntary action.

TAXATION

With the nation in the grip of depression and the federal government in need of additional sources of revenue, a tax on pipeline transportation was revived. During World War I an emergency tax had been placed on transportation of freight by water, rail, and mechanical motor power, and on express, oil, passengers, and messages moved over common-carrier facilities.[77] The 5 per cent tax, increased to 8 per cent in 1918, was incident on the shipper but was collected by the carrier. It applied to all transportation of oil by pipeline, thus affecting private as well as common carriers. In 1921 this tax had been repealed.

In the early years of the Great Depression the profitability of pipeline operations, suggested by large dividend payments, invited congressional attention to pipelines as a source of tax revenue. Accordingly, under Title V of the Revenue Act of 1932, a new tax was to apply to the transportation of "crude petroleum and liquid products thereof," making it applicable to both gasoline and crude-oil pipelines. Unlike the World War I tax, it was levied against the carrier instead of the shipper and did not apply to other forms of transportation. The tax rate was set at 4 per cent, which penalized the continuation of high pipeline rates.

Although the tax was supposedly adopted as a temporary measure, it was continued. In 1940 an additional 0.5 per cent was added to the rate as a defense revenue measure. Railroad tank cars, tank trucks, and boats transporting oil for hire were subjected to a 3 per cent tax in 1942, but it was collected from the shipper instead of the carrier. Thus, relative to other vehicles of oil transportation, pipelines were subjected to discriminatory taxation.

Inevitably many problems arose from this specialized tax. Initially, for example, the Internal Revenue Service attempted to collect the tax on 100 per cent of the volume that entered a pipeline at its origin. Because pipelines had always required and been permitted deductions for evaporation, losses in transit, and so on, Internal Revenue authorities were finally persuaded to levy the tax on volume delivered at destination.[78] There were other problems, as well. Did movement of oil by pipeline within the confines of a refinery or adjacent premises fall under the tax? What was a "fair" rate to use when a pipeline issued no tariffs because it was carrying oil as a private operation? [79] Since the Constitution prohibits export taxes, what conditions had to be met to prove that pipeline movements of petroleum and its products were destined for overseas and therefore exempt from tax?

The Internal Revenue Act of 1934 attached an additional penalty to concentrating large bookkeeping profits in pipeline subsidiaries of integrated companies. This practice was one of long standing, and critics attacked it on the grounds that pipeline "profits" subsidized other branches of the business. One element of the tax law that had allegedly encouraged this practice was the opportunity it offered integrated oil companies to file consolidated tax returns. With a consolidated return, the losses in one branch of the business, such as marketing, could for tax purposes be set against profits in another, such as pipelining, to reduce the over-all tax rate to which the integrated group was liable.

Periodically, efforts had been made to end the consolidated filing privilege, and in connection with the NIRA the tax penalty for filing such returns had been increased. In 1934, with the encouragement of Senator William Borah,* the privilege was entirely withdrawn except for railroad corporations.[80] While this move was not directed specifically against oil companies, it did affect many of them. Reinforced by the Public Utility Act of 1935, it appears to have been significant in the decisions of several companies to reorganize their pipeline activities as departments of the parent organization, a development reflected in ICC statistics for the first time in 1936.[81]

Regardless of the subsidy argument, there was no gainsaying that, with high rates, pipeline companies' books showed large profits. By ending the privilege of filing consolidated returns, Congress forced pipeline companies to pay their income taxes directly and therefore subjected their profits to higher tax liabilities.

Permissive filing of consolidated returns was restored in 1942, but both the transportation tax and the consolidated income tax problem continued to be important after World War II. In the early 1930's, however, they provided additional incentives for the management of integrated oil companies to reappraise the organization of their pipeline operations and prevailing rate structures.

*On March 8, 1934, Borah had also introduced bills to apply the commodities clause to pipelines (S. 2995) and to divorce pipeline ownership from other operations in the oil industry (S. 2994). Two days later their counterparts were introduced in the House (H.R. 8572 and H.R. 8576).

CONGRESSIONAL PETROLEUM INVESTIGATION, 1934

The petroleum industry had been at the center of government-business controversy at the turn of the century, and it seemed destined for the same role again as Congress and the Executive Branch continued to probe for answers to the Great Depression. In 1934 a subcommittee of the House Committee on Interstate and Foreign Commerce held extensive hearings on the petroleum industry, again raising the issues of pipeline divorcement and the role of pipelines in integrated operations. Although the subcommittee, headed by Congressman William P. Cole of Maryland, was primarily concerned with conservation problems, it heard a parade of witnesses representing independent refiners, producers, and integrated companies give their views on pipelines.

The basic position of such integrated companies as Sun Oil, Texas, Phillips, Sinclair, and Humble Oil & Refining was that pipelines built by them furnished services and advantages to independent producers that would not be available if the industry were structured differently. To the extent that this might not be the case, representatives of integrated companies argued that relief lay in more effective action by the existing regulatory body, the ICC.

Clearly, the regulatory body once feared by pipeliners had now come to be regarded as a bulwark against the dangers associated with unpredictable congressional action. The ICC had shown no disposition to question pipeline practices or to upset existing pipeline relationships. If anything, the existence of the regulatory statute had strengthened them by accepting the integrated framework as given. What was to be feared, then, was that Congress might, without fully comprehending the consequences, decide to force an alteration in the integrated structure with which the ICC was accustomed to working.

The integrated oil industry's case was best summarized by J. Edgar Pew of Sun Oil and the Sun Pipe Line Company. After making standard references to the distinction between railroads and pipelines, the "plant facility" findings of the Splawn report, and the lack of complaints to the ICC about pipelines, Pew proceeded to outline the advantages that accrued to the independent producer as a result of ownership of pipelines by integrated companies. His presentation centered on the fact that integrated companies built pipelines to obtain oil, not to perform common-carrier transportation services. Important benefits to the producer derived from this fact, he claimed. Competition for supplies of oil was keen. Therefore, numerous lines offered alternative markets for the producer's oil. Integrated concerns built pipelines into the field earlier than would be the case if transportation was the only purpose of their construction, and the pipelines of integrated companies remained in the field longer because the parent's need for oil justified it where transportation revenues alone would not. Under the existing system, Pew maintained, the producer was provided with a dependable purchaser, could count on his pipeline connection, was relieved of the necessity for providing expensive storage facilities, and benefited from competition between major companies to keep their lines full by improving pipeline service and prices paid for oil. According to Pew, these advantages would not be possible with an independently owned pipeline, and the specialized character and risks of such an undertaking would not attract investors.[82]

Qualifications to this presentation were offered by some independent producers and refiners, while others denied that it had any validity whatsoever. The general complaint by producers was that the pipeline, while it created the market, also controlled the price in that market. For example, Carl Weiner, president of the Kansas Stripper Well Association, stated that he had to take the posted price for oil if he wanted to move his production.[83] When Congressman Charles A. Wolverton attributed this fact to the character of pipeline operations by integrated companies, Weiner concurred but without noticeable enthusiasm. In fact, he reinforced Pew's argument by declaring that he preferred to sell to pipeline companies because this practice was convenient and eliminated losses and the need for capital expenditures on his part.[84] Reversing a complaint voiced on other occasions by producer in the Southwest, the witness's chief dissatisfaction seemed to be that the posted price of crude was uniform for oil of specific gravities regardless of where located. This, Weiner felt, deprived him of sharing in transportation savings that accrued to the purchaser of his oil from the fact that his wells were located 300 miles closer to midwestern refineries than those in east Texas.[85]

Joseph Danciger of the Danciger Oil & Refining Company, which had been involved in one of the key cases testing Texas conservation laws, took a stronger stand. He supported divorcement on the grounds that pipelines of integrated companies refused to perform as common carriers and gave their parents an "unfair advantage" over nonintegrated competitors. Citing his own experience, he reported to the subcommittee that the Texas-Empire Pipe Line had refused to accept two of his shipments from east Texas to the Gulf. Danciger admitted, however, that he had not complained to the Railroad Commission at the time. The reasons, he said, were that the shipments in question were urgent, tankers were being kept waiting, and there was no time to seek governmental intervention. The movements were therefore made by tank car at a cost he estimated to be some $9,000 more than would have been the case at pipeline rates.[86] Danciger's concern about this episode seemed minimal since he could not recall whether a subsequent complaint had been lodged with the commission or what penalties, if any, were provided by Texas law for a pipeline's refusal to transport a legal cargo of oil.

Danciger was more concerned about the general advantages that ownership of pipelines gave to integrated companies. As he saw it, "If they sustain a loss in the production business, it is offset by the profit in the pipeline business. If they sustain a loss in the refining business, it is likewise offset by the profit in the pipe-line business. They thus put the 'squeeze' to their competitors, especially the independent refiners." [87] Although he maintained that pipeline profits were excessive and subsidized other parts of integrated operations, he did not offer — nor was he asked — to substantiate this contention. His complaints that major companies carried almost exclusively for themselves and that the level of their rates was simply a question of "transferring the money from one pocket to the other," [88] seemed to contradict his "subsidy" case.

The pipeline "profits" and "transportation rebates" that Danciger mentioned might have accrued to the owner of a pipeline used by a nonintegrated shipper, but this situation by his own testimony was atypical. If one regarded pipeline investment as a riskless common-carrier proposition, to the extent that outside shippers paid more than "cost" rates, they could perhaps be said to be helping to "subsidize" their competition. This point of view was adopted by J. Edward Jones of New York, a dealer in royalties on oil-producing properties, when he said: "Now, if the independent . . . under present conditions, is forced to pay that major company for transporting his thousand barrels, the major company transports the thousand that belongs to him at less cost than what the independent paid because the transportation line is operated at a profit and just in that margin is that independent damaged in the sale of that product." [89]

This argument, of course, ignored the question of whether there was any opportunity cost (i.e., other favorable investment opportunity foreclosed) in the construction of a pipeline by an integrated company. For Danciger it was enough that the integrated concern had an advantage in the ownership of pipelines and this advantage, he thought, could be overcome by governmental action to divorce pipelines from other branches of the oil industry. A few other witnesses took substantially the same position, using the large pipeline dividends to parent companies as examples of the profitability of pipelines per se.

In questioning Wallace E. Pratt, geologist and vice-president of Humble Oil & Refining, Congressman Carl Mapes of Michigan tried to get at the reason for concentrating large profits in the pipeline sector of integrated operations. The exchange was as follows: [90]

Mapes: I would like to ask you one further question, Mr. Pratt.

What is the justification for [the] integrated company that carries nothing through its pipe lines except its own oil keeping its books, or whatever is necessary to do, so as to make such excessive profits on the pipe-line business when you say it is conducting its refining and marketing end on a very small margin?

Pratt: I do not know that I can answer that question; I do not think I know enough about it.

In a subsequent written statement, Pratt made an additional explanation. [91]

Most of the profit is merely interdepartmental, merely a bookkeeping entry. It is not, as Mr. Pennington declared it to be, a profit levied on the independent producer who sells his oil to Humble Oil & Refining Co.; nor can it be used from the transportation of oil for others than Humble Oil & Refining Co. to balance off, or to reimburse itself for losses sustained in the production of oil. It is a real cost of Humble Oil & Refining Co. just as much as though it had been paid to some other pipe line company.

This statement, however, did not go to the next step, involving the payment of dividends by the pipeline company to its parent. When this transfer took place, Humble Oil & Refining Co., like other companies that assumed the risks of pipeline construction in the hope of lowered transportation costs, presumably received its pipeline transportation at cost. In this respect the transaction differed significantly from payment to "some other pipe line company."

The "Subsidy" Question

Advocates of the "subsidy theory" never spelled out their charge in detail in the 1934 investigation and the area was so confusing that even Harry Sinclair endorsed the theory.[92] The charge became so important to public policy decisions, however, that it is worth further consideration.

The subsidy idea seems to have been suggested by the high-rate policy of oil pipelines prior to the 1930's. High rates and high minimum tender requirements generally denied use of pipelines owned by large, integrated companies to small, nonintegrated shippers. On the one hand, this gave rise to the charge that possession of pipelines, the lifeline to markets, allowed integrated companies to depress the price of crude bought from independent producers; on the other hand, control of this transportation bottleneck allegedly secured major marketing areas against the competition of independent refiners. Adopting the latter view, which involved some large assumptions that were typically ignored, critics of high pipeline rates seem to have attributed to them a central role in transferring some of the parent company's returns from the retail market to subsidiary pipeline companies, which built up substantial surplus accounts. The subsequent payment of large amounts of money to the parent in the form of pipeline dividends thus gave the appearance of a "subsidy" to make up for any marketing losses. Some advocates of the "subsidy theory," however, mistook these payments for a transfer of profits derived from transportation and concluded that pipelines as transportation facilities were in themselves the most profitable part of the oil business. In fact, of course, the pipeline's "profitability" rested on its place in the integrated structure, and it was integration — not pipelines per se — that many critics of pipelines were attacking in 1934 without making an explicit connection between the two.

If there was a significant relationship between pipeline rates, practices, and profits, and the alleged need for divorcement, the critics should have been able to demonstrate that possession of pipelines had actually insulated integrated companies from competition at the producing and marketing ends of the business. Although there were many assertions to this effect, proof of them was much more difficult than a demonstration of pipeline "profits." This probably accounts for the apparently naïve emphasis placed on profits by a number of pipeline critics. Their approach, however, was facilitated by the practice of keeping pipeline companies' capitalization low in relation to physical assets. Splawn, it will be recalled, had made these very points.

Whether pipeline divorcement would have had the consequences predicted by either defenders or attackers of integration in 1934 seems questionable. No industry experience indisputably gave more support to one position than the other, but defenders of integration had the fact of the industry's development on their side in arguing against the unpredictable consequences of divorcement.

The Divorcement Question

Actually, the Cole subcommittee had difficulty in finding forthright advocates of divorcement. With virtually every witness, Congressman Wolverton tried, generally without success, to gain a positive statement of concurrence with the President's April 1933 endorsement of divorcement. From Ernest O Thompson of the Texas Railroad Commission, however, he finally received an enthusiastic response — this time from the producer's standpoint. The following exchange is illustrative:

> Wolverton: Are you in favor of the President's recommendation that there should be a divorcement of pipe lines from companies having other branches of the industry?
>
> Thompson: Most assuredly.
>
> Wolverton: You are the first one that has said so.
>
> Thompson: I am heartily in accord with it.
>
> Wolverton: Can you mention some of the inequitable practices that have grown up that influence you to have that opinion?
>
> Thompson: Yes. Pipe lines prorate fields themselves. The reason is this: In most instances the company that owns the pipe line also purchases oil in the field. Through the control of the pipe line you absolutely control the production, in the new fields, where only one pipe line is connected with the field. It costs a good deal of money to build another pipe line, unless there is very large production, and the individual producer, without the aid of the State, is wholly at the mercy of the pipe line.[93]

Wolverton asked Thompson how he would account for the lack of enthusiasm for divorcement among independents as well as representatives of major companies who had appeared before the committee. The Texan replied: "That is because you are getting into a very tender subject and something that they are afraid to talk about, because they are afraid of reprisals."[94] Thompson did not believe that there would be any lack of purchasers for pipelines if they should be divorced from major companies. "There would be a wild scramble for the pipe-line stock," he said. "It is the choice plum of the business." [95] Thus, the Texan, although experienced in oil matters, also seemed to take pipeline profits at their face value.

Although adopting a general position in favor of divorcement and criticizing the excessive profitability of pipelines resulting from practices that he condemned, Thompson was somewhat more restrained when the questioning became more specific. Asked to comment on a statement that there was no competition for the output of a well once it had been connected by a major pipeline company, Thompson replied: "Well, we had an instance about a month ago where a pipe-line company cut the price to 60 cents and lost 38 of his connections the next day. It went to other people who were paying $1." [96]

One independent oil producer, Jake Hamon of Ardmore, Oklahoma, gave pipelines his unqualified endorsement. Although he thought that there had been past abuses in pipeline rates, "It has been my experience with the pipe lines they have gone out of their way in a good many instances to extend their lines to small stripper wells and to old fields, and I would certainly hesitate to contemplate the divorcement of pipe lines." Hamon opposed federal intervention in the industry beyond curbing the shipment of hot oil. Since this step had been taken, he saw no need for further "bureaucratic" actions. [97]

Senator Thomas P. Gore of Oklahoma, whose interest in federal pipeline legislation extended back to Healdton days, straddled the fence on the divorcement issue. He believed that the desired ends might be achieved short of such drastic action and he feared that venture capital would not be attracted to pipelines in the event of divorcement. [98] Since Gore had mentioned his colleague Congressman E. W. Marland in a context that made it seem that the latter favored divorcement, Marland intervened to say that he had never advocated such a step. Instead, he declared, "I believe that if the Interstate Commerce Commission would exercise the authority it now has under the Interstate Commerce Act over pipe lines, great good could come from such regulation." [99]

Although there was more testimony on pipelines before the Cole subcommittee, it did not add materially to that already described. There was general agreement on what pipelines had done in the past, but, depending on the witness, there was a difference of opinion about what had motivated that behavior and its significance. The predominant opinion, even among critics of pipelines in an integrated context, seemed to favor divorcement only as a last resort. The fact that rate reductions had already been made and that the ICC was at last beginning to take action with respect to pipelines apparently carried considerable weight with both witnesses and members of the Cole subcommittee. When these considerations were added to the opposition of integrated companies to affirmative legislative action with respect to divorcement, little progress in this direction was realized.

In retrospect, then, Congress did not deal harshly with the integrated oil industry from 1930 to 1935 as far as its pipeline sector was concerned. The divorcement threat of the NIRA had evaporated, but its conservation provisions had survived. Nevertheless, critics of the industry both inside and outside congressional circles had been afforded new opportunities to air their charges, which gained something merely from repetition. Tax legislation was important but not critical. The management of integrated companies had been put on the defensive by these developments; yet they found a surprising amount of support among those whom they were accused of exploiting.

In oil-producing states adjustments had to be made to new regulatory requirements, but the national administration's position on oil remained ambivalent. That the environment of business decision-making was changing was beyond question, and it posed some major problems of adaptation for the oil industry and its pipeline sector.

CHAPTER 13

MANAGERIAL ADAPTATION TO CHANGE: CRUDE-OIL PIPELINES

The managers of crude-oil pipelines encountered complex problems of adaptation to the changing business and industry environment during the 1930's. Among the major new factors relevant to their decisions were state and federal action to deal with the problem of flush production, new taxes, and, above all, a brisk new initiative at both state and federal levels seeking to regulate crude-oil pipeline rates and practices.

For integrated companies, renewed threats of divorcement formed the background for consideration of how many and what kind of changes to make in traditional methods of pipeline operation. These questions involved the strategy and tactics of dealing with governmental bodies, identification of areas particularly vulnerable to attack, and decisions on a course of voluntary action, consistent with protection of the parent company's interests, to reduce this vulnerability.

MANAGERIAL ADAPTATION TO CHANGING CONDITIONS IN TEXAS

For many decades, managers of pipeline companies had generally been able to ignore both state and federal regulatory commissions in the setting of rates. In Texas, however, a combination of flush production and obvious indications of forthcoming pipeline rate regulation in the early 1930's led to managerial initiative in making significant changes in pipeline rate polcies. Humble Pipe Line Company provides an example.

Humble Pipe had enjoyed the same high rate levels as its competitors, and, despite occasional prodding from Jersey, Humble for a decade had declined to initiate major rate cuts. With the situaton that developed in Texas after 1930, however, there was reason to re-examine this policy. The outpouring of oil from the east Texas field meant that west Texas crude had to compete with the new production on the basis of a laid-down cost of 50 cents a barrel at dockside on the Gulf of Mexico. This price was less than combined gathering and trunk-line charges for the west Texas product. Therefore, Humble, which had substantial interests in west Texas, introduced a general reduction in pipeline tariffs of about 20 per cent in June 1931 and, outside east Texas, also cut the posted price.

236

Although the imbalance between the laid-down cost of crudes from the two regions was not eliminated,[1] Humble transported such a temendous volume of oil during 1931 that pipeline earnings on gross investment after taxes amounted to approximately 25 per cent.[2] Apparently to decrease vulnerability to attack on this score, Humble Oil & Refining's Crude Oil Department in 1932 took over the gathering of Humble's own production in a number of fields. This move deprived Humble Pipe Line Company of 7.5 cents a barrel revenue on some 30,000,000 barrels annually.[3]

Like other pipeline companies operating in Texas, Humble Pipe's income was also affected by the Texas Railroad Commission's 1933 reduction in the amount allowed for losses in gathering. Under the commission's 1919 rules, this 2 per cent deduction had made it possible to run 100 barrels of oil and be obligated to deliver only 98, on the theory that the difference was lost through evaporation, leakage, and such. In practice this had once been the case, but with the introduction of steel tanks in place of wooden ones and improved standards of pipeline operation that guarded against such losses, this deduction became a substantial source of income to pipelines. Humble Pipe Line had annually derived between one and two million dollars revenue from the sale of oil which passed into its hands in this way. By cutting the approved pipeline gathering allowance, the 1933 order bit deep into this source of pipeline revenue.

Other pipeline companies also reduced Texas tariffs before they were ordered to do so by the Railroad Commission. In June 1933, for example, on shipments between Troup Station and Sinco Station on the Gulf, Sinclair-Prairie cut its east Texas gathering charge from 10 cents per barrel to 5 cents and its trunk-line rate from 20 cents to 15 cents. These reductions meant that east Texas oil could be transported from the well to shipside for 20 cents[4] — or 2.5 cents less than the maximum that the Railroad Commission specified in its order of August 31. Sinclair-Prairie also made cuts in gathering and trunk-line rates in the Panhandle and west Texas. Shell and other companies followed suit.

Aside from actual or anticipated regulatory action, other considerations led pipeline managements to reduce intrastate rates in Texas. As in the case of Humble, the need to keep pipelines full and to equalize laid-down costs of crude from different areas under the pressure of flush production was important. Efforts by integrated companies to keep their costs of transportation in line with one another's and with the low price of oil, and to offset the impact of increased taxation, were additional factors. As officials of Stanolind Pipe Line explained to the ICC in justifying rate reductions in 1934, "It is apparent that under existing tax laws the respondent is faced with the necessity of providing the service furnished by it to its parent company at no greater cost or burden than would be necessary in the case of any outside customer or customers, and that the lower rates of competitive pipelines cannot well be met by respondent without similar reductions in its own rates."[5]

In replying to subsequent charges of discrimination through such reduction of rates, integrated companies operating in Texas emphasized the fact that their interstate rates were affected by the intrastate rates prescribed by the Railroad Commission. For example, Stanolind had reduced system-wide gathering charges by 5 cents in December 1933, except for east Texas where it depended on Humble Pipe Line Company for gathering service. It did not lower the gathering charge in joint tariffs applying to shipments from east Texas to northern interstate destinations when pipeline companies running south to the Gulf had done so to comply with Railroad Commission orders. The resulting competition, however, induced Stanolind in conjunction with its connecting carrier to drop this gathering charge from 10 cents to 7.5 cents in June 1934. Other carriers cut theirs still further, from 7.5 cents to 5 cents, a move met in turn by Stanolind's joint tariff of August 8, 1934. Slashing of gathering charges was not alone sufficient to meet the competition from shipments moving to the Gulf Coast from east Texas under the Railroad Commission's ceiling of 22.5 cents per barrel. Accordingly, an adjustment had to be made in Stanolind's trunk-line rate to northern points. The net result was a 5-cent gathering charge in east Texas, and a trunk-line rate decreased by 17.25 cents.[6] Such were the important but indirect results of the Railroad Commission's 1933 intrastate rate order.

Rate reductions had obvious relevance to a new movement to secure outside business. Depressed conditions in the oil industry during the early 1930's induced the managements of integrated oil companies to look increasingly to pipeline transportation for others as a source of income. Both the Humble and Texas companies adopted this new viewpoint. The latter's pipelines, for example, served the Conroe field near Houston, where the Texas Company itself had no production. Humble Pipe Line began carrying crude from Reagan County to Houston for the account of Continental Oil Company. An unidentified but obviously influential official of Shell Petroleum, noting the aggressiveness with which these companies were seeking outside business, wrote in January 1933 to the company's Houston representative.

> I wish to emphasize as strongly as possible the importance which I attach to developing our transportation business particularly as we have surplus capacity in our Texas pipe line system for both northern and Gulf movement. I suggest you set aside a member of your staff to make a complete study of the problem and to review the monthly pipe line reports obtainable from the Railroad Commission which gives particulars of all pipe line movements originating within the State . . . I am just afraid that on account of the pressure of proration matters, etc., that our interests in this direction may not be receiving all the attention which I should like them to have.[7]

That this directive was not merely a temporary aberration was shown by the fact that it was repeated again in November 1936 in these words:

> As in the past, we must continue to look to the Pipe Line for a considerable part of our revenue. With this in mind, the necessity for making every effort to increase its business is very apparent. The development of potential

outside transportation must be made mostly, if not entirely, through contacts of your office with other concerns.[8]

Behind such statements lay the fact that pipeline transportation for others, even at reduced rates, was profitable while the physical and economic characteristics of pipelines made the existence of excess capacity in a line expensive to the owner. The concept of a pipeline as a "plant facility" did not, as these letters showed, preclude its devotion to common-carrier use where excess capacity existed. The advent of prorationing with its enforced reduction of production helped in some instances to create such excess capacity, suggesting that public policy applied in one area of the oil business had repercussions in another just as pressure on intrastate rates affected rates for interstate business.

ADAPTATION TO FEDERAL LEGISLATION

The pipeline tranportation tax imposed by the 1932 Internal Revenue Tax Law, the provisions of the NIRA, and the end of consolidated tax filing in 1934 all called for managerial evaluation and adaptation with respect to rates and practices. Looking at the divorcement provisions of the NIRA, for example, President J. C. Hilton of Louisiana Standard in June 1933 recommended to the top management of Jersey Standard that trunk-line rates, gathering charges, and minimum tenders be reduced. The financial impact of such a move, he pointed out, would largely be absorbed through savings in the federal transportation tax. Except for a reduction of five cents in Oklahoma Pipe Line Company's gathering charge, however, Jersey did not approve this suggestion. In the spring of 1934, with the ICC about to investigate crude-oil pipeline rates, with other companies reducing rates in response to the Texas Railroad Commission order and with Petroleum Administrator Ickes' demand for action under provisions of the NIRA, Jersey's position changed. Both the Oklahoma Pipe Line and the Standard Pipe Line companies reduced their gathering charges and trunk-line rates with the concurrence of their parent company.[9]

In view of the changed consolidated tax situation, there was, after 1934 a penalty for accumulating profits in pipeline subsidiaries of integrated companies. Reduction of rates was one answer to this problem; absorption of the pipeline company by its parent was another. Notable examples of the latter strategy are provided by Louisiana Standard, into which Standard Pipe Line Company was merged in August 1936,[10] and by Sinclair Refining Company, which took over the Sinclair-Prairie Pipe Line Company (of Texas).[11] In both instances pipeline activities became the responsibility of pipeline departments in the former parent company.

The desirability of this organizational rearrangement was enhanced by the ICC Bureau of Accounts' decision in 1935 to confine its reporting requirements solely to interstate pipeline operations. This removed the fear of oil company management that a federal agency would be probing production, refining, or marketing operations under the guise of pipeline regulation when pipeline subsidiaries were merged into the parent company. This fear, it will be recalled, had contributed to the decision to separate pipeline activities from other integrated operations in several companies following the Supreme Court's 1914 decision in The Pipe Line Cases.

RELATIONS WITH THE ICC

Cooperation in Pipeline Valuation

Cooperation as well as conflict characterized pipeliners' relations with the ICC during this period. The need for cooperation arose in connection with the valuation of common-carrier property of pipeline companies subject to the ICC.

The ICC began valuation work with respect to railroads prior to World War I and had arrived at tentative valuations for practically all of them by 1920. However, the roads — as was their right under the law — objected to the final valuations, and negotiation and litigation continued until 1933. As a result, the ICC had taken no action on pipeline valuations at the time the NIRA was enacted. When pipeline rates came into question the following year, Petroleum Administrator Ickes urged the ICC to order the valuations as a necessary foundation for rate determination.[12]

The ICC had found that cooperation with railroad representatives expedited agreement on valuation facts and principles, and this procedure, authorized by statute, was followed with pipelines. Repeating an approach adopted earlier in connection with depreciation accounting, the ICC's Bureau of Valuation in September 1934 requested the American Petroleum Institute to aid in this new work. On September 28, 1934, Clark Kountz, chairman of the Institute's Central Committee on Pipe Line Transportation (organized in 1932), appointed a Committee on Pipe Line Valuation with Colonel H. T. Klein of the Texas Company as its chairman. Later that fall at a meeting of the API in Dallas, Texas, a special subcommittee of engineers and accountants was appointed by the Valuation Committee to work with the ICC. Ralph B. McLaughlin of the Texas Pipe Line Company was named its chairman. A year later, in December 1935, the ICC recognized these industry groups as representatives of the pipeline carriers.[13]

At the November 1934 meeting of the API, it was reported that the ICC wanted the industry to select a typical pipeline system that might be used in developing inventory forms for valuation purposes. The committee was reluctant to name any one system and therefore suggested six or seven. ICC field work got underway in 1935 and the first tentative valuation was issued in November 1936. The fact that Atlantic Pipe Line was the first to receive this distinction surprised the industry since it had not been among the test group suggested by the Valuation Committee.[14]

By the end of 1939 substantially all the valuation work for major pipelines reporting to the ICC had been completed. However, pipeline companies were entitled to, and did, take exception to tentative findings. In the case of Atlantic Pipe Line Company, for example, the final valuation as of

December 31, 1934, was not decided until December 8, 1937. Issuance of final valuations as of 1934 for other companies extended down to June 1945.[15]

The significance of industry cooperation in the valuation process lay in the elements considered to have a bearing on pipeline valuation. These included cost of reproduction new, cost of reproduction less depreciation, original cost, working capital, present value of lands and rights, plus an allowance for the value of a going concern.[16] The first element was a concession to the peculiar economic characteristics of pipelines, including the fact that they service a diminishing resource.[17] However, to arrive at cost figures, prices had to be established for all items employed in conducting a common carrier business. Considering the innumerable items involved and the fluctuations of their prices over time, the cooperation of the pipeline companies in arriving at mutually satisfactory figures was considered important by the ICC.[18]

Initiation of ICC Docket 26570

In the same year that pipeline valuation work began, the ICC ordered its first investigation of pipeline rates and gathering charges. Ironically, after years in which high pipeline rates were the object of repeated attacks, the proposed reduction in rates by certain pipelines running from the Mid-Continent to Chicago led in the spring of 1934 to the first formal complaint against pipelines submitted to the ICC since the Brundred case of the early 1920's. Again, it was a case of an interest group being adversely affected — in this instance, independent refiners.

A protest asking for suspension of certain proposed pipeline rate reductions was filed with the ICC on June 11, 1934, in the name of the Louisiana-Arkansas Refiners' Association, of which John E. Shatford, a member of the Planning and Coordination Committee of the Petroleum Administration, was president.[19] The group he represented was an unincorporated association consisting of some 18 refineries located at or near producing fields in Arkansas and Louisiana. Specifically, Shatford asked that reductions in trunk-line rates and gathering charges proposed by Stanolind, Shell, Texas, and Texas-Empire pipeline companies be suspended from becoming effective on or before July 1, 1934, as the companies had requested.

The essence of Shatford's complaint was that the rate reductions would hurt field refiners trying to compete in the same market with refiners served by crude-oil pipelines and that railroad tonnage and revenue would be seriously affected. Among other things, the petition charged that the rate reductions were inspired by a desire to avoid the impact of the federal transportation tax and to offset the elimination of benefits previously available through consolidated tax returns. But the heart of the matter was contained in two sentences. "Continuation of the present status pending investigation will work no injustice on respondents. Change of this status by allowing the reductions to become effective will cause severe injury to protestant and the members of its association — an injury difficult to remedy however severe it may be after it has once been caused." Harold Ickes, as Administrator of the Code of Fair Competition for the petroleum industry, in a letter to the ICC added his support to this request for suspension and investigation of the proposed rate reductions.[20]

After years of being criticized for maintaining high rates, the pipeline affiliates of integrated oil companies now found themselves forced to defend rate reductions. Some coordination of protests to the ICC was made among the pipeline companies, which had to tread the difficult line between justifying rate reductions without at the same time admitting that prior rate levels had been unjustifiably high.

A telegram from one company to the Secretary of the ICC, June 15, 1934 set forth the following preliminary explanations. First, rate reductions were made in response to "vigorous and repeated demands of numerous independent producers and refiners." Second, one purpose was to equalize interstate rates with Texas intrastate rates. Third, reductions would benefit common-carrier business, which was substantial. Fourth, the reductions were in line with Secretary Ickes' letter of April 10, 1934, to the chairman of the Planning and Co-ordinating Committee suggesting that criticisms of high pipeline rates were not unfounded. Stanolind Pipe Line sent a wire on June 18, 1934, covering the same points and others. Besides pointing out that it was meeting rate reductions which others had put into effect earlier without provoking protest, the Indiana Standard subsidiary noted: "During past years pipe line rates have been materially decreased because of traffic volume increase and have not caused any rate wars between pipe lines on crude and railroads on gasoline and there is no rate war now contemplated or indicated." [21] Emphasizing that pipelines were uniquely adjuncts of the oil industry, the Stanolind telegram denied that the ICC had any need, power, or duty to suspend tariffs in the name of protecting railroads.

These protests were apparently effective, for on June 20, 1934, Division 2 of the ICC announced that it was denying the request for suspension of the protested tariffs. At the same time, however, the ICC indicated that, on its own motion, it was considering an investigation of rates covered by the tariffs in question.[22] Ten days later this investigation was ordered, and it was broadened by a supplemental order of September 26, 1934, to include additional companies that had reduced their rates in the interim. As a result, the investigation covered 37 out of the 49 pipeline carriers reporting to the ICC for the year 1933. Although subsequently three companies were excused from the probe, those remaining represented most of the gathering line mileage and four-fifths of the trunk-line mileage subject to federal regulation.[23]

To obtain information on which to proceed, the ICC sent a detailed questionnaire to respondent pipeline companies covering physical facilities, shippers, rate histories, and financial data. These questions were to be answered before December 1, 1934, and primarily in terms of the situation existing at the close of the preceding calendar year.

Hearings

On July 23, 1935, a hearing was held before ICC Commissioner Clyde B. Aitchison. Although in announcing the hearing notice was given that the ICC would accommodate any interested party desiring to cross-examine officers of respondent pipeline companies, no such requests were received. In fact, this first federal pipeline rate hearing drew only 25 people. Although 34 pipeline companies had responded to the questionnaire, which was the only documentary evidence introduced in the record, the hearing was attended by only a handful of company representatives.

Only one witness, John E. Shatford, testified. Even he declared that he "hoped to be able to dodge in and out of this hearing with ׳ a general statement of effect," and he disclaimed any particular interest in the specific rates at issue.[24] His testimony was generalized and emphasized the hurt to the field refiner and to the railroads if reduced pipeline rates were allowed to stand. At times he seemed to contradict himself. For example, at one point he admitted that, despite large pipeline profits, there was in the nature of their business an inherent relationship between pipelines and the existing structure of the oil industry.[25] At another point he appeared to be advocating divorcement, saying that he could not make any useful recommendation "if the pipeline companies are to remain in the hands of their present owners." [26]

Respondents' replies to the ICC questionnaire had revealed a state of affairs that was familiar to anyone who had followed the numerous federal investigations of oil pipelines in the preceding few years. The rate-histories showed that rates had gradually been reduced since 1931; yet earnings in relation to capitalization of pipelines affiliated with large companies remained very substantial. Minimum tender requirements differed widely, but 100,000 barrels was not unusual. Diversity as well as uniformity was found in these and other areas covered by the questionnaire.

Taking this information into account, Commissioner Aitchison posed six key questions that were to become the basis for continuing the investigation. First, were rate schedules or individual rates excessive in terms of aggregate earnings, or in comparison with other rates, costs of service, or effect on movement of traffic or value of service? Second, should the rates be considered with respect to the respondents individually and should their effect on other pipelines or rail or water carriers be considered? Third, were the disparities and differences in rates justified and what accounted for them? Fourth, were varying minimum tenders justified and was any violation of the Brundred decision involved? Fifth, if earnings of carriers were found to be unduly high, what rate or other action was required? Sixth, was it desirable or necessary to have greater uniformity in rules governing shipments? Aitchison stated that these questions were merely suggestions and did not preclude consideration or introduction of additional pertinent data.[27] On this basis, respondent pipeline companies were invited to submit briefs. The same invitation was extended to Shatford, and the hearing was adjourned.

Up to this point the pipeline companies had not viewed the rate proceedings with alarm. The poor attendance of their representatives at the initial hearing was one evidence of their lack of concern. However, whether by design or accidentally, Commissioner Aitchison's questions had created a real dilemma for the companies by extending the range of investigation far beyond what it had initially appeared to be. While company lawyers generally agreed among themselves that the existing record was legally insufficient to justify a rate order by the ICC, there was always a possibility that the Commission itself might not think so. In fact, if the companies emphasized the insufficiency, the lawyers feared that they might cause the ICC to reopen the hearing and take additional evidence that could prove damaging. In the end, only Shell Pipe Line Corporation decided to file a brief.

The Examiner's Report

In April 1936, ICC Examiner J. Paul Kelley issued a proposed report. Primarily on the basis of the evidence provided by the questionnaries, Kelley recommended three actions by the ICC. First, future minimum tender requirements in excess of 10,000 barrels of crude oil as a single shipment should be held to be unreasonable. Second, because the first pipeline questionnaire had covered only the years 1929–1933, the proceeding should be reopened to obtain additional information for 1934 and 1935. Finally, as part of the reopened hearing, the ICC should require respondents "to show cause why the rates charged by them for the transportation of crude petroleum oil by pipeline should not be found to be unreasonable for the future to the extent that they may exceed 65 per cent of the rates in effect on December 31, 1933." Application was made by the pipeline companies to extend the time for filing exceptions to the report, and this request was granted.

Company Reaction

The examiner's first two recommendations met no strenuous opposition from the companies, but the third aroused objections. Shell Pipe Line, for example, did not oppose the reduction of rates but the basis on which it was asked. An internal company document reported: "This proposed reduction would be very much in line with our own thought on the matter, except that we object to having these further reductions established by an order whose sole support is that pipe line earnings have been too liberal in the past. This recommendation was made without any information as to the effect of the June, 1934, reductions on the earnings for the years 1934 and 1935, and no consideration has been given to the relation between present earnings and fair return on the value of the properties." [28] Stanolind Pipe Line took much the same position. Neither of these companies filed exceptions to Kelley's proposed report, but 19 others did.[29]

A number of pipeline companies adopted a strategy seemingly based on the hope of delaying ICC action. The Jersey-owned pipeline companies, for example, took major exceptions to Kelley's proposed report. In briefs filed in June 1936, they argued that the examiner had acted prematurely on an inadequate record from which he made erroneous assumptions and therefore drew erroneous conclusions. Any conclusions about rates were premature, according to these briefs, because ICC depreciation and valuation proceedings for pipelines were still in progress. The examiner also erred, it was claimed, in recommending a reduction in rates based on earnings in relation to the capital stock of pipeline companies rather than on the value of their property. Furthermore, "the Examiner seems not to have taken into account the extraordinary hazards of the pipeline business, some of which were referred to in the Brundred case and recognized by the Commission itself." On these and other grounds, the briefs urged that the report be rejected and further action postponed until rates of depreciation were fixed in accordance with ICC Order 19200 and valuation proceedings concluded in accordance with Orders 26 (relating to original cost) and 27 (relating to inventories of all physical carrier property).

The unity of the integrated oil industry with respect to the rate proceedings was rudely shattered at this point by the intervention of the Standard Oil Company (Ohio) and the National Refining Company in support of Examiner Kelley's recommendations. Both companies utilized pipelines on a common-carrier basis to move Mid-Continent crude to their refineries located in Kentucky and Ohio. Since gathering charges already had been reduced to the level recommended by Kelley, the complainants concentrated their fire on the level of trunk-line rates. They maintained that average costs of pipeline transportation per barrel-mile to the points in which they were interested were far below the rates charged. In the words of the brief:

> It must be obvious that when there is such a wide spread between the costs of pipeline transportation and the published rates for this transportation, those refining companies which own pipe lines are in a most enviable position. They are not only enabled through this wide spread to secure their raw materials on a much lower costs basis than are the companies who are not only in theory but in fact required to pay the published rates, but through their pipe line subsidiaries they can and do make handsome profits on the raw materials transported for their competitors . . .
>
> The margin between the costs of pipe line transportation and the published rates must be narrowed, or else those refiners who do not own pipe lines will be forced out of existence.[30]

Citing the evidence on earnings provided in the questionnaire returned to the ICC by respondent pipeline companies, Ohio Standard and National Refining maintained there was no need to postpone implementation of Kelley's recommendations. "Whether the earnings of the pipeline companies as reflected in the dividends paid be compared with capital stock or with their recorded book investment, those earnings are extravagently high," the brief declared. "Clearly the pipeline transportation business of the respondents above listed cannot be considered particularly hazardous for the future, judged by the only guide which we have, namely, past experience." [31]

One of the points made by pipeline company representatives in filing exceptions to Examiner Kelley's proposed report was that generalization about pipeline rates was unwarranted since conditions differed materially between companies. That this position accurately reflected the actual situation within the integrated oil industry is indicated by the variety of views and objectives reflected in subsequent discussions among company representatives on procedure with respect to the rate case. A Pipe Line Committee of Fifteen tried to map common strategy but found it difficult to satisfy the varied interests. At a meeting of this committee in New York on September 24, 1936, it was agreed that the rate case should be taken seriously, that the Commissioners needed to be familiarized with the nature of pipeline operations, but that otherwise the various companies would have to work out representation before the ICC to suit their individual needs.

Oral argument before the full Interstate Commerce Commission on October 22, 1936, was confined to the existing record, and industry meetings on strategy continued. A steering committee for the case was appointed at a meeting of the Committee of Fifteen in New York on February 10, 1937. At a subsequent meeting in Washington, the only point on which there seemed to be a consensus was that a mandatory and uniform reduction of pipeline rates should be opposed. Tactically, the problem was to keep any one company from taking steps that would undermine the position of the others. There was also a question of whether, in view of the persistent demands in Congress for divorcement, a policy of delay with respect to rate reductions was still desirable. On balance and in view of the deliberate speed with which the ICC was proceeding, however, company representatives agreed not to push for an early hearing.[32] Meantime, the ICC had issued questionnaires for operations in 1934–35 and was actively engaged in valuation work.

While formal action before the ICC was postponed, more than a year slipped by and changes in company attitudes began to take place. Some companies still opposed rate reductions; others had made or were proposing substantial ones by August 1938. At a Pipe Line Rate Conference held at the Drake Hotel in Chicago early that month, "Cap" Finney of Oklahoma Pipe Line announced that the Jersey pipelines moving crude north and south from Oklahoma proposed to reduce trunk-line rates to a point close to the Kelley report's recommended level.* Other companies had already taken such action, but there was still a diversity of viewpoints on whether this kind of move was good strategy, just as there were apparently differences over whether pipelines should be presented to the ICC and the public as common carriers or as plant facilities of an integrated industry.[33] The

---

*This move, executed in the fall of 1938, was influenced by the need to meet competition from the new Illinois production. *Pipe Line News* (October 1938), 14.

familiar charge before congressional committees that pipelines of integrated companies acted in close concert is given little substantiation from the record of this meeting.

The variety of considerations involved in a voluntary rate reduction was reflected in a study of the matter prepared at Shell Pipe Line Corporation in the summer of 1938. The question was whether Shell should further reduce major trunk-line rates to the level advocated by Examiner Kelley. An analysis of Shell's rates showed that between Oklahoma-Kansas points and East Chicago, for example, the rate in effect at the end of 1933 had been 46 cents a barrel. A reduction in June 1934 had brought the rate to 38.5 cents. Kelley's recommendation, based on 65 per cent of the December 31, 1933, rate, would have made the figure 30 cents. The proposed rate under consideration would be 31 cents. The latter figure was based on an across-the-board reduction designed to yield 6 per cent on Shell Pipe's capital investment, operating the system at 95 per cent of capacity, or 9 per cent on the "fair value" established by the ICC. Such a reduction would cause an estimated $2,500,000 drop in pipeline earnings, of which only $562,500 would be offset by savings in federal and state taxes.

The study also considered the anticipated results of the proposed rate reduction outside the Shell organization. First, it was expected that one or more competitors might protest but eventually they would meet the reductions. Second, although independent refiners at pipeline terminals might benefit initially from the reduced rates, it was likely that a decline in product prices would eventually reflect decreased crude-oil transportation costs thus eliminating this advantage. Third, the analysis expressed doubt that the lowering of pipeline rates would affect crude prices generally, though maintenance of the established differential between east and west Texas prices and the relationship of prices for the recently discovered Illinois crude to those for Mid-Continent crude were involved. Finally, the capacity at which the pipeline system actually operated would have an important effect on earnings.[34] Here, in a single memorandum, was an example of the range of factors to be considered in any major rate reduction. In the end, however, Shell was not prepared to upset the rate structure between the Mid-Continent and Chicago by initiating a further round of rate reductions.

More Hearings and a Decision

In November 1938 another ICC hearing was held, information contained in the updated questionnaires was made part of the record, and pipeline representatives tried to educate the ICC anew in the intricacies of pipeline operations and rate-making. Several companies, notably Oklahoma Pipe Line and Ajax, reported they were already experiencing difficulties through loss of business.[35] These arguments apparently had some effect on Examiner Kelley, for his second report, issued in February 1939, contrasted sharply with that of three years before. In his latest version he accepted pipelines as plant facilities, acknowledged the "paper" character of many rates, and found no basis on which the ICC could declare that rates were unreasonable or rules and regulations unlawful or discriminatory. He therefore recommended that the proceeding be terminated. Understandably pipeline companies filed no exceptions to this report.

Examiner Kelley's recommendations were not accepted by the full Commission. Although no shipper had appeared to challenge pipeline rates or practices, and Kelley found no basis for continuing the proceeding, a majority of the ICC decided that further action was required. Undoubtedly the scrutiny which pipelines and ICC inaction with respect to them were receiving elsewhere in the government contributed to this decision.

The ICC entered a preliminary order on December 23, 1940.[36] In doing so it acknowledged the plant facility argument but brushed its relevance aside in terms of the ICC's statutory responsibility. "Every carrier subject to the act must maintain a schedule of just and reasonable charges," the ICC declared, "regardless of whether the public generally has been or is in a position immediately to avail itself of the service." [37]

In paving the way for this order, the ICC reviewed the pipeline picture during the preceding decade as it had been developed in questionnaires and hearings. While noting that individual lines or groups of lines differed very considerably in the character of their operations, most of those involved in the proceeding were devoted primarily to serving the needs of large, integrated companies. Many factors besides rates — type of haul, distance, volume — were found to affect their revenues. Although rates were found to have been reduced appreciably since 1933, the effect of these reductions on revenue had been offset in some measure by an increased volume of shipments, especially in 1937. Pipelines in existence for more than ten years were found to have earned enough to repay their owners' full investment.

While the hazards of exhausting sources of oil supply or having new fields undermine existing pipeline investment were not negligible, they appeared to the ICC to have been amply provided for. The case of Ajax Pipe Line was cited by the Commission. The decrease in volume transported by Ajax to less than 25 per cent of capacity as new-found Illinois production challenged that from the Mid-Continent had been advanced by the industry as illustrative of pipeline hazards. However, the ICC found that Ajax, by its own admission, had already paid dividends that exceeded the owners' investment.[38] Over-all, the ICC concluded, "The industrial risks urged upon us to justify the relatively high earnings shown, and as necessary to attract capital for the construction of pipe lines, have been fully met in the past, and are now being met in spite of rate reductions." [39] Furthermore, that these reductions were the result of changes in the tax laws was "practically admitted on the record."

The ICC found the unit cost of pipeline transportation to be low. Humble Pipe Line, for example, showed 88,088,733 barrels transported in its trunk lines during 1929 at a cost per barrel-mile of $0.00030332 cents; in 1937 146,671,047 barrels were moved at a cost per barrel-mile of $0.00030492.

Volume transported had increased 66.5 per cent, but unit cost had remained virtually constant.[40] Operating costs had not decreased, first because of the increased volume of oil handled and second because both labor costs and taxes had risen. Losses in revenue due to rate reductions were offset to a large extent by increased business.

Humble Pipe Line also supplied the only specific data on contamination to be studied by the ICC in considering reasonable minimum tenders. The data were for the year 1937 and particularly for the month of December. Humble had transported 42 different grades of crude, and in only 10 of them, whether for the month or the year, did contamination exceed 2 per cent. However, an inverse correlation was shown to exist between the size or quantity of shipment and the amount of contamination. During 1937, Humble Pipe Line transported a total of 163,949,854 barrels, with an average contamination of 1.402 per cent, and a range of contamination from .029 to 15.158 per cent.[41]

Division 2 of the ICC in the Brundred Brothers case had found 10,000 barrels as a reasonable minimum tender, and in the present instance the Commission reaffirmed the view that anything more was unlawful and unreasonable. Again, however, the decision was made without the benefit of any evidence on behalf of any shipper or interested party. Respondents were given 60 days to show why the finding should not be entered.[42]

Since the beginning of the case, the lack of data on which to make regulatory decisions had been partially offset by the completion of ICC valuation proceedings for a number of the respondent pipeline companies as of December 31, 1934. Over the objections of some carriers, these data were made part of the record in the rate case. In many instances the ICC's valuation was found to be less than the carrier's investment; in a few cases there was a close resemblance; and in a few others the ICC's valuation exceeded investment in carrier property. On this basis, the ICC found 14 respondents to have earned less than 8 per cent on valuation as of December 1934; 21 respondents earned more. Pure Transportation Company, with a 46.86 per cent return on ICC valuation, topped the list.[43]

Having elsewhere in the preliminary order denied the more extreme claims of the oil industry concerning the hazardous character of pipeline operations, the ICC in arriving at a basis for evaluating rates gave these claims some recognition. Accordingly, it adopted an 8 per cent annual return on ICC valuation as a yardstick, saying, "The hazards and uncertain future of the common-carrier business of the pipe lines suggest the fairness of a somewhat larger rate of return than it would be reasonable to expect would be applied in industries of a more stable character." [44]

In applying this yardstick, the ICC proceeded with caution. First, the majority made clear that its reading of the record showed that companies had seemingly not adjusted rates with respect to one another and this strengthened the majority's view that pipelines did not compete. Therefore, no uniform or flat percentage readjustment of rates seemed justified. Second, while the respondents with a return of more than 8 per cent on their

1934 valuation were found to have an unjust and unreasonable level of rates, the ICC, especially in view of Examiner Kelley's second report, hesitated to enter a final order for reduction. Instead, it gave the 21 carriers 60 days in which to show cause why their interstate rates should not be reduced by a percentage sufficient to produce an 8 per cent maximum return on valuation.

Commissioners Charles D. Mahaffie and William J. Patterson dissented from this order. Mahaffie pointed out that the use of earnings to show that rates were excessive ignored such other factors relevant to earnings as volume of traffic, management, and taxes. Furthermore, he questioned whether the maintenance of different rates for the same services rendered by competing companies was possible. To illustrate, the Commissioner used the majority's own example of the four trunk pipelines between the Mid-Continent and Chicago. As of October 1, 1938, their rates were identical for the same haul.* Applying the ICC's order, the rates could range from 33.5 cents in the case of Sinclair to 17.5 cents for Texas-Empire. Unless the other companies met this latter rate, Mahaffie argued, Texas-Empire's business would be likely to increase to the point where, using the majority's criterion, a further rate reduction (because increased volume would lower unit costs and increase earnings) would be required. In his view, "The theory that rates may properly be based on individual net earnings has a place in regulating a public-service company in a position to exercise a monopoly. It is not practicable in the competitive field." [45]

Since the ICC had not yet entered a final order, the way was still clear for the companies affected by the preliminary decision to take exception to it. In point of fact, the case dragged on until after World War II. However, the ICC was now on record as favoring rates set to return not more than 8 per cent on crude-oil pipelines' ICC valuation. This fact was to be of major significance in connection with an indirect form of regulation that shortly emerged from a contemporary revival of antitrust interest in the integrated oil industry. More immediately, however, the ICC had to decide what should constitute the maximum reasonable rate of return on a new form of pipeline transportation.

*In early 1934 all the pipelines serving this route — Shell, Sinclair, Stanolind, and Texas-Empire — had had a rate of 46 cents. As of October 1, 1938, they all had the same rate of 38.5 cents, which Shell had established on June 28, 1934.

CHAPTER 14

INNOVATION AND ITS REPERCUSSIONS: GASOLINE PIPELINES

Between 1906 and the late 1920's no major innovations had changed the basic role of pipelines or the methods of operating and using them. However, beginning in 1929 such an innovation was introduced — the pipeline transportation of gasoline and other refined products. During the ensuing decade this new use of pipelines developed rapidly. The repercussions touched many areas of the oil industry and competing forms of oil transportation. This innovation also led to a demand from the disadvantaged that the ICC take a hand in cushioning the impact of change.

RAILROADS AND MID-CONTINENT REFINING: THE HISTORICAL BACKGROUND

The introduction of the gasoline or products pipeline in the 1930's had an impact on the oil industry comparable to that of crude-oil trunk lines in the nineteenth century. Where early crude-oil lines had become competitive weapons with respect to the railroads, this rivalry had been quickly decided in favor of the lower cost carrier with consequences that accrued to the benefit of the Standard Oil combination. Nevertheless, products continued to be shipped by tank car, and this was one reason the railroads had been willing to continue their cooperation with Standard Oil despite the loss of their crude-oil traffic. Leading competitors of the Standard Oil combination, as well as its own major elements after dissolution, had found it increasingly necessary to build their own crude-oil pipelines. There were others, however, who lacked the resources — or the vision — to embrace this alternative by building their refineries in marketing centers and supplying them by pipeline. Among this group, which was constantly renewed as new flush fields invited new entrants to the oil business, were smaller Mid-Continent field refiners who began shipping their products into northern marketing areas by tank car prior to World War I.

Although the output of crude oil in Kansas had appeared to be declining in 1915, production of flush fields elsewhere in the Mid-Continent field was mounting and refinery output was increasing even in Kansas.[1] The spurt in refining, which intensified competition among the smaller

251

refineries, was attributable to such factors as lower prices of crude oil because of the abundant supply, the increased demand for gasoline for automotive use, and the success of William Burton's new cracking process which greatly increased the amount of gasoline that could be obtained from a barrel of crude oil. In 1914, gasoline production by United States refineries totaled 1,500,000,000 gallons compared with 1,935,000,000 gallons of kerosine; in 1916 the proportion was 2,059,000,000 gallons of gasoline to 1,455,000,000 gallons of kerosine.[2] In this changing context, the small refineries located in Kansas and Oklahoma not only had to compete with each other in marketing their products but also with Indiana Standard refineries using the efficient Burton process. Indiana's large refineries at Sugar Creek, Missouri, Wood River, Illinois, and Whiting, Indiana, of course, received their supply of crude via pipeline. To offset this advantage the Mid-Continent refiners had demanded lower rail rates. In 1915 their complaints culminated an ICC review of Mid-Continent oil rates.[3]

According to Commissioner James S. Harlan, who presented the decision of the ICC in the 1915 proceeding, the rates on petroleum and its products in carloads from the Mid-Continent field had been a "prolific source of complaint" for many years.[4] Among such complaints a number had been filed attacking the rates in effect from Kansas and Oklahoma to points in Illinois, Iowa, Nebraska, Missouri, Colorado, Utah, and elsewhere, as "unreasonable per se and relatively."[5] The defendants in the 1915 case requested that these complaints be consolidated and that numerous previously decided cases be reopened in order that the entire structure of oil rates throughout the territory involved might be considered. This suggested course of action was adopted by the ICC.

The consolidated record brought under review the rates on petroleum and its products from shipping points in the Mid-Continent field to all important points in western trunk-line and trans-Missouri territories. Under the arrangements then in effect, Kansas producing and refining points were grouped together for rate-making purposes, and in the case of many destinations they took lower rates than oil traffic from Oklahoma points. Oklahoma producers and refiners therefore asked that all shipping points in the Mid-Continent field be accorded the Kansas rates. While the evidence was confined almost entirely to the higher grade oils, such as naphtha, gasoline, and kerosine, special attention was given to rates on the lower grades when necessary.

The complainants asked for a rate of 15 cents to St. Louis from both Oklahoma and Kansas refineries, with corresponding rates to other points. At the hearing the defendant railroads countered with a plan of rates that they asserted was just and reasonable.[6] They proposed to divide the Mid-Continent field into two groups, the Kansas points included in one, and the Oklahoma points in the other. To St. Louis the Oklahoma group was to take rates 2 cents higher than the Kansas group; to Kansas City, the Mississippi River, Chicago, St. Paul, Des Moines, Denver, and Salt Lake

City, the Oklahoma group's proposed rates were to be 5 cents higher than the Kansas group's; and to Omaha, 3 cents higher.

The ICC did not accept the rates suggested by either the complainants or the railroads. It increased some rates, lowered others, and left some unchanged. For example, in addition to grouping all origin points in the Mid-Continent field with respect to St. Louis as a destination, the ICC found that the existing rate of 17 cents per 100 pounds was too low and that 20 cents was a reasonable maximum rate for the future. But the ICC took a different view of the Chicago gateway, where the existing rate for oil originating in both Kansas and Oklahoma was 27 cents. The carriers had proposed to continue this rate from Kansas and establish a higher rate of 32 cents from Oklahoma. The ICC's decision was that 25 cents per 100 pounds would be reasonable to Chicago, to the territory then taking the Chicago rate, and to the territory proposed by the defendants in western Indiana and eastern Illinois. On the shorter hauls from Kansas and Oklahoma points to Kansas City, the ICC's opinion was that a difference in rates was justified and that those then in effect were reasonable maximum rates for the future.

This decision was the one to which all subsequent controversy over Mid-Continent oil rates referred, and such controversy flared periodically as the oil-carrying railroads sought to relieve their financial distress by raising rates. This remedy was facilitated by national policy outlined in the Transportation Act of 1920, which affirmed governmental support for the rail carriers. Therefore, railroad management had ICC approval for increasing rates, including those on refined products moving from Mid-Continent refineries into major midwestern markets.

The rising level of railroad rates in the late 1920's and early 1930's provided one important stimulus to the construction of gasoline pipelines. As these lines multiplied, the railroads lost an increasing proportion of their products business to the newcomers. Based on tonnage, gasoline shipments originating on Class I railroads declined from 86.6 per cent of the domestic demand for motor fuel in 1930 to 44.3 per cent in 1939. Comparable percentages for gasoline pipelines rose from 0 to 17.1 per cent.[7]

The plight of oil-carrying railroads was also worsened by the rise of barge and tank-truck movements in the 1930's. Railroad managements did not reduce long-haul rates to meet the new competition; instead, they tried to keep the short-haul business by cutting rates from refineries and gasoline pipeline terminals to distribution points. This response, of course, aided the integrated companies that had transferred long-haul gasoline shipments to pipelines. Consequently, the Mid-Continent field refiner dependent entirely on rail transportation found himself at a growing disadvantage in his efforts to market in the upper Midwest.

The discovery of large quantities of oil in Illinois in 1937 further aggravated the Mid-Continent refiner's distress by reducing the transportation costs of his midwestern competitors like Ohio Standard which previously had relied on southwestern crude delivered by pipeline. In short, the refiner in Oklahoma, Kansas, or Missouri seeking a market in Indiana, Illinois, or Kentucky had to ship long distances by rail into a territory where his competition by the late 1930's was drawing on local production, using long-haul gasoline pipelines, or moving products comparatively short distances by rail, barge, truck, or pipeline from refineries served by affiliated crude-oil lines. This situation precipitated a new round of complaints to the ICC, this time attacking gasoline pipelines as well as railroads.

INTRODUCTION AND GROWTH OF GASOLINE PIPELINES

Although gasoline had for a long time been transported by pipeline within refineries and from them to loading racks and docks,* east of California this medium of transportation was not employed over longer distances before 1929. The large integrated companies, as already shown, had moved crude by pipeline and water transportation and did their refining close to major markets. In short, the companies best able to finance the gasoline pipeline innovation had lacked the incentive to pioneer it.

Quite aside from the financial problem, however, there were technical obstacles to building gasoline lines. When Mid-Continent refiners in the 1920's had considered a cooperative venture in gasoline pipelining as an answer to their difficulties with the railroads, they had been deterred by the fear that the various grades of gasoline would be mixed in transit and no shipper could count on withdrawing gasoline of the same specifications as he had shipped. This problem was in part resolved by the publication of United States government master specifications for liquid fuels and methods for testing and sampling them.[8] Subsequent experimentation showed that contamination could be controlled more easily than had been anticipated.

Another problem that contributed to the long-standing reluctance to move gasoline long distances by pipeline was that of leakage. To prevent economic loss and fire danger in moving this volatile fuel, it was believed desirable to have pipe and joints of a higher quality than were generally necessary for crude-oil lines. Improved seamless and welded pipe met the first requirement, and electric welding of pipe joints, introduced in the late 1920's, met the second.

Because of the volatility of the product it was also desirable to eliminate tankage at intermediate pump stations wherever possible. This called for automatic (mechanical) means to control the flow of gasoline through such stations and for safety devices to shut down operations in case of malfunction. Such controls had been developed by the late 1920's and pro-

---

*The use of pipelines to transport natural gasoline over distances from 2 to 30 miles had been developed in California before World War I. C. P. Bowie, *Transportation of Gasoline by Pipe Line,* U.S. Dept. of Commerce, Bureau of Mines, Technical Paper 517 (Washington, 1932), 4-5. See also, John W. de Groot, "History and Development of Products Pipe Lines," API, *Proceedings of the Twenty-Ninth Annual Meeting* (Chicago, Ill., November 7-10, 1949), Section V, 41.

duced satisfactory results on a 100-mile natural gasoline pipeline built by Shell between Ventura and Wilmington, California.[9] By 1930, then, technical obstacles to operation of long-distance gasoline pipelines had been largely overcome.

As so often with invention, necessity also provided the specific stimulus to innovate. Since the early 1920's, the overland movement of crude oil from the Southwest to the Atlantic seaboard had been adversely affected by the growth of tanker transportation. Among the lines most hurt by this competition was Jersey Standard's Tuscarora pipeline that for many years had carried Mid-Continent and Pennsylvania crude oil to Bayonne and Bayway. Despite the efforts of Jersey management to favor this line when it could, Tuscarora by 1929 had reached the end of its economic usefulness as a crude-oil carrier. Instead of junking it, however, Jersey management decided to reverse the flow in the 370-mile line and to convert it to carry refined products inland to the vicinity of Pittsburgh. The experiment proved such a technical and financial success that it was quickly emulated by other companies.

With the success of Jersey's Tuscarora experiment, Sun Oil felt the need to protect its position. This company had been considering a gasoline line for several years and had taken active steps to create a market that would support one. Before making a final decision on construction, however, Joseph Pew, Sun vice-president, approached the railroads and asked for a rate cut to meet the new pipeline competition. This request was refused on the grounds that it would upset every rate in trunk-line territory like a stack of falling cards.[10] Accordingly, Sun Oil undertook construction of a gasoline pipeline from its Marcus Hook refinery west and north to Pittsburgh and Cleveland with a branch to Syracuse. By late June 1931 this line was delivering Blue Sunoco to Cleveland.[11]

Legal title to the Sun lines was vested in three different companies — Susquehanna Pipe Line Company in Pennsylvania, Sun Pipe Line (Inc.) in New York, and Sun Oil Line Company in Ohio. Susquehanna filed tariffs with the Interstate Commerce Commission, and the other two companies joined in them for movements to New York and Ohio respectively. A minimum tender of 75,000 barrels was established, and during the first six months of operation no gasoline was carried for outsiders.[12]

The Tuscarora and Susquehanna lines posed a direct threat to Atlantic Refining, whose marketing territory they crossed. To meet this challenge, Atlantic built the Keystone pipeline system in 1931. Originally confined to the eastern part of Pennsylvania and limited to gasoline transportation, the system proved so successful that it was expanded during 1935–1937. The lines were pushed west to Pittsburgh and north to the New York state line, where the Buffalo Pipe Line Corporation continued the movement to Buffalo and Rochester. The economy of the products pipeline enabled Atlantic to expand marketing activities in New York state while protecting its home territory in Pennsylvania. Furthermore, in 1933 — only a year after the system went into operation — Atlantic found it practical to move kerosine and furnace oil, as well as gasoline, through the same line. Both the Keystone and Buffalo companies were common carriers under state law and eventually developed a profitable business for outside shippers.[13]

While these developments in products pipelining were taking place in the East, Mid-Continent refiners had also embraced the innovation. As early as 1920, a group of refiners in the Tulsa area had discussed the possibility of building a 6- or 8-inch products line northward to the Great Lakes and southward to New Orleans.[14] Nothing came of the proposal at that time, but a decade later advancing rail rates gave the gasoline pipeline a new appeal for these refiners seeking to compete in markets served from Chicago refineries that obtained their crude by pipeline from the Mid-Continent.

One of the first companies to take action was Phillips Petroleum Company. Founded in 1917, it had not become fully integrated until the late 1920's. In 1930 Phillips decided to build a gasoline pipeline from its refinery at Borger, in the Panhandle of Texas, through Wichita and Kansas City, Kansas, to East St. Louis, Illinois. For this purpose the Phillips Pipe Line Company was organized and in 1931 completed a 681-mile, 8-inch gasoline pipeline. By the end of that year the line was in full operation with actual earnings exceeding estimates.[15]

Meantime, another significant venture had been undertaken by a group of Mid-Continent refiners. Taking their lead from the organizational and financing techniques employed with the Texas-Empire and Ajax Pipe Lines, these refiners created a joint-venture pipeline, organized in corporate form. Ownership in the new Great Lakes Pipe Line Company (Delaware) was represented by 60,000 shares of no-par stock, of which 55,000 were issued initially.

This undertaking had its beginnings in the summer of 1930 when Continental Oil Company and Barnsdall Corporation discussed plans for a gasoline pipeline from Oklahoma to the Great Lakes.[16] Other Mid-Continent refiners soon joined in the ownership, and when the new line was opened from Ponca City, Oklahoma, to Kansas City in early 1931, their roster, in addition to Continental and Barnsdall, was composed of Skelly, Mid-Continent Petroleum, Phillips Petroleum, and Pure Oil.[17] In July 1931 the Great Lakes line was completed to Chicago, and in the summer of 1933 both the Texas and Sinclair companies became part owners.[18]

The main stem of the Great Lakes system ran from Tulsa — where branches connected with refineries at Ponca City, Muskogee, Tulsa, Barnsdall, and Okmulgee, Oklahoma, and El Dorado, Kansas — to Minneapolis-St. Paul, with a branch to Omaha from Osceola, Iowa, and another to Chicago, beginning at Des Moines. A subsidiary, Great Lakes Pipe Line Company (Illinois), owned the line built across Illinois from the Iowa border to Chicago.[19] The Phillips gasoline line was interconnected with the Great Lakes system near Kansas City, and Phillips "66" gasoline moved northward from there over Great Lakes, while other owners of that

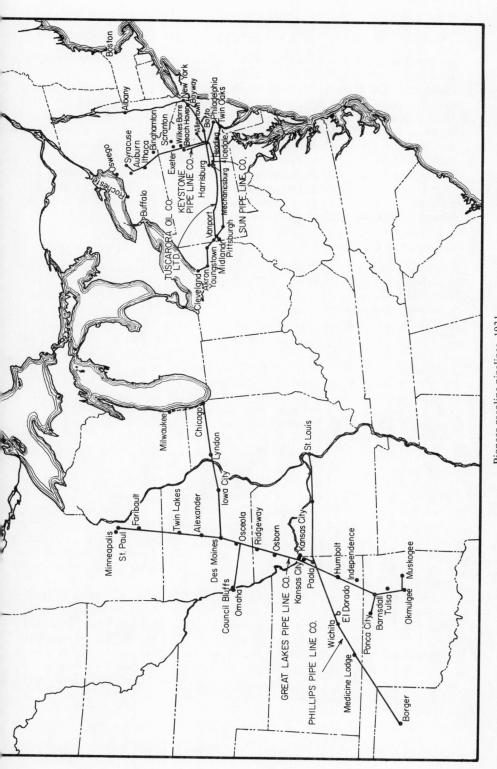

Source: C. P. Bowie, *Transportation of Gasoline by Pipe Line,* U.S. Department of Commerce, Bureau of Mines, Technical Paper 517 (Washington, 1932), facing p. 4.

Pioneer gasoline pipelines, 1931.

system used the Phillips facility for movements from Paola, Kansas, to St. Louis.[20]

As interstate common carriers, both Phillips and Great Lakes filed tariffs with the ICC. The first ones showed that an effort was being made to keep pipeline rates and pipeline-plus-railroad rates equal to all-rail rates between origin and destination points named in the tariff.[21] As had been the case with the early crude-oil lines, this policy met the statutory requirements for common carriage yet offered no advantage to nonowners of the line. Furthermore, without more shipper-owners, it limited somewhat the impact of this new competition for the railroads' oil traffic, though this did not prevent angry complaints from railroad managements who, as noted in Chapter 11, looked to Congress for redress.

The Impact of Gasoline Pipelines

Although in absolute terms the growth in mileage and barrel-miles of transportation performed by crude-oil pipelines in the 1930's was large compared to gasoline pipelines,[22] the percentage growth of the latter was extremely impressive. Between 1929 and 1938, the number of barrels transported by gasoline lines increased 30 times, while barrel-miles multiplied 500 times.[23] In 1931, gasoline pipelines had originated the movement of only 4.78 per cent of the amount of refined oil originated on Class I railroads.[24] In 1938, this figure had risen to 24.04 per cent.[25]

The increased use of pipelines — both crude and refined — had a severe impact on railroad revenues from petroleum traffic. According to ICC calculations, railroad revenue from the transportation of crude oil between 1928 and 1941 dropped 49.5 per cent while that from refined oil fell 45.5 per cent.[26]

The benefits of this change accrued to oil companies that had the resources to build or share in pipelines, and their number was necessarily limited. Thus, seventeen companies reportedly owned 96.1 per cent of the gasoline pipeline mileage in the United States as of January 1, 1938.[27] However, the handful of companies mentioned so far in this chapter owned about 80 per cent of this mileage, including their holdings in Great Lakes.[28] The largest so-called "independent" concern owning a gasoline pipeline was Champlin Refining Company, which completed a 250-mile, 6-inch pipeline from its refinery at Enid, Oklahoma, to Superior, Nebraska, in 1935.[29]

The savings that accrued to oil companies by virtue of owning gasoline lines appear to have been passed on to consumers of the product. Chart 1, prepared for presentation to a subcommittee of the House Interstate and Foreign Commerce Committee in 1941, indicates the impact of gasoline pipelines in Pennsylvania during the 1930's by comparing the yearly average tank wagon price of gasoline for 6 cities in that state with that in 50 representative cities across the country. To show that the relationship between pipelines and gasoline prices was causal rather than accidental, a

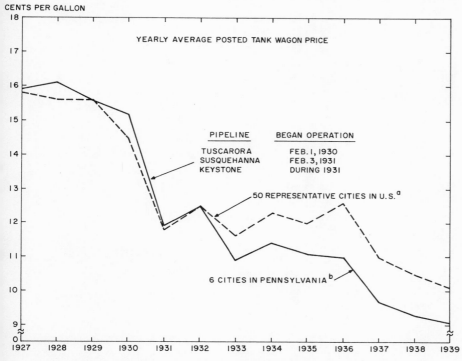

Chart 1. Gasoline prices in six Pennsylvania cities served by gasoline pipeline compared to fifty other cities, 1927-1939.

Source: Statement of R. T. Haslam before Special Subcommittee on Petroleum Investigation of the Committee on Interstate and Foreign Commerce, U.S. Congress, House of Representatives (1941).

[a] Includes cities coast to coast and border to border receiving gasoline primarily by rail or water.

[b] Allentown, Altoona, Erie, Philadelphia, Pittsburgh, and Scranton, receiving gasoline primarily by pipeline after 1931.

similar approach was adopted for eight cities near the Great Lakes Pipe Line. These results are depicted in Chart 2.

The Spread of Innovation: The Shell Case

The economic and strategic considerations leading to entry into gasoline pipelining by the large, integrated companies are illustrated by the case of Shell Petroleum. This St. Louis-based company had sustained significant losses from 1927 through 1935,[30] and in 1936 the whole operation was subjected to searching examination in terms of what might be expected in the next five years. One conclusion of this study was that in every state where the leading competitor had lower costs than Shell, it was due to

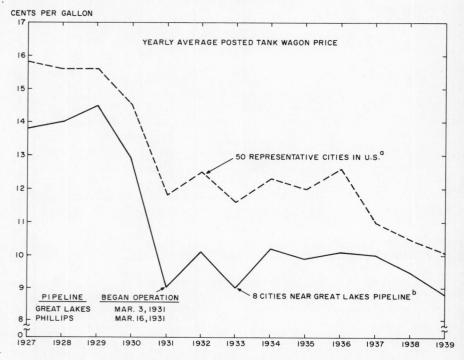

CENTS PER GALLON

YEARLY AVERAGE POSTED TANK WAGON PRICE

50 REPRESENTATIVE CITIES IN U.S.[a]

PIPELINE   BEGAN OPERATION
GREAT LAKES   MAR. 3, 1931
PHILLIPS   MAR. 16, 1931

8 CITIES NEAR GREAT LAKES PIPELINE[b]

Chart 2.   Gasoline prices in eight cities near Great Lakes Pipe Line compared to fifty other cities, 1927-1939.

Source: Statement of R. T. Haslam before Special Subcommittee on Petroleum Investigation of the Committee on Interstate and Foreign Commerce, U.S. Congress, House of
Representatives (1941).
  [a] Includes cities coast to coast and border to border receiving gasoline primarily by
rail or water.
  [b] Chicago, Illinois; Davenport and Des Moines, Iowa; Kansas City, Missouri; Minneapolis, Minnesota; Muskogee, Oklahoma; Omaha, Nebraska; and Tulsa, Oklahoma.

transportation savings — either in terms of the location of refining facilities or because the competitor could ship products into the area by pipeline.[31] While the study committee recommended that Shell withdraw from
marginal marketing territory, it also urged that a gasoline pipeline be
built from the Wood River refinery into Ohio to protect Shell's heavy
marketing investment in that area. Although the line would cost an estimated $5,440,000, transportation savings were expected to pay it out
within five years.[32] The logic of this move was enhanced by the expectation
that the pipeline would take some of the load off Shell's East Chicago
refinery and utilize excess cracking capacity available at Wood River.
  The problems posed by innovation were evident in the building of this
line. Initially, responsibility was placed in Shell Pipe Line Corporation

because of its long experience with crude-oil lines. However, when the planners decided that, in addition to gasoline, the line should transport other refined products such as kerosine, fuel oil, and naphtha, design and operational problems took on novel dimensions. Although Shell Pipe had obtained a right of way and even let bids for pipe and pumping equipment, responsibility for design and construction were transferred to Shell Petroleum in January 1938.

After studying the experience of existing gasoline lines, S. S. Smith, who was put in charge of the project, decided that Sun Oil's Susquehanna line was the one on which to model the new Shell line. There were good arguments for a closed, automatic system such as the Sun line had. The dangers of contamination when pumping multiple products, the need to control product movements closely, and the necessity of maintaining flexibility of throughput all dictated the use of a closed system. This decision in turn meant that electrically-driven centrifugal pumps suitable for automatic operation were preferable to diesel-driven positive displacement pumps. Automatic features of the new system included start and stop with change-of-flow rate, and automatic shutdown in response to bearing temperature, gland temperature, low suction pressure, motor overload, and so on.* [33] Benefits of automatic station control included maximum throughput, uninterrupted operation, and savings in labor costs.[34] Because of the switch to this type of operation, diesel-driven pumps, some of which were already installed, had to be discarded and equipment not originally contemplated had to be acquired.[35]

As planned, Shell's welded 8-inch line was to run from Wood River, Illinois, to Lima, Ohio, where it would divide — one branch going to Toledo and the other to Columbus. However, since Standard Oil of Ohio already had a products line running from Toledo to Fostoria, Shell proposed — and Ohio Standard agreed — to extend the latter's line from Fostoria to Lima. Shell thereby avoided the cost of constructing a duplicate facility. By mid-June 1938, the trunk line was completed from Wood River to Lima, and in 1939 the 6-inch spur to Columbus was finished. The total cost came to $4,785,000, an amount substantially less than anticipated. Initially capable of moving 16,000 barrels of different grades of gasoline a day, the line's capacity was raised another 8,000 barrels daily by the addition of pumping stations during 1939.[36]

The wisdom of this pipeline investment was soon demonstrated. In August 1939, before the Columbus spur was completed, the Transportation and Supplies Department of Shell Oil (successor to Shell Petroleum) estimated annual freight savings and profits of $1,100,000.[37] And this estimate was prepared under unfavorable circumstances. A large gasoline surplus had developed at East Chicago and dictated that shipments from Wood River over the Toledo line be reduced. Even though Shell was not

---

*Apparently the first automated pump station was one installed on the Empire Pipe Line's crude-oil trunk system between Cushing, Oklahoma, and Kansas in 1929.

making full use of this spur, under the agreement with Ohio Standard it had to meet minimum payment guarantees.[38]

Crude and products pipelines figured prominently in decisions to reorganize and consolidate over-all Shell operations in the United States. In March 1938 Shell Petroleum decided to abandon its marketing operations west of the Mississippi River. In connection with this move, refining operations at Arkansas City, Kansas, and East Chicago came under review. The former refinery, built in 1923, was virtually obsolete and no combination of crude or products lines could be found to justify its continued operation. While Shell did not propose to abandon the markets served from East Chicago, the refinery there needed modernization, and increased capacity would require provision of additional crude-oil pipeline space from Wood River. By concentrating refining operations at the latter point, however, substantial operating economies and economies of scale could be realized. Moreover, the existing crude-oil pipeline could be turned into a products line which, without enlargement, could carry the volume of products then being originated at East Chicago.[39]

As far as the pipeline was concerned, this decision was implemented in May 1940 when Shell Pipe turned the Wood River-East Chicago line over to Shell Oil's products pipeline department. To save further capital expenditures, as much use as possible was made of existing equipment, including the diesel-driven reciprocating pumps. Early in June 1940 the first shipment of products reached East Chicago over this route.[40]

A year earlier Shell Oil Company on the West Coast, Shell Eastern, and Shell Petroleum Corporation had been merged to form Shell Oil Company, Incorporated, with Shell Union as the sole stockholder of the merged companies.[41] Although the Shell companies east of the Rockies had shown a net loss of some $40,000,000 in 1931, they were well in the black by 1940 despite a continuing low price for gasoline. The reorganization and revamping of operations to cut costs had made this possible, and the flexibility and economies of pipelining both crude oil and products had contributed significantly to the favorable outcome.

The significance of the products pipeline and of even lower cost water transportation which supplemented this development was summed up by President Alexander Fraser of the new Shell Oil Company. "Ten years ago," he said early in 1941, "over 90% of our products were transported by rail throughout the Middle West. Today we are practically off the rails." [42] And Shell's experience was by no means the exception.

STATUS OF GASOLINE LINES

The introduction of gasoline pipelines raised technical, legal, and organizational problems for oil company management. The new lines's status with respect to federal regulation was not settled in the 1930's. Organizational relationships therefore reflected the owning company's views on this question. The distinction between the common-carrier status of crude-oil lines and the private status of products lines was emphasized in Shell's case by the fact that the former were owned by Shell Pipe Line Corporation and the latter were assigned to Shell Oil. A similar arrangement existed in Indiana Standard, which built a gasoline line from Sugar Creek to Council Bluffs in 1939 and vested ownership in the parent company rather than in Stanolind Pipe Line. As of December 31, 1941, however, 18 pipeline companies carrying refined oil were reporting to the ICC.[43]

THE PETROLEUM RAIL SHIPPERS' ASSOCIATION CASE

The spread of both crude-oil and gasoline pipelining under the auspices of large companies like Shell, combined with high long-distance rail rates on petroleum products, accentuated the plight of the Mid-Continent field refiner seeking to market at a distance. Adversely affected by declining refiners' margins, these refiners felt that the only alternative to the destruction of their position in distant markets was remedial action by the Interstate Commerce Commission. In 1938, independent refiners, marketers, and jobbers, banded together as the Petroleum Rail Shippers' Association and sought aid from the federal regulatory body. While the target of their action was primarily the railroads,[44] 14 companies operating both crude-oil and gasoline pipelines were made parties to the case.

Although antitrust charges were included in the complaint, the presiding examiner limited the issues to alleged violations of the Interstate Commerce Act. Hearings were conducted in the fall of 1939, oral testimony was heard by the ICC in July 1940, and the case was reopened to include gasoline pipeline cost, valuation, and earnings data. The final decision was handed down in March 1941 and became effective June 11 following.

Railroad Rates

Since the ICC was not required to make shippers' distress a primary consideration in forcing rate reductions, it was necessary for the complainants to show that lower rates would not be detrimental to railroad revenues. Admitting that the cost of rail movements from the Mid-Continent would not permit railroad competition with crude-oil pipelines to major refining points throughout the Midwest, the shippers nevertheless claimed that the rail carriers could meet long-haul pipeline competition in the greater part of that destination territory. By their calculations, rail costs — including a 5.75 per cent return on investment — to 40 selected destinations in the upper Midwest averaged 29.2 cents for 100 pounds at carload rates. They compared this figure with the average published rate to the same destinations of 29.3 cents that had emerged in the wake of the ICC's 1915 decision. Existing rates, however, averaged 45.2 cents.[45] The complainants therefore argued that a reduction from this level to that of 1916 would still be compensatory and yield a return to which the railroads were entitled.*

The complainants showed that railroad revenues from petroleum had fallen faster than tonnage during the 1930's because the roads had reduced short-haul rates from various midwestern refining points to meet competition — actual or potential — from alternative forms of transportation. Thus, there had been cuts in 1931 and 1932 from Chicago and Wood River to various Illinois points to meet truck competition. This pattern was subsequently repeated elsewhere, and to meet threatened pipeline competition it had culminated in a reduction of 48.6 per cent on rates for the haul between Superior, Wisconsin, and Minneapolis, Minnesota, in 1937.[46]

During the course of the proceedings before the ICC, still further reductions were made in rail rates from marine and pipeline terminals to a variety of points in western trunk-line territory. Nevertheless, the railroads seemed to be fighting a losing battle. To cite but one example, motor truck movements into South Dakota from pipeline terminals and other points in Kansas and Wyoming increased from a mere 250,000 gallons in 1937 to an impressive 26,500,000 gallons in 1939.† [47]

Although in the Rail Shippers' case the railroads attacked the complainants' figures on rates and costs as unrepresentative or inaccurate and argued that the reductions requested could be offset only by an impossibly large increase in petroleum traffic, the ICC rejected these contentions. It decided that the roads could not maintain even existing revenues from this traffic unless rates were reduced, and it further found as a fact that the contested rates were unreasonable.[48] In the words of the 1941 decision, "the value of the service to the shipper has materially decreased. Rates which were reasonable . . . have with the change in conditions ceased to be reasonable." [49]

The examiner had recommended consideration of multiple-car rates as one way of meeting both the railroads' cost problems and pipeline competition. However, the railroads objected, as did several large oil companies and some of the ICC commissioners. As a result, this remained an area for further investigation.

Gasoline Pipelines: Tenders

Gasoline pipelines came in for their share of attention in these proceedings. Specifically, Great Lakes Pipe Line, operating over 2,000 miles of

---

*Shell and Indiana Standard intervened in the proceedings with the claim that if this reduction in rates were made, they would have to request reductions in rail rates from their Wood River and Whiting refineries, respectively, into the destination territory.

†Truck and barge competition and shifting centers of oil production had also hurt pipeline traffic. For example, the increased Illinois production had caused crude-oil lines from the Mid-Continent to reduce runs as much as 50,000 barrels a day, while gasoline lines suffered from increased use of barge transportation and the lengthening of truck hauls.

products lines, and Phillips with about 800 miles, were the targets of complaint by several independent refiners who challenged the size of minimum tender requirements and the reasonableness of pipeline rates.

Both Great Lakes and Phillips had initially imposed a 50,000-barrel minimum tender requirement, but by the end of August 1939 Great Lakes had cut this requirement in half and Phillips did likewise following the recommendations of the ICC examiner's proposed report. These reduced tenders, equivalent to 125 carloads of 8,000 gallons each, were defended as the minimum amounts compatible with acceptable contamination for the various grades of gasoline and other products transported through the lines.[50] However, if only one grade of gasoline was involved, instead of the six actually being moved, Great Lakes stated that it was prepared to accept a 10,000-barrel tender.[51]

Actual experience up to June 1, 1940, with the 25,000-barrel tender showed that only 25 of 169 tenders to Great Lakes were of this minimum size. Even so, that company announced at the last hearing on the Rail Shippers' case that it would accept tenders at any one receiving point from two or more consignees in amounts of not less than 12,500 barrels each.[52] The ICC concluded that for a pipeline of Great Lakes' size, 25,000 barrels was a practical operating minimum but that smaller amounts, if tendered subject to delay in movement, might also be reasonable.

Gasoline Pipelines: Rates

Gasoline pipeline rates were also involved in the complaints. It was shown that Great Lakes's and Phillips' published rates equalled all-rail rates whether the rate was from one of their receiving stations to a pipeline terminal or to the ultimate destination. The complainants objected to the way in which the rates were constructed. Since all-rail rates direct from points of origin to ultimate destination did not necessarily equal the rail rate via the pipeline route plus the rail rate from pipeline terminal to ultimate destination, the pipeline companies used varying proportional rates. For example, from origin points in Group 3 territory (Mid-Continent) to Kirksville, Missouri, the all-rail rate was 35 cents per barrel. The pipeline rate between the same points was broken down into a charge of 14 cents for the pipeline movement from point of origin to the Kansas City terminal plus 21 cents for rail shipment from there to Kirksville. On the other hand, when the ultimate destination was North Platte, Nebraska, where the all-rail rate was 50 cents, the charges broke down to 9 cents for the same pipeline movement to Kansas City plus 41 cents for the rail movement to North Platte. In other words, pipeline rates from Group 3 territory to Kansas City differed according to railroad rates to the ultimate destination — not according to the cost of the pipeline movement plus some percentage of return on investment.

Given an objective of minimizing friction with the railroads, pipeline managers' use of varying proportional rates made good sense. When the pipeline did not serve the ultimate destination, the distance from the pipeline terminal to that destination had to be covered in some way. Assuming that railroad tank cars were used, then the cost of this service had to be subtracted from the all-rail rate direct to the destination in order to arrive at the pipeline charge. This, of course, produced the varying proportional pipeline rates, and the practice was not unknown in railroad rate-making.

This method of rate-making was, however, a matter of choice. The complainants showed that in the East, the Keystone, Susquehanna, and Sun Oil gasoline lines did not attempt to equalize pipeline-plus-rail rates with all-rail rates.[53] Clearly, the shippers believed that this practice was adopted by the Mid-Continent lines as an exclusionary tactic against outside shippers — a fact suggested not only by the rate level but by Great Lakes's refusal up to the time of the complaint to load trucks at its pipeline terminals and by Phillips' insistence on quoting all-rail rates even when trucks were employed to complete the haul to the ultimate destination.[54]

It appears that, like most innovators, the Mid-Continent gasoline pipeline owners had sought to maximize for their own benefit innovational advantages that they possessed. These advantages presumably accrued from lower transportation costs than their competitors, whether integrated or not. (It was significant that only one of Great Lakes's original owners was fully integrated.) The gasoline pipelines, even more than crude-oil lines, in fact, had been built not for common-carrier service but as a means of lowering their owners' transportation costs while improving their competitive position. Only where these expectations were disappointed, or where outside pressures required it, could major changes in rate and tender policy be expected.

Barge and truck competition, the continued spread of gasoline lines, as well as the initiation of the Rail Shippers' case, provided the context for change. For example, deliveries out of Great Lakes's Chicago terminal dropped 43 per cent in 1939 compared with 1937,[55] partly as a result of Phillips' construction of its own line into the area. Volume of operations throughout the Great Lakes system also suffered. As the result of increased trucking of gasoline from Kansas and Oklahoma into Nebraska, products arriving by this mode of transportation rose from 22 per cent of consumption in 1934 to 51 per cent in 1939.[56] Comparable situations, reflecting movements by truck or barge or both, affected adversely pipeline movements to Wisconsin, North Dakota, and Minnesota. Furthermore, competition from large integrated companies was increasing. Shell had turned to truck movements from water terminals along the Mississippi to supply Minnesota, Iowa, and western Illinois; and Indiana Standard was moving products by truck from its Whiting and Sugar Creek refineries. In short, quite aside from the proceedings in the Rail Shippers' case, Great Lakes's management had cause to reappraise policies adopted to fit an earlier situation. However, neither Great Lakes nor Phillips voluntarily lowered its rates.

Using cost figures supplied by these defendants and relating them to ICC valuations, the ICC found in March 1941 that existing local rates, and in many instances proportional rates, were unreasonable. It therefore suggested that proportionate rate-making be dropped and reasonable rates to destinations served by Great Lakes and Phillips Petroleum (successor to Phillips Pipe Line Company) be set. Underlying this determination was the adoption of a maximum 10 per cent return on ICC valuation of gasoline pipelines as a yardstick. Commissioner Splawn observed in his concurring opinion that maximum reasonable gasoline pipeline rates so determined seemed close to the minimum reasonable rail rates.[57] Finally, with respect to pipelines, the existing 25,000-barrel minimum tender was found reasonable under normal conditions, though on gasoline and kerosine subject to delay in movement a requirement for more than a 5,000-barrel tender was ruled unreasonable for the future.[58]

For the Great Lakes's management and for their shipper-owners, the ICC's decision proved to be a blessing in disguise. This was so because of the way in which ownership was exercised. As in the Ajax line, dividends had been paid to shipper-owners on the basis of their share of ownership — not on the basis of their use of the facilities. An owner who used the line proportionately more than his share of ownership lost part of his transportation savings, recovered through dividends, to those who used it less. With pipeline rates set at railroad levels, then, there had been an incentive for some owners in Great Lakes to keep down their utilization of its facilities. When rates were dropped in compliance with the ICC decision, these owners had a new incentive to use the line since they could now make direct savings through the lowered rates as well as indirectly through dividends. As a result, tonnage and revenues increased rapidly after June 1941.

The year 1941, then, saw the end to one phase of a continuing battle between a variety of elements in the oil industry employing competing modes of transportation for petroleum products. The products pipeline had established itself beyond question as a new competitive weapon in the never-ending search to reduce transportation costs and to create and protect marketing areas. The ICC had with comparative dispatch established a basis for determining maximum reasonable rates on such lines, allowing a somewhat larger return than on crude lines. By this time, however, pipeliners were far more concerned with an antitrust threat that overlapped and overshadowed their regulatory problems.

CHAPTER 15

THE REVIVAL OF ANTITRUST INTEREST
IN INTEGRATED OIL OPERATIONS

The judicial condemnation of the National Industrial Recovery Act in 1935 had ended an experiment with industry self-regulation and suspension of antitrust enforcement. When a major setback to the economy followed two years later, some economists and politicians came to the conclusion that concentration of private economic power was an important causal factor. Economists wrote and talked of the mature economy and the decline of competition. Franklin D. Roosevelt lent a sympathetic ear to these explanations for continued economic distress, and with his encouragement Congress in 1938 authorized a comprehensive investigation of private economic power. The oil industry became one focal point of the inquiry, and pipelines came under fire once more because of their relationship to integrated oil operations. Meantime, under the direction of Thurman Arnold, a former Yale law professor, the Antitrust Division of the Department of Justice was rejuvenated and a flurry of antitrust suits followed. For the first time since 1911 the firms in the integrated oil industry, accustomed to being on the defensive, had to face a clearly serious threat of dissolution by legal action.

THE MOUNTING ATTACK ON THE INTEGRATED OIL INDUSTRY

Legislative Proposals for Divorcement

The political appeal of attacking the oil industry as an exemplar of monopoly was reflected throughout the 1930's, especially in renewed proposals to break up integrated companies. Within the industry, independent marketers increasingly led the attack, which found expression in a succession of bills introduced in both the House and Senate, where a small number of Congressmen and Senators became identified with the anti-integration movement.

Senator William E. Borah of Idaho was one of those who expressed continuing concern about the relationship of pipelines to integrated companies. In 1934, for example, in introducing a bill to prevent stock ownership in pipelines by oil companies, he said: "One of the most important items in the oil industry which looks toward monopoly and enables the major com-

268

panies to control the situation and to effectuate complete monopoly is the fact that the pipe lines transmitting the oil are owned by the major companies or some of them." [1] In that session,[2] and others in 1935,[3] 1937,[4] and 1939,[5] Borah introduced bills to extend the commodities clause of the Hepburn Act to pipelines. In the bill submitted on April 17, 1939, he acted not only for himself but for Senator Guy M. Gillette of Iowa,[6] who, since 1937, had been seeking to divorce marketing from the integrated oil industry. Comparable measures had been introduced in the House.[7] The Borah-Gillette bill, for example, had its counterpart in a divorcement proposal advanced on July 11, 1939, by Congressman E. V. Izac of California.[8]

None of these bills progressed far, but the integrated oil industry had to be alert to the potential threats they posed and also to efforts to extend the powers of the ICC. For example, Section 12 of the proposed Transportation Act of 1939, as introduced, extended the commodities clause to all forms of transportation under ICC jurisdiction. Although Senator Burton K. Wheeler, chairman of the Senate Interstate Commerce Committee, had been a sponsor of the bill, he changed his mind about including an expanded commodities clause in it. During the hearings he announced that the repercussions of such a step would be so widespread that the proposal deserved extended study and separate consideration.[9] Though the threat to pipelines in this section was thus sidetracked, other provisions of the proposed Transportation Act seemed to place pipeline securities under ICC jurisdiction and to make all pipelines, regardless of their employment, more clearly common carriers than was the case under existing law and judicial interpretations.

After the Wheeler bill passed the Senate, representatives of leading pipeline companies marshalled their forces to fight the offensive provisions in the House Interstate and Foreign Commerce Committee.[10] The bill went no farther at that session, but it provided the basis for the Transportation Act of 1940, which omitted the features objectionable to pipeliners.

The Elgin Case

It will be recalled that the commodities clause had been adopted in the Hepburn Act of 1906 primarily to prevent coal-carrying railroads from favoring mines allied with them over independent mines. The ICC had subsequently applied the clause in a case involving the Elgin, Joliet & Eastern Railroad, which was owned by United States Steel Corporation and transported for its subsidiaries as well as for outsiders. On May 25, 1936, the Supreme Court handed down a 6-3 decision that found no violation of the law in this relationship. In the words of the decision: "It is impossible for us now to declare as matter of law that every company all of whose shares are owned by a holding company necessarily becomes an agent, instrumentality, or department of the latter. Whether such intimate relation exists is a question of fact to be determined upon evidence." [11] Although the ICC called congressional attention to this problem in applying the commodities clause, no legislative action was taken to remedy it until the Wheeler bill of 1939, and this particular provision of the bill, as noted above, was eliminated during the legislative process. The Elgin decision therefore remained an important legal bulwark for the corporate organization and control of pipeline subsidiaries by integrated oil companies.

The Madison Case

The Antitrust Division of the Justice Department had meanwhile undertaken prosecution of 18 large oil companies, 5 of their subsidiaries, a number of individuals, and several oil trade journals, charging them with criminal conspiracy to violate the Sherman Antitrust Act. The brief interlude of suspended antitrust action that had accompanied the National Industrial Recovery Act experiment was clearly at an end.

The charges filed in 1936 by the Justice Department grew out of jobber complaints against alleged fixing of gasoline prices in the Midwest, which followed a pattern begun in conjunction with a distress gasoline buying program sanctioned by the National Recovery Administration and continued after its demise. The trial began at Madison, Wisconsin, in October 1937. The first case, which involved the buying program, ended on January 21, 1938, with a verdict for the government. However, the presiding judge decided to set aside the verdict as it applied to some individuals, to hold a new trial for some of the defendants, and to dismiss others. After some complicated legal proceedings, the Supreme Court in a decision handed down in May 1940, sustained the lower court judge.[12] A companion case covering the policies of integrated companies with respect to jobbers ran a varied course until 1941.

In this case the integrated oil industry had again been placed in the limelight as a major offender under the antitrust laws. There was understandably a feeling among the defendants and in some financial and industry quarters that the government had unilaterally changed the rules of the game and that industry cooperation with the government under the NIRA had been ill repaid.

THE TNEC INVESTIGATION

By 1938 the integrated oil industry was under critical scrutiny or defending itself from attack in several branches of the federal government. The recession that hit the economy late in 1937 contributed to this hostile environment. The setback cast doubt on New Deal recovery policies and led in some quarters to the suspicion that the existing structure and ownership of American industry stood in the way of further progress. In the spring of 1937 the Attorney General had recommended a study of government antimonopoly policies, and the following spring the President called for the most comprehensive investigation of the economy since the turn of the century.

On April 28, 1938, a few months after the Madison case was launched,

Franklin D. Roosevelt sent a special message to Congress on "monopolies." In it he directed congressional attention to two developments that he considered of major importance: the increase in private economic power and the inability of private industry to provide adequate employment for labor or capital. He raised the questions of whether these developments had passed beyond the remedy of the antitrust laws and whether they reflected a decline in competition as a result of a concentration of ownership and banker control of key corporations and industries in the United States. He asked Congress to authorize an investigation of these and related matters, especially as they affected the functioning of the price system and price policies of major industries. Congress responded with a joint resolution, signed by the President on June 16, 1938, authorizing the creation of a Temporary National Economic Committee to study "monopoly and the concentration of economic power in and financial control over production and distribution of goods and services."

The TNEC was composed of three Senators (including Senator Borah), three Congressmen, and one member each from the Departments of Justice, Treasury, Labor, and Commerce, the Securities and Exchange Commission, and the Federal Trade Commission. The chairman of the committee was Senator Joseph C. O'Mahoney of Wyoming. Assistant Attorney General Thurman Arnold represented the Justice Department, and members of his staff — Hugh B. Cox, W. B. Watson Snyder (who had taken part in the Madison case) and F. E. Berquist — were active in the proceedings. From the standpoint of pipeliners, it was significant that the ICC — the federal agency assigned statutory jurisdiction over their activities — was not represented on the committee.

The hearings devoted to the oil industry covered 25 days between September 25 and October 25, 1939. They produced 3,116 pages of testimony by 48 witnesses and 986 charts, graphs, and tables. While pipelines were involved in only part of this record, they received thorough coverage, much of it retracing ground familiar to anyone who had followed the charges and countercharges of the past decade. Attention was focused on a group which the committee designated "the 20 major integrated oil companies," though the TNEC questionnaire that was the cornerstone of the proceedings had been sent to 49 companies, 41 of whom replied. Witnesses appeared only with the committee's permission to do so, and once again the issues of public policy were defined by interested parties.

The American Petroleum Institute managed the presentation to the committee for the integrated oil industry. The case for pipelines as part of integrated operations was handled in general terms by Fayette B. Dow, the chairman of API's committees on railroad transportation and pipeline accounting regulation. Representatives of integrated oil companies, appearing under API auspices, also touched on pipelines to a greater or lesser extent. Among them, J. Howard Pew, president of Sun Oil, and William S. Farish, president of Jersey Standard, were especially prominent.

The Independent Refiner's Position

Like the ICC, the TNEC investigators drew much of their information from questionnaires sent to companies in industries covered by their probe. One part of the TNEC questionnaire to oil companies had dealt with "pipeline policies," and at the hearings a leading witness was John E. Shatford, the complainant against pipeline rate reductions who had helped to trigger the ICC's investigation of this question in 1934.

Shatford had a long association with the oil industry. His father had acquired an old varnish plant in Chicago in 1904 and converted it into an oil refinery. Faced with the refusal of Standard Oil pipelines to transport crude for him from the Mid-Continent, the elder Shatford had supplied his refinery by rail. Flush production in Oklahoma in 1914 gave him a chance for favorable purchases on a long-term contract. Successful in this venture, he retired from the business. The son, however, became an independent field refiner and served in the NRA first as a member of the oil industry's Planning and Coordination Committee and later as National Coordinator of Refining under the Petroleum Code.[13]

In Shatford's opinion, restrictive pipeline practice had helped to shape the structure of the refining end of the oil industry. With the development of oil production in the Southwest and lack of access to crude-oil pipelines to move the oil to major marketing centers, producers with excess crude had built their own field refineries. According to Shatford, at that time "the organic structure of the refining industry was developed, the die was cast, there was no turning back, the small refiner was there [in the field] for better or for worse, and there he has been from that day to this, in a constantly recessive struggle, in a continuous retreat against increasingly unfavorable transportation circumstances relatively speaking." [14] His approach to oil transportation problems started from this point, and his attack was focused more on the policies of the Interstate Commerce Commission than on the integrated oil companies owning pipelines.

The ICC was a logical target for Shatford because it had power over rates for the rail shipment of petroleum products, and the southwestern nonintegrated refiner depended on tank car shipments to reach northern and central markets. Citing ICC Docket 17000, Part 4A, "Rates of Refined Petroleum Carload, from, to and Between Points in the Southwest," Shatford showed that refiners in Kansas and Oklahoma in 1927 had asked rail carriers and the ICC for lower freight rates as an alternative to building gasoline pipelines from the Mid-Continent to northern and central states. The rail carriers agreed not to invoke the proposed advance in rates, but the ICC, according to Shatford, "juggled the matter indefinitely without decision and in the end disregarded the carriers' request." [15] In his judgment, "Having made the mistake which created the gasoline pipe lines, the Commission sat with folded hands and did nothing of mentionable effect to make them common carriers. And they have done nothing since except raise rail rates to the further disadvantage of those who are tied to the raise by the Commission's inept policies." [16] The witness further testified that he believed ICC railroad rate decisions tended to favor large marketers, who moved gasoline long distances by pipeline. This was shown, he thought, by ICC approval of reduced rail rates for short hauls from pipeline terminal points to offset competition from trucks. On the longer hauls important to small refiners, the ICC seemed to favor raising rail rates.[17] In essence, then, Shatford recapitulated the charges then pending before the ICC in the Petroleum Rail Shippers' case.

In the light of such charges, Shatford's own position with respect to common-carrier use of gasoline pipelines was surprising. Though he said that he believed these lines were subject to the Hepburn Act, he conceded that they were loaded to capacity and were not able "as a practical operating matter to carry gasoline of anybody else." [18] Furthermore, in his statement he declared that it was "indisputable" that both crude-oil and gasoline pipelines had resulted in lower costs to consumers.[19]

Shatford believed that a fairly systematic policy of excluding outside shippers had been followed by crude-oil pipelines in the past but that it was being modified and, in any event, was no longer as significant as it once had been.[20] He stated that gathering lines uniformly performed as common carriers. Pipelines of integrated companies carried for other integrated companies as matters of convenience or accommodation or to forestall construction of a competing pipeline. When lines were short of tonnage, they might also carry for small refiners and he cited the case of the Texas Pipe Line Company supplying the Globe Oil & Refining Company in connection with movements to the Texas Company's refinery at Lockport, Illinois.[21]

Shatford's position on the significance of pipeline rates brought him into conflict with Willis Ballinger of the Federal Trade Commission. Ballinger, apparently reflecting complaints to the FTC by independent marketers, took the position that common-carrier use of pipelines created profits that could be used to subsidize marketing. In his view, the appropriate remedy was divorcement.[22] Shatford took issue with this conclusion. In 1934 he had opposed reduced pipeline rates on the grounds that the transportation savings to integrated companies would allow them to extend their markets in competition with rail shippers. He now had a different view. If outside shippers, like Globe, were admitted to the lines, they could make the same use of these savings as the lines' owners. Under these conditions, his objection to reduced pipeline rates disappeared. When Ballinger maintained that the pipeline owner would still be making profit at the outside shipper's expense, Shatford countered by maintaining that the latter could extend his market, cut his prices, and force the integrated concern to dissipate any pipeline profit in meeting this competition.[23] Also, with common carriage, small refiners could locate more advantageously with respect to markets. Then, as Shatford put it, "I think they would cut the major companies' throats." [24]

In trying to reconcile theoretical and practical considerations, Shatford found much difficulty, but in the end he approached the pipeline question from the standpoint of the existing field refiner. First, he made it clear that he did not consider pipelines responsible for small refiners' difficulties in obtaining crude oil; rather he placed the blame on prorationing.[25] Second, access to crude lines would be of little help to the field refiner — he was located close to crude already; what he needed was cheap transportation to markets for refined products.[26] Opening the crude-oil lines might lead to construction of new refineries closer to markets but it would ruin existing field refiners. He also brushed off the importance of making gasoline lines common-carriers, and he thought application of the commodities clause to pipelines would create chaos in the oil industry.[27]

It seems clear that Shatford was personally most interested in securing reductions in rail rates for the transportation of petroleum products. If this could be done, he had no quarrel with pipelines as such. If the ICC would do its job with respect to both pipelines and railroads, divorcement would be unnecessary.

What Shatford would have liked, in fact, was restoration of the 1916 schedule of rail rates into Western Freight Association Territory. On that basis he believed that tank car shipments would become competitive with gasoline pipeline rates.[28] The fact that this would involve a rollback of 35 per cent from existing rail rates did not bother him. However in view of the ICC's disposition, as he interpreted it, to foster railroad earnings, he suggested the establishment of a "control authority" to enforce the Hepburn Act and maintain equitable relations between rail and pipeline rates.[29]

The Independent Producer's Position

A more intractable position was taken by Karl A. Crowley, a Fort Worth lawyer who appeared as a friend of independent producers. He insisted that only divorcement of pipelines from integrated operations would meet the problem of monopoly that he saw in the oil industry. His primary emphasis was on the alleged subsidies that pipelines provided for other parts of integrated operations and the size of the dividends that pipelines paid. He singled out Shell Pipe Line especially, emphasizing that the Shell companies were owned abroad but enjoyed the same benefits as a full-fledged American institution.[30]

Crowley attacked the use of the 1933 Splawn report to defend integration with respect to pipelines. To make his point he quoted from a letter written by Splawn, who had made the famous 1933 "plant facility" statement. In this letter Splawn declared: "Of course, the report to which you refer speaks for itself. I have never thought it supported some of the arguments which have been put forward by representatives of various groups. This, though, is a free country in which views are published whether they be logical or illogical, well or ill founded." [31]

The Fort Worth lawyer also charged that the ICC did not render the protection to small shippers by pipeline that the Hepburn Act required. He pointed out that challenging pipeline rates before the ICC was expensive and time-consuming, and independents did not dare to challenge large companies.[32] This view was shared by another witness who estimated the cost of filing a rate complaint at $20,000 to $30,000.[33] Fayette Dow for the industry challenged this estimate as many times too high. Furthermore, he maintained, an interested party could intervene in an ex parte proceeding at no cost whatsoever.[34]

The question of who would buy pipelines if they were divorced from integrated operations had been raised by Splawn and a whole generation of oilmen, but the answer offered no problem for Crowley. If there was an economic function to be performed, he maintained, someone would purchase them. He cited the case of railroads and of packing houses forced to divest themselves of certain operations as a result of antitrust action. In the case of oil companies, pipeline stock could be distributed to shareholders of the parent concern.[35] He pointed out that members of the Northern and Southern Groups of pipelines divorced from Standard Oil as a result of the 1911 decision were publicly owned, had a lower capitalization per mile, and had very much lower earnings than 15 pipeline companies 100 per cent owned by large integrated concerns. They were, to his mind, evidence of the feasibility and desirability of divorcement.* [36]

The Question of Pipeline Rates

The profitability of pipelines became a continuing subject of discussion because it was relevant to both regulatory and divorcement considerations. Therefore, the "numbers game" figured prominently in the testimony both to prove and to refute the charge that pipeline rates were excessive. Many different sets of figures entered the picture, but the committee was seemingly most interested in those that showed the rate of return on depreciated investment for all pipelines in 1938 as 28.4 per cent; a rate of return of 26.5 per cent for major company crude-oil lines; and a 29.7 per cent rate of return for gasoline lines.

Industry representatives attacked these figures. J. Howard Pew emphasized that the figures in question showed return only after an allowance had been made for depreciation. In his view, the return for integrated company crude lines should more properly have reflected original investment. On this basis the figure of 26.5 per cent would have fallen to 11.7 per cent for 1938, while the same approach applied to gasoline lines would have produced a figure of 20.7 instead of 29.7 per cent. W. S. Farish argued that the net investment in pipelines alone was a misleading base on which to determine the reasonableness of rates. Since a pipeline depended on both the producing and marketing ends of the business, he felt that some account should be taken of the investment in them. Dow and Farish added further to the confusion by arguing that ICC valuation figures, which took into account both original investment and original investment after depre-

---

*For an appraisal of the experience of independent common carriers, see Chap. 9.

ciation, should have been used. On this basis the average net income of the lines would have been 13.6 per cent of value.[37]

As a second line of defense, the integrated oil industry representatives fell back on the argument that high rates of return on pipeline investment were necessary to protect against the risks of oil fields declining and to provide capital for new lines in the face of such hazards. Finally, both Pew and Farish admitted that pipeline rates had been somewhat high in the past, but they joined Dow in maintaining that this was no longer the case.[38]

The Subsidy Question Again

Representatives of the Department of Justice and the Federal Trade Commission were not content with the industry's rationale. Wendell Berge put the problem in these words: "Isn't a larger question posed here than merely the question whether the rate that the shipper pays is in itself fair? I think we can assume that it is if it is regulated, but isn't the question rather whether a set-up is fair which requires that a shipper pay even a reasonable rate to his competitor?" [39] He maintained that the commodities clause as applied to railroads should be equally applicable to pipelines, and he had already introduced the idea that pipeline profits offset losses in other branches of the integrated oil business.* [40] F. E. Berquist supported this line of argument and felt that its merit was confirmed by the significance of pipeline income in relation to the total operating income of large integrated companies as well as by comparison with the small role that pipeline earnings played in the income of nonmajor companies.[41]

The industry replies to the subsidy charge were as varied as the witnesses, though they had a common theme — the subsidy argument was groundless. Pew maintained that in an integrated company, one could not properly determine the profitability of any one activity and he cited the fact that one-third the capital in his company was not specifically applicable to any single activity.[42] When Ballinger of the FTC pursued this question further, Pew seemed to admit that the "subsidy" argument might have some validity if pipeline rates were unreasonable. But, in Pew's opinion, this was not the case. In any event, the pipelines of his company, Sun Oil, carried little for outsiders. "Why," he asked, "should we set up a fictitious profit on our pipeline operations?" [43] Ballinger, however, maintained that if the pipelines showed a profit, then it must be a real one and Pew could find it. Pew replied that this was not so; pipeline rates could double but competition on the marketing end would prevent any increase in receipts that would convert pipeline "paper profits" into real ones. It seems clear that the interrogators and the witness were talking about different situations. Government representatives had been discussing rates charged outside ship-

---

*The idea of pipeline "profits" as a competitive weapon against small independent marketers had also been advanced in a much criticized report of the National Recovery Review Board, headed by lawyer Clarence Darrow, in 1934. *Oildom,* July 2, 1934.

pers; Pew's argument was based on a situation where only a shipper-owner used the pipeline.

One alleged example of the outside shipper aiding his competitor through payment of pipeline charges was given by Louis J. Walsh of Eastern States Petroleum Company. His company had built a refinery at Houston in 1935 and supplied it from pipelines affiliated with three large, integrated companies. Walsh had no complaint about the service rendered, but he figured that pipeline charges represented a 50 per cent profit to the pipeline companies. Under detailed questioning, however, he had no data to support the charge and seemed unsure of whether his profit figure applied to investment or gross revenue.[44]

When W. S. Farish of Jersey Standard appeared before the committee, he was asked to explain the high rate of pipeline profit compared to other branches of the oil industry. Farish replied: "I think the reason for it . . . is that the pipeline rates are a service rate that is fixed, and we all pay, those of us that use the pipelines, and mind you, the owners do most of the using, they all pay that rate in good times as well as bad ones. Therefore there is a constant earning to the pipelines where there isn't a constant earning in the other branches of the industry." [45] He attributed the downward movement of rates during the preceding eight years to: the advent of prorationing, the discovery of new sources of low-cost crude as in east Texas, and competition from other means of oil transportation such as barge and tanker. In his view, pressure from regulatory bodies was "of relatively little importance," though the ICC's recent actions had strengthened the business pressures to reduce rates.[46] However, Farish elsewhere in his testimony conceded that except for competition between producing areas, government regulation rather than competition had "a lot" of influence on rates and profits of pipelines.[47]

Asked to comment specifically on the subsidy argument, Farish declared that pipelines carried chiefly for their owners and therefore their earnings were mostly a bookkeeping transaction. "How you could subsidize yourself by moving money from one pocket to another is a little disturbing to my way of thinking," the Jersey president said.[48] Senator O'Mahoney challenged the aptness of the comparison since, even if it was an internal pricing device, the results affected "literally thousands of retailers who have no opportunity to produce and no opportunity to transport." [49] Farish replied that the marketing end of Jersey's business operated at a profit and "we don't put anybody out of business." [50] As had been the case in the 1934 congressional investigation, neither the Senator nor the oilman carried his analysis into a specific situation.

The subsidy question was also put to Dr. Robert E. Wilson, president of Pan American Petroleum and Transport Company, an affiliate of Indiana Standard. He analyzed the problem in terms of its complexity and in terms of the time element. In his opinion, refining and marketing generally operated at a profit, though he also pointed out that it was sometimes difficult to unscramble one branch from another simply because of the way companies were organized. Admittedly in some years marketing might operate at a loss, but unless it were carried along in some manner — which might be interpreted as a "subsidy" — the only alternative was to go out of the business. He could not say whether such losses were made up from reserves, pipeline profits, producing profits, or marketing profits of the previous year.[51]

The Integrated Companies' Position

Despite variations between oil-company witnesses appearing before the TNEC, some fairly well defined positions emerged. Representatives of large oil companies took the position that ownership of pipelines by integrated concerns was beneficial to the public; they were available to, but little used by, outside shippers; rates had been high but were being reduced and, in the absence of outside business, were of little significance in any event. To maintain this position it was necessary to argue on the one hand that it was virtually impossible to separate out the profitability of any one branch of integrated operations; on the other hand it was necessary to maintain that the cost savings of pipelines and the profitability of marketing operations could be ascertained. The testimony suggested that important companies really did not know in any detail what the profitability of their separate branches was, though some companies were in a better position than others to ascertain it. From the testimony one also gets the definite impression that the integrated oil industry had simply evolved and that its professional managers had reacted to new situations in pragmatic ways within certain traditions, such as high pipeline rates. It seems equally clear that in appearing before the TNEC the integrated oil industry was on the defensive and its representatives at a disadvantage in replying to questions which moved from one topic to another in an almost random manner. Accordingly the easiest defensive strategy was to defend the *status quo*, stress the fact that change was taking place which would correct any abuses of the past, emphasize the fact that public policy had already provided a regulatory agency for pipelines, and otherwise take a stand on the basis of individual experience which indicated the impossibility of exact analysis.

The Integration Issue and Gasoline Pipelines

Although committee investigators denied it, integration of oil-company operations was on trial before the TNEC — not pipelines as such. Unlike previous congressional investigations, no parties appeared who had specific grievances resulting from their treatment by pipeline companies. Rather, government officials led the attack on pipeline rates and practices. Apparently recognizing that changes were taking place on crude-oil lines, they concentrated more on alleged abuses by gasoline pipelines. Great Lakes Pipe Line, a pioneer in this field and a corporate joint-venture owned by large companies marketing in the Midwest, was a favorite target.

The charges against Great Lakes were the standard ones made so familiar by previous investigations of crude-oil lines: high rates, high minimum tenders, collaboration with the railroads, undue advantages to owners, and deliberate exclusion of outsiders. In addition, one witness maintained that certain tariffs put into effect on the Great Lakes system in March 1936 had failed to comply with ICC requirements. Rates were said to be high because, despite the economies of pipeline transportation, they matched rail rates to the same destinations. Tenders were called high because they specified a minimum of 25,000 barrels. (For a time questioning proceeded on the assumption this figure was 50,000 barrels.)* Undue advantage to owners was suggested by citing an article from *Fortune* on Continental Oil stating in part that, over a period of years, Continental figured that dividends from the pipeline "have been largely offset by losses suffered by its marketing division in expanding its operations in the Chicago and North Central areas." [52]

Most of the objections to Great Lakes's rates and regulations were of a hypothetical character, for apparently no outside shipper had actually asked to use these facilities. Of course, the latter fact could be and was interpreted as the result of a successful exclusion policy. As a government questioner suggested, there was no advantage to be gained by an outside shipper if pipeline rates equaled all-rail rates. Farish, however, took the position "that there is no one [outside party] who has a refinery tributary to it that could use it." [53] Shatford, who could scarcely be considered a friend of the gasoline lines, made the same point. "I think many of the suggestions relating to the correction of the pipeline situation obscure the practical problem that to merely impress upon present gasoline pipelines the character of common carriers wouldn't solve anything, because they don't go where they need to go to reach the small man's product." [54]

For virtually every witness, pipelines had a different significance in relation to integration. One witness who strongly favored divorcement was Paul Hadlick, secretary of the National Oil Marketers Association, and formerly secretary of the Division of Marketing, API. Hadlick believed firmly in the "subsidy" theory. He had already testified earlier in the year on a bill to divorce marketing from the integrated industry. Before the TNEC he advocated the same procedure for pipelines. "I am principally interested in divorcement of marketing," he said. "I do think that part of it might be accomplished by divorcement of pipelines because it would take away these large profits that they have." [55]

Hadlick also maintained that the railroads set their rates to favor large, integrated companies and that the ICC was not keeping up with its job.[56] To support his position on railroad relations with these companies, he cited the fact that the railroads had refused to cut rates when a gasoline pipeline (Great Lakes) served Minneapolis, but quickly reduced them under the threat of a short pipeline being constructed from Superior, Wisconsin, to

*See above, Chap. 14. Great Lakes, involved in the Rail Shippers' case and suffering from the competition of barges and trucks, had reduced its tender requirement on the eve of the TNEC oil-industry hearings.

Minneapolis.* [57] Shatford had mentioned the same example, but neither man was asked to produce evidence to support his conclusions about the motivation for railroad action or inaction in relation to the oil industry.

Hadlick was asked what difference it would make whether pipelines were independently owned or not in the light of what he had just said. The witness replied that it might make no difference as to rates, but the consumer would benefit because pipeline profits would not be "siphoned" into marketing. Again he did not specify exactly what he meant.

The formal industry position on oil transportation was presented to the TNEC by Fayette B. Dow. Dow was a graduate of Amherst College and Columbia Law School. After serving on the Columbia faculty and practicing law in New York City, he had joined the ICC as an attorney and examiner. Upon leaving the ICC, he became associated with API as chairman of its General Committee on Railroad Transportation and its Committee on Pipeline Accounting Regulations. He also served on the API's Pipeline Valuation Committee, and for 20 years had acted as counsel for the International Apple Association, appearing in its behalf before the ICC on numerous occasions.[58]

Dow's prepared statement was in response to the committee's invitation to discuss trends of the past ten years with respect to the movement of oil transportation from the railroads to private pipeline, truck, and water carriers, the reasons for these trends, and the question of whether the savings involved were being passed on to consumers. His report covered the history of oil transportation, the movement toward pipeline transportation because of its lower costs, and developments of the preceding decade in terms of rates and investigations. These and many other topics were presented in a manner that reflected favorably on the development of pipeline transportation.

From his investigation of the record, Dow concluded that noncontroversial aspects of pipelining were numerous. Pipelines had been built with private capital, which was applied economically and efficiently. They were extended in adequate capacity to new fields and in the process provided the producer with a market where he wanted it — at the wellhead. Pipeline companies had reduced their costs of construction, operation, and maintenance, and provided the lowest cost overland transportation for petroleum. Service was safe, efficient, and dependable, and pipelines had occasioned no financial losses of significance to public investors.[59]

Under questioning, however, Dow seemingly handicapped himself by taking an overly defensive position and by attempting to anticipate and answer all kinds of criticisms of pipelines. As divorcement seemed to him to be the big issue, on his own initiative he had prepared a statement on the subject and kept returning to it. Senator O'Mahoney denied that this was a primary concern of the committee. In this connection, he told Dow, "There is no case here and you are not in any sense speaking for a de-

*See above Chap. 14.

fendant. I want that clearly understood." [60] Again, a short time later, the chairman declared, "You do seem to have the feeling you are here on the defense. You are not." [61] But of the two views, the witness's evaluation of the hearing was probably the more correct.

On specific points, Dow sometimes found himself in trouble. For example he was trapped between the argument that pipelines were solid financial performers and the argument that they were hazardous. His favorite examples of risk due to changing conditions were the impact of the Illinois field on existing pipeline investment and the decline in Great Lakes Pipe Line revenues as evidence of the uncertainty surrounding pipelining. Justice Department representatives Snyder and Berquist jumped on such statements. The following exchange was typical:

> Mr. Berquist: Just to make the record clear on that risk element, let's look at the Great Lakes Pipeline. In 1937 its net income was $5,088,000 and its investment in carrier property $23,759,000. In 1938 its net income was $4,552,000, and its net income in 1935 was $4,459,000, and in 19 — there was another one here; well, for five years it has been averaging about 20 per cent of its total investment, so it has about paid out in income and also in dividends the total investment of the pipelines. It has substantially paid out in its short life already, has it not?

> Mr. Dow: Well, if the figures show it, it has. I hadn't figured it from that standpoint. I didn't know whether this was a question or a statement. Either one is all right with me.

> Mr. Berquist: They are ICC figures and I got from that the indication that the risk involved the pipeline and I wanted to raise whether you thought that was an undue risk in terms of what earnings it had paid for the preceding years.

> Mr. Dow: Did you take a look at the Ajax line, with 60 per cent less traffic this year than last and 71 per cent less income? I don't think either of us can prove things much from individual cases. I think the pipeline business is not as good a business as you think it is unless you have got an assurance of traffic, and then it is a swell business.[26]

As we shall see, this sparring over Great Lakes may have had far greater significance than appeared at the time of verbal encounter. In any event, Dow's admission that it was impossible to prove much by individual cases was a condemnation of his own tactics as well as those of his questioners. But generalization based on statistics could be equally misleading.

The Hearings in Perspective

The diversity of testimony, the manner in which it was elicited, and in many instances, the obvious biases of both witnesses and questioners were shortcomings of the TNEC invetigation. In the case of pipelines it was established that ownership conferred economic benefits, that large integrated companies were dominant in this area of transportation, and that it was a profitable part of the integrated oil business. Beyond this, all sorts of questions arose and the answers depended on the viewpoint of the individual examining the testimony or data, as well as the manner in which testimony was prepared or offered and its intended purpose.

In an effort to give the proceedings on the oil industry some semblance of order, the American Petroleum Institute prepared a digest of the testimony, added the formal statements of API witnesses, and published the results in 1942 under the title *Petroleum-Industry Hearings Before the Temporary National Economic Committee*. The consequences of the proceedings had already been felt, the TNEC had completed its work, and the nation's attention was turned to problems of war instead of depression, but the organization of the API volume gives some indication of the integrated oil industry's appraisal of the hearings.

The API digest concluded that integration was the central issue in which pipelines were involved.

> To some extent the whole integration controversy revolves around the question of pipe-line ownership. Pipe lines seem to account for the greater part of the 'profits' (i.e. economies) which are allegedly used to 'subsidize' refining and marketing operations. Many of the witnesses who insisted upon complete disintegration would probably be satisfied if pipe lines alone were divorced. The questions asked and the views expressed by the Committee members show that they were more interested in the divorcement of pipe lines than in any other phase of disintegration.[63]

Testimony against divorcement was found to have centered on two themes: first, it would be unworkable; and second, where the consequences might be anticipated, divorcement would be damaging to the very interests that it was supposed to help. Thus the record showed that two of the three independent refiners who appeared before the TNEC opposed divorcement, as did the Independent Petroleum Association of America, representing some 10,000 producers.[64]

Testimony of industry representatives was found to have contrasted what had actually happened under integrated operations with what might happen after divorcement. While admitting that integrated company pipelines carried little crude oil for outsiders and no nonowner refiner had tendered to gasoline lines, industry spokesmen argued that the consumer had not suffered. Dow's testimony, for example, was to the effect that the public paid some $800,000,000 less for gasoline in 1937 than a similar amount of the fuel would have cost in 1928 and he suggested that this situation was tied to transportation savings. In the words of the API summary: "The implication of Dow's testimony seems to be this: There is no way of determining the extent to which this record is *attributable to* integrated-company operation of pipe lines. But, it is certain that this record *was made under* integrated-company operation. Whether any other system could have given a comparable performance is problematical."[65]

In retrospect, the TNEC hearings developed little that was new concerning pipeline operations. The charges against integrated companies' lines and the rebuttals and countercharges were familiar ones in a long tradition.

The similarities to testimony before the United States Industrial Commission at the turn of the century were more striking than the differences, though the object of attack had shifted from a single combination to a group of 20 companies. Reflecting the changing times, the marketing element had become the most aggressive critics of pipelines, and gasoline pipelines figured more prominently in the hearings than did crude-oil lines. On the other hand, no witnesses appeared before the TNEC to complain specifically of their treatment by pipelines. The most vigorous critics were government officials, especially those from the Justice Department. The chief significance for pipelines of the TNEC hearings was to lie in this fact.

TNEC Monograph on the Oil Industry

To supplement oral testimony, the TNEC also published monographic studies of various problems coming under its purview. These monographs, though published at the committee's expense and for its use, were specifically attributed to their authors. TNEC endorsement of their conclusions was not signified by the fact of publication. Nevertheless, the form of publication could easily give the impression that these were official documents.

The monograph on the petroleum industry was significantly entitled "Control of the Petroleum Industry by Major Oil Companies," and its author, Roy C. Cook, was identified by Senator O'Mahoney as an "expert" in the Antitrust Division of the Department of Justice. The letter of submittal by Thurman Arnold of the department in January 1941 pointed out that Cook's work was actually undertaken as a research project at George Washington University and was not to be considered as representing the opinions or policies of the department. On the other hand, Arnold characterized the study as "a definite contribution to the hearings and literature on The petroleum industry." Whether the capital "The" was in Arnold's letter or a printer's mistake, it was clear that Cook considered 20 major companies as The industry. The preface frankly stated that the author intended to investigate "the more important monopolistic conditions" in the industry and that he proposed to do so from the standpoint of the "independent oil man." Given these premises, the results were predictable.

Setting the scene with quotations from FTC and ICC reports of the pre-World War I period, Cook recapitulated all the standard charges against pipelines. They were controlled by major companies; pipeline profits were large and used to subsidize marketing; independent shippers were denied access to pipelines because of high minimum tenders; possession of pipelines made it possible for major companies to fix the price of crude. These charges were not analyzed. Instead they were presented primarily in the form of assertions, buttressed with suitable statistics and quotations.[66]

Cook's monograph spurred W. S. Farish of Jersey Standard and J. Howard Pew of Sun Oil to prepare a review and criticism, based largely on testimony, including their own, before the TNEC. They charged that Cook's use of statistics was misleading and that he had not included all pertinent data. Among other things, the oilmen pointed out that Cook had neglected to mention that pipeline rates had been substantially reduced during the 1930's prior to the ICC's preliminary order of 1940.[67] They also specifically challenged his statement that the "typical minimum tender on crude oil is 50,000 barrels." According to Farish and Pew, the most common minimum tender was 10,000 barrels, used by over one-third of 48 interstate crude-oil pipeline companies.[68] Furthermore, Cook had not noted that contamination problems made a minimum tender necessary.

In his rejoinder, Cook did not spend much time on pipelines. For the most part he stuck by his earlier statements, pointing out that Farish and Pew had not in some instances specifically answered or denied them. On other points, such as the minimum tender question, he showed that 100,000 barrels minimum tender was required as of January 1, 1940, by five large companies and that statistics as of that year sustained his original statement. While he admitted that pipeline rates had been reduced during the 1930's, he quoted the ICC as authority that lines in existence for ten years or more had already paid for themselves and that this was especially true for large companies. As in the case of oral testimony before the TNEC, this exchange did not constitute a meaningful dialogue because neither side was prepared to admit that the other had a case. However, portions of the pipeline commentary by Dow and Farish were reprinted by the National Association of Manufacturers in 1942 as part of a book entitled *Fact and Fancy in the T.N.E.C. Monographs* containing reviews of the 43 monographs issued.[69] Meantime, the Justice Department had set out to prove in the courts that there was more fact than fancy to charges against the integrated oil industry.

FROM INVESTIGATION TO ACTION

For a decade the integrated oil industry and its pipeline sector had been criticized, investigated, and attacked by members of Congress, independent oilmen, and public administrators, but all this was only a prelude to one of the most comprehensive antitrust actions in American history. In September 1940, the Justice Department filed an antitrust suit against 22 integrated oil companies, their subsidiaries and affiliates, and the industry's leading trade association — the API. In addition, three cases were filed charging violation of the Elkins Act in the payment of pipeline dividends to parent companies. Because of its wide-ranging indictments of the integrated oil industry, the antitrust case was known as the "Mother Hubbard" case. The Justice Department's press release of September 30, 1940, said: "This proceeding is being instituted under the Department's policy of taking up in a single investigation or proceeding all of the restraints which affect the distribution of a product from the raw material to the consumer. Only in this way can economic results be achieved." The Elkins Act cases were described as "representative proceedings to clarify the law with respect to all cases where pipelines are owned by the major oil companies."

A new era in the oil industry's relations with the federal government was about to begin. Belated action both by oil-company management and by the ICC had not been sufficient to allay the suspicions of Justice Department officials, encouraged by some segments of the industry, that pipeline power and integration in the oil industry had been used to the disadvantage of nonintegrated concerns and the public. The Roosevelt administration's increased interest in the use of antitrust policy as a remedial device, coupled with the opportunity afforded by the TNEC investigation to review the operation of the integrated oil industry, provided the impetus for the Justice Department to challenge the results of three decades of oil-industry growth since the Standard Oil dissolution of 1911. From this initiative were to flow important consequences for the pipeline sector of the industry.

CHAPTER 16

ANTITRUST CONFLICT AND COMPROMISE

A complicated sequence of events brought interstate oil pipelines in late 1941 under a new form of governmental supervision — a consent decree. Growing out of the antitrust action launched against the integrated oil industry by Thurman Arnold's Antitrust Division, the consent decree was the product of the actions and decisions of the parties directly at interest — the Justice Department and the oil industry — and of political pressures and national security considerations generated by the deepening involvement of the United States in defense preparations and finally in war itself. Not only was there conflict between various government agencies and departments and the oil industry, but within each group there was controversy over specific objectives, strategy, and tactics. Unlike the situation that had prevailed before the TNEC, where it was possible for opponents to maintain a relatively consistent role and position from start to finish, flexibility characterized the position of all participants in the new proceedings. The entire episode provides a fascinating case-study of government-business relations.

INITIATION OF ANTITRUST ACTION

At least as early as the spring of 1939, a general antitrust action against the integrated oil industry was being contemplated by the Justice Department. The appropriations bill to cover antitrust enforcement in the coming fiscal year contained an increase of $520,000 over fiscal 1939. Testifying in support of this request for increased funds, Arnold forecast a "cover-all suit" against the oil industry. Attorney General Frank Murphy declared that under a new concept of antitrust enforcement, unlawful restraints would be attacked broadly enough to cover the entire industry.[1]

The TNEC investigation provided Justice Department attorneys with an opportunity to familiarize themselves with the oil industry and to assess its vulnerabilities to antitrust action. As indicated in the preceding chapter, during the fall of 1939 government lawyers led the attack before the TNEC on existing practices in the industry.[2]

While the Justice Department prepared for action against the integrated oil industry, Senator Guy Gillette of Iowa was attempting to interest his colleagues in legislative divorcement of marketing from other integrated operations. In January 1938 Gillette had introduced a bill for this purpose, and in March of that year he joined with Senator Borah of Idaho in proposing a pipeline divorcement bill. Congressional involvement in neutrality legislation and the death of Senator Borah prevented action on these measures, but in the spring of 1940 Gillette reintroduced them on his own. At that time, he later told the Senate, Arnold approached him and stated that the Department of Justice was preparing antitrust action against the integrated oil industry. The Assistant Attorney General apparently asked Gillette to postpone hearings on the divorcement proposals, as a favor to the department, until they could be coordinated with the antitrust action. The Senator agreed to cooperate, but months passed without further word from Arnold, and Gillette grew impatient.[3]

The proposed action of the Antitrust Division against the oil industry had been complicated by insertion of defense considerations into the picture. The outbreak of war in Europe in September 1939 had raised important questions on the United States's defense preparedness. To consider these matters the President appointed a Council of National Defense. An Advisory Commission of eleven members, the majority of them representatives of large oil companies, aided the council in considering problems relating to the oil industry. Since antitrust action relating to the oil industry would have a bearing on the industry's ability to perform defense functions, the Justice Department asked the council for comment.

The draft complaint, as mentioned in Chapter 15, was directed primarily against 22 major companies, their subsidiaries, and affiliates. In addition to charging price-fixing and similar abuses, the draft asked that the companies named be forced to divest themselves of their transportation and marketing facilities. For a number of weeks in the summer of 1940 the Defense Council's Oil Industry Advisory Commission reviewed these proposals in terms of defense requirements. Finally, the commission endorsed legal action to remove restraints on competition, but it opposed divorcement of marketing and transportation facilities. In the commission's opinion, such attempts to force structural changes by antitrust action would "becloud relationships between the Government and industry," result in complications and delays in defense preparations, and threaten efficient management of a vital industry.[4] These recommendations were accepted by Attorney General Robert H. Jackson,[5] who in the interim had been under mounting pressure from Gillette to expedite antitrust action.

On Monday, September 30, 1940, the Justice Department announced that it had filed suit in the Federal District Court for the District of Columbia against 22 major oil companies, their subsidiaries, and affiliates, and against the industry's trade association, the American Petroleum Institute. The action against the oil companies and API charged violation of Sections 1, 2, and 3 of the Sherman Antitrust Act and of Sections 2 and 3 of the Clayton Act. The government claimed that the companies, with the assistance of API, had conspired to fix the price of crude and control petroleum transportation, distribution, and sales. As a remedy for these and other alleged violations of the antitrust law, the complaint asked for an injunction against continuation of these practices and dissolution of the API. On the subject of pipelines, the government alleged that the defendants had conspired to force independent producers to sell at the well under controlled conditions rather than providing them with common-carrier facilities. This pressure was brought to bear, the government charged, by the defendants' failure to provide common-carrier terminal facilities, by their maintenance of oppressive and onerous rates, by requirements for unreasonably large minimum tenders, and by other devices to limit use of pipelines to the advantage of the defendants. Similarly, they were charged with restricting the common-carrier use of gasoline pipelines. The defendants also allegedly received as refunds and rebates a substantial part of the revenue from their pipeline operations.[6]

The Elkins Act Pipeline Cases

In addition to the main action, the Justice Department simultaneously filed three pipeline cases alleging violation of the Elkins Act of 1903. The government's charge was that in paying dividends, the pipeline companies in question gave illegal rebates on published transportation rates to their shipper-owners. In December 1940, Arnold stated that the department's objective in this action was merely to force rates down to a point which would yield a "reasonable return." If this and other adjustments could be made to facilitate common-carrier usage, the government had no desire to press the rebate or penalty issues.[7] In January 1941, perhaps for bargaining purposes, Arnold took the more extreme position that the law forbade a shipper from accepting *any* dividends from a subsidiary carrier. However, he conceded that the law on this point was not settled.[8] Viewed in these terms, a "rebate" consisted of the difference between the costs of pipeline operation and the corresponding tariff rates.[9]

Elkins Act complaints had been prepared against 59 pipeline companies,[10] but 3 were selected as representative when it came to actually filing charges. One complaint was against Phillips Petroleum Company and Phillips Pipe Line Company,[11] representing a situation where a common-carrier pipeline facility, previous to July 1, 1940, a separate corporate entity, had been transferred to departmental status in the shipper-owner company. Among other things, the complaint alleged that this organizational change was a mere device to permit continuation of illegal rebate practices. Another complaint was against Standard Oil Company (Indiana) and involved a case where the pipeline was a 100 per cent subsidiary of the parent company.[12] The third case, against Great Lakes Pipe Line,[13] involved a situation where the pipeline was a separately incorporated concern with eight shipper-owners. In the actions against Phillips and Indiana Standard, the government sought forfeiture of triple the amount of alleged rebates since January 1, 1939. In the Great Lakes case the government asked only that an injunction be issued prohibiting payment of dividends or other considerations

that represented rebates, refunds, or offsets and that the company be permanently enjoined from unjust discrimination against shippers.

To make the best possible case, the Antitrust Division took full advantage
of the undercapitalization of the pipeline companies and the large dividends
paid in terms of this base. Thus Phillips was charged with having paid
dividends in 1938–39 representing an average annual return of 89 per cent
on its capital stock.[14] Over the nine years preceding the complaint, Great
Lakes's dividend payments were said to have exceeded a 34 per cent annual
return on the paid-in price of its capital stock,[15] while Stanolind Pipe Line's
payments were claimed to have exceeded 36 per cent.[16]

The rebate idea as applied to pipelines was apparently a by-product of
the preparation of the over-all industry case. Justice Department staff members noted the large dividends paid to parent companies by pipeline affiliates or subsidiaries and the comparatively small amount of operating expense compared to total transportation revenue. Whether credit for the
rebate idea in connection with these transactions properly belongs to Justice
Department staffers or to a representative of independent marketers and a
close associate of Senator Gillette is not clear.[17] In any case, by the spring
of 1940 the idea was also in the public domain. Forrest R. Black, writing
in the *Cornell Law Quarterly* in June 1940, put the pipelines' alleged violation of the Elkins Act in terms of pipeline owners shipping at cost while
others paid the published transportation rate.[18]

Whether the Elkins Act cases represented an antitrust or regulatory action assumes some significance in view of their outcome, which required
leading pipeline companies to report annually to the Justice Department as
well as to the ICC. The background of the Elkins Act provides some clues
to its interest and use in this connection. Because the intense rivalry between
railroads in the nineteenth century had led to special rates, rebates, and
other devices to attract and retain business despite the discrimination
against shippers who did not enjoy this favored treatment, the Interstate
Commerce Act of 1887 declared common carriers who engaged in such
practices to be guilty of unjust discrimination.[19] The weakness of this provision in practice led in 1903 to the adoption of the Elkins Act which made it
a misdemeanor, subject to substantial fines, to grant or accept rebates or
similar concessions that resulted in property being transported at a lesser
rate than the one named in tariffs.[20] The Hepburn Act of 1906 further
amended the Elkins Act to make the shipper who received or accepted
rebates subject to forfeiture to the United States of triple the amount of
money or value of other considerations so received. Imprisonment, dropped
in the 1903 act, was restored as a penalty. Initiative in such proceedings
could come from either the Attorney General or the ICC.[21] Thus, despite
the primary jurisdiction of the ICC over pipelines, the Justice Department
could maintain that rates and rebates were also properly matters for its
concern.[22]

The circumstances under which the Elkins Act pipeline cases were introduced certainly suggest that they were conceived as adjuncts to antitrust

enforcement. The fact that the same alleged offenses were also included as part of the conspiracy charges in the over-all Mother Hubbard antitrust case strengthens the case for this interpretation.

NEGOTIATIONS FOR SETTLEMENT

Arnold's conception of these cases was presented to industry representatives in December 1940. Atlantic Refining Company, one of the defendants in the Mother Hubbard case, had retained the Philadelphia law firm of Ballard, Spahr, Andrews & Ingersoll to represent its interests. A casual dinner table conversation between Sturgis Ingersoll, one of the partners, and another member of the Philadelphia bar, Francis Biddle, who was then Solicitor General of the United States, led to Biddle's suggestion that Arnold be approached directly. "I'm sure Mr. Arnold would welcome the opportunity to talk," the Solicitor General reportedly told Ingersoll.[23]

On December 20, 1940, a meeting arranged by Biddle took place between Arnold and members of his staff and three members of Ingersoll's firm, including Charles I. Thompson, who played an important part in subsequent negotiations. On this occasion the Assistant Attorney General proposed exploration of both the Mother Hubbard and pipeline cases on the basis of negotiation.[24] Although a consent decree was not mentioned, it probably figured in the department's offer to negotiate.

The consent decree device, first used in 1906, had gained considerable popularity as a means of settling civil antitrust suits. The product of negotiation between government attorneys and antitrust defendants, the decree can be entered with a Federal Court and stand as the court's judgment. On the other hand it does not represent a trial of the issues on their merits, it is usually cheaper and quicker to negotiate a decree than to settle the same problem by litigation, and it gives each side some control over its concessions to the opposing group. A decree normally does not represent evidence or admission of alleged offenses and it cannot be used as prima-facie evidence to substantiate triple damage suits by private parties under the antitrust laws. As a result, over half the antitrust equity actions initiated by the government between 1906 and 1940 had been settled on this negotiated basis. Arnold presumably had a similar solution in mind for the oil industry and pipeline cases. However, by early 1941, neither side was committed to more than exploratory negotiations.

At the December 1940 meeting with oil company representatives, Arnold declared that he was not interested in the divorcement of pipelines but only in making them conform more closely to the common-carrier role specified for them by Congress. In short, he seemed to be advocating that the Justice Department perform the role assigned by Congress to the ICC. Although he conceded that pipelines were different from railroads and could be regarded as plant facilities, he maintained that tariffs should be revised downward "so that the pipelines would earn no more than a reasonable return, plus some reasonable adjustment as respects tender requirements and terminal facilities available for independent shippers." [25] In entering the area entrusted by law to the ICC, Arnold was apparently most interested in general leverage to force a settlement of the Mother Hubbard case. In fact, he indicated that if the objectives he outlined could be obtained, the government would be happy to postpone the pipeline suits and would not attempt to collect penalties.[26]

To use the pipeline cases to force the oil industry to settle the Mother Hubbard case by consent decree required emphasis on the size of the triple penalties that might be collected as a result of the Elkins Act proceedings. The department estimated the penalties at 1.6 billion dollars while the industry placed the figure as high as 2.5 billions.[27] If the government actually litigated these cases and won a favorable verdict even in a lower court, the results could have been financially catastrophic for the industry and embarrassing to the government which wanted to discipline, but not to ruin, a key industry. Even though later set aside, the size of the fine levied by Judge Kenesaw Landis in his decision in the 1908 Elkins Act case against Indiana Standard must have been in the minds of both government and industry representatives.[28] In comparison with the stakes in the pending case, that fine had been a trifle. Arnold's initial strategy seemed to be to keep this kind of threat hanging over the defendants in the hope that it would induce settlement on other issues, but at the same time not to let the Elkins Act cases get into the courts if this could be avoided.

To maintain this position was not easy. The view that pipelines were merely a side issue was not shared by some members of Arnold's staff and certainly not by Senator Gillette. The Senator had been induced to postpone his legislative divorcement proposals on the basis of the Justice Department's proposed legal action. When the divorcement provisions of the antitrust case were dropped in deference to the views of the Council of National Defense, Gillette was far from pleased.[29] As a result it seemed probable that any arrangements worked out between the Justice Department and the integrated oil industry would have to be approved by Gillette.

Since the entire integrated oil industry had been attacked, determination of over-all strategy by consultation and cooperation in its execution was to be expected. By January 1941 industry representatives had decided that it was advisable to negotiate with the department if it could be done on acceptable terms. A number of considerations led to this decision. The attitude of the courts was judged to be such that the government could be expected to win at least some of the points in the Mother Hubbard case. While such an outcome was less clear with respect to the pipeline rebate charges, the size of the penalties involved made it advisable to take the least possible risks and presumably negotiation was less risky than litigation. Since the ICC had issued its preliminary rate order in December 1940 and the Justice Department seemed to share somewhat the same objectives as the ICC, negotiation might lead to a solution satisfactory to both agencies and put the implementation into the hands of the ICC. In short, negotiation offered the hope that regulatory action could be substituted for antitrust action. Industry representatives considered it significant and favorable that Arnold was willing to negotiate, and by following this path the industry could possibly fend off adverse publicity and perhaps forestall more drastic legislative action at a future time.[30]

After another meeting with Arnold on January 29, 1941, where the Assistant Attorney General declared that the department would not insist on the usual form of a decree making the signatories punishable for contempt, representatives of the oil companies decided to accept his suggestion and appoint a small committee to work with the department. That afternoon the committee was selected. Colonel Harry Klein of the Texas Company was named chairman. The other members were Edwin S. Hall of Jersey Standard, John E. Green, Jr., of Gulf Oil, Buell F. Jones of Indiana Standard, Don Emery of Phillips Petroleum Company, James J. Cosgrove of Continental Oil Company, and Charles I. Thompson, outside counsel for Atlantic Refining Company.[31] For the next 11 months this group worked to find a settlement that would be acceptable to their principals and to the Justice Department, whose negotiating staff was headed by Mac Asbill.

The first of the exploratory meetings took place February 10, 1941. At that time department representatives, headed by Asbill, submitted proposed topics for discussion and outlined their view of the case. Although conveniently reserving final decisions to higher authority in the department, the staff proposed to treat the antitrust and pipeline rebate cases as a single issue to be settled in a single decree.[32] The staff maintained that the economic objectives of the department were twofold: (1) to force pipelines to be operated as common carriers in fact as well as form and (2) to force a reduction in rates so that independent producers could seek their own markets via pipeline if they so desired.[33] The staff did not feel that the exercise of the ICC's authority to establish maximum reasonable pipeline rates was any barrier to Justice Department action on the rebate question.[34]

While there was some indication that rebate penalties might be dismissed, the staff's position on the future level of acceptable rates had not crystallized. In their initial working paper they had suggested that rates be set on a basis that would "not produce gross revenues in excess of costs of operation and such funds and moneys as may be necessary to secure continued and efficient operation of each pipeline." [35] But what this meant specifically was not clear — even to them. The industry committee indicated that it would end negotiations if this provision were interpreted to mean pipelines could charge only "cost" rates, but the staff neither affirmed nor denied that this was their objective.

During February and March 1941, each side explored the limits to which the other could be pushed. The Asbill group was firm that it would not settle for transfer of the pipeline question to the ICC, and the industry committee was equally firm that it would not accept litigation of the pipeline cases in order to settle the Mother Hubbard case.[36] Both groups agreed that the problem of products lines was substantively different from that of crude-oil lines, but neither came up with satisfactory means of acknowledging the difference.[37] Nevertheless, the government and industry groups developed a working relationship that seemed mutually satisfactory.

Further progress was temporarily threatened in early March by the intervention of Arnold, who reappeared on the scene, apparently at the urging of Dr. George Stocking,* adviser to the department's consent decree group. This element of Arnold's staff wanted to take a sterner stand than the negotiators led by Asbill, whom industry negotiator Charles Thompson described as "cooperative, constructive, and reasonably sympathetic toward the industry points of view which we presented." [38] After inquiring into the procedure being used by Asbill, however, Arnold permitted negotiations to continue as before.[39] By this time Asbill and his associates, Watson Snyder and Frederick Berquist, had seemingly conceded that they were not so interested in pipeline rates or tariffs per se as in the alleged rebates. For its part, the industry committee had concluded that any consent decree as to pipelines should only be directed against payment of an excess over a reasonable return to a shipper-owner out of rates paid by him and that profit derived from transporting for third parties was not an issue.[40]

The ICC's decision in the Petroleum Rail Shippers Association case became relevant to these negotiations. The Commission had indicated that maximum reasonable rates for products lines should not return more than 10 per cent on carrier valuation and that such lines should accept minimum tenders of as little as 5,000 barrels to be held in storage until a 25,000 barrel batch was ready for movement.[41] Thus the ICC was on record as to what constituted a maximum reasonable return on valuation of both crude (8 per cent) and products (10 per cent) pipelines. Apparently encouraged by these decisions, the Asbill group in early April 1941 proposed that the pipeline section of the Mother Hubbard complaint be settled on the basis that a yet-to-be-specified percentage of return on the latest final ICC valuation of carrier property would not be considered a rebate, concession, or other form of discrimination.[42] This basic decision underlay all subsequent negotiations.

There were still complications. Phillips Petroleum, with its major interest in products lines, felt that rate of return was only one factor to be considered when setting rates. Phillips' position was that the ICC was not only empowered but also best equipped to decide such matters, and it was prepared to leave the decision in the ICC's hands without right of appeal. However, the Justice Department staff was not willing to have the regulatory agency decide the question of what level of rates would result in rebates.[43] On the other hand, the staff was willing to concede that an acceptable rate of return should be considered in terms of an entire system and not in terms of its various segments.[44] Although the industry committee was ready to proceed further on this basis, Arnold again gave Thompson and his colleagues pause by declaring that he would have to show whatever

---

*Dr. Stocking's analysis of the oil industry (*The Oil Industry and the Competitive System: A Study in Waste* [Boston: Houghton Mifflin, 1925]) won the Hart, Schaffner & Marx economic essay contest in 1924.

decree materialized to such industry critics as Senator Gillette, Congressman John M. Coffee, and Paul Hadlick before the decree was entered. Edwin S. Hall of the negotiating committee indicated that such a procedure would be unacceptable, at least at that stage of the proceedings, and Arnold did not insist on it.[45]

However, the framing of a decree was not to be resolved so easily. While the industry committee worked with Asbill and his colleagues, another group in the Justice Department was preparing a more restrictive document. When it was presented in the latter part of May, industry negotiators were dismayed to find that it contained provisions contrary to their understanding with Arnold, as they interpreted it, and apparently directed toward divorcement of pipeline and marketing facilities — a matter that they thought had been disposed of months before. In view of these developments, the negotiating committee terminated its work and sought the aid of Solicitor General Biddle and Attorney General Jackson. This decision was reached amidst lowering war clouds and a fast-growing national emergency.

The Issue of a Defense Pipeline

Although the United States was not yet involved in overt hostilities, it was committed to aiding the powers fighting Hitler, and oil was becoming an increasingly vital resource in the conflict. In March, Congress had passed the Lend-Lease Act; on May 27, President Roosevelt declared an unlimited national emergency, and on the following day appointed Secretary of the Interior Harold L. Ickes, whom many oil men feared as an advocate of federal control of their industry, to the post of Petroleum Coordinator for National Defense. Industry fears were relieved somewhat on June 4, 1941, when Ickes named Ralph K. Davies of Standard Oil of California as Deputy Coordinator with authority coequal to his own.[46]

As these developments took place, Schofield Andrews and Charles Thompson of Atlantic's outside counsel discussed the latest impasse in the consent decree negotiations with Solicitor General Biddle and Attorney General Jackson. The latter promised to do what he could to straighten out the problem,[47] and on June 3 he wrote to Ickes that the Justice Department would take no final stand on negotiations with the oil industry until the Petroleum Coordinator had been consulted. Similarly, no new antitrust actions would be taken without consultation.[48] On June 16, Ickes replied: "As you suggest, both pending and prospective litigation involving alleged violations of the antitrust laws by units of the oil industry should be examined in the light of their economic aspects and their effect upon national defense." [49]

While the Justice Department had been negotiating over the pipeline cases, other branches of the government were becoming increasingly impressed with the need for additional pipeline facilities. Since the summer of 1940, the Interior Department had been studying the problem of supplying the East Coast with crude and refined products in the event that tanker transportation was adversely affected as the result of war emergency. In the spring of 1941 two major privately financed pipeline projects were under way. Jersey Standard, Standard of Kentucky, and Shell already had made significant progress on the Plantation Pipe Line, designed to transport products between Baton Rouge, Louisiana, and Greensboro, North Carolina. Gulf and Pure had a products line under construction from Port St. Joe, Florida, to Chattanooga, Tennessee. However, in each instance opposition from the railroads and the intransigence of the Georgia state legislature in granting pipelines the right of eminent domain had made it impossible to complete the rights of way over railroad property. This crisis became a matter of national concern when, in April 1941, 50 American tankers were diverted from their regular runs to a "shuttle" service for the benefit of the British, who picked up the cargoes of products from the Caribbean and Gulf Coast in New York and Halifax and transported them across the Atlantic in their own bottoms. With the strong urging of the President, therefore, Congress adopted a bill, sponsored by Congressman William Cole of Maryland, that enabled interstate pipeline companies to exercise the right of eminent domain when the President determined that such action was in the interest of national defense. This act became law on July 30, 1941.[50]

These fast-moving events furnished the immediate background for industry and government strategy with respect to the pending Mother Hubbard and Elkins Act cases in the summer of 1941. The industry defendants hoped to make their contribution to the accelerating defense effort impregnable to future antitrust action and at the same time to use the need for additional tankers and pipeline facilities as a basis for reaching some settlement of the pending cases. Therefore, in late June the negotiating committee suggested a settlement of the pipeline cases by transferring the question of reasonable rates to the ICC for determination and by getting the defendants to agree to pay no more than 8 per cent dividends on crude-oil lines and 10 per cent on products lines until the ICC came up with a final rate order. In return the government was asked to discontinue the existing suits and to state that the proposed level of dividends did not violate the Elkins Act.[51] This settlement was to be accompanied by a partial or final decree in the antitrust case. However, neither the Justice Department nor Ickes was amenable to these suggestions. Asbill declared that the industry representatives' draft had emasculated key points on which the Justice Department staff had to insist.[52] A representative of Ickes reported that the Petroleum Coordinator would not tolerate any effort by the industry to trade off pipeline construction for dismissal of the Elkins Act cases. Before he would be a party to such an agreement, he would ask that the government itself build the necessary pipelines.[53]

By early August 1941 it was clear that the rapidity of changes taking place in connection with the defense emergency might make it impossible to settle the Mother Hubbard case, but there was still a possibility that the Elkins Act cases could be cleared up in connection with the industry's construction of government-approved emergency pipelines. For some months a group of East Coast oil companies, with Ickes' encouragement, had been considering the possibilities of a 20-inch or larger crude-oil pipeline from east Texas to the Philadelphia-Bayonne area. An industry-financed engineering study was in progress during the summer under the direction of W. R. "Cap" Finney, a leading pipeline engineer, and two companion products lines were also under consideration.[54] Colonel Klein, chairman of the negotiating committee, reported on August 5, 1941, to Robert H. Colley, president of Atlantic Refining, that the defense pipeline project had been successfully attached to a proposed settlement of the Elkins Act cases.[55] This development had come about primarily as a result of Ickes' initiative in asking the oil industry to build a very expensive emergency pipeline. To finance it, however, the East Coast oil companies had to be allowed to earn a rate of return that the Justice Department had seemingly condemned in bringing the Elkins Act cases.[56]

To meet the respective needs of the government and the oil industry, some adjustment of their positions was necessary. In July, Ickes' representatives, together with Arnold and the industry negotiating committee, had arrived at what seemed to be a mutually satisfactory basis for drawing a final pipeline decree. It was to be based on a limitation of dividend payments. The only major obstacle was determination of what rate of return could be paid to shipper-owners in the form of pipeline dividends. For their yardstick, industry representatives again turned to the ICC findings of 10 per cent on ICC valuation for products lines and 8 per cent for crude-oil lines. The Justice Department started at a low figure and gradually came up to 6 per cent, while the industry representatives finally agreed to 8 per cent for both crude and products lines. At this point neither side was willing to make further concessions, but the impasse was quickly broken by Francis Biddle, now the Acting Attorney General. Informed by Arnold that negotiations had come to a halt over a question of two percentage points, Biddle suggested the obvious: split the difference. Both sides then agreed to accept 7 per cent on valuation as the figure for permissible dividend payments.[57]

While the Executive Branch of the government was growing increasingly anxious to settle with the oil industry, Senator Gillette continued to express reservations. Arnold had kept the Senator informed of progress towards a decree, but the Iowan only went along reluctantly. According to Charles I. Thompson of the industry negotiating committee, Gillette disliked abandonment of the government's claim for penalties under the Elkins Act and he felt that the principle of the decree — a limitation on dividends — was wrong because it left both rates and earnings unregulated. In the end, Gillette's agreement to the proposed decree was obtained only on the understanding that the industry would build and finance the national defense pipeline.[58]

The industry's construction of this pipeline posed some difficult problems. Participating companies naturally wanted protection against antitrust action in connection with their collective effort; but, such approval by the Justice Department would in effect confirm situations that it had under attack in the existing Mother Hubbard case. The agreement signed by 11 East Coast oil companies on September 5, 1941, to form National Defense Pipelines, Inc., raised the antitrust issue specifically. The preamble stated that implementation was contingent on a written request from the Petroleum Coordinator for provision of the facilities, qualification for the benefits conveyed by the recent Cole Act, approval by the Assistant Attorney General in charge of antitrust, and a decree from the court holding jurisdiction over the Mother Hubbard case "wherein it is adjudged and decreed that the concerted activities of the parties hereinafter set forth are not in violation of the Anti-Trust or other laws of the United States." [59] When later questioned as to whether the last provision in effect legitimatized activities under attack in the API case, Charles Thompson replied affirmatively. "The lawyers who permitted the industry without such a condition to build that pipeline should have had their heads examined," the lawyer said. [60]

At this point it still appeared that industry difficulties with the Justice Department could be resolved by two separate actions. Acceptance of a consent decree stipulating a maximum return of 7 per cent on ICC valuation to be paid shipper-owners in the form of dividends would end the Elkins Act cases. A stipulation and decree in the Mother Hubbard case as part of the defense pipeline operation would postpone or eliminate that problem. Accordingly, counsel for defendants met at the Raleigh Hotel in Washington on September 16, 1941, and with a few exceptions signed the pipeline decree. Gulf, Jersey, and Humble were the hold-outs, but tactical considerations — not opposition to the decree — apparently dictated their position. [61] The signatures obtained on September 16 were left in the possession of Colonel Klein, chairman of the negotiating committee, pending further developments.

In the interim several events had taken place that jeoparadized the settlement that industry members thought had been achieved earlier in the month. On September 11 a Senate committee studying the gasoline and fuel-oil picture on the East Coast reported that it found no cause for alarm. Its report left the strong implication that the zeal of the Petroleum Coordinator was chiefly responsible for the view that government should take immediate measures to encourage construction of a transcontinental pipeline as a defense measure. [62] This interpretation was given added validity by the decision of the Allocations and Priority Division of the Office of Production Management not to grant the necessary steel priorities to the proposed pipeline. [63] When this news reached Gillette's ears, he withdrew his approval of the consent decree in the Elkins Act cases, and without the Senator's consent, no decree was possible, according to Arnold. [64]

As a result of external events, a complex situation had developed. Virtually all the defendants had already signed their agreement to a consent decree in the pipeline cases, and figuratively the chief industry negotiator had the signatures in his hip-pocket ready to lay on the table at any time.

The chief of the Antitrust Division had not renounced the earlier agreement, but he would not go further without the approval of Senator Gillette. The Senator was unwilling to give this approval unless there was a *quid pro quo* — industry construction of the defense pipeline. The Petroleum Coordinator believed that such a line was essential, but congressional investigators disagreed. Thus, for a variety of reasons there was no opportunity for progress. Accordingly all parties simply marked time during the fall of 1941, waiting for something beyond their control to break the logjam. As it was becoming increasingly obvious that the nation's involvement in the war as a belligerent was only a matter of time, Thompson took the position that time was running in the industry's favor. The government would scarcely take drastic action against the defendants in the face of a national struggle for survival.[65]

One unanticipated development, however, shook both the industry and government negotiators. Phillips Petroleum Company had taken the position that determination of pipeline rates and common-carrier status were matters subject to ICC jurisdiction, not the Justice Department's.[66] Phillips apparently had not had time to assess the full implications of the industry's movement toward a consent decree. In any event, Phillips Petroleum had filed a request with the ICC in August 1941 to be relieved of its common-carrier pipeline status.[67] On the same day that other industry members signed the consent decree, the Justice Department learned of Phillips' action. To the antitrust group and to Senator Gillette this maneuver suggested a serious loophole in the proposed consent decree. Signatories could escape its obligations simply by giving up their common-carrier status. Gillette was outraged, and the industry was distressed by this apparent defection from a united front. The staff insisted that the loophole must be closed: Phillips would be excluded from the decree, but subject to separate action.

The Final Act

Intermittent industry contact with the Justice Department continued throughout the fall. On December 5, 1941, the negotiating committee submitted new draft decrees for both the Mother Hubbard and Elkins Act cases. The Justice Department staff seemed reluctant to consider them, and the industry was unwilling to take further steps. Two days later, however, the Japanese attack on Pearl Harbor changed the whole context of negotiations. Colonel Klein suggested to Mac Asbill on December 9 that the only feasible course would be to dismiss or postpone the Mother Hubbard case and to enter the pipeline consent decree that the defendants had signed on September 16. Asbill, much agitated by the war news, seemed favorably impressed with this solution to a situation that now clearly conflicted with national needs.[68]

Decisions were made quickly as the nation moved into a wartime situation. On December 11, Arnold informed Klein that the December 5 draft of a pipeline decree might be acceptable with a few changes, but it would also have to include additional provisions relating to minimum tenders and common-carrier failities.[69] Four days later, however, the Assistant Attorney General asked for a meeting with the negotiating committee on December 17. At that time he reported that the draft proposed to settle the Mother Hubbard case was "unsatisfactory" and that his staff was urging substantial changes in the proposed pipeline decree signed on September 16. Then, without further discussion, he proposed that a final settlement be reached on the basis of the September document without further changes. When this proposal was communicated to the industry, they accepted it unanimously.[70]

One can only speculate what had gone on behind the scenes in Washington. It is not too much to imagine that after the catastrophe of Pearl Harbor strong pressures for settlement of the pipeline controversy came from the very top levels of the administration. Francis Biddle, who had suggested the negotiations in the first place, had been elevated to Attorney General. He had intervened at another critical point — the determination of the percentage of return to be allowed by the draft decree — and he was clearly regarded by the oil industry as a friend at court. On November 3, for example, Thompson reported: "It does seem advisable to everybody that if, as, and when the opportunity arises, Biddle should be informed of the present status of the situation." [71] It appears quite likely, therefore, that by the middle of December he had been apprised of the deadlock in the negotiations. The industry also had support in the Petroleum Administration for War, which would have to handle the problem of supplying the military forces and the home front with oil.

Within the Justice Department, on the other hand, opposition to signing the decree in its existing form did not subside on the staff level. Mac Asbill, W. B. Watson Snyder, and H. Douglas Weaver, who had been engaged in the negotiations, declined to sign the judgment for reasons that have never been made clear.[72] As a result, the government signatories were Biddle and Arnold, plus Edward M. Curran, United States Attorney, whose participation was merely formal.[73]

The speed and manner in which the negotiations were brought to a sudden close were particularly galling to Representative Coffee of the state of Washington. On April 23, 1942, he introduced a resolution in the House of Representatives asking for an investigation.[74] Among other things, he wanted to know why an "appropriate" committee of Congress was not consulted, why the test cases were not adjudicated, who had participated in the decision, "what inducements" were offered to the Justice Department to agree to the decree, and what action would be necessary to recover the fines and penalties that the government had foregone. However, this request was lost amidst the press of other business.

The formal conclusion of the proceedings took place in the District Court for the District of Columbia on December 23, 1941. The government entered its complaint and prayed for relief. The court then accepted the draft decree of September 16, 1941, as its final judgment "without trial or adjudication of any issue of fact or law herein and without admission by any party in respect of any such issue and in final settlement of all claims herein on issue." [75]

PROVISIONS OF THE CONSENT DECREE

The decree applied to defendant common-carrier pipelines engaged in carrying crude oil, and petroleum products (excluding natural gas) in interstate commerce, where the shipper-owner employed the line for transportation and was entitled to share in its net earnings. No defendant common-carrier was to "credit, give, grant, or pay, directly or indirectly, through or by any means or device whatsoever" to a shipper-owner for any calendar year, commencing January 1, 1942, "any earnings, dividends, sums of money or other valuable considerations derived from transportation or other common carrier services which in the aggregate is in excess of its share of seven percentum (7%) of the valuation of such common carrier's property," if the carrier had transported for its shipper-owner during that calendar year.

Valuation, which subsequently became a source of controversy, was to be based on "the latest final valuation" of the ICC brought down to date by the carrier in accordance with specified methods, about which controversy also developed. In the absence of a final ICC valuation, methods were set forth for approximating it. Amounts within the permitted 7 per cent that were earned but not paid could be distributed in any subsequent year unless they had been invested in common-carrier facilities and included in valuation. Earnings above 7 per cent could be invested in such facilities but not included in the valuation on which future dividends could be paid. Such excess earnings were to be segregated in a surplus account. Except to retire debt already in existence and incurred for common-carrier facilities, or to build and acquire facilities which could not be included in the valuation for dividend purposes, or to maintain working capital, these funds were effectively "frozen" until the sale, dissolution, transfer, or divorcement of the carrier. If a defendant pipeline did not earn the permitted 7 per cent, an amount equal to the difference could be paid to the shipper-owner in any one or more of the next three suceeding years, but not thereafter.

Other provisions of the decree were primarily procedural. Each defendant common carrier was to report annually, on April 15, to the Attorney General financial information relevant to the decree. Knowing violation of the decree's restrictions subjected the violator to a penalty of three times the amount of the prohibited payment. The government's rights in the Mother Hubbard case were specifically protected, while the defendants were specifically safeguarded in their rights under the Cole Act. The District Court retained jurisdiction over the case for the purpose of construing, modifying, and enforcing it.

The ambiguities of the decree were later to create major problems of interpretation for the companies subject to it. In fact, a substantial part of the remainder of this study will be concerned with such questions. However, as of December 1941 the decree provided a welcome solution to a problem that had to be resolved in order to meet the war crisis.

The decree was signed by 20 major oil companies, 52 pipeline companies, and 7 affiliates or subsidiaries of major companies.[76] Phillips Petroleum Company was among the group, as were Gulf, Humble, and Jersey Standard. The suits against Phillips, Great Lakes, and Indiana Standard were dismissed simultaneously. The court also signed an order which extended the time for filing answers, motions, and other pleadings in the Mother Hubbard case, until July 20, 1942, and the case was subsequently continued from time to time until it was finally dropped. Meantime in 1943 Arnold was quietly boosted onto the federal bench as the Roosevelt administration sharply curtailed antitrust activity in favor of more pressing cooperation with business in the war effort.

THE CONSENT DECREE NEGOTIATIONS IN PERSPECTIVE

The government's side of the consent decree negotiations has never been made public. Therefore, the preceding account comes primarily from the files of industry negotiators and, most specifically, from those of Charles Thompson, now deceased. Since he supplemented these written records with his own testimony before the Celler Committee investigating the consent decree program in 1957, the account of the proceedings is presumably accurate as far as it goes. From them, directly and by inference, it is possible to reconstruct what took place on the government's side as well as on the industry's. In view of the significance of the results, it is well worth reviewing the over-all record for insights on objectives, strategy, and accomplishments of both the government and the defendants.

Arnold's strategy seems somewhat inconsistent with his stated objectives. Formally he maintained that the action against pipelines was designed to make them common carriers; however, he admitted that they were essentially plant facilities. Logically, then, to achieve his formally stated objective he should have pressed for divorcement; yet he specifically renounced this course, partly, it must be assumed, because the Council of National Defense had opposed such drastic action as contrary to the national interest. In any event, Arnold stated in December 1940 that his aim was to reduce the rate of return on pipelines to the point where common carriage would be encouraged, and a year later he was still insisting that any settlement of the controversy must provide for reduced minimum tender requirements and easy access to common-carrier facilities. The industry position throughout the negotiations was that determination of rate questions and common-carrier obligations were matters already assigned by statute to the ICC. Consequently the basic strategy of its negotiations was to get the regulatory commission into the picture.

But the real objectives of both sides seem to have been somewhat different from the formal positions that they took. An examination of the record suggests that Arnold was primarily interested in using the pipeline cases as a lever to force settlement of the Mother Hubbard case. By comparison, the pipeline issue was a minor one. What gave it importance in the eyes of both the government and the industry was the size of the penalties involved if the cases were litigated. The industry's basic objective appears to have been to minimize the risk of incurring even a part of these penalties. Arnold wanted to keep the maximum threat before the industry but not to invoke a test of it.

Elkins Act violations were clearly within the jurisdiction of the Justice Department under the terms of the Hepburn Act of 1906, and by equating dividends with rebates the department was able to thrust itself squarely into the whole complicated relationship between pipeline rates, earnings, dividends, and the carriage of proprietary and nonproprietary traffic. Although the industry challenged the department's claim that it had jurisdiction in these areas, the industry could ill-afford to press its case to a legal determination that might have catastrophic repercussions. Since Arnold admitted the dividend-rebate argument represented a new and untested interpretation of the law, negotiation offered an "out" to each side. For the Justice Department it offered the possibility that the industry might agree to settle the Mother Hubbard case without a court battle. For the industry, negotiation offered the possibility of avoiding a court's finding that the Justice Department's rebate contentions were justified and awarding large fines and penalties on that basis.

As negotiations progressed, the department negotiators seemed increasingly willing to confine their demands to the rebate question viewed in terms of the relationship of dividends to ICC valuation. If the department had any case and jurisdiction, the Hepburn Act put it on the strongest ground in this area. A settlement based on rate of return was also the least painful to the industry because it still left room for a broad range of decision-making. For example, a limitation on dividends, especially when applied with respect to the valuation for a whole system instead of its component parts, left the matter of specific rates to managerial discretion. By April 1941 negotiators had begun to focus on this possible area of agreement.

Neither the industry nor the department moved toward their respective objectives in a direct line, partly because within each group there was disagreement over what the objectives should be. Both sides attempted to preserve maneuvering room by turning day-to-day negotiations over to small working committees. Thus, for practical purposes, Asbill represented contact with the department as far as industry negotiators were concerned. This situation gave Arnold the opportunity to intervene periodically to confirm, deny, or supplement what his representatives were doing. At the same time, by raising him above the level of routine negotiations, this tactic gave the staff considerable importance in the determination of specific objectives.

It is quite obvious that one group in the department felt that no concessions should be made to the industry while the group actually entrusted with negotiations was more inclined to entertain industry arguments. Arnold's sporadic intervention in the proceedings and shifts in his own position probably reflected the pulling and hauling of these two elements of his staff, not to mention the pressures brought to bear by Senator Gillette and his followers.

The industry succeeded generally in maintaining a common front and consistent position, though using the same flexible negotiating tactics as the opposition. The Phillips' unilateral decision to seek relief from common-carrier status was the single notable exception.

The times also had a great deal to do with the actual course of negotiations, and generally this factor favored the industry's position. If Arnold had a lever in the size of the potential penalties under the Elkins Act, the industry had a countervailing force in the form of the deepening defense emergency. No responsible administration would deliberately create chaos in the oil industry in the face of an all-out war threat, and the industry knew it. In essence, this became the trump card in the game the negotiators were playing. In fact, the conflicting objectives of the Petroleum Coordinator and the Justice Department, both representing the government in different capacities, were brought into sharp contrast in connection with the national defense pipeline. To build the line under private auspices for national purposes required government approval of practices which one branch of government was condemning. Such were the inconsistencies forced on public policy by the realities of the changing situation.

While the industry attempted to make the most of the national defense pipeline issue, there were limits beyond which even Ickes, who favored the line, could not be pushed. In the end, two exogenous events — the Maloney committee's finding that fears of an East Coast gasoline and fuel oil shortage were exaggerated, and the refusal of an allocation of steel for the pipeline — deprived this industry weapon of much of its effectiveness.

One cannot but feel from a review of the record that, at least from midsummer 1941, officials in the higher levels of the Executive Branch were seeking ways to hasten a conclusion of the proceedings against the oil industry. The whole defense pipeline episode can be interpreted logically on this assumption. What was needed was some device that would allow the Justice Department to show interested Congressmen like Gillette that the national interest could be served by measures that fell short of changing the structure of the oil industry either directly by antitrust action or indirectly by means such as the Elkins Act prosecutions. The defense pipeline offered this opportunity and it was seen as such by Gillette. When its future was put in doubt, industry strategy was even more expressly geared to the idea that, in view of the worsening war situation, time was running in its favor. The attack on Pearl Harbor vindicated this strategy and in a little over two weeks led to a settlement.

Again reading between the lines, it seems likely that the speed with which the whole affair was brought to a close reflected pressure from the top level of the Roosevelt administration. The abruptness with which Arnold agreed to accept the draft of September 16 over the opposition of his staff, plus the unwillingness of his negotiating staff to sign the decree, lend credence to this interpretation. The fact that this draft was in existence and had already been accepted by most of the defendants, of course, was an important argument for adopting it. Yet it contained many ambiguities and cloaked many an unresolved question. Whether or not this feature, which conceivably could help as well as harm either side, was regarded as a positive reason for adopting that particular draft must remain an interesting speculation.

The consent decree climaxed a decade of sporadic conflict and cooperation between various arms of the federal government and the pipeline sector of the integrated oil industry. During those years both federal and state legislation had brought a measure of stability to the producing end of the industry threatened by the flood of oil from the Southwest. The Interstate Commerce Commission had taken the initiative to implement its pipeline regulatory responsibilities and had established criteria for reasonable maximum pipeline rates. Pipeline managements had been spurred by both industry and governmental developments to lower rates in important instances. The threat of legislative action to break up integrated oil operations, remained ever-present, however, though antitrust initiative to this end had been slowed, if not blunted, by the events of 1940–41. Pipeline managements had been confronted with many problems of adapting to a changing environment and, on the whole, they had succeeded in preserving more freedom of decision-making than many had first thought possible. Within the industry itself the introduction of gasoline pipelines had added a whole new dimension to transportation and marketing strategies. These changes formed the background against which the oil industry met the severest test in its history — supplying a vital resource in unprecedented volume to a nation engaged in global war.

PART

IV

The Wartime Experience,

1941-1946

CHAPTER 17

PIPELINES IN THE WAR EFFORT

When war challenges the great American industrial complex to prove its productive capacity, American businessmen have typically responded with enthusiasm. Under the stress of national emergency, differences between public officials and businessmen are suppressed in the common interest; businessmen even become government bureaucrats. Within industries, as well as between industry and government, competitive relationships give way to cooperative endeavors to achieve common goals. Such was the case during World War II.

The difficulties of supplying the East Coast with crude oil and refined products by tanker in a war emergency focused governmental and public attention on the strategic importance of overland pipeline transportation. The need for such facilities, as noted earlier, was the major factor leading the industry and the government to settle the Elkins Act charges against major pipelines on the basis of a consent decree. This decision also made it easier for the government to postpone further action in the antitrust case against the integrated oil industry. The same executives whom the Justice Department had lately accused of conspiring to violate public policy were soon being applauded by other branches of government for their constructive and successful contributions to the war effort.

In the endeavor to meet the demand for crude oil and petroleum products on the East Coast, government-financed pipelines embodied technological innovations — particularly with respect to diameter of pipe — that were to have a lasting impact. Private industry efforts also changed the nation's pipeline map appreciably. For these and other reasons, the World War II era marked a major turning point in the history of American petroleum pipelines.

OIL TRANSPORTATION ON THE EVE OF WAR

The general contours of the nation's pipeline system were well established by 1940 and had changed but little during the decade of national depression. Crude-oil trunk lines radiated from interior points in Texas, Louisiana, Oklahoma, and New Mexico toward the Gulf and major mid-western refining centers. Some oil from the Mid-Continent moved to these destinations. However, practically all the petroleum used in states along the eastern seaboard was delivered by tanker, with 90 per cent of it originating in Texas. Tanker deliveries of 64.3 million tons in 1940 consisted of 42 per cent crude oil, 24 per cent gasoline, 20 per cent fuel oil, and the remainder was composed of various products like kerosine and gas oil.[1] In the first quarter of 1941, pipelines (Illinois and Buckeye) were delivering only 46,000 barrels a day to the East Coast.[2]

The number of pipeline companies reporting to the ICC climbed from 49 in 1931 to 66 in 1940. In the latter year 100,000 miles of pipeline (trunk and gathering) moved nearly 283,000,000 barrel-miles of crude oil, and 23,700,000 barrel-miles of refined products flowed through trunk lines. Most of the gathering line mileage of that era was 2- or 4-inch diameter; most trunk-line was 8-inch. As of December 31, 1941, for example, 68.62 per cent of all trunk crude-oil lines had a diameter of 8 inches or less.[3] Over 95 per cent of refined-oil trunk lines fell into the same category.[4] Total refined-oil trunk-line mileage rose from just over 1,000 miles in 1930 to 9,000 in 1940.

Despite the volume of pipeline movements of petroleum and its products, barges and railroads were also important oil carriers in certain areas. A rapid development of barge movements of petroleum and its products took place on the Mississippi between 1937 and 1940. The 4,800,000 tons of crude oil and products moved on the river in 1940 was more than double comparable movements three years earlier. There was also some barge activity on the Ohio and Illinois rivers. The movement of both crude and products along the Gulf Intracoastal Waterway between Corpus Christi, Texas, and St. Marks, Florida, was very substantial and increased dramatically between 1937 and 1940.[5]

Railroads did not fare well in the petroleum trade, but in 1940 they were still a significant factor, especially in products shipments. Although railroad crude-oil originations dropped in the early 1930's, they were running between 5,000,000 and 6,000,000 tons in 1939 and 1940. Refined-oil rail shipments decreased from 47,400,000 tons in 1930 to 34,200,000 tons in 1940.

When large oil companies could see substantial transportation savings in building a pipeline, the railroads generally could do little to stop them. An important exception came to national attention in 1940–41, and for a time it threatened to delay the accelerating defense effort. The resolution of this difficulty by federal legislation provided one important cornerstone of the wartime pipeline effort.

THE SOUTHEASTERN AND PLANTATION PIPELINE PROJECTS

Before the war emergency developed, several large oil companies conceived and began to execute plans to transport refined products by pipeline into areas of the South and Southeast that later developed major defense significance. Gulf and Pure Oil combined their resources to build a products line from Port St. Joe, Florida, on the Gulf of Mexico northward to Tennessee, with numerous branches in Georgia. This 462-mile line was named the Southeastern Pipe Line. Jersey Standard undertook a more ambitious project in 1939 when it mapped an 812-mile gasoline line to run from Baton Rouge, Louisiana, to Greensboro, North Carolina. The Plantation Pipe Line, as it was later called, was projected to run from Louisiana Standard's Baton Rouge refinery via Birmingham and Atlanta to Greensboro, with 449 miles of laterals to various intermediate points such as Columbus and Macon, Georgia, and Chattanooga, Tennessee. Initially, Jersey had as a partner in this project Standard Oil of Kentucky, a marketing concern that bought its refined products from the Jersey-affiliated Louisiana Company.

Apparently to help reduce its investment and subsequent operating costs for this line, Jersey late in 1939 invited Shell Oil to take an interest. Shell responded with enthusiasm. Assuming a 25 per cent interest in the line, Shell analysts estimated that transportation savings over existing railroad rates would amount to $1,000,000 a year. On this basis the investment would be paid out in three and a half years.[6] Quite aside from protecting Shell's interests in Kentucky and Tennessee markets, participation in the pipeline also promised to give much-needed flexibility in refining operations. Shell's southern refinery at Norco, Louisiana, for example, could supply northern markets via Plantation while some of the load could be taken off the Wood River facility where midwestern refining was being concentrated.

As mentioned earlier, the Southeastern line ran into trouble in Georgia. Attempting to preserve their petroleum products business, the railroads refused to grant rights of way for the pipeline to cross their property. Southeastern fought back by initiating a civil antitrust action against seven railroad companies in the federal district court at Atlanta.[7] The railroads countered with a request for an injunction against the Georgia Highway Board to prevent its granting the pipeline the right to cross under state highways. A ruling by Georgia's Superior Court in April 1940, upholding the interpretation of the state's attorney general in favor of the Highway Board, dissolved the injunction.[8] However, in the absence of a Georgia law conferring the right of eminent domain on petroleum pipelines, the railroads were still able to block completion of the new products line. The backers of the Plantation project watched these developments with mounting concern, for their plans could not be completed until this obstacle was removed.

In the winter of 1940–41 the scene shifted from the courts to the Georgia state legislature, where Southeastern Pipe Line sought to obtain passage of a law giving it the right of eminent domain. The United States was becoming increasingly involved in efforts to aid hard-pressed Great Britain. Accordingly, the Southeastern and Plantation projects found support in Washington on the grounds that they were essential to the defense effort. Secretary Harold Ickes of the Interior Department, Secretary Frank Knox of the Navy Department, and finally the President himself appealed to

Georgia authorities to adopt the pending legislation. But these efforts were to no avail. The Georgia legislature voted down the eminent domain bill in March 1941.

As the intransigence of the railroads and the Georgia legislature seemed to be threatening the defense effort, Representative William Cole of Maryland introduced a bill in Congress to permit interstate pipeline companies to exercise the right of eminent domain when the President found it in the interest of national defense for them to do so. Such proceedings were to be initiated in the federal district court for the region where the land in question was located.

The Cole bill dealt with more than the matter of eminent domain. Under its provisions, private interests building pipelines needed for national defense were entitled to financial aid from the government. If private interests could not construct, complete, or extend essential pipelines, the government was specifically authorized to undertake this work. The President was also empowered to designate the agency or department to operate any such line. Unless otherwise specified by the President, a pipeline built in accordance with the act was subject to the relevant provisions of the Interstate Commerce and Natural Gas acts.

The sweeping powers conferred on the President by the House version of the Cole bill worried the Interstate Commerce Commission, for the Chief Executive could indefinitely suspend the application of the Interstate Commerce Act with respect to emergency pipelines. Accordingly, Chairman Joseph Eastman of the ICC requested that the Senate add a limiting amendment. Under its provisions, the powers of the President over pipelines were to terminate on June 30, 1943. This constituted a concession to the ICC. A companion provision, which limited government operation and maintenance of any emergency pipeline to a maximum of one year after the termination of the unlimited national emergency declared May 27, 1941, was a clear concession to the oil industry.

The amendment also required a proposed defense pipeline from east Texas to the Northeast, to become a common carrier after June 30, 1943. Although this provision introduced the possibility that the original shippers might have to share space with newcomers, the industry committee negotiating the consent decree thought that the short-run benefits of the pipeline outweighed the possible long-run disadvantages.[9] In any event, the Senate amendment was part of the law as finally adopted on July 30, 1941.[10]

When the Cole Act was passed, the Southeastern Pipe Line was already completed except for the crossings of railroad property; the Plantation Pipe Line was ready to start construction. The newly established Office of the Petroleum Co-ordinator recommended to President Roosevelt that both pipeline projects be accorded the right of eminent domain under the new legislation. By the end of August 1941 the appropriate steps had been taken. The Southeastern Line was quickly completed. Construction of Plantation began on September 1, 1941, and the line was in operation by the turn of the year.

One other line was an immediate beneficiary of the Cole Act. During 1941 Jersey Standard had conceived the idea of building a crude-oil pipeline from Portland, Maine, to Montreal, Canada. The reasons were the same as those that had dictated a railroad connection between the two cities many decades before: avoidance of the bottleneck created when the St. Lawrence froze over in winter months, plus a reduction of the distance — and therefore the cost — involved in connecting Montreal with the sea. In this instance, a pipeline would also help to conserve tanker space by eliminating the long voyage via the St. Lawrence. The Montreal line was certified under the Cole Act as essential to national defense and was completed before the end of the year. By that time the United States was at war.

ORGANIZING THE EMERGENCY PIPELINE EFFORT

Oil provided the sinews of the war effort; without it, the vast industrial and military machine of the United States would have ceased to function. At the same time, of course, the requirements of America's allies and of the domestic population had to be met. An elaborate structure of government and industry committees, boards, and agencies was created during 1941 to meet this challenge.

The fact that the handling of oil problems was to be a cooperative government-industry effort was signalized by the appointment on May 28, 1941, of Interior Secretary Harold Ickes as Petroleum Co-ordinator and later of an industry representative, Ralph K. Davies of California Standard, as his deputy. The organizational philosophy behind all subsequent moves was that government responsibilities and activities involving oil should be centralized in a single agency as much as possible. Initially, the Office of Petroleum Co-ordinator (OPC) was this agency. It had an independent status and was directly responsible to the President. The same was true of its successor, the Petroleum Administration for War (PAW) created in December 1942. A second principle of organization for the government oil agency was that it should be functional. Thus on the national level the OPC organization resembled that of the head office of an integrated oil company.

A Transportation Division was established in OPC on August 1, 1941, and a Supply Division was added to it in March 1942. Their functions, like those of other divisions, were to determine requirements for their particular areas and to find the best ways to meet them. The Transportation Division was broken down into sections — among them, Pipeline Operations, Pipeline Engineering and Materials. The responsibility of the pipeline sections was to make the most effective use of existing lines in meeting operating requirements and to promote, select, and expedite pipeline projects needed for the war effort. H. A. Gilbert, J. R. Parten, and G. A. Wilson were the successive directors of the Transportation Division, and various experienced pipeliners like R. B. McLaughlin of the Texas Company and W. C. Kinsolving of Sun served in top capacities. Veteran pipeline experts were contributed by all major pipeline companies to staff the government agency, and during their terms of service they were full-fledged government employees.

Another basic principle of the government's wartime oil organization was decentralized administration and primary reliance upon voluntary industry cooperation. For administrative purposes, therefore, OPC divided the country into five districts. District offices became the points of direct contact between the government and the industry in administering the oil program. The industry counterpart to the government district office was the district committee, organized along the same lines. These committees became operational in July 1941. Out of the work of the district committees evolved a national oil industry committee and the realization that continuing industry contact with the policy-making activities of OPC was necessary.

In May 1941 President W. S. Farish of Jersey Standard had called a meeting of senior oil company executives to discuss the possibility of building emergency pipelines to the East Coast for crude and/or products. At the same time the American Petroleum Institute reported that steps should be taken to promote voluntary cutbacks in petroleum consumption in the East and to increase shipments to that region. Meetings on these and other matters continued during the summer of 1941 and brought together chairmen of the newly established district committees. Recognizing the benefits derived from such top-level discussion and coordination of industry moves in the defense effort, industry leaders organized a Petroleum Industry Council for National Defense, renamed the Petroleum Industry War Council (PIWC), on November 28, 1941. Headed by William R. Boyd, Jr., president of the API, the council initially consisted of 66 members, including 30 representatives from district committees and 13 from industry trade associations. The council's Committee on Supply and Transportation included two subcommittees on various aspects of pipelining: the Pipe Line Management Subcommittee headed by W. Alton Jones of Cities Service and the Pipeline Engineering Subcommittee headed by W. R. Finney of Jersey, who had led the engineering study during the summer of 1941 for the emergency pipeline. By mid-June 1942, PIWC was described as "the supreme policy-making body, almost a governing body, of the oil industry." [11]

PLANNING THE PIPELINE PROGRAM FOR WAR

Although Pearl Harbor came as a shock to the whole nation, the oil industry and the government had taken preliminary steps to cope with such an eventuality. While much remained to be done to meet the problems of supplying oil for war purposes, much had already been accomplished. A government organization had been established to coordinate the mobilization of oil resources, and it had been paralleled by an industry organization. The Cole Act had given a statutory basis for building whatever emergency pipelines might be required, and industry surveys of a route for one such major undertaking from Texas to the East Coast had been completed.

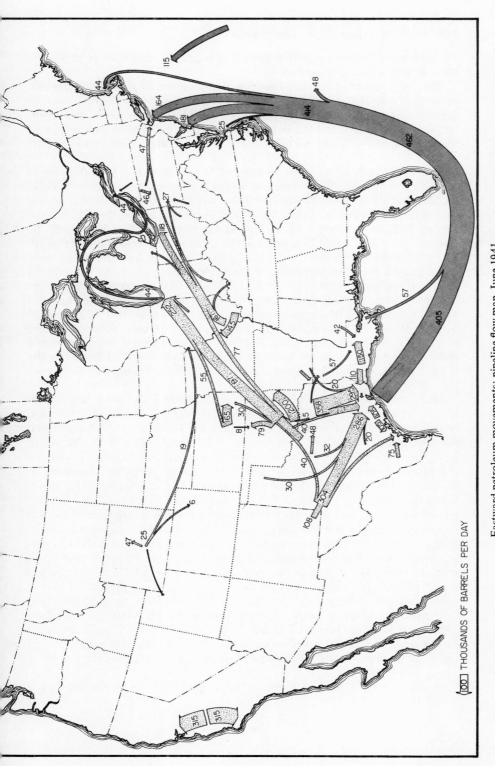

Eastward petroleum movements: pipeline flow map, June 1941.

Source: Shell Pipe Line Corporation, Report to Interstate Commerce Commission Regarding Depreciation of Crude Oil Pipe Line Carrier Property, August 12, 1953.

Two privately financed products lines that might be important in this same service were also completed.

The only unsettled conflict between the government and the integrated oil industry at the time of Pearl Harbor was the unsatisfactory state of negotiations on the pipeline consent decree. Within three weeks this problem was disposed of, and the industry's attention, manpower, and resources were focused on making oil available where and when needed to win the war.

The basic domestic pipeline strategy of World War II was laid down at a meeting of pipeline executives and engineers at the Mayo Hotel in Tulsa on March 23–26, 1942. This meeting was called as mounting tanker losses, slow-ups, and diversions created a major oil emergency on the East Coast. During February alone, a dozen United States tankers had been sunk by German submarines that had become the scourge of the Atlantic seaboard. The Petroleum Economics Committee of the Petroleum Industry War Council estimated that the minimum rationed petroleum needs of the eastern part of the United States were about 1,300,000 barrels per day; yet, as the nation's leading pipeliners convened in Tulsa, the tanker movements that would normally have supplied this amount with ease had been cut in half. Tank cars, made up into full trains running on tight schedules, were helping to overcome the deficit, but only with difficulty. Pipelines could reduce both train and barge hauls, operate continuously, and release badly needed manpower for other war duties. The Tulsa meeting was to investigate these possibilities.

In light of the worsening transportation situation, the need for coordination between industry districts had become manifest to W. Alton Jones, chairman of the Transportation Committee for District 1, which embraced the blockaded East Coast. Accordingly on March 12, 1942, he wired E. C. Seubert of Indiana Standard, chairman of District 2, which embraced the Midwest, and H. C. Weiss of Humble Oil & Refining, chairman of District 3, which covered the oil-producing Gulf states, asking for a meeting at the earliest opportunity. A Temporary Joint Pipe Line Sub-Committee consisting of two members from each of these districts was quickly organized,* and invitations were sent to 112 companies engaged in pipelining crude oil or products to attend the meeting called in Tulsa. Representatives of 67 companies gathered in response to this request and spent four full days discussing pipeline problems and their solutions. The formal report of their proceedings was released in New York on April 2, 1942.

Basically, the subcommittee's work was focused on the problem of developing transportation projects that would meet the demand for petroleum and its products in Districts 1 and 2 if the entire Gulf-to-Atlantic seaboard tanker fleet were taken out of service. The approach adopted was to match the forecast demand for oil in these districts against all possible means of

*District 1, W. R. Finney, B. J. Hanks; District 2, C. Bunje, C. H. Kountz; District 3, B. E. Hull, T. E. Swigart.

moving supplies from District 3. The subcommittee found that various companies had already taken emergency action to increase their capacity for moving oil northward and eastward. For example, Gulf Refining Company had looped its line northward so that capacity had been increased from 45,000 barrels to 56,000 barrels per day between Oklahoma points and Dublin, Indiana. Its east Texas-Port Arthur line, built to serve tanker loading facilities on the Gulf, had been reversed to move coastal crude northward. The Texas Company had reversed its Oklahoma-Texas line; Sinclair had looped its line to eliminate a bottleneck; Stanolind had increased its capacity northward from Kansas; and Oklahoma Pipe Line had reconditioned an idle line making it possible to move 40,000 barrels a day into Districts 1 and 2 with the cooperation of Humble Pipe Line, Ajax, Standard of Louisiana, and Illinois Pipe Line.[12]

The subcommittee's first recommendation, therefore, was to increase deliveries into District 1 by utilizing existing pipelines with the adjustments necessary to re-establish routes that had functioned before tankers took over the Gulf-East Coast business in the 1920's. A modicum of changes and improvements, involving primarily industry decisions, could bring additional crude into the Chicago-Lima area. By relaying some of its line, Illinois Pipe could feed the Northern and Southern Group lines for deliveries to Bayway, New Jersey. Another route could be provided via Tuscarora Pipe Line, which had been taken out of crude service as shipments from the Mid-Continent declined in the 1920's and had been used to move products west. The subcommittee recommended that flow in this line again be reversed in order to perform its original function. If this program could be carried out — and it appeared feasible because the pipe and equipment were on hand or could be obtained without disrupting vital services — 25,000 barrels a day of east Texas and Kansas crude could be delivered to the East Coast entirely by pipeline. This would free some 1,700 tank cars for other service.

The subcommittee's second recommendation related to the newly-built Plantation Pipe Line. Between Baton Rouge, Louisiana, and Bremen, Georgia, it could handle 60,000 barrels a day; between Bremen and Greensboro, 42,000 barrels. By increasing the pumping units on this line, the subcommittee believed that 90,000 barrels a day could be moved out of Baton Rouge, making an additional 30,000 barrels available at Greensboro.

Two new projects grew out of this proposal. One, which later developed into the so-called Bayou system, was to supply 60,000 barrels a day to Baton Rouge from refineries at Beaumont and Baytown, Texas, utilizing reclaimed pipe from west Texas lines, especially those of Illinois Pipe Line Company. The other project was to extend the Plantation line to a point on an inland waterway northwest of Norfolk, using secondhand 8-inch pipe. This line would then deliver to barges for further movement the extra 30,000 barrels a day made available at Greensboro. Thus, scarce tank cars would be freed to deliver still more oil from Texas to New York.

The subcommittee's third recommendation involved Shell's products line from Wood River to Lima, which was being enlarged to handle 24,000 barrels per day, and Sun's Susquehanna line from Pennsylvania that terminated at Akron. In the late 1930's, it will be recalled, Ohio Standard had furnished Shell with the means of reaching Toledo via a branch line between Lima and Fostoria, Ohio. The subcommittee suggested that the two companies could "trade out" on these north-south movements and extend the Fostoria line to a connection with the Susquehanna system at Akron. It was hoped that such arrangements would result in the daily movement of some 15,000 additional barrels of products into District 1, specifically, into western Pennsylvania.

Another recommendation proposed to increase tanker movements on the Great Lakes in order to deliver more products to Buffalo. From there they could be moved to the seaboard by barge or by pipeline. In the latter case, the Keystone-Atlantic system, the Socony line, and the Sun line to the Philadelphia refining complex were available. The impact of these plans, however, was in part contingent on what additional steps could be taken to deliver east Texas crude into the Midwest.

The indicated decline of the Illinois field and the need to shorten tank car and barge hauls wherever possible lay behind the recommendation that a new crude-oil pipeline be laid between east Texas and Salem, Illinois. It would require an estimated 114,000 tons of steel and new pumping units aggregating about 50,000 horsepower. To move the maximum amount of oil per pound of steel, use of 20-inch diameter pipe was suggested — a radical departure from existing industry practice. Although priorities on scarce steel were involved and the project might cost as much as $30,000,000, the subcommittee felt that this line was essential.

A products line from east Texas to a tank car and barge loading terminal on the Ohio River near Paducah, Kentucky, was also suggested. This plan assumed that Pan-American's new crude-oil line from east Texas to Texas City could be converted to products use and tied into the complex of refineries in the Houston area. Secondhand 12- and 14-inch pipe could be used to complete the route to a point near Paducah. By these means about 75,000 barrels per day of products could be delivered to a location that would cut in half the existing tank-car haul from District 3 to District 1. Barge movements could also be employed to serve the Pittsburgh area from the Ohio River terminal, thus freeing for crude service lines carrying products from the seaboard to the interior.

Trainload shipments of crude to the East Coast at that time were being assembled in the Tinsley Field in Mississippi. To shorten this haul, the subcommittee recommended that an 8- or 10-inch line be built north to the Memphis area.

All of these projects if carried through as proposed would still have left District 1 far short of its estimated minimum daily oil requirements. Accordingly the subcommittee concluded: "There does not seem to be any solution but to build *two big pipe lines* from the Texas area thru to the Atlantic Coast if tankers are not going to be available." [13] This was a momentous conclusion. In it lay the genesis of the big-inch pipelines that were to help win the war and revolutionize postwar American pipelining.

The subcommittee's conclusions gave new importance to the question of the National Defense Pipe Line, soon known as the Big Inch. Before Pearl Harbor the line had merely seemed desirable; it was now deemed essential. The 1,400 miles of 24-inch pipe from east Texas to New York with a branch to Philadelphia would permit the delivery of 300,000 barrels a day into Salem, Illinois, where 50,000 barrels would be drawn off for local refining needs to replace declining Illinois production. From Salem east, the line would carry 250,000 barrels a day.

Such a project would be large and expensive. It would require an estimated 450,000 tons of steel, of which 422,000 would be in the form of pipe alone. Because of price increases the preceding year, the estimated cost of the project mounted from $68,000,000, the figure used earlier in industry planning, to close to $95,000,000. Estimated operating costs rose similarly — from 30 cents a barrel to 45 cents. Nevertheless, in arguing for the pipeline the subcommittee pointed out that under existing conditions tankers required more steel per barrel of oil moved than did the pipeline, and tanker operating costs were higher. In the last analysis, however, costs were not the basic criteria for building the line. There was, according to the industry group, simply no alternative to the pipeline if tankers were not going to be available.

In the event that the Big Inch crude-oil line was built, the subcommittee suggested that the proposed 20-inch line from east Texas to Salem, Illinois, be assigned to products service and extended to the New York-Philadelphia area. This was the genesis of the Little Big Inch. The complete line from Texas to the East Coast would cost an estimated $80,000,000 but would permit 200,000 barrels of products per day to be delivered in the major consuming areas of District 1. If this plan were carried out, the proposed 12- and 14-inch line to deliver products from east Texas to Paducah could be freed for crude-oil use, delivering an additional 50,000 barrels a day to southern Illinois. The sum total of all these projects would meet the estimated minimum daily requirements of District 1.

In making its recommendations, the subcommittee had a time-phased plan of implementation in mind. Rearrangements of existing lines and projects involving secondhand pipe could be completed in six months or so by the industry. The larger projects involving the use of new steel would take a year to 18 months, though the long lines could be laid in sections as materials became available. The striking thing about the recommendations, however, was their reversion to pipeline patterns of the 1920's in connecting existing pipeline systems to provide an all-pipeline route from the Southwest to the East Coast and their forward look in the ready acceptance of large-diameter pipe as essential to meeting the oil shortage that would still exist.

These proposals, it must be remembered, emanated from an industry group, a point which the group took pains to emphasize in the concluding section of its report on the Tulsa meeting.

> If the projects proposed by this Committee are accepted and the program carried thru in whole or in part, the work must necessarily be handled by the Pipe Line and Oil Companies. They are the only ones who can supply the men with the required knowledge and experience and, above all, the ability to manage this highly-specialized pipe line construction and operation. These Companies can act singly or in cooperative groups, but must be allowed freedom of action with protection against loss on the huge expenditures involved. The consent and approval of the Department of Justice, the Interstate Commerce Commission, and other Governmental agencies will be required. This must be recognized as an emergency program brought about by the effect of the War, and if so viewed, the Committee believes it can be carried through to successful completion without further delay.[14]

IMPLEMENTATION OF THE TULSA PLAN

The Tulsa plan recommendations were accepted by the PAW with only slight modifications. Approval was contained in a PAW recommendation dated May 11, 1942. Where industry initiative and existing pipelines were involved, it was possible to proceed almost immediately under the supervision of an Industry Pipe Line Management Committee. Where government financial support or priorities for scarce materials were involved, some delays were inevitably experienced.

The industry's project to use existing lines to create an all-pipe route from Texas to the East Coast was started in the summer of 1942 and completed before the end of the year. It was necessary to make changes in the existing pipelines of 12 companies in order to complete the job. Looping of lines, the reversal of two lines, conversion of one from gasoline to crude oil, the addition of pumps and pumping stations, and new river crossings in some instances, were among the required changes. Over 3,200 miles of pipe had to be dug up, reconditioned, and relaid, and various problems relating to rate-schedules and coordination of operations had to be overcome.

THE UNDIVIDED INTEREST PIPELINE

The industry also undertook significant new projects. The Bayou Pipe Line System, organized and constructed to supply the Plantation Pipe Line with products from the Texas Gulf Coast, represented a major organizational innovation. Bayou was the first line in the United States to be built and operated by several different common-carrier pipeline companies acting through an agent, with each owning a fractional undivided interest in the facilities.

The advantages of the undivided organization, which was later copied in a number of instances, are several. An undivided interest pipeline can be conceived as a single line consisting of a bundle of different-sized lines, each with a different owner. Participants enjoy the economies of large-diameter pipe which they might not be justified in building just for themselves. Each owner exercises full control over tenders, tariffs, and other requirements on his share of the line. He is entitled to throughput in proportion to his percentage of ownership. Allocation of costs, with the exception of those that vary directly with throughput, is likewise based on this percentage. If an owner has more throughput than his share of the line can accommodate, he must offer it to other owners as though they were operating a separate pipeline. Construction, maintenance, and operation of an undivided interest line can be by contract, and the contractor need not be — but generally is — an owner-participant. Each owner reports on his share of undivided interest lines as though they were part of his wholly-owned facilities, and this share can be included in his valuation base for consent decree purposes. The name, such as "Bayou System," simply identifies physical facilities, not a separate organization.

Compared to a corporate form, like Plantation, where a new organization owned by several companies is established, an undivided interest system offers several advantages. For example, a new corporate entity by virtue of the fact that it is a corporation incurs such costs as income tax and some administrative expense. Also, with the corporate form there are greater problems of coordinating the interests of large and small ownership holders on matters such as declaration of dividends, extension, and throughputs. However, the corporate form has certain advantages with respect to financing, where large amounts are borrowed. In the Bayou system case, organization of a separate corporation to own the Bayou properties would not have been acceptable to some of the oil companies that already owned stock in a pipeline corporation, because Texas law at that time prohibited an oil company from owning stock in more than one such corporation.*

Initially there were six participants in the Bayou system — Humble Pipe Line Company, Pan American Pipe Line Company, The Texas Pipe Line Company, Pure Transportation Company, Crown Central Pipe Line and Transportation Corporation, and Shell Pipe Line Corporation. The refineries affiliated with these companies were to provide the products to be carried by the line, while the participating pipeline companies underwrote the cost of constructing it in proportion to their ownership shares. Shell Pipe Line Corporation acted as agent for the other owners in building and op-

---

*At the time the Bayou system was constructed, Article 1499, Texas Revised Civil Statutes, provided that no corporation could engage in the oil and gas producing business "while owning or operating oil pipelines in this State." Articles 1500 and 1501 provided for the ownership of such oil pipelines in corporations separate from the corporations engaged in production operations. Article 1502 provided that such corporation engaged in the producing business "shall not own the stock of more than . . . one pipeline corporation, organized under the laws of this or any other single State." Although these specific articles were repealed in 1955 when the Texas Business Corporation Act was adopted, Article 201 of that act prohibits organization of a corporation for a combination of "The business of engaging in the petroleum and producing business in this State and the business of engaging directly in the oil pipe line business in this State."

erating the system, which in effect consisted of six different common carriers.[15]

Shell Pipe commenced work on the new system in the summer of 1942 and finished it in February 1943. Working primarily with secondhand and reclaimed materials, the crews laid 8-inch pipe from Baytown to Port Neches and 10-inch from Port Neches to Baton Rouge. The line could handle 40,500 barrels a day between Baytown and Port Neches, Texas, and 64,000 barrels a day between the latter terminal and Baton Rouge.[16] Bayou, in short, provided a very sizable input of products to Plantation Pipe Line for further movement northward.

GOVERNMENT-FINANCED PROJECTS

The federal government through the Reconstruction Finance Corporation and its subsidiaries provided the financing for five wartime pipeline projects. In addition to the Big Inch lines to the East Coast, government-financed projects included the Florida Emergency Pipe Line, the extension of the Plantation system, the Ohio Emergency Pipe Line, and the Southwest Emergency Pipe Line.

The trans-Florida line was considered essential to save tanker space and to avoid the hazards of tanker movements through submarine-infested waters around the tip of that state. Products could be moved by barge along the protected Gulf Coast to Florida's west coast and then transported 200 miles across the state to Jacksonville, whence they could be distributed along the intracoastal waterway. A reclaimed 8-inch line that had been used by the American Liberty Oil Company from east Texas to the Gulf was acquired for this project, and the first delivery through the new line was made on June 17, 1943.

Meanwhile the capacity of Plantation Pipe Line had been increased and its extension from Greensboro, North Carolina, to Richmond, Virginia, had commenced. Fourteen booster stations were installed along the original line and completed in February 1943. Capacity was thus raised from 60,000 barrels to 90,000 barrels daily between Baton Rouge and Bremen, Georgia, and from 42,000 to 63,000 barrels between there and Greensboro. Government funds underwrote the extension from Greensboro to Richmond. This 8-inch line, built with secondhand pipe, was completed in April 1943 at a cost of some $4,096,000. Plantation Pipe Line operated the extension as agent for the Defense Supplies Corporation.

The Ohio Emergency Pipe Line was a means of connecting Ohio Standard's pipeline system with the Sun-Susquehanna Products system running east. It consisted of some 80 miles of reconditioned 8-inch pipe which linked Tiffin and Doylestown, Ohio. From the latter point another Ohio Standard line completed the connection to Randolph, Ohio, on the Susquehanna system.

Still another government-owned line supplied both the Houston refinery area and the War Emergency Pipe Line with crude. Known as the South-

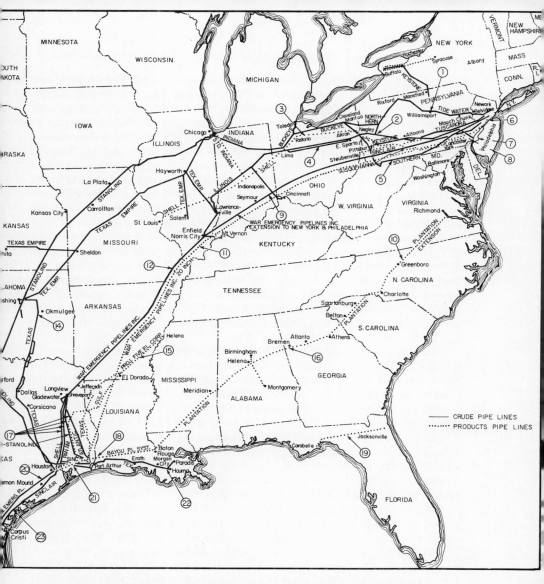

Emergency pipeline projects for delivery of petroleum to the East Coast, 1943.
Source: Adapted from T. E. Swigart, "Oil's War-Time Achievement in Transportation," map to accompany address to Southwestern District of the American Petroleum Institute, April 29, 1943.

Project Characteristics

1. Crude 2,000 B/D
2. Crude 20,000 B/D
3. Products 15,000 B/D
4. Crude 15,000 B/D
5. Crude increase 5,000 B/D
6. Products 15,000 B/D
7. Crude 25,000 B/D
8. Products 15,000 B/D
9. Crude 300,000 B/D
10. Products 30,000 B/D
11. Products 235,000 B/D
12. Crude 300,000 B/D
13. Lay 54.2 miles, 12 loops
14. Reverse and loop Texas Pipe Line and increase capacity of Texas-Empire Pipe Line to deliver 30,000 B/D to Chicago area
15. Products 55,000 B/D
16. Products 30,000 B/D
17. Reverse feeder lines, crude 175,000 B/D
18. Products 60,000 B/D
19. Products 30,000 B/D
20. Convert gas line to crude, 75,000 B/D
21. Products 37,000 B/D
22. Crude and products 45,000 B/D
23. Crude 20,000 B/D

west Emergency Pipe Line, it consisted of 149 miles of 14- and 16-inch pipe converted from gas service between Refugio and Pierce Junction, Texas. Humble Pipe Line, as agent for the RFC's Defense Plant Corporation, took charge of this project, which included an extension from Pierce Junction to Houston where connections were made with reversed Shell and Pan American lines running to east Texas and with the Shell refinery at Deer Park on the outskirts of Houston. Humble Pipe Line also operated the line as agent for the Defense Supplies Corporation. Beginning in October 1943, about 80,000 barrels of crude a day were moved from southwest Texas to Houston. In contrast to these projects, the construction of the new large-diameter lines from Texas to the East Coast was a mammoth undertaking.

As previously described, the idea of a major pipeline from the Southwest to the Atlantic seaboard had been under consideration in both government and industry circles since the summer of 1940, but numerous factors had postponed positive action on it. In September 1941, 11 companies had agreed to finance and build a 24-inch line, using the newly organized National Defense Pipelines, Inc., as their agent. Denied a steel allocation, this project was at an end when that agreement expired two days before Pearl Harbor.

The industry's Tulsa plan again stressed the importance of building such a line if tankers were to be unavailable, and the mounting record of tanker losses made this assumption not overly pessimistic. Tanker deliveries to the East Coast in May 1942, for example, were only 173,000 barrels daily, or 18 per cent of what they had been in the month of Pearl Harbor.[17] This worsening situation led Petroleum Administrator Ickes to press the War Production Board to issue a steel allocation for the pipeline. Finally, on June 10, 1942, the WPB agreed that 137,500 tons of steel should be assigned for the construction of a 24-inch pipeline from Longview in east Texas to Norris City, Illinois, where provision would be made for loading tank cars for the remainder of the journey to New York and Philadelphia.[18]

Where earlier the industry had proposed to finance the line, the estimated $35,000,000 cost of this first segment of the new line was to be provided by the government through the Reconstruction Finance Corporation. Ownership was to be vested in the Defense Plant Corporation. To provide an organization to handle construction and operation, Emergency Pipelines, Inc., which had been organized in Delaware in September 1941 to facilitate emergency industry projects, was renamed War Emergency Pipelines, Inc. (WEP). Eleven eastern oil companies each subscribed to ten shares of the $100-par stock of the pipeline.* W. Alton Jones became president of the new organization; Burt E. Hull was vice president and general manager. The amended charter included a stipulation that the industry participants

---

*The companies were Cities Service Company, Standard Oil Company (New Jersey, Atlantic Pipe Line Company, Gulf Refining Company, The Texas Company, Socony-Vacuum Oil Company, Inc., Sinclair Oil Corporation, Shell Oil Company, Incorporated, Pan American Petroleum & Transit Company, Tidal Pipe Line Company, Sun Pipe Line Company (Texas).

would not pay dividends or accrue profits based on government contracts.[19] On June 26, 1942, a formal construction agreement was concluded between the Defense Plant Corporation and War Emergency Pipelines, Inc.[20]

Under the WPB steel allocation, the Big Inch line had to be built with pipe made from steel billets. Therefore, unlike electric-weld pipe which was made from sheet steel, the pipe had to be seamless. The National Tube Company had the only mill in the country that could produce 24-inch seamless pipe.[21] The first order was placed with this company on July 2, 1942, and 16 days later the first trainload of this pipe was dispatched from the mill. Meanwhile, contractors had been selected and had signed cost-plus-fixed-fee contracts. On August 3, construction work actually got underway at a point near Little Rock, Arkansas. While work went ahead on eight sections of the Big Inch, tankage and feeder lines were provided in the Longview area. At Norris City, Illinois, tankage was also erected and the terminal was tied into Ohio Oil's pipeline moving crude eastward.

On the last day of 1942, the WEP began to feed crude oil into the newly completed line. The oil was preceded by a "slug" of water 50 miles long to test for leaks, but no major defects were found. Considering the speed with which the large-diameter pipe had been laid, this was a remarkable achievement. On February 13, 1943, the first oil from Longview was received at Norris City. Six days later the first trainload of this oil moved eastward from the Norris City loading racks.

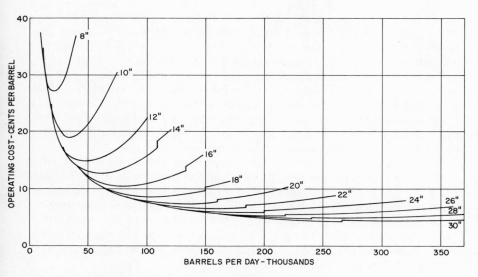

Chart 3. Pipeline diameters and operating costs per barrel, 1943.

Source: War Emergency Pipelines, Inc.

While the first leg of the over-all project was still under construction, the WPB agreed to another allocation of steel to complete the 24-inch line to the seaboard. The next day, October 27, 1942, the RFC made a commitment to finance the extension, which would cost an estimated $60,000,000. Work on the eastern extension of the Big Inch started in December 1942. As contractors finished their jobs on the Texas-Norris City segment, they moved their "spreads" to new sites on the more challenging terrain of the extension. Plans called for 24-inch pipe from Norris City to Phoenixville, Pennsylvania. There the line would divide, with one 20-inch line going to New York and another to Philadelphia. The branches were constructed of electric-weld pipe supplied by Youngstown Steel and Tube Company.

Despite the more rugged terrain, the unfavorable time of year, and the greater distances involved, work on the extension went comparatively smoothly. On July 14, 1943, the first oil was turned into the line east of Norris City. The first shipment of crude arrived at Phoenixville Junction on August 14, 1943, and was delivered to Sinclair and Sun refineries in the Philadelphia area on the same day. Although some crude was delivered to Linden, New Jersey, on August 20, leaks in that branch line caused it to be shut down almost immediately. The repaired facility was not restored to service until the following October. While these developments had been taking place, rearrangement of pipeline facilities in Texas had permitted west Texas crude oil to be delivered directly to the Big Inch. The first batch of this oil arrived at Norris City on June 22, 1943, showing contamination of less than one-half of 1 per cent.[22]

A products line from Texas to the East Coast had been considered as a possibility at least since 1941. After the Tulsa meeting in March 1942, this project was accorded a lower priority than the Big Inch in view of the steel shortage.* In addition, the shortage of heavy equipment for construction and the unique experience acquired by the organization that built the Big Inch made it both necessary and desirable to wait until the equipment and the contractors were available for use on the products line. In October 1942, when WPB was asked for steel to complete the Big Inch to the seaboard, PAW indicated that a second line might be necessary. In January 1943, steel was requested and granted for the 20-inch products line, the "Little Big Inch," to run from Beaumont, Texas, to Seymour, Indiana.

Meanwhile, the tanker crisis had become increasingly serious. By May 1943, tanker deliveries to the East Coast hit their low point of 63,000 barrels a day, or a little more than half a load for a T-2 tanker.[23] It became apparent, then, that the Little Big Inch should be extended from Indiana to the seaboard, and approval was granted for the entire line on April 2, 1943. The revised estimated cost of the undertaking was placed at $75,000,-000.[24] Again, the Defense Plant Corporation provided the capital and War Emergency Pipelines, the know-how.

*Consideration was given to converting a 20-inch natural gas line from Boldman, Kentucky, to Coatesville, Pennsylvania, but the resulting impact on gas-using communities and industries was judged too severe to warrant adoption of this expedient.

Table 17. Key physical characteristics, Big Inch and Little
Big Inch pipelines.

Characteristics	Big Inch	Little Big Inch
Length of main lines (miles)	1,254	1,475
Length of feeder and distribution lines (miles)	222	239
Total length of pipe in systems (miles)	1,476	1,714
Weight of pipe in systems (tons)	358,000	287,000
Number of pump stations	28	31
Number of main and branch line pumping units	81	86
Electric motors (total rated horsepower)	130,000	120,000
Daily power consumption, full load (kilowatt hours)	2,040,000	1,885,000
Volume of oil required to fill system (barrels)	3,836,000	2,870,000
Daily designed throughput (barrels)[a]	300,000	235,000
Peak daily throughput achieved (barrels)	334,456	239,844

Source: 79 Cong. 1 Sess., Senate Special Committee Investigating Petroleum Resources, "War Emergency Pipe-Line Systems and Other Petroleum Facilities," *Hearings,* 15.

[a]Design throughputs were based on east Texas crude oil for Big Inch, and gasoline for Little Inch. Big Inch averaged 317,000 barrels daily from May 1944 through August 1945, a remarkable record.

After proceeding in a northeasterly direction from Beaumont, the route of the products line paralleled that of the Big Inch from Little Rock, Arkansas, to Linden, New Jersey. Construction was by sections, with work beginning on the southern end of the line first. A total of 1,475 miles of 20-inch pipe was required. A combination of seamless and electric-weld pipe was used, but the latter type developed leaks and delayed progress.[25] The final weld in the products line was made on December 8, 1943, or 225 days after the actual start of construction. The first gasoline shipped from Beaumont entered the pipe on January 26, 1944, and was immediately followed by No. 2 heating oil. The head of the gasoline stream reached Linden on March 2, 1944, and during the succeeding ten days sufficient heating oil arrived to alleviate the shortage that had been threatening the New York City area.[26] Another major pipeline contribution to the war effort had begun to prove its worth, and the feasibility of using large-diameter pipe had been conclusively demonstrated.

Both Big Inch lines cost less than anticipated and performed beyond expectations. The Big Inch actually cost approximately $77,000,000 and up to June 30, 1945, carried 244,700,000 barrels of crude oil. As of the same date, the Little Big Inch, which cost about $65,000,000 had delivered

101,400,000 barrels of products to Linden, New Jersey, with less than a third of it destined for civilian use.[27]

Because the cost of laying down crude and products pipelines in the East under emergency conditions was higher than would have been the case if normal transportation had been possible, the government made appropriate adjustments to cover the differences. Under a subsidy program initiated in August 1942, the Reconstruction Finance Corporation paid distributors of oil on the eastern seaboard the excess of wartime transportation costs over normal ones, provided they refunded to RFC the amount of government-approved price increases on gasoline. Normal rates for transportation to the East Coast were figured as 55 cents a barrel for crude and 45 cents for refined products. However, the RFC placed tariffs on the emergency pipelines at 80 cents and 65 cents respectively. Thus, under the subsidy program, oil companies paying these rates became eligible for refunds of 25 cents a barrel on crude and 20 cents a barrel on products. Even so, because of the efficiency of the pipelines, the RFC figured that as of June 30, 1945, after paying subsidies on pipeline shipments amounting to $81,000,000, the lines showed a net profit of $54,000,000.[28]

PIPELINES' CONTRIBUTION TO THE WAR EFFORT

To separate pipelines from other forms of oil transportation in their contribution to the war effort is perhaps unfair, for every branch of petroleum transportation performed at comparably high levels. However, from the standpoint of the public, the pipeline for the first time became a mode of transportation as familiar as the railroad. As the official PAW history put it with respect to the Big Inch, "people began to look upon it as an inanimate knight in shining armor." [29] Moreover, during their brief existence as petroleum carriers, the two Big Inch lines delivered over 350,000,000 barrels of crude and refined products. It would be difficult to measure what the availablility of this amount of petroleum and petroleum products meant to the war effort, both overseas and at home. But clearly it was a major contribution.

Although the Big Inch lines were the most dramatic examples of the wartime pipeline program, without the rearrangement of existing lines, construction of new feeder lines, and so on, the big lines would have been unable to perform their roles. And, of course, systems that had nothing to do with the big lines also contributed to the war effort and had to be expanded, maintained, and rearranged.[30]

The pipeline sector of the oil industry also contributed directly to the success of military operations. For example, a portable pipeline developed by Sidney S. Smith, manager of the Shell products pipeline department, was adopted by the Army in 1942 and saw service on virtually every front. It was inexpensive, could be assembled and operated by relatively inexperienced personnel, and could be adapted to transport water as well as gasoline.[31] The most dramatic applications of the pipeline in theaters of military operations were the 1,500-mile installation along the Burma Road and the network that supported the invasion of Europe, where at the height of operations 3,800,000 gallons of gasoline were pumped inland daily from the ports of France.[32] Pipeliners not only manned Washington offices and domestic installations, but also served throughout the world wherever their specialized skills were needed.

If pipelines and pipeliners contributed significantly to the war effort, the war also helped to advance pipelining. Under the stress of the emergency and the need to move large volumes of crude oil and petroleum products safely and efficiently, innovation was encouraged and government was justified in financing it. The success of the Big and Little Big Inch lines, both technically and financially, more than vindicated their proponents and provided an example and an incentive for emulation by privately-financed projects in the postwar era. Perhaps the shift to large-diameter pipe would have come about without the wartime stimulus, but the dramatic example of the war-built lines undoubtedly accelerated the movement by demonstrating its possibilities on a large scale.

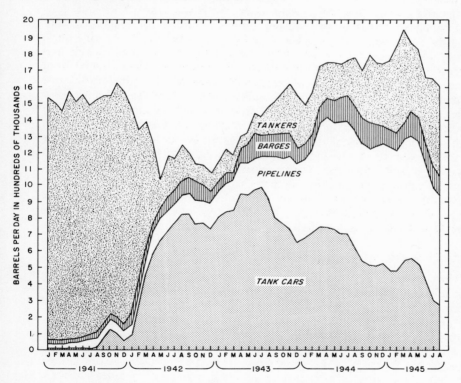

Chart 4. Deliveries of petroleum into PAW District No. 1 (East Coast), 1941-1945.

Source: Petroleum Administration for War.

CHAPTER 18

PIPELINE MANAGEMENT PROBLEMS

═══

While government-industry planning on oil transportation shaped the broad contours of pipeline managements' wartime decision-making, managers were also confronted with numerous specific problems that had an impact on their contribution to the war effort and the postwar position of their concerns. At the operating level they faced the problem of how to maximize each company's contribution to the war effort. Such questions had to be answered in the face of serious shortages of manpower and material and involved decisions on increasing the efficiency of existing lines, construction of new ones with or without government financial aid, and relocation or elimination of lines whose usefulness or efficiency had been decreased by the shifts in oil movements occasioned by wartime conditions. A premium was therefore placed on management's ability to make the most efficient allocation and utilization of available and existing resources. In addition, management faced a major problem of determining how the recently-adopted consent decree affected both the form and the substance of oil pipeline financing and traditional relationships between owners and users of pipeline facilities. Decisions made on these questions could potentially affect each pipeline company's postwar position in terms of its profitability and usefulness as well as its relationship to the government bodies that had jurisdiction over it. Thus, decisions made under the pressure of wartime conditions had long-run peacetime implications.

PRIVATE WARTIME PIPELINE CONSTRUCTION

One important result of the wartime emergency was an increase in pipeline mileage and capacity, quite aside from government-sponsored construction. Changes in mileage were accompanied by changes in the amount of oil moved and the direction in which it was transported. Larger diameter pipe was used in many instances and products lines received new emphasis.

Privately financed construction, conversions, and reversals of trunk pipelines during World War II aggregated some 9,850 miles of pipe and an expenditure of about $127,000,000.[1] In addition, pipeline companies laid some 2,200 miles of gathering lines and provided auxiliary facilities for pumping, storing, and transferring crude from pipelines to tankers or tank cars.[2] A significant proportion of new construction involved products pipelines, which increased in total from about 9,000 miles in May 1941 to 15,-000 miles by September 1945.[3]

Early in the war effort it was necessary to increase the capacity for movements of crude, primarily through existing systems, north and east from the Texas Gulf and Mid-Continent areas. This endeavor, authorized and coordinated by the Petroleum Administration for War, was undertaken in the summer of 1942 and completed in February 1943. It involved the cooperation of 12 companies. To increase capacity for crude-oil movements from Texas into Oklahoma, for example, the Texas Pipe Line Company reversed its 333-mile, 8-inch line between Port Arthur and West Dallas and added an additional pump station. Meanwhile, with secondhand pipe, the capacity of the trunk line between West Dallas and Stuart, Oklahoma, was increased by a series of loops. Stanolind looped its Graford, Texas-Healdton, Oklahoma line to increase its capacity, and Oklahoma Pipe Line constructed an 8-inch line from Healdton to Hewitt, Oklahoma, to take 10,000 barrels a day from Stanolind destined for the East Coast. By such means, these companies and others increased the flow of crude oil into the Illinois area from Texas and the Mid-Continent by 40,000 barrels a day in the space of a few months.

More than half this increased northward flow continued on to the East Coast. As detailed in the preceding chapter, the old pattern of Standard Oil movements from the Souhwest was revived. In the Midwest, Buckeye increased its trunk-line capacity eastward by installing new pumping facilities and, pending completion of the War Emergency Pipe Line, supplemented eastbound pipeline deliveries by loading as many as 40,000 barrels a day into tank cars for rail shipment to East Coast refineries. Illinois Pipe Line (Ohio Oil) looped its line between Lima and East Sparta, Ohio. The Tuscarora line, which had been moving gasoline westward from Bayway, New Jersey, was reversed to move crude eastward from Negley, Ohio, as it had done in its early days. National Transit, Southern Pipe Line, Northern Pipe, and Tide Water Pipe Line improved and enlarged their facilities in various ways.

In Texas, major alterations in the existing pipeline network were required to feed the War Emergency Pipe Line. To a large extent the prewar lines had been oriented from inland points toward the Texas Gulf Coast. For example, of the 330,000 barrels being produced daily in the east Texas field in July 1941, 210,550 barrels moved to the coast. Shell, Sun, Stanolind, Atlantic, and Humble pipelines all funneled east Texas crude into the Houston-Beaumont area. With the construction of the Big Inch, however, it was necessary to reverse some of these lines, work out new connections, and in some instances to add new pump stations. Other lines had to be built, rearranged, or reversed to keep crude flowing into the coastal refineries.

The one major Texas area where there was excess crude-oil producing capacity in existing fields was west Texas. New pipelines soon began to tap this source of crude. Stanolind Pipe Line constructed a 385-mile, 16-inch line from the Slaughter field in Hockley County, west Texas, to Drumright, Oklahoma. Using new pipe, this project was completed in March 1944 at a cost of about $8,000,000. Its initial capacity of 65,000 barrels daily could be raised to an estimated 116,000 barrels by the addition of more pump stations.[4] Magnolia Pipe Line Company increased its capacity out of west Texas by construction of a 12-inch line from Midland to Corsicana, paralleling an existing 8-inch line. This project, also completed in March 1944, cost about $6,000,000 and enabled Magnolia to move daily about 85,000 barrels of west Texas crude compared to about 30,000 barrels before the war.[5] Gulf Refining increased the capacity of its Judkin-Ranger line by a series of six 10-inch loops.[6] The Texas-New Mexico Pipe Line, a corporate form of joint venture (Texas Co., Sinclair, Cities Service, Tide Water) dating from 1937, gathered and delivered crude from west Texas and New Mexico to the Houston area. The capacity of its west Texas line was increased by looping before the end of the war.

THE PACIFIC WAR EMERGENCY PIPE LINE

A proposal to give west Texas production an outlet to the West Coast failed to win government approval. The Pacific War Emergency Pipe Line was conceived during the war as a private venture to transport crude oil from west Texas and New Mexico to California. The 20-inch line was to run from Monahans, Texas, to Los Angeles, California. As proposed, it would have been 986 miles long and would have required 204,833 tons of pipe. With 17 pump stations it would have had a capacity of 175,000 barrels per day and cost an estimated $47,203,122.[7]

To obtain the necessary materials and financial support, promoters of the line sought PAW approval. An application for a necessity certificate filed May 1, 1944, was denied consideration. In reporting this fact to the secretary of the company, Petroleum Administrator Harold Ickes pointed in June 1944 to the following considerations: inadequate crude oil in west Texas to support the line, a proposed pipeline capacity in excess of surplus refinery capacity in California, the time needed for construction, and lack of provision for gathering facilities in Texas and of distributing facilites in California.[8]

The proposal was reconsidered and again turned down in the summer of 1945 as the war was drawing to a close. This decision, following extensive review by the PAW and its appropriate functional and geographical subdivisions, was severely attacked by Chairman Olin Culberson of the Texas Railroad Commission, which had not been overly pleased with PAW intervention in oil and gas matters over which the commission had previously exercised jurisdiction.[9] According to Culberson: "Those in authority in such matters in Washington, many of whom are dollar-a-year men on leave from the organizations they represent, invariably rule against extending any consideration to those rugged individuals and groups who seek to make their contribution toward winning the war by proposing to enter the competitive field of business controlled by monopolistic groups." [10]

Such comments, pleasing to small operators, indicated one drawback of the integrated oil industry's wartime collaboration with government. The alliance exposed participants to attack and invited easy misrepresentation of their motives. In this instance, however, the ending of the war emptied Culberson's attack of its patriotic element. Furthermore, as Congress, Ickes, and the military, as well as the PAW's industry people, had a hand in the decision on the Pacific War Emergency Pipe Line, it was scarcely accurate for the Texan to lay all the blame on the industry group for torpedoing the project.

The significance of the episode was not limited to the wartime proposal. The possibilities of connecting the west Texas with California continued to have allure after the close of the war. Although the project was seriously advanced by independent groups on several occasions, it never materialized.

TAX RELIEF FOR EMERGENCY PROJECTS

Wartime pipeline projects required government approval even when privately financed. This requirement cut two ways. First, it might prevent the construction of facilities that private promoters considered desirable, as in the case of the Pacific War Emergency Line. On the other hand, if a project received official approval, it gave private management a claim on government for tax relief and allocation of scarce resources. Since meeting the war emergency was necessarily a cooperative endeavor between government and business, there was an obvious justification for government to offer incentives to private business to expand facilities for war production. There was an equally obvious justification for businessmen to request such assistance before making major capital commitments expressly to meet an emergency situation. These considerations weighed heavily in management decisions in many areas of importance to the war effort, and pipelines were no exception.

Specific decisions on the commitment of capital funds to emergency pipelines projects hinged not only on the attitudes and policies of wartime agencies but also those of the Interstate Commerce Commission, Internal Revenue Service, and Justice Department. For example, decisions on rates for new facilities had to give consideration to the yardsticks applied by the ICC; decisions on payment of permissible dividends involved consideration of the ICC-determined valuation base and the attitude of the Justice Department. Finally, the tax implications of these decisions had to be analyzed in the light of Internal Revenue Service rulings. Therefore pipeline managements had good reason to evaluate proposed courses of action in terms of several agencies of government.

The tax picture was relatively favorable for new construction. Before Pearl Harbor, Congress had acted to help overcome the reluctance of private capital to invest in emergency facilities under peacetime tax burdens. The second Revenue Act of 1940 took cognizance of this problem, and Section 124 of the Internal Revenue Code was amended to permit accelerated amortization of defense facilities. Under its provisions, a taxpayer investing in a government-approved project could write off its cost for tax purposes in a period of five years (or in less time if the emergency ended sooner) contrasted with a much longer period under normal conditions. In effect, this treatment of amortization amounted to an interest-free government loan.[11] Restoration of the consolidated tax filing privilege in 1942 was also a favorable development for pipeline companies. On the other hand, pipeline revenues were subjected to a new tax levy with an increase in the transportation tax.

To qualify for accelerated amortization, the taxpaying corporation had to obtain a certificate of necessity from an appropriate government agency. Initially the granting of such certificates was in the hands of the War Department or Navy Department, depending on which of them had the greater contractual interest in the product involved. Later, the responsibility for granting these certificates was transferred to the War Production Board (WPB). The Petroleum Administration for War was generally asked for its recommendations on facilities within its jurisdiction, but these recommendations were not required by, nor binding on, the WPB.[12]

An exchange of letters between Attorney General Robert Jackson and John Lord O'Brian of the Office of Production Management (later the WPB) in June 1941, provided antitrust immunity to companies acting in compliance with government requests.[13] Activities of the Petroleum Industry War Council, the industry counterpart of PAW, were later granted antitrust immunity by certificates issued by WPB, after consultation with the Justice Department, under provisions of section 12, Small Business Mobilization Act.[14]

To meet the problem that was raised by the fact that the usefulness of a wartime project might end before hostilities did, "nonnecessity certificates" were also issued. Under their authority, a taxpayer could write off a facility between the time it was initiated and the time its wartime usefulness ended. For petroleum industry projects, the PAW advised on such cases as well as on amendments to certificates of necessity resulting from discrepancies between original plans and estimated costs and the actual results.[15] In all, the PAW approved 39 privately financed pipeline projects of varying magnitudes, and 27 were completed by September 30, 1945.[16]

THE CONSENT DECREE PROBLEM

Although governmental tax policies adopted to meet the war emergency aided new construction, the consent decree had introduced an important new variable into financial decisions. The decree had been rushed through in December 1941 to allow both the government and the oil industry to get on with the tasks of war, but compliance with it became a matter of immediate and continuing concern.

From the managerial standpoint, the meaning of the consent decree could be established in only three ways, each of them potentially dangerous in the sense that adoption of any one of them might bring in its wake penalties or restrictions that were not explicit in the decree itself. First, clarification might be sought directly and formally from the Justice Department. However, members of the department's staff had opposed the decree in the first place, and there was more than a slight chance that they would have an influential part in any interpretations rendered by the department. Second, clarification might be sought from the courts, but the Justice Department would be a party to any such proceeding and could widen the area of inquiry and interpretation beyond that contemplated by the industry parties starting the action. An additional disadvantage of an approach via the courts was the differing position of each company subject to the decree. A substantive question vital to one might be a matter of indifference to others under existing conditions, though a court ruling on the matter might open new areas of uncertainty for all of them. Consequently, any company that took the initiative in seeking formal court interpretation of the decree ran the risk of disturbing the *status quo* under which all companies operated.

The most feasible alternative in terms of flexibility was for each company subject to the decree to interpret the document for itself, report to the Justice Department what the company had done or proposed to do, and attempt to clarify the decree in terms of specific, limited problems as they were encountered. The widespread adoption of this approach encouraged many different industry interpretations of what was and was not permissible under the decree and resulted in sporadic Justice Department interpretations that were not available to all companies except as they took the initiative to obtain them.

The questions faced by each company ranged from determination of the intended meaning of specific words in the decree to the possible application of this terminology to situations that did not seem to have been anticipated in the decree yet were not clearly beyond its reach. For example, did a pipeline's purchases from a shipper-owner have to be deducted from the permissible 7 per cent payable to the parent? Could excess earnings as defined in the decree be loaned to affiliates of the pipeline company's parent? To outsiders? The possible variations on such questions, depending on the size and extent of multifaceted operations by large, integrated oil companies, was virtually limitless. For this reason, if not for others, each company had to rely heavily on the advice of legal counsel. Even here there was a significant question. Was consultation with counsel and proceeding in accordance with his advice a protection against the decree's condemnation of "knowingly" violating its provisions? Although the industry negotiating team attempted to clarify certain aspects of the decree as they understood them, individual companies still had to decide what they should do.

The number of company approaches to the Justice Department during the war years was limited, but the results were significant. In early 1942, for example, the department approved — and the court accepted — a significant move by the owners of Great Lakes Pipe Line Company to refinance that concern.

The Great Lakes Case

The Great Lakes Pipe Line Company had been included in the government's three Elkins Act cases because Great Lakes, a pioneer products system, represented the somewhat unusual situation for that era of a pipeline system with a number of owners. Before the final consent decree negotiations, the eight shipper-owners had decided to withdraw some 82 per cent of their $13,722,300 investment in Great Lakes.[17] Apparently because it seemed that this move might result in the offering of Great Lakes stock to the public, in effect achieving voluntary divorcement, the Justice Department did not oppose this move. The industry committee therefore authorized James J. Cosgrove to negotiate separately with the department on behalf of Great Lakes.[18] Although it was anticipated that the results of this negotiation might be added to the general industry decree, the sudden change of events after Pearl Harbor made this plan impractical. Instead, it was decided to petition the court under section X of the decree, and with the approval of the Justice Department, for a special order authorizing the refinancing.

The shipper-owners of Great Lakes proposed to sell $12,000,000 in 15-year 3.25 per cent debentures and withdraw $11,252,286 from the capital surplus resulting from a write-down of the stated value of the stock. The debentures were to be retired with funds set aside from the company's depreciation fund. The Justice Department approved this procedure, subject to four conditions designed to protect owners of the debentures and to keep permissible payments to shipper-owners within the 7 per cent limitation of the consent decree.[19] Interest on bonded indebtedness was to be subtracted from the 7 per cent permitted to be paid shipper-owners.* No dividends were to be paid to shipper-owners if interest charges were not fully earned or until any such deficiency was eliminated. Sinking fund payments could be made out of cash funds from depreciation allowances, but unearned depreciation in an amount not to exceed current sinking fund payments was to be transferred to a special deficit account. No dividends were to be paid until this deficit was made up. The recapitalization, in short, allowed Great Lakes's owners to borrow indirectly against their equities but did not allow them a greater share of future profits than if the recapitalization had not taken place.

The federal district court for the District of Columbia approved these arrangements on August 3, 1942. Private sale of the debentures to five insurance companies and one savings bank was completed on September 4, and distribution to Great Lakes' shipper-owners was made on September 9.

---

*Great Lakes had a surplus of only about $386,000 as of January 1, 1942, so interest payments necessarily had to be made from transportation revenues. This was not true of some other companies with large earnings who had to decide whether interest fell within the 7 per cent dividend restriction.

A successful refinancing of a corporate-form joint-venture pipeline had been completed, substituting debt for equity and within the approved terms of the consent decree. It was a precedent of some importance for later pipeline development, though not widely copied at the time. Its primary importance lay in the demonstration of possibilities for using debt instead of equity to finance pipeline construction. This procedure, as will be shown subsequently, represented a major innovation and significant adaptation to the requirements of the decree.

Paragraph III of the Consent Decree

Meanwhile, the provisions of Paragraph III of the consent decree gave oil company and pipeline management and their legal advisers new problems. This key paragraph provided that if the signatories had carried any crude or products for their shipper-owner during the year, they could not "credit, give, grant, or pay, directly or indirectly, through or by any means or device whatsoever," to the shipper-owners any revenues derived from transportation or other common-carrier services in excess of the shipper-owner's share of 7 per cent of the valuation of the common-carrier's property. This paragraph had to be interpreted in conjunction with Paragraph V, which required that net earnings from transportation or other common-carrier services in excess of the permissible 7 per cent be placed in an identifiable surplus account. This account could be drawn on for working capital for a maximum period of one year following the year in which the excess was earned, for retiring debt outstanding at the time of the decree if it had been incurred to acquire or construct common-carrier property, or for acquiring, constructing, or extending common-carrier facilities. However, the latter facilities were not to be included in the valuation on which future dividends could be paid.

The effect of these provisions on dividends paid by pipeline companies to shipper-owners was further related to the valuation used to figure the permissible return. Paragraph III (a) defined valuation as "the latest final valuation of each common carrier's property owned and used for common carrier purposes as made by the Interstate Commerce Commission." To this valuation were to be added additions and betterments made after the latest final valuation, from which were to be deducted "appropriate" amounts for physical depreciation on, and retirement of, common-carrier property used for common-carrier purposes. Such additions and subtractions were to be made in accordance with ICC procedures. In the event the ICC had not made a final valuation of a defendant common carrier's property, the carrier was to determine the valuation for consent decree purposes from its records and accounts kept in compliance with the accounting methods prescribed by the ICC.

Valuation was a complicated process. Accordingly, from the start of valuation procedures — going back to 1934 — the oil industry had assisted the ICC by supplying basic data needed for valuation processes. At the time of the consent decree, 52 pipeline companies had received final ICC valuations only as of December 31, 1934.[20] Obviously, then, there was need to update them considerably for consent decree purposes; yet, because of the war, the ICC's Bureau of Valuation was too short-handed even to assemble or evaluate cost data submitted by the API's Pipe Line Valuation Committee.[21] By August 1943 valuation work was so far behind that the head valuation engineer of the Bureau of Valuation sought clerical help from the carriers.[22] In 1944, for lack of funds, pipeline valuation work stopped completely.

The valuation problem for consent decree purposes was further complicated by the fact that the ICC had never formally revealed its valuation procedures, nor could it be forced to do so. Thus, to meet the requirements of the consent decree, pipeline companies were supposed to rely on the ICC, which was not in a position to perform the valuation work required. Confronted with this problem, each company had to use its own discretion in arriving at a valuation figure for consent decree purposes. To preserve the best profits position possible, it was desirable for management to claim the maximum permissible dividend by making the most favorable interpretation of valuation procedures. On the other hand, to be safe from penalties under the decree, it was necessary to pay the shipper-owner no more than would be permissible under the narrowest interpretation of Paragraph III.

The problem confronting management was exemplified in the first annual report of Shell Pipe Line Corporation to the Attorney General in compliance with the decree. It stated that: "The management of Shell Pipe Line Corporation has not been able to secure the official formula or full description of methods used by the Interstate Commerce Commission in bringing pipe line valuations down to date. The accompanying tabulations, therefore, represent the management's best interpretation of the intent of Section III (a) of the aforementioned Final Judgment." [23] The question of how to arrive at valuation in the absence of ICC action continued to plague all companies subject to the decree and resulted in amended or revised reports as they changed their ideas about appropriate procedures. The Justice Department routinely accepted the reports for file but did not thereby specifically acknowledge the correctness of the methods used.

Paragraph V of the Consent Decree

The provisions of the decree relating to pre-decree debt as specified in Paragraph V were subject to the same conflicting interpretations as those relating to valuation. Prior to 1941 pipelines for the most part had been conservatively financed. Many large oil companies abhorred public borrowing, and they did not need to resort to it for pipeline purposes. Thus their pipeline affiliates were financed either through equity investment or with the aid of loans from the parent company.

The consent decree made special provision in Paragraph V to cover repayment of existing intercompany debts. Repayment by a pipeline company of debt outstanding and owed to a shipper-owner as of December 23, 1941, the date of the decree, was permissible. However, there was a potential conflict here with provisions of Paragraph III, which forbade annual payments to shipper-owners in excess of 7 per cent of the carrier's ICC valuation. Could a company which paid a 7 per cent return to its shipper-owner also repay pre-decree debts and interest owed to the same owner? The industry negotiators apparently thought that Paragraph V, for the purposes stated, constituted an acknowledged exception to Paragraph III. The Justice Department staff, especially after they learned the magnitude of intercompany debt, disagreed.

This question arose after the first annual reports required by the consent decree had been submitted in the spring of 1943. The Antitrust Division asked for a further analysis of indebtedness by certain pipeline companies to their shipper-owners and an explanation of the way that it was being handled. The position of the department, as stated by Assistant Attorney General Wendell Berge to one company, was that "all payments of every kind by the carrier to the shipper-owner in excess of its share of 7% of the valuation of the carrier's property" were forbidden. This interpretation appeared to contradict the provisions of Paragraph V of the decree.

Some industry analysts believed that the department was not nearly so firm in its position on pre-decree debt as its formal letters indicated. Furthermore, it was possible that Berge had deliberately taken an extreme position so that the companies in reacting to it would go to the courts and thus allow the department to raise new issues that it hesitated to bring up on its own initiative. Consequently, there was a strong disposition among pipeline companies to let the debt repayment question ride unless and until the department took the initiative and meantime to keep in touch with developments through informal contacts.

While these questions were still pending, Senator Guy Gillette renewed his interest in pipeline matters. On February 7, 1944, he wrote to Attorney General Francis Biddle asking whether action taken by the Justice Department had ended the practices that the Senator had attacked some three years before. In reply, Biddle pointed to the existence of the consent decree but professed ignorance of the specific results that it had produced. He noted, however, that 22 carriers had put $15,500,000 in their special surplus accounts for 1942, and this action suggested to him that they had not reduced their tariffs significantly.[24] Gillette reported this correspondence to his Senate colleagues on March 28, 1944, and promised to reintroduce his bill after the war emergency had passed.

About this time, presumably in response to congressional pressures,[25] the FBI conducted an investigation of the pipeline companies, focusing on their accounting procedures. No court action resulted, though reportedly pleadings were drawn up.[26] Meanwhile, Price, Waterhouse & Co. had surveyed accounting procedures of several companies subject to the decree and made recommendations concerning them. The industry negotiating committee helped to coordinate company interpretations and in June 1944 a clearing committee was established to keep those subject to the decree informed about Justice Department moves and proposed company actions.

Financing Pipelines Under the Consent Decree

The ambiguities and prohibitions of the consent decree created financial as well as legal challenges for management. As interpreted by most companies, the decree stopped further expansion out of profits. It appeared to require that annual net earnings in excess of 7 per cent of ICC valuation for practical purposes be "frozen." This was so because, while such funds could be invested in carrier property, this property could not be included in valuation for purposes of determining the 7 per cent payable in future years to shipper-owners. Whether depreciation taken on these properties was subject to the same limitation was not clear.

Given such uncertainties, the financial alternatives open to companies subject to the decree varied. One possibility was to invest no earnings in new property but to borrow the necessary capital, repaying it primarily from depreciation allowances. This practice would increase the base on which permissible dividends could be paid while reducing equity commitments and thus freeing capital for other employments. Another possibility was to invest allowable earnings in carrier property, freezing excess earnings (i.e., over 7 per cent of ICC valuation) in cash or noncarrier investments. Over time, this procedure increased the base on which permissible dividends could be paid but at the cost of accumulating relatively unproductive funds. In addition, this procedure created a problem under the Internal Revenue Act of 1942, because undistributed earnings were taxable. Alternatively it was possible to invest only excess earnings while paying out all allowable profit. This maximized, within the decree, immediate returns to shipper-owners but offered no long-run prospects of their increase. Finally, some combination of these approaches was also a possibility.

The advantages of debt financing exemplified in the Great Lakes case did not immediately become apparent to most pipeline managements, but within a few years its possibilities were widely appreciated. Facilities financed by borrowing could apparently be added to the valuation base on which permissible dividends could be paid. Interest on the resulting debt could be deducted from transportation revenues as an expense, and the debt retired through depreciation allowances. Adoption of such a policy, however, involved uncertainties that warranted cautious exploration.

There were at least two major obstacles to adopting debt financing: the negative attitude of shipper-owners toward debt and uncertainty about the reactions of the Justice Department. The war years automatically restricted the possibilities of putting the parent companies' attitudes toward debt to an acid test. Meantime, as already indicated, there was a limited opportunity to test the Justice Department's reactions to various financial arrangements. Although the Assistant Attorney General took a "hard" line, the Antitrust Division failed to back up his letters and words of warning with stronger action. As a result, the use of debt to finance pipeline expansion remained an attractive alternative as the oil industry faced the problems of postwar readjustment.

THE POSTWAR FRAMEWORK FOR GOVERNMENT-INDUSTRY COOPERATION

Although the integrated oil industry had its problems with the Justice Department during the war years, close and effective cooperation had existed with other branches of the government, reflected most spectacularly in the construction of the Big and Little Big Inch pipelines. Looking to the return of peacetime conditions, industry members considered ways of continuing the collaboration among themselves and with the government. The nucleus for possible action existed in the Petroleum Industry War Council. This group, in early 1943, appointed a Sub-Committee on Post-War Readjustment, of which Paul Ryan, formerly president of National Refining Company, was made chairman.

In September 1943 the subcommittee began to consider possible topics for study. Among them were such matters as supply and demand for petroleum products in the United States after the war, examination and analysis of crude-oil resources in terms of recovery and transportation, examination and analysis of changes in petroleum transportation resulting from the war, disposition and utilization of war-created transportation facilities, the status and changes in marketing, and re-employment of demobilized personnel.[27] The proposed approach was to accumulate and study factual information, not to recommend specific courses of action. Aware of the possible antitrust implications of even such limited collaborative activities, however, the subcommittee appointed its own counsel and arranged for outside counsel to review its work. A number of circumstances, among which was difficulty in defining a specific program of action and apparently some negative reactions in the PAW, led to the dissolution of the subcommittee in February 1944.[28]

Although it was a foregone conclusion that the PAW would itself be liquidated after the war,[29] the benefits of government-industry cooperation on war problems had been such that continuation of the Petroleum Industry War Council in some form was still under serious consideration after V-E Day.* In December 1945, a 23-member committee of PIWC, headed by W. Alton Jones, proposed a specific plan for a postwar organization. Its purpose was defined in terms of advising and consulting with the federal government on matters, national in scope, relating to or affecting the oil industry. It was also to take the initiative in such matters where it seemed

---

*Samuel B. Eckert, marketing vice-president of Sun Oil Company and wartime chairman of the distribution and marketing committee of PWA District 1, warned that extension of wartime cooperation into peacetime could possibly lead to charges of collusion and to imprisonment. He pointed to the industry's experience with the NRA and its aftermath in the *Madison* case as a lesson not to be overlooked in planning for the future. *Platt's Oilgram,* November 30, 1944.

desirable in terms of national defense or national welfare. Active membership was to be limited to executive heads of companies and major associations.[30] To implement these proposals it was agreed that 75 per cent of the former members of PIWC would have to approve. A poll of 75 members was taken early in 1946, and of 70 replies only 46 endorsed the proposal. Since this number was less than the requisite percentage, the Jones plan for a National Petroleum Council was shelved.[31]

The initiative in establishing a framework for government-oil industry liaison then passed to President Harry S. Truman. On May 3, 1946, he wrote to Secretary of the Interior J. A. Krug: "I have been impressed with the great contribution of government-industry cooperation to the success of the war petroleum program, and feel that the values of such close and harmonious relations between Government and industry should be continued. I, therefore, suggest that you establish an industry organization to consult and advise with you." [32] The President also urged that the Interior Department establish an agency to coordinate and unify federal policy concerning petroleum. To implement this suggestion, Secretary Krug on May 6, 1946, issued an administrative order establishing an Oil and Gas Division in the department "with a view to the conservation of oil and gas resources of the Nation and the achievement of petroleum security."

Adopting substantially the same approach as the one recommended by the Jones committee of PIWC in December 1945, Secretary Krug also took the initiative in creating a National Petroleum Council. Its primary functions were to advise and inform the Secretary of the Interior or the director of the Oil and Gas Division on matters relating to petroleum or the industry, to raise matters within the purview of President's Truman's letter of May 3, 1946, and, upon approval by the Secretary or director, to take appropriate action.

These arrangements were cleared with the Attorney General, and the National Petroleum Council was formally organized on September 26, 1946. It has continued to function, performing a variety of services as a point of contact between government and the oil industry. Members of the pipeline sector of the oil industry naturally became involved, providing, for example, data on the capacity of the underground carriers in time of national emergency and otherwise keeping government officials informed of the status and plans for these vital transportation arteries.

During this same period the groundwork was also laid to present the pipelines' case in a coordinated manner to government bodies, or other groups, who might have an interest in the lines. This development grew out of a need to answer questionnaires sent out by the House Interstate and Foreign Commerce Committee in response to a national transportation inquiry sponsored by its chairman, Clarence F. Lea, in 1945. A committee composed of pipeline company officials and representatives of their parent companies was formed to handle the questionnaires and to prepare a statement for the House committee. This work extended over the next few years and led in 1947 to the establishment of a voluntary, unincorporated association of common-carrier oil pipeline carriers, known today as the Association of Oil Pipe Lines.

DISPOSAL OF THE BIG INCH LINES

The fruits of wartime cooperation with the government in building the Big Inch lines posed a major problem for the oil industry as it looked to the return of peacetime conditions. To meet an emergency situation the government, with the aid of the industry, had launched itself directly into the pipeline business. Furthermore, the purchase, scheduling, and sale of oil transported by the Big Inch was handled by government agencies of which the War Emergency Pipelines, Inc., though staffed by industry representatives, was one. Thus, in addition to operating a key transportation facility, the government was deeply involved in transactions antecedent and consequent to oil transportation. Anticipation of such a development had undoubtedly inspired the industry proposals of 1941 to build the emergency facilities as an industry project, but as things had worked out, this plan was not followed.

With the completion of the Big Inch, industry representatives began to consider ways in which the government could be kept from exploiting in peacetime the foothold that war had given it in the oil business. One element of protection already existed in the Cole Act, which required the government to cease operation of emergency pipeline facilities within a year after the end of hostilities. Still, additional precautions seemed justified.

During the spring of 1943, some members of the oil industry gave considerable thought to the advisability of substituting a private corporation for the government agencies in buying and selling oil transported through the Big Inch. Late in March, for example, Charles F. Roeser, chairman of the General Committee, District 3, wrote to the Deputy Petroleum Administrator that: "Under any plan of operation, the basic arrangements for purchase and sale [of oil] should be made by the industry with the approval of the Petroleum Administrator for War."[33] The question was discussed within the War Emergency Pipelines and the various companies participating in the wartime arrangements. As the system was then operating, WEP, Inc., actually owned the oil moving through the Big Inch lines, purchasing it at the Texas end and selling it to the refineries on the other end. Thus no question of common carriage was involved. The reluctance of some companies to endorse conversion of the War Emergency Pipeline to postwar common-carrier operations acted as a brake on precipitant industry action to make changes in existing procedures.

Despite discussion of numerous alternatives designed to minimize the government's oil buying and selling role, it was apparent by June 1943 that no industry action should or could be taken. The PAW had taken a strong stand that its protective mantle was essential to guard the industry against "any possibility of a scandal or charges of collusion."[34] While claiming to save the industry from itself, the PAW was also clearly unwilling to surrender its control over the movement of oil. Upon mature consideration, industry representatives concluded that the PAW had a point. Disturbance of the *status quo* in an endeavor to head off future difficulties, which might never materialize, could be more harmful to industry interests than to let events take their course.

Postwar ownership of the Big Inch lines rapidly became a matter of pressing concern. If the industry failed to make the disposition of these lines fit the prevailing structure of the business, large investments in privately owned pipelines, refineries, and marketing organizations could be upset. On March 2, 1943, the Petroleum Industry War Council adopted, and Secretary Ickes and Deputy Petroleum Administrator Davies endorsed, a resolution that declared:

> The Petroleum Industry War Council recommends that, at the end of the tanker emergency and/or the end of the war, but not less than 6 months thereafter, the Office of Petroleum Administration for War or its successor agency call into conference the petroleum industry in districts 1, 2, and 3 to determine the disposition and future use of all oil pipe lines built with government money.[35]

A short time previously, on February 26, 1943, in response to fears expressed by independent companies about the disposition of the government-owned lines, Ickes had stated that he hoped, and would try to insure, that no action or inaction by the PAW would change the competitive position between companies.[36] However, virtually any action that was taken in disposing of the lines would have competitive implications. As a result, some industry representatives suggested that after the war the lines should simply be left full of oil, sealed, and kept inactive until some future national emergency should call for their use.[37] But obviously an investment of over $142,000,000 was not going to be abandoned by the government in this fashion.

An alternative solution to the problem of postwar use was to convert these lines into carriers of natural gas, thus removing them as a competitive factor from the oil business. However, this alternative had its drawbacks. Gas would presumably displace coal to some extent, and coal companies and mine workers would be adversely affected, as would railroads transporting that fuel. Therefore, these groups went on record as opposed to such a solution.[38]

From the standpoint of the oil industry, one of the major problems in taking a position on pipelines was that of ascertaining the peacetime economics of their operation. Under wartime pressure, cost had been no object. In determining the lines' possible postwar value to the industry, however, costs became a basic consideration. And costs had to be analyzed in the light of the privately owned pipeline network and compared with the alternatives of shipping by tanker and barge. Tankers had an advantage over small-diameter lines as was clearly attested by prewar patterns of oil transportation. But was the same true for the large-diameter lines?

T. E. Swigart, president of Shell Pipe Line Corporation, addressed himself to these questions in a paper prepared for the February 1944 meeting of the American Institute of Mining and Metallurgical Engineers and published in the September 1944 issue of *Petroleum Technology*. His findings affected much of the subsequent industry discussion about the Big Inch lines.

After careful consideration of relevant factors which, of course, involved a number of assumptions about postwar conditions, Swigart concluded that at best the oil industry could probably use only one segment of one war-built line to economic advantage. This conclusion was based on the very large size of shipments that would have to be made over the lines to realize their full economies, the costs of transporting over feeder lines into Longview, Texas, where the Big Inch lines originated, and the problems of distribution on the northern and eastern ends of the lines. When these considerations were put in the balance against the flexibility of and investment in tankers, plus the weight of customized private pipelines already serving fields and refineries, the presumed attractions of the big-inch lines began to pall.

Swigart assumed that no group of nonshippers would be interested in acquiring the government-built lines as they would have no means of guaranteeing the throughputs necessary to insure a return on their investment. However, shippers who might be interested in acquiring them already had investments in existing pipelines and tankers and were reluctant to acquire additional facilities that could not show very substantial cost-saving advantages. These he failed to find. In addition, the return on such new investment would in part be governed by the 7 per cent limitation on dividends imposed by the consent decree, further decreasing the attractiveness of major new commitments. He therefore concluded that under the best of conditions:

> The 20-in. line could not compete with tankers for Gulf to East Coast products transportation on a marginal or out-of-pocket basis; the 24-in. line could meet tanker costs only if enough East Texas crude or combined East and West Texas (by direct pipe line haul) were tendered for transportation to give it a high load factor. It is within the realm of probability that enough total petroleum business could be obtained to give one segment of one line an economic load into District 2 and it may be possible for industry to utilize a segment of one line for this purpose.[39]

Swigart's conclusions about the relative advantages of pipelines versus tankers were indirectly challenged in a statement by Secretary of Commerce Jesse Jones in November 1944. Asserting that pipelines could compete with tankers after the war, Jones pointed out that total costs (including gathering and delivery to Longview) for shipping crude to New York through the 24-inch line amounted to 38 cents a barrel compared to 60 cents in tankers. Comparable figures for products moving through the 20-inch line were 24.3 cents as against 40 cents.[40] However, as one industry analyst noted, Jones in predicting postwar competition had apparently neglected to figure the effect of taxes on private operation of the pipelines, and, more important, the 40-cent tanker tariff was double what prewar tanker charter rates had been.[41] Certainly, hundreds of new, efficient tankers had been added to the nation's fleet during the war,* and they promised to depress tanker rates.

Wallace Finney, Chairman of the Special Emergency Committee, PAW, and J. B. Adoue of Jersey Standard had earlier examined the question of postwar use of the Big Inch and had concluded that it would be operated permanently. These views were expressed in an article appearing in *Mining and Metallurgy* in October 1943. According to their calculations, the total cost of transportation over the Big Inch, including allowance for taxes, depreciation, and a 7 per cent return was 20 cents a barrel. Although these calculations were estimates and involved arbitrary decisions, they contrasted most favorably with existing rail rates of $1.46 a barrel and 67.5 cents for small-diameter lines making substantially the same haul.† [42] Without really analyzing tanker costs, they put that figure as being close to the net cost of the Big Inch transportation. In their view, then, the postwar operation of the Big Inch in petroleum service seemed assured. "It will provide not only low-cost transportation," they said, "but will have the further beneficial effect of acting as a cushion on tanker rates, which in years past have fluctuated widely."[43]

But Finney and Adoue wrote without consideration of oil industry reactions to the big pipelines. Both large and small companies became increasingly alarmed at what might happen if these lines developed into major factors in the postwar oil transportation picture. Swigart had given convincing reasons why large, integrated companies could not expect to benefit from them. Smaller, independent concerns, particularly those marketing in the Midwest, did not want their markets upset by the competition that would be added with private operation of the lines. In short, the oil industry, integrated and otherwise, was generally anxious that the lines should not continue in petroleum service.[44]

Some industry position had to be taken on disposal of the lines when Senator Joseph C. O'Mahoney indicated in the spring of 1945 that he would hold hearings on the full range of problems involved. Accordingly, leaders of the most prominent national trade associations in the oil and gas industries appointed a committee on postwar disposal of pipelines, refineries, and tankers. The chairman was W. Alton Jones, who had been intimately associated with the Big Inch from the start. Members included

---

*Between 1938 and June 30, 1944, the U. S. Maritime Commission had let contracts for 523 ocean-going tankers, four-fifths of which could individually carry 137,500 barrels of gasoline or 116,000 barrels of 30° crude as a full load.

†Sam G. Spal of the Interstate Commerce Commission added his estimates to the controversy in August 1944. Assuming a postwar valuation of $60,000,000 for the Big Inch and allowing an 8 per cent return on depreciated investment, Spal found the cost of moving crude from Longview to New York ranged from 16.0 cents per barrel at full capacity to 25.5 cents at half capacity. For tanker movements he found a total cost of 18.3 cents per barrel. Sam G. Spal, "War-Built Pipe Lines and the Post-War Transportation of Petroleum" (Washington, D.C., August 1944), 92-94. (mimeo).

Finney and Swigart. A subcommittee on pipelines was headed by B. I. Graves, vice-president of Tide Water Associated Oil Company. A panel group headed by Fayette B. Dow was appointed to consider the Big Inch pipeline systems' postwar effect as oil carriers. Another panel, composed of natural-gas industry representatives, was to consider the prospects for conversion of the lines to natural-gas use. Still other panels dealt with the smaller government-owned pipelines and with water and motor-truck oil carriers. During the fall of 1945 these groups made the formal industry presentation to a Special Committee Investigating Petroleum Resources and also to the Surplus Property Subcommittee of the Senate Committee on Military Affairs, both of which were headed by Senator O'Mahoney.

From the studies and discussions of the industry groups there emerged agreement on certain points concerning disposition of the large-diameter lines. First, because of their military importance, the lines should not be scrapped. Second, they should not be used for transportation of crude oil or refined products to the East Coast or the interior. Third, it might be feasible to convert the lines to natural gas service. Finally, if they could not be so converted, they should be removed from use entirely and held as a "military asset." [45]

To get an outsider's analysis of the problem with which the industry had been wrestling, the RFC hired the New York engineering firm of Ford, Bacon and Davis to make an independent study.[46] This firm's report, issued in August 1946, tended to support the oil industry's position. It concluded that the government could recover more of its investment from conversion of the lines to natural-gas use than in any other way. Their engineers believed that the Big Inch could compete with tankers if eastern refiners could use it at from 83.3 to 100 per cent of capacity. But this possibility seemed remote. Like the industry analysts, these consultants thought that tankers would be preferred because of their greater flexibility. The Little Big Inch, they felt, could not possibly compete with tankers and its only alternative economic use lay in natural-gas service.

Numerous views, both for and against conversion of these pipelines to natural-gas conduits, were received by the Senate committee considering the disposal problem. The Independent Natural Gas Association, for example, took the position that the lines should be sold or leased by competitive bidding and without restrictions on their subsequent use. The Commission for Conservation of Oil and Natural Gas stated that natural gas was a "drug on the market" in Texas and should be transported to the East. The Association of American Railroads opposed use of the lines for this purpose because of its impact on railroad transportation revenues. The Eastern States Retail Solid Fuel Conference and the National Coal Association, echoed by the United Mine Workers, favored shutting the lines down and holding them for future military use.[47] The whole affair was a classic clash of interest groups.

Although it had seemed that the oil industry had succeeded in directing disposal toward natural-gas use, the Surplus Property Administration

(SPA) headed by W. Stuart Symington created new problems. In a report to Congress on January 4, 1946, this body, or at least the authors of the report, challenged all findings to date by declaring that both the Big Inch and the Little Big Inch should be kept in petroleum service — by the government if necessary.* According to the report, the crude-oil line had distinct cost advantages over tankers; this advantage was more questionable with respect to the products line, but both were unequalled in their efficiency in serving the interior. After specific reference to the Mother Hubbard antitrust case and familiar charges that pipelines were important instruments of control in the oil industry, the report declared that disposal of the lines to the petroleum industry should be geared to the requirement that they be operated as "true common carriers." [48] Presumably this meant that preference should be given to independent producers, refiners, or cooperatives who were mentioned as potential purchasers. It was disturbing to industry representatives that the authors of the report had not consulted the industry for the "facts." [49]

In the absence of contrary action by Congress, the policy suggested by the Surplus Property Administration became the official governmental one on February 13, 1946. It meant that an effort was to be made to sell the big-diameter pipelines to members of the petroleum industry before their conversion to natural gas was considered. This operation soon got underway. Advertisements were placed in newspapers in cities and towns along the route of the lines indicating that July 30, 1946, was the closing date for making bids. These bids, or more properly proposals, were opened in August of that year and came from 16 individuals and companies. Some proposed to use the lines for petroleum; others asked for their conversion to natural gas. The only large oil company represented as such was Sinclair Refining, whose vice-president A. E. Watts indicated an interest in the products line from Phoenixville to New York, the 10-inch crude lines from Phoenixville into Philadelphia, and the products distribution system at New York harbor.[50]

Before taking action on the bids, the Administrator of the War Assets Administration established a special board to advise him, and asked two representatives of the Department of the Interior to join it. The department was committed to the oil industry's view that use of the lines for natural gas was the most desirable employment for them. When it developed that no further action was possible on the policy represented by the SPA's January 4, 1946, report to Congress, the Interior Department men withdrew from the Advisory Board. On November 19, however, the War Assets Administrator rejected all bids for the lines and started anew, this time with the cooperation and advice of the Interior Department.[51] Behind this

---

*Later questioned by Congressmen about this report, Symington admitted that he was not personally familiar with the underlying data. The principal author of the report was discovered to be a young man with no experience in business, transportation, or the oil industry. 79 Cong., 2 Sess., House. Second Interim Report of the Select Committee to Investigate Disposition of Surplus Property, 3-4.

change on the part of the WAA was a shift in the position of the Army-Navy Petroleum Board. Its representative had earlier stated that the board favored sale of the lines for petroleum use. In mid-October 1946, however, it became clear that the board did not feel strongly on this point.[52]

Once this difficulty was cleared away, the steps toward final disposition of the lines accelerated. Following a House investigation early in December, the WAA reopened bidding. Meantime it had awarded temporary operation of the lines to Tennessee Gas Transmission Company as an emergency measure during a serious coal strike. On February 10, 1947, the bids were opened (eight had qualified for consideration) and Texas Eastern Transmission Corporation was found to be the high bidder, with $143,127,000 offered for both lines — only $2,700,000 less than their total initial cost and nearly twice the highest prior bid. Among those interested in this new corporation were E. Holley Poe of New York, Everett De Golyer of Dallas, and George R. Brown of Houston.[53]

The sale was approved by the Attorney General and by November 1947 the final payment was made. Thus the lines that had contributed so magnificently to the war effort and threatened to upset the postwar picture in the oil industry finally passed into natural-gas service, ending the threat that had concerned so many for so long. Disposition of the other government-built lines — by sale or salvage — went smoothly and uneventfully in contrast to the struggle over the fate of the Big Inch lines.*

Although the Big Inch lines had been neutralized as a force in the postwar oil industry, it was virtually inevitable that new privately-financed construction in the postwar era would draw on their wartime lessons. They had shown the value of cooperative endeavors and thus paved the way for postwar joint ventures in laying big-inch pipe. Wartime needs had also resulted in the construction and interconnection of numerous pipeline systems in the interest of moving oil as directly and efficiently as possible to its destination. These connections were not all abandoned when the pipeline map began to be reshaped to meet postwar demands.

On the public policy side, the war emergency had given the oil industry welcome respite from attack by antitrust authorities. The consent decree settlement of the Elkins Act cases, or at least the form that it took, can be attributed to the coming of war, and in the postwar era it was to play an important role in the financing and management of oil pipelines. Meantime, the oil industry's outstanding performance under pressure had refurbished a public image that had been tarnished by such prewar episodes as the Madison case and the TNEC investigation.

Many problems relative to the consent decree remained unresolved at war's end; yet it seemed that it might not prove so restrictive on new con-

---

*The Plantation Extension, Greensboro to Richmond, was purchased by Keystone Pipe Line for removal. The Southwest Emergency Pipe Line was acquired by a gas pipeline company. The Florida Emergency Pipeline was sold for salvage, and the Ohio Emergency Pipeline was bought by Ohio Standard. U.S. War Assets Administration, *Quarterly Progress Reports to the Congress*, 1947–1948, passim.

struction as first feared. Pipelines had been brought to favorable public notice as a result of their wartime achievements, and a fund of good will had been built up in the top levels of the Truman administration. Provision had been made to continue government-industry liaison, and pipeliners had developed a framework for cooperation in meeting their common problems in government-business relations. All of these changes added up to a new environment for postwar pipelining and new managerial attitudes toward the pipeline's role and functions.

PART

V

The Transformation
of Pipelining,
1946-1959

CHAPTER 19

POSTWAR PIPELINE EXPANSION:
THE FIRST ROUND

The experience of World War II gave a new orientation to American petroleum pipelining. The size of investment and technical problems associated
with the adoption of large-diameter pipe, rising costs of labor and all materials, and an unexpectedly steep rise in postwar demand for petroleum and
its products provided major challenges for the managers of petroleum pipelines. The shortage of steel pipe after the war, the inability to foresee how
large the boom would be in demand for pipeline services, and later the
complications arising from the Korean emergency, further aggravated the
problems of adjustment to the new era. But over-all it was clear even by
1946 that this was a new era, that many prewar pipeline policies and practices had been outmoded, and that new ones would have to be evolved to
meet the intensified competition for new markets and retention of old ones.
As a result, the years after World War II saw an unparalleled expansion in
pipeline mileage of large diameter, a new burst of products pipeline construction, increased emphasis on cooperative undertakings, a downward
trend in the unit costs of pipeline transportation, and an upward trend in
outside usage of lines owned by integrated companies. Pipelining was never
more dynamic or challenging.

PIPE LINE GROWTH AND TECHNOLOGY

The rapid growth in demand for petroleum products in this country
after World War II was unforeseen, but once recognized it was matched by
increased imports and increased domestic production, necessitating major
additions to the nation's pipeline network. In 1946, average domestic demand for petroleum and its products was 4,912,000 barrels per day; by
mid-1952 it had reached 7,000,000 barrels. In this period domestic crude-oil
production rose from a daily average of 4,751,000 barrels to over 6,000,000.
Domestic pipeline mileage grew correspondingly. In terms of percentages, the largest part of this increase was in products pipelines, whose mileage in operation — as reported to the ICC — increased 78 per cent, from
9,000 miles in 1944 to 16,000 in 1950. In absolute mileage terms, however,
crude-oil trunk lines with some 65,000 miles in 1950, and gathering lines

with some 48,000 miles were more impressive, though their increase, 1944 to 1950, was only 11 and 12 per cent respectively.

The capacity of this pipeline network is suggested by the amount of liquid required to fill it. As of January 1, 1950, line fill for the nation's crude-oil trunk lines amounted to over 35,300,000 barrels; for refined products, over 6,000,000 barrels; and for gathering lines, over 5,400,000 barrels.[1]

Equally impressive was the increase in the diameter size of crude-oil trunk lines. Between 1941 and 1950, lines of 10-inch diameter or more increased 8,749 miles. The explanation for this trend lies in the fact that pipeline capacity rises almost by the cube of the diameter while the requisite investment increases more slowly. Since there is more volume per unit surface area in a large than in a small pipe,[2] the percentage increase in crude-oil trunk-line mileage was far surpassed by the percentage increase in its carrying capacity.

Table 18. Crude and product pipeline mileage by sizes, 1936, 1941, 1950.

| | Trunk lines | | | | | Gathering lines | |
| | Crude oil | | | Products | | | |
Size[a]	June 30 1936	May 1 1941	Jan. 1 1950	May 1 1941	Jan. 1 1950	June 30 1936	Jan. 1 1950
2-inch	—	—	—	—	—	19,620	17,249
3-inch	—	—	—	—	—	9,220	9,655
Below 4-inch	1,270	1,050	1,233	162	391	—	—
4-inch	3,990	3,590	2,768	692	1,366	13,550	20,940
6-inch	10,460	12,570	12,254	3,781	6,696	7,680	9,224
Over 6-inch	—	—	—	—	—	2,690	3,492
8-inch	27,060	29,380	27,780	4,230	9,979	—	—
10-inch	9,450	11,710	13,500	68	1,628	—	—
12-inch	5,510	6,710	9,027	68	817	—	—
Over 12-inch	80	170	4,811	—	4	—	—
Total U.S.	57,820	65,180	71,373	9,001	20,881	52,760	60,560

Source: Oil and Gas Journal (November 2, 1950), 32.
[a]Data for odd sizes are included in next smaller size listed.

Although initial investment in a large-diameter line is bigger, unit cost per barrel is lower than in a smaller diameter line over the same distance. The heavy investment characteristic explains the need for joint undertakings, which characterized many postwar big-inch projects, while the lowered operating costs explain the incentive to join in them. These economic characteristics were recognized at least as early as 1934,* but it took the war experience with big-inch construction and the postwar demand for petroleum to justify putting them to a practical test. Products lines did not show as pronounced a shift toward the larger diameters, but two-thirds of the mileage built in the late 1940's was 8-inch diameter or larger.

The postwar shift to large-diameter pipe was facilitated by new techniques for making, handling, and laying it. Pipe manufacturers contributed to progress by improved methods of rolling, pressing, welding, expanding, and testing large-diameter pipe. During the war a new cold-bending machine for large-diameter pipe was developed for use on the Big and Little Big Inch lines. In 1945 came the internal lineup clamp, in 1946 X-ray inspection of welds, and in 1948 a hydraulic bending machine for large-diameter, thin-wall pipe.

Developments in pipeline construction† were complemented by improvements in scheduling, pumping, and remote control of pipeline movements. Progress was made in improving pumps (largely centrifugal) and associated power sources, which were increasingly electrified in the interests of economy and automatic operation. Installation of remote-reading gauges, automatic pumping stations, and improved safety devices were among the innovations or improvements made to keep pace with the demands of the new era.

Communications were central to efficient, coordinated operation of pipelines. Over the years the pipeline telegraph had been supplemented or superceded by teletype and A.M. radio. By the early 1950's microwave radio systems, less expensive than telegraph and more versatile and reliable than A.M. radio, began to be widely used.** This innovation provided an important new means for remote control of pipeline operations.

A veritable technological revolution had overtaken the pipeline business. Industry recognition of the sweeping character of accelerating technological change was reflected by the fact that the API's Transportation Division began in 1949 to hold annual pipeline conferences and devoted a special three-day conference to products-pipeline technology in September 1950.

The pipeline business was done with greater efficiency as a result of these postwar technological developments. Pipelines moved 683,000,000,000 barrel-miles of crude and products in 1950, or 34 per cent more than in 1944; yet they did this business with only a 12 per cent increase in the number of pipeline employees. Reflecting the increased efficiency, average trunk-line

*F. R. Young, "Applied Design and Economics of Pipe Lines," *Oil and Gas Journal* (November 8, 1934), 38 ff.

†For a discussion of petroleum pipeline construction, see Harold S. Bell, ed., *Petroleum Transportation Handbook* (New York, 1963).

**Microwave communications, developed during the war, broke the log-jam of a limited number of channels for point-to-point land use. Keystone Pipe Line introduced microwave to pipeline use in November 1949 with a system that provided 23 voice communication channels on one system. E. B. Dunn, "Microwave Communications for Pipeline Use," paper given at API Products Pipe Line Technology Conference, St. Louis, Missouri, September 11-13, 1950. (mimeo).

tariffs filed with the ICC during this period showed an increase of only 2.6 per cent — or a rise from 4.70 to 4.82 cents per barrel per 100 miles. During this same period of rising prices, other vehicles for oil transportation, including barges and tankers, showed increased costs of from 13 to 80 per cent.[3]

Table 19. Innovations or improvements in constructions
and operation of pipelines, 1950.

1. Large diameter pipe — 20–22-inch — giving larger volume capacity.
2. Use of electrical or diesel power dual-fuel pump installations.
3. Use of micro-wave radio-relay communication systems.
4. New methods of cutting and tapping lines.
5. New mechanical sealing machine.
6. New methods for making hydraulic calculations.
7. Automatic or push-button operation of stations.
8. Use of radioactive tracers to direct products to proper storage tanks.
9. Handling of greater variety of products in same line — kerosine, gasoline, liquid petroleum gas, and others.
10. Automatic devices for detecting leakages.
11. Quicker assembly through double jointing and arc welding of pipes.
12. Use of six-stage centrifugal pumps to give more steady pressure.
13. Use of seamless pipe.
14. New longer-lasting pipe coatings.
15. New batching methods.

CRUDE OIL LINES

The supply of both crude and products pipelines naturally responded to changing supply and demand conditions in the oil industry. Therefore immediate postwar expansion of pipelines was inhibited by pessimistic wartime forecasts on the peacetime demand for petroleum products. In the months following V-J Day, however, these forecasts were proved wrong, and the oil industry was soon engaged in an accelerating race to meet unexpectedly large requirements for petroleum products.

The rise in demand for products in turn required enlarged sources of crude supply and more transportation facilities. Expanded refining requirements on the East Coast were met by imported crude and by tankers moving over prewar routes from the Gulf Coast. Midwestern demand for products also rose sharply and this rise increased the demands of midwestern refineries for domestic crude. Although the Illinois field had provided an important, nearby source of crude during the late 1930's, it was now in decline. Therefore, midwestern refiners looked initially to new production in the Southwest, where output and exploration boomed, and later to the Rocky Mountain area. To move this crude to refineries, new crude-oil trunk lines were needed.

After a slow start because of uncertainty about the future demand for products, plus a shortage of materials, pipeline managements implemented a sweeping program of large-diameter crude-oil trunk-line construction. Stanolind Pipe Line led the way in the spring of 1946 when it began to

Table 20. Total domestic demand for all petroleum products, 1944–1953.
(thousands of barrels)

Year	Total demand
1944	1,671,263
1945	1,772,685
1946	1,792,786
1947	1,989,803
1948	2,113,678
1949	2,118,250
1950	2,375,057
1951	2,569,827
1952	2,664,407
1953	2,775,321

Source: API, *Petroleum Facts and Figures*, 1959, pp. 209–210.

parallel its multiple small-diameter trunk lines from Drumright, Oklahoma, to Whiting, Indiana, using 20-inch pipe. A year later Magnolia Pipe Line commenced a 20-inch line from Corsicana, Texas, to Patoka, Illinois. This line, planned even before the end of the war, was the first completely new postwar crude-oil trunk line. It linked Magnolia's Texas system with the network of lines serving Socony-Vacuum refineries in the Midwest and as far east as Buffalo, New York.[4] These projects supplemented wartime construction by both Stanolind and Magnolia to move increased amounts of crude out of west Texas.

Other companies adopted the same strategy of improving transportation from the Permian Basin of west Texas and New Mexico to the upper Midwest. Early postwar crude production in the basin greatly exceeded existing pipeline capacity out of the area. Among the companies feeling the resulting transportation pinch was Shell Oil. Shell Pipe Line's existing facilities could move 85,000 barrels a day out of west Texas, but in addition to this quantity, Shell Oil Company was daily moving 15,000 barrels by rail and up to 75,000 barrels over the lines of other companies.[5] The Sinclair and Cities Service companies, which lacked trunk-line facilities from west Texas to the Midwest, faced similar transportation problems. Together with Shell Pipe Line, the pipeline affiliates of these companies, plus the Texas Pipe Line Company, agreed to build an undivided interest line, known as the Basin system, from Jal, New Mexico (a point on the Texas-New Mexico Pipe Line) via Wink, Midland, Westbrook, and Wichita Falls, Texas (points where one or more of the sponsoring companies already had pipeline connections) to Cushing, Oklahoma. The line consisted of 20–22-inch diameter pipe from Jal to Wink and 24-inch pipe from Wichita Falls to Cushing.* [6]

---

*Ownership in the Basin system was also divided by segment, with the Texas Pipe Line Company and Shell Pipe Line Corporation holding the largest interests in each instance.

Increasing deliveries to Cushing called for additional facilities to move this oil to the Midwest. Prior to the Big Inch era, it had been customary to lay parallel lines when other means of increasing existing capacity were exhausted. Shell had adopted this approach with its 10-inch Cushing-Wood River line of World War I vintage, which was paralleled by another 10-inch pipe in 1937. However, they were inadequate to handle the anticipated flow of west Texas oil. Accordingly, an integral part of Shell's plan for the Basin system was to supplement or replace these 10-inch lines to the Midwest with a large-diameter one. Since the Texas Company also had need for additional transportation facilities northward, it joined with Shell to build the 22-inch Ozark system from Cushing to Wood River. Construction of both systems took place between 1947 and 1949. Even before Ozark was completed, the demands on it required the addition of five pump stations beyond those originally planned.* [7]

New connections were also built to move Basin-Ozark crude into Chicago area refineries. The Texas Pipe Line Company in 1949 laid a 22-inch line from Wood River to Patoka, Illinois. Together with the pipeline affiliate of Cities Service, it extended an 18-inch line from Patoka to Wilmington, Illinois, serving the Texas Company refinery at Lockport, and to East Chicago, where Cities Service had a refinery. Thus, both companies' refineries could be supplied with west Texas crude from the new Basin-Ozark system as well as via the older 12-inch Texas-Empire line.

Pipe shortages, especially in the larger diameters, hampered these projects and forced the deferral of others by as long as several years. Construction of large-diameter natural-gas lines was booming at the same time as crude-oil and petroleum products lines, and the resulting pressure on pipe manufacturers proved overwhelming. In mid-summer of 1947, for example, the A. O. Smith Corporation of Milwaukee, one of the major pipe manufacturers, reported a backlog of orders for 6,000 miles of pipe.[8] To meet the demand for large-diameter (26-inch) seamless pipe, National Tube rebuilt its Lorain, Ohio, pipemill in 1948 and had already booked orders well into 1952.[9]

By 1950, the pipe log-jam seemed to have been broken and pipeliners looked forward to resumption of more normal sequences between planning new projects and executing them. Although midway in the year the Korean emergency intervened and caused some delays, the pipeline network continued to expand. The largest and longest of the lines completed was Mid-Valley, a corporate joint-venture form, owned by Ohio Standard and Sun. This 20- and 22-inch line was a logical response to the other large-diameter lines, like Stanolind's and Magnolia's, which gave their parent companies transportation savings in moving oil to refineries in the same territory as Ohio Standard's and Sun's. To a large extent supplanting upstream barge

*One 10-inch line was left in place but its pumping equipment was electrified. The other (World War I) line was taken up, reconditioned, and used in a Shell line between Elk City, Oklahoma, and Cushing to feed Basin-Ozark. *Pipe Line News* (April 1950), 27.

movements for its owners on the Mississippi and Ohio rivers, Mid-Valley stretched 1,000 miles from Longview in east Texas to Lima, Ohio. It added 157,000 barrels-per-day capacity to the pipeline network between Texas and the Midwest, and it could be expanded to 235,000 barrels per day by the addition of pump stations and similar devices.[10] Meanwhile, Buckeye built a 22-inch line from Lima, where Mid-Valley ended, to Toledo refineries, replacing existing 8- and 10-inch lines, and laid a 12-inch line from Cygnet, Ohio, to Ohio Standard's Cleveland refinery.

In the Northeast, the 12-inch line running from Portland, Maine, to Montreal was looped with 18-inch pipe.[11] Built by Jersey Standard in 1941,* the original line was sold in 1946 to British American Oil Company, Ltd., Imperial Oil, Ltd., McColl-Frontenac Oil Company, Ltd., and Shell Oil Company of Canada, Ltd. They exercised their ownership through the Portland Pipe Line Corporation, which owned and operated the system to the international border, and Montreal Pipe Line Company, Ltd., which owned and operated the remainder of the route.[12]

In Texas, there were comparable developments. Humble Pipe Line, for example, completed in 1950 an 18-inch line connecting west Texas with Houston and almost tripled previous delivery volume over that route.[13] Atlantic also improved its position as a purchaser in west Texas by building a new 10-inch line from Midland to Harbor Island, near Corpus Christi.[14]

In the early 1950's Sinclair and Ohio Oil† also turned to large-diameter pipe to replace or supplement existing lines. Sinclair put in a 660-mile, 22–24-inch line from Cushing, Oklahoma, to East Chicago in 1952–53, replacing existing parallel small-diameter pipes.[15] In 1952, Ohio Oil opened a 20–22-inch line between Wood River and Lima, Ohio, replacing multiple lines.[16]

During this period west Texas crude began to move in ever greater volume to the Gulf as well as the Midwest. The West Texas–Gulf line was begun in January 1951 and completed in May 1953. It consisted of 26-inch pipe from Colorado City (west Texas) to Worthham, and 24-inch from Worthham to Sour Lake. A 20-inch spur from Worthham to Longview connected with the new Mid-Valley route northwards. Ownership was shared by Gulf, Sun, Standard of Ohio, Pure, and Cities Service.[17]

Plans for yet another west Texas line to the Houston refinery area were announced in July 1951. The so-called Rancho system was to be an undivided interest line connecting McCamey with the Houston Ship Channel and its owners' facilities. Construction of the 457-mile, 24-inch line began in March 1952 under the supervision of Shell Pipe Line; dedication of the

---

*See Chapter 17.
†Effective January 1, 1943, Illinois Pipe's operations had been taken over by the Pipe Line Department of Ohio Oil, except for the Texas properties which were transferred to the Illinois Pipe Line Company of Texas. In this new relationship, the Ohio company's pipelines were operated under the charter of Ohio Oil until 1960, when tax and other consideration dictated the re-establishment of a separate pipeline company.

completed line took place in April 1953. Rancho's initial capacity was planned at 210,000 barrels per day, which could be expanded to 345,000 barrels per day. Like other new lines, Rancho had the latest technological features, including automatic controls.

Meanwhile, the discovery of new production in the Rocky Mountain area created a need for moving this new crude to market in competition with Mid-Continent and Texas oil. Low-cost transportation was essential, and this requirement led to construction of the Platte Pipe Line, a corporate-form joint-venture of five companies (Sinclair, Continental, Ohio, Pure, and British American Oil Producing). Laying of the $60,000,000, 1149-mile, 20-inch line was scheduled to start in 1951. However, the Korean emergency and accompanying steel shortages, accentuated by the steel strike of 1952, delayed construction. Once appropriate steel priorities were obtained, tight scheduling enabled contractors to build the line as rapidly as pipe could be delivered. The route between Big Horn Basin in northern Wyoming and Wood River, Illinois, was opened December 1, 1952. Like the other new systems, Platte had the latest automatic operation features, including 44 microwave stations along its route.*

PIPELINES FROM CANADA

Far to the north, the discovery of large oil reserves in Edmonton, Alberta, led to the construction of pipeline facilities to move this crude both east and west. To provide the requisite transportation facilities westward, the Trans Mountain Pipe Line Company was organized in April 1951 under the auspices of Imperial Oil, Ltd. (a Jersey Standard affiliate) and Canadian Bechtel.[18] Invitations were extended to other oil companies to join in the venture; a number, including Canadian Gulf, Shell of Canada, and Standard of British Columbia, accepted. Backed by the "deficiency agreements" of these potential users to cover servicing of its first-mortgage bonds,[19] Trans Mountain began construction of a 24-inch line in the spring of 1952. Following a route southwestward from Edmonton to Vancouver, the 718-mile facility, costing some $94,000,000, was ready for use by the fall of 1953. The first oil to reach Vancouver refineries by this means arrived that October.[20]

Comparable developments had already provided an eastward outlet for the new Alberta crude. Interprovincial Pipe Line Company, also sponsored by Imperial Oil but jointly owned with other companies, began to move the Canadian crude to Superior, Wisconsin, in October 1950. The United States segment of this line, from Gretna, Manitoba, to Superior, was built by Lakehead Pipe Line Company, a wholly-owned subsidiary of Interprovincial. Initially, oil moving through this system was loaded aboard Great Lakes tankers for delivery to refineries throughout the upper Midwest dur-

*See *Oil and Gas Journal* (April 6, 1953) for a detailed description of this communications and control system.

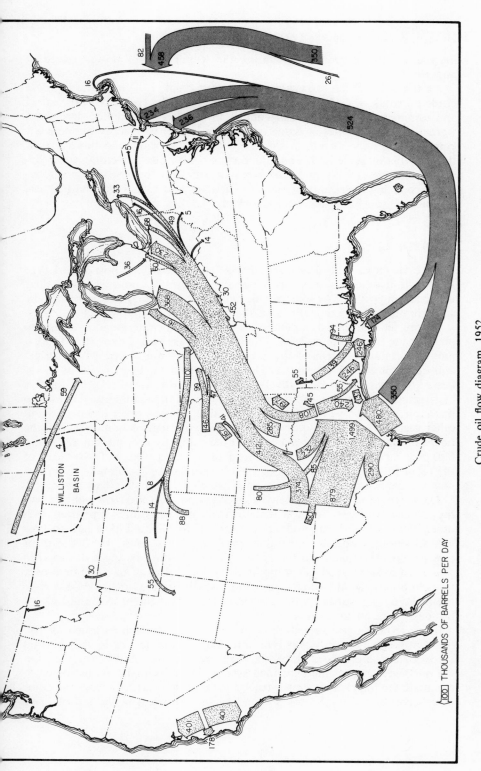

Crude oil flow diagram, 1952.

Source: Shell Pipe Line Corporation, Report to Interstate Commerce Commission Regarding Depreciation of Crude Oil Pipe Line Carrier Property, August 12, 1953.

ing the months of navigation; during the winter months it was stored at Superior.[21]

As these examples show, the oil industry created a great interregional crude-oil trunk-line network in the years between the end of World War II and termination of the Korean conflict in 1953. By the latter date there were over 32,000 miles of crude trunk lines 10 inches or more in diameter, compared to only 18,500 at the time of Pearl Harbor, and more than a third of this increase had been added since 1949. Supplementing these developments were many new feeder or take-off lines to serve newly discovered producing areas and to increase capacity into refineries. The new era of crude-oil pipelining was well launched.

PRODUCTS LINES

Like the expansion of crude-oil trunk-line mileage, the post-World War II growth of products lines was impressive. There was no question of their increased importance as weapons in the struggle to build and maintain the strength needed for competition in the booming postwar products markets.

Before the war ended, a number of products pipeline operators began to plan for the future. Among the earliest to act was Great Lakes Pipe Line, a pioneer products system of the corporate joint-venture type whose origin and development have been traced in prior chapters. Even while its facilities were being strained to the limit by wartime demands, Great Lakes's management was looking to the return of peacetime conditions. Anxious to maintain and improve its competitive position vis à vis other companies and other means of products movement, the management recommended to the board of directors in October 1944 that the company undertake a $20,000,-000 postwar expansion program. This plan was approved, and two-thirds of the requisite capital was to be obtained by borrowing — the new pattern of pipeline financing and another area in which Great Lakes had pioneered.

Underlying the proposed new extensions and relevant tariff policies was top management's recognition that to retain gallonage in competition with other means of postwar products transportation, Great Lakes had to provide its shippers with demonstrable transportation savings. The location of new pipeline terminals and the applicable tariffs were therefore designed to give southwestern products shippers using Great Lakes an advantage over transportation by any other means to most destinations in the Midwest — even where river transportation, a significant prewar threat to Great Lakes's business, was an alternative.[22]

The expansion program took several years, but though as much as 100 per cent reserve capacity was built into some of the new lines, they proved inadequate to meet the skyrocketing demand for Great Lakes's service. On the northwest arm of the expanded system beyond Omaha (constructed to eliminate the long rail or motor-truck haul into that territory from the company's prewar terminals) the demand became so great in the fall of 1947 that 12-cylinder, V-type Allison aircraft engines had to be installed as emergency prime movers on an overloaded system.[23]

As a result of its expansion program, Great Lakes alone made nearly one-third the total investment reported by both crude and products lines to the ICC for 1945–46.[24] A total of $30,000,000 was expended, and 1,200 miles 6- and 8-inch pipe were added to the Great Lakes network. Net operating capacity of the Great Lakes system reached 39,790,000 barrels of gasoline in 1947. Nine nonowners originated shipments on the system, in addition to its eight owners.

Shortly it became apparent that still further building would be required to meet the foreseeable demands of the 1950's. In 1949, therefore, Great Lakes embarked on a new round of expansion. At a cost of some $55,000,-000, the system's capacity was doubled once again, enabling it to deliver approximately 65,000,000 barrels annually for 18 shippers over a large part of the Midwest.[25]

Great Lakes was far from alone among products pipelines in its aggressive approach to postwar demands. In fact, expectation of severe competition for products movements had spurred its management to early action. This expectation was soon fulfilled, partially in response to Great Lakes's own construction. For example, as agent for Indiana Standard, Stanolind Pipe Line began in August 1946 to lay a line (10-inch and 8-inch) from Indiana's big Whiting refinery 662 miles to Moorhead, Minnesota, via the Twin Cities. And the same pipeline company was already planning to build an 8-inch products line southward from Casper, Wyoming, to Cheyenne and Denver as agent for Wyco Pipe Line (owned by Indiana Standard, Texas Company, and Socony-Vacuum).[26]

It was now clear that no important marketing center would long remain without one or more products line connections. Thus, for example, the Denver market also became the objective of the Phillips-Shamrock 6-inch line built northwards from Borger and Sunray, Texas, to La Junta, Colorado, in 1947. Although delayed by the pipe shortage, this line was completed to Denver in 1951.

Similar developments took place in Texas. Products pipelining from coastal refineries to major interior marketing and distribution points developed as rapidly as the availability of pipe permitted. Humble Pipe Line led this postwar movement when, in September 1946, it completed construction of a products line from its Baytown refinery to the Dallas–Fort Worth area. Although this project involved expenditures of over $6,000,000, it quickly proved its worth. Within a year of its completion, the line was delivering over half the gasoline sold by the parent company's sales department and was doing so at a considerable savings over rail or truck costs.[27]

Sinclair was another integrated company that moved aggressively into postwar products pipelining. Sinclair's management had made the initial decision to enter this field of transportation shortly before Pearl Harbor, moving products from Marcus Hook, Pennsylvania, to Baltimore and Pittsburgh. This line was expanded during the war and extended to Steubenville,

Ohio. To meet wartime needs, the line flow was reversed and products brought by barge from the Gulf Coast to Steubenville were moved by the pipeline to the seaboard. In October 1945, the line flow was again reversed and, in accordance with the original plan, products were once more moved westward over it from Marcus Hook. Meanwhile, to avoid dependence on lake transportation, a products line built from salvaged pipe and materials had been completed from Sinclair's East Chicago refinery to the Toledo area. In late 1946 and early 1947 this line was tied in with Detroit and Columbus, Ohio. Next, a connection was made with Steubenville, resulting in an 820-mile pipeline link between Sinclair's Marcus Hook and East Chicago refineries.[28]

While expanding its products pipeline operations in the East, Sinclair, like Humble, also began to build north from the Texas Gulf Coast. Starting at the Sinclair refinery in Corpus Christi, an 8-inch line built of reclaimed and reconditioned pipe was constructed to San Antonio and Austin in 1947. In November of the same year, work began on a 10-inch products line from Houston to Arlington, Texas, between Fort Worth and Dallas. During 1948 this line was extended to Kansas City, using reclaimed 8-inch pipe between Arlington and Panova, Oklahoma, and converted crude lines from there to the Kansas City terminal. By October 1949 Sinclair products refined in Chicago were also moved south to this point via converted crude pipelines.*

These developments contributed to Sinclair's decision to close down four smaller refineries in the Southwest. By concentrating on larger refinery units, whose crude supplies and products distribution were handled by pipeline, refinery costs were reduced and greater flexibility in output was achieved.

In 1950 Sinclair acquired a refinery at Wood River especially designed to refine sulphur-laden Wyoming crude. This input was soon being supplied by the new, large-diameter Platte Pipe Line. By converting a crude line from Wood River to Carrollton, Missouri (the old Prairie route), Sinclair tied the new refinery's output into its expanding products system, eliminating backhauls from Chicago to its marketing area in Kansas and surrounding states. Thus, in a few short years Sinclair had created an interconnected products system that stretched from Houston on the Gulf Coast to Marcus Hook on the Delaware River over 2,000 miles distant.[29] As a result of these moves, Sinclair's products lines in 1950 moved 35,000,000 barrels, a startling 33 per cent increase over the preceding year.

The decision to move ahead at this speed involved calculated risks. Sinclair management had been faced with the choice of delaying construction until new pipe could be obtained or making use of reclaimed pipe and con-

*The conversion of the Chicago-Kansas City line involved only the use of water pressure to blow out pits and weak sections before turning the line to products use. Earl W. Unruh. "Converting a Pipe line from Crude Oil Service to Refined Products Service," API, Division of Transportation, Products Pipe Line Conference, Atlanta, Georgia, May 21, 1951. (mimeo.)

verted crude lines already in place. It chose the latter alternative and was able to pipeline products extensively several years earlier than would otherwise have been possible. Transportation savings made possible by early completion of the Sinclair products system were expected to far more than compensate for any problems resulting from use of secondhand rather than new pipe.

As in past periods of pipeline expansion, a move by one company that promised significant transportation savings was quickly met by its competitors. Like Humble and Sinclair, therefore, the Texas and Magnolia companies also decided to supply products to the Dallas–Fort Worth area by pipeline. In 1947 Magnolia Pipe Line laid a 12-inch line from Beaumont to Hearne, Texas; from there Texas Pipe Line laid a 10-inch line into Fort Worth.

By the start of 1950, gasoline had resumed its controlling position in the operation of most refineries, but demand was rising for all products. Since pipeline costs were not rising as fast as those of alternative means of transportation, a new round of products pipeline construction was planned. Representative projects involved the rebuilding of the venerable Tuscarora, construction of the new Miami Valley Pipe Line, and the expansion of Plantation Pipe Line.

In July of 1950 Esso Standard Oil Company announced that the 300-mile products pipeline system owned by its affiliate Tuscarora Oil Company, was to be increased in capacity according to a reconstruction and expansion program.* The Tuscarora line began at Esso's Bayway Refinery in New Jersey, and served the Pennsylvania area through five terminals near Reading, Altoona, Johnstown, Harrisburg, and Pittsburgh. It also had a water terminal in West Virginia with barge-loading facilities from which it served cities along the Ohio River. Under the expansion plan, the daily capacity of the system, then amounting to 25,000 barrels of gasoline and distillate fuels, was to be raised initially to 45,000 barrels per day with a potential future capacity of 80,000 barrels per day. The existing pipe, which was of varying sizes, was to be replaced with 10- and 12-inch, and the nine pumping stations then in operation were to be replaced with four new, more efficient ones.[30]

Among the new products pipeline projects also announced in 1950 was one projected by the Miami Valley Corporation, a firm jointly owned by Ohio Standard and Pure Oil Company. This venture involved building a 58-mile, 8-inch line between Dayton and Cincinnati.[31] Construction, estimated to cost $1,400,000, was to start in mid-August and be completed in October. At Dayton, the new Miami Valley line connected with Ohio Standard's 6-inch products line from Springfield, Ohio, which in turn was connected by other lines to Toledo, where both parent companies had modern

---

*Tuscarora, it will be recalled, had been built 40 years before as a crude-oil carrier for Standard Oil. Retained by Jersey Standard after the 1911 dissolution, the line was converted to products use in 1929. During World War II it had been returned to its original role but was reconverted after the emergency ended.

refineries of considerable size. The Miami Valley line also connected at Dayton with a new terminal linked to Pure's Newark, Ohio, refinery by a 6-inch line.

Expansion of large multiple-ownership systems such as Great Lakes and Plantation added still more mileage to the burgeoning products pipeline network. Plantation Pipe Line, owned jointly by Jersey Standard, Kentucky Standard, and Shell Oil, embarked on a major expansion program in 1950.[32] Originally built in 1941, the Plantation system consisted of 1,261 miles of pipeline with 31 pump stations, including 456 miles of 12-inch, and 356 miles of 10-inch pipe and laterals. The new construction program announced by Plantation's president, C. R. Younts, contemplated a total expenditure of $52,000,000. The added facilities consisted of a parallel line of 18-inch pipe, 432 miles long, from Baton Rouge, Louisiana, to Bremen, Georgia, and 275 miles of 14-inch pipe from Bremen to Charlotte, North Carolina. Pipe specifications for the entire route called for 3/8-inch wall, grade B seamless. In view of the Korean emergency, government approval was sought and obtained for the pipe needed in construction.

A new arrangement of pumping station facilities provided for spacing at 120-mile intervals. This would give the Plantation system a capacity of 167,000 barrels per day (67,000 barrels-per-day existing and 100,000 barrels-per-day new line). By reducing station spacing to 60 miles on the new line, however, future capacity could be boosted to 221,000 barrels per day. The latest in equipment was installed. Pumping equipment at the four stations on the 18-inch section (Baton Rouge, Collins, Akron, and Silver Run) was composed of three single-stage centrifugal pumps in series.* Three of the stations on the 14-inch section employed two multistage centrifugal pumps in series, driven by 3,600 r.p.m. electric induction motors. New manifolds, filtering, and metering equipment were also installed. The importance of accurate controls is suggested by the fact that there were normally in transit over the Plantation's main line 30 or more different batches of products, of at least 25,000 barrels each.

Like other companies, Plantation borrowed the bulk of the money needed to build these new facilities. In this case, $40,000,000 in 20-year sinking fund debentures was sold by Morgan, Stanley & Company. An additional $12,000,000 came from bank loans.[33]

In the opposite corner of the country, Billings, Montana, had developed as a refining center using Wyoming and Montana crude. Products turned out by Continental Oil, Farmers' Union, and Carter Oil refineries were shipped from Billings into the Northwest by rail. In 1953, Carter Oil, Continental Oil, Union Oil Company of California, and the H. Earl Clack Company decided to cut their transportation costs and to enlarge their markets by building a joint-venture products line to Spokane. In July 1953 Yellow-

*A centrifugal pump employs an enclosed wheel or "impeller" which throws oil received through the shaft outward. Each impeller is called a stage. A series installation provides greater stability, flexibility, and efficiency than a parallel installation, where one pump may tend to take the load from others.

stone Pipe Line Company was organized for this purpose. Carter Oil's share was taken over by another Jersey affiliate, Interstate Oil Pipe Line Company, and Continental Oil assumed construction and operational responsibilities on contract. Construction of the 540-mile, 10-inch line was commenced in the fall of 1953 and completed a year later.* [34]

Spokane also received products from Salt Lake City via the Salt Lake Pipe Line, completed in 1953. And Salt Lake City, in turn, was connected to refineries at Sinclair, Wyoming, by the Pioneer Pipe Line (jointly owned by Continental and Sinclair).

A similar strategy of locating refineries near crude-oil sources was exemplified by Indiana Standard, which established a refinery at Mandan, near Bismarck, North Dakota, after oil was discovered in the Williston Basin. From Mandan, an 8-inch products line was laid in 1953 to Indiana's Moorhead products terminal outside Fargo, North Dakota, on the Minnesota state line. At that point it connected with Indiana's extensive midwestern products system.

As a result of construction and conversion, total products line mileage at the end of 1952 topped 27,000, and was almost triple what it had been a decade earlier.[35] This record growth far from exhausted the possibilities for expansion, which were increasingly recognized during the remainder of the decade.

THE IMPACT OF CHANGE ON INDEPENDENT PIPELINE COMPANIES: BUCKEYE AND NATIONAL TRANSIT

The competitive scramble and capital-intensive character of pipeline development in the immediate postwar period posed difficult problems for systems not affiliated with integrated companies. Buckeye Pipe Line and National Transit, two of the independent common-carrier pipeline companies left to fend for themselves as a result of the 1911 dissolution of Standard Oil, offer cases in point.

After 1911 Buckeye had been associated in common management with the Indiana Pipe Line Company, Northern Pipe Line Company, and New York Transit Company. As a group, they formed an interconnected crude-oil pipeline network extending from Griffith, Indiana, on the west to Buffalo, New York, on the east, serving such important refining centers as East Chicago, Toledo, Detroit, and Cleveland.

Although close working arrangements had existed for many years between these companies with consequent savings in overhead expenses, it appeared to the management early in World War II that formal unification would permit more effective strategy with regard to possible postwar developments. This view may have been influenced in part by the fact of a

---

*The Office of Defense Mobilization found in August 1953 that the Yellowstone line contributed to national defense. Accordingly accelerated amortization was authorized on 25 per cent of the capital outlay. *Oil and Gas Journal* (September 14, 1953), 75.

stockholders' suit over the allocation of joint expenses among the Northern Group and a June 1941 court decision that New York Transit had paid more than the court deemed its proper share.[36] In addition to eliminating such problems, unification would also permit distribution of some funds locked in for working capital or reserves as long as each company remained a separate entity.[37] Accordingly the capital stock of Buckeye was increased from 200,000 shares, $50 par, to 1,352,000 shares of no-par stock that was exchanged in various ratios for the stock of the other companies. By February 1943 these transactions had been completed, formalizing a managerial relationship that had existed for many decades.

During this same period, Buckeye's management made the important decision to move into products pipelining. The difficult first step was made easier by the unanticipated availability of a newly completed facility. To eliminate long truck hauls, the Ohio Oil Company had undertaken construction of a products pipeline between its Robinson, Illinois, refinery and Indianapolis, Indiana. The line, constructed with new 8-inch pipe under PAW authorization, had a capacity of 16,000 barrels daily.[38] At Indianapolis, tankage and a four-truck loading rack were constructed. For undisclosed reasons, perhaps related to uncertainty about the nature and future extent of the ICC's jurisdiction over gasoline lines, Ohio Oil decided in 1944 to sell the new line to Buckeye.[39] With the aid of a $1,000,000 loan from the National City Bank of New York, Buckeye management launched the company into the products pipeline business.

By providing service to shippers who would not find it economic to build their own products lines, Buckeye hoped to build a place for itself in a postwar pipeline world populated by large companies. Under the leadership of P. R. Applegate (1939–1948), J. H. Peper (1948–1952), and George S. Patterson (1952–   ), the company not only increased its crude-oil pipeline operations but also found, secured, and expanded a niche in the products transportation field. By 1952 it was moving products from refineries in Illinois, Michigan, and Ohio to destinations throughout that area,[40] utilizing not only new products lines that it had constructed but also small-diameter crude lines that it had converted to products service.

In the 1950's, Buckeye's management found opportunities for common-carrier products pipelining in the populous East, where refining was concentrated in the Philadelphia–New York area. Buckeye's Eastern Products Division was created in 1952–53 to move products from these refineries, and service was provided to points in Pennsylvania and in upper New York state for a number of shippers over a 440-mile refined products system of 16-, 14-, and 10-inch pipe built at a cost of $24,000,000. This system originated at Linden, New Jersey, and furnished an outlet from the Philadelphia refining area through a connection with Harbor Pipe Line System constructed by Texaco, Gulf, and Sinclair at the same time.

As an independent common carrier, Buckeye had no special claim on those who might employ its services; its business depended on salesmanship, efficient, reliable operations, and an eye for opportunities that others had overlooked or could not exploit economically. By meeting these challenges imaginatively, Buckeye's management found that it could obtain adequate financing. The company's long experience and the strategic location of its system were also important factors in winning financial support and shipper interest. The satisfactory results of the system's resulting expansion were reflected in a steady upward movement of daily average deliveries of products, which climbed from 20,000 barrels in 1951 to 182,000 in 1959.*

The National Transit Company, another of the common-carrier pipeline companies broken out of the Standard Oil combination in 1911, lacked the strategic advantages of its one-time protegé, Buckeye. The company's business consisted of gathering from thousands of small wells in the heartland of the early American oil industry plus the operation of two trunklines — one from the Bradford district to Pittsburgh and another from Kane to Philadelphia. At the end of World War II it also still owned the National Transit Pump & Machine Company, an asset of substantial value.

Wartime demands for trunk-line service across Pennsylvania had, of course briefly revived the importance of the routes that had given National Transit its early greatness. But the return of peacetime conditions emphasized once again the company's dependence on a limited area of high-quality crude-oil production. Despite such developments as water-flooding of low-yield fields to stimulate their output, the pipeline company was tied to areas of "fruit-jar production" that offered little incentive to expansion.

The company's future was thrown in doubt by two major changes in its ownership shortly after the war. The Rockefeller Foundation, as part of its endowment, held a very substantial interest in the pipeline companies separated from Standard Oil in 1911. In 1946 the Foundation decided to dispose of these holdings. Over 126,000 shares of National Transit stock were acquired by Wertheim & Company, a New York securities firm, and the Graham-Newman Corporation. In May 1947 the results of this transfer were manifested in the decision to reduce the par value of Transit stock from $12.50 to $1 per share; to separate the Pump & Machine Company from its parent, reducing its stock par value from $25 to $5 per share; and to make a distribution of stock plus cash from reserve funds.[41]

These developments apparently caused some alarm to the refining in-

---

*Fittingly, in view of the origins of the two pre-1911 Standard companies, Buckeye in 1960 acquired the renovated Tuscarora Pipe Line from the Esso Standard Division of Humble Oil & Refining Company. This acquisition permitted Buckeye to link its Eastern and Midwest Products Division, giving seaboard shippers access to new points on Buckeye's system, and more particularly to the Cleveland market. It had also acquired in 1953 from Imperial Oil Company another former Standard company, the Transit and Storage Pipe Line system which extended from Cygnet, Ohio, to Port Huron, Michigan. Buckeye's performance matched that of the largest integrated companies' pipeline systems. It was one of six companies, including such giants in the industry as Service and Humble, which moved over 200,000,000 barrels of crude oil in 1958. And it was one of the nine products systems that delivered more than 30,000,000 barrels of products in that year.

terests of western Pennsylvania who were dependent on the pipeline system for crude deliveries. Acting individually, a group of these companies by January 1948 had acquired about one-third of National Transit's outstanding shares.[42] After 37 years of operation as a nonaffiliated common carrier, the Transit Company thus had its relation to refining interests formally confirmed in this manner.

By 1956, National Transit was participating in products movements from Philadelphia to Pittsburgh, thus following general industry trends not only in ownership but in use of pipeline facilities. The story was substantially the same for the Eureka Pipe Line Company (also acquired by Pennsylvania refiners), South West Pennsylvania Pipe Lines (merged into National Transit in 1952), and the Southern Pipe Line (sold to Ashland Oil & Refining Company).

Both Buckeye and National Transit were long-established companies, and their adjustment to postwar conditions, though not without difficulties, was facilitated by this fact. More substantial barriers confronted those who sought to enter the pipeline business on the wave of postwar prosperity and rising demand for petroleum.

THE KOREAN EMERGENCY AND PROMOTION OF INDEPENDENT PIPELINES

The Korean emergency, with the accompanying opportunity it offered pipeline promoters to seek governmental financial assistance, revived interest in building major trunk lines as independent ventures. However, the obstacles to financing and operating them solely "for the tariffs," especially where the project was a large one and the promoters themselves not potential shippers, remained as significant in the postwar era as before. They were well illustrated in the failure of numerous plans to build a line from west Texas to the West Coast.

The Pacific War Emergency Pipe Line had been suggested late in World War II and shelved, but the idea did not die. The heavy postwar demand for west Texas crude in the Midwest and on the Gulf Coast, plus changes in the California supply picture, made a pipeline to the West Coast appear marginal from the standpoint of the large, integrated companies that looked into it. From time to time, however, various proposals for a large-diameter line were made by independent pipeline promoters. In 1948, for example, Texas-Western Oil Lines, Inc., proposed a 24-inch line from west Texas to the vicinity of Los Angeles under a plan that, to secure throughput, offered ownership to producers on the one hand and refiners on the other.[43] The problem of financing the line, involving some $100,000,000, proved insuperable, and the supply of crude in west Texas relative to existing demands on it remained too tight to warrant its shipment westward.

With the advent of the Korean emergency, the question of supplying crude to the West Coast from west Texas arose again. The Progress Company of Los Angeles proposed a 24-inch crude line from, and a 10.75-inch products line to, west Texas; a Dallas group proposed a 22-inch crude line under the auspices of the West Coast Pipe Line Company.[44] It still seemed questionable whether the price of west Texas crude plus transportation charges would make it competitive with California crude of comparable gravities, and independent California producers did not welcome this proposed influx of Texas crude. On the other hand, the possibility that the Korean emergency might spread, putting additional pressures on the West Coast's petroleum supply, indicated that government authorities allocating steel should consider these projects seriously.

The administration of defense responsibilities with respect to petroleum and gas was delegated to the Secretary of the Interior by Executive Order 1016, pursuant to the provisions of the Defense Production Act of 1950. Under this authority, the Petroleum Administration for Defense (PAD) was established by the Secretary on October 3, 1950. While the organization of the PAD was patterned after that of the PAW in World War II, it was dissimilar in several respects because of added responsibilities — including, among other things, jurisdiction over natural gas — and the differences between a world war and a defense mobilization program. Following the World War II precedent, the Act of 1950 made provision for financial incentives to encourage private industry to expand production. Among these incentives was accelerated tax amortization, and by April 1952, 350 applications on pipeline and terminal-storage facilities had been received.[45] Unlike World War II, however, no domestic pipelines were built with government funds during the Korean emergency.

The oil industry's National Petroleum Council, as well as the PAD's Supply and Transportation Division, made detailed surveys of the nation's petroleum supply, the requirements expected to be placed on it, and the transportation facilities needed in this context.* Based on these and other findings, the PAD submitted claims for steel to the Defense Production Administration, which allocated this scarce material among competing uses. With its share, the PAD decided how much steel should be allotted to natural gas lines and how much to crude and products pipelines.†

To some observers it appeared more logical for the PAD to encourage a pipeline connection to the Pacific Northwest from the new Canadian oil fields than a west Texas–California link. Such a line would save steel compared to a west Texas line, release tankers which were supplying the Puget Sound area, and reduce demands on California crude. In fact, as noted earlier, Trans Mountain Oil Pipe Line Company was already at work on a line between Edmonton, Alberta, and Vancouver, British Columbia. Taking such factors into consideration, the PAD in early 1952 recommended against building a Texas–California pipeline.

In September 1952, the PAD changed its mind and made an allotment of

---

*See, for example, Petroleum Administration for Defense, *Transportation of Oil* (Washington, 1951).

†Coordination functions between the PAD and oil pipeline companies were performed by a representative of the Committee for Pipe Line Companies. Gas lines were actively represented before the PAD by a committee organized for this purpose.

pipe to the West Coast Pipe Line Company, as well as to the United States Pipe Line Company which, as an independent venture, proposed to build a products line from Texas to New Jersey tidewater.* [46] Both these projects ran into opposition from groups who would be adversely affected by them. They also experienced the familiar difficulty of finding shippers who had markets for the oil that would enable them to commit sufficient shipments in advance to justify construction of the line.

The United States Pipe Line proposed to offer five-year guaranteed tender contracts to interested shippers and received Department of Justice clearance in November 1952 that such contracts would be immune from criminal antitrust proceedings. No immunity from civil proceedings was promised, nor was any opinion given on the possible application of other federal laws.[47] Within a month, four barge companies, whose business would be adversely affected if the line were built, tried to get the Justice Department to change its opinion. Failing that, they initiated court action against execution of the contracts, claiming they invited combination contrary to the Sherman Antitrust Act and discriminated against small marketers and refiners.[48]

Meanwhile, the West Coast Pipe Line had also run into difficulty in signing up shippers. Union Oil Company of California was regarded as a key prospect, but in a letter released to the press early in 1953, president Reece Taylor of that company made it clear that, although interested, Union Oil was not prepared to make any advance promises about its use of the proposed line.

This development triggered a familiar reaction in Texas. The executive committee of the Texas Independent Producers and Royalty Owners Association adopted a resolution blaming the West Coast pipeline's difficulties on the large importing oil companies. Instead of meeting California's demands with Texas crude, the Texans claimed, the international oil companies were increasing imports from abroad. Olin Culberson of the Texas Railroad Commission, who had been critical of the government's failure to approve the earlier Pacific War Emergency Line, reportedly charged that the refusal of West Coast refiners to commit themselves to the new line looked "like a repression or restraint on the West Texas crude oil market." In Midland, Texas, a group of business and civic leaders met to consider ways in which they could aid the West Coast line.[49]

The whole episode was colored by a mounting friction between domestic producers and oil companies importing crude, as well as by Justice Department interest in the antitrust aspects of the West Coast petroleum situation.† Quite aside from these elements relevant to time and place, large

---

*The promoters of the United States Pipe Line had been encouraged to undertake the project because of a recent increase in tanker costs compared to pipeline operating costs.

†See below, Chap. 23 and 85 Cong., 1 Sess., Subcommittee on Antitrust Monopoly, *Petroleum, The Antitrust Laws and Government Policies,* Report on S. Res. 57 of the Senate Committee on the Judiciary, (1957).

potential shippers were reluctant to guarantee shipments to lines still in the planning stages and over which they would have no control if and when completed. In the absence of such guarantees there was no basis, other than government subsidy, on which such a capital-intensive undertaking as a large-diameter, long-distance pipeline could be financed. Denied this help, the West Coast pipeline project lay dormant.

The emergency government controls were terminated in mid-1953. The oil industry and its pipeline sector had weathered the "heating up" of the Cold War with a minimum of dislocations, and the machinery for government-industry cooperation had proved its worth.

THE CHANGING PICTURE

The Korean emergency had added impetus to the postwar trend toward use of large-diameter pipe. Total petroleum pipeline mileage rose from 158,472 miles in December 1950 to 179,023 three years later. In each year more total mileage was added than in the year before. However, crude-oil trunk-line mileage reported to the ICC was affected by the completion of pre-1950 building programs and the resulting substitution of single large-diameter for multiple small-diameter lines. As a result, crude-oil pipeline mileage remained virtually constant in 1950–1952 and actually declined in 1953, though capacity increased.[50]

In addition to strengthening the existing patterns of pipeline transportation,* the construction of this period indicates new trends and geographic emphases. Texas' development is particularly noticeable. The increase in Texas mileage between 1946 and 1953 accounted for nearly all the net gain in crude-oil pipeline mileage for the United States, and for 15 per cent of the increase in products mileage. West Texas alone had five new crude lines — four to the Gulf and one north to Chicago. But the Northwest's participation for the first time in the pipeline revolution was even more dramatic. Although eight western states† did not report a single mile of products lines in 1946, they had a total of 1,581 miles in 1953. Crude was coming into the Northwest for refining from Canada, and refineries built near new sources of crude in Wyoming and Montana were points of origin for products distribution to the western states.

Many factors helped to change the nation's pipeline map between 1945 and 1953. Chief among them was the need of integrated companies and other producers to obtain outlets for new crude discoveries and for refiners to improve their access to major crude supplies. This need plus the possibilities for achieving increased economies in the pipeline transportation of petroleum and its products led to an impressive amount of new pipeline construction. But further changes were yet to come, building on and extending the lessons learned during the early postwar period.

*Of the total increase in products mileage from 1946 to 1953, the increase in Ohio, Michigan, Indiana, and Illinois accounted for over 22 per cent.

†Washington, Oregon, Idaho, Montana, Wyoming, Colorado, Utah, and Nevada. Of these, only Nevada and Montana had no products lines in 1953.

CHAPTER 20

POSTWAR PIPELINE EXPANSION:
THE SECOND ROUND

During the years following the end of hostilities in Korea in 1953, crude and products pipeline construction continued vigorously. The proliferation of products lines was particularly impressive, and they were put to new uses by companies that entered this dynamic field of transportation for the first time. The trend toward automated pipeline operations accelerated, and new producing areas were knit into the national pipeline network. Although steel shortages and rising costs characterized the period, new records were set in the addition of pipeline mileage and capacity.

The Rocky Mountain area, North Dakota and Montana, and the Four Corners region of Utah, Arizona, Colorado, and New Mexico were the scenes of major crude oil discoveries that brought significant new crude trunk lines into existence during the 1950's. Again, big-inch construction generated competitive pressures that further expanded the pipeline network and reduced pipeline tariffs.

CRUDE LINES

Rocky Mountains and Williston Basin Construction

The 1,300-mile large-diameter Platte Pipe Line connecting Casper, Wyoming, with East St. Louis, had inaugurated the new era of big-inch pipelining from the Rockies to Mid-Continent refineries. Platte was in direct competition with Service Pipe Line (name changed from Stanolind in 1950), which previously had offered the only common-carrier pipeline service from the Rocky Mountains to the Midwest. The basic Service Pipe Line system for moving Rocky Mountain crude was laid in 1924 between Wyoming and Freeman, Missouri. Although Service had expanded capacity over this route by replacing 10-inch pipe with 16-inch in 1947 and 1948, Platte's 20-inch pipe permitted lower operating costs than even the modernized Service system and therefore could undercut the latter's rates. This did not become a matter of serious concern to Service management until early 1954 when, for the second time, Platte increased its capacity, reaching a total of 190,000 barrels per day. By then the Service lines from the West were being operated at capacity, additional crude reserves had been found in the

372

Denver-Julesburg Basin of northeast Colorado and western Nebraska, and a new large-diameter line (Arapahoe), jointly owned by Pure and Sinclair, had been announced to serve this production.

Because there were still further possibilities of increased traffic from new production in the Williston Basin of eastern Montana, Service management decided that the time had come to build a new large-diameter line from the Rocky Mountain area. Completion of this 625 miles of 20-, 22-, and 24-inch pipe enabled the Indiana Standard subsidiary to post competitive tariffs, and to make further reductions in rates in 1956.

In February 1957, Service also confirmed its place as the largest crude-oil pipeline system in the country by taking over the properties of the American Oil Pipe Line Company, another Indiana Standard subsidiary. Inheriting American's share in the Rancho system, as well as its east and west Texas and Rio Grande Valley lines, Service increased its daily crude capacity by 187,000 barrels to a total of more than 750,000 barrels, and its 13,000-mile system by an additional 10 per cent.[1] Although this was but one of a series of moves by Indiana Standard to consolidate the activities of existing subsidiaries, it added to the "visibility" of Service as a target for a congressional investigation to be described later.

The Butte Pipe Line provided both the Platte and Service big-inch systems with a link to the important Williston Basin at mid-decade. Butte's development was yet another instance of the pipeline's role in providing an outlet for the production of new oil fields.

By 1953 the problem of transporting crude from the Williston Basin had become acute; the Platte and Service lines out of Wyoming were 300 miles away. A combination of truck and tank-car shipment was a temporary transportation expedient, but the number of Williston producers requiring service and the expense of moving oil long distances by surface transportation made the construction of a trunk pipeline seem desirable. Accordingly, a committee of interested parties was formed. It canvassed various possibilities — on a strategic level comparing such alternatives as moving crude to the West Coast, to the Twin Cities, and to the Kansas City–Chicago–St. Louis areas; on a tactical level, considering the alternatives of building a major new trunk line eastward or constructing a shorter one to a connection with the Wyoming common-carrier lines to the Midwest.

As agent for this committee, Shell Pipe Line Corporation made a basic research study of six possible pipeline routes. By mid-1954, it appeared that no single scheme would satisfy the requirements of all the interested parties. Therefore the so-called Sioux Pipe Line System proposal was dropped, and each participant sought answers to his transportation problem in his own way. Several proposals were made by parties outside the Sioux Group interested in providing the facilities. In the end, however, Shell, Murphy Corporation, Placid Oil Company, and a subsidiary of Northern Pacific, all of which had production in the area, decided to build a joint-venture, common-carrier line through the eastern Montana producing district to a connection with Platte and Service at Fort Laramie and Guernsey, Wyoming. For this purpose the Butte Pipe Line Company was organized in 1955 and laid a 450-mile, 16-inch line to connect with the lines to the Midwest.[2]

Construction projects such as these increased appreciably the proportion of large-diameter pipe in total crude-oil trunk-line mileage. During 1953–1955, for example, crude trunk-line mileage of 12-inches diameter and over increased 24 per cent and at the end of 1955 represented 30 per cent of the total main line mileage.[3] This proportion continued to rise in the succeeding three years,* receiving a significant boost from new construction to connect the Four Corners producing area (Utah, Arizona, Colorado, and New Mexico) with established markets.

Outlets from the Four Corners Area

Oil was discovered in the Four Corners area in 1956, and even before the fields were well defined, various proposals to pipeline their production were being considered. Since the new producing area was closer to Los Angeles than to the Gulf Coast, Shell Oil and Standard Oil of California considered building a line to Los Angeles to overcome some of the 165,000 barrels-per-day deficit then being met by imports. At the same time, Texas–New Mexico Pipe Line (Tidewater, Texaco, Sinclair, Cities Service) was weighing a connection with Jal, New Mexico, to link up with its trunk line from the Permian Basin to the Texas Gulf Coast. Also, Pacific Northwest Pipe Line Corporation had announced its intention of building a line to Salt Lake City.

Production in the Bisti (N.M.)–Aneth (Utah) fields was then only beginning and it appeared that — even with good prospects for more output — there would be considerable risk in building one, let alone two, trunk pipelines out of the Four Corners area. Since steel pipe was once again in short supply, the company that first found the steel for its project would win the race. Shell located sufficient steel (which had been scheduled for automobile production) and contracted to have it fabricated into 16-inch pipe.[4] As agent for the new Four Corners Pipe Line Company, owned by Shell Oil, California Standard, Gulf Oil, Continental Pipe Line, Richfield Oil Corporation, and Superior Oil Company, Shell Pipe Line Corporation undertook to build and operate the 600-mile line between Aneth, Utah, and Los Angeles.[5] Construction began in June 1957, and the first crude was delivered to Los Angeles over this line in April 1958.

Late in the fall of 1957, Standard of California and Shell Oil posted a price of $3.15 a barrel for high quality (40° plus gravity) crude in the Four Corners area. This raised immediate problems for the promoters of the Texas–New Mexico line which was then under construction and reportedly had a firm shipping commitment from only one of its owners.[6] The competition created by the Four Corners line had increased the price of

---

*The most popular size for new crude-oil trunk-line construction in this period was 16-inch diameter (1,591 miles); the next most common was 20-inch (657 miles). U.S. Bureau of Mines, *Information Circular 7942* (1959), 2.

Four Corners crude to such an extent that refiners in the Southwest were reluctant to commit themselves to the new area. This problem was eventually overcome, and the Texas-New Mexico extension proved successful. In the process these pipelines, built primarily to further their owners' production interests, had created a situation that benefited independent producers, encouraged exploration, and stimulated competition for common-carrier traffic.*

The discovery of new sources of crude oil in the Williston and Denver basins, plus the construction of new lines to serve them and the recently discovered Canadian fields, resulted in the funneling of large amounts of crude oil into the midwestern refining area. In 1955, for example, Platte was bringing 100,000 barrels per day from the Rocky Mountains plus an equal amount from Kansas and Nebraska; Service Pipe Line was moving 178,000 barrels per day from Wyoming; Arapahoe 80,000 barrels per day from Colorado; and Lakehead Pipe Line was moving twice this amount into the Sarnia refinery area.[7] Each line could also be expanded if the need arose.

GOVERNMENT ATTITUDE TOWARD FINANCIAL AID TO PIPELINES

The new oil discoveries in the western part of the country and private postwar big-inch construction raised the question of whether government-financed Gulf–East Coast pipeline facilities should be available to offset a reduction in tanker movements in the event of a national emergency. The National Security Council was insisting that there should be no repetition of the World War II oil transportation crisis resulting from submarine attacks on domestic tanker routes, so the evaluation of additions to the nation's pipeline network had a high priority with defense planners. They were confronted with a specific problem in 1955 when the Texas Eastern Transmission Company and American Pipe Line Company asked for government assistance in proposed pipeline projects.

Texas Eastern wanted government approval and aid for its plan to convert the Big Inch from natural gas back to crude service between the Gulf of Mexico and the vicinity of Pittsburgh; American Pipe Line wanted government help to build a products line and a stand-by crude line from Texas to the East Coast. After consideration, both these requests were turned down by the Office of Defense Mobilization. ODM and its advisers in the Oil and Gas Division of the Interior Department apparently believed that the volume and location of privately financed pipeline construction were changing the crude supply picture rapidly enough to preclude the need for commitment of any government guarantees or funds to oil pipelines for the time being.[8]

This view did not change during the next three years. In 1958, the ef-

---

*The Four Corners line began deliveries to Los Angeles in April 1958 at the rate of 53,000 barrels per day. In June the Texas-New Mexico line began operations at a comparable level of volume. *Petroleum Week*, April 11, 1958, July 11, 1958.

Petroleum transportation patterns in the United States, crude-oil pipelines, 1958.

forts of two perennial applicants for government aid in building pipelines were denied for the last time. The West Coast Pipe Line Company, it will be recalled, had obtained a tax amortization certificate and steel allocation during the Korean conflict, to build a line from west Texas to the West Coast. Unable to obtain enough shipper commitments to support this endeavor, the project had languished. In 1958, however, West Coast was asking the government to guarantee loans for $139,000,000 of its proposed $146,000,000 line from Wink, Texas, to Norwalk, California. American Pipe Line, disappointed in its 1955 application, now sought government guarantees for $35,000,000 of the estimated cost of a products line from Beaumont, Texas, to Newark, New Jersey. After review by both Defense and Interior Departments, these applications were rejected by Defense Mobilizer Gordon Gray. While he termed both projects "desirable," he did not find them sufficiently essential for mobilization needs to warrant government aid.[9] Although West Coast's tax-amortization certificate was extended into 1959, its fate had been sealed.

Never since the beginning of the American oil industry, except during World War II, had the federal government financed oil pipeline construction directly. Consequently, denial of such aid to launch new pipelines in the 1950's was in keeping with a long and consistent policy. In this same period, however, government action curbing crude-oil imports provided welcome aid to domestic producers and protection to existing domestic crude-lines investment.

IMPORT OIL QUOTAS

The upward trend of oil imports in the early 1950's led to demands for their curtailment, and Congress took notice. Under the Trade Agreements Extension Act of 1955, the director of ODM was empowered to advise the President when oil imports imperiled national security. If the President agreed, he could take the requisite action to limit them. This mild provision proved inadequate and had to be strengthened in 1958, when total imports rose to 24.7 per cent of domestic crude production compared to the 16.6 per cent of 1954.[10] Finally, mandatory oil import controls were imposed by President Eisenhower in March 1959.[11] Since most of the leading crude-oil pipeline owners in the United States were also crude importers, the new import controls gave increased importance to their domestic producing and pipeline subsidiaries, as well as relieving the fears of domestic oil operators generally. The resulting repercussions on oil-company strategy, although they affected pipelines to some extent, are beyond the scope of this study.

OIL FROM CANADA

The threatened imposition of United States controls on imported oil was a matter of concern to Canadian producers and to investors in the pipelines that moved their oil into this country. Between 1953 and 1959 this investment had increased appreciably.

Predictably a use for Canadian crude had been found in the United States Pacific Northwest, a fast-growing area of the country that up to the early 1950's had lacked major refining capacity. In 1954 a spur pipeline was built off Trans Mountain Pipe Line, which terminated at Vancouver, British Columbia, to serve a refinery at Ferndale, Washington. Meanwhile, Shell Oil had decided to build a new refinery at Anacortes, Washington, on Puget Sound, accessible to ocean-going tankers.[12] The availability of Canadian crude was also a consideration in locating the Shell refinery, which was linked to Trans Mountain in August 1955.

The Interprovincial-Lakehead system running southeast from the Canadian oil fields to the United States was so successful that its capacity was soon increased and the line extended. To eliminate the costly storage and inventory investments necessitated by seasonal navigation of the Great Lakes, the pipeline was pushed from Superior, Wisconsin, to the Sarnia, Ontario, refining complex near Detroit. When this section of 30-inch pipe was completed in 1953, the Edmonton-Sarnia line was the longest in the world — 1,750 miles.[13] The following year the Minnesota Pipe Line Company tapped the Lakehead line at Clearbrook, Minnesota, to bring Canadian crude to refineries in the Twin Cities. In 1957, Lakehead was further extended 156 miles from Sarnia to Port Credit, Ontario, near Toronto, where it served British-American and Regent plants.[14] By 1959 the Interprovincial-Lakehead system covered some 2,000 miles and represented a $250,000,000 investment.*

A mandatory limitation on imports of Canadian oil to the United States was obviously a threat to these large pipeline investments. After a flurry of diplomatic activity, this threat was removed by exempting imports of oil by land transportation from the import-control program.

TECHNOLOGICAL ADVANCES

Technological advances continued during this period, but they were more evolutionary than revolutionary. There was continued emphasis on reducing costs in all areas, particularly by improving construction practices and by developing still further the remote and automatic operation of pipelines. The construction of the Four Corners line can be taken as typical of the most advanced industry practice in the late 1950's.[15]

Construction was by contract, involving four major contractors along the main line. Ditches for the 16-inch pipe were 30 inches wide and depth was such that minimum cover was 36 inches, except 12 inches in rock where blasting was required. Where the bottom of the ditch contained rock or other hard objects, a minimum pad of 6 inches of backfill material free of hard objects was placed in the bottom of the ditch before lowering the pipe. After the pipe was in place, another 6 inches minimum of backfill material

* In 1960 the Interprovincial-Lakehead system was interconnected with Buckeye's system at Port Huron, Michigan, affording Detroit and Toledo refiners access to Canadian crude via pipeline.

free of hard objects was placed around and over the pipe. During the lowering-in process, protective shields were placed alongside walls of any ditch containing rock or other hard objects. Block valves and insulating flanges were installed on both sides of the Colorado and Little Colorado rivers, on the south side of the San Juan River, at pump stations, at delivery junctions in the Los Angeles area, and at several intermediate locations along the line.

Approximately 45 miles of pipe in the Los Angeles area was shop-coated to a nominal thickness of 9/16 inches with "Somastic" coating. Buried pipe not coated with "Somastic" and not placed in casing or under rivers and small water courses (where pipe was pushed into place) was coated with a single layer of asphalt or coal tar enamel with a minimum thickness of 3/32 inches, into which a layer of glass fiber reinforcing was drawn, followed by a layer of impregnated asbestos felt. Pipe which was pulled into place across water courses and into casing had three alternating coats 2/32 inches thick of enamel and glass fiber reinforcing followed by a layer of felt. Pipe for the Colorado River crossing was given a double coat of coal tar enamel and glass fiber reinforcing, and a single layer of felt wrapper followed by a concrete sheath with a minimum thickness of 1 inch.

Pipe thickness varied over the route, but the longest stretch (492.5 miles) was 1/4-inch X-52 electric weld pipe. Water crossings took heavier pipe, and 1/2-inch wall, Grade X-42 seamless steel pipe was installed at these points. The Little Colorado River crossing was installed on an existing highway bridge at Cameron, Arizona, and the Los Angeles River crossing on the Union Pacific Railroad bridge. All other major crossings were placed under ground.

The latest in communications systems was provided. A General Electric Type UA-1-D microwave system with talking, supervisory control and telemeter channels extended from Farmington, New Mexico, to Los Angeles, California. General Electric VHF Radio Base Stations were located at each of the five microwave junctions and three repeater stations, and mobile radio units were supplied for automotive equipment.

There were three pump stations on the main line and two pressure reducing stations. The pump stations were equipped with centrifugal pumps powered by electric motors, while the pressure-reducing stations employed double acting piston power injection pumps. Initial capacity of the line was 70,000 barrels per day, which the pumps could move at the rate of 2.36 miles per hour. Additional pump stations, contemplated in the engineering design, could raise daily capacity to 160,000 barrels.

Automation which characterized the Four Corners system had its counterpart even in gathering operations. In this area, one of the most significant developments of the 1950's was the introduction of lease automatic custody transfer (LACT) of crude oil. Standard practice since the early days of the industry had been for gaugers to visit leases, test the quality of oil in lease tanks, and measure the volume released into the pipeline. This was a time-consuming, arduous job and also required a considerable investment in tankage to hold oil awaiting the gauger's visit. LACT, first introduced in 1955, began to change all this. LACT units performed the gauger's job electronically, automatically determining the quality of the oil and releasing it to the pipeline when the lease tank was full. This approach to saving manpower and money was so successful that the number of LACT-served leases in this country rose to 100 by 1958.[16] During this period there were also comparable efforts to put deliveries to refineries on an automatic basis.

Perhaps the most outstanding example of the result of aggressive management efforts to reduce maintenance costs and improve labor productivity was the record of Service Pipe Line. In 1946, it had employed 780 maintenance personnel while moving 292,000 barrels per day through a 9,500-mile system. In 1957 the system's mileage had risen to 14,000 and daily deliveries to 800,000 barrels, but the number of maintenance personnel had declined to 589.[17] Behind these changes, of course, were large amounts of capital investment in big-inch pipe and accompanying sophisticated equipment.

Table 21.   Productivity of pipeline employees, 1946–1953.
(1929 = 100)

Year	Output	Persons engaged	Output per person
1946	232.6	110.0	211.5
1947	255.5	115.5	221.2
1948	284.6	121.9	233.5
1949	279.8	116.8	239.6
1950	324.7	111.7	290.7
1951	388.0	116.0	334.5
1952	406.1	117.7	345.0
1953	430.3	113.4	379.5

Source: John W. Kendrick, *Productivity Trends in the United States*, NBER #71, General Series (Princeton, 1961), 556.

QUANTITATIVE MEASURES OF CRUDE-OIL PIPELINE PROGRESS

As a result of postwar construction, a vast interconnected crude-oil trunk pipeline network was in existence in 1959. Although there were over 70,000 miles of these lines, the figure had actually dropped 1,000 miles since 1950, principally because of the replacement of multiple small-diameter pipe with single big-inch pipes.* With the continuing shift to large-diameter pipe, barrel-miles of crude provides a more meaningful measure of pipeline progress than mileage. These figures had become literally astronomical.

Despite some departures from the upward trend in 1957 and 1958, crude-oil barrel-miles climbed from nearly 715,000,000,000 in 1952 to over 980,000,000,000 in 1958.[18]

Even more significant from the standpoint of the individual oil company and its customers was the fact that great flexibility and economy characterized these vast movements. To take an extreme example, crude from Poplar Creek, Montana, in the Williston Basin, could be moved more than 2,000 miles to a refinery in upper New York state over the lines of seven connecting pipeline carriers at a cost of only 81 cents a barrel, or under two cents a gallon.[19] This achievement had been possible by pipeline investment (much of it since the Korean conflict) which offered this refinery, and others, varied types and sources of crude at low transportation costs.

PRODUCTS LINES

Mileage reported to the ICC in the 1950's is an even less reliable indicator of growth for products lines than for crude lines, because roughly one-third of products mileage was for private carriage. Total products line mileage increased nearly a third between 1953 and 1958, with particularly large spurts in 1953–54 and 1955–56. At the end of 1958 there were nearly 45,000 miles of these products carriers.[20] In terms of barrel-miles moved, products line utilization doubled each five years, and the figure stood at 260,000,000,000 barrel-miles in 1958.[21]

A gradual shift to larger diameter products lines took place during this period, repeating on a smaller scale and after a considerable time lag the experience with crude lines. The U.S. Bureau of Mines reported that as of 1955 most products lines were only 8 inches in diameter and that there were but 443 miles of 18-inch diameter products lines, the largest size then in products use.[22] However, the basic strategy that had governed products line construction since the early 1930's was already beginning to change. A number of factors were involved, ranging from improved pipeline technology, particularly in the automation area, to reconsideration of refinery locations in the light of expanded products lines' use.

Refinery Locations

Standard Oil in its early days had set a widely followed precedent by locating its refineries in major marketing and export centers. Market-oriented refining in a relatively limited number of these centers had permitted volume shipments of crude, thus encouraging the use of pipelines which were ideally suited to this kind of operation. Products, on the other hand, were shipped out over wide areas in smaller amounts and were therefore less suited to pipelining. Where long-distance volume shipments could be assembled, pipelining products offered transportation economies that

*Between January 1, 1956, and the same date in 1959, some 5,600 miles of new and secondhand pipe were put in crude-oil trunk-line service. But 13,867 miles were taken up! Bureau of Mines, *Information Circular 7942* (1959), 4.

eventually encouraged the building of such multi-ownership products systems as Great Lakes in the 1930's. With a few such significant exceptions, however, development of products lines even after World War II had been on an individual company basis for which a line 8 inches or less in diameter provided ample capacity. Moreover, many small-diameter crude lines, as noted earlier, were converted to products service as their owners moved into big-inch crude pipelining.

By the mid-1950's products lines were no longer so completely the stepchildren of individual market-oriented refineries served by big-inch crude lines. With new oil discoveries in the interior of the country and the advances that had been made in products pipelining, there was also less justification than previously for moving crude-oil long distances by pipeline to a refinery and then shipping the refined products by rail back into the area whence the crude came. Even where back-hauls were not a factor, products pipelines offered demonstrated savings compared to railroad shipment if volume movements were involved. Accordingly a new emphasis on crude-oriented refining, relying on volume distribution by jointly-owned products lines, was superimposed on the traditional market-oriented locational strategy based on supply by crude lines.

New Construction

The basic pattern of building products lines from long-established refining centers to large marketing centers also continued. In 1954, for example, the Sinclair, Gulf, and Texas companies combined their resources to build the 16-inch diameter Harbor Pipe Line system from Woodbury Junction near Philadelphia to Trembly Point, New Jersey, on New York harbor,[23] thus joining the nation's second largest refining area with its largest marketing area and also affording a connection at Linden, New Jersey, with Buckeye's eastern products system to upper New York state. A year earlier, Harbor Pipe Line's owners had also cooperated to build the Evangeline Products system, linking the Port Arthur refining area with Baton Rouge, whence products could move into the Plantation system or barges for further distribution.[24]

Significant new products lines were built into and out of the Chicago area at this time. In 1953, Shell, Cities Service, and the Texas Company opened the Wolverine Pipe Line from the East Chicago refining complex to Detroit and Toledo. The following year, the last two named companies, plus Pure and Sinclair, built the Badger Pipe Line westward to Madison, Wisconsin.[25] A few years later the new Wabash Pipe Line (Ohio Oil and Continental Oil) was moving products along the familiar route from the Wood River refinery center into the Chicago marketing area. Meanwhile, such well-established common-carrier products systems as Great Lakes, Buckeye, and Phillips expanded their existing products facilities and added to them.

Outmoded crude lines continued to be converted to products use. In 1954, for example, Jersey Standard sold Ajax Pipe Line to the newly-formed

Cherokee Pipe Line, owned by Continental Oil and Cities Service. Ajax, it will be recalled, had been built in 1930–31 to move crude north through twin 10-inch lines from the Mid-Continent. Under the new ownership, one of these lines was immediately converted to products service and the other followed in 1958.[26]

The outstanding example of the movement to big-inch products pipe-lining was the Laurel Pipe Line, built in 1958. Laurel was a joint-venture project of the Gulf, Texas, and Sinclair companies, each of which had a refinery at tidewater in the Philadelphia area. Their common interest in westward products shipments from there justified construction of a jointly-owned large-diameter line through the interior of Pennsylvania and across the northeast corner of Ohio to Cleveland.[27] The segment from Eagle Point, New Jersey, to Mechanicsburg, Pennsylvania, consisted of 24-inch diameter pipe, an increase of 6 inches in diameter over the largest pipe in products service only three years before. From Mechanicsburg the pipe diameter was gradually sized down to 14 inches for the final segment from Aliquippa, Pennsylvania, to Cleveland. Numerous marketing terminals along the line, of course, reduced the line's required carrying capacity as the distance from Philadelphia increased. Sixteen grades of products could be assembled at the initial storage point, whence they were dispatched in separate batches to sales terminals and connecting carriers.[28]

In its purpose and geographical orientation, Laurel was not significantly different from the pioneering Tuscarora, Keystone, and Sun products lines of the 1930's which traversed much of the same territory. But Laurel's initial capacity of 100,000 barrels per day and 24-inch diameter showed that advances in products pipelining were now following close on the crude lines' big-inch example.

In this same year, 1958, the first big-inch products line, known as the Little Big Inch in World War II, was being returned to products service. It will be recalled that, much to the relief of the oil industry, both this line and the Big Inch had been assigned to natural gas use after the war. As noted earlier in this chapter, Texas Eastern had planned in 1955 to convert the Big Inch back to crude but had been rebuffed in its quest for government aid. This did not change the management's decision to turn the Little Big Inch from Beaumont, Texas, to Moundsville, West Virginia, back to its original use. Over the objections of barge and other interests who feared the results of this change, the Federal Power Commission approved it in October 1956. An appeal to the federal courts and further review by the commission did not alter this decision. Texas Eastern therefore went ahead with the project, which cost about $35,000,000.[29]

The initial products capacity of the remodeled Litte Big Inch was 185,000 barrels per day. This meant that aviation and motor gasoline, jet, tractor, and diesel fuel, kerosine, and liquid petroleum gas (LPG) could be moved from Texas, Louisiana, Oklahoma, and Arkansas to markets in eleven states. A new 14-inch lateral from Seymour, Indiana, to Chicago served Indiana-polis and intermediate points. Like Laurel, the Little Big Inch was highly automated. For example, attendants at four main stations operated twelve unattended pumping stations by remote control. Test shipments over this line began in May 1959, and regular operations commenced the following October.[30]

New Uses

While products lines were being expanded, the uses to which they were put became more varied. One of the most significant developments of the late 1950's was the extensive pipelining of LPG. The liquefied products of natural gas processing found a growing postwar demand for home heating and cooking uses, and as an additive in refining processes. In the 1950's LPG demand moved steadily ahead, improving its percentage of total domestic demand for petroleum products from 3.6 in 1950 to 6.4 in 1960. (By way of contrast, gasoline demand as a percentage of total domestic products demand moved upward less than 1 per cent in the same period.) In terms of barrels demanded, of course, there was a significant absolute increase in all products, with LPG daily demand rising from 234,000 barrels at the start of the decade to 621,000 barrels at the end.[31]

It was not until 1955 that a pipeline was built especially for LPG use.* In that year, the Warren Petroleum Company, a pioneer in LPG tank-car movements, constructed a 6-inch, 140-mile LPG facility between Liberal, Kansas, and Tulsa. From this small start, pipelines made steady inroads on rail transportation of LPG. Phillips Pipe Line, for example, batched LPG in regular products lines from Borger, Texas, to Denver and Chicago; this company, Magnolia Pipe Line, Gulf Refining, Shell Pipe Line, and others also moved LPG comingled with crude-oil streams.[32] Outmoded crude lines, as well, were pressed into LPG service. Phillips, for example, took over from Shell a 10-inch crude line made obsolete by completion of the Rancho system and converted it to LPG movements between west Texas and Houston.[33]

Despite the mounting pipeline challenge, railroads still moved most of the LPG. It was not surprising therefore that the Missouri-Kansas-Texas Railroad and the New York Central were reported in October 1957 to be considering an LPG pipeline from Houston to New York.[34] These plans, considerably altered in sponsorship and destination, finally materialized in the Mid-America Pipe Line. It commenced operation in 1960, delivering LPG from Texas and New Mexico to points as distant as the Twin Cities and Janesville, Wisconsin. The significance of the mounting LPG traffic was reflected by the fact that half the products-line mileage added to the existing network in the four years after September 30, 1957, was for LPG use.[35] A leading railroad owner, the Southern Pacific Company, also entered the products pipeline business during this period. Among the customers

---

*There was previous experience with LPG movements by pipeline. For example, Humble Pipe Line converted a 300-mile crude facility to this use in 1936. It could move 16,000 barrels per day from east Texas to Baytown. *The Story of Humble Pipe Line Company,* published by the company.

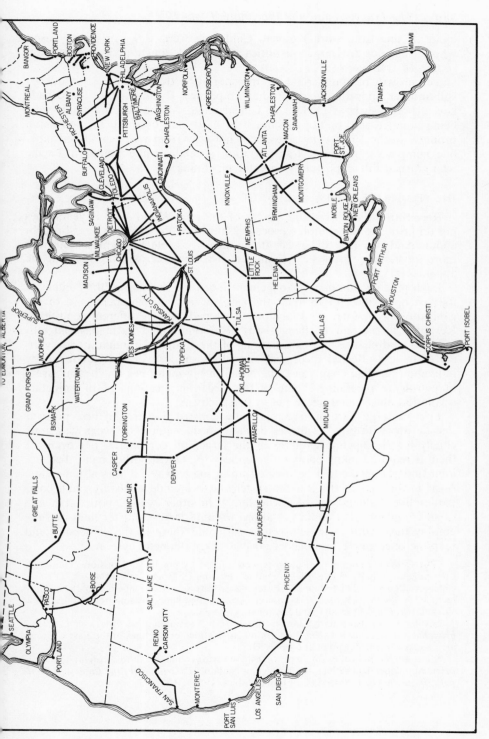

Petroleum transportation patterns in the United States, products pipelines, 1958.

Source: Adapted from American Petroleum Institute, *Petroleum Facts and Figures, Centennial Edition, 1959,* facing p. 113.

along its line from west Texas to California were U.S. Air Force bases, whose demands for large quantities of jet fuel constituted an important source of traffic.

The growth of commercial air transportation during the 1950's offered still another opportunity for products pipelines. By the end of the decade key airports, such as O'Hare at Chicago and Miami International, were being supplied with fuel by pipeline.* In short, new demands for petroleum products in the 1950's met a response not only from well-established pipeline companies but from transportation specialists like Southern Pacific who grasped this opportunity to enter pipelining.

THE RESULTS OF POSTWAR CHANGE

Recounting these over-all changes of the post World War II years does not do justice to the complex processes by which the changes were brought about. And, for lack of space, it has been possible to mention only the more outstanding projects. A complete list, however, will be found in the appendices.

Each pipeline company management faced the new era in the context of its past operations, of its relations with owners and shippers, and of organization, work force, and facilities developed to meet different conditions. Response to the new challenges was also conditioned by managerial attitudes toward change and expectations of the future. Although a wide variety of factors affected the speed and kinds of postwar changes made by individual pipeline companies, the boom in big-inch lines touched all areas of petroleum pipelining. Some of the larger implications of this pipeline revolution must therefore be put in perspective.

First, a large part of trunk pipeline construction in the first postwar decade was with pipe 12 inches or more in diameter. This work was done chiefly by the pipeline affiliates of the larger oil companies, but even for them it required many cooperative endeavors. On the other hand, because joint undertakings could be divided up in many ways, it was also possible — as in the case of the Rancho system — to include relatively small companies like Ashland in the ownership.† In other words, both large and small companies that could not afford to build large-diameter lines or fully employ them with their own resources, could share in the ownership and reap the operating economies of postwar large-diameter system.**

*The following commercial airports were served by pipelines: Houston (Humble), Los Angeles (Shell), Love Field, Dallas (Humble), Miami (Everglades), O'Hare, Chicago (Badger). Thirty-one Air Force bases were served by pipeline in 1959. They included bases in such places as Tuscon, Arizona; Spokane, Washington; Rome, New York; Great Falls, Montana; and Savannah, Georgia.

†Ashland was also a participant in the 20-inch Tecumseh Pipe Line which in 1957 provided a direct link between the terminus of big-inch crude lines in the East Chicago area and a key transfer point at Cygnet, Ohio.

**For a hypothetical example of what these savings could mean to a potential market-oriented independent refiner, see Leslie Cookenboo, Jr., *Crude Oil Pipe Lines and Competition in the Oil Industry* (Cambridge, Mass. 1955), 132-133.

Second, since large-diameter construction outmoded many existing multiple-line, small-diameter systems, there was an opportunity to convert the latter to new productive uses at less expense than would otherwise have been the case. The initial development of the Sinclair products system using a large amount of converted or reclaimed pipe is a case in point.

Third, the spread of products pipelining encouraged the discontinuance of outmoded refining facilities and concentration on the distribution of products from strategically located and optimum-size refineries supplied by large-diameter crude lines. Before the war, for example, Shell had shown the possibilities by discontinuing its Chicago refinery and using a converted crude line to supply that area with products from Wood River. After the war, Sinclair's Products system, combined with new large-diameter crude lines, had made it possible to close down Sinclair refineries at Fort Worth, Texas; Sand Springs, Oklahoma; and Coffeyville and Kansas City, Kansas.

Fourth, in the classic sequence of innovation dispersion in an enterprise economy, the construction of a major new pipeline system, or conversion of an older one to a more efficient large-diameter operation, induced imitation by other companies moving crude or products over competitive routes. A number of such examples have been given in this chapter.

Fifth, the pipeline business became more complex. Automated systems were sophisticated and pipeline investments were large. The complexity and magnitude of technical and financial decisions called for engineering and managerial skills developed by formal training rather than "up from the ditch" experience. These requirements led to a gradual and then accelerated shift toward increased specialization of decision-making functions and increased emphasis on highly skilled personnel.* Thus there was a slow but steady decline in the number of pipeline employees, especially those in nonsupervisory positions, with an accompanying increase in average weekly earnings.[36]

Sixth, the large-diameter lines required full loads to realize their maximum operating efficiency and this fact encouraged new interest in common-carrier business. Although large companies for the most part constructed the new lines, all the interstate crude lines and many of the products lines were common carriers. This had also been true in a formal sense of their prewar counterparts, but large minimum tender requirements and high rates had limited common-carrier use. In the new era, outside business was welcomed. Some companies, like Service, eliminated the tender requirement completely and others had minimal ones. Similarly, there was a downward trend in rates stimulated by competitive building of large-diameter systems.

The present chapter has touched only the highlights of pipeline devel-

---

*Since long before the war, actual pipeline construction work had been done by specialized contractors according to plans and specifications prepared in pipeline company engineering departments. With the advent of large-diameter pipe and automated systems, the demands for professional engineers in these departments rose rapidly. To prepare estimates of reserves to which a pipeline connection was proposed, several pipeline companies even had their own geologists.

opment in the late 1950's, for the closer one comes to the present, the more difficult it is to view events in adequate perspective. Even so, it is clear that the pipeline revolution commenced during World War II was still in progress a decade and a half later, though the emphasis had gradually shifted from crude to products lines. In the latter area, especially, significant newcomers got a firm hold in the 1950's.

Private capital and initiative since World War II had supplied pipeline facilities to move large volumes of petroleum and its products at lower costs, despite the price inflation characteristic of the era. Operating costs, based on ICC statistics, fell from 2.72 cents per 100 barrel-miles in 1953 to 2.48 cents in 1957. This achievement was in large measure the result of cooperative undertakings in expensive but efficient big-inch pipelining, the dominant theme of postwar development.

Inevitably, some oil industry interests were hurt as well as helped by these changes, and some government officials still refused to believe that the revolution in pipeline technology had been accompanied by any change in the pipeline policies of integrated companies. These fears, suspicions, and allegations of abuse of pipeline power came to a head in the late 1950's against a background of tension over access to world oil supplies and domestic producer discontent. In the succeeding governmental investigations and administrative and legal actions, managerial adaptation to economic and public policy constraints of two decades were subjected to an acid test.

1. Gauging a lease tank, early 1920's. Determination of the amount of oil in a producer's tank before it was run into a pipeline was the basis for paying the producer. This important task was performed by the gauger with a long pole. Establishing the depth of oil, he could find the volume from "tank tables." The gauger also determined the quality of the oil, which usually figured in its price.

2. Lease Automatic Custody Transfer (LACT) unit, 1950's. The gauger's pole was superseded by a steel tape and then by this LACT unit. It automatically records the amount of oil run from a producer's lease tanks and is read periodically by the gauger.

3. Steam pumping station, 1920's. On some oil trunk pipelines, pumping stations were powered by steam until the mid-1940's. The scale of these installations is suggested by this picture, with the boiler house at the left and the pump station on the right.

4. Steam-powered pump at a pipeline station, Fort Madison, Iowa, 1920's.

5. Diesel-powered pump station, 1948. The number of workers employed in manning this station and its connecting facilities is suggested by the cottages at the right.

6. Diesel engine used to power pipeline pumps, Martinsville, Illinois, 1947.

7. Electrically powered centrifugal pumps, early 1950's. This type of installation dramatically reduced labor requirements at pump stations.

8. Evolution of pump stations. In the picture below, pumps have moved outdoors but are still protected from the weather. Note microwave relay tower used to relay signals for automatic operation.

9. A typical main-line pump station of the 1950's with weatherproof electric pumping units eliminating the need for station house.

10. Control panels for electric pumping station, Martinsville, Illinois, 1958.

11. Modern dispatching and control centers. In the picture above, the nerve-center of a products pipeline system of the 1950's is shown. From here, aided by mechanical display, the operation of an entire division is controlled.

12. The same type of operation, aided by electric display of the situation throughout a system, is shown in the picture below.

PART

VI

The Public Policy Parameter,
1941-1959

CHAPTER 21

THE ICC AND PETROLEUM PIPELINES

As the pipeline sector of the oil industry faced the postwar era with a fresh outlook, its relations with the Interstate Commerce Commission took on a new significance. After a long period of no regulatory activity, the immediate prewar period was characterized by a series of ICC decisions affecting pipelines. One of them — the Reduced Pipe Line Rates and Gathering Charges case, initiated in 1934 — remained open as the war ended. Resumption of pipeline valuation work by the ICC became increasingly urgent in view of the consent decree's provisions basing permissible dividends to pipeline shipper-owners on ICC valuations. Yet Congress procrastinated about making appropriations to meet the requirements of valuation work. Accounting provisions specified by the ICC, and particularly those involving depreciation rates, also became a matter of heightened concern to pipeline management in view of the trend toward expansion of facilities through debt financing. In these areas a basis for postwar industry-agency cooperation was eventually found, and cordiality marked most of the relationships.

The conflict between regulator and regulated was not, however, completely eliminated. The large, integrated companies had been forced in 1914 to accept ICC jurisdiction as a fact of business life and, since then, most had learned to live with it comfortably. But the Commission proved unexpectedly anxious to extend its jurisdiction over smaller companies, and this raised new questions that affected all pipelines. Some of the resulting controversies came before the United States Supreme Court, which gradually clarified its criteria for determining the applicability of the federal pipeline statute. These decisions had particular relevance to the common-carrier status of some of the postwar products pipeline systems.

COOPERATION OF OIL-COMPANY MANAGEMENT IN ICC VALUATION WORK

Oil industry cooperation with the ICC in postwar pipeline valuation work was based on both necessity and mutual self-interest. Valuation of common-carrier property assumed great importance for regulated pipeline carriers subject to the 1941 consent decree because the decree related allowable dividends to ICC valuation. Initial pipeline valuations were made as of

December 31, 1934, but for the most part they were not decided until just prior to World War II.* Carriers thereafter filed annual reports on changes in their properties as originally valued. The ICC, however, lacked the personnel and funds to keep valuations current.

Major amendments were made to the Interstate Commerce Act by the Transportation Act of 1940, but no change was made in section 19a. Paragraph (f) of that section required the ICC to keep itself informed on all new construction, extensions, improvements, retirements, and such; to learn the cost of all additions and betterments; and to have information available "at all times" that would enable the Commission to revise and change its previous inventories, classifications, and valuations. In the very year of that new statute, however, the ICC reported that its valuation work was already "from 2 1/2 to 10 years short of being current," and this "lag" was accumulating. The Commission recognized that lack of progress in bringing valuations up to date was a serious matter because currency of information was the key to practical use of valuation data and was essential to the integrity and usefulness of ICC records. Increased appropriations for securing these data, the Commission's 1940 report stated, offered the only solution.[1]

Increased appropriations for pipeline valuations, however, were not forthcoming. Instead, as the country became involved in global war, the ICC's Bureau of Valuation was called upon for aid by the Departments of Agriculture, Interior, Justice, Labor, Navy, Treasury, and War, as well as by various subsidiary or independent agencies.[2] As a result, on July 1, 1944, the ICC suspended work on assessing current values of pipelines by determining original cost and bringing forward changes in land and other property.[3]

Since the ICC did not reveal its formula for determining specific company valuations,† pipeline carriers that had to have a valuation figure for purposes of the consent decree sought to approximate the ICC formula as best they could. Close study of past valuations suggested that five elements were considered by the ICC in arriving at a "fair value" for pipeline properties. They were:

1. Property other than land or right of way, valued on a weighted average of original and reproduction costs, less depreciation.
2. Land valued at an average of original cost and appraised current value.

*The basic program of pipeline valuation was completed in 1940. Under this program, the properties of 52 operating companies and 1 lessor were valued as of December 31, 1934. The values found by the ICC of the properties of these pipelines, excluding working capital of $7,589,194, aggregated $564,654,534 for property owned and $542,158,198 for property used. As of December 31, 1934, these companies had outstanding $381,908,987 for capitalization, consisting of $84,137,676 of long-term debt and $297,771, 311 of capital stock. Their total recorded investments amounted to $835,683,565, of which $766,371,364 represented carrier property. ICC *Annual Report* (1940), 133.

†For an explanation of the ICC's approach in its first valuation of a pipeline, see Valuation Docket 1203, Atlantic Pipe Line Company, 47 *ICC Valuation Reports* 541, Appendix 4, pp. 584-598.

3. Rights of way valued at original cost less depreciation based on probable life of the facilities.

4. Working capital determined by a formula to reflect needs for maintenance of stocks and cash to meet current operating expenses.

5. Going concern value determined in a way that produced an amount equal to about 6 percent of item one.[4]

Using data such as these, each company subject to the consent decree arrived at a valuation figure to be used in its reports to the Justice Department and in calculating permissible dividend payments to shipper-owners.

The situation that had developed by 1944 was unfair both to the ICC, which had a statutory obligation but no funds to maintain valuations, and to the pipeline companies, which had legal obligations to fulfill based on such valuations. Although the ICC annually called congressional attention to the suspension of pipeline valuations,[5] no appropriation to resume this work was made until fiscal year 1949. At that time an additional allotment of funds to the ICC permitted the Bureau of Valuation to resume work in part.[6]

In the absence of congressional appropriations for pipeline valuation work, and in view of its importance for consent decree purposes, pipeline company representatives in 1948 suggested to Senator Clyde M. Reed that he sponsor legislation permitting the companies to pay for this work themselves.[7] When Reed consulted Commissioner Charles D. Mahaffie of the ICC about this proposal, Mahaffie argued against such a step. Among other things, the Commissioner pointed to the relatively small amount of money involved in relation to the bookkeeping problems that would be created, not to mention the inequities that might be caused with respect to the valuation of other types of carriers subject to the act.[8] As a result, no further action was taken on the companies' offer.

Without ICC pipeline valuation work, pipeline managers had looked to the Commission's railroad decisions for guidance. What they saw was not encouraging. In July 1948, for example, the ICC in an industry-wide railroad rate case adopted original cost less book depreciation reserve in valuing railroad property.[9] Although it was by no means clear that this formula would also be applied to pipelines, such a change — by omitting reproduction cost (i.e., the current cost of construction) from pipeline valuation calculations — could have resulted in significant decreases in valuations for consent decree purposes. As it turned out, when work was resumed on pipelines, the ICC did not apply the 1948 railroad rate valuation formula.[10]

Assured of at least some funds for pipeline valuations, the ICC in July 1948 ordered 55 pipeline companies for whom earlier valuations had been found, plus 10 new companies, to submit data on their inventory and its original cost as of December 31, 1947, the new base date set for pipeline valuations.* By October 1949 these data had been submitted and work

---

*The decision to do a thorough revaluation of pipeline properties was occasioned by the vast property charges and price-level increases that had occurred since the last final valuations as of 1934. *Ajax Pipe Line Corporation* (50 ICC *Valuation Reports* 1, 1949).

commenced on valuing all regulated pipeline carriers, property as of the end of 1947.

In 1952 this work had progressed to the point where the Bureau of Valuation could begin to issue annual valuation reports on all pipeline companies subject to the ICC. In 1954 it was brought to a current status and was continued on that basis thereafter.[11]

As in the past, and as authorized by the Interstate Commerce Act, the ICC and representatives of the oil industry cooperated in developing the new valuations. In arriving at reproduction prices for pipeline property, for example, it was necessary to establish price indices showing the movement of prices relative to 1934, the date of the last final valuations. This was an important topic of discussion between industry and ICC representatives in view of the postwar inflationary trend. The higher the level of prices applied to the reproduction element of the valuation formula, the higher the valuation itself would presumably be. On the other hand, industry representatives recognized that if they pressed too hard for recognition of higher prices, the ICC might consider the result inflationary and, drawing on its 1948 railroad rate decision, drop the reproduction element from pipeline valuation. It was finally decided that a composite cost index of 162 (with 1934–100) should be applied to the 1947 price situation.

The allowance for depreciation was another important variable affecting valuation, and from the standpoints of both the ICC and pipeline managements, it involved a number of considerations. The service life of pipe and its salvage value (i.e., value and physical condition of property) were key elements. Related to them were depreciation rates for accounting purposes (i.e., recovery of cost property) and for federal income tax. In arriving at the 1934 valuations, the Bureau of Valuation had dealt with pipeline companies individually on figures for pipeline service life and salvage value; the Bureau of Accounts did likewise for accounting purposes. Depreciation rates for income tax purposes were handled individually with the Bureau of Internal Revenue.

With the new valuation work under way, these questions arose again and were complicated by lack of precedent for the new large-diameter, thin-wall pipe that was coming into widespread use. In its work with the API Valuation Sub-Committee, the Bureau of Valuation proposed that the service life of new steel pipe be considered as 40 years and that it be assumed to have a salvage value equal to 25 per cent of its original cost. Both these figures represented increases over past allowances, but the implications of accepting them were more than first met the eye. The "service life" question is a case in point.

Factors other than physical deterioration entered into the determination of a pipeline's service life. The peculiar characteristics of a specialized oil carrier had long been called to the attention of the ICC and were declared by some pipeline companies to be relevant to service life. These characteristics included obsolescence of small-diameter pipe which was not fully depreciated when replaced by larger diameter pipe that was more efficient;

decline of oil fields resulting in increased operating costs or abandonment of feeder lines; and loss of business as a result of factors over which the pipeline had no control, such as a shipper taking his patronage elsewhere because of shifts in the cost, availability, or quality of crude.*

Because of the different situation in which each pipeline company found itself with respect to the size, age, and use of pipe, there was a diversity of managerial reactions to the proposal to lengthen the service life of pipe for valuation purposes. Companies engaged in rapid pipeline expansion programs largely financed by borrowing did not want their depreciation allowances to be reduced through use of long service life criteria. This would have decreased an important source of funds for debt retirement. Companies with a preponderance of old, small-diameter lines, fully depreciated or near it, welcomed an extension of service life criteria because it maintained their valuations and in turn allowed higher dividend payments under the consent decree. In the light of such considerations, each company made its own case with the Bureau of Valuation, which then made the final determinations.

INTERPRETATION OF THE FEDERAL PIPELINE STATUTE

While cooperating with pipeline companies in valuation work, the ICC was raising some novel interpretations of the scope of its pipeline jurisdiction and demonstrating that pipeline rate regulation could be more than nominal. In these two areas, the ICC adopted a somewhat more active role than before World War II, though the results produced no constraints on pipeline management comparable to those of the consent decree.

The Minnelusa Case: Rate Regulation

In 1944, thirty years after the constitutionality of the pipeline amendment to the Hepburn Act was upheld by the United States Supreme Court, the ICC decided the first pipeline rate case in its history brought by bona fide shippers over the defendant pipelines. Minnelusa Oil Corporation, a producer and marketer of crude oil in the Rocky Mountain area, and Wasatch Oil Refining Company, a small refining company at Woods Cross, Utah, filed the complaint in February 1942. They charged that the rates of the defendants — Continental Pipe Line Company, Rocky Mountain Pipe Line Company, Stanolind Pipe Line Company, Utah Oil Refining Company, and Wasatch Oil Refining Company — were unreasonable, unjustly discriminatory, and unduly prejudicial, as they related to the transportation of crude oil by pipeline from Lance Creek, Salt Creek, and Rock River Station, Wyoming, to Woods Cross, Utah, near Salt Lake City. The complainants also alleged that gathering charges of 7.5 cents per barrel were unreasonable and that undue preference was shown by the defendants to Utah Oil

---

*In 1927 substantially the same points were made in testimony before the ICC on depreciation. See above, Ch. 11.

Refining Company and the large oil companies that Utah served from its refinery at Salt Lake City.

Utah's pipeline into Wyoming was the first to cross the Rocky Mountains and had been built in 1939 under the supervision of Stanolind Pipe Line, a wholly-owned subsidiary of Indiana Standard. Stanolind Pipe Line also operated this line under contract for Utah Oil Refining Company, about three-quarters of whose capital stock was owned by Indiana Standard.

Failing to obtain an ownership interest in Utah's new line, Wasatch had laid a short connecting spur from its Woods Cross refinery to Wasatch Junction. Therefore, Wasatch, one of the complainants, was also a defendant because it participated in the joint tariffs from Wyoming to Woods Cross. Continental, Rocky Mountain, and Stanolind pipelines were involved as defendants because they supplied the connections between the Wyoming fields and Utah's trunk line.

Including gathering charges, the defendants had charged 48 cents per barrel from Rock River station and 79 cents from the Salt Creek and Lance Creek fields to Woods Cross. For providing transportation over its spur line into its refinery, Wasatch received 0.5 cents per barrel as its share of the through rate on this traffic.

In reviewing these rates, the ICC affirmed that just and reasonable ones should reflect the cost of service, taxes (excluding excess-profits taxes), and a fair return on value. Citing the 10 per cent annual return allowed on products lines in the Petroleum Rail Shippers' case,[12] Stanolind and Utah had maintained that the character of Rocky Mountain operations justified recognition of at least this percentage of return for crude lines in that area. The ICC acknowledged that crude-oil pipelines confronted risks and hazards not reflected in operating expenses, mentioning specifically changes in the volume of shipments due to factors over which a pipeline had little or no control.[13] However, complainants had argued, and the ICC agreed, that defendants in this case had been substantially compensated in the past for any risks of the industry involved in the area under consideration.[14] The ICC, therefore, reaffirmed the 8 per cent maximum return for crude-oil lines that it had applied in the Reduced Pipe Line Rates and Gathering Charges case.

The ICC also found that Wasatch was a common carrier by virtue of its participation in the joint trunk-line tariff. Commissioner J. Haden Alldredge dissented from this finding on the grounds that Wasatch had been forced to build the spur pipeline, which was only half a mile long, in order to obtain service for itself. Hence, in his opinion, this pipeline was in the same category as a railroad spur track which the ICC had never found to impose common-carrier status per se on a shipper-owner.* [15]

Although the defendants argued that Wasatch had originally concurred

*Where a *railroad* extended a spur line on order of a public service commission and used the right of eminent domain, the Supreme Court had held the track, though built to serve only one shipper, to be part of a public carrier. *Union Line Company v. Chicago and Northwestern Railway*, 233 U.S. 211 (1914).

in the rates of which it subsequently complained, the ICC dismissed this argument on the grounds that Wasatch took what Utah and its connections offered in the way of rates and had no real voice in setting them.[16] In reaching this decision, the ICC apparently attached some significance to Indiana Standard's ownership in Utah Refining and Stanolind Pipe Line, as well as to the fact that the defendants other than Wasatch were subject to the provisions of the consent decree.[17]

The ICC concluded that the challenged rates to Woods Cross were unreasonable to the extent that they exceeded 37 cents a barrel from Rock Creek Station, 55 cents from Lance Creek, and 68 cents from Salt Creek. It therefore ordered reparation, with interest, of the difference between these rates and those actually paid on shipments since the date of complaint. However, the decision dismissed the complaints that gathering charges were unreasonable and that Utah enjoyed an undue advantage in trunk-line rates through its pipeline ownership.[18] Railroad objections to the reduction of the pipeline rates were likewise dismissed.

Reduced Pipe Line Rates and Gathering Charges

In the 1940 order used as a yardstick in the Minnelusa case, the ICC had announced that a maximum annual return of 8 per cent of the fair value of common-carrier properties used in transportation of crude petroleum oil by pipeline was reasonable. At that time it found 21 of 35 respondents to be earning in excess of this amount. Therefore, they were ordered to show cause why they should not be required to reduce their rates to the designated level. All respondents were also ordered to show cause why 10,000 barrels of crude of a single shipment should not be the maximum amount specified for a minimum tender.

At a hearing on December 18, 1941, less than two weeks after Pearl Harbor, representatives of the respondents appeared and a start was made on updating rate and operational data. Since company representatives were not then equipped to provide all the required information and since the war seemed likely to change the whole picture, this hearing was adjourned sine die. Thus the ICC had indicated its position on pipeline rates and minimum tenders but the matter was not formally closed.

When the proceedings on pipeline rates were reopened in 1948, the number of respondents had declined from the original 35 to 26, the difference representing chiefly consolidations.* Of the 26, six operated only trunk lines; the remainder operated both trunk and gathering lines.

The evidence presented to the ICC showed that significant changes had taken place in the pipeline business since the outbreak of World War II. By comparison with the situation in the mid-1930's, these changes were star-

---

*Gulf Refining Company, Ohio Oil Company, and Sinclair Refining, for example, had consolidated their pipeline activities in the parent company; Buckeye Pipe Line Company had absorbed Indiana Pipe Line Company; Interstate Oil Pipe Line Company had been formed by a consolidation of Oklahoma Pipe Line Company and the Pipe Line Department of Standard Oil Company of Louisiana, and so on.

tling. Gathering line mileage operated by the respondents in 1947 had declined 1.3 per cent compared with 1935, but trunk-line mileage had increased 20.9 per cent. Technological developments and improved operating techniques had permitted an increase of 104.4 per cent in the amount of oil transported in 1947 compared to 1935 and an increase of 14.8 per cent over even 1944, when pipeline facilities had been strained to the utmost.[19]

This increase in traffic was found to have been accompanied by a decline in trunk-line rates. Analyzing tariffs covering movements involved in the original investigation, the ICC discovered 69 still in effect between the same origin and destination points. They showed an average decline of 17.7 cents per barrel compared to those in effect on December 31, 1933, or an average rate reduction of 43.2 per cent. To illustrate this change, Commissioner Clyde Aitchison cited the rate which had given rise to the original action. It covered transportation between the Mid-Continent and Chicago. Since 1933 that rate had been reduced in a series of steps from 40 cents until it stood at 25 cents.[20] Gathering rates also had fallen. They were typically stabilized at half what they had been at the end of December 1933.

Aggregate operating revenues for 1947 (reflecting the increased volume of shipments even at lower rates) were 45 per cent above 1935, but total operating expenses plus taxes (reflecting, among other things, a general price rise) had increased 106 per cent. As a result, total pipeline operating income of respondents in 1947 was 44.5 per cent less than it had been in 1935.[21]

A review of minimum tender requirements for crude-oil shipments showed that all but seven of the respondents had adopted the 10,000-barrel figure suggested by the ICC in 1940. Five of the respondents required 25,000 barrels as a minimum, two required 100,000 barrels as a shipment but the tender could be offered jointly by several shippers of the same grade oil. Some had agreed to accept 10,000-barrel tenders but would only make shipments of 100,000-barrel lots of the same grade of oil. However, with deliveries coming from common stock, the latter provision did not necessarily delay service to outside shippers, and it reportedly offered protection against contamination. Those respondents who had not accepted the 10,000-barrel minimum tender amount were asked to do so within 90 days or inform the ICC so that it might consider appropriate action.

Changes made during and after World War II appeared to the ICC to have eliminated past rate problems as the subject for further action. In the words of the decision, which was announced by Commissioner Aitchison:

> The record shows that the reductions in rates which were the primary cause of this investigation were but the beginning of a continuing process which, as shown herein, had resulted in a decrease of more than 40 per cent in the present rates below those which were in effect on December 31, 1933. This is the more remarkable, as every other type of common carrier in the same period has been forced to make general increases in rates — often successive increases of material size — to cover their mounting costs of operation.[22]

As a result of these findings, the ICC concluded that, with the exception of the several respondents involved in the minimum tender question, the rates, rules, regulations, and practices of respondents concerning interstate transportation of crude petroleum oil were not unlawful. Therefore, the rate investigation was closed.

The clean bill of health given the pipeline companies by this decision was the product of a number of factors, of which ICC action was only one. It will be recalled that the situation giving rise to the investigation of rates originated with a voluntary reduction of them by some pipeline companies. By the time the ICC adopted an 8 per cent return on the fair value of crude-oil pipelines as its yardstick, a number of companies were already earning less. For practical purposes even that figure became almost academic when the consent decree imposed a limitation of 7 per cent on the dividends that integrated pipeline companies could pay shipper-owners. Finally, changing conditions in the oil industry and in pipeline technology, plus the impact of public policy, had made high rates less feasible and less desirable than they had once been from the standpoint of pipeline management. The same was true with minimum tenders. With higher investment in larger diameter pipe and with the proliferation of competitive routes, reduced rates and tenders were increasingly viewed as means of attracting outside use and additional revenue, which helped to lower the pipeline owner's costs. ICC attention to such matters dated from an earlier era, but the Commission re-enforced and encouraged revision of tariff policies that were outmoded by industry developments.

The Valvoline Case: The Question of ICC Jurisdiction

In connection with its original pipeline valuation work, the ICC provoked the first of a series of cases that, extending into the postwar era, were to clarify the extent of its pipeline jurisdiction. Basically, this question hinged on an interpretation of the Hepburn Amendment of 1906 to Section I of the Interstate Commerce Act. It read that: "The provisions of this Act shall apply to any corporation or any person or persons engaged in the transportation of oil or other commodity, except water and except natural or artificial gas, by means of pipelines, or partly by pipelines and partly by railroad, or partly by pipelines and partly by water, who shall be considered and held to be common carriers within the meaning and purpose of this Act."

When the pipeline statute was put to a judicial test in 1914, the Supreme Court had made only one exception to the apparent intent of the literal language. In the Uncle Sam Oil Company case the fact that the company produced its own oil and transported it through its own pipeline to its own refinery seemed to a majority of the Court to differentiate Uncle Sam from the other cases at issue, even though the oil crossed a state line. As no outside producer or owner of oil was involved, the Court decided that transportation was incidental to the end-use and that the company was exempt from the act. This decision became the basis for subsequent controversy over the implementation of the federal pipeline statute, and the Uncle Sam exception was invoked by the Valvoline Oil Company in 1936 when the ICC served that concern with a valuation order.

Valvoline was a New Jersey corporation authorized to engage in production, transportation, and marketing of petroleum and its products. It owned a refinery at Butler, Pennsylvania, where it specialized in the manufacture of lubricating oils. In order to meet the industrial specifications for these oils, the Valvoline Company required crude of a clear, amber color relatively free from impurities.

Valvoline purchased high-grade crudes from producers in Pennsylvania, West Virginia, and Ohio, and transported them by its own pipelines to its East Butler refinery. The company did not own any of the 9,000 wells it served but maintained accounts with some 3,000–4,000 operators of leases and owners of wells. Producers were not under written contract to sell their oil to Valvoline, and at least one common-carrier pipeline company served each of the fields reached by Valvoline. Crude in excess of the company's own requirements was sold to two small refineries, one in Pennsylvania and the other in West Virginia.

Subsequent to receipt of the ICC valuation order, the company ceased supplying the West Virginia refiner with Ohio crude. Because its Pennsylvania customer was receiving only Pennsylvania crude, Valvoline maintained that it was engaged only in intrastate carriage for others and that so far as transportation for itself was concerned, its status was the same as that of the Uncle Sam Oil Company (i.e., that of a private carrier). In 1938 the company asked the ICC for a rehearing on the question of filing valuation information and on the question of whether it was a common carrier within the meaning of the Interstate Commerce Act. The petition was granted, and a decision was announced on July 6, 1938.[23]

After reviewing the evidence, the ICC announced that Valvoline was a common carrier of oil by pipeline within the meaning of the Interstate Commerce Act. In support of this conclusion the ICC relied on the broad language of the statute, noting that there was no explicit requirement that actual common carriage be performed before a pipeline became subject to the act. Valvoline differed from the Uncle Sam Oil Company, the ICC said, in its relations with producers and owners of oil in the producing fields. The Uncle Sam Company had produced its own oil whereas Valvoline purchased crude. Although Valvoline did not have a monopoly of such purchases, a situation which Congress had sought to reach in adopting the pipeline section of the Hepburn Amendment, the ICC held this point was irrelevant in view of the statute's comprehensive language.[24] Accordingly, the ICC ordered Valvoline to comply with the request for valuation information.

The Valvoline Company asked the federal district court for an injunction against enforcement of the ICC's order. This request was denied by the court, and the denial was sustained by the United States Supreme Court in 1939. Like the ICC, the highest Court differentiated this case from that of the Uncle Sam Company on the basis that Valvoline purchased its crude. Therefore, the Court found that Valvoline was a common carrier within the meaning of the Interstate Commerce Act to the extent that it could be required to submit valuation data.[25]

Although the Supreme Court did not pass on other aspects of Valvoline's obligations under the act, the company apparently interpreted them to mean that it was also required to file tariffs.[26] This issue was specifically raised for adjudication in a subsequent case brought by the ICC against the Champlin Refining Company.

The Champlin Cases: The Status of Gasoline Pipelines

The rapid growth of refined products lines in the 1930's had raised a question about their status under the federal pipeline statute. Many of these lines had been built and operated as private carriers, and in 1941 the ICC decided to bring a test case against one of them to establish the limits of its valuation jurisdiction.[27] For this purpose, it chose the Champlin Refining Company which operated a gasoline pipeline from its refinery in Enid, Oklahoma, to bulk terminals that it owned in Kansas, Nebraska, and Iowa. Through this 6-inch line it transported only gasoline that the company owned.

Champlin had never sought outside shippers, and its line was equipped to receive petroleum products only at Champlin's Enid refinery. The pipeline had been built by the Cimarron Valley Pipe Line Company, a wholly-owned Champlin subsidiary possessing the right of eminent domain. This power was not used directly in obtaining right of way, though the fact that it existed may have been a factor in the minds of the property owners who settled with the company. In any event, the line was sold to Champlin before it began operations, and the refining company regarded it as a private products line.[28]

Champlin I

Like Valvoline a few years earlier, Champlin was asked by the ICC in May 1941 to file information for valuation purposes in compliance with section 19a of the Interstate Commerce Act. The company refused to file the information from the standpoint of a statutory common carrier. After a hearing in December 1942 and reargument in June 1944, the ICC ordered Champlin to comply with the valuation orders within 90 days.

The ICC maintained that the Interstate Commerce Act had declared that all pipeline companies transporting oil or its products in interstate commerce were common carriers and that this interpretation had been upheld by the Supreme Court in the 1914 Pipe Line Cases and in the 1939 Valvoline decision.[29] Champlin argued that its situation was different from both these cases because it did not purchase from others the product that it transported.[30] However, the ICC, citing Champlin's pricing formula (f.o.b. refinery price at Enid plus the through rail rate to destination minus charges borne by the purchaser between the pipeline terminal and his bulk plants), held that Champlin was in effect performing common-carrier services for hire.[31]

Champlin sought an injunction against execution of the ICC valuation orders, but the federal district court for the western district of Oklahoma dismissed the request. On appeal, the United States Supreme Court on November 18, 1946, upheld the lower court. A majority of five justices of the Supreme Court found that Champlin's delivered pricing formula, which involved transportation charges, and the fact that Champlin moved its products interstate to a market for sale rather than into a refinery for its own use,[32] was "transportation" within the meaning of the act. Hence Champlin was in a different category from Uncle Sam.

Although the majority held that the ICC's assertion of jurisdiction for valuation purposes was justified, they did not rule on whether Champlin was a common carrier for other purposes set forth in the Interstate Commerce Act. Instead, they avoided the issue by emphasizing that Congress had extensive authority over private carriers under the interstate commerce power and that this extended to requiring information from a carrier, whether it be a private or common-carrier facility.

A minority of four justices stated their belief that the applicability of the statute's various provisions to pipelines hinged on first finding that a carrier was a common carrier engaged in the transportation of oil under Section 1 of the act. In their view, "If a line does not carry oil of others, it is not transporting within the contemplation of the act." [33] In this respect, Champlin seemed to the minority of the Court no different from Uncle Sam, and a fresh opportunity to examine this position arose a few years later.

Champlin II

Having gained a victory on the filing of valuation data by Champlin, the ICC followed it up early in 1948 with an order that the company also file annual reports, institute a uniform system of accounts in accordance with Section 20 of the Interstate Commerce Act, and publish and file rates and charges for transportation of petroleum products in compliance with Section 6 of the act. From Champlin's standpoint, the latter requirement was equivalent to an order to become a common carrier for hire.

Subsequent to the initiation of these proceedings by the ICC, Champlin changed its method of pricing, which the company apparently felt had been a prime source of vulnerability in its first case. Beginning on May 9, 1948, Champlin posted a pipeline terminal price for its products and made allowances from this price for the purpose of meeting competition. Although the pipeline transportation charge was not shown separately, the selling price included it. The end results, according to a witness for the carrier, were substantially the same as those achieved by the earlier pricing method.[34]

In contesting the ICC order, Champlin again argued that its operations were not clothed with a public interest but were clearly in the same category as that of Uncle Sam Oil Company and recognized in The Pipe Line Cases as private carriage. Champlin demonstrated that it moved only its own products and that its sales were to a very small portion of the market it served. Only about 1.98 per cent of the gasoline consumed in that area (Oklahoma, Kansas, and Nebraska) moved through Champlin's pipeline, which was the smallest in the territory. Furthermore, alternative means of pipeline shipment were available to other refiners in the area. In the ICC's own words, "Apparently, common-carrier pipe-line transportation is available to any small refiner in this area desiring such transportation." [35] Nevertheless, in June 1949 the ICC reaffirmed its order for Champlin's compliance with Sections 6 and 20 of the Interstate Commerce Act.

Commissioners Walter Splawn and Richard Mitchell dissented from this order as it applied to Champlin's publishing, posting, and filing tariffs. Splawn pointed out that Champlin had not and did not hold itself out as a common carrier and that it carried an inconsequential part of the total volume of products moved by pipeline in its area. While he agreed that the carrier might properly be required to file reports and valuation data, the requirement that it file tariffs and thereby obligate itself to perform as a common carrier was a different matter. In requiring the independent company to turn this line into a common carrier, Commissioner Splawn argued, the ICC was threatening the very purpose of the pipeline provisions of the Hepburn Act, the protection of small, independent producers from monopoly power. Commissioner Mitchell also dissented from the order on much the same grounds.

Champlin took the ICC order to court. This time a three-judge district court, with one dissent, decided the ICC had gone too far. The court therefore enjoined the ICC from enforcing its order. This decision was appealed and in May 1951, the Supreme Court handed down its second Champlin decision.[36] A majority found that the change in Champlin's method of pricing products had not substantially altered the situation: the company was still transporting products by interstate pipeline and receiving remuneration for it. However, noting that in the prior case the court had declined to make a blanket ruling with respect to Champlin's being a common carrier under Section 1 of the Interstate Commerce Act, the majority drew a line between the requirement for submitting information under Sections 19a and 20 and the filing of tariffs for common carriage under Section 6. The former they found acceptable for general purposes of improving regulation or avoiding the need for more regulation. But the latter requirement could "make common-carriers for hire out of private pipe lines whose services were unused, unsought after, and unneeded by independent producers, and whose presence fosters competition in markets heavily blanketed by large 'majors.' " [37] Champlin, therefore, could not under the conditions shown be required to file tariffs.

Several justices took this occasion to express concern about the Supreme Court's position on the meaning of the federal pipeline statute. Justice Felix Frankfurter, although concurring in the majority decision, would have overruled the earlier Champlin decision. Justice William Douglas, speaking for himself and Justices Stanley Reed and Harold Burton, pointed to the need for a consistent definition of "common carrier." In his reading of both the Uncle Sam case and Champlin I, he felt that products pipelines carrying only for their owners and between the owners' refineries and their storage tanks for marketing should not be subject to the act. As he saw it, Section 1 of the Interstate Commerce Act did not apply to Champlin; consequently neither did Sections 6 or 20. The same argument had been applied by the minority in Champlin I with respect to Section 19.

Justice Hugo Black, however, read a different meaning into The Pipe Line Cases and the earlier Champlin decision. He interpreted them to mean that the Court had decided that Congress had intended to make common carriers for hire of *all* pipeline companies engaged in transporting oil or other commodities across state lines. Now the Court had drawn back. For him it made no sense that the majority should have found in Champlin I that this company was not entitled to the Uncle Sam exemption, and then in Champlin II to rule that it was different from Valvoline because it moved only its own products (i.e., like Uncle Sam). As he saw it, there was no significant difference between the Valvoline and Champlin companies as far as this question was concerned. Both were common carriers. "That Champlin is a common carrier within the literal language of this provision is shown by the unchallenged findings of fact made by the I.C.C.," Black wrote.[38] In his view, the Court had been inconsistent and illogical in its treatment of the Champlin cases to the extent that, instead of clarifying, it had created genuine uncertainty about the Hepburn Act's meaning and potential efficacy for pipelines.

Implications of the Supreme Court Decisions

The basic problem involved in these cases was the all-embracing language of the pipeline statute in Section 1. As an administrative agency, the ICC made use of the full implications of the law. The Supreme Court, on the other hand, apparently felt that the language was broader than the intent of Congress had required. Consequently, there could be cases — complete or partial — where the statute did not apply, and the Court reserved for itself this determination in the light of specific circumstances. A majority, nevertheless, persistently declined to admit that a finding of common-carrier status in accordance with Section 1 of the statute necessarily required the offering of pipeline services for hire, or that such an interpretation was a necessary condition for determining the applicability of subsequent sections.

By the early 1950's, then, although the jurisdiction of the ICC had been subjected to several important judicial reviews, significant gray areas still remained. The Pipe Line Cases had established that interstate pipeline transportation of crude oil purchased from, as well as owned by, others was common carriage within the meaning of the Interstate Commerce Act. This seems to have been so in the Court's view because, in purchasing crude from independent producers, a company owning pipelines automatically affected the market situation in the area of its purchases. Had the Uncle Sam Company purchased instead of producing the oil moved by its pipeline, it would — under this test — have been forced to become a common carrier like the Standard lines.

Behind this comparatively easy purchase test was a basic position of the Supreme Court — that Congress had been trying to protect the independent producer in enacting the pipeline statute. Because large, integrated companies inevitably bought as well as produced their crude, there was after 1914 no question about the common-carrier status of their interstate crude-oil lines. After the Valvoline decision, it was clear that the same test applied to small companies as well.

In Champlin I the Supreme Court took the position that a common-carrier operation might be inferred from the method of pricing and selling products moved by their owner's interstate pipeline; yet in Champlin II, on substantially the same evidence, the Court proved unwilling to state that such carriage provided a basis for requiring that the pipeline service be offered to the public for hire. This approach of "when is a pipeline common carrier not a common carrier" was apparently forced on the Court by its unwillingness to make Section 1 govern all remaining provisions of the Interstate Commerce Act.

For practical purposes, it seemed that products lines used solely for carriage of their owners' products through and between facilities owned by them were exempt from obligations to file rates and tariffs as common carriers. However, the Court had also suggested that, to remain in the category of private carriers, such facilities must be "unused, unsought after, and unneeded by independent producers." Consequently, the Court left it to the owners and managers of each interstate products line to determine whether these conditions existed or were likely to exist in the areas served by them. If so, voluntary adoption of common-carrier status seemed indicated. If not, their private carriage could be continued until challenged. Despite the somewhat tortured way that this conclusion was reached by the Court, it had again left room for managerial interpretation and adaptation to the federal statute. This proved sufficient to avoid further controversy over the ICC's pipeline jurisdiction for the remainder of the decade.

THE ICC AS ARBITER BETWEEN COMPETING CARRIERS

Pipelines continued to pose a threat to other types of oil carriers, and this threat led to adversary action before the ICC in the early 1950's. The Texas Company and its pipeline affiliate announced in 1951 that they intended to build a refined products line from the company's El Paso refinery to Tucson and Phoenix, Arizona. California Standard, which also operated a refinery at El Paso, indicated that it would use such a pipeline. If implemented, this plan would threaten the rail movement of products from El

Paso into Arizona. Accordingly, the ICC was asked to authorize a reduction in rail rates sufficient to discourage construction of the pipeline.*

The railroad-pipeline issue was complicated by the fact that tank trucks had been operating in effective competition with railroads from the Los Angeles Basin into Arizona. The railroads asked that the requested rate reductions also extend to this eastbound rail traffic, although it was not threatened by any pipeline at the time. Their reasoning was that if the rates from El Paso were reduced while those from Los Angeles remained unchanged, the latter traffic would dry up. The truckers, on the other hand, could not meet the reduction requested in the Los Angeles rail rates and survive. Accordingly they petitioned the ICC to deny the request.

On January 12, 1953, the ICC approved the reduction of railroad rates. A majority, citing Gasoline From Superior, Wisconsin (222 ICC 487), maintained that it was justifiable to act in anticipation of pipeline competition because no effective redress could be offered after a pipeline was constructed. It found that "the proposal to build a pipeline from El Paso poses a real threat to continued participation in this traffic by both the rail and the motor carriers." [39] This left the question of whether the proposed rail rates were below reasonable minima, which the majority found not to be the case.

A significant minority of the ICC dissented from this decision. Speaking for himself and two others, Commissioner James K. Knudson argued that if pipelines were more economical than rail transportation it was not the function of the ICC to neutralize that advantage. Furthermore, he could not see the justification for reducing the Los Angeles rates, which he felt would result in putting common-carrier tank-truck lines out of business.[40]

This reduction of rail rates approved by the ICC did, in fact, forestall construction of the proposed pipeline by the oil companies. However, it opened the way for the Southern Pacific Company to provide pipeline as well as rail service. A wholly-owned subsidiary, Southern Pacific Pipelines, Inc., was organized in 1955 to move products west from El Paso and east from Los Angeles. Intended to serve ten oil companies and various Air Force bases, the El Paso–Phoenix segment of the line was opened in December 1957.[41] The ICC's 1953 decision to preserve rail traffic in petroleum products had the unanticipated result of encouraging railroad initiative in entering products pipelining.

THE ISSUE OF POOLING

The development of undivided-interest lines posed a problem for the managements of some companies in the mid-1950's. It will be recalled that this arrangement allowed several companies to participate in the ownership

---

*About the same time, Congressman Christopher C. McGrath of New York introduced a bill (H.R. 5632, October 5, 1951) requiring certificates of public convenience and necessity for pipeline construction. Adoption of such a requirement, of course, might have proved an obstacle to the building of pipelines in areas already served by other carriers.

of a large-diameter line that was treated as though it consisted of multiple individual lines each completely under the control of its owner. Leading examples of this form of organization were Bayou, the first to employ it, and the postwar Basin, Ozark, Rancho, Evangeline and Harbor pipeline systems. Obviously, counsel for companies participating in these systems felt that there was no danger of violating Section 5(1) of the Interstate Commerce Act which banned the pooling of traffic, service or earnings. However, this question had never been reviewed by the ICC up to 1954.

Since 1920 the Interstate Commerce Act had authorized pooling under conditions approved by the ICC, and such approval was obtained by pipeline companies in specific instances. One instance involved the Great Lakes and the Augusta and Kaneb Pipe Lines. The pressure of traffic was such in 1954 that Great Lakes was forced to utilize an emergency route of its own, depriving the other two companies of their normal share of a joint through rate. Accordingly, permission was sought and obtained from the ICC in June 1954 for Great Lakes to make the same payments to Augusta and Kaneb as it would if the traffic had actually moved through its normal channels.[42]

While this case was pending, two pipeline companies routinely filed notice with the ICC of the adoption of tariffs in connection with their acquisition of a share of ownership in an existing undivided-interest system. Apparently the combination of circumstances led the ICC's Bureau of Traffic to raise the question of whether such systems might fall within the pooling provisions of the Interstate Commerce Act, and this question was referred to the Commission's General Counsel. After ascertaining the facts, a process in which the Committee for Pipe Line Companies proved helpful both to the ICC and to its own members, the General Counsel ruled that Section 5 (1) did not apply to undivided-interest pipeline systems. Accordingly, any doubts that may have existed on this point were relieved, and the path remained open to employ this organizational innovation where it seemed appropriate.

Clearly, the federal pipeline regulatory body came to occupy a more prominent position with respect to postwar pipeline activities than had been the case prior to World War II. In part this role was forced on the ICC by the provisions of the consent decree, in part it reflected interest in testing the extent of the ICC's authority over pipelines, and in part it flowed from increased adversary action. However, contrasted with the number of proceedings involving rail and motor carriers, those involving pipelines were almost infinitesimal. Furthermore, aside from demonstrating that pipeline regulation could be more than nominal, none of the ICC's actions during this period imposed significant new constraints on managerial decision-making. Where such problems did arise, as in valuation and jurisdictional areas, they had largely been resolved by the mid-1950's.

CHAPTER 22

THE PUBLIC POLICY PROCESS AND PIPELINE MANAGEMENT: KEY ISSUES

In dealing with the various facets of the complex public policy process, pipeliners in the postwar era had the advantages of greater unity and better organization than had characterized their conduct of business-government relations before the war. Out of the wartime experience, the need for meeting the consent-decree problem, and the cooperative requirements of big-inch pipelining had come a growing recognition of the need for common action on common problems in the public policy area. Within the pipeline sector of the oil industry, the formation of the Committee for Pipe Line Companies gave concrete evidence of this new awareness. In addition to representing its members in Washington and keeping them abreast of developments there, the committee provided useful liaison with other transportation interests. It was also the vehicle through which pipeliners joined forces in seeking relief from the federal transportation tax by taking an unaccustomed initiative in legislative action.

Public policy problems consumed far more management time and demanded more continuing attention than before the war. One key issue was the interpretation of the consent decree. Another issue was the appropriate weight to attach to new criticisms of the integrated oil industry and a flurry of proposals for public policy to affect the pipelines' place in it. For example, just as pipeline management was meeting postwar demands with new policies and practices, the integrated oil industry was brought under attack by an important academic critic of the old ones. Because the massive governmental assault on Standard Oil early in the century had come from just such beginnings, this new manifestation of outside interest in integrated pipeline operations warranted continuing appraisal by pipeliners. In short, the public policy process from the well springs of legislation to the role of administrative discretion in implementing its outcome took on new meaning for pipeline management.

INTERPRETATION OF THE CONSENT DECREE

Whatever the difficulties experienced by pipeline managers in dealing with the ICC, they could at least be handled on a basis of established procedures, recognized channels, and accustomed relationships. The same was not true for other areas of public policy as they impinged on postwar pipeline management. An outstanding example of these uncertainties was represented by the consent decree of 1941. It posed a threat of triple damages for knowing violation; yet the provisions of the decree as they applied to specific postwar pipeline problems were far from clear-cut. By the very nature of the situation, the Justice Department could scarcely be regarded as an ally in straightening out the resulting difficulties. Appeal to the courts could have opened new difficulties. As a result, managerial adaptation to this public policy had to be cautious; but at the same time, to get on with the business of meeting postwar demands for pipeline service, it was necessary for managers to take calculated risks in interpreting the decree.

From the Justice Department's standpoint, the consent decree was aimed at eliminating any advantage that a shipper-owner might have over an outside shipper by virtue of pipeline ownership. The contention of the department in 1941, it will be recalled, was that pipeline dividends to shipper-owners should be considered rebates, constituting illegal discrimination against outside shippers. However, it was finally agreed between the negotiators for the industry and the department that shipper-owners could receive up to an annual 7 per cent return on a carrier's ICC valuation without being considered to violate the decree.

The department apparently reasoned that a limitation on the payout of pipeline earnings would exert a downward pressure on pipeline rates. This reasoning appeared valid because excess earnings would either have to be frozen until a pipeline company was liquidated or, if invested in common-carrier property, would not be permitted to earn a return for the shipper-owner. The decree did not fobid the excess earnings; only their payment to the parent company was subject to penalty. In addition, their inclusion in the valuation base for dividend-computing purposes was forbidden. The ICC's 1940 decision in the Reduced Pipe Line Rates and Gathering Charges case, which had set an 8 per cent maximum return on the fair value of common-carrier property, therefore constituted the formal postwar ceiling on a company's over-all rates for crude-oil transportation.

Within these constraints, management was free to determine rate policy. Reduced unit costs as a result of larger volumes of crude-oil shipments, for example, could conceivably increase pipeline earnings beyond what could be paid out in dividends under the consent decree. Thus, it would theoretically have been possible to: (1) increase net earnings by reducing unit costs while holding rates constant at a level producing an 8 per cent return on ICC valuation, (2) pay out earnings to a shipper-owner to the extent of 7 per cent of valuation, and (3) freeze the remainder in a surplus account to be recaptured when the pipeline company was liquidated.

Adoption of such a strategy would have emphasized maintenance of rates at the maximum level permissible under the 1940 ICC decision. While this strategy might have been in keeping with some pre-World War II ideas about discouraging outside business, it did not fit the postwar situation.

A high-rate policy primarily directed to barring outside shipments would have sacrificed important incremental contributions that such shipments could make to pipeline overhead and operating costs. With expensive big-inch lines, these were major considerations. By charging maximum rates, a shipper-owner not only risked insufficient utilization of its lines, but also, even if able to keep them fully loaded, would have been forced to pay excessively for its oil transportation. In the postwar years when capital for expansion of pipelines and other facilities was in short supply, adoption of a high-rate policy for exclusionary purposes would only have aggravated the problem. In fact, it was an alternative that was not generally available, but not for the reasons the Justice Department had anticipated in 1941.

As shown in the coverage of postwar pipeline expansion, there was an important competitive aspect to postwar big-inch construction. For example, Service Pipe Line found that it could not provide competitive transportation service from the Rocky Mountains to the Midwest with a system less modern than Platte's new one. This meant that its parent, Indiana Standard, had to pay more for its transportation of Rocky Mountain crude than Platte's owners. Consequently, Service built a new line and reduced its tariff rates. Although these decisions were based on competition between pipelines owned by integrated companies, they obviously had significance for actual and potential outside shippers. Increased pipeline capacity meant increased interest in outside shipments.

The postwar aim of most pipeline companies subject to the consent decree was to reach a 7 per cent return on ICC valuation. Surprisingly, this goal was difficult to define in practical terms, let alone achieve under increasingly competitive conditions.

In the absence of current ICC valuations during the early postwar period, pipeline managers were forced to take a position on the decree's valuation provisions. Obviously, different approaches could expand or contract valuation and therefore the size of permissible dividends. One question was whether "latest final valuation" should be interpreted in the time perspective of 1941. In view of the heavy equity element in pipeline financing that had existed at that time, ICC valuation had been a reasonably close approximation of the shipper-owner's pipeline investment in most cases. Possibly, for this reason the Justice Department accepted it as a base for dividend calculations. Because pipeline valuation as determined by ICC methods made allowance for reproduction cost and other factors, it was also more favorable to the companies in a period of inflation than "investment" would have been.* This situation may have been a reason for the industry negotiators advocating this base. In any case, the Justice Department, apparently recognizing that "investment" and "valuation" could be substantially different, sought belatedly to minimize that difference by insisting that the 1934 ICC final valuation was to be the point of departure for all future time in calculating dividends. However, the language of the

---

*In the case of one company, reproduction cost was 88.5 per cent of book cost as of December 31, 1934, but this figure had risen to about 130 per cent 14 years later.

decree was sufficiently unclear to encourage pipeline managements to interpret it in its most favorable light in determining maximum valuation for reporting purposes, and to make the department hesitant to challenge such interpretations.

Another key question which later confronted pipeline management, though it was not thought to be a problem until it was raised by the Justice Department, was whether, under the decree, dividends could be paid on the debt-financed element of valuation. Pipeline debt had grown large in view of the competing postwar demands for capital and the limited return on equity investment permitted by the consent decree.* Yet, ambiguity remained in Paragraph III of the decree, which referred to payment of dividends on the shipper-owner's "share" of valuation. The interpretation that the Justice Department subsequently placed on this term was that it meant the shipper-owner's equity contribution to valuation; companies subject to the decree took the contrary position that it referred to "share" in joint-ownership lines — not equity as opposed to debt. Accordingly they claimed the right to pay dividends up to 7 per cent on total valuation, not just on their equity share of it.

Where a problem of procedure in reporting under the decree seemed particularly difficult, it was frequently referred to the Justice Department for an opinion. Thirty-one of these opinions were rendered between 1942 and 1957, some oral and some in writing.[1] However, these interpretations were not disseminated by the department to all companies subject to the decree, presumably because the opinions dealt with individual company situations. The frequent turnover of top-level department personnel, and eventually the disappearance from the department of all staff members who had participated in the decree's negotiation, was an invitation for conflicting opinions to issue from the department. The chief value of such interpretations, then, was protection for the company soliciting them against "knowing" violation of the decree.

Just as pipeline companies confronted uncertainties as a result of the decree, the Justice Department was also placed in a difficult position. If it detected some matter of concern in an annual report made by a pipeline company to the Attorney General in compliance with the decree, it could — and did — question the company's interpretation of that document. Similarly it could warn against practices that it regarded as in contravention of the decree. However, unless it was prepared to take the matter to court, there was little that the department could do but accept the company's explanation. Thus, although numerous letters emanated from the department questioning or warning companies about compliance with the consent decree, they were typically not followed by anything more. Lack of action

*In terms of sources of funds, long-term debt of pipeline companies reporting to the ICC constituted 42.5 per cent of the total for 1946–1950 and 33.7 per cent for 1951–1955, compared to 5.9 per cent for 1941–1945 and only 3.7 per cent for 1931–1935. Based on ICC, Bureau of Transport Economics and Statistics, *Statistics of Oil Pipe Line Companies Reporting to the Interstate Commerce Commission,* 1929–1956.

suggests that the department itself was not sure how the decree would be construed by the courts. Therefore it was unwilling to force the issue of interpretation.

With the passage of time, this policy of relative passivity by the department gave increased validity to the procedures adopted by pipeline managements in complying with the decree. In order to meet both their business and legal obligations, they had to take the initiative in interpreting it. These interpretations were eventually subjected to scrutiny by the courts and upheld. Meanwhile, the very uncertainty of the meaning of the decree plus the magnitude of penalties for knowingly violating it, formed an important and worrisome parameter of decision-making by pipeline managers in the postwar period.

ACADEMIC CONTROVERSY OVER DIVORCEMENT

While pipeline managements were wrestling with the problems of interpreting and complying with the consent decree, they unexpectedly found themselves under fire from an academic critic writing in the antimonopoly tradition of Henry Demarest Lloyd and Ida Tarbell, the great antagonists of the Standard Oil Trust. The new attack came in a study of national oil policy published in 1948 by Eugene V. Rostow of the Yale Law School. His key indictment of pipelines was framed in these words: "The chief weapon of the major companies for protecting their position in the market for crude oil is their ownership of pipe lines, the indispensable link . . . between the oil well and the refinery." [2]

Declaring that the prewar charge (highlighted in the TNEC hearings) that pipeline "profits" subsidized other integrated company operations "will not bear inquiry," Rostow made it clear that he was concerned about the more subtle effects of integrated-company pipeline ownership. "The level of pipe-line rates is a measure of the forces required to keep posted prices for crude at an appropriate minimum," he wrote, "and above all to keep independent refiners, who must depend on independent sources of crude, on relatively short and expensive rations of supplies." [3] Correctly observing that pipelines were still being built to transport their owner's oil, Rostow emphasized his belief that pipeline rates were also still being used to discourage the independent producer from "paying the costs of carriage on his oil in order to reach a wider market in the refinery area." [4] Apparently, in his view, nothing had changed since the days of The Pipe Line Cases.

Writing in 1946–47 before the trend of postwar pipelining had become clear, Rostow necessarily drew largely, if selectively, on experience with pipelines in the pre-World War II era. Even so, his charges were not buttressed by specific evaluation of primary sources. There was, for example, no analysis of even one situation where an integrated company's pipeline ownership had forced a reduction in the price of crude to an independent or had enabled an integrated company to maintain a market position that would otherwise have been vulnerable to competition.

Rostow's interpretation involved an implicit assumption that so-called "major" (i.e., large, integrated) companies made a consistently united front against "independents" (i.e., small, nonintegrated) operators. He did not assess the evidence that independent producers preferred to sell their oil in the field. There was no suggestion that large companies willingly reduced pipeline rates, or that in the past pipelines had enabled previously nonintegrated companies to become "majors" themselves. In fact, as the ICC reported, rates had been declining since 1933. But, unquestionably, there was some evidence to support the basic Rostovian position, and much of the evidence has been reviewed in previous chapters of this book.

Although Rostow claimed that high pipeline rates were a barrier to entry into refining, he recognized that lower ones would not necessarily change the situation. Thus he suggested that even with substantially reduced rates the independent's position would not be "radically improved" because pipeline service available to him would also bring other independents into the common market place. Then he modified this position to suggest that a "significant" improvement in the crude-oil producer's position might result.[5]

Rostow was correct in his view that major pipelines were not built for the revenue to be derived from common-carrier transportation service under published tariffs but to move their owners' (purchased or produced) oil. It followed for him, and again correctly, that pipeline "profits" insofar as they were based on the owner's shipments were not profits at all but book-keeping charges in a single family of companies. It was also logical, though not necessarily correct, to conclude that pipeline rates were most significant as a device to deny or control access by nonowners to the cheapest mode of overland oil transportation. It was again logical, though again not necessarily correct, to hypothesize that such a control device allowed the integrated companies more profits than what they would receive in an alternative structuring of the industry where transportation was no barrier to entry. Rostow accepted this hypothesis as proved. Therefore, pipeline divorcement appeared to him a logical remedy.[6]

Without an opportunity to actually try divorcement, however, there was little except hypothesized future conditions that Rostow or other advocates of industry reorganization could point to in support of their contentions. Defenders of integration could challenge these assumptions and they could stress past achievements under integrated operations. Here, as in the past, there was ample room for speculation and argument.

As an alternative to divorcement, statutory public policy as established in the Hepburn Act of 1906 had attempted to deal with the problem that concerned Rostow by bringing pipelines under federal regulation. This economic regulation was indeed of questionable effect in terms of forcing rate reductions, at least until the 1930's; even then, other factors, such as taxation, contributed to the gradual reduction of pipeline rates.

Reviewing this record in a cursory manner, Rostow's appraisal of pipelines came to the 1940 ICC decision in Reduced Pipe Line Rates and Gathering Charges. By applying the concept of a "fair return on a fair value" to pipeline rate regulation in this case, he charged, the ICC had envisioned "a fantastic rate structure" resulting in different rates in different areas for the same service. Thus, he said, rates were made to depend "largely upon the historical accident of what the various pipe lines happened to cost when they were built." [7]

As Rostow pointed out, the United States Supreme Court in the 1944 Hope Natural Gas case[8] had noted that "fair value" was a faulty concept when used as the basis for determining a reasonable return, because value depends on the return. Applied to pipelines, a given rate yielding a reasonable return on fair valuation at one level of volume may yield a higher return on investment at a larger volume because of lowered unit costs.[9]

Leslie Cookenboo, Jr., in a study of pipelines published in 1955, gave a practical example of how this relationship worked. He found that for a selected group of large companies owning pipelines, pre-federal tax pipeline earnings on depreciated investment increased 10.2 (after tax 2.5) per cent from 1948 to 1951, while rates rose 8 per cent.[10] These upward changes were possible within the unchanging ICC limitation of an 8 per cent maximum return on valuation (i.e., this figure permitted a return on *more* than depreciated investment). The explanation for the increased earnings, Cookenboo claimed, lay primarily in the larger volumes of oil transported in 1951 compared to 1948. For him, as for Rostow, this difficulty under public-utility regulation showed the inadequacy of the approach.[11]

This conclusion was not necessarily warranted. Among other things, it ignored the incentive offered under existing rate regulation to increase private investment in more efficient pipeline facilities. Between 1949 and 1950, for example, net investment (current dollars) in pipelines reporting to the ICC increased $130,000,000; revenues rose about $65,000,000 with an average rate increase of only 0.7 cents per 1000 barrel-miles.[12] In other words, new capital expenditure, undertaken within the framework of "fair-value" rate regulation, had contributed to more efficient movement of larger volumes of oil. Although this increase in volume was also accompanied by a slight increase in *average* rates, the rates that increased the average were not necessarily those charged for movements over the new facilities.

Should average rates have fallen to reflect the increased economies made possible by the new investment? Would they have been reduced under any alternative mode of regulation? Would the new lines have been built at all, or as rapidly, under these conditions? These kinds of questions interested academic commentators as well as those directly involved in the public policy process.

Given the reduction of rates as a primary goal, it seems doubtful that such a radical step as divorcement would have forced rates below those charged under "fair value" regulation as it existed in 1948. Independent pipeline operators would have wanted to recover their investment and earn a return on it, and it is a fair assumption that their cost of obtaining capital would have been higher than a large integrated company's. Therefore, they might well have required a higher level of rates than those that satisfied the needs of an integrated concern providing equivalent facilities. Rostow, however, did not explore this problem.

In comparing the desirability of integrated versus independent pipeline operations, the cost of capital is not the only factor to be considered. The failure of an integrated company to earn a compensatory return on pipeline investment per se may be more than offset by the access it gains to valuable sources of crude or markets. Therefore, even with "cost" rates, which would presumably encourage outside shippers, an integrated company might still have an adequate incentive to continue pipeline construction. Consequently, the country might be better supplied with pipelines charging lower rates under integrated ownership than would be possible under divorcement and independent pipeline ownership.

This was substantially the view adopted by George S. Wolbert, Jr., whose book *American Pipe Lines* (1952) first appeared in article form in the *Oklahoma Law Review* during 1951. In this carefully documented study, Wolbert seemed to agree with Rostow that pipelines had been built to move their owners' oil and that rate policies for many years had discouraged outside usage.[13] Unlike Rostow, however, he did not see market control as a primary objective of integrated companies' pipeline ownership, but rather a logical response by private capital to conditions encountered.[14] He argued that it was a matter of record that many of the policies and practices for which prewar pipelines were attacked were exaggerations of the facts, and past abuses had been or were being eliminated. He flatly rejected divorcement as a cure for any that remained.

Like the proponents of divorcement, Wolbert hypothesized the possible consequences of such action, adding to those already mentioned some of the pragmatic considerations that would affect business decisions. In essence, he maintained that such a drastic alteration of existing relations would not in and of itself eliminate the pre-existing advantages of size, established position, and resources of large companies. Independent pipeline operators would be as inclined to favor large shippers as integrated pipeline management was; independent producers would still prefer large customers; independent refiners who gained access to metropolitan refining areas would (as Rostow had also suggested) meet the competition of others there, and field refiners would suffer, again perhaps benefiting large companies.[15]

Discarding divorcement as a remedy and arguing that pipeline regulation was a proper function of the ICC, not of the Justice Department under the consent decree, Wolbert advocated the use of "cost rates."[16] Such rates would presumably compensate the pipeline owner yet keep the level of rates low enough to encourage, or at least not discourage, independent shippers. This proposal, however, had its drawbacks.

In addition to covering operating costs and the usual fixed costs, a cost rate would also have to compensate the investor for other opportunities foreclosed by the pipeline investment. Looking at over-all integrated company operations, for example, Cookenboo found their after-tax earnings averaged about 10 per cent in 1951.[17] Using this figure, he concluded that pipeline cost rates, taking opportunity costs into account, would have been higher than those actually in effect and consequently would have been of little benefit to independents.[18] For these reasons, among others, Cookenboo rejected "cost rates" as unworkable. On the other hand, he pointed out that under integrated operations, opportunity costs might be virtually zero for a company building a pipeline to realize a return on capital committed to an area other than transportation.[19] Thus, divorcement was no answer to rate problems either.

The appearance of Wolbert's book provided Professor Rostow and a student associate, Arthur S. Sachs, with a new opportunity to review the Rostovian position on pipelines. They did so in a 1952 *Yale Law Journal* article devoted to the question of entry into the oil refining business.[20] The article made it clear that Rostow had not changed his mind, though he had shifted his position somewhat to acknowledge that pipeline rates had dropped consistently from 1933 to 1948 (a fact blinked in the Rostow book). The authors made vertical integration "the" key factor in large companies' influencing the price of crude, limiting independents' access to consuming markets and thereby maintaining "a semblance of order in the pricing of final products." [21] The authors would not concede that either rate regulation or the consent decree had done very much to improve the independents' position since 1941.[22] In effect, they rejected cost rates as unworkable and, even if they could be established, as producing too low (in the absence of an opportunity cost element) a return to receive regulatory sanction.[23] Otherwise, Rostow and Sachs contested Wolbert's version of what would happen in the event of pipeline divorcement.[24]

Basic to the position adopted by Rostow and Sachs was the assumption that pipeline ownership by integrated companies was a primary obstacle to entry into the refining business. Such matters as large capital requirements for efficient refining operations were dismissed on the basis that plant size, not company size, was the crucial factor and that an efficient refinery need not be on the scale typical of those belonging to the large companies. Again, the evidence offered was extremely limited.[25]

These questions were taken up by Cookenboo in his *Crude Oil Pipe Lines and Competition in the Oil Industry* (1955). In appraising the role of pipelines and other facets of integrated operations, Cookenboo's book had the benefit not only of Rostow's and Wolbert's work but also of a research study done by John G. McLean and Robert W. Haigh of the Harvard Graduate School of Business Administration and published in 1954 as *The Growth of Integrated Oil Companies*.[26]

McLean and Haigh, as part of their examination of the integration process over time, reviewed the position of the small refining firm in the oil industry and found that it had declined substantially (from 28 per cent to 15 per cent of the total) in the period 1920–1950. However, rather than attributing the decline to exclusionary pipeline tactics, they found the explanation to lie in the rapid advance of refining technology and its attendant capital requirements.[27] These findings impressed Cookenboo.

> It is only by demonstrating that divorcement would appreciably assist those independents large enough to promote more vigorous price competition in the refined products market that a program of dis-integration can be justified — especially when such a program carries with it danger of higher transportation costs. This demonstration has not yet adequately been made by the proponents of divorcement. Indeed, the cost data of McLean and Haigh indicate that new plants must be large to compete with large plants.[28]

If capital costs of new plants would constitute a barrier to independents' competition in major refining centers even assuming pipelines could be made as freely available as Rostow wanted, it was just as doubtful that divorcement of pipelines would be of material assistance to owners of existing independent refining capacity. Independent refineries were typically crude-oriented; that is, they were already located near crude supplies. Such refineries therefore would have little to gain from pipeline divorcement. This fact was overlooked by Rostow when, relying on the TNEC hearings, he suggested in his book that the disappearance of supposedly efficient east Texas refineries between 1935 and 1941 might have been prevented by divorcement.[29]

This problem intrigued Cookenboo, and he set out to examine it systematically. From a locational analysis of all independent refining capacity, he concluded that the owners of only about 20 per cent of this capacity, or 4 per cent of total refining capacity, could be helped by divorcement of integrated company pipelines. When he applied a yardstick of efficient independent refining capacity, Cookenboo concluded that pipeline divorcement would affect only some 2.4 per cent of total United States refining capacity, given the location of existing independent refineries.[30] Such a finding clearly did not support the drastic public policy prescriptions of Rostow and Sachs.

As already indicated, Cookenboo agreed with Rostow that public-utility regulation of pipelines was inappropriate, and he also dismissed Wolbert's suggestion of cost rates. Instead, he proposed an interesting combination of an economics textbook answer and an adaptation of the joint-venture device. As developed in the oil industry, the ownership of joint-venture pipelines had involved chiefly large companies. Cookenboo in essence suggested that United States public policy should require an extension of this device to require that all who wished admittance to ownership in a joint-venture pipeline be accepted.[31] By such means the most efficient size lines could replace competing systems and maximum operating economies would be achieved, all who had a need for pipeline services would be accommodated, and the inadequacies of regulation would be circumvented.

As a model for the direction in which public policy should move, Cookenboo employed a "blown up" and rationally designed (from the standpoint of economic theory) version of what private enterprise was already creating. But for all his obvious display of technical competence in analysis,

Cookenboo's recommendations for public policy seem almost utopian when applied to the whole industry.

Just what the specific significance of these works was for the development of public policy is no more clear in retrospect than it was at the time. At a minimum, however, they provided some provocative discussion of the postwar alternatives of public policy for dealing with pipelines and the strengths and weaknesses of various implementing devices. On balance, they seem to have shown that, whatever the problems of nonintegrated oil concerns, divorcement of pipelines per se would provide no answers. Whatever the theoretical drawbacks of fair-value rate regulation, in practice it probably worked better than any alternative suggested by academicians. Nevertheless, the possibility that Rostow's views would find a sympathetic reception in Congress worried many a pipeline executive.

REPEAL OF THE FEDERAL TAX ON TRANSPORTATION OF OIL BY PIPELINE

Pipeline executives were accustomed to being on the defensive in public policy matters, but in the 1950's they took an unaccustomed initiative to obtain repeal of the federal tax on transportation of oil by pipeline. This tax had been adopted as an emergency revenue measure in the depths of the depression but had been continued and its rate increased from 4 to 4.5 per cent in 1941. Since the tax was levied on the carriers' revenues, and since transportation charges were largely paid by the shipper-owners of the pipelines, the tax increased their costs except as it could be offset by reducing rates and therefore the tax base, or by increasing rates and ultimately passing the tax forward to consumers in the price of petroleum products. Most managements chose the first alternative. Thus, rather than increasing pipeline rates, the imposition of the transportation tax had tended to decrease them. The Eastman Report of 1940 on "Public Aids to Transportation," for example, pointed out that pipelines had not depended on public subsidy and had been instrumental in reducing the price of refined products.[32]

On several occasions the undesirable and discriminatory character of the transportation tax had been noted in reports made by groups and individuals outside the oil industry. In 1944 the Board of Investigation and Research established under the Transportation Act of 1940 stated in its staff report that the pipeline transportation tax had no counterpart in the peacetime taxes on other transportation agencies."[33] Secretary of the Treasury Henry Morgenthau in 1942,[34] and one of his successors, John W. Snyder, in 1950, without singling out pipelines specifically, opposed transportation taxes because they raise costs to consumers by pyramiding handling costs in a most undesirable way.[35] However, nothing came of their recommendations.

The drive to repeal federal transportation taxes was revitalized after the Korean conflict. The spearhead for the oil industry's efforts to obtain repeal of the pipeline transportation tax was the Committee for Pipe Line Companies.* In July 1953 the committee's staff, headed by Gordon C. Locke, was authorized and directed to cooperate with other groups in any concerted effort to obtain relief from the transportation tax.[36] This strategy was in keeping with the new effort to identify pipeline problems with those of the transportation industry rather than with the oil industry.

In December 1956, Locke appeared before the House Ways and Means Committee in support of a statement by the National Committee for Repeal of Taxes on Transportation,† favoring repeal of transportion excise taxes. He pointed out that the pipeline tax was 50 per cent higher than the general freight transportation tax and that the movement of more than three-fourths of the crude oil in the country was subject to this tax, while the remainder was either subject to a lower one if moved by other types of common carriers, or to no tax at all if moved by private carriers. He noted that $35,600,000 dollars was paid by pipeline companies in transportation taxes during 1956, or 22 per cent of total federal taxes paid by pipelines. In his view there was clear discrimination against the common-carrier oil pipeline, which at a minimum should be treated on a par with other carriers. Like representatives of other transportation media whose cause he also endorsed, Locke took the broad position that transportation taxes imposed as an emergency measure were no longer justified.[37]

These arguments and others like them met a favorable reception in Congress. Consequently the Tax Rate Extension Act of 1958 removed taxes on the transportation of property via pipeline, effective August 1, 1958. A major tax burden had finally been lifted from the pipeline sector of the oil industry as a result of a cooperative legislative endeavor with other transportation interests.

Removal of the pipeline tax led counsel for the Independent Refiners Association of America to note in a bulletin to members that they might expect pipeline rates to be reduced. However, Locke quickly issued a statement that this result was unlikely. Pointing out that pipeline rates were set on an individual company basis, he stated that pipelines had always absorbed the transportation tax. In view of the current business recession, which had adversely affected pipeline movements, costs had risen to the point where rate increases had been contemplated. Therefore, rather than looking for a general reduction of pipeline rates, he implied, the refiners should be pleased if the removal of the tax made such an increase unnecessary.[38]

This chapter has included a few examples of the most important facets

---

*The American Petroleum Institute assigned the tax question to the Pipe Line Study Committee, established as a subcommitee of the API Executive Committee in April 1945.

†The conference was supported by 50 associations or organizations as varied as the Associated Traffic Clubs of America, Brotherhoods of Locomotive Engineers, Firemen and Enginemen and Sleeping Car Porters, Traffic Bureau of Sioux Falls, and West Coast Lumbermen's Association. 84 Cong., Sess., House Committee on Ways and Means, "Excise Taxes," *Hearings* (Washington, 1957).

of public policy that affected postwar pipeline management directly or indirectly. Clearly, the consent decree, like ICC regulation, had to be accepted as a continuing constraint on the freedom of managerial decision-making. From the standpoint of management, the problem was how to maximize a company's position within its provisions. In addition to this challenge, the integrated oil industry faced a new generation of critics, who drew their ammunition from charges that management believed were long outdated. However, as shown in the handling of the transportation tax question, pipeliners had become more politically sophisticated than had been the case prior to World War II. Furthermore, they displayed both greater autonomy and more unity in handling public policy matters than in the prewar era. A concatenation of events in the later 1950's, however, posed problems of dealing with administrative and legislative bodies for which even this experience was a minimal preparation.

CHAPTER 23

THE CONTINUING ATTACK
ON INTEGRATED OPERATIONS

Although the pipeline consent decree of 1941, combined with the nation's involvement in World War II, ended an era of sustained congressional attack on integrated oil operations, the respite proved temporary. A small group of Congressmen kept up a drumfire of divorcement proposals, and their suggestions for legislative action received sporadic encouragement in the postwar years from congressional investigations of increasingly complex oil problems. These manifestations of congressional interest in integrated oil operations formed a backdrop for occasional legal and administrative forays by government agencies, with inevitable repercussions for the pipeline sector of the integrated industry. The Suez crisis of 1956 and its aftermath brought many of these strands together in a way that occasioned more concern among pipeline managements than any development since the late 1930's.

LEGISLATIVE PROPOSALS FOR PIPELINE DIVORCEMENT

Proposals for legislative divorcement of pipelines were filed almost routinely in Congress from the early 1930's on, but they made no more progress in the 1940's and 1950's than before. In the Congress before Pearl Harbor, Senator Guy M. Gillette of Iowa and his colleague in the House, Congressman Vincent F. Harrington, introduced pipeline divorcement bills. The railroads also supported a 1940 proposal (S. 3753) by Senator Edwin C. Johnson of Colorado proposing that, as in the case of the rail carriers, the ICC should have authority to grant or deny certificates for pipeline extensions, construction, or abandonments.[1] The Association of American Railroads' Subcommittee on Pipeline Transport made substantially the same recommendation in a 1944 report, which also implied that pipeline divorcement might be desirable.[2]

The active involvement of the United States in World War II and the ensuing negotiation of the pipeline consent decree temporarily ended legislative divorcement efforts. The war did not, however, prevent Congressman Edouard V. M. Izac of California from reintroducing in 1943 his divorcement bill of 1939,[3] and in 1944 Senator Gillette indicated on the floor of the Senate that he was concerned about the effectiveness of the consent decree.[4] In 1945, Congressman Izac renewed his divorcement proposal (H.R. 55) but it got no further than his previous two.[5] The same was true of H.R. 6972 introduced by Congressman H. J. Voorhis of California in 1946.[6]

Senator Gillette remained discontented with what he viewed as the Justice Department's inaction with respect to the oil industry. In January 1949, therefore, he introduced bills for the divorcement of pipelines, marketing, and tankers.[7] Again, no substantive action was taken, and the same fate befell yet another move for pipeline divorcement submitted by the Senator in 1954.[8] Aside from this bill and the attempt of Senator William Langer of North Dakota to resurrect it two years later in connection with an unsuccessful effort to exempt natural gas production from federal price regulation,[9] senatorial proposals for pipeline divorcement temporarily languished.

The House was not completely inactive on pipelines during this period. In 1949–50 Congressman Emanuel Celler, a long-time Democratic Congressman from Brooklyn, became chairman of the House Committee on the Judiciary. He also headed the committee's Subcommittee on Monopoly Power. In this capacity he heard testimony in May 1950 from Commissioner Clyde Aitchison of the ICC on a proposal to extend the commodities clause to new forms of transportation, including pipelines. Aitchison diplomatically but firmly took the stand that such a step would be ill-advised.[10] Again, no legislative action was taken.

CONGRESSIONAL INVESTIGATIONS, 1946–1949

For active legislative interest in measures that would change the structure of the oil industry, there had to be more than an occasional Congressman's interest. Traditionally, congressional investigators had helped to create such an environment.

As the war came to an end, congressional committees resumed their inquiries into the functioning of the oil industry. During 1945–46, for example, a special Senate committee, headed by Senator Joseph C. O'Mahoney of Wyoming, heard extensive testimony on the nation's petroleum resources and the place of the independent operator in the oil industry.[11] In these hearings there seemed to be little concern with oil pipelines per se, or even discontent with the power of integrated companies, though Justice Department representative W. B. Watson Snyder introduced evidence tending to show that large companies had improved their position during the war.[12]

A much less sympathetic view of pipelines was reflected in the report of an extensive investigation conducted by the Senate Special Committee to Study Problems of American Small Business, chaired by Senator Kenneth Wherry of Nebraska.[13] This probe originated in response to complaints arising out of the postwar shortage of crude and refined products, which pinched independent operators. Among this group were Chicago peddlers of fuel oil obtained from integrated companies. Their complaints led the

Wherry Committee to appoint a special committee on oil in August of 1947. After a year and a half of hearings, the report of its findings was made in January 1949. Not unexpectedly, given the function of the Senate Small Business Committee as a legislative guardian of small enterprise,* the conclusions were not favorable to large, integrated oil companies.

Independent refiners had testified in a familiar vein that they experienced difficulty in using the pipelines of integrated companies, and, when they could use them, in obtaining deliveries where they wanted them.[14] Although at least one of these refiners recognized that the postwar shortage of pipeline facilities was a factor in his difficulties, other witnesses, incensed at the unwillingness of integrated companies to sell them crude oil in a time of shortage, were understandably more concerned with their own problems. One independent refiner, for example, declared: "Pipe lines post rates and get all the benefits of being common carriers, but we think it is time that they become common carriers in fact instead of only in name." [15]

Despite these complaints, other testimony showed that the independent refining industry had not made strenuous efforts to take advantage of such possibilities as refining-in-transit rates on crude oil, or to secure joint through rates on crude transportation by pipeline, water, and rail.[16] The independents explained this lack of initiative in terms of their dearth of resources to pursue such matters, and they asked the committee's aid in getting the ICC to look into commodity rates on crude oil and refined products.[17]

The Wherry Committee reported the independents' charges without qualification. It declared that there "is no open market for crude oil such as there exists in other commodities; for example, grains and cotton." [18] Also, the committee accepted uncritically the charges — recently broadcast in Rostow's book of 1948 — that control of pipelines enabled integrated companies to control crude oil at its source and that integrated companies enjoyed advantageous transportation rates because of pipeline ownership, plus "a draw-back or kickback of the profit on the crude oil transported for the account of others." [19] Although acknowledging that trunk pipeline rates had shown a downward trend, the report did not analyze the impact of the consent decree.†

The committee apparently accepted at face value the charge of one refiner that there was no industry other than oil where it was necessary to control the raw material from the ground to the consumer.[20] This assertion obviously overlooked the fact that complete vertical integration characterized in varying degree a number of other extractive industries, such as lumber, rubber, steel, and aluminum. The report also charged that pipelines were

---

*The Special Committee on Small Business Problems was first established by the Senate in 1941 and under various names has continued in existence.

†Senator Wherry had contacted the Justice Department inquiring about compliance with the decree, but Assistant Attorney General Peyton Ford had replied only that the department was investigating and needed the benefit of more experience with it for a proper appraisal.

no different from railroads, thus ignoring, and therefore failing to evaluate, years of oil industry claims, testimony, and evidence presented to Congress on such differences. The committee report even went out of its way to suggest that ICC Commissioner Aitchison, who had been intimately involved in the pipeline rate case, was singularly blind to the pipelines' competitive significance.[21] In the light of such one-sided evidence and conclusions, it was inevitable that the committee's report should recommend separation of crude-oil pipelines from their parent shipper-owners.[22]

Similar conclusions were reached on products lines. The report was critical of the operation of these lines as private carriers, citing Champlin I in this connection. While admitting that shipper-owned, common-carrier products lines served others than their owners, independents as well as large companies, the report charged that the shippers were all refiners (i.e., not jobbers, and such) and that rail rates were the basis for pipeline transportation charges.[23]

As exemplified in Champlin I, this last charge involved the refiner's policy of setting product prices f.o.b. refinery and adding to them rail charges even though the transportation was done by lower-cost pipeline. In the committee's view this amounted to "phantom freight." Though the Federal Trade Commission's attention was called to the matter, its response was noncommittal.[24]

For common-carrier products lines, the phantom freight charge was probably ten years out of date. The 1939 Petroleum Rail Shippers' case, of course, had indicated that rates producing more than a 10 per cent return on ICC valuation would be considered unreasonable. Using the rule of that case for a given haul, therefore, the difference between rail charges and pipeline costs plus a 10 per cent return on the pipeline's valuation would have constituted phantom freight. However, no specific evidence was introduced to substantiate a claim that any common-carrier products pipeline was still charging rail rates.

For private products carriers, the phantom freight charge was perhaps more pertinent. However, as the Supreme Court later found in Champlin II, ownership of a private products pipeline had enabled Champlin, a comparatively small refiner, to survive in competition with large companies, promoting the very kind of competition desired by the Wherry Committee. Although Champlin's method of pricing had been accepted by the Court as a justification for an assertion of limited ICC jurisdiction in Champlin I, thus perhaps justifying the Wherry Committee in raising the phantom freight question, the same Court later found in Champlin II that this did not justify a requirement that Champlin perform as a common carrier for hire. It seems that congressional hearings tended to be long on allegations and short on critical examination of them.

REVIVAL OF ANTITRUST ATTACKS ON THE INTEGRATED OIL INDUSTRY

Complementing congressional interest in oil matters, there was a revival of antitrust interest and action against the integrated oil industry during the early 1950's. The Mother Hubbard case, of which the pipeline consent decree had been an offshoot, was suspended during the war because the government needed the cooperation of the oil companies that Thurman Arnold had felt should be broken up. Arnold, of course, had advocated an attack on the whole integrated oil industry. In reconsidering this strategy after the war, the Justice Department, now under different leadership, concluded that such a wide-ranging indictment might be difficult to sustain compared to a segmented approach focused on specific areas of the industry. Accordingly, the Mother Hubbard case was dropped in 1950 and replaced by an attack on conditions in the West Coast segment of the industry.*

Traditionally, the West Coast area had been a self-contained petroleum province, with local production as the principal source of supply. In *United States v. Standard Oil Company of California*, inaugurated on May 12, 1950, the Justice Department charged this company and six others on the Pacific Coast with a conspiracy to monopolize and suppress competition at all levels of operations. The complaint alleged that the conspiracy covered 94 per cent of production, 97 per cent of crude-oil trunk pipelines, 77 per cent of gathering pipelines, 100 per cent of marine transportation, 90 per cent of gasoline refining capacity, 86 per cent of the retail outlets, and 90 per cent of total marketing in this area.[25]

With this case still in progress, the Justice Department in June 1953 also launched a major attack on five large international oil companies. They were charged with conspiring over a period of nearly 30 years to secure and maintain control over foreign production and supplies of petroleum, to maintain prices at agreed levels throughout the world, and to divide producing and marketing territories. Much of this conspiracy was alleged to have been accomplished through the joint ownership of 33 companies created for that purpose.[26]

Although neither case had been settled when pipelines came under fresh attack later in the decade, the very fact of their existence provided ammunition for critics of the integrated oil industry and its pipeline sector. Meanwhile, Congress assigned a new "watchdog" function to the Justice Department that carried this agency still deeper into the affairs of the oil industry.

CONGRESSIONAL PROVISION FOR CONTINUING REVIEW OF THE PETROLEUM INDUSTRY

Since the federal support of oil conservation measures had been adopted in 1933 there had been congressional concern with its possible implications for price stabilization and monopolization in the domestic oil business. For

*In 1947 the Justice Department had initiated suits against California Standard and Richfield Oil Company in connection with distribution-level practices. Assistant Attorney General Peyton Ford pointed this out to Senator Gillette in May 1949 in response to the Senator's expression of concern about the disposition of the Mother Hubbard case. Ford said of that case that it was "so large and unwieldy" as to prevent clear presentation of issues of law. *Cong. Rec.,* August 30, 1949, p. 12700.

this reason the Interstate Oil Compact between oil-producing states enforcing oil conservation was made the subject of continuing congressional review and was periodically renewed for only limited periods of time.

The compact, like integrated pipeline ownership, came in for heavy criticism from the Wherry Committee in 1949, and it received another critical review by the House Committee on Interstate and Foreign Commerce in 1951. At that time a minority report suggested that the Attorney General be required to conduct a continuing study of action taken under the compact to insure that it was not inconsistent with the interests of the "consuming public."[27] Although this amendment was not adopted at the time, its equivalent was added in the Senate in 1955 when the compact came up for renewal. After some alteration in the House, the Joint Resolution of July 28, 1955, directed the Attorney General to make "an annual report to the Congress for the duration of the Interstate Compact to Conserve Oil and Gas as to whether or not the activities of the States under the provisions of such compact have been consistent with the purpose set out in Article V of such compact." [28]

This directive was sufficiently broad to encourage the Attorney General to make his own interpretation of its intended thrust. In his first report under the directive, submitted September 1, 1956, Herbert Brownell, Jr., stated that he interpreted the Joint Resolution to call for "an examination of the petroleum industry to determine if it evidences the existence of anti-competitive practices, including monopolization and price stabilization" and, then, on this basis to establish whether any such results were the product of the regulatory system.[29]

Adoption of this approach automatically shifted emphasis from an examination of the operation of the Interstate Oil Compact Commission to the operation of the petroleum industry. Inevitably this also increased the scope of inquiry and provided a basis for continuing close scrutiny of the industry by the arm of the Executive Branch entrusted with antitrust enforcement. As a result, it was also virtually inevitable that the ownership and operations of integrated pipelines would receive attention.

For lack of time and the resources to do an extensive research study, the Attorney General's first *Report* was largely historical, reviewing the development of conservation practices and regulation and the over-all structural characteristics of the oil industry. Relying heavily on McLean and Haigh's study of integrated oil companies, the report showed that in 1950 there were 179 companies operating refineries and 54 of these were completely integrated. These 54 companies owned about 80 per cent of gathering and crude-oil trunk-line mileage and about 90 per cent of products-line mileage.[30] The report also showed that refining capacity was concentrated in the hands of the large companies — the six largest holding 46.2 per cent of total domestic capacity in 1950; the top eight accounting for 57 per cent; and the top 19, some 81 per cent. The remainder was divided among 160 companies, 96 of which had less than 5,000 barrels a day capacity.[31] Here, of course, was grist for critics such as Rostow, though McLean and Haigh also provided the elements for rebuttal.*

THE SUEZ CRISIS AND RENEWED ATTACKS ON INTEGRATED PIPELINES

Brownell's first report appeared just as an international crisis focused congressional attention anew on the integrated oil industry. In late July of 1956 Egypt, under the leadership of President Nasser, seized the Suez Canal. This development, quite aside from its international diplomatic implications, posed a serious threat to western Europe's oil supplies, much of which came from the Middle East in oil tankers that provided about 50 per cent of the canal's traffic. The holdings by United States companies of Middle East oil reserves constituted a major share of the world's proved oil reserves. To meet the problems created by the Suez crisis, a group of these companies in mid-September 1956 formed a so-called Middle East Emergency Committee (MEEC).

Within two months the British and French had taken retaliatory action against Nasser, and the canal was completely closed. As a result, Europe was cut off from its main source of crude and rationing of the stocks on hand was necessary. With Justice Department clearance on industry cooperation, MEEC undertook to meet the emergency. By early December, emergency shipments to Europe from the American Gulf Coast totaled 8,874,500 barrels, and shipments were being maintained at a rate of 600,000 barrels a day.[32] This high level was short-lived, and for the week ending January 16, 1957, daily shipments fell to 275,000 barrels, of which only 75,000 came from Gulf ports.[33] Though this was less than the amount promised by the United States, the companies continued to import high-grade Venezuelan crude for domestic use rather than ship it to Europe for use as fuel oil.

The Texas Railroad Commission, which had jurisdiction over the only readily available source of increased domestic production, became the storm center of controversy in the resulting situation. The commission did not want to hike production allowables only to find that a surplus existed if the emergency should suddenly evaporate.[34] Instead, the commission advocated a curtailment of imports. This position was not disagreeable to independent Texas producers because it shortly created a rise in crude prices, a movement initiated by Humble Oil which maintained that, in the crisis, it could not otherwise obtain sufficient crude.[35] Eventually, the Texas Commission was persuaded to boost allowables for March 1957;[36] shipments to Europe were increased; and the critics were calmed. In April the canal reopened, the pressure for emergency actions was relieved, and the commission cut back production.[37] However, the brief crisis had important repercussions both in Texas and in Washington.

THE TEXAS UNCONNECTED WELLS CONTROVERSY

Under Texas law, the Texas Railroad Commission is charged with preventing the "waste" of oil or gas, which, among other things, means pro-

*See Chap. 22.

duction in excess of transportation or market facilities or reasonable market demand." [38] In executing this responsibility, the commission fixes the basic allowable production for individual wells in the state on the basis of MER (Maximum Efficient Recovery) or other criteria. At monthly meetings held by the commission, major crude purchasers in the state give estimates of their needs for the coming month. Weighing these cumulative estimates against such other factors as U.S. Bureau of Mines' estimates of demand, and existing oil stocks, the commission determines the market demand for Texas crude production for the next month. It then fixes the maximum monthly allowable production of each well in the state. These decisions become binding on producers because federal law forbids interstate transportation of oil produced in excess of amounts authorized by state authorities. In 1956, "allowables" were expressed in terms of days of production per month.

As the regulator of output in the nation's largest oil-producing state, the Texas Railroad Commission became in that year a focal point for controversy between independent producers and large crude-oil purchasers. The buyer-seller relationship was affected by producers' claims that they had the right to a market for oil produced in accordance with state regulation. The purchasers, typically integrated companies, took the position that they should not be required to buy oil that they did not want or need.

The geographical distribution of Texas production assumed major significance in this controversy. East Texas had produced 32.8 per cent of the state's crude output in 1940 but only 11.4 per cent in 1956. West Texas, on the other hand, had increased its share of the state's production from 17.2 per cent to 41.7 per cent in the same period.[39] The amount of Texas production subject to daily shutdown increased by nearly 274,000 barrels between August 25, 1956, and August 24, 1957, and a major portion of this increase reflected added productive capacity in west Texas that could not be marketed.[40]

This situation gave special importance to the pipelines running from that area to the Gulf Coast, whence Texas oil moved into markets where it encountered imported oil. In this connection it was relevant that ten integrated companies accounting for about 42 per cent of Texas production were also importers of crude.[41] When these companies asked for increased allowables, they prompted the question of whether west Texas crude was being "shut in" by lack of pipeline facilities to move it to the Gulf, and whether the lack of such facilities reflected decisions by companies with foreign production or import interests to favor foreign crude over the west Texas product. The question was presented at the commission's statewide hearings on December 19 whether allowables should be increased before an alleged pipeline bottleneck out of west Texas was eliminated. This question became entangled in the issue of connecting unconnected wells and the relationship that Texas production should bear to imported oil.*

*For the problem of national public policy with respect to imported oil, see above, Chap. 20.

Some of the affiliates of the companies forming the MEEC asked at the December hearings that allowable Texas production be increased by several days. Humble Oil & Refining's representative, for example, requested increased production because his company's Gulf Coast stocks of crude had been exhausted in meeting the Suez emergency.[42] These requests were protested by independent producers, especially from north and west Texas. They maintained that currently allowable production from their areas was not reaching the Gulf for lack of pipeline transportation facilities. It was pointed out, for example, that some crude had to move north to St. Louis by pipeline and then be transferred to barges for movement southward to the Gulf.[43]

What was needed, these producers claimed, was not more allowable production but more pipeline connections for existing wells. In essence, they accused the affiliates of large international oil companies of seeking a temporary increase in Texas allowables for their own benefit while good Texas crude was still available from wells that lacked pipeline connections.

Although most pipelines did not actually purchase oil, they were the visible means through which the oil was moved from the wells. Accordingly they made obvious targets for the discontented producers' criticism. Pipelines were charged with failure to connect wells that they did not choose to, with favoritism toward the wells of shipper-owners, and with failure to take the full allowables from independent wells. Rather than "purchaser proration," which was the more accurate term, the last approach was called "pipeline proration" by the producers, and this term was used interchangeably with the other — even by members of the commission.

Obviously, the pipeline companies resented the implication that they did not perform as common carriers and their critics' confusion of this role with that of a common purchaser. However, producers regarded the affiliates of an integrated company — in this case its purchasing and pipeline arms — as acting in concert under unified direction.

At the very start of the December statewide hearings of the commission, the West Central Texas Oil & Gas Association presented a petition charging discrimination by Texas common-carrier pipelines. The petition alleged that, for lack of pipeline connections, trucking of oil from wells in the state had increased 50 per cent between September 1955 and September 1956. Since trucking costs had to be borne by the producer, this development was said to reduce the profitable operation of wells to the point where they might be shut-in, resulting in economic waste. The pipelines were accused of not extending their lines or increasing their capacity commensurate with the needs of the oil industry or national defense. Furthermore, the carriers were charged with selective purchasing and favoring affiliated companies and producers. The association therefore asked for a full investigation by the commission.[44]

This request was granted on February 19, 1957. At that time the Railroad Commission issued an order requiring pipeline common carriers of crude oil in Texas to show cause why they should not offer connections to all wells requesting such connections and why certain carriers should not be required to increase their trunk-line capacity out of west, north, and central districts of Texas. Hearings were held on April 1–3, 1957, at which time the complainants presented their case, and again on May 13–15, 1957, when the pipeline companies presented their response.

The first set of hearings centered on examples of specific situations where wells were unconnected and on general charges of evasion of Texas requirements by pipeline companies. The independents introduced statistics purporting to show that since 1936, total Texas production, the number of producing wells, and the amount of crude-oil reserves had increased percentagewise faster than the total length and cubic capacity of gathering lines, except during 1949–1955. They also demonstrated that imported crude oil, understandably the Texas producer's bête noire, had risen from an amount equal to only 14 per cent of total Texas production in 1948 to 22.5 per cent in 1956.[45] And, among other things, the producers also claimed (erroneously, as a pipeliner pointed out) that nine common-carrier pipeline companies operating in west, north, and central Texas had averaged a 30 per cent net return on their capital stock for 1948–1956.[46] Counsel for the petitioners stressed that there were over 8,000 unconnected wells in the Lone Star State and about two-thirds of them were located in fields that already had pipeline connections* [47]

Producers in various fields told of their difficulties in obtaining pipeline connections and the costs and troubles to which the lack of such connections put them. The gist of their testimony was that pipeline companies acted arbitrarily and in defiance of state law. They claimed that when an unconnected well owner asked for a pipeline connection, the pipeline representative stressed the need for a market for the producers' crude; when the producer contacted the pipeline's purchasing affiliate, it declined to purchase on the grounds that the producer did not have a pipeline connection. The dissatisfied producers maintained that pipeline companies were not willing to make reasonable arrangements to provide gathering service. As a result, to reach a market, these producers had to truck oil to a pipeline terminal.† That expense lowered their net wellhead receipts compared to other producers in the same area with pipeline connections.[48]

The very severity of the attack on pipeline practices constituted an implicit tribute to the importance of these carriers in bringing a market to the producer in the field. No complainant, for example, asked for divorcement of pipelines. If a pipeline of an integrated company could be induced — or forced — to connect a well or field, the producer there had a virtually guaranteed market by virtue of the Texas common-purchaser law. Therefore, what the unconnected producers seemed to want was a pipeline con-

---

*Understandably, the petitioners did not deal in percentages, which would have revealed that only 4.97 per cent of the 168,930 wells in the state as of December 1956 were unconnected. *Shell Pipe Line Brief*, 1-2.

†Only 3.19 per cent of total Texas production in 1956 was trucked. *Ibid.*, Exhibit 41.

nection with an integrated company which would be required to purchase their oil* — not a common-carrier facility to some distant market.

The producers' testimony before the commission made it clear that a variety of selling arrangements had developed in the oil fields. Truckers, for example, provided a market for oil from unconnected wells and sold it at the pipeline terminal, deducting transportation costs of 5 to 30 cents a barrel from the posted price when they paid the producer.† In some instances, large companies had sold their gathering systems to independent operators, thus relieving themselves of the necessity to purchase oil that they did not want by virtue of owning the gathering system and therefore becoming subject to the common-purchaser law. There were also "swapouts" between companies, one having production that it did not need in a given area, and another having a need for it and an equivalent amount of oil to swap at another location. The complexity of these arrangements suggested that no simple generalization about marketing conditions for crude oil would cover all cases.

In their presentation, representatives of the pipeline companies rebutted specific allegations of discrimination, stressed their view that producers were primarily interested in obtaining a market for crude rather than transportation, and raised questions as to the extent of their companies' obligation under Texas law to furnish uneconomic pipeline connections. In general, the pipeline companies took the position that they were justified in extending gathering facilities only when there was a market for the crude and a reasonable prospect of recovering the specific investment. (In this connection, the consent decree's limitation on dividends was said by the petitioners to be a relevant factor.)[49] However, there was some testimony that where a system was already connected in a field, gathering lines were extended to new wells even though that specific investment might not be recovered.[50] In decisions on connecting a new field, estimates of its reserves — in some instances made by pipeline company geologists — were important. Each company had its own criteria, but in the last analysis construction of any pipeline connection that did not promise to pay its way was dependent on the management's view of its moral rather than legal obligations to producers.

The legal obligations of common-carrier pipelines in Texas were defined in Article 6049a of *Vernon's Annotated Statutes of Texas*. Section 7 stated that the Railroad Commission, on its own motion or on complaint, could require any common carrier to extend or enlarge its lines or storage capacity

---

*The Oklahoma Corporation Commission had ordered every purchaser of oil in that state to take the full allowable from every connected well and lease for October and November 1953. Similar orders were adopted in July 1956 and July 1957. Gulf Oil Corporation was adjudged in contempt of the latter order by the Corporation Commission, and Gulf appealed to the Oklahoma Supreme Court. The order was held invalid by that court in 1961. *Gulf Oil Corporation v. State of Oklahoma, et al.* (Okla. Sup. Ct. 1961), 360 Pac. 2d 933.

†The specific charges depended on the distance the oil was trucked and whether or not the trucker acted as a broker between the producer and refiner.

subject to various conditions. The chief of these were that the action requested be reasonable, be in the public interest, and not be such as to impair the ability of the carrier to perform its function. Section 8 dealt with "common purchasers," who were defined as crude buyers affiliated with a common-carrier pipeline. Such a purchaser was forbidden to discriminate in the same field in favor of its own production and was required to purchase ratably on the basis of total production in the field.* Section 11d authorized the commission to investigate connections and in the event of discovering discrimination, to order common purchasers to remedy them.[51] †

The pipeline company briefs maintained that Sections 8 and 11 applied only to common purchasers and therefore were not relevant to the existing proceedings, which had summoned only common carriers. At this point, only Section 7 had not yet received a judicial interpretation in Texas.

The pipeline lawyers argued that because of the similarity of Section 7 to Section 1 (Par. 21) of the Interstate Commerce Act the interpretation of the latter statute in the federal courts[52] should govern the Texas law. The gist of these decisions was that a state commission could not require extensions of existing facilities that would in effect become new undertakings, nor (and this was particularly relevant to the requested enlargement of trunk lines from west Texas) could a commission have unfettered discretion to order large capital investments.

In essence, the pipeline companies maintained that the law protected the exercise of the companies' discretion in making pipeline connections, subject to Railroad Commission review only in particular cases. The independent producers, on the other hand, argued that leaving pipeline connections to the discretion of private oil companies in effect deprived the commission of its power to regulate because the connections determined the amount of marketable production.[53]

Taking these various contentions into account, the commission rendered its decision on June 4, 1958.[54] The resulting order denied the request for an enlargement of common-carrier lines from west Texas to the Gulf and also denied the request that all wells in Texas be connected unless the carrier showed cause for not complying. However, the order did direct that pipeline connections should be furnished when they were in the general area served by a common carrier affiliated with a common purchaser, or when a carrier possessed the only line serving a field or common reservoir.[55] But the conditions on which such connections were required made it clear

---

*In Col-Tex Refining Co. v. Railroad Commission (1950 Tex. 340; 240 S.W. 2d 747 [1951]) the highest court of Texas held that Section 8a applied only to discrimination in the same field, not discrimination between fields. The statute itself barred only "unreasonable" discrimination between fields.

†Section 11 also authorized the commission to relieve a common purchaser from the duty of buying inferior oil. This provision was upheld in the Court of Civil Appeals and the Supreme Court of Texas in 1943. Agey v. American Liberty Pipe Line Co. 141 Tex 379; 172 S.W. 2d 972 (1943).

that the commission was largely restating existing law. The order announced that the commission would take into account "evidence relating to ability of the pipeline carrier to transport the quality of oil, the market or lack of market for the tendered oil, and the period required to return the capital investment for the connection." [56]

Although the commission's order was hailed as a victory by the producers, this does not seem actually to have been the case. In the next session of the Texas legislature several bills were introduced to accomplish by legislative action what had not been obtained through administrative action. The proponents of this alternative approach were again disappointed. By focusing attention on the unconnected well problem, however, they undoubtedly gave pipeline managers a new incentive to examine very carefully any decision not to connect a well in compliance with a producer's request. Meanwhile, as in many prior instances, producers' complaints on the state level were repeated in Washington for the benefit of national legislators.

PIPELINES AND THE CONGRESSIONAL INVESTIGATION OF THE OIL LIFT TO EUROPE

Concurrently with the Texas proceedings, pipelines were receiving scrutiny from congressional investigators of the Suez crisis. The price of gasoline as well as crude had been raised, taking the first upward swing in several years. This fact, the increased flow of imported oil into the United States while domestic crude went to Europe, and the cooperative activities of the large international oil companies in the oil lift, gave critics of the integrated oil business a new opportunity to call for a congressional investigation. From February 5 to March 22, 1957, the Subcommittee on Antitrust and Monopoly of the Senate Judiciary Committee held hearings jointly with the Subcommittee on Public Lands of the Senate Committee on Interior and Insular Affairs.[57] Senator O'Mahoney was asked to conduct the hearings by the Antitrust Subcommittee's chairman, Senator Estes Kefauver. Representatives from all branches of the oil industry as well as numerous government officials testified.

It was clear from the start that the cooperation of the Eisenhower administration with the oil companies — some of whom were under antitrust indictments for their international activities — in meeting the European oil emergency was going to be one focal point of the investigation. It was equally clear that the impact of the handling of the emergency on the independent oil producer and refiner in this country was to be another. These were not left as matters of conjecture, for Senator O'Mahoney made the points in his opening remarks at the hearings.[58] Inevitably, also, the conduct of domestic pipeline operations by integrated companies and the efficacy of public policy with respect to them were subjected to review.

In an unusual departure from customary procedure the subcommittee's proposed report was presented by staff members at a public session on

June 12, 1957. The recommendations of two other staffers were submitted without the opportunity for full review by members of the subcommittee. Subsequently, Republican Senator Everett Dirksen, a minority member of the subcommittee, charged that "Certain of the staff's facts, conclusions, and recommendations were erroneous or ill-founded." [59] Among these, he found the majority's statements about pipelines. Before turning to the statements themselves, however, it is necessary to review the testimony briefly.

Representatives of independent oil producers repeated the same criticisms of pipelines that they presented to the Texas Railroad Commission. First, they alleged that some pipeline companies refused to extend gathering lines to connect wells. Second, in some fields that were connected, they claimed, there was pipeline "prorationing" — that is, pipelines of large, integrated companies would not take the full allowable production of small producers. Third, they charged there was indirect price discrimination involved when some producers had to pay for trucking their oil to a pipeline, thereby reducing their net receipts compared to producers with pipeline connections.[60] Still another charge was that at least one integrated company used the highest posted prices in the fields where it was the dominant producer and the lowest posted prices where independents dominated the production.[61] The explanation for this behavior was claimed by the independents to lie in the efforts of *international* oil companies[62] (a significant shift in emphasis from the charges of the 1930's relating chiefly to domestic *integrated* operations) to maximize their returns on foreign crude-oil investment at the expense of domestic producers.

The Texas unconnected well problem was brought to the attention of the O'Mahoney subcommittee by several witnesses, including Lester Clark, who spoke for four Texas associations of independent producers. The thrust of his testimony was that in increasing their posted prices at the time of the Suez crisis, the large companies had discriminated by raising prices more in areas where they had large production and less in areas where independents were the leading producers. When the question of the relative quality and therefore value of the crudes was raised, Clark claimed that the long-standing differentials in value between sweet and sour crudes had been upset.[63] Asked by Senator O'Mahoney to provide more authoritative evidence than mere assertion, Clark promised to do so. However, in a subsequent letter to the Senator, included in the hearings record, he still dealt in generalities.[64]

Close questioning put some of Clark's statements in useful perspective. For example, it was established that his own storage facilities were connected by at least six integrated company pipelines and that they were taking his allowables.[65] Senator John A. Carroll of Colorado asked several perceptive questions of the witness, leading up to this exchange:

> Senator Carroll. May I ask a question?
> It has been running through my mind all through the testimony here —

you have made it very clear to me, much clearer than I had in my mind before — why don't some of you independents get together and build your own pipelines?

Mr. Clark. You mean our own marketing facilities? The pipelines would not do any good, Senator, without the marketing facilities.[66]

Senator Carroll then suggested that the independents might look to the West Coast and supplying the Navy's demand for petroleum products there. In reply, Clark said:

We have talked to various people that have been interested, but it is such a tremendous job that those of us who are just in the business of producing oil and do not have unlimited capital, Senator — it is just a great undertaking that most of us just cannot do. I do not even know enough about pipelines to know if it would be profitable or not.[67]

In microcosm, this exchange summarized the very reasons that the oil industry had come to depend on trunk lines built by large, integrated companies. Unquestionably, however, this fact also gave such companies significant power in dealing with the small operators whose problems were being explored by the O'Mahoney subcommittee.

Charges concerning unconnected wells and price discrimination by integrated companies against independents were also made by W. A. Delaney, Jr., of Ada, Oklahoma, a lawyer with natural gas and oil interests. He challenged the adequacy of regulation to deal with pipeline problems, maintaining that administrative procedures were not understood by independents and that, in any case, they were reluctant to invoke them for fear of retaliation by major purchasers of their crude.[68] He agreed that there was a difference in size between independents, ranging from very substantial independent interests to the industry's "sharecropper," with whom he was most concerned. Such individuals lacked the financial resources or credit to obtain capital on favorable terms for long periods of time [69] and, according to Delaney, they had to take what the purchaser (i.e., the large, integrated company) offered him.

Like Lester Clark, Delaney felt that control of terminal markets would have to be a condition for construction of a West Coast pipeline, which he believed was justified. "No man with sense enough to get the capital or credit together to justify the construction of a pipeline to carry oil without ownership of the terminal markets would be fool enough to invest it in an oil pipeline in an attempt to compete with oil of Kuwait, Sumatra, origin in the California market. He just cannot do it." [70]

The question of a pipeline from west Texas to the West Coast was taken up in detail by representatives of the West Coast Pipe Line Company — Lowell M. Glasco, vice-president, and H. Graham Morison, former Assistant Attorney General in charge of the Antitrust Division. The thrust of their testimony was that $22,000,000 in equity capital was available to build the independent line, but that to obtain the remainder a certificate of essentiality from the government was necessary. This certificate had been denied. The lack of progress in this undertaking, claimed by its backers to be of major importance to national security as well as to the welfare of "shut-in" west Texas producers, was attributed to opposition and pressure of large, integrated companies operating on the West Coast and to their close relations with government agencies making oil policy.[71] These charges even extended to the assertion that one of the officers of the West Coast Pipe Line Company, a former employee of a large company, had been denied just claims for taking on this new, independent connection.[72] This allegation was later denied and refuted in writing by the company concerned,[73] but the charge was typical of the wide-ranging assertions of undue pressure made by the proponents of the independent line.

Whereas both the independents, Clark and Delaney, had maintained that a major obstacle to building an independent line to the West Coast was the lack of independents' control of market terminals, the economic necessity for such an interrelationship was seemingly discounted by the former Assistant Attorney General. Referring to a controversy that had developed earlier between Shell Oil and an independent pipeline promoter in connection with the Butte Pipe Line, Morison referred to the testimony of Shell Oil president Burns before the Kefauver committee:

> ... Burns said — and he reflects the policy of the major oil companies — oil pipelines have got to be owned by people who have interests at both ends — meaning you have got oil production, wells, and refineries, and distribution facilities for products. Those pipelines are built, significantly, to carry the oil of the majors who build the pipelines. And this thing of saying that such pipelines are substantial avenues of transportation, free avenues of transportation for independent crude, is nonsense.[74]

As Clark and Delaney recognized, long trunk pipelines had to have a sure market for the oil transported in order to justify the transportation investment. Morison recognized the point but appeared to turn it on its head, leaving the impression that the interdependence between pipelines and other phases of the oil industry was an invention of the "majors" — not a product of an economic reality which any pipeline promoter had to recognize. Whether independents' crude was moving through integrated companies' lines was a different question that Morison did not pursue beyond his generalization.

Morison denounced virtually every government agency dealing with the oil industry and pipelines. By refusing to guarantee throughput to the West Coast Line, he said, the "majors" had barred private financing for the venture.[75] Then, by their influence in government through various liaison groups, as well as in industry-oriented government departments and agencies, the former Assistant Attorney General claimed, the large companies had blocked issuance of a certificate of necessity to the company he represented.[76] He reserved his most acid criticism for the Interstate Commerce Commission. It "is a receptacle for the filing of papers with reference to tariffs, it has never so far as I know ever raised its finger or inquired or done anything about the transportation of oil by pipelines." [77]

Statements such as these, and Delaney's incorrect written one that the Standard Oil combination had been broken up in 1910 by order of Justice Kenesaw M. Landis,[78] casts some doubt on the accuracy of the witnesses' other information. Clearly, in the case of the ICC, Morison had overlooked or forgotten such cases as Reduced Pipe Line Rates and Gathering Charges, Minnelusa, and both Champlin cases. His information on independent pipelines seemed equally vague, though he mentioned Buckeye as one he had at least heard about. From a layman such a lack of information about pipelines and their regulation would be understandable, but coming from the former head of the Antitrust Division it was surprising. Moreover, Morison had volunteered to prescribe public policy and to frame a piece of suggested legislation to cope with problems whose details seemed unfamiliar to him.

The information, misinformation, charges, and countercharges about pipelines were considered by the O'Mahoney subcommittee staff in the manner described earlier. The majority report recommended that the Justice Department examine the ownership and control of pipelines by large companies, with particular reference to possible monopolization of common-carrier pipeline transportation, use of pipelines to deny independent producers a competitive market for crude and independent refiners access to crude, discriminations in price against independents, and the alleged practice of pipeline prorationing.[79] On a broader scale the subcommittee also recommended investigation and recommendations by an appropriate congressional committee to meet the problems involved in oil imports, the West Coast crude shortage, and other problems raised in the hearings.[80]

Senator Dirksen, as already noted, rejected most of the staff's findings, pointing out that responsible representatives of the pipeline sector of the oil industry had not even been offered an opportunity to rebut the charges brought against them.[81] Dirksen, it developed, was armed with protests and information from the Committee for Oil Pipe Lines, as well as a memorandum from the Independent Producers Association of America sent to Senator O'Mahoney and critical of "every conclusion and accusation made by the staff report." [82]

The Republican Senator reviewed the case for integrated pipelines in a manner made familiar over generations of congressional investigations of the subject. He pointed out that there was a necessary relationship between carriers and other phases of the oil business, that pipelines were regulated, that complaints to regulatory bodies were virtually nonexistent, and that in the recent past subsidiaries of railroads had found it possible to enter the business on a nonintegrated basis. Dirksen also noted that pipelines did not purchase oil; therefore they could not be guilty of the price discrimination charges leveled against them. Affiliated purchasing companies were subject to state common-purchaser laws that forbade discrimination in favor of the purchaser's production. There was a confusion of so-called "pipeline prorationing," he said, with purchaser ratable taking. In times when more oil was available than existing pipelines could handle, they were legally required to haul for all customers alike, taking ratably from their owners' and independent's production.[83] He explained that trucking oil from wells to a pipeline connection was an economic question — the availability of oil in relation to the investment required in gathering lines. Pipelines did not own or control such trucking operations, and large companies operating in unconnected fields had to truck their own oil just as the independents did.[84]

On the subject of the West Coast Pipe Line, Dirksen noted that the project had been reviewed by the Office of Defense Mobilization and by congressional subcommittees. The promoters' complaints, therefore, "can only be of the Government's decision that there is no justification for governmental financial aid for the building of their pipeline." [85] To demonstrate that the review had not been conducted by individuals in government with close ties to the integrated oil industry, the Senator included a letter from the Director of ODM, Gordon Gray, naming the review group and their affiliations.[86] Senator Alexander Wiley in another minority report concurred in Senator Dirksen's view of the West Coast Pipe Line, but he also concurred in the majority view that the charges against pipelines warranted Justice Department investigation, which he felt should also include natural-gas lines.[87]

Meanwhile, in the House, the Committee on Interstate and Foreign Commerce headed by Oren Harris of Arkansas, had looked into the oil lift to Europe and concluded that a good job had been done. In the words of its preliminary report, issued in April 1957," the success of the suddenly enforced alternate operation cannot but be hailed as a stupendous achievement on the part of the oil industry." [88] While it was critical of the timing of the price increases in connection with the Suez crisis, the Harris committee appeared to recognize that increased costs of finding, developing, and producing oil in the United States warranted recognition. In view of these conclusions, there was no mention in the Harris report of any domestic pipeline problems.

In retrospect, a decade of congressional interest in oil pipelines had moved from a series of relatively routine gestures toward divorcement to a more general questioning of integrated operations in an environment that was perhaps more favorable to adverse legislative or legal action than any since the 1930's. In significant respects, however, the situation was different from what it had been in the depression decade. Whereas earlier the context of controversy had been domestic operations, it now shifted to the international scene. Domestic producers found themselves confronted with the importation of lower-cost foreign crudes, and the integrated American companies that reached out to obtain them inevitably set themselves up as targets for attack. Accordingly, domestic pipelines owned by these companies found themselves at the center of a new controversy. The complaint of small producers during this period was the unwillingness of pipeline companies to connect uneconomic wells. The inability of independent pipeline promoters to win either governmental support or commitments from integrated companies for major new trunk lines added fuel to the fire. Academic commentators at this time brought up new charges of monopolization against the role of pipelines in integrated operations. The cooperation of the Executive Branch and oil companies to meet an international crisis in the Suez Canal area which was quickly over, gave congressional critics fresh ammunition.

In the O'Mahoney hearings, charges by various interested parties were mingled in a new onslaught on alleged abuses of private economic power. In each instance, the complainants and the investigators seemed to see only what they wanted to see, and in the O'Mahoney subcommittee's report — whose conclusions had been foreshadowed in the Senator's introductory remarks to the hearings — pipelines assumed an importance that had not been attributed to them since TNEC days.* This time, however, the integrated oil industry was better prepared to meet attack. As Dirksen's minority report showed, the Committee for Oil Pipe Lines (the name had been changed from Committee for Pipe Line Companies to avoid needless confusion over its relation to gas lines, the center of another controversy) was ready with evidence and arguments to counter the one-sided charges made before the O'Mahoney subcommittee. However, these pieces of information had to find their way into the proceedings via a minority report rather than through the appearance of pipeline representatives before the subcommittee. In early 1957, then, the integrated oil industry and its domestic pipeline sector had clearly been put on the defensive, and the situation was shortly to grow worse.

*O'Mahoney, of course, had been chairman of the TNEC.

CHAPTER 24

FROM CONGRESSIONAL INVESTIGATION
TO JUDICIAL DECISION

In 1957 the unconnected wells issue at the state level, the Suez crisis at the international level, and the O'Mahoney hearings at the national level had focused both public and congressional attention on the integrated oil industry, though to a far lesser extent than in the days of either the Republican or the Democratic Roosevelt. Nevertheless, a new and relatively favorable opportunity for action had been presented to congressional critics of big business in general and of the oil industry in particular.

One specific area staked out for a 1957 congressional probe of consent decree practices was the enforcement of the oil pipeline consent decree. Congressman Emanuel Celler's Antitrust Subcommittee of the House Committee on the Judiciary called the managers of a leading pipeline company to account for their policies and practices under the decree. Top officials of the Justice Department and the Interstate Commerce Commission, the two federal bodies that were involved directly or indirectly in the implementation of the decree, were also subjected to critical questioning. Obviously the proceedings invited conflict between an arm of the Republican Eisenhower administration and an independent regulatory body, as well as between both of them and Democratic representatives of the legislative branch. Reacting at least in part to this political pressure, the Justice Department initiated the first legal action in 16 years to test the consent decree, leading to a judicial decision on past managerial adaptation to the decree's requirements.

ORIGINS OF THE CELLER INVESTIGATION

One of the functions of the House Antitrust Subcommittee, suggested by its name, was that of watchdog over the antitrust area of public policy. On April 3, 1957, Chairman Emanuel Celler informed Assistant Attorney General Victor R. Hansen that the Antitrust Subcommittee proposed to investigate and "ascertain how effective consent decrees have been to eliminate the conditions that caused the Government to institute its antitrust proceeding, and to restore a competitive climate in the industries concerned. In addition, the committee is interested in the effects of consent decrees upon competitors of the defendants." [1] For this purpose it selected as case-studies the negotiation of the recent A. T. & T. decree and the enforcement of the oil pipeline consent decree.

Shortly before public hearings on these questions were commenced in October 1957, the Justice Department initiated four court proceedings involving the decree. The first of these cases was against Arapahoe Pipe Line Company, owned jointly by Pure Oil Company and Sinclair Pipe Line Company. The motion asked the court to direct Arapahoe to deduct from its calculation of valuation for computing permissible dividends to its shipper-owners that part of the valuation obtained from third parties to finance common-carrier facilities.[2] This action was aimed against payment of dividends to shipper-owners greater than 7 per cent of their paid-in investment. In other words, the Justice Department objected to the inclusion in their rate base of property acquired by use of loans.

Another motion was against Service Pipe Line Company and its parent Standard Oil Company (Indiana). The charge here was that Service had violated Section III of the decree by its method of calculating valuation for consent decree purposes.[3] Section III specified valuation be brought up to date "as of the close of the next preceding year." It further provided that in the event dividends were unearned in a given year they might be paid within any one or more of the next three succeeding years (in addition to permissible dividends payable for those years). Beginning in 1951, the government claimed, Service Pipe Line, in determining its valuation for dividend purposes, had adopted the practice of adding pro rata additions and betterments made after the close of the next preceding year and subtracting from them pro rata depreciation and retirements. This method decreased valuation in some years and increased it in others. The complaint charged that the use of the method in 1952 had increased valuation for that year beyond what the decree permitted and that unearned carry-forward based on this excessive valuation was improperly used to justify dividends in excess of 7 per cent in 1955 when the company had earned in excess of its permitted valuation as interpreted by the department.

A third action involved the Tidal Pipe Line Company and its shipper-owner Tidewater Oil Company. This complaint alleged that Tidal had included in its valuation for consent decree purposes, all property used by it for common-carrier purposes, whether owned or not.[4] The Justice Department maintained that this practice was in violation of Paragraph III, which referred to valuation of property "owned and used" — not owned *or* used. That is, property used by Tidal also had to be owned by it if the property were to be included in valuation for dividend-computing purposes under the decree. The complaint maintained that the method employed by the defendant had increased Tidal's valuation in specified years beyond that recognized in the decree, resulting in excess earnings that were paid to the shipper-owner instead of being placed in a surplus account.

The fourth action involved Texas Pipe Line Company, which was alleged to have followed a valuation procedure comparable to Tidal's. However, the Texas case differed from Tidal's, because the dividends which the Justice Department claimed were excess earnings had not actually been paid to the shipper-owner.[5]

On the first day of the Celler hearings, Assistant Attorney General Hansen reported the initiation of these cases and enumerated a number of other Justice Department moves that reflected an active interest in the pipeline sector of the oil industry. In addition to the West Coast oil case, where antitrust charges against pipeline use in a relatively isolated area of the business had reflected allegations made by critics against the main body of the industry, Hansen reported extensive research in connection with the Attorney General's annual report on the Interstate Oil Compact, research and conferences with regulatory officials in Texas, Oklahoma, and Louisana, and research in the files of the ICC, the Department of the Interior, and so on.[6] Finally, he stated, "We have launched a full-scale FBI investigation of all crude and products pipelines jointly owned by the major oil companies to detect any anticompetitive aspects of the joint ownership." [7] In his testimony, Hansen seemed to be anticipating criticism by the Celler subcommittee of the Justice Department's inactivity during the first 16 years of the oil pipeline consent decree. If this was indeed the expectation that underlay his strategy, it proved to be firmly grounded.

An early exchange between Hansen and the subcommittee chairman made it clear that enforcement activities of the Justice Department, as well as the terms of the oil pipeline consent decree itself, were at issue. Celler maintained that the Assistant Attorney General had been dilatory in replying to requests for information on the pipeline decree and that the statement finally submitted was both brief and evasive.[8] Although Congressman Kenneth Keating, a New York Republican, took the side of the department, it was evident that veteran Democrat Celler was not going to miss any chance to score the Republican Executive Branch.

A case in point was the heated controversy over the department's interpretations of the pipeline consent decree to signatories of that decree. On July 2, 1957, the Antitrust Division had informed the Celler subcommittee that 31 "official" interpretations, some oral and some in writing, had been made by the department.[9] However, it declined to provide these interpretations for the congressional investigators. The grounds cited in a subsequent department letter were that the interpretations were specific ones in response to company problems that were sometimes unique, and that the department might want to take the position in some future action that these interpretations had no bearing.[10] At the October congressional hearings, the representatives of the Antitrust Division reiterated that this was their position, and they felt it was now even more justified in view of the pending litigation over the decree.[11] Congressman Celler was incensed that those subject to the decree should receive from the Justice Department information that was denied to his subcommittee, but he also indicated in the course of questioning that he was scoring the department rather than actually seeking the interpretations, many of which the subcommittee had already obtained from the companies involved.[12]

The Assistant Attorney General likewise refused to disclose the results of FBI investigations of pipeline company books. Here his argument was that the government's cases might be prejudiced and possible defendants might be damaged. The following exchange between Hansen, Celler, and Congressman Keating exemplified the problem and their respective attitudes toward it:

> Mr. Hansen: This is shocking to me. I cannot understand how a committee here would want to try the lawsuit, prejudice the Government in the cases we have pending, asking us to give confidential files of results of the FBI investigation, damage possible innocent defendants or possible defendants and just tie our hands in the prosecution. It is just beyond me.

> Mr. Keating: It is equally shocking to me, Judge Hansen. I do not think this is an area that we ought to go into at all with this litigation pending. It may prejudice the Government. It may prejudice one of these defendants that is now brought into court.

> Mr. Hansen: That is correct.

> The Chairman: I do not agree with that, and I think we have a perfect right to go into it. We are not prejudicing anybody in this case. We want to know how this situation developed.[13]

The Justice Department representatives also refused to give any information about differences of opinion within the department over the consent decree, including most specifically the unwillingness of MacAsbill and W. B. Watson Snyder to sign it. Assistant Attorney General Hansen's position was that difference of opinion within the department was healthy, but that public display of it would adversely affect enforcement activities in the courts. Consequently the subcommittee was unable to obtain the internal Justice Department records that it desired on this aspect of the decree's origin and enforcement.[14]

The sessions involving the Assistant Attorney General revolved chiefly around the question of whether the Antitrust Division had been as active as it should have been in policing the pipeline consent decree. It was developed that enforcement action had been contemplated at various times but that, for one reason or another, the department had not decided to go into court until 1957. W. D. Kilgore, Jr., Chief of the Judgment and Enforcement section of the Antitrust Division, maintained that action of this kind could not be taken lightly and that the amount of time involved was not inordinate in view of the complexity and significance of the issues.[15]

Hansen himself had been on the job for only a little more than a year, and he was unwilling to play Congressman Celler's game by giving opinions on the work of his predecessors. The clear implication of questioning by the subcommittee's chairman and counsel was that the pipeline companies, and Service Pipe Line in particular, had interpreted the decree to their own benefit and that the Justice Department had either passively or actively supported them. Hansen's position was that whatever the situation in the past, he had no direct knowledge of it; that he had already demonstrated his own determination to test the decree in the courts; and that the Congressman's line of questioning and production of company documents to underscore his points threatened the success of the litigation already in progress. On most points he had the active support of Republican Keating, who seemed anxious to show that the Eisenhower administration had been more active in consent decree enforcement than the Truman administration had been.

Chairman Owen Clarke of the Interstate Commerce Commission followed Hansen to the witness chair. He was questioned closely about methods of valuing pipeline properties. The questioners' emphasis was on the fact that whereas the ICC used original cost valuation for rate-making in the case of railroads, it included reproduction cost in the valuations used for pipeline rate and consent decree purposes.[16] Clarke accounted for the difference on the grounds of the "hazards of the pipeline business with a diminishing source of supply and limited amount of traffic, which eventually dries up, and the fact that it is just a one-way haul and one product." [17] He also stated that ICC regulation of pipelines was "in effect limited to the question of rates," [18] but he noted that complaints with respect to them had been few and the same was true of the minimum tender requirement.[19]

Under pointed questioning, Clarke admitted that there was no formal ICC liaison with the Antitrust Division on oil pipeline matters. With the ICC's jurisdiction limited to rate matters, however, he saw no need for such liaison. But he also took the position that collaboration with the API Engineers-Accountants Valuation Subcommittee was authorized, indeed required, by the Interstate Commerce Act; that the practice of requiring carrier assistance had proved necessary and workable in earlier railroad valuation work; and that no complaints against this procedure in the case of pipelines had reached his ears. Therefore, he saw no need to change this practice.[20]

Although pipeline companies' representatives had performed some mechanical tasks in cooperation with the ICC in the process of postwar valuation work, Clarke maintained that no conflict of interests was involved. Chairman Celler was not satisfied. "As I see it," he said, "there is no doubt that the industry is meeting parts of the costs of its own regulation by following this procedure." [21] Clarke was forced to concede that no other carrier regulated by the ICC had actually provided personnel to perform tasks of the kind assigned to pipeline company employees.[22]

On the whole, it seemed from the exchanges between Chairman Celler and the ICC commissioner that the regulatory body had probably worked more closely with pipeline companies in establishing valuations than with other transportation media subject to the ICC's jurisdiction. In view of the unique requirements of the pipeline consent decree and the postwar shortage of ICC personnel and funds for pipeline valuation work, there seemed to be a justification for it. Congressman Celler, however, left the impression in his questioning and comments that he believed the ICC, like the Justice Department, had given the pipeline companies distinctly favorable treatment.

Fayette Dow, a veteran Washington hand on oil matters, was discouraged by the picture that emerged from the early testimony. Appearing before the subcommittee, he declared almost wistfully: "There was a good deal said in criticism of Justice and Justice had its replies, and nobody all day long said a good word for pipelines. Nobody all day long . . . Your committee, able as it is, admirable as it is, doesn't transport any oil and neither does the Justice Department. I was disheartened last night at the fact that the virtues, if there are any, of pipelines were completely neglected." [23] Because Dow was an "old hand," he had a wealth of acquaintances in the Washington community, excellent rapport with ICC commissioners,[24] and long experience with congressional investigators. Unlike the witnesses who preceded and followed him, he was not subjected to extensive questioning. Apparently for old time's sake, the report of Dow's testimony before the TNEC nearly 20 years before was accepted for the record.

The hearings heated up again when J. L. Burke, president of Service Pipe Line, appeared before the subcommittee on Thursday, October 24, 1957. Burke was a long-time pipeliner, having entered the business with Sinclair (predecessor of Stanolind and Service) Pipe Line in 1920. He had become traffic manager of that system in 1924 and president in 1948.[25] As the chief executive of the pipeline company that came under the heaviest fire from the subcommittee, he had a difficult assignment.

His opening statement stressed that great changes had taken place in the pipeline business since the 1930's. He emphasized that technological change, alterations in industry structure, and changes in the national economy had transformed pipelines from plant facilities to common carriers.[26] Citing Service's experience in being forced to lay a new line from the Rocky Mountain area to the Midcontinent to meet the threat posed by Platte and Arapahoe, Burke pointed out that technology (e.g., the economics of big-inch lines) and competition were prime factors in keeping rates down. In fact, he said, Service's rates were lower than they had been in 1950, no minimum tenders were imposed, and his company alone served 73 refineries, almost a quarter of all those in the nation.[27]

The witness's testimony then turned to the amended reports submitted to the Attorney General in the early 1950's by his company in complying with the consent decree. The changes in these reports had involved several different valuations for the same year. The implication of earlier questioning of Justice Department witnesses had been that the primary purpose of these changes was to increase the company's dividend base, but this motive was emphatically denied by the witness. Further, he stated that the Justice Department had been informed of the pro rata method of valuation, which was under attack in the pending litigation. He also denied the charge that the company kept two sets of books and explained that annual reports to the Justice Department under the decree showed that his company did not pay to its parent all dividends that the management believed were legally payable. These dividends reported to the Justice Department as payable were based on a maximum valuation (i.e., the most favorable interpretation of the decree), but dividends were actually paid on a minimum valuation (i.e., the most restrictive interpretation).* He made it quite clear that in view of the penalties for any misstep, the policy of his company had been to follow the most conservative course in paying dividends while preserving its position on the record.[28]

Burke spelled this out in some detail, indicating that Service Pipe Line had been put in a difficult position by virtue of its conservative policy on decree matters. For example, to finance expansion, he said, it had been necessary to borrow from banks while there was still held in the company's name amounts that management believed payable as dividends (i.e., also available for investment in common-carrier facilities) yet whose disbursement might be challenged under a different interpretation of valuation.[29]

The controversy over the valuation procedures was in large measure the result of managerial adaptation to the ICC's failure to provide annual pipeline valuations during the early years of the consent decree. This inaction, of course, explained the companies' eagerness to obtain postwar congressional appropriations for valuations by the ICC and also their aggressive cooperation in the valuation work that was hampered by lack of federal funds. Each company, faced with the penalties of the consent decree yet also with the need to declare dividends, had calculated valuation as best it could.

Uncertainty about the appropriateness of empirical procedures had been finally relieved with the publication of a new set of ICC final valuations as of December 31, 1947. When Service's new valuation appeared in 1950, the pipeline company found that one of its assumptions about ICC methods for determining valuation had been incorrect; the ICC had used period prices while Service had used annual prices. In August 1950, therefore, Service filed its first amended reports for the years 1942–1949, using period prices and reaching a slightly lower valuation base than that given in the original reports.[30]

Service then sought an interpretation from the Justice Department to clarify the meaning of "latest final valuation," and to establish the proper procedure for bringing its valuation down to date for those years for which no ICC valuation was on record.[31] Assistant Attorney General Bergson replied in September 1950, holding that "latest final valuation" as used in the decree referred to the ICC valuation closest in time to the submitting of annual reports, not to the time of the consent decree itself.[32] Thus, the

---

*Apparently other companies followed this course, although the Jersey companies reportedly followed the most conservative policy of freezing earnings in excess of 7 per cent of minimum valuation while the Texas Company went to the other extreme and classified as earned and payable, dividends based on a maximum valuation. *Celler Report,* 197.

recent 1947 valuation could be used for calculating the base for dividends after that date, rather than the original (and lower) 1934 figure. Bergson went on to indicate that, contrary to the company's past practice, interest paid on borrowed funds should be deducted before calculating earnings available for distribution. The Bergson letter was open to interpretation, but it seemed to suggest that the correct procedure for bringing the latest final valuation down to date would be to hold the ICC valuation figure constant, dealing with additions and betterments and physical depreciation and retirements on a current basis. Since Service had depreciated its whole property in both sets of reports for 1942–1949, this new method resulted in significantly higher valuation figures for those years and produced the second amended reports which Service filed in March 1951.[33]

In preparing these reports, Service considered several ways in which the Bergson letter could be interpreted. It finally adopted an interpretation that inside counsel did not consider correct but which they did not oppose in view of the conservative dividend policy adopted by the company. Burke, however, felt the interpretation was defensible.[34] With ICC final valuation held constant (i.e., without depreciation or appreciation), additions and betterments (using period prices) were adjusted for depreciation and retirements. Facilities retired or withdrawn from service were deducted at net depreciated value. These calculations included the pro rata feature.[35]

This approach had been applied retroactively to reports for 1942–1949 and on a current basis for 1950–1952.[36] When in 1953 the ICC supplied annual valuations for 1949 and subsequent years, Service again amended its reports, discarding the plan adopted after the Bergson letter as the ICC was now providing on a current basis the required final valuation information.

In the hearings, Burke made clear that although the pro rata approach to valuation was explained to the department, no ruling was given on it. He took full responsibility for adopting it but pointed out that again, in pursuing a conservative policy, no dividend payments had actually been made on a pro rata valuation basis. He also maintained that the dividend payments of 1955 challenged by the department in the pending litigation would have been permissible even without the pro rata approach.[37]

Hammond Chaffetz, outside counsel for Standard Oil Company (Indiana), Service's parent, intervened in support of Burke's contention that the Department of Justice was improperly engaged in regulatory activities that properly belonged to the ICC. He characterized the decree as "born of an illegitimate union of antitrust and ICC."[38] Chaffetz stated that his firm had advised Indiana Standard in 1941 not to sign the decree,* whose basis in the Elkins Act he challenged as lacking any foundation in law. However, he agreed that in view of the time that had passed since the industry's accep-

---

*Chaffetz later denied that he was personally familiar with the complaint filed against Indiana Standard in 1940 alleging violation of the Elkins Act. He explained that although his firm had handled the matter, "I had nothing to do with this case at that time." *Cellar Hearings,* 1158.

tance of the decree, this question was now primarily academic and histori-cal. He also established that on at least one, and possibly two occasions, letters similar to the Bergson letter to Service Pipe Line had been sent to other companies by succeeding Assistant Attorney Generals.[39] In other words, the policy enunciated in that letter, at least with respect to the meaning of the crucial term "latest final valuation," had received subse-quent support in the department.

Further questioning was directed to the fact that dividends paid by Service to its parent in some years represented very signficant percentages of transportation revenues. (The lean years were ignored by the ques-tioners.)[40] It was then developed that through the postwar growth of com-mon carriage for outside shippers, Service's transportation revenues came from outside shippers, as well as from Indiana Standard affiliates. This led to the key question of whether dividends paid from revenues derived from carriage for outsiders did not constitute discrimination in favor of Indiana Standard. This question, of course, went to the heart of the Elkins Act charges, and understandably no direct reply to it was offered. The lack of actual complaint by shippers and the availability of the ICC to hear such complaints, however, seemed to answer the question in practice.*[41]

A considerable amount of questioning centered on the reporting to the Justice Department of maximum valuation by Service and the payment of dividends on a minimum valuation. Subcommittee counsel tried to show that the consent decree called for a different method of figuring valuation from that employed by the ICC, that Service management was aware of the difference, and that reporting a maximum valuation and simultaneously reporting payment of dividends based on a minimum one might constitute a false report. Burke's position did not change: in view of the ambiguity that surrounded the decree's provision on valuation, his company had fol-lowed a prudent and legally defensible course by paying dividends on its most conservative interpretation and keeping its position on the record by reporting the maximum valuation.[42] He maintained that the department had been informed, and in any event could easily have deduced, the nature of his company's approach.

The investigators were clearly suspicious of these varied moves. Their questions indicated their belief that Service Pipe Line had interpreted the decree to its own advantage and that the company's approach, if not in technical violation of the decree, was at least not in keeping with their inter-pretation of the decree's intended thrust. They ignored, however, the fact that the Service approach diminished as well as increased valuations used for figuring dividends.

*One answer might well have been that the largest dividends paid still represented 7 per cent or less on the most conservative valuation of common-carrier properties. As suggested in Chap. 22, outside shippers were probably paying less than if the facilities had been provided under independent auspices, and 7 per cent probably would not have compensated them any more than Indiana Standard for the opportunity costs in building pipelines, except as the lines facilitated their own access to crude.

Company witnesses relied for the evidence of their good faith on the act that their interpretations had been made available to, and in some cases after consultation with, the Justice Department. This, of course, brought the hearings back to the point where they had started: namely, the relations between the department and companies subject to the pipeline consent decree.

THE CELLER SUBCOMMITTEE REPORT

As might have been anticipated, the report by the majority of the Celler subcommittee was critical of the Justice Department. The opening pages of the report, which did not appear until January 1959, pointed out that the oil pipeline consent decree had been singled out for examination not only because it shed light on problems of industry-wide decree negotiations but also because it "delineated the Antitrust Division's procedures and the enforcement problems that arise when a consent decree's provisions become the standard for an entire industry." [43] The report then went on to criticize the department for failure to cooperate in the investigation, forcing the subcommittee to turn to private corporations for records that the government arm could have easily provided.

The majority report conceded that the language of Paragraph III of the consent decree was not entirely clear, but the report adopted a different interpretation from the pipeline companies. There was, for example, some evidence to suggest that Justice Department representatives in negotiating the decree had wanted to specify that the permissible 7 per cent dividends were to be based on the shipper-owner's "investment" but that "valuation" had been used instead at the industry's suggestion.[44] As the majority report pointed out, with the shift to postwar debt financing, "valuation" (which made allowance for reproduction costs and therefore inflationary developments) was no longer an index to the shipper-owners' investment.* [45]

The majority found that, despite active efforts at policing the pipeline consent decree (involving among other things three FBI investigations), the Justice Department's enforcement record was "bad." [46] The record showed that alleged violations of the decree had been repeatedly noted in the department yet no administrative or judicial action had followed.[47] In fact, the majority emphasized, no legal action was initiated until after the subcommittee started its probe of Justice Department enforcement activities.[48]

The report explained that Service Pipe Line had been selected for special attention because in terms of mileage it was the largest pipeline system in the country. In addition, Service presented a particularly interesting case because it had solicited and received the Bergson letter of 1950 which, the majority claimed, in effect had nullified proposed contempt proceedings prepared by the antitrust staff in the wake of 1944 and 1949 FBI investigations.[49] (How an interpretation in 1950 could have precluded action be-

*See Chap. 22, for a discussion of this point.

tween 1944 and 1950 was not explained.) Further, the majority charged that the fact that a Service Pipe Line representative had been active in the API Engineers-Accountants Valuation Subcommittee since 1934 and was its chairman after 1950 made Service privy to the actions taken by other companies and placed it in a position to "coordinate industry action with respect to the ICC." [50] The majority stressed the number of amended reports filed by Service but also had to note that other companies had done the same.[51] Therefore, the Justice Department was again faulted for failure to take corrective action.[52]

The majority was equally critical of the ICC. Although charging that the regulatory commission had permitted the pipeline sector of the oil industry to participate in the framework of its own regulation,[53] the majority also conceded that the extent of ICC statutory jurisdicton over pipelines was limited.[54] They were, however, critical of the lack of liasion between the ICC and the Justice Dpartment, as well as of Chairman Clarke's unconcern on this score as expressed in his testimony.[55] The same critical attitude was adopted with respect to the Commission's willingness to depend on pipeline company personnel for certain elements of valuation information.[56]

Apparently Clarke felt some vulnerability on this score. He reported to the subcommittee in December 1957 that procedures had been changed to eliminate the use of company personnel in ICC offices in connection with pipeline valuation work.[57] He also announced discontinuance of ICC cooperation with the Engineers-Accountants Valuation Subcommittee and the establishment in its place of an industry advisory committee headed by an ICC employee.[58] Despite these changes, the majority of the Celler subcommittee barely softened its criticism of the ICC and recommended that it perform pipeline valuation work only as it, not the companies subject to the consent decree, had need for it.[59] This recommendation of course blinked the fact that lack of current ICC valuations had given rise to the very actions about which the majority complained.

The majority made other wide-ranging recommendations. On the one hand they suggested the need for a reappraisal of federal regulatory policy with respect to oil pipelines;[60] on the other, they suggested amending the Elkins Act to prohibit payment of dividends to shipper-owners based on transportation charges paid by shipper-owners and nonowners.[61] They likewise recommended that the Justice Department revise its consent decree procedures to provide more publicity and to afford an opportunity for outsiders to file their reactions with the court before a decree could go into effect.[62]

A minority of three members of the subcommittee criticized the majority's report as "much chaff with very little wheat."[63] The minority even questioned whether the "report" could be regarded as a formal one since it was "only the report of 4 of the 6. Democratic members of the Antitrust Subcommittee" and had not been submitted to the full Judiciary Committee.[64] The minority took the position that the majority had created a political document, had seized on two consent decrees (AT&T and pipeline) that were calculated to embarrass the administration, and charged that the recommendation to amend the Elkins Act was not supported by the evidence and was not in keeping with the proclaimed purpose of the inquiry.[65] On the other hand, the minority agreed that 16 years was a long time for the Justice Department to take before deciding to seek a court interpretation of the oil pipeline consent decree,[66] and it also agreed that a further investigation of the need for more publicity in connection with the filing of decrees might be helpful.[67] The minority advocated reopening the hearings, this time approaching them more positively with a specific focus on the Attorney General's administrative decision-making powers under the antitrust laws.[68] No comment was offered on the ICC's relations with the oil pipeline companies.

Looking back at the Celler hearings, one is inclined to view the minoritys' verdict as the more balanced one. The majority of the subcommittee seemed more interested in showing up deficiencies in the enforcement of specific decrees and in scoring political points than in broader questions of public policy. Nevertheless, their criticisms of administrative and enforcement procedures seem well placed, though there were extenuating circumstances. It seems equally apparent that the majority attributed an element of motivation to the activities of pipeline managements which was based more on preconceived ideas of business behavior than on an objective weighing of alternative explanations.

The hearings showed that discontinuities in governmental processes, the turnover of government personnel, congressional economizing with the ICC, and the resulting dependence of the ICC on the carriers for significant amounts of valuation information and assistance, created a difficult situation for all concerned with the decree. Testimony and documents indicate that Service Pipe Line's management had been acutely aware of the penalties for violating the consent decree and had taken the most conservative course in complying with it. This approach had not precluded taking advantage of ambiguity in the decree, where this could be done without danger of incurring penalties. The failure of the ICC, however, to provide annual valuations had invited, perhaps necessitated, aggressive and imaginative managerial action to deal with this problem. The relative passivity — if not explicit approval — of the Justice Department with respect to resulting procedures, had provided further encouragement for adopting them.

Given the circumstances in which they found themselves, the pipeline companies subject to the decree had reacted pragmatically. If the congressional subcommittee had spent more time in determining the causes and objectively assessing the economic consequences of this behavior, it would have performed a valuable service. As it was, the majority's report constituted primarily an indictment underscoring the deficiencies, some real and some imagined, of a pragmatic approach to problems of government-business relations. Although it emphasized the costs of this approach to the public interest, the majority report did not evaluate them specifically. Moreover, managerial problems of working in a framework of governmental uncertainty were heavily discounted or disregarded.

COURT ACTION

Some of the issues of the oil pipeline consent decree raised in the Celler subcommittee hearings had already been placed before the courts in the Tidal, Service, Texas, and Arapahoe cases. Thus there was an opportunity for a judicial review and decision on the arguments advanced at the Celler hearings for conflicting interpretations of the decree. In fact, the trial court had already announced its decision by the time the subcommittee's report appeared.

The motion against the Texas Pipe Line Company had been dropped in February 1958 when the company agreed to transfer to surplus some $100,000 previously classified as earned and payable to the shipper-owner on a basis challenged by the Justice Department.[69] The three remaining motions were placed before the federal district court for the District of Columbia on March 24–25, 1958.

Appearing for the Justice Department was Alfred Karsted. In the Service Pipe Line case he argued that the company had not complied with the government's interpretation of the consent decree in ascertaining valuations for dividend purposes. He conceded, however, that the company had not "rigged" its returns. In fact, he stated, Service had been scrupulously consistent in its application of its pro rata formula, and he admitted that — disregarding his interpretation of the literal language of the decree — there was much merit in the approach adopted by the defendant.[70] It almost seemed from his presentation to the court that the government lawyer did not feel strongly about the role he was playing as a complainant.

The government's formal position was that a common-carrier pipeline facility completed in the year for which dividends were being reported to the Attorney General could not be included in the valuation base used in computing these dividends.[71] Similarly, common-carrier property retired during that year could not be deducted from the valuation. Thus, for example, dividends reported for 1944 should be based on a valuation determined as of December 31, 1943, without including any property changes made during 1944. The Service Pipe Line position was that the decree required a facility contributing to revenue be included in valuation on a pro rata basis.[72] In reports to the Justice Department these values had therefore been included with valuation as of December 31 of the year immediately preceding the one for which dividends were being reported. (The actual reporting date of valuation adopted by Service was January 1 of the year reported on.) Following a consistent interpretation, this approach meant that retirements in the year reported on were also deducted pro rata from valuation as of the end of the preceding year.[73]

Appearing for the defendant, Service Pipe Line, Hammond Chaffetz explained his client's approach and maintained that it had been adopted from the start, that the Justice Department had not questioned it before 1951, that an explanation had been made at that time and subsequently, and that it had not been challenged until the motion under consideration had been filed.[74] He declared that Service had under-earned its permissible 7 per cent dividends for several years in the early 1950's and stated that the dividends at issue before the court involved $240,000 claimed on the pro rata basis in 1952 but not earned at that time.[75] In 1955, however, Service had earned in excess of 7 per cent, even though it had deducted from its valuation (in accordance with a consistent application of its pro rata procedure) some $14,000,000 that the government's interpretation would have allowed. Against these 1955 earnings there was a carry-forward of several million dollars in dividends previously payable but unearned.[76]. Although these dividends were not based on the pro rata procedure, only a fraction of the total amount was actually paid.[77]

The government charged that the $240,000 Service claimed as payable in 1952 was wrongfully included in the 1955 dividends actually paid. Chaffetz denied the charge. "We were entitled to pay out millions more than we actually did pay out for moneys that were uncontroverted, that were not tainted, even, by the government's theory of pro rata," he said.[78] He argued that if there was no merit to the pro rata theory, then the $14,000,-000 subtracted by Service Pipe Line from its valuation base for 1955 should be restored, making even more dividends payable.[79]

Karsted maintained that "valuation" as used in the decree had to be construed in terms of 1941 when the document was drawn up; therefore "the latest final ICC valuation" meant the one established for 1934.[80] He argued that the decree's provisions for handling additions and betterments, depreciation and retirements, as of the close "of the next preceding year" had been framed, in the absence of current valuations, to bring the latest final valuation down only to the end of the year preceding the one reported on.[81] Chaffetz insisted that the decree was plain on its face that additions and betterments and depreciation and retirements for the year reported on should be included on a pro rata basis in determining the valuation on which dividends could be paid.[82] Otherwise, for example, revenue from a line installed in the reporting year could create earnings that would have to be "frozen" indefinitely under the decree, while property taken out of service would be included improperly in the base on which dividends were figured.[83] To Karsted, however, this interpretation was like that of including the value of an addition built on a house in September in determining the value of that house at the end of the preceding year.[84]

Federal District Court Judge Richmond B. Keech found that Service and Indiana Standard had not violated the decree. In reaching this decision he admitted that the government's case was not without merit but that a literal interpretation of the decree as advanced by Karsted might be inequitable. He also took into account the length of time that the Justice Department had concurred in the Service pro rata practice, as well as the fact that the defendants had made complete and full disclosure of it over a period of time.[85] For substantially the same reasons, he dismissed the motion against Tidal.* [86] Since the Texas Pipe Line Company case had already been settled, only the Arapahoe issue remained to be decided.[87]

Arapahoe Pipe Line Company had been incorporated in June 1954, with Sinclair Pipe Line Company and The Pure Oil Company holding all of its $2,900,000 par value capital stock. Two months later, $16,000,000 of First Mortgage Pipe Line bonds were issued to the Metropolitan Life Insurance Company, and they were followed later in the fall of 1954 by a $10,000,000 issue taken by the same company. Including in its valuation the property 90 per cent financed with this borrowed capital, the pipeline company had reported a total of $3,749,748 payable as dividends for 1954–1956, though it actually paid a dividend of only $580,000 (i.e., 7 per cent on equity investment for three years) in 1956.[88] The government action filed in October 1957 charged that in figuring dividends payable the company had wrongfully included the valuation attributable to loans from third parties, resulting in a rate of return on the owners' equity investment of 3.9 per cent in 1954, 52.6 per cent in 1955, and 72.7 per cent in 1956.[89] The motion asked that Arapahoe be required to deduct from valuation for dividend purposes that part attributable to loans from third parties.[90]

Other companies under the consent decree, of course, had a vital interest in the outcome of the Arapahoe case, for postwar pipeline construction had relied heavily on borrowed funds. Appearing before Judge Keech on January 27, 1958, Justice Department attorney Karsted said that Arapahoe had been chosen for a test action because its case was relatively simple and the department was seeking only an interpretation of law. Under Rule 5 of the Federal Rules of Procedure, the motion had been served only on Arapahoe. He therefore took the position that other companies under the decree would not be bound by the Arapahoe decision.[91] The lawyers of these companies felt differently, and a few days later twelve companies entered the case with the Judge approving a stipulation of their interest, provided that additional questions of fact should not be introduced.[92] Lawyers for Jersey Standard affiliates, Interstate Oil Pipe Line, and Tuscarora Pipe Line, did not participate in the negotiation of the stipulation, and they advised their clients not to sign it with the qualification that it included. These companies filed a motion on February 5, 1958, to dismiss the government's motion and to confirm their interpretation of the decree, but this motion was consolidated with that of the other companies.[93]

The government's brief in the Arapahoe case argued that the clear intent of the Elkins Act (and therefore of the decree) was to prevent discrimination between shippers;[94] that there was legal precedent for the claim that dividends could constitute rebates;[95] that the decree had allowed a return (7 per cent) because it was equivalent to a "service" provided by the car-

---

*The government had contended that the decree permitted valuation only of common-carrier property "owned and used." Tidal included property used but not owned. The defense argued that the decree was based on latest ICC valuation, which included *all* property employed in common-carrier service.

rier,[96] but that anything over 7 per cent on equity investment violated the decree.[97] "Congress," the brief said, "recognized that when a shipper supplies something to a carrier, an illegal rebate results if the shipper receives more than a reasonable amount in return for that which he supplies." [98]

Karsted clarified the Justice Department's view of shipper-owner loans. Those made before the decree were regarded as part of the owner's investment and therefore were not repayable under Paragraph V. Loans made after the decree but not included in valuation for dividend purposes were entitled to interest and repayment.[99] "The one thing that the Department has been adamant on," he said, "is that the shipper-owner cannot receive both 7% on the valuation resulting from or attributable to the loan, and, in addition, interest on and the repayment of the loan." [100]

In the light of previous indications of the Justice Department's attitude on debt, the shipper-owners of Arapahoe had understandably used their credit to obtain a third-party loan for Arapahoe. They had signed a throughput agreement which committed them to ship enough oil, or in the event of any deficiency to supply sufficient cash, to enable the pipeline company to meet its debt obligations.[101] This was, of course, a condition of the lender in supplying the borrowed funds. As the resulting agreement involved the shipper-owners' credit, they argued that this was justification for including the properties thus financed in valuation for dividend purposes.[102] The government brief contended, however, that it was illogical to permit a 7 per cent return for guaranteeing a loan when the lender was receiving only a little over half this percentage for supplying the capital.[103] The brief, of course, rejected the carrier's interpretation that the decree authorized payment of dividends on that part of ICC valuation which included properties financed by third parties.[104]

The government brief had difficulty in meeting the defense argument that for 16 years the carriers had been allowed to follow the practices now challenged.[105] Karsted acknowledged that this defense might protect against imposition of penalties for past actions but argued this was no guide for the future.[106] His brief conceded that government inaction had contributed to the decision by defendants to borrow funds, but he also maintained that sound public policy did not permit estoppel of action on these grounds, however regrettable the results for the defendants.[107] In any case, the government attorney said, the Court could not tolerate a violation of the Elkins Act, which was what the government charged.[108]

The carriers argued that the Great Lakes 1942 supplemental judgment* supported their interpretation of the decree,[109] the government brief claimed that it did not.[110] The brief interpreted that judgment to mean that the owners of Great Lakes had been authorized to recover some 82 per cent of their equity investment for whatever use they wished but that in return they were to forego the 7 per cent dividend on their remaining 18 per cent equity for a period of 15 years, the life of the debentures.[111] That is, in the Great

*See Chap. 18.

Lakes refinancing, interest payments took precedence over dividends and for the first half of the period, interest payments had exceeded the 7 per cent dividend on 18 per cent equity; in the latter half the reverse was true. This approach ingeniously explained why the department had sanctioned the substitution of debt for equity. However, this argument was a weak one since the government brief claimed that Great Lakes (against which no action had been taken) had also consistently violated the decree by paying dividends on its entire valuation.[112]

As with the Service and Tidal motions, Judge Keech found the defense of Arapahoe more persuasive than the government's counterarguments. In rendering his decision, the Judge declared of the decree: "I think it is clear upon its face; but even if there had been ambiguities, I certainly would be constrained to hold that ambiguity had been resolved through the practice of the defendants, acquiesced in by the Government after full disclosure throughout the 16 years." [113]

The government's suits seemed to the judge a unilateral and unwarranted effort to rewrite the decree.[114] Accordingly on March 25, 1958, he denied the government's motion with respect to Arapahoe. Affirmatively he ordered "that the valuation of common carrier's property on which the shipper-owner's permissible dividends may be computed is the valuation of the carrier's property as provided in the judgment entered December 23, 1941 without deducting the amount of any indebtedness from such valuation; and it is further ORDERED that defendant common carriers are permitted to pay dividends to their respective shipper-owners on the basis of such computation." [115] Thus, the government lost all of its motions at the district court level. However, this reverse for the Justice Department could not be considered final until it had been appealed to the United States Supreme Court.

Apparently there was widespread feeling among pipeline executives that much more was at stake in the appeal of the Arapahoe case than in either the Tidal or Service Pipe Line cases. To allow the Justice Department to take the latter two to the Supreme Court, therefore, might divert defense energies and unnecessarily complicate a clear-cut decision on the highly important debt issue. Accordingly the companies involved in these two subordinate proceedings sought and reached an understanding with the department, which agreed that no further action would be taken in return for Service's dropping its claims to the pro rata approach for the future and Tidal's agreeing to exclude leased property from its valuation for dividend purposes. Once this had been accomplished, the stage was set for the nation's highest court to review the district court's decision that pipeline companies operating under the consent could properly include debt-financed property in their valuations when determining permissible dividends under the consent decree.

The final decision in the Arapahoe case was announced on June 8, 1959. In a 6-to-1 decision, the Supreme Court sustained Judge Keech. In the words of the court:

Where the language of a consent decree in its normal meaning supports an interpretation; where that interpretation has been adhered to over many years by all the parties, including those government officials who drew up and administered the decree from the start; and where the trial court concludes that this interpretation is in fact the one the parties intended, we will not reject it simply because another reading might seem more consistent with the Government's reasons for entering into the agreement in the first place.[116]

At last the pipeline sector of the integrated oil industry had an unambiguous declaration, based on the full exploitation of the legal process, that they had not violated the consent decree.

The extent of this victory was clearly related, at least in part, to the Justice Department's prolonged failure to challenge the procedures adopted by pipeline management and reported over a long period of time. In retrospect, it appears that Assistant Attorney General Hansen in initiating the motions for a judicial interpretation of the decree had been acting under political pressure. On this hypothesis it is not surprising that the Supreme Court took the view that the government's construction of the decree was at odds with that intended by the negotiators in 1941 and accepted by Hansen's predecessors. In essence, then, the Court held that if any fault was involved, it lay in the terms of which the decree was originally accepted by the government. In this sense, the verdict of the Celler subcommittee, both majority and minority, that more publicity should accompany decree negotiations was partially vindicated. However, the implication that the companies subject to the decree had conspired to violate it was emphatically rejected by the very language of the Supreme Court's decision.

PART

VII

Conclusions

CHAPTER 25

PIPELINING IN PERSPECTIVE

Looking back over the history of American petroleum pipelines in this century, one is impressed by the elements of both continuity and change in their story. Of the two, continuity is unquestionably the stronger. The pipeline's basic transportation role — the movement of a fluid through a pipe with all that this implies in terms of heavy capital requirements and continuous, large inputs — has not changed. Consequently, the great changes in pipelining have predominantly been in degree rather than in kind. They have been reflected in the spread of pipeline systems, the increased size of pipe, automation, reduced rates per barrel-mile, plus more varieties of petroleum and its products that can be carried. But these changes have for the most part only increased the scale of the technological and financial problems that were familiar to pipeliners at the turn of the century.

There has been remarkable continuity, too, in the amount of attention given pipelines by arms of government from local to national levels. The era covered by this study started with both the executive and legislative branches of the federal government condemning the alleged use of pipelines by Standard Oil to preserve a dominant position in the oil industry. The era ended with the United States Supreme Court reviewing and upholding the industry's interpretation of a consent decree dating from the days of antitrust furor just prior to the country's active involvement in World War II. At almost any place between these two points in time one can find some kind of agitation to place the constraint of public authority on the freedom of decision-making by pipeline managers.

The remarkable thing about this long period of governmental interest in oil pipelines, however, is that it did not of itself produce basic changes in the modes of pipeline operation or significantly alter the yardsticks applied in making private pipeline investment decisions, This it not to say that changes did not occur, and in many instances changes of major importance, but virtually without exception they were the result of private industry rather than public policy decisions.

Larger pipe, more efficient prime movers, better control of oil movements, and similar technological developments of the twentieth century left unaltered the basic economic framework that governed private decisions on pipeline investment and employment. The pipeline was first a conduit from

461

the oil fields to the refinery and later from the refinery to distribution points, but in both instances, and in 1959 as in 1906, its economies as a transportation medium rested on large, assured inputs and continuous flow. The question confronting oil-company management was always the same: Can we obtain access to new sources of crude and/or cheaper transportation for crude or products by making this pipeline investment?

This question concerned primarily large, integrated oil companies both at the start and at the end of the period, though in the interim the number of companies had grown substantially. Pipelines helped some of them to get their start; others were forced to enter pipelining to preserve their existing position in other phases of the oil industry; and all had to expand their pipeline operations to remain competitive. Although the context of the key question concerning pipelines was different for different companies, the overriding element of continuity lies in the fact that in 1959 as in 1906 the great-majority of pipeline investment decisions were made in the light of the investing company's position in the oil industry.

In special situations, and particularly after World War II, non-integrated oil companies and companies interested in the revenue to be derived from transportation also made pipeline investments. In the former instance, the investment was most typically undertaken to obtain an outlet from some oil field not served by a large integrated oil company. In the latter instance, some transportation companies, like the Southern Pacific, found pipelining, primarily of products, attractive and remunerative in the context of their other interests. Such developments came relatively late in the period covered by this study, and they did not alter the position of large oil companies as the principal owners of American petroleum pipelines. Accordingly, any meaningful analysis of pipeline progress and problems in this century must start from this understanding: petroleum pipelines were more closely linked with the oil industry than with the transportation industry in the years 1906–1959. While the degree to which this was true was reduced appreciably in the interim, the basic balance between the two orientations of pipeline management was not reversed.

A great amount of empirical data on these points has been presented in preceding chapters; the function of the present chapter is to summarize and evaluate this material in terms of its over-all significance. To do so, one must begin with the fact that Standard Oil pioneered in large-scale pipeline operations and left a legacy of both business accomplishments and public policy problems that conditioned pipeline development in the period from 1906 to 1959.

THE LEGACY OF STANDARD OIL

By a series of astute strategic decisions and careful business management, Standard Oil moved from horizontal combination to full but not balanced vertical integration by 1890. In the process it confirmed its leading place in an otherwise disorganized industry. It would be difficult to overemphasize the importance of pipelines, where Standard's dominance was most pronounced, in achieving this leading position.

As the vital links between oil fields and refineries, pipelines gave Standard Oil a transportation advantage over competitors and would-be competitors that was never seriously challenged as long as oil production remained relatively concentrated in the Appalachian and Lima-Indiana fields. Standard Oil was therefore the training ground for pipeliners active during the first half of the period covered by this study, just as it was the originator of many, though not all, of the business practices and techniques that characterized oil pipelining down to World War II.

The key to Standard's strategy of overland oil movement lay in its construction and operation of pipelines as parts of an integrated structure. This strategy recognized that the essence of the oil industry is the continuous movement of oil from the places where nature has secreted it to the consumer. In this flow process, of course, oil is stored and oil is processed, but to provide profits it must move efficiently, continuously, and therefore in volume.

For Standard Oil, as for those who followed in its wake, these considerations added up to a need to control pipelines as part of an integrated structure and to make decisions on their employment in this context. As a result, pipelines were not built as public transportation facilities but as facilities to reduce the transportation costs of the company that supplied the capital and assumed the risks associated with pipelining. To insure efficient pipeline usage, minimum tenders of substantial size were required. To recover pipeline investment as rapidly as possible, high rates relative to operating costs were charged. Within an integrated company, of course, these were largely bookkeeping matters, but they posed a formidable barrier to outside users.

Pipelines are significant competitive weapons, and there is no question that Standard Oil exploited them fully in this way before the turn of the century. By entering early the limited number of new oil fields and by using its pipeline power to protect and augment its position in these and older fields, Standard slowed — though it did not halt — inroads on its commanding position. Such a strategy, however, was vulnerable to discovery of new fields where heavy transportation investment was not a barrier to entry. This situation, of course, accounted for the basic significance of the Spindletop oil discovery of 1901, for Spindletop was located within easy reach of ocean-going oil carriers and therefore world markets.

It is unnecessary to recapitulate here the rise of the new integrated oil companies based first on the heavy crude of the Texas Gulf Coast and later on the rich production of the Mid-Continent. They benefited not only from the accessibility of the new fields but also from an expanding market for fuel oil and motor gasoline. The significant fact for present purposes is that the new companies treated the construction and operation of their pipelines in much the same way as Standard. Pipelines for them, as well as for the pioneering Standard combination, were a lifeline to changing sources of production, and the uncertainties of that production dictated policies of protecting and recovering pipeline investment as rapidly and fully as possible. In addition, of course, these companies feared that if rates or tenders were reduced, Standard or other competitors would capitalize on such opportunities to demand access to the new conduits.

If the Standard Oil combination of 1906 left a legacy of pipeline know-how to the oil industry, it also left significant public policy problems as well. The legislative and antitrust triumphs of the Progressive Era suggest that the managers of Standard Oil (and other combinations) had underestimated the potential power of the federal government to affect private business decisions. Theodore Roosevelt, at least for political purposes, made a contest between the power of the federal government and that of large private corporations the central theme of his administration, albeit in the name of saving big business from itself. Standard Oil, the largest owner of oil pipelines, became his bête noire.

In his campaign to establish the supremacy of the federal government in dealing with big business, Roosevelt actively strove to strengthen the regulatory powers of the Interstate Commerce Commission and to revive selective antitrust prosecutions as a weapon for dealing with alleged monopoly and "unfair" methods of competition. His efforts helped to bring oil pipelines under the ICC and eventually the dissolution of Standard Oil. Both developments affected oil pipelines over the entire period under consideration in this study, and they had their counterparts on the state level as well. To them was added the always present possibility of divorcement of integrated oil operations by legislative action, the least predictable public policy process of all because of the varied political considerations that affect congressional action. This legacy, as well as the example of how to run a pipeline business efficiently, was left by the pioneering oil combination and its pipeline element to their successors.

FEDERAL REGULATION

In the heat of the excitement whipped up by Roosevelt against Standard Oil and the railroads in 1906, Congress precipitately placed pipelines under the Interstate Commerce Commission. The legislators made virtually no study of pipeline problems as such and no analysis of how these privately built carriers differed from other carriers with which they were lumped for regulatory purposes. The action was only partially anticipated by Standard Oil, was not sought by the Interstate Commerce Commission, and created difficult problems for both the regulated and regulators. Accordingly, every legal remedy was exhausted before the constitutionality and applicability of the statute was established beyond question eight years after its passage.

One conclusion of this study is that managerial evaluations of the potential power of government to make or alter private decisions on the construction and employment of pipelines tended to swing from one extreme to the other. For example, after the 1914 Supreme Court pipeline decision, several large companies, in the expectation that the decision portended rigorous implementation of the statute reorganized their pipeline operations and one even sold its pipelines to stockholders. In retrospect it appears that these companies took more action than was necessary in light of the circumstances. The ICC already had its hands full with railroads, and after the court decision it showed no disposition to take the initiative on pipeline regulation.

As it became clear that the ICC did not pose the threat anticipated, pipeline managers settled into a comfortable routine of complying with the limited number of formal federal regulatory requirements. Indeed, this approach seemed warranted by the lack of complaints about pipeline operations, and it apparently suited the ICC which, in the absence of such complaints, had more pressing concerns to occupy its attention.

During 20 years of treating federal regulation as a formality, pipeliners allowed misconceptions about pipelines to accumulate and outmoded practices to continue. Consequently, even though industry changes had begun to dictate revision of rates and practices in many instances, pipeliners were placed very much on the defensive when outside pressures finally moved the ICC to begin its own investigation of pipeline rates and gathering charges in 1934.

As it turned out, the time-consuming process of federal administrative procedure gave pipeliners adequate opportunity to adjust their operations to the new regulatory threat. Six years passed before the investigation initiated in 1934 reached the stage of even a preliminary ICC order. Thus, managerial alarm centered more on the possibility that active regulation might be extended into new areas than on the prospect of enforced rate reductions. In point of fact, conditions in the oil industry, not fear of the ICC, were already bringing about such reductions.

Although the ICC was more active in the post-World War II years than previously, the results were not substantially different from those of the earlier era for pipeliners. Again, the implications of the handful of ICC pipeline decisions rather than the decisions themselves worried management most. For example, there was the question of ICC jurisdiction over private products pipelines. The issue was not raised in connection with any leading company's operations, and the more assertive claims of the ICC were struck down by the courts. Since there was no final decision in this area, pipeline owners had the choice of disregarding the question or voluntarily declaring their products lines available to outside shippers.

Unquestionably, after 1945 pipeliners were more alert to possible difficulties with the ICC than they had been before the war. The establishment of the postwar Committee for Pipe Line Companies evidenced a new industry-wide interest in keeping in touch with Washington developments, including the views of the ICC. The exchange of information between the private and public bodies proved mutually valuable, and the opportunities to promote understanding of one another's problems was equally helpful.

If one conceives pipelines as integrated parts of a long production line, the lack of complaints against them before the ICC comes into better focus. In the first place, only those with oil to move had any direct interest in using pipelines. This fact automatically limited complainants to members of the oil industry. Fully integrated companies could largely be eliminated from this group because they had their own pipeline facilities. Partially integrated companies in times of scarcity might become complainants, as was the case with Ohio Standard in the early 1930's. But it was the independent producer or refiner who was most likely to seek regulatory action — the first because he could not sell all the oil he wanted or at the price he wanted, and the latter because he could not get all the oil he wanted at the price he wanted.

Conditions of this kind were not widespread except in depressed times. Hence, the coincidence of industry complaints against pipelines with decline in the general price level or in the price of oil as the result of overproduction is not surprising. Under ordinary conditions the integrated companies appear to have made the market for crude oil on terms that were acceptable to non-integrated operators. When the latter's supply or market, or the security of an established niche, were threatened, however, complaints were voiced.

DEMANDS FOR GOVERNMENTAL ACTION

Most efforts to invoke governmental power to make pipelines more available to nonowners were initiated by elements of the nonintegrated oil industry. This fact was true in the era of Standard Oil's dominance and was typically the case throughout the period from 1906 to 1959. The process was substantially the same in each instance. A discontented element (or even individual) in the industry would seek redress through one or more branches and at one more levels of government. The typical progression was from the state level, where often complaints were first addressed to a regulatory commission and then to the legislature, to the federal level, where this tactical procedure was frequently reversed.

The variety of industry interests generally proved an obstacle to the successful employment of such tactics. The simple division of the industry into integrated and nonintegrated concerns, though appealing to politicians and to some integrated industry critics, oversimplified the interests represented. The geographical spread of the oil business, the diversity of functions embraced by it, and the interdependencies of its various elements, not to mention competitive relationships, made sustained unity of attack on pipeline ownership or practices via government channels extremely difficult to achieve. Unity of support for positive governmental action to correct alleged inequities proved even more troublesome to maintain, for no single public policy would affect in the same way all those seeking change.

Although the integrated industry almost by definition controlled the bulk of the nation's oil pipelines and derived from this fact a certain unity of purpose and action in public policy matters, this unity often proved fragile in specific situations. The same diversity of opinion on strategy and tactics appeared in the ranks of integrated concerns as in the camp of their attackers, and for much the same reasons. The larger the arena of controversy, as in moving from the state to the federal level, the more the chances of diversity among the elements supposedly committed to a single cause.

In the light of these industry conditions, legislative action on pipelines generally had to come out of some larger concern of politicians or the electorate. Although industry elements might formulate specific legislative issues, a conjunction of deep public and political concern about the functioning or distribution of economic power in the economy, plus depressed conditions in particular sectors of the oil industry, over the years brought about the major changes in statutory public policy affecting oil pipelines. The conjunction of such circumstances was limited and periodic, however, so there were few statutory changes directly and solely affecting oil pipelines at the federal level throughout this period.

Understandably, in oil-producing states like Texas there were more frequent and explicit movements for pipeline legislation. To the extent that they were successful, the results tended to spread beyond state borders and made federal action in the same areas less appropriate or necessary than might otherwise have been the case.

CONGRESSIONAL INTEREST

Repeated proposals by a few Congressmen to divorce pipelines from integrated oil operations produced no restrictive legislative action of consequence. In fact, with the short-lived exception of the pipeline provisions of the National Industrial Recovery Act, the only significant federal oil pipeline legislation of this century was the 1906 act placing the carriers under the ICC. In that instance there were no congressional hearings at all on pipelines. In succeeding decades one congressional investigation after another inquired into pipeline practices as part of the integrated industry, but in no instance were the consequences noteworthy.

The explanation for this phenomenon appears to lie not only in the diversity of the oil industry and the nature of the federal system, but in the nature of the political and legislative processes themselves. They provide arenas for the airing of problems, some of which are put to rest by discussion while others pass on to a test of votes. At particular times various Congressmen, responding to their constituents, seeking an issue that would appeal to their constituents, or taking on a problem they considered genuinely important to the national welfare, selected the integrated oil industry and its pipeline sector for attack. Senators La Follette, Borah, O'Mahoney, and others come quickly to mind. The lack of support they found among their fellow Congressmen in these matters, plus the disinterest of the Executive Branch and the ICC with but few exceptions, suggests that drastic federal legislative action directed to reorganization of the oil industry lacked widespread appeal. Even assuming that active lobbying against measures deemed unfavorable to the integrated industry played a role in this result, it cannot explain the failure of one divorcement measure after another even to find a place on a committee calendar over a period of decades.

The cumulative weight of past congressional inaction appears to have contributed significantly to this outcome. Divorcement of pipelines in 1906 from common ownership with other stages of the oil industry might conceivably have changed the structure of the modern oil industry, which at that time was still in its formative period. Independent oil operators, however, intervened to prevent application of the commodities clause to pipelines because they deemed it harmful to their own interests. By 1911, when limited restructuring was accomplished by judicial decree directed against the leading concern, it was too late to change the direction that the new industry had taken. The economics of the industry, competition, and the legacy of Standard Oil had fastened an integrated structure, to which pipelines were central, on the industry that had emerged from the Spindletop discovery. From that time on, the likelihood of Congress attempting to restructure an industry proliferating with firms based on integrated operations grew steadily less. The dislocations and losses would have far outweighed the most optimistic expectations of gain.

The argument that congressional inaction in 1906 conditioned subsequent possibilities for divorcement could be toppled by giving great weight to accident or irrationality in the historical process. Nevertheless, the historical record of oil pipeline companies' relations with the Executive Branch, Congress, and independent regulatory commissions sustains the thesis that the passage of time was on the industry's side in its governmental relations. This situation led management in some periods to underestimate potential public policy threats and in others, when familiar relationship patterns suddenly became tinged with uncertainty, to feel undue anxiety. But it is worth reemphasizing that time-consuming governmental processes relative to the dynamics of the oil industry and the economy diminished the consequences of miscalculations by managements in either direction.

Over time, Congress also provided assistance to the oil industry in various forms, ranging from depletion tax allowances to the federal ban on interstate oil shipments in excess of state-authorized oil production. The relative ease with which such measures passed congressional muster in contrast to the disinterest or insurmountable obstacles encountered by restrictive measures is explained by the factors already mentioned, plus the role of Congress in melding private interests with the national interest. Against the background of a society basically committed to economic progress through private enterprise, there was a presumption more favorable to aiding such enterprise than restricting it. Although this presumption was severely challenged and significantly modified during the period 1906–1959, it remained viable, and nothing in the history of congressional treatment of oil pipelines or the oil industry refutes it.

THE PUBLIC POLICY PROCESS AND MISCONCEPTIONS ABOUT PIPELINES

If there was continuity in the key economic elements governing the construction and management of pipelines, there was equally persistent misunderstanding of them both in the nonintegrated oil industry and in government. This was so in large measure because pipelines were so deeply imbedded in a complex industry. The general public had little or no direct knowledge of these underground carriers. The explanation of their role was therefore up to their owners, who, prior to World War II, did little publicly to explain their pipeline operations except when put under attack; to nonintegrated producers or refiners with a vested interest in attacking integrated operations; to representatives of competing forms of transportation seeking to share the carriage of petroleum and its products; and to public officials who approached pipeline problems from the standpoint of assigned administrative responsibilities or of less explicit political considerations or pressures. In the efforts of these various groups to simplify the pipeline picture for their own purposes, one misconception bred another.

The persistence of the same kinds of charges from one generation of pipeline critics to another, however, suggests that the misconceptions must have had some basis in fact. The explanation appears to lie in one or more of the following areas: (1) the appearance of integrated pipeline operations belied their reality, (2) the reality of integrated pipeline operations under some conditions did in fact work to the disadvantage of one or more elements of the oil industry, (3) there was something to be gained from the exploitation of the situations created by either or both of these two preceding circumstances.

One can certainly conclude from the present study that the way in which pipeline operations were geared into integrated company complexes invited fundamental misconceptions about their functions, and that these misconceptions colored the relations of pipeline managers with both industry and government. On the most elementary level, for example, was the producer's frequent misconception that because a pipeline physically took his output, it was the actual purchaser. When pipeline space was in short supply, this misconception time and again brought attacks on so-called "pipeline prorationing." This approach blinked the facts that in most, if not all, instances, pipeline management had no control over oil purchases and that pipelines were required to allocate space equitably among those who employed their services. In the case of integrated companies, of course, these customers usually included an affiliated purchasing agency, but a pipeline's management had no more control over this agency than over those of other companies it served. In attacking pipeline prorationing, then, producers were really complaining about the purchasing policies of integrated concerns, though they focused their fire on pipeline management. How much of this was a deliberate tactic and how much a case of mistaken identity is not clear.

On another level, the pre-World War II accumulation of large surpluses or the payment of large dividends by a pipeline company was commonly mistaken for evidence that pipelines were extremely profitable in their own right and that their profits subsidized other areas of integrated operations such as marketing. As pointed out, although pipelines were generally operated as common carriers to meet governmental requirements, they were built primarily for the benefits conferred on the owning company. For most lines of this type, outside patronage before World War II was negligible or insignificant. The only way in which pipeline "profits" could properly have been said to subsidize other parts of the integrated company would have been if possession of the lines allowed that company to sell its products for more than would otherwise have been the case. Generations of critics alleged that this was so because, they claimed, high pipeline rates and high minimum tenders kept potential competitors from reaching major markets on the same terms as the integrated company. However, this claim by its very nature could never be really substantiated, and it also overlooked the fact that there was significant competition among integrated companies for products markets as well as for sources of crude. And, even in the era of high pipeline rates, there was also energetic competition in numerous markets from nonintegrated companies.

If a nonintegrated company was dissatisfied with its transportation costs, it was free to build its own pipelines — and a number of them did. Indeed, this was the process by which the pipeline network expanded from the days when Standard Oil controlled it to the modern era characterized by wide dispersion of pipeline ownership throughout the industry.

The alternatives available to nonintegrated companies were ignored in the late 1930's when critics charged that outside users of pipelines were in effect contributing to rebates enjoyed by the parent shipper-owner company. Interestingly, the charge came from academicians and government officials, notably in the Justice Department, much more than from nonintegrated industry spokesmen.

The rebate argument claimed that when an outside shipper paid more than the "cost" (it was never quite clear whether this included return on capital) of pipeline transportation, he was in effect contributing to the profits of the pipeline's shipper-owner and therefore reducing the latter's cost of transportation. This argument had an obvious appeal, but it ignored the question of the shipper-owner's opportunity cost in providing the pipeline in question, or what the outsider's cost would have been in providing equivalent service for himself. Statutory public policy which treated pipelines as part of the transportation industry rather than as part of the oil industry contributed to this confusion over alleged rebates. Oil-company managements compounded the confusion by keeping their pipeline subsidiaries undercapitalized. This practice, begun by Standard Oil, was perpetuated into the modern industry for reasons that still are unclear. In any event, the practice gave ammunition to pipeline critics, who seized on the size of pipeline dividends in relation to capital stock as evidence of the great profitability of pipeline operations.

Perhaps the most persistently popular misconception of all was that any company with "Standard" in its name was in fact acting as it had before the dissolution of 1911. Although certain predissolution relationships, as in the use of pipelines, persisted for a time out of necessity, even these limited ties between the former members of the combination were severed long before government agencies finally accepted the separation as a fact. Whether the general public, brought up on Ida Tarbell's business history, ever fully believed dissolution was accomplished is questionable. The significance of such a misconception for those attacking pipelines is obvious.

Allegations of abuse of pipeline power must be viewed in perspective. Unquestionably there were occasional specific situations where an integrated company's possession of a pipeline worked to the disadvantage of one or more elements dependent on, or in competition with, that concern. However, nothing in this study, which has attempted to embrace the majority of formal complaints on this score at both state and federal levels, appears to substantiate any general charge that exercise of pipeline power went beyond protection of the shipper-owners' legal rights. That these rights were fully exploited is equally true, but the latitude for managerial discretion in this area was far more tightly circumscribed than was the case for those who exploited the numerous misconceptions about the role of pipelines in the oil industry.

Since neither federal regulation nor legislative action succeeded in working any basic changes in the relationship of pipelines to integrated operations, the final avenue open to those who desired change was antitrust policy. It was here that public policy impinged most sharply on the pipeline sector of the integrated oil industry.

ANTITRUST POLICY

The threat of antitrust prosecution as a major weapon that the federal government held over the pipeline sector of the integrated oil industry dates back to Theodore Roosevelt's day. The indictment obtained during his administration against Standard Oil resulted in the 1911 court victory which put the potentialities of pipeline divorcement to a limited test.

Although the 1911 decision eventually added to the number of independent, integrated companies, it could not — and did not — end the interdependence of pipelines and refiners. None of the refining companies divorced from the combination remained without pipelines of their own two decades later, and most had found it necessary to integrate backward sooner than that. The pipeline companies separated from the combination found themselves just as dependent on Standard companies' patronage as before the dissolution. Because initially the dependence was reciprocal, they made few changes in operating practices and rates. This policy, plus the changing location of oil production and consumption centers, contributed to the decline or demise of most of the independent disaffiliated pipeline companies by the early 1930's.

Limited disintegration of the most powerful element in the oil industry by antitrust action, then, failed to produce a viable, independent pipeline sector. The separated pipeline companies could not afford to tap new centers of oil production without guarantees of throughput to justify the investment. Concerns in a position to offer such guarantees preferred to control their own transportation and this meant building their own lines. Thus a new integrated oil industry composed of numerous firms, some newcomers and others offshoots of the dissolution, appeared to replace the dominant one of the early 1900's.

The conjunction of the Great Depression with troubled conditions in some quarters of the oil industry, plus the crusading zeal of Assistant Attorney General Thurman Arnold, brought the new integrated industry under major antitrust attack at the end of the 1930's. In the Temporary National Economic Committee hearings of that era, the charges against the pipelines of integrated companies resembled closely those made at the turn of the century against Standard Oil's. Again, familiar misconceptions, arguments, and rebuttals passed across the committee room, but the TNEC did not advocate pipeline divorcement. The Justice Department therefore turned to legal action on its own initiative to accomplish this result.

A complicated series of negotiations, ending under the pressure posed by the national crisis of Pearl Harbor, led to the pipeline consent decree. In the interim the emphasis had been shifted from divorcement, an antitrust action, to a limitation of dividends payable by the pipeline subsidiaries of integrated companies that also carried outsiders' traffic, a regulatory function. Aside from the pressure to get on with wartime tasks, the magnitude of possible penalties for alleged past offenses seems to have been the key factor in the industry's decision to accept the relative certainty of the decree in preference to the uncertainty of litigation at a future time.

From that time on, avoidance of the penalties involved in any knowing violation of the consent decree consumed a far larger share of managerial thought and time than ICC regulatory questions ever had. No major pipeline investment decision could be made without consideration of the implications of the decree for return of that investment. This concern formed one direct and important stimulus to the resort to debt financing in the postwar era, and the 7 per cent limitation on dividend payments by pipeline companies subject to the decree for practical purposes put an over-all ceiling on rates.

Despite the relative passivity with which the Antitrust Division treated the filing of annual reports required by the decree, occasional severe letters to pipeline companies made their managers keenly aware that a mis-step in their handling of an apparent formality could have very serious consequences. In this sense, the decree was self-enforcing and the initiative in interpreting it was left to pipeline management. Because interpretations were understandably influenced by managerial evaluations of Justice Department attitudes, as well as by the decree itself, the department's antitrust staff enjoyed a significant amount of undelegated power under the decree. However, in terms of possible enforcement by formal legal action, the staff's actual power was limited by the unclear language of the decree.

The problems of interpretation were manifold and have been discussed at some length in this study, but basically they turned on the question of what base should be used for calculating permissible dividend payments to shipper-owners. This problem arose from a degree of ambiguity in the decree, plus the fact that for a period of some years the ICC lacked the funds to prepare up-to-date pipeline valuations. Although industry relations with the ICC were such that pipeline companies could work with it to remedy this defect partially, reports had to be filed with Antitrust Division for nearly a decade on the basis of a company's best guess as to its valuation.

Adding to the confusion was the question of whether the decee permitted dividend payments on total valuation or only on the equity-financed element of it. Full equity financing of pipelines, with returns on that capital limited by the consent decree to a maximum of 7 per cent, became increasingly unattractive as oil companies confronted mounting postwar demands for capital in other areas of integrated operations that promised a higher return. Their response was substitution of debt for equity in pipeline financing, a decision influenced by the belief that the decree permitted pipeline dividends to be computed on total valuation rather than on solely its equity component. Obviously a 7 per cent dividend on the valuation of a pipeline financed with 75–90 per cent debt represented a better return to equity than if the dividend were calculated only on the equity portion. The pipeline companies generally claimed the right to pay such dividends, though actual payments were usually made on a most conservative interpretation of the decree. And, of course, payments of any kind were dependent on earnings that were not necessarily large enough to constitute a dividend problem.

The Justice Department did not see fit to raise these issues on a general basis until it was put under pressure from congressional investigators of the department's consent decree program. Finally, the debt-equity question was brought into the courts for adjudication, and in 1959 the companies' position was upheld. In the view of Lee Loevinger, head of the Antitrust Division under President Kennedy, this result ended even the limited usefulness of the decree as a restrictive device.

Testifying before Congressman Celler's House Antitrust Subcommittee in June 1961, Loevinger declared that the decree as drawn originally had only limited potential and that the Supreme Court's 1959 decision had emptied it of even this. He pointed out that the decree had not put a ceiling on earnings. Accordingly a company could maintain high rates as long as it did not pay out the resulting earnings; it was also free to balance high rates in one segment of a pipeline system with low ones elsewhere to its own advantage. "Under the Supreme Court decision," he said, "the decree no longer has even a limited effectiveness in the case where the shipper-owner investment is a small part of the total property." He noted, however, that the ICC had become more effective in pipeline regulation and that "for several years we have received no serious complaints on pipeline rates." His net conclusion was that time spent on enforcing the decree would largely be wasted and that other actions were more promising in attacking any monopoly advantages accruing from ownership of transportation facilities.

Loevinger appeared to be playing his role as head of the Antitrust Division without qualification. Lacking from his testimony was any acknowledgment that pipeline companies might find it in their own best interests to maintain low rates, solicit outside business, and otherwise seek to serve producers and refiners alike as responsible common carriers. For economic reasons there were in fact strong postwar incentives to behave in this way. Unquestionably the existence of the consent decree provided an additional incentive based on managerial evaluation of its potential threat rather than aggressive enforcement by the Antitrust Division. Although pipelines were still built primarily to further their owners' interests in 1959, it seems clear that there was far less conflict between these interests and those of outsiders than there had been in 1939.

Antitrust enforcement played a limited role in this result and for the most part by indirection. Given the situation and the decree as drawn in 1941, the pipeline sector of the integrated oil industry probably benefited more than it suffered from this expression of public policy. If nothing else, it won time to adjust to a new era free from the uncertainty of antitrust litigation. And in this adjustment, not in antitrust action, lay the real benefits of oil pipelines to the whole oil industry and the economy.

On balance it seems warranted to conclude that neither federal regulation nor antitrust action between 1906 and 1959 substantially altered the development of the pipeline sector of the integrated oil industry. This conclusion appears to have been so: (1) because the concept of railroad regulation was not well suited to the realities of pipeline operation and (2) because regulation was incapable of achieving the antitrust goal that Congress seems to have had in mind in imposing it. Similarly, the consent decree as the outcome of proposed antitrust action proved more ineffectual than anticipated primarily because it sought to achieve an antitrust goal by regulatory means. Thus, the choice of public policy weapons seems to have been inappropriate for the ends sought, even if we disregard the appropriateness of the ends themselves.

Given this interpretation, the relative passivity of enforcement by federal agencies concerned with pipelines is at least partially explicable on the basis of this built-in conflict between ends and means. There was, in short, an incentive for government officials to let events take their course, and it is notable that neither the ICC nor the Justice Department, with the exception of the Arnold era, took aggressive action except under pressure from some other branch of government. Even when they did, the complexities of administrative and legal processes worked against them. The net result of these characteristics of public policy as applied to pipelines at the federal level was a continuing opportunity for management to shape pipeline policies primarily in the light of industry requirements, which reflected general supply and demand conditions for petroleum and its products.

The present study indicates that this situation was conductive to achieving the goals of public policy via private decision-making within limited governmental constraints. In the amount of time involved in effecting changes, perhaps lies the key distinction between public policy employed to force rapid change and business policy oriented to evolutionary change.

It took decades for the oil industry to achieve in its pipeline sector what public policy advocates had hoped would be accomplished overnight. Had they succeeded in realizing their hopes, the oil industry might have looked quite different today. Whether the results would have been any better in terms of the public interest is certainly debatable but it is also irrelevant. For reasons already discussed, the weight of history and of the public policy process in a free society were on the side of privately-directed evolutionary change.

WORLD WAR II

Aside from the great oil strikes of the early 1930's and the subsequent efforts to stabilize production with the aid of governmental controls, perhaps the most significant exogenous event affecting the oil industry and therefore pipelines was World War II. The demands it generated for petroleum and its products accelerated change in the oil pipeline business beyond anything known before. Ending the threat of prosecution for alleged past offenses, the war gave integrated oil companies and their pipeline affiliates an unprecedented opportunity to demonstrate their capacity to meet a national need quickly and efficiently. Their response was so effective that it virtually transformed the business of moving oil by pipeline. In the process, the relevancy of charges leveled against pipelines in the prewar era was largely eliminated.

In many respects, World War II was a watershed in the relations between oil pipeline companies and government and in the relations of companies with one another. Under the pressure of a common peril to the nation's existence, pipeliners and government officials met the most demanding crisis that ever confronted the domestic oil industry and they did so as partners.

Planned by the oil industry and substantially, though by no means completely, financed by government, the nation's arteries of oil flow were transformed in direction, size, and efficiency in a remarkably short time. The short-run results were impressive; the long-run consequences were no less so. The huge demand for oil justified experimentation with large-diameter pipeline systems, and the government's need for oil justified its bearing the financial risks of this innovation. The experiment proved a brilliant success, and the government's big-inch investment was more than fully recovered.

The technical lessons learned in this wartime experience were applied in peacetime, resulting in a transformation of the pipeline network under private auspices. Moreover, the cooperation among pipeline companies to meet war needs was perpetuated into the new era in order to execute projects beyond the capabilities or resources of a single firm.

POSTWAR PIPELINES

The postwar demand for petroleum and its products encouraged and sustained the boom in large-diameter pipeline construction which in turn fostered innovation in organizational and financial arrangements as well as operating policies. The joint-venture pipeline, financed in large measure by long-term borrowing from financial institutions, became more typical of new construction than the single-company, equity-financed, small-diameter projects of prewar days. When one of these new lines tapped an area, other companies operating there were put under pressure to realize comparable transportation economics. Thus competitive pressures generated still further new construction, forcing down rates and encouraging solicitation of outside traffic for the marginal contribution it could make to the reduction of operating costs.

The prewar trend toward use of pipelines to move petroleum products was further accelerated by postwar developments which, among other things, made outmoded small-diameter crude lines available for products movements. Consequently there was a rapid proliferation of products systems, some utilizing converted lines and others building *de novo*.

Although results of these postwar changes seemed revolutionary, they were in fact the product of rapid evolutionary change. Joint-ventures, use of debt financing, and movement of products by pipeline had all existed before the war on a limited scale. What was new in the postwar era was the extent to which they came to dominate the pipeline sector of the integrated oil industry.

From the standpoint of public policy, these changes were significant. Although most new postwar construction was under the auspices of large, integrated companies — a fact which in itself was cause for suspicion by many traditional pipeline critics — the availability of pipelines to nonowners was substantially increased. Again, the trend toward lowered rates and smaller minimum tenders had begun before the war, but it was greatly accelerated by the economics of the postwar industry, reinforced by the constraints of the consent decree and a new managerial alertness to public policy pressures. By 1948, in fact, the ICC found that the level of rates had dropped to the point where continuation of the rate investigation begun in 1934 was unjustified.

IMPACT OF CHANGE ON PIPELINE MANAGEMENT

Although it would be difficult to document this conclusion irrefutably, one apparent outcome of these developments was considerably more autonomy for managers of pipeline companies owned by integrated companies than had been the case before the war. The consent decree encouraged arm's length dealings between shipper-owners and their pipeline companies; the borrowing of large amounts of money in the name of a pipeline company, though in effect guaranteed by the parent, gave pipeline management a new and significant financial aspect; the responsibility for construction of new pipelines, plus the search for partners in and users of such facilities, was frequently delegated to pipeline managers, further enhancing their stature. The impression of autonomy is further heightened by the fact that pipeline companies formed their own association to handle legislative and public relations problems of common interest rather than relying on the more comprehensive activities of the American Petroleum Institute. And this approach was supplemented by pipeliners' participation in transportation groups like the Transportation Association of America and cooperation with other transportation interests in seeking relief from the federal transportation tax.

Without denying that the pipeline subsidiaries of integrated companies in the 1950's still owed their first allegiance to their parent shipper-owners, it is equally valid to say that the typical pipeline manager saw himself as responsible for conducting a soundly managed common-carrier operation. This conclusion emerges not only from the concrete data presented in this study but also from personal and extended contact with the present generation of pipeline managers.

Of course, interesting questions would come up if the course of action dictated for a common-carrier enterprise conflicted with the interests of the shipper-owner. As already explained, however, a basic conclusion of this study is that such situations in the postwar period were rare. The factors that argued for granting pipeline managers greater autonomy were premised on an increasingly greater identity of interest between individual shipper-owners and the oil industry generally. When brought down to specific places and circumstances, there might be important qualifications to this generalization. Presumably the Texas unconnected wells controversy would be a case in point. Even there, however, the outcome after all appropriate public policy processes were exhausted, sustains the general thesis that common-carrier pipeline transportation by an affiliate of an integrated oil company would be provided if the economics of the situation warranted it, the interests of the parent company apart.

These conclusions are basically favorable to integrated and pipeline company management, but they appear to be justified on the evidence. The purpose of this study was to examine historical data as exhaustively as possible with a view to evaluating the effects of public policy on pipeline management as opposed to the effects of economic and business factors. It has been shown that although both generally worked in the same direction, the latter clearly dominated. The data suggest that an integrated structure was the key element in pipeline operations and that those who disliked its implications chose the wrong public policy instruments for dealing with it, applied them at the wrong times, and in general entertained exaggerated expectations of their potential.

These conclusions do not argue that pipeline managers and those to whom they were responsible in parent companies pursued consistently enlightened policies. The fact seems to be that they fully recognized the advantages conferred by pipeline ownership and did not relinquish any of them except under pressure, which in virtually all cases was more economic than governmental. By refusing to acknowledge a valid public interest in the reduction of pipeline rates before it was forced on them by overcapacity, by following capitalization and dividend policies that fostered misconceptions, and by reacting to rather than anticipating attack, pipeline management invited the investigations, the hearings, and the criticism to which it was subjected. This passivity with respect to external relations was a direct inheritance from Standard Oil days, encouraged and perpetuated by the comparatively protected position of pipelines relative to other parts of the oil industry.

The range of factors that saved the pipeline sector of the integrated oil industry from reaping the full fruits of perpetuating outmoded policies has already been discussed. Voluntary corrective action beginning belatedly in the early 1930's, plus the outbreak of World War II, blunted an intensifying and varied attack on pipeline ownership and operating policies. Emerging from this conflict with a solid record of accomplishment and new viewpoints, pipeline management placed a new value on its public image and adjusted easily to conditions favoring the adoption of policies to sustain it. Here, if anywhere, there was a revolutionary as opposed to evolutionary change.

The postwar transformation of managerial attitudes and policies was not complete nor completely embracing, but it was highly significant. It was more than sufficient to justify the conclusion that, given time, private, decentralized decision-making produced a national pipeline network operating in a fashion that approximated the goals sought by earlier proponents of rapid, enforced change via public policy. This result was not solely the product of enlightened management nor of public policy but of a sustained interaction between the two, with technology and supply and demand conditions in the oil industry determining the major turning points in the relationship.

Appendixes

Bibliography

Notes

Index

APPENDIX A

Principal large-diameter[a] crude-oil pipelines constructed in the United States, 1946–1958.

Pipeline or oil company name[b]	Year completed	Diameter (inches)	Mileage	Connecting points
Standard Oil Company (Calif.)	1946	18–20	176	San Joaquin Valley — San Francisco
Stanolind Pipe Line Co.[1]	1946	8–20	202	Loops in Missouri and Illinois
Humble Pipe Line Co.[2]	1947	20	50	Satsuma — Baytown, Tex.
Sinclair Refining Co.[3]	1947	18	50	Looping of trunk lines in Kansas
Stanolind Pipe Line Co.[1]	1947	20	178	Drumright, Okla. — Freeman, Mo., looping
Texas Pipe Line Co.[4]	1947	16	60	West Columbia — Houston, Tex.
Basin Pipe Line System[5]	1948	20–22	345	Jal, N.M. — Midland and Wichita Falls, Tex.
Magnolia Pipe Line Co.[6]	1948	20	650	Corsicana, Tex. — Patoka, Ill.
Stanolind Pipe Line Co.[1]	1948	8–16	208	Pilot Butte — Fort Laramie, Wyo.
	1948	12–16	250	Loops in Nebraska and Kansas
	1948	16–20	250	Loops in Oklahoma
	1948	10–16	111	West Texas construction
Texas Pipe Line Co.[4]	1948	20	87	Houston — Port Arthur, Tex.
Basin Pipe Line System[5]	1949	24	275	Wichita Falls, Tex. — Cushing, Okla.
Buckeye Pipe Line Co.[7]	1949	22	82	Lima — Toledo, O.
Ozark Pipe Line System[8]	1949	22	440	Cushing, Okla. — Wood River, Ill.
Texas-Empire Pipe Line Co.[9]	1949	18	183	Patoka — Wilmington, Ill.
Texas Pipe Line Co.[4]	1949	22	55	Wood River — Patoka, Ill.
Stanolind Pipe Line Co.[1]	1949	16	75	Loops, Washington, Kan. — Freeman, Mo.
Humble Pipe Line Co.[2]	1950	18	373	West Texas (Satsuma) — Baytown, Tex.
Lakehead Pipe Line Co.[10]	1950	18	321	Neche, N.D. — Superior, Wis.

APPENDIX A — *continued*

Principal large-diameter[a] crude-oil pipelines constructed in the United States, 1946–1958.

Pipeline or oil company name	Year completed	Diameter (inches)	Mileage	Connecting points
Mid-Valley Pipe Line Co.[11]	1950	20, 22	1,053	Longview, Tex. — Lima, O.
Portland Pipe Line Co.[12]	1950	18	236	South Portland, Me. — U.S.-Canada line (near Highwater, Que.)
Richfield Oil Corporation	1950	10–16	60	Cuyama Valley — Newhall, Calif.
Texas-Empire Pipe Line Co.[9]	1950	16	45	Wilmington, Ill. — East Chicago, Ind.
Ohio Oil Company	1951	20, 22	245	Wood River — Martinsville, Ill. and Sheridan, Ind.
Cities Service Pipe Line Co.	1952	18	64	Sour Lake, Tex. — Lake Charles, La.
Humble Pipe Line Co.[2]	1952	18	201	Hawkins — Baytown, Tex.
Interstate Oil Pipe Line Co.[13]	1952	16–20	147	Flora — Bunkie — Melville, La., and Sunset — Anchorage, La.
Ohio Oil Co.	1952	22	117	Sheridan, Ind. — Lima, O.
Pan American Pipe Line Co.[14]	1952	26	27	Genoa — Texas City, Tex.
Platte Pipe Line Co.[15]	1952	16–20	1,100	Chatham, Wyo. — Wood River, Ill.
Service Pipe Line Co.[1]	1952	16–20	83	Bowie, Tex. — Drumright Okla. — Sugar Creek, Mo.
Texas-Empire Pipe Line Co.[9]	1952	18	30	Wilmington — Lockport, Ill.
Texas Pipe Line Co.[4]	1952	22	319	Louisiana points — Port Arthur, Tex.
	1952	16	175	Corsicana — Houston, Tex.
Cities Service Co.	1953	20	64	Sour Lake, Tex. — Lake Charles, La.
Humble Pipe Line Co.[2]	1953	16, 18	71	Hawkins, Tex. — Texas-Louisiana state line, near Shreveport
Interstate Oil Pipe Line Co.[13]	1953	8–22	222	Shreveport — Baton Rouge, La.
Lakehead Pipe Line Co.[10]	1953	30	643	Superior, Wisc. — Sarnia, Ont.
Magnolia Pipe Line Co.[6]	1953	16	155	Ringgold — Corsicana, Tex.

Company	Year	Diameter (in.)	Miles	Route
Mesa Pipe Line System[26]	1953	24	80	Midland, Tex. — Colorado City
Pan American Pipe Line Co.[14]	1953	16	43	Arden Jct. — Colorado City, Tex.
Rancho Pipe Line System[16]	1953	24	457	McCamey — Houston, Tex.
Service Pipe Line Co.[1]	1953	16	163	Bowie, Tex. — Drumright, Okla.
	1953	12–16	170	Williston Basin — Mandan, N.D.
Sinclair Pipe Line Co.[3]	1953	22, 24	666	Drumright, Okla. — East Chicago, Ind.
	1953	18	45	Panova — Cushing, Okla.
West Texas Gulf Pipe Line Co.[17]	1953	20–26	577	Colorado City — Beaumont and Port Neches, Tex. with 20-inch branch to Longview, Tex.
Arapahoe Pipe Line Co.[18]	1954	18, 20	494	Merino, Col. — Humboldt, Kan.
Humble Pipe Line Co.[2]	1954	12, 18	201	East Texas — Gulf Coast
Lakehead Pipe Line Co.[10]	1954	26	186	Loops, Canada-U.S. line — Superior Wis.
Magnolia Pipe Line Co.[6]	1954	20	208	Corsicana — Beaumont, Tex.
Service Pipe Line Co.[1]	1954	20, 22, 24	625	Fort Laramie, Wyo. — Freeman, Mo.
Sinclair Pipe Line Co.[3]	1954	12, 16	20	Moner — Blue Island, Ill.
Trans Mountain Oil Pipe Line Co.[19]	1954	16, 26	47	Canada-U.S. line — Ferndale, Wash.
Butte Pipe Line Co.[20]	1955	16	450	Poplar and Glendive, Mont. — Guernsey and Fort Laramie, Wyo.
Magnolia Pipe Line Co.[6]	1955	12–16	215	Expansion of line, Midland — Corsicana, Tex.
Minnesota Pipe Line Co.[21]	1955	16	260	Clearbrook — Hastings, Minn.
Lakehead Pipe Line Co.[10]	1956	26	51	Looping in conjunction with Interprovincial P.L.
Magnolia Pipe Line Co.[6]	1956	12, 16	50	Ringgold — Addington, Tex., and Andrews — Midland
Pasotex Pipe Line Co.[22]	1956	20	127	Wink, Tex. — El Paso, replacement of 8-inch lines
Sinclair Pipe Line Co.[3]	1956	18	152	Jacksboro — Teague, Tex.
Humble Pipe Line Co.[2]	1957	18	94	Ector — Kemper stations, west Texas

APPENDIX A — *continued*

Principal large-diameter[a] crude-oil pipelines constructed in the United States, 1946–1958.

Pipeline or oil company name	Year completed	Diameter (inches)	Mileage	Connecting points
Tecumseh Pipe Line Co.[23]	1957	20	201	East Chicago, Ind. — Cygnet, O.
Union Oil Co. (California)	1957	12, 16	225	San Joaquin Valley — San Francisco Bay, Calif.
Four Corners Pipe Line Co.[24]	1958	16	750	Aneth, Ut. — Los Angeles, Calif.
Lakehead Pipe Line Co.[10]	1958	24, 26	185	Looping, U.S.-Canada line — Superior, Wis.
Magnolia Pipe Line Co.[6]	1958	12–20	250	Expansion and looping, west Texas — Corsicana and Beaumont
Service Pipe Line Co.[1]	1958	20	76	Looping, Fort Laramie — Glendo Jct., Wyo., and Casper — Welch
Sinclair Pipe Line Co.[3]	1958	20	150	Teague — Houston, Tex.
Texas-New Mexico Pipe Line Co.[25]	1958	16	515	Southeast Utah — Jal, N.M.

Source: Compiled from various published sources, including *Oil and Gas Journal*, *The Oil Record*, *Petroleum Week*, and company annual reports.

[a]New construction, 16 inches or more in diameter.

[b]Ownership of the pipeline company as of date shown is indicated by arabic numeral referring to the list of parent companies on the next page.

(continued on next page)

List of Pipeline Company Owners in Appendix A

Detail on ownership, which was exercised through a variety of organizational arrangements, varies according to availability of information from published sources. Affiliations of immediate or intermediate owners are shown in parentheses wherever possible. In the case of multiple ownership lines, especially where more than two companies are involved, percentage shares of ownership may vary considerably.

1. Standard Oil Co. (Ind.)
2. Humble Oil & Refining Co. (SONJ)
3. Sinclair Oil Corp.
4. The Texas Co.
5. Cities Service, Shell, Sinclair, Texas Co.
6. Magnolia Petroleum Co. (Socony-Vacuum)
7. Independent common carrier
8. Shell, Texas Co.
9. Empire Gas and Fuel Co. (Cities Service), Texas Co.
10. Interprovincial Pipe Line Co., (Canadian Shell, Canadian Oil, Imperial (SONJ), etc.)
11. Standard Oil (Ohio), Sun
12. British American Oil, Canadian Shell, Imperial (SONJ), McColl Frontenac (Texas Co.)
13. Standard Oil (N.J.)
14. Pan American Petroleum & Transport Co.
15. British American, Continental, Ohio Oil, Pure, Sinclair
16. Ashland, Crown Central, Nantucket (Eastern States Pet. Co.), Pan American, Phillips, Shell, Sinclair
17. Cities Service, Gulf, Pure, Standard Oil (Ohio), Sun
18. Pure, Sinclair
19. Canadian and U.S. oil companies, producers, investors, etc.
20. Murphy Corp., Northwestern Improvement Co. (Northern Pac. Ry. Co.) Placid Oil Co., Shell
21. Southern Production Co., Woodley Oil Co., and private interest
22. Standard Oil Co. of Texas
23. Ashland, Pure, Sinclair
24. Continental, Gulf, Richfield, Shell, Standard Oil of Calif., Superior Oil
25. Cities Service, Sinclair, Texas Co., Tidewater
26. Cities Service, Gulf, Pure, Standard Oil (Ohio), Sun

APPENDIX B

Principal products[a] pipelines constructed in the United States, 1946–1958.

Pipeline or oil company name	Year completed	Diameter (inches)	Mileage	Connecting points
Great Lakes Pipe Line Co.[1]	1946	6–8	602	El Dorado — Humboldt, Kan. Kansas City — Omaha, Neb. Minn. — N.D.
Humble Pipe Line Co.[2]	1946	8	276	Baytown — Dallas — Fort Worth, Tex.
Phillips Petroleum Co.	1946	12	75	Borger — Wichita, Tex.
Socony-Vacuum Oil Co., Inc.	1946	8–10–12	300	Huntingdon — Pittsburgh, Pa.
Tuscarora Pipe Line Co., Ltd.[3]	1946	10–12	360	Reconversion and looping, New Jersey — Pittsburgh
Warren Petroleum Corp.	1946	6–8	82	Houston area
Wood River Oil & Refining Co.	1946	8	67	Peru — Rockford, Ill.
Great Lakes Pipe Line Co.[1]	1947	8	54	Ponca City — Barnsdall, Okla.
Magnolia Pipe Line Co.[4]	1947	10–12	178	Beaumont — Hearne, Tex.
McKee-La Junta pipeline[16]	1947	6–8	269	McKee, Tex. — La Junta, Col.
Phillips Petroleum Co.	1947	8	120	Borger, Tex. — Richmond, Kan.
Socony-Vacuum Oil Co.	1947	8–10–12	350	Paulsboro, N.J. — Midland, Pa.
Standard Oil Co. (Ind.)	1947	8–10	662	Joliet, Ill. — Moorhead, Minn. — Fargo, N.D.
Sunray Oil Corp. and Wilcox Oil Co.	1947	8	53	Allan — Bristow — Tulsa, Okla.
Texas Pipe Line Co.[5]	1947	10	172	Hearne — Dallas — Fort Worth, Tex.
Great Lakes Pipe Line Co.[1]	1948	8	580	El Dorado — Humboldt, Kan. Barnsdall, Okla. — Kan. City Kan. City — Grand Forks, N.D.
Phillips Petroleum Co. and Shamrock Oil & Gas Corp.	1948	8	115	Borger, Tex. — Paola, Kan., loops
Shell Oil Co.	1948	8	250	Restationing program on North Products pipeline

Company	Year	Diameter	Miles	Route
Sinclair Refining Co.[6]	1948	10	264	Houston — Fort Worth, Tex.
	1948	8	185	Fort Worth — Panova, Okla.
	1948	8	290	Panova, Okla. — Redel, Kan. reconditioning crude line for products
Socony-Vacuum Oil Co., Inc.	1948	8	147	Malvern, Pa. — Binghamton, N.Y.
Texas Pipe Line Co.[5]	1948	10	143	Hearne — Dallas, Tex.
	1948	8	26	Dallas — Fort Worth, Tex.
	1948	6–8	107	Hearne — Austin — San Marcos, Tex.
Triangle Pipe Line Co.[7]	1948	8	141	Carthage, Tex. — Shreveport, La. — El Dorado, Ark.
Wyco Pipe Line Co.[8]	1948	8	267	Casper, Wyo. — Denver, Col.
Alamo Refining Co.	1949	8	23	Sweeney — Freeport, Tex.
Buckeye Pipe Line Co.[9]	1949	8	140	Speedway City, Ind. — Lima, O.
Plantation Pipe Line Co.[10]	1949	8	12	Helena, Ga.
Salt Lake Pipe Line Co.[11]	1949	8	168	Salt Lake, U. — Burley, Id.
	1949	8	152	Burley — Boise, Id.
Sinclair Refining Co.	1949	8	25	Marcus Hook — Philadelphia, Pa.
Standard Oil Co. (Ohio)	1949	8	38	Toledo — Fostoria, O.
Tuscarora Pipe Line Co., Ltd.[3]	1949	10	21	East Waterford, Pa. — West
Buckeye Pipe Line Co.[9]	1950	8	140	Speedway City, Ind. — Lima, O.
Great Lakes Pipe Line Co.[1]	1950	12	1,298	Looping, Tulsa — North
	1950	12	224	Tulsa, Okla. — Kansas City, Kan.
	1950	12	54	Ponca City — Barnsdall, Okla.
	1950	8	48	Tulsa — Cushing, Okla.
	1950	12	77	Sioux City — Hawarden, Ia. — Sioux Falls, S.D.
	1950	12	100	St. Paul — Minn. state line
	1950	12	47	Irvington — Decatur, Neb.
	1950	12	37	Osceola — Des Moines, Ia.
	1950	12	57	South of Bethany across Mississippi R.
	1950	12	142	Atchison, Kan. — Falls City, Neb. — Omaha
	1950	12	253	Kansas City — Des Moines, Ia. and North
Inland Corporation[12]	1950	8	57	Lima — Springfield, O.
Miami Valley Corporation[13]	1950	8	58	Dayton — Cincinnati, O.

APPENDIX B — *continued*

Principal products[a] pipelines constructed in the United States, 1946–1958.

Pipeline or oil company name	Year completed	Diameter (inches)	Mileage	Connecting points
Salt Lake Pipe Line Co.[11]	1950	8	63	Mountain Home — Boise, Id.
	1950	6–8	242	Boise, Id. — Pasco, Wash.
	1950	8	140	Boise, Id. — Baker, Ore.
Susquehanna Pipe Line Co.[14]	1950	8	126	Toledo, O. — Sarnia, Ont. Can.
Tuscarora Oil Co., Ltd.[3]	1950	10	68	Shirley — East Freedom, Pa.
	1950	12	60	Reading — Harrisburg, Pa.
Great Lakes Pipe Line Co.[1]	1951	12	355	Kansas City, Kan. — Omaha, Neb. — Sioux City, Ia. — Sioux Falls, S.D.
	1951	8	107	Des Moines — Iowa City, Ia.
Miami Valley Corp.[13]	1951	8	58	Dayton — Cincinnati, O.
Phillips Pipe Line Co.[15]	1951	10–12	300	Looping, Borger, Tex. — Buffalo, Okla. — Wichita, Kan.
	1951	10	40	Monteau, Cole, Osage, and Gasconde counties, Ill.
	1951	8	198	Looping, East St. Louis — Decatur, Ill.
Phillips-Shamrock Pipe Line[16]	1951	6	155	La Junta — Denver, Col.
Plantation Pipe Line Co.[10]	1951	14–18	707	Baton Rouge, La. — Charlotte, N.C., additional parallel line
Socony-Vacuum Oil Co.	1951	6–8	175	Augusta, Kan. — Kansas City, Mo.
Standard Oil Co. (Ind.)	1951	10	56	Lawrenceville, Ill. — Mount Vernon, Ind., parallel line
Triangle Pipe Line Co.[17]	1951	10	85	El Dorado, Ark. — Mississippi R.
Tuscarora Oil Co., Ltd.[3]	1951	10–12	329	Replacement of line, Tuckerton — Midland, Pa.
U.S. Army Engineers	1951	6	190	Searsport — Limestone, Me.
Buckeye Pipe Line Co.[9]	1952	16	77	Linden, N.J. — Macungie, Pa.
Gulf Refining Co.	1952	6–8	136	Orange — Port Arthur — Texas City, Tex.
Keystone Pipe Line Co.[18]	1952	12	60	Point Breeze, Pa. — Montello

Company	Year	Diameter	Miles	Route
Ohio Oil Co.	1952	8–10	279	Wood River — East St. Louis, Ill. — Indianapolis
Phillips Oil Company	1952	12	27	Sweeney — Freeport, Tex.
	1952	8	50	Goldsmith — Spraberry, Tex.
	1952	8	104	Odessa — Borger, Tex.
Phillips Pipe Line Co.[15]	1952	10	137	Paola, Kan. — East St. Louis, Ill.
Salt Lake Pipe Line Co.[11]	1952	8	329	Salt Lake City, Ut. — Boise, Id.
Shell Oil Co.	1952	8–14	365	Wood River, Ill. — East Chicago, Ind.
Sinclair Pipe Line Co.[6]	1952	6–8	310	Sinclair, Wyo. — Salt Lake City, Ut.
Socony-Vacuum Oil Co.	1952	6–8	175	Augusta, Kan. — Kansas City, Mo.
Standard Oil Co. (Ind.)	1952	12	316	Sugar Creek, Mo. — Dubuque, O.
	1952	8	122	Neodesha, Kan. — Belton, Mo.
Susquehanna Pipe Line Co.[14]	1952	6–8	125	Fostoria — Randolph, O.
Tuscarora Oil Co., Ltd.[3]	1952	12	27	Allentown — Reading, Pa.
Augusta Pipe Line Co.[19]	1953	8	43	Arkansas City — Augusta, Kan. (where connection with Kaneb Pipeline)
Buckeye Pipe Line Co.[9]	1953	8–16	280	Allentown, Pa. — Auburn — Syracuse — Caledonia, N.Y.
Continental Pipe Line Co.[20]	1953	8	593	Billings, Mont. — Spokane, Wash.
Evangeline Pipe Line System[21]	1953	16	194	Baton Rouge, La. — Port Arthur, Tex.
Indiana Farm Bureau Coop. Assoc.	1953	4–8	230	Mount Vernon — Indianapolis — Peru, Ind.
Kaneb Pipe Line Co.[19]	1953	8–10	246	Wichita, Kan. — Fairmont, Neb.
Phillips Petroleum Co.	1953	6–8	36	Spraberry, Tex. — west Texas plant of Plymouth-Beneduum (natural gasoline)
Phillips Pipe Line Co.[15]	1953	12	63	Borger, Tex. — Paola, Kan. loop
	1953	10	44	Loops, Paola, Kan. — East St. Louis, Ill.
Pioneer Pipe Line Co.[22]	1953	8	290	Sinclair, Wyo. — Salt Lake City, Ut.
Plantation Pipe Line Co.[10]	1953	14	82	Charlotte — Greensboro, N.C., loop
Salt Lake Pipe Line Co.[11]	1953	8	140	Pasco — Spokane, Wash.

APPENDIX B — *continued*

Principal products[a] pipelines constructed in the United States, 1946–1958.

Pipeline or oil company name	Year completed	Diameter (inches)	Mileage	Connecting points
Sinclair Pipe Line Co.[6]	1953	12	83	Houston — Port Arthur, Tex.
Standard Oil Co. (Ind.)	1953	10	207	Mandan, N.D. — Moorhead, Minn.
Sun Pipe Line Co.[14]	1953	8	50	Toledo, O. — Inkster Jct, Mich.
Tuscarora Pipe Line Co., Ltd.[3]	1953	12	27	Allentown — Tuckertown, Pa.
Wolverine Pipe Line Co.[23]	1953	16	200	Chicago — Detroit, Mich. — Toledo, O.
Badger Pipe Line Co.[24]	1954	10–12	195	East Chicago, Ind. — Madison, Wis.
Bell Oil and Gas Co.	1954	6–8	140	Ardmore — Cushing, Okla.
Buckeye Pipe Line Co.[9]	1954	8	80	Lima — Columbus, O.
Great Lakes Pipe Line Co.[1]	1954	12	188	Kansas City, Kan. — Des Moines, Ia., loop
	1954	8	130	Iowa City, Ia. — Middlebury, Ill.
	1954	8–12	266	Minneapolis, Minn. — Fargo, N.D., loop
	1954	8	130	Nebraska City — Grand Island, Neb.
Harbor Pipe Line System[21]	1954	16	86	Woodbury Jct. (Phila. area) — Trembly Point, N.J. (N.Y. harbor area)
Inland Corporation[12]	1954	10	38	Toledo — Columbus — Dayton, O.
Cherokee Pipe Line Co.[25]	1954	8	70	Conversion of a purchased crude line (Ajax) to products and 8-mi. extension, Ponca City — Wichita, Okla.
Oil Basin Pipe Line Co.[19]	1954	8	234	Laurel — Billings — Glendive, Mont.
Oklahoma Miss. R. Products Line, Inc.[26]	1954	10–12	475	Duncan, Okla. — West Memphis, Ark.
Phillips Petroleum Co.	1954	8	72	East St. Louis — Kankakee, Ill.
Triangle Pipe Line Co.[17]	1954	12	560	Arkansas City, Ark. — Covington, Ky.
Wyoming-Nebraska Pipe Line Co.[27]	1954	6	220	Cheyenne — North Platte, Neb.
Yellowstone Pipe Line Co.[28]	1954	10	540	Billings, Mont. — Spokane, Wash.

Company	Year	Diameter (in.)	Length (mi.)	Description
Buckeye Pipe Line Co.[9]	1955	8	120	Conversion of crude-oil line Toledo — Cleveland, O.
	1955	8	60	Lima, O. — Fort Wayne, Ind.
	1955	10	14	Wayne — Detroit, Mich.
Great Lakes Pipe Line Co.[1]	1955	12	106	Des Moines, Ia. — Tulsa, Okla.
Keystone Pipe Line Co.[18]	1955	8	49	Westchester — Allentown, Pa.
Okan Pipeline Co.[29]	1955	6	140	Liberal, Kan. — Tulsa, Okla., natural gasoline line
Shell Pipe Line Corp.[30]	1955	12	65	Norco, La. refinery — Baton Rouge, connecting with Plantation Line
Southern Pacific Pipe Lines, Inc.[31]	1955	8	424	El Paso, Tex. — Phoenix, Ariz.
	1955	12–16	418	Los Angeles, Calif. — Phoenix, Ariz.
Standard Oil Co. (Ind.)	1955	8–10	114	Humboldt — Wichita, Kan.
Standard Pipe Line Co.[32]	1955	6–8	248	El Paso, Tex. — Albuquerque, N.M.
Texas-Cities Service Pipe Line Co.[33]	1955	6–8	106	West Tulsa — Cushing — Ponca City, Okla., connecting with Cherokee Pipe Line
Magnolia Pipe Line Co.[34]	1956	8–10	540	Conversion of crude-oil line to L.P.G., Midland — Beaumont, Tex.
	1956	12–20	203	Looping, Midland — Beaumont, Tex.
Phillips Petroleum Co.	1956	12	139	Looping, Borger, Tex. — St. Louis, Mo.
Plantation Pipe Line Co.[10]	1956	18	327	New line, Baton Rouge, La. — Helena, Ala.
Sohio Petroleum Co.[35]	1956	8	37	Mogadore — Girard, O.
Southern Pacific Pipe Lines, Inc.[31]	1956	6	176	Laterals from main system Los Angeles — Phoenix, to supply air bases
Sun Pipe Line Co.[14]	1956	14	109	Marcus Hook, Pa. — Newark, N.J., replacement
Atlantic Pipe Line Co. Eureka Pipe Line Co. National Transit Co. Southern Pipe Line Co.	1957	—	—	Linkage of these 4 lines to carry products from Philadelphia to Pittsburgh as of Jan. 15, 1957. First use of Eureka, National Transit, and Southern Pipe Line as products carriers. Atlantic tie-in with Southern at Brookhaven, Pa., Southern Pipe Line joining Eureka near Morgantown, W.V. Eureka tie-in with National Transit at Waynesburg, Pa.

APPENDIX B — *continued*

Principal products[a] pipelines constructed in the United States, 1946–1958.

Pipeline or oil company name	Year completed	Diameter (inches)	Mileage	Connecting points
Buckeye Pipe Line Co.[9]	1957	8	116	Huntington — Griffith, Ind., conversion to products line.
	1957	8	32	Conversion of crude-oil line between Mantua and Youngstown, O.
Emerald Pipe Line Corp.[36]	1957	6	120	Sunray, Tex. — Tucumcari, N.M.
Great Lakes Pipe Line Co.[1]	1957	8	165	Minneapolis, Minn. — Superior, Wis.
Gulf Refining Co.[37]	1957	10	530	L.P.G. line from Waddell, Tex. — Houston, conversion of crude-oil line.
Northwest Pipe Line Corp.[38]	1957	8–10	350	Products and crude-oil carrier, Four Corners area — Salt Lake City, Ut.
Southern Pacific Pipe Line Co.[31]	1957	6–8–10	315	Richmond, Calif. — Fallon, Neb.
Yellowstone Pipe Line Co.[28]	1957	8	22	Spokane area, Wash.
Buckeye Pipe Line Co.[9]	1958	10	51	Syracuse — Utica, N.Y.
	1958	8	70	Wayne — Durand, Mich.
Clark Oil and Refining Corp.	1958	8	15	Blue Island — Hammond, Ind.
Cherokee Pipe Line Co.[25]	1958	12	78	Ponca City — Tulsa, Okla.
Conn.-Mass. Pipe Line, Inc.[19]	1958	6–8	69	New Haven, Conn. — Springfield, Mass.
El Paso Natural Gas Co.	1958	6	240	Odessa — El Paso, Tex.
Everglades Pipe Line Co.[39]	1958	10	60	Port Everglades, Fla. — Miami International Airport and terminals south
Laurel Pipe Line Co.[21]	1958	14–24	440	Philadelphia, Pa. — Cleveland, O.
Little Big Inch Pipe Line[17] conversion to products	1958 1958	20 14	1,168 230	Baytown, Tex. — Moundsville, W. Va. Lateral to Chicago
Ohio Oil Co.	1958	12	350	Wood River and Robinson — Chicago, Ill.

Salt Lake Pipe Line Co.[11]	1958	8	80	Loops, Adams — Ontario, Ore.
Wabash Pipe Line[40]	1958	12	265	Wood River — Chicago, Ill.
West Emerald Pipe Line[36]	1958	6	300	Albuquerque, N.M. — Tucumcari, with branches to McKee and Amarillo, Tex.

Source: Compiled from various published sources, including *Oil and Gas Journal, The Oil Record, Petroleum Week,* and company annual reports.

[a]New construction, 8 inches or more in diameter. In a few instances 6-inch diameter construction is shown where the line served a new market.

[b]Ownership of pipeline company as of date shown is indicated by arabic numeral referring to the list of parent companies on the next page.

(continued on next page)

List of Pipeline Company Owners in Appendix B

Detail on ownership, which was exercised through a variety of organizational arrangements, varies according to availability of information from published sources. Affiliations of immediate or intermediate owners are shown in parentheses wherever possible. In the case of multiple ownership lines, percentage shares of ownership may vary considerably.

1. Cities Service, Continental, Mid-Continent Petroleum, Phillips, Pure, Sinclair, Skelly, Texas Co.
2. Humble Oil & Refining Co. (SONJ)
3. Esso Standard Oil Co. (SONJ)
4. Magnolia Petroleum Co. (Socony-Vacuum)
5. The Texas Co.
6. Sinclair Oil Corp.
7. Chicago Corp. and Triangle Refineries, Inc.
8. Socony-Vacuum, Standard Oil (Ind.), Texas Co.
9. Independent common carrier
10. Shell, Standard Oil (Ky.), Standard Oil (N.J.)
11. Salt Lake Refining Co. (S.O. Calif.)
12. Shell, Standard Oil (Ohio)
13. Pure, Standard Oil (Ohio)
14. Sun Oil Co.
15. Phillips Petroleum Co.
16. Phillips Petroleum Co., Shamrock Oil and Gas Corp.
17. Texas Eastern Transmission Co.
18. Atlantic Refining Co.
19. Privately owned
20. Continental Oil Co.
21. Gulf, Sinclair, and Texas Co.
22. Continental, Sinclair
23. Cities Service, Shell, Texas Co.
24. Cities Service, Pure, Sinclair, Texas Co.
25. Continental, Cities Service
26. Sunray-Midcontinent and private interests
27. Frontier Refining Co.
28. Continental, Interstate Pipe Line Co. (SONJ), Union Oil Co. of Calif., and private interest
29. Warren Petroleum Co.
30. Shell Oil Co.
31. Southern Pacific Co.
32. Standard Oil Co. of Calif.
33. Empire Oil & Gas Co. (Cities Service), Texas Co.
34. Magnolia Petroleum Co. (Socony-Mobil)
35. Standard Oil Co. (Ohio)
36. Shamrock Oil and Gas Corp.
37. Gulf Oil Corp.
38. Pacific Northwest Pipe Line Corp.
39. Buckeye Pipe Line Co., Cities Service
40. Continental Oil, Ohio Oil

BIBLIOGRAPHY

BOOKS AND PAMPHLETS

Adams, Walter, and Horace M. Gray. *Monopoly in America: The Government as Promoter.* New York : Macmillan, 1955.

American Petroleum Institute. *Petroleum Facts and Figures: Centennial Edition, 1959.* New York: American Petroleum Institute, 1959.

————. *Petroleum-Industry Hearings Before the Temporary National Economic Committee.* New York: American Petroleum Institute, 1942.

Arnold, Ralph, and William J. Kemnitzer. *Petroleum in the United States and Possessions.* New York: Harper, 1931.

Bain, Joe S. *The Economics of the Pacific Coast Petroleum Industry,* Part I: *Market Structure.* Part II: *Price Behavior and Competition.* Part III: *Public Policy Toward Competition and Pricing.* Berkeley: Bureau of Business and Economic Research, University of California, 1944, 1945, and 1947.

Beard, William. *Regulation of Pipe Lines as Common Carriers.* New York: Columbia University Press, 1941.

Beaton, Kendall. *Enterprise in Oil: A History of Shell in the United States.* New York: Appleton-Century-Crofts, 1957.

Bell, Harold S., ed. *Petroleum Transportation Handbook.* New York: McGraw-Hill, 1963.

Buckeye Pipe Line Company. *The Flow of Oil: The Story of the Buckeye Pipe Line Company and Its 75 Years of Service to the Petroleum Industry.* New York: The Company, 1961.

Connelly, W. L. *The Oil Business As I Saw It: Half a Century with Sinclair.* Norman, Okla.: University of Oklahoma Press, 1954.

Cook, Roy C. *Control of the Petroleum Industry by Major Oil Companies.* TNEC Monograph 39. Washington: Government Printing Office, 1941.

Cookenboo, Leslie, Jr. *Crude Oil Pipe Lines and Competition in the Oil Industry.* Cambridge, Mass.: Harvard University Press, 1955.

Dow, F. B., and D. C. O'Hara. *The National Petroleum Association, 1902–1952.* Washington: National Petroleum Association, 1952.

Farish, W. S., and J. Howard Pew. *Review and Criticism on Behalf of Standard Oil Co. (New Jersey) and Sun Oil Co. of Monograph No. 39 with Rejoinder by Monograph Author.* TNEC Monograph 39-A. Washington: Government Printing Office, 1941.

Gibb, George S., and Evelyn H. Knowlton. *History of the Standard Oil Company (New Jersey): The Resurgent Years, 1911–1927.* New York: Harper & Bros., 1956.

Giddens, Paul H. *Standard Oil Company (Indiana): Oil Pioneer of the Middle West.* New York: Appleton-Century-Crofts, Inc., 1955.

Hardwicke, Robert E. *Antitrust Laws, et al. v. Unit Operation of Oil or Gas Pools.* New York: American Institute & Mining and Metallurgical Engineers, 1948.

Hidy, Ralph W., and Muriel E. Hidy. *History of Standard Oil Company (New Jersey): Pioneering in Big Business, 1882–1911.* New York: Harper & Bros., 1955.

Hildebrand, Ira P. *The Law of Texas Corporations.* Kansas City, Mo.: Vernon, 1942.

Humble Pipe Line Company. *The Story of Humble Pipe Line Company.* Published by the company, n.d.

496 / Bibliography

Humphrey, William D. "The Ohio Oil Company, 1887–1937." Findlay, O.: n.d. (mimeo)

Ickes, Harold L. *The Secret Diary of Harold L. Ickes: Vol. I, The First Thousand Days, 1933–1936.* New York: Simon and Schuster, 1953.

James, Marquis. *The Texaco Story: The First 50 Years, 1902–1952.* New York?: The Texas Company, 1953.

Johnson, Arthur M. *The Development of American Petroleum Pipelines.* Ithaca, N.Y. Cornell University Press, 1956.

———. *Government-Business Relations: A Pragmatic Approach to the American Experience.* Columbus, O.: Charles E. Merrill Books, 1965.

Kendrick, John W. *Productivity Trends in the United States.* National Bureau of Economic Research #7, General Series. Princeton, N.J.: Princeton University Press, 1961.

Knowles, Ruth S. *The Greatest Gamblers: The Epic of American Oil Exploration.* New York: McGraw-Hill, 1959.

La Follette, Belle Case, and Fola La Follette. *Robert M. La Follette, June 14, 1855 — June 18, 1925.* 2 vols. New York: Macmillan, 1953.

Larson, Henrietta M., and Kenneth W. Porter. *History of Humble Oil & Refining Company: A Study in Industrial Growth.* New York: Harper & Bros., 1959.

Editors of *Look. Oil for Victory.* New York: McGraw, 1946.

Loos, John L. *Oil on Stream! A History of the Interstate Oil Pipe Line Company, 1909–1959.* Baton Rouge: Louisiana State University Press, 1959.

McLean, John G., and Robert W. Haigh. *The Growth of Integrated Oil Companies.* Boston: Harvard University Graduate School of Business Administration, Division of Research, 1954.

Massie, Joseph L., *Blazer and Ashland Oil: A Study in Management.* Lexington, Ky.: University of Kentucky Press, 1960.

Mathews, John J. *Life and Death of an Oilman: The Career of E. W. Marland.* Norman, Okla.: University of Oklahoma Press, 1951.

Mellon, W. L. *Judge Mellon's Sons.* Pittsburgh: privately printed, 1948.

Murphy, Blakely M., ed. *Conservation of Oil and Gas: A Legal History, 1948.* Chicago: Section of Mineral Law, American Bar Association, 1949.

National Petroleum Council. *A Unique Experience in Government-Industry Cooperation: The First Seven Years, 1946–1953.* Washington: National Petroleum Council, 1961.

Pogue, Joseph E. *The Economics of Petroleum.* New York: John Wiley & Sons, 1921.

Rister, Carl C. *Oil! Titan of the Southwest.* Norman, Okla.: University of Oklahoma Press, 1949.

Rosenam, S. I., ed. *The Public Papers and Addresses of Franklin D. Roosevelt.* 13 vols. New York: Random House and others, 1938–1950.

Rostow, Eugene V. *A National Policy for the Oil Industry.* New Haven: Yale University Press, 1948.

Scoville, John, and Noel Sargent, comp. *Fact and Fancy in the T.N.E.C. Monographs.* New York: National Association of Manufacturers, 1942.

Sharfman, I. L. *The Interstate Commerce Commission.* 5 vols. New York: The Commonwealth Fund, 1931–1937.

Spence, Hartzell. *Portrait in Oil.* New York: McGraw-Hill, 1962.

Thompson, Craig. *Since Spindletop: A Human Story of Gulf's First Half-Century.* Pittsburgh?: Gulf Oil Corporation, 1951.

Warner, C. A. *Texas Oil and Gas Since 1543.* Houston: Gulf Publishing Company, 1939.

Werner, Morris R., and John Starr. *Teapot Dome.* New York: Viking Press, 1959.

White, Gerald T. *Formative Years in the Far West: A History of Standard Oil Company of California and Predecessors through 1919.* New York: Appleton-Century-Crofts, 1962.

Williamson, Harold F., and Arnold R. Daum. *The American Petroleum Industry: The*

Age of Illumination, 1859–1899. Evanston, Ill.: Northwestern University Press, 1959.

Williamson, H. F., R. L. Andreano, A. R. Daum, and G. C. Klose. *The American Petroleum Industry: The Age of Energy, 1899–1959.* Evanston, Ill.: Northwestern University Press, 1963.

Wilson, Neill C., and Frank J. Taylor. *The Building of Trans Mountain: Canada's First Oil Pipeline Across the Rockies.* Vancouver, B.C.: Trans Mountain Oil Pipe Line Company, 1954.

Wolbert, George S., Jr. *American Pipe Lines.* Norman, Okla.: University of Oklahoma Press, 1951.

Zimmermann, Erich W. *Conservation in the Production of Petroleum: A Study in Industrial Control.* New Haven: Yale University Press, 1957.

ARTICLES

Atwood, Albert W. "The Greatest Killing in Wall Street," *McClure's Magazine*, XXXIX (August 1912), 409–419.

Barde, F. S. "The Oil Fields and Pipe Lines of Kansas," *The Outlook*, LXXX (May 6, 1905), 19–32.

Black, Forrest R. "Oil Pipe Line Divorcement by Litigation and Legislation," *Cornell Law Quarterly*, XXV (June 1940), 510–536.

Blum, John M. "Theodore Roosevelt and the Hepburn Act: Toward an Orderly System of Control," in Elting E. Morison, ed. *Letters of Theodore Roosevelt.* 8 vols. Cambridge, Mass.: Harvard University Press, 1951–1954, VI, 1558–1571.

Bruce, Andrew A. "The Supreme Court and the Standard Oil Case," *Central Law Journal*, LXXIII (August 18, 1911), 111–119.

Ellsworth, Catherine C. "Integration Into Crude Oil Transportation in the 1930's," *Business History Review* XXXV (Summer 1961), 180–210.

Finney, Wallace R., and J. B. Adoue. "The 'Big Inch' Pipe Line," *Mining and Metallurgy* (October 1943), 440–445.

German, W. P. Z. "Legal History of Conservation of Oil and Gas in Oklahoma," in *Legal History of Conservation of Oil and Gas, A Symposium.* Chicago: American Bar Association, 1938, pp. 110–213.

Jenks, Jeremiah W. "Economic Aspect of the Recent Decisions of the United States Supreme Court on Trusts," *The Journal of Political Economy*, XX (April 1912), 346–357.

Johnson, Arthur M. "Theodore Roosevelt and the Bureau of Corporations," *Mississippi Valley Historical Review*, XLV (March 1959), 575–584.

Kahle, Loren F. "Continued Increased Petroleum Demands," *Oil and Gas Journal*, LI (October 13, 1952), 198–200.

Platt, Warren C. "Oil Business Too Big For Probers To Grasp," *National Petroleum News,* XV (January 24, 1923), 23.

Ralph, Henry D. "Investigations Reflect Policy of Department of Justice," *Oil and Gas Journal,* XXXVIII (May 25, 1939), 20–21.

Ralph, Henry D. "Petroleum Industry War Council at Work," *Oil and Gas Journal,* XLI (June 11, 1942), 16–19, 30.

Rostow, Eugene V., and Arthur S. Sachs. "Entry into the Oil Refining Business: Vertical Integration Re-Examined," *Yale Law Journal,* LXI (June-July 1952), 856–914.

"The Standard Oil and Tobacco Trust Decisions," *Bench and Bar,* XXV (June 1911), 89–95.

"Standard Oil at 900," *Literary Digest,* XLIV (March 30, 1912), 664.

"The Standard Oil Decision," *The Green Bag,* XXIII (June 1911), 279–284.

Swigart, T. E. "Postwar Uses of the War Emergency Pipe Lines for Petroleum Transportation," *Petroleum Technology* (September 1944).

Williamson, Harold R., and Ralph L. Andreano. "Competitive Structure of the American Petroleum Industry, 1880–1911: A Reappraisal," in *Oil's First Century.*

Papers given at the Centennial Seminar on the History of the Petroleum Industry, Harvard Business School, November 1959. Boston: Harvard University Graduate School of Business Administration, 1960, pp. 71–84.

Young, F. R. "Applied Design and Economies of Pipe Lines," *Oil and Gas Journal,* XXXIII (November 8, 1934), 38–42.

INDUSTRY PAPERS, PAMPHLETS, AND REPORTS

American Petroleum Institute, Division of Transportation. "Design Features of the Laurel Pipe Line System." *Report on the Annual Pipe Line Conference,* May 1959.

Association of American Railroads, Railroad Committee for the Study of Transportation. "Report by Subcommittee on Pipe Line Transportation." Washington: 1944. (mimeo)

Boice, John E. (Special assistant to the Director, Supply and Transportation Division, Petroleum Administration for Defense). "Keeping Oil Flowing for National Defense." API Conference on Products Pipeline Technology, Fort Worth, Texas, April 21, 1952. (mimeo)

De Groot, John W. "History and Development of Products Pipe Lines." American Petroleum Institute, *Proceedings of the Twenty-Ninth Annual Meeting.* Chicago: November 7–10, 1949.

Dunn, E. B. "Microwave Communications for Pipeline Use." Paper given at API Products Pipe Line Technology Conference, St. Louis, September 11–13, 1950.

Ferris, R. E. "Texas Corporation and Anti-Trust Law, 1895–1917, and Their Effect on the Oil Industry, Particularly the Humble Oil and Refining Co. and Standard Oil (N.J.)." Paper presented at the Business History Foundation Conference, Saybrook, Conn., September 18, 1948.

Lennart, R. P., Service Pipe Line. "Pipelining Crude Oil." Paper at 15th Joint Technical Meeting, April 20, 1957.

National Petroleum Council. *Report of the Committee on Oil and Gas Transportation Facilities.* Washington: October 4, 1962.

Planning and Coordination Committee for the Petroleum Industry. "Report upon Pipe Line Practices, Rates and Related Subjects." 1934. (mimeo)

Swigart, T. E. "Oil's Wartime Achievements in Transportation." Paper presented at Southwestern District Meeting of American Petroleum Institute, April 29, 1943.

Unruh, Earl W. "Converting a Pipe Line from Crude Oil Service to Refined Products Service" American Petroleum Institute, Division of Transportation, Products Pipe Line Conference, Atlanta, May 21, 1951. (mimeo)

War Emergency Pipelines, Inc. *Fuel for the Fighting Fronts . . . via "Big Inch" and "Little Big Inch."* New York: War Emergency Pipelines, Inc., 1944.

CONGRESSIONAL DOCUMENTS

59 Cong., 2 Sess. H. Document 606. *Railroad Discrimination and Monopolies in Coal and Oil.* Washington: Government Printing Office, 1907.

63 Cong., 2 Sess. House Committee on Interstate and Foreign Commerce. "Transportation of Oil by Pipe Lines." *Hearings.* Washington: Government Printing Office, 1914.

67 Cong., 2 and 4 Sess. Senate Subcommittee of the Committee on Manufactures (La Follette Committee). "High Cost of Gasoline and Other Petroleum Products." *Hearings.* 2 vols. Washington: Government Printing Office, 1923.

70 Cong., 1 Sess. S. Doc. 61. *Petroleum Industry: Prices, Profits, and Competition.* Washington: Government Printing Office, 1928.

71 Cong., 3 Sess. House Committee on Interstate and Foreign Commerce. "Pipe Lines." *Hearings* on H.R. 16695. Washington: Government Printing Office, 1931.

72 Cong., 2 Sess. House Committee on Interstate and Foreign Commerce (W.M.W. Splawn). *Report on Pipe Lines* (House Report No. 2192). 2 vols. Washington: Government Printing Office, 1933.

73 Cong. Recess. House Subcommittee of the Committee on Interstate and Foreign Commerce. "Petroleum Investigation." *Hearings*. Washington: Government Printing Office, 1934.

76 Cong., 1 Sess. Senate Committee on Interstate Commerce. "Transportation Act of 1939." *Hearings*. Washington: Government Printing Office, 1939.

77 Cong., 2 Sess. Senate Committee on Finance. "Revenue Act of 1942." *Hearings*. Washington: Government Printing Office, 1942.

78 Cong., 1 Sess. House Select Committee to Conduct a Study and Investigation of the National Defense Program in Its Relation to Small Business in the United States. "A Study and Investigation of the National Defense Program in Its Relation to Small Business." *Hearings*. Washington: Government Printing Office, 1943.

79 Cong., 1 Sess. House Select Committee to Investigate Disposition of Surplus Property. "Investigation, Disposition of Surplus Property." *Hearings*. 3 vols. Washington: Government Printing Office, 1946.

79 Cong., 2 Sess. House Select Committee to Investigate Disposition of Surplus Property. *Second Interim Report*. Washington: Government Printing Office, 1946.

79 Cong., 1 Sess. Senate Committee on Military Affairs. "War Emergency Pipe-Line Systems and Other Petroleum Facilities." *Hearings before the Special Committee Investigating Petroleum Resources and the Surplus Property Subcommittee . . .* Washington: Government Printing Office, 1945.

79 Cong., 1 Sess. Senate Committee on Military Affairs. "War Emergency Pipe-Line Systems and Other Petroleum Facilities." *Report to the Special Committee Investigating Petroleum Resources and to the Surplus Property Subcommittee of the Committee on Military Affairs*. Washington: Government Printing Office, 1945.

79 Cong. 1 Sess. Senate Special Committee Investigating Petroleum Resources. "Investigation of Petroleum Resources." *Hearings, June 1945*. Washington: Government Printing Office, 1946.

79 Cong., 2 Sess. Senate Committee on Military Affairs. "War-Plants Disposal: Bids for Big Inch and Little Big Inch Pipe Lines." *Report of the Surplus Property Subcommittee*. Washington: Government Printing Office, 1946.

79 Cong., 2 Sess. Senate Special Committee Investigating Petroleum Resources. "The Independent Petroleum Company." *Hearings, March 1946*. Washington: Government Printing Office, 1946.

81 Cong., 1 Sess. Senate Special Committee to Study Problems of American Small Business (Wherry Committee). "Oil Supply and Distribution Problems." *Final Report*. Washington: Government Printing Office, 1949.

81 Cong., 2 Sess. House Committee on the Judiciary, Subcommittee on Study of Monopoly Power. "Study of Monopoly Power." *Hearings*. Washington: Government Printing Office, 1950.

81 Cong., 2 Sess. House Committee on Ways and Means. "Revenue Revision of 1950." *Hearings*. Washington: Government Printing Office, 1950.

82 Cong., 1 Sess. House Committee on Interstate and Foreign Commerce. *Report . . . Consenting to Extension of the Interstate Compact to Conserve Oil and Gas*. Washington: Government Printing Office, 1951.

84 Cong., 2 Sess. House Committee on Ways and Means. "Excise Taxes." *Hearings*. Washington: Government Printing Office, 1957.

85 Cong., 1 Sess. House Committee on Interstate and Foreign Commerce. "Petroleum Survey: 1957 Outlook, Oil Lift to Europe, Price Increases." *Preliminary Report*. Washington: Government Printing Office, 1957.

85 Cong., 1 Sess. House Committee on the Judiciary. "Consent Decree Program of the Department of Justice." *Hearings before the Antitrust Subcommittee* (Subcommittee No. 5). Part I, *Oil Pipelines*. 2 vols. Washington: Government Printing Office, 1957–1958.

85 Cong., 1 Sess. House Committee on the Judiciary. *Report of the Antitrust Subcommittee (Subcommittee No. 5) on Consent Decree Program of the Department of Justice*. Washington: Government Printing Office, 1959.

85 Cong., 1 Sess. Senate Committee on the Judiciary, Subcommittee on Antitrust and Monopoly. "Petroleum; the Antitrust Laws and Government Policies." *Report . . . with Minority Views*. Washington: Government Printing Office, 1957.

85 Cong., 1 Sess. Senate Subcommittee of the Committee on the Judiciary and Committee on Interior and Insular Affairs. "Emergency Oil Lift Program and Related Oil Problems." *Joint Hearings*. Washington: Government Printing Office, 1957.

UNITED STATES GOVERNMENT PUBLICATIONS

Attorney General. *First [and Second] Report[s] of the Attorney General Pursuant to Section 2 of the Joint Resolution of July 28, 1955, Consenting to an Interstate Compact to Conserve Oil and Gas*. Washington: Government Printing Office, 1956, 1957.

Bureau of Corporations. *Conditions in the Healdton Oil Field*. Washington: Government Printing Office, 1915.

————. *Report of the Commissioner of Corporations on the Petroleum Industry,* Part I: *Position of the Standard Oil Company in the Petroleum Industry*. Washington: Government Printing Office, 1907.

————. *Report of the Commissioner of Corporations on the Transportation of Petroleum*. Washington: Government Printing Office, 1906.

Bureau of Mines. *Information Circulars:* No. 6011 (1926), No. 7769 (1956), No. 7942 (1959). Washington: Government Printing Office.

————. *Transportation of Gasoline by Pipe Line*. Technical Paper 517. Washington: Government Printing Office, 1932.

————. *United States Government Specifications for Lubricants and Liquid Fuels and Methods for Testing*. Technical Paper 323A. Washington: Government Printing Office, 1924.

Congressional Record. Washington: Government Printing Office, irregular.

Department of the Interior. *An Appraisal of the Petroleum Industry*. Washington: Government Printing Office, 1965.

————. *Oil Lands in Indian Territory and Territory of Oklahoma*. Hearings before the Secretary of the Interior on Leasing of Oil Lands and Natural-Gas Wells in Indian Territory and Territory of Oklahoma. Washington: Government Printing Office, 1906.

Federal Co-ordinator of Transportation, Office of. *Public Aids to Transportation*. 2 parts, 4 vols. Washington: Government Printing Office, 1940.

Federal Trade Commission. *The Advance in Price of Petroleum Products*. Washington: Government Printing Office, 1920.

————. *Foreign Ownership in the Petroleum Industry*. Washington: Government Printing Office, 1923.

————. *Investigation of the Price of Gasoline*. Washington: Government Printing Office, 1916.

————. *Pacific Coast Petroleum Industry*. 2 parts. Washington: Government Printing Office, 1921.

————. *Petroleum Industry of Wyoming*. Washington: Government Printing Office, 1921.

————. *Petroleum Trade in Wyoming and Montana*. Washington: Government Printing Office, 1922.

————. *Report on Pipe-Line Transportation of Petroleum*. Washington: Government Printing Office, 1916.

————. *Report on the Petroleum Industry: Prices, Profits, and Competition*. Washington: Government Printing Office, 1928.

————. *Report on the Price of Gasoline in 1915*. Washington: Government Printing Office, 1917.

Frey, John W., and H. Chandler Ide, eds. *A History of the Petroleum Administration for War, 1941–1945.* Washington: Government Printing Office, 1946.

Geological Survey, *Mineral Resources of the United States.* Washington: Government Printing Office, 1906–1915.

Interstate Commerce Commission. *Annual Reports.* Washington: Government Printing Office, annually.

———. *ICC Activities, 1937–1962: Supplement to the 75th Annual Report.* Washington: Government Printing Office, 1962.

———. *A Review of Statistics of Oil Pipe Lines, 1921–1941.* Washington: Government Printing Office, 1942.

———. *Selected Financial and Operating Statistics from Annual Reports of Pipe Line Companies.* Washington: Government Printing Office, 1921–1959.

———. *Statistics of Oil Pipe Line Companies.* Washington: Government Printing Office, annually.

Petroleum Administration for Defense. *Transportation of Oil.* Washington: Government Printing Office, 1951.

Petroleum Administration for War. *A History of the Petroleum Administration for War, 1941–1945.* Washington: Government Printing Office, 1946.

———. "History, Petroleum Pipeline Transportation as of September 30, 1945." Washington: October 1945. (mimeo)

Surplus Property Administration. *Government-Owned Pipe Lines: Report . . . to the Congress* (January 4, 1946). Washington: Government Printing Office, 1946.

Temporary National Economic Committee. *Verbatim Record of the Proceedings of the Temporary National Economic Committee.* 14 vols. Washington: Government Printing Office, 1939.

War Assets Administration. *Quarterly Progress Report to the Congress.* Washington: Government Printing Office, 1946–1947.

COURT CASES

Alfred MacMillan et al. v. Railroad Commission of Texas, 51 F 2d 400 (1931).

Associated Pipe Line Company v. Railroad Commission of California, 176 Cal. 518 (1917).

Atchison, Topeka & Santa Fe Railroad v. Railroad Commission of California, 173 Calif. 577 (1916).

Champlin Refining Company v. United States et al., 329 U.S. 29 (1946).

Danciger Oil and Refining Company v. Railroad Commission of Texas et al., 49 S.W. 2d 837 (Texas Civ. App., 1932).

Federal Power Commission v. Hope Natural Gas Company, 320 U.S. 591 (1944).

ICC v. United States ex rel. Los Angeles, 280 U.S. 52, 74 L. Ed. 163 (1929).

In re Champlin Refining Company, 129 Okla. 166, 264 Pac. Rep. 160 (1927).

Missouri Pacific v. Nebraska, 164 U.S. 403, 17 Sup. Ct. 130 (1896).

National Pipe Line Co. v. United States, 48 F. Supp. 655 (1934).

National Transit Co. v. Weston et al., 121 Pa. 485 (1888).

Northern Pacific Railroad v. North Dakota, 236 U.S. 585, 35 Sup. Ct. 429 (1915).

Northern Securities Co. v. United States, 193 U.S. 197 (1904).

Panama Refining Co. v. Ryan, 293 U.S. 388 (1935).

Pierce Oil Corporation v. Phoenix Refining Co., 259 U.S. 125 (1922).

Prairie Oil & Gas Co. v. United States, 204 Fed. 789 (Com. Ct., 1913).

Producers' Transportation Company v. Railroad Commission of California, 251 U.S. 228 (1920).

Ramsey et al. v. Tod, 69 S.W. 133 (1902).

Samuel Griffin v. South West Pennsylvania Pipe Lines, 172 Pa. 580 (1896).

Standard Oil Company of New Jersey et al. v. United States, 221 U.S. 1 (1911).

Standard Oil Company of New Jersey et al., Appellants, against United States of America, Appellee, Brief for Appellants. 2 vols. New York, 1909?

State v. Humble Oil and Refining Company, 263 S.W. 319 (Texas Civ. App., 1924).
State of Washington ex rel. Oregon Railroad and Navigation Company v. Fairchild et al., 224 U.S. 510, 32 Sup. Ct. 535 (1912).
The Pipe Line Cases, 234 U.S. 548 (1914).
United States v. Atlantic Refining Co. et al., 360 U.S. 19 (1959).
United States et al. v. Champlin Refining Co., 341 U.S. 290 (1951).
United States v. Socony-Vacuum Oil Co., 310 U.S. 150 (1940).
United States v. South Buffalo Ry. Co., 333 U.S. 771 (1948).
United States v. Standard Oil Co. of New Jersey et al., 173 Fed. Rep. 177 (1909).
United States of America, petitioner, v. Standard Oil Company of New Jersey et al., defendants . . . 23 vols. Washington: Government Printing Office, 1908–1910.
Valvoline Oil Co. v. United States, 308 U.S. 141 (1939).
W. W. Cargill Co. v. Minnesota, 180 U.S. 452 (1901).

CIVIL ACTIONS

United States v. The Atlantic Refining Company et al., Civil Action No. 14060. Final Judgment (D.C., District of Columbia, December 23, 1941) and Official Transcript, March 25, 1958.
United States v. Great Lakes Pipe Line Co., Civil Action No. 183 (D.C., Delaware, September 30, 1940).
United States v. Phillips Petroleum Company and Phillips Pipeline Company, Civil Action No. 182 (D.C., Delaware, September 30, 1940).
United States v. Standard Oil Company of California, Civil Action No. 11584-C (Southern District of California, May 12, 1950).
United States v. Standard Oil Company (Indiana), Civil Action No. 201 (D.C., Northern District of Indiana, Hammond Division, September 30, 1940).
United States v. Standard Oil Company of New Jersey, Civil Action No. 86-27 (Southern District of New York, June 8, 1953).

ICC DECISIONS

Brundred Brothers v. Prairie Pipe Line Company et al., 68 ICC 458 (1922).
Champlin Refining Company Accounts and Reports, 274 ICC 409 (1949).
Crude Petroleum Oil from Kansas and Oklahoma, 59 ICC 483 (1920).
Depreciation Charges of Telephone Companies; Depreciation Charges of Steam Railroad Companies, 118 ICC 295 (1926).
In Re Conditions Affecting the Production, Transportation, and Marketing of Crude Petroleum, 36 ICC (1915).
In the Matter of Pipe Lines, 24 ICC 1 (1912).
Increased Freight Rates, 270 ICC 403 (1948).
Mid-Continent Oil Rates, 36 ICC 109 (1915).
Minnelusa Oil Corporation et al. v. Continental Pipe Line Company et al., 258 ICC 41 (1944).
Petroleum From Los Angeles and El Paso to Arizona and New Mexico, 287 ICC 731 (1953).
Petroleum Rail Shippers' Association v. Alton & Southern Railroad et al., 243 ICC 589 (1941).
Reduced Pipe Line Rates and Gathering Charges, 243 ICC 115 (1940); 272 ICC 375 (1948).
Winona Oil Company v. Director General, Atchison, Topeka & Santa Fe Railway Co., 57 ICC 152 (1920).

ICC VALUATION REPORTS

Ajax Pipeline Company, 48 ICC Valuation Reports 153 (1939).
Champlin Refining Company, Valuation of Pipe Line, 49 ICC Valuation Reports 463 (1942).

Champlin Refining Company, Valuation of Pipe Line, 49 ICC *Valuation Reports* 542 (1944).
Gulf Pipe Line Company, 47 ICC *Valuation Reports* 774 (1938).
Gulf Pipe Line Company of Oklahoma et al., 48 ICC *Valuation Reports* 501 (1939).
Magnolia Pipe Line Company, 48 ICC *Valuation Reports* 775 (1939).
Petition of the Valvoline Oil Company in the Matter of the Valuation of Its Pipe Lines, 48 ICC *Valuation Reports* 10 (1938).
Sinclair Prairie Pipeline Company et al., 47 ICC *Valuation Reports* 613 (1937).
Stanolind Pipeline Company, 48 ICC *Valuation Reports* 678 (1939).
Texas-Empire Pipe Line Company et al., 48 ICC *Valuation Reports* 327 (1939).

STATE REGULATORY COMMISSIONS

Louisiana Public Service Commission Order No. 118. *Louisiana Public Service Commission v. Standard Oil Company of Louisiana et al.* April 14, 1923.
Railroad Commission of Texas. *Before the Railroad Commission of Texas. In re: In the Matter of the General Inquiry into the Status, Facilities, Extensions, Capacities, and Practices of Common Carriers of Crude Oil In Texas and Related Matters. Brief for Petitioners,* 1957.
————*Special Order Pertaining to the General Inquiry into the Status, Facilities, Extensions, Capacities, and Practices of Pipe Line Common Carriers of Crude Oil in the State of Texas, June 4, 1958.*
————Oil and Gas Docket 138. Order Amending Rule Number Nine, Oil and Gas Circular Number Ten. August 31, 1933.
————Oil and Gas Docket 139. Order Fixing and Establishing Rates of Charges for Gathering, Transporting, Loading, and Delivering Crude Petroleum by Common Carrier Pipe Lines in this State. August 31, 1933.
————"The Statewide Hearing," December 19, 1956. Transcript of Testimony.

INVESTMENT ADVISORY SERVICE PUBLICATIONS

Moody's Manual of Railroad and Corporation Securities. New York: Poor's Publishing Company, 1912–1924.
Poor's Manual of Industrials: Manufacturing, Mining and Miscellaneous Companies. New York: Poor's Railroad Manual Co., 1914–1918.
Redmond, G. F., and Company. *Sinclair vs. Cosden.* Boston, ca. 1921.
Smith, Lyman D., & Co., *The Sinclair Consolidated Oil Corporation of New York: Its Present and Potential Position in the Oil World.* New York, September 1919.
Smithers, F. S., & Co. *Standard Oil Companies.* New York, 1912, 1913. (pamphlets, unpaginated)
Standard Corporation Records. New York: Standard & Poor's Corporation, 1914-1932.

NEWSPAPERS AND JOURNALS

American Petroleum Institute, *Daily Oil News,* 1948.
Boston *Evening Transcript,* May 5, 1906.
Central Law Journal (Central Law Journal Co., St. Louis, Mo.), 1911, 1914.
Columbia Law Review, 1914.
The Gasoline Retailer, 1944.
Harper's Weekly, September 1912.
Harvard Law Review, 1914.
Houston *Post,* 1945.
The Law Journal (London, Eng.), 1911.
The Law Times (London, Eng.), 1911.
Literary Digest, 1911–1912.
Living Age (Philadelphia, Pa.), 1911.
National Petroleum News (McGraw-Hill Publication, New York, N.Y.), 1923–1930.

New Orleans *Times-Picayune,* 1920–1923.
New York Times, 1916–1941.
New York World, 1906.
Oil and Gas Journal (Petroleum Publishing Co., Tulsa, Okla.), 1911–1959.
Oil City Derrick (Oil City, Pa.), 1948.
Oildom (Oildom Publishing Co., Bayonne, N.J.), 1914–1919.
Our Sun (Sun Oil Co., Philadelphia, Pa.), 1961.
The Outlook, 1905–1906.
The Petroleum Almanac (National Industrial Conference Bd., New York, N.Y.), 1946.
The Petroleum and Natural Gas Register, 1917–1918.
The Petroleum Register, 1921.
Petroleum Week (McGraw-Hill Publication, New York, N.Y.), 1955.
Philadelphia *Press,* 1906.
Pipe Line News (Oildom Publishing Co., Bayonne, N.J.), 1931–1950.
Platt's Oilgram (McGraw-Hill Publication, New York, N.Y.), 1945.
Railroad Gazette, May 1906.
Railway Age, July 1944.
The Sinclair Pipeliner (Sinclair Pipe Line Co., Independence, Kan.), 1954.
The Texaco Star (Texaco Co., Houston, Tex.), 1933.
Texas State House Reporter (Austin, Tex.), 1957.
World Oil (Gulf Publishing Co., Houston, Tex.), 1953.
World's Work (Doubleday, Page & Co., New York, N.Y.), 1911.

COMPANY REPORTS

Buckeye Pipe Line Company. *Annual Report* (1927).
Great Lakes Pipe Line Company, *Annual Reports* (1946, 1947).
Interprovincial Pipe Line Company. *Annual Report* (1954).
National Transit Company. *Annual Reports* (1915–16, 1925, 1927, 1928, 1931).
New York Transit Company. *Annual Report* (1941).
The Ohio Oil Company. *Annual Report* (1952).
Phillips Petroleum Company. *Annual Reports* (1931, 1954).
Sinclair Oil Corporation. *Annual Report* (1952).
Southern Pacific Company. *Annual Reports* (1955–1957).
Texas Eastern Transmission Company. *Annual Report* (1958).
Trans Mountain Oil Pipe Line Company. *Annual Reports* (1953, 1954, 1955).

COMPANY RECORDS

The author and his research associates had access to records in the files of the following pipeline companies:
Buckeye Pipe Line Company, New York, New York.
Humble Pipe Line Company, Houston, Texas.
Marathon Pipe Line Company, Findlay, Ohio.
National Transit Company, Oil City, Pennsylvania.
Service Pipe Line Company, Tulsa, Oklahoma.
Shell Pipe Line Corporation, Houston, Texas.
Sinclair Pipe Line Company (papers relating to Prairie Pipe Line Company), Independence, Kansas.

NOTES

PREFACE

1. Arthur M. Johnson, *The Development of American Petroleum Pipelines: A Study in Private Enterprise and Public Policy, 1862–1906* (Ithaca, N.Y., 1956).

CHAPTER 1: Crude-Oil Pipelines in an Expanding Industry

1. H. F. Williamson, R. L. Andreano, A, R. Daum, G. C. Klose, *The American Petroleum Industry: The Age of Energy, 1899–1959* (Evanston, Ill. 1963), 65.

2. *Ibid.*, 74.

3. *Ibid.*

4. U.S. Bureau of Corporations, *Report of the Commissioner of Corporations on the Petroleum Industry,* 2 vols., Part I, *Position of the Standard Oil Company in the Petroleum Industry* (Washington, 1907), 100–101.

5. Harold F. Williamson and Ralph L. Andreano, "Competitive Structure of the American Petroleum Industry, 1880–1911: A Reappraisal," in *Oil's First Century,* papers given at the Centennial Seminar on the History of the Petroleum Industry, Harvard Business School, November 1959 (Boston, 1960), 75.

6. The story is told in detail by Ralph W. and Muriel E. Hidy, *History of Standard Oil Company (New Jersey): Pioneering in Big Business, 1882–1911* (New York, 1955).

7. Harold F. Williamson and Arnold R. Daum, *The American Petroleum Industry: The Age of Illumination, 1859–1899* (Evanston, Ill., 1959), 581–582. See also Johnson, *Petroleum Pipelines,* 110–111.

8. For the rise of Pure Oil, see Williamson and Daum, *Age of Illumination,* 576–581.

9. Williamson and Andreano, in *Oil's First Century,* 74.

10. Hidy and Hidy, *Pioneering,* 176.

11. Williamson and Daum, *Age of Illumination,* 563.

12. Hidy and Hidy, *Pioneering,* 177.

13. Quoted *ibid.,* 181.

14. *Ibid.,* 182.

15. *Ibid.*

16. *Ibid.,* 183.

17. *Ibid.,* 186–187.

18. For methods used by Standard Oil's competitors, see *ibid.,* 378.

19. Quoted *ibid.,* 377–378.

20. Quoted *ibid.,* 379.

21. *Ibid.*

22. *Ibid.,* 380. See also U.S. Bureau of Corporations, *Report . . . on the Petroleum Industry,* pt. I, 169–173.

23. U.S. Bureau of Corporations, *Report . . . on the Petroleum Industry,* pt. I, 137.

24. Hidy and Hidy, *Pioneering,* 374.

25. Quoted *ibid.,* 279.

26. Williamson and Daum, *Age of Illumination,* 597.

27. Quoted in Hidy and Hidy, *Pioneering,* 158.

28. *Ibid.,* 159.

29. Williamson and Daum, *Age of Ilumination,* 602–603.

30. *Ibid.,* 603.

31. Hidy and Hidy, *Pioneering,* 187.

32. *Ibid.,* 166.

33. Williamson and Daum, *Age of Illumination*, 612.
34. *Ibid.*, 613.
35. *Ibid.*
36. Carl C. Rister, *Oil! Titan of the Southwest* (Norman, Okla., 1949), 58.
37. Hidy and Hidy, *Pioneering*, 394.
38. *Ibid.*
39. *Ibid.*, 393; Rister, *Oil*, 46–47.
40. Williamson, Andreano, et al., *Age of Energy*, 85–86.
41. For a table of early pipeline construction in these areas, see *ibid.*, 77.
42. Hidy and Hidy, *Pioneering*, 393, 696.
43. C. A. Warner, *Texas Oil and Gas Since 1543* (Houston, 1939), 45.
44. Rister, *Oil*, 63.
45. U.S. Bureau of Corporations, *Report . . . on the Petroleum Industry*, pt. I, 148.
46. *Ibid.* See also map facing p. 148.
47. *Ibid.*, 149.
48. Warner, *Texas Oil*, 118.
49. U.S. Bureau of Corporations, *Report . . . on the Petroleum Industry*, pt. I, 148.
50. Rister, *Oil*, 33–34.
51. Hidy and Hidy, *Pioneering*, 275.
52. Rister, *Oil*, 38.
53. Hidy and Hidy, *Pioneering*, 394.
54. *Ibid.*, 395, 396.
55. *Ibid.*, 399. Paul H. Giddens, *Standard Oil Company (Indiana): Oil Pioneer of the Middle West* (New York, 1955), 67. U.S. Bureau of Corporations, *Report . . . on the Petroleum Industry*, pt. I, 146.
56. Hidy and Hidy, *Pioneering*, 399.
57. *Ibid.*
58. U.S. Bureau of Corporations, *Report . . . on the Petroleum Industry*, pt. I, 146.
59. Giddens, *Standard Oil Company (Indiana)*, 69–70.
60. Hidy and Hidy, *Pioneering*, 399–400.
61. U.S. Bureau of Corporations, *Report . . . on the Petroleum Industry*, pt. I, 43.
62. See Gerald T. White, *Formative Years in the Far West: A History of Standard Oil Company of California and Predecessors through 1919* (New York, 1962); Joe S. Bain, *The Economics of the Pacific Coast Petroleum Industry*, 3 vols., Part I, *Market Structure*, Part II, *Price Behavior and Competition*, Part III, *Public Policy Toward Competition and Pricing* (Berkeley, 1944–1947).

CHAPTER 2: The Pipeline Amendment to the Hepburn Act

1. The law of eminent domain applied to pipelines in 1906 in the following states: California, Colorado, Indiana, Kentucky, New York, Ohio, Pennsylvania, Texas, West Virginia, and Wyoming. 40 *Congressional Record* 6365 (May 4, 1906).
2. See George S. Wolbert, Jr., *American Pipe Lines* (Norman, Okla. 1951), 114–115.
3. *Samuel Griffin v. South West Pennsylvania Pipe Lines,* 172 Pa. 580 (1896); *National Transit Co. v. Weston et al.*, 121 Pa. 485 (1888).
4. U.S. Bureau of Corporations, *Report . . . on the Petroleum Industry*, pt. I, 156–157.
5. *Ibid.*, 156.
6. *Ibid.*, 157.
7. *Ibid.*, 156.
8. *Ibid.*, 185.
9. *Ibid.*, 186–187.
10. *Ibid.*, 186.
11. *Ibid.*, 159.
12. Hidy and Hidy, *Pioneering*, 672.

13. F. S. Barde, "The Oil Fields and Pipe Lines of Kansas," *The Outlook*, LXXX (May 6, 1905), 23.

14. Hidy and Hidy, *Pioneering*, 672.

15. *Ibid.*

16. Johnson, *Petroleum Pipelines*, 214.

17. Hidy and Hidy, *Pioneering*, 674; Johnson, *Petroleum Pipelines*, 214–215.

18. Quoted in *The Outlook* (February 10, 1906), 283.

19. 58 Cong., 3 Sess., H. Res. 499.

20. For the formation and early history of the Bureau of Corporations, see Arthur M. Johnson, "Theodore Roosevelt and the Bureau of Corporations," *Mississippi Valley Historical Review*, XLV (March 1959), 575–584.

21. See I. L. Sharfman, *The Interstate Commerce Commission, 5* vols. (New York, 1931–1937), I, 23–26.

22. See Johnson, *Petroleum Pipelines*, 219; John M. Blum, "Theodore Roosevelt and the Hepburn Act: Toward an Orderly System of Control," in Elting E. Morison, ed., *Letters of Theodore Roosevelt*, 8 vols. (Cambridge, Mass., 1951–1954), VI, 1558–1571.

23. H. Res. 15438, 59 Cong., 1 Sess. In December 1905, Congressman W. R. Hearst proposed pipeline regulation in H. Res. 468, 59 Cong., 1 Sess.

24. 40 *Cong. Rec.* 9337–9338 (June 26, 1906).

25. *Ibid.* Rhinock pointed out that the offering was for oil at a terminal, and from it transportation charges were deducted.

26. *Ibid.*, 9337. See *W. W. Cargill Co. v. Minnesota*, 180 U.S. 452 (1901).

27. See Johnson, *Petroleum Pipelines*, 220.

28. U.S. Bureau of Corporations, *Report of the Commissioner of Corporations on the Transportation of Petroleum* (Washington, 1906), xx.

29. 40 *Cong. Rec.* 6358 (May 4, 1906).

30. *New York World*, May 5, 1906.

31. Philadelphia *Press*, May 11, 1906.

32. 40 *Cong. Rec.* 6358 (May 4, 1906).

33. Boston *Evening Transcript*, May 5, 1906.

34. 40 *Cong. Rec.* 6361 (May 4, 1906).

35. *Ibid.*, 6365–6366, 6368–6369.

36. *Ibid.*, 6368.

37. *Ibid.*, 6373.

38. *Ibid.*, 6365.

39. Quoted in *New York Tribune*, May 5, 1906.

40. *The Outlook* (May 12, 1906), 50.

41. *Railroad Gazette* (May 25, 1906), 528–530.

42. *Ibid.*

43. S.R. 32, H. J. Res. 101, 59 Cong., 1 Sess. and Jt. Res. 8 (March 7, 1906).

44. 40 *Cong. Rec.* 6456 (May 7, 1906).

45. *Ibid.*, 6456–6461.

46. *Ibid.*, 9108 (June 25, 1906).

47. *Ibid.*, 9251 (June 26, 1906).

48. *Ibid.*, 9108–9109 (June 25, 1906).

49. *Ibid.*, 9252 (June 26, 1906).

50. *Ibid.*, 9253.

51. *Ibid.*

52. *Ibid.*, 9101 (June 25, 1906).

53. *Ibid.*, 9107.

54. *Ibid.*, 9104.

55. *Ibid.*, 9340 (June 26, 1906).

56. *Ibid.*, 9584 (June 28, 1906).

57. *Dictionary of American Biography*, 22 vols., (New York, 1931), VI, 503.

58. 40 *Cong. Rec.* 9107 (June 25, 1906).

59. *Ibid.*, 9255 (June 26, 1906).
60. *Ibid.*, 9108 (June 25, 1906).
61. *Ibid.*, 9101.
62. 34 U.S. Stat. 584 (1906).

CHAPTER 3: New Fields, New Companies, and Old Pipeline Practices

1. William D. Humphrey, "The Ohio Oil Company, 1887–1937," 95. Marathon Pipe Line Company files, Findlay, O. (mimeo)
2. *Ibid.*, 90–96, esp. 92, 96.
3. *Ibid.*, 98.
4. "Historical Outline and Development of our Lines, Comprising the Illinois Gathering Lines," undated summary in Marathon Pipe Line Company files.
5. *Ibid.*
6. Giddens, *Standard Oil Company (Indiana)*, 71.
7. Hidy and Hidy, *Pioneering*, 406.
8. *Moody's Manual of Railroad and Corporation Securities, 1912*, p. 3448.
9. For costs of pipeline construction in the Gulf area, see Wiliamson, Andreano, et al., *Age of Energy*, 88.
10. See in W. L. Mellon, *Judge Mellon's Sons* (Pittsburgh, 1948), 278–288.
11. American Petroleum Institute, *Petroleum Facts and Figures: Centennial Edition, 1959* (New York, 1959), 238–239.
12. Craig Thompson, *Since Spindletop: A Human Story of Gulf's First Half-Century* (Pittsburgh, 1951), 23.
13. Mellon, *Judge Mellon's Sons*, 279–288.
14. *Gulf Pipe Line Company*, 47 ICC *Valuation Reports* (1938), 774, 777–778.
15. Williamson, Andreano, et al., *Age of Energy*, 92.
16. *Gulf Pipe Line Company of Oklahoma et al.*, 48 ICC *Valuation Reports* (1939), 520.
17. *Ibid.*, 516.
18. Williamson, Andreano, et al., *Age of Energy*, 92; Marquis James, *The Texaco Story: The First 50 Years, 1902–1952* (New York?, 1953), 32–33.
19. James, *The Texaco Story*, 27.
20. U.S. Federal Trade Commission, *Report on Pipe-Line Transportation of Petroleum* (Washington, 1916), 4.
21. Rister, *Oil*, 78. For a full account see Sun Oil Company, *Our Sun*, Special 75th Anniversary Issue (Philadelphia, 1961).
22. Rister, *Oil*, 79; 72 Cong., 2 Sess., House Committee on Interstate and Foreign Commerce, W. M. W. Splawn, *Report on Pipe Lines*, 2 vols. (Washington, 1933), I, 241, 247.
23. *Ibid.*, 342–347; U.S. Bureau of Corporations, *Report . . . on the Petroleum Industry*, pt. I, 168.
24. *Ibid.*
25. 72 Cong., 2 Sess., W. M. W. Splawn, *Report on Pipelines*, I, 342–345.
26. For list of Oklahoma-Kansas independents, 1906–1911, see Williamson and Andreano, et al., *Age of Energy*, 95.
27. Rister, *Oil*, 91.
28. *Ibid.*, 93.
29. Hidy and Hidy, *Pioneering*, 400–401.
30. *Ibid.*, 401.
31. By 1907, the Gulf and Texas companies were running 20 per cent of Oklahoma-Kansas production. Williamson, Andreano, et al., *Age of Energy*, 92.
32. This account is from John L. Loos, *Oil on Stream! A History of Interstate Oil Pipe Line Company, 1909–1959* (Baton Rouge, 1959), 52–53.
33. According to George S. Davison, president of the Gulf Pipe Line, Standard Oil

wrote a letter to President Taft on the question, and Gulf Oil challenged the facts presented. *Oil and Gas Journal* (September 28, 1911), 14.

34. Loos, *Oil on Stream*, 53, 55, 57.

35. Prairie Oil & Gas Co. purchases had in fact declined steadily since 1907. See *In Re Conditions Affecting the Production, Transportation, and Marketing of Crude Petroleum*, 36 ICC (1915), 481.

36. Loos, *Oil on Stream*, 56.

37. *Oil and Gas Journal* (October 5, 1911), 8.

38. See Interstate Commerce Commission, *In the Matter of Pipe Lines*, 24 ICC (1912), 6–7.

39. U.S. Bureau of Corporations, *Report . . . on the Petroleum Industry*, pt. I, 184.

40. *Ibid.*, 185–186.

41. *Ibid.*, 184.

42. *Ibid.*, 186.

43. *Ibid*

44. *Ibid.*, 186, 188.

45. U.S. Bureau of Corporations, *Report . . . on the Petroleum Industry*, pt. I, 241–242.

46. *Ibid.*, 242.

47. *Ibid.*, 190–191.

48. *Ibid.*

49. *Ibid.*

50. Testimony reported in *Oil and Gas Journal* (September 28, 1911), 10.

51. *Ibid.*, 12; *ibid.* (October 5, 1911), J. S. Cullinan testimony, 6; *ibid.* (September 28, 1911), Davison testimony, 14.

52. *Ibid.* (September 28, 1911), Leovy testimony, 10. Compare with 36 ICC 429 (1915), 453–454 as to deliveries by Gulf Company pipelines in this area.

53. *Oil and Gas Journal* (September 28, 1911), Leovy testimony, 10.

54. *Ibid.* (October 5, 1911), Cullinan testimony, 6.

55. *Ibid.*

56. *Ibid.* (September 28, 1911), Leovy testimony, 10, 12.

57. *Ibid.*, Davison testimony, 14.

58. Quoted *ibid.* (October 5, 1911), 20.

59. *Ibid.* (September 28, 1911), 14.

60. *Ibid.* (October 5, 1911), Cullinan testimony, 8.

61. *Ibid.* (September 28, 1911), Davison testimony, 14.

62. *Ibid.*, 18.

63. *Ibid.* (October 5, 1911), O'Neil testimony, 8.

64. *Ibid.*, 9–10.

65. Williamson, Andreano, et al., *Age of Energy*, 83–84.

66. *Oil and Gas Journal* (October 5, 1911), Sharp testimony, 10.

67. *Ibid.*, 12.

68. *Ibid.*, 20.

69. *Ibid.*, 6.

70. *Ibid.* (September 28, 1911), 10.

71. *Ibid.* (October 5, 1911), 16.

CHAPTER 4: Antitrust Policy and Standard Oil Pipelines

1. *Northern Securities Co. v. United States*, 193 U.S. 197 (1904).

2. See Arthur M. Johnson, "Theodore Roosevelt and The Bureau of Corporations," *Mississippi Valley Historical Review*, XLV (March 1959), 583–589.

3. 59 Cong., 2 Sess., H. Doc. 606, *Railroad Discriminations and Monopolies in Coal and Oil*, letter from the Chairman of the ICC Submitting a Report of an Investigation of Railroad Discriminations and Monopolies in Oil (Washington, 1907), 5–6.

4. George S. Gibb and Evelyn H. Knowlton, *History of the Standard Oil Company (New Jersey): The Resurgent Years, 1911–1927* (New York, 1956), 174.

5. 59 Cong., 2 Sess., H. Doc. 606.

6. U.S. Bureau of Corporations, *Report . . . on the Petroleum Industry*, pt. I, xix.

7. *Ibid.*, pt. II, 640.

8. *Ibid.*, 643.

9. *Ibid.*, 639.

10. *Ibid.*, pt. I, 196 ff.

11. *Ibid.*, 193–195.

12. *Ibid.*, 34.

13. Hidy and Hidy, *Pioneering*, 691.

14. Supreme Court of the United States, October Term, 1909, *Standard Oil Company of New Jersey et al., Appellants, against United States of America, Appellee, Brief for Appellants*, 2 vols. (New York, 1909?), II, 109.

15. *Ibid.*, 119.

16. *Ibid.*, 120.

17. *Ibid.*, 122 ff.

18. *Ibid.*, 124–126.

19. *Ibid.*, 123.

20. *Ibid.*, 123, 126.

21. *Ibid.*, 122–123.

22. *Ibid.*, 116.

23. *Ibid.*, 117.

24. *Ibid.*, 110.

25. *Ibid.*, 113.

26. *Ibid.*, 115.

27. *Ibid.*, 111–112.

28. *Ibid.*, 113.

29. *United States v. Standard Oil Co. of New Jersey et al.*, 173 Fed. Rep. 177 (1909), 193–200.

30. *Standard Oil Company of New Jersey et al. v. United States*, 221 U.S. 1 (1911), 45.

31. *Ibid.*, 47.

32. See *Living Age*, CCLXIX (June 24, 1911), 812–814; *World's Work*, XXII (July 1911), 14547–14549; and a summary of newspaper reactions in *Literary Digest*, XLII (May 27, 1911), 1035–1038.

33. "The Standard Oil and Tobacco Trust Decisions," *Bench and Bar*, XXV (June 1911), 95.

34. "The Standard Oil Decision," *The Green Bag*, XXVIII (June 1911), 284.

35. Jeremiah W. Jenks, "Economic Aspect of the Recent Decisions of the United States Supreme Court on Trusts," *Journal of Political Economy*, XX (April 1912), 354–355.

36. *The Law Journal*, XLVI (May 20, 1911), 321.

37. *The Law Times*, CXXXI (May 20, 1911), 49–50.

38. Quoted in *Literary Digest*, XLII (May 27, 1911), 1036, citing the *New York Tribune*.

39. *Ibid.*, 1037.

40. *Ibid.*, 1038.

41. Andrew A. Bruce, "The Supreme Court and the Standard Oil Case," *Central Law Journal*, LXXII (August 18, 1911), 112.

42. *Ibid.*, 114.

43. *Harper's Weekly*, LVI (September 14, 1912), 4.

CHAPTER 5: Managerial Response to the Hepburn Act

1. *In the Matter of Pipe Lines*, 24 ICC 1 (1912), 10.

2. See *Prairie Oil & Gas Co. v. United States*, 204 Fed. 798 (Com. Ct., 1913), 803–804.

3. 24 ICC 1 (1912), 10.

4. U.S. Bureau of Corporations, *Report . . . on the Petroleum Industry*, pt. I, 53–54.

5. *Ibid.*, 31.

6. *Ibid.*, 193.

7. *Ibid.*, 193–195.

8. *Ibid.*, 195.

9. *Ibid.*, 160.

10. 24 ICC 1 (1912), 11.

11. See *The Pipe Line Cases*, 234 U.S. 548 (1914), 561–562.

12. See ICC, *Annual Report* (Washington, 1907), 118–119.

13. *Oil and Gas Journal* (May 9, 1912), 3.

14. *Ibid.*, 2.

15. *Ibid.*

16. *Ibid.*

17. 24 ICC 1 (1912), 3.

18. *Ibid.*, 7.

19. *Ibid.*, 8.

20. *Ibid.*

21. *Ibid.*, 9.

22. *Ibid.*, 9–10.

23. *Ibid.*, 10.

24. 204 Fed. 798 (1913), 803–804.

25. *Ibid.*, 812.

26. *Ibid.*, 813–816.

27. *Ibid.*, 817.

28. 234 U.S. 548 (1914), 549–552.

29. See *ibid.*, Brief on Behalf of Ohio Oil Co., 21–26; Brief on Behalf of Standard Oil Co., 15–20; Brief on Behalf of Standard Oil Co. of Louisiana, 8–12.

30. See *ibid.*, Brief on Behalf of the Prairie Oil & Gas Co., 12–13, 68–87, and Brief on Behalf of Appellees, Robert D. Benson *et al.*, doing business under the partnership name of the Tide Water Pipe Company Limited.

31. See *ibid.*, Brief on Behalf of the Uncle Sam Oil Company, 32–48, esp. 44.

32. 234 U.S. 548 (1914), 559.

33. *Ibid.*, 560.

34. *Ibid.*, 562–563.

35. *Ibid.*, 565–567.

36. *Ibid.*, 571.

37. *Ibid.*, 573–574.

38. *Central Law Journal*, LXXIX (July 10, 1914), 20.

39. *Harvard Law Review*, XXVIII (November 1914), 86, 87.

40. *Columbia Law Review*, XIV (December 1914), 664.

CHAPTER 6: The Impact of Public Policy on Standard Pipelines

1. *Oildom* (January 1915), 35–36.

2. Albert W. Atwood, "The Greatest Killing in Wall Street," *McClure's Magazine*, XXXIX (August 1912), 414.

3. "Standard Oil at 900," *Literary Digest*, XLIV (March 30, 1912), 664–665.

4. Hidy and Hidy, *Pioneering*, 608.

5. Gibb and Knowlton, *Resurgent Years*, 18.

6. Hidy and Hidy, *Pioneering*, 608.

7. F. S. Smithers & Co., *Standard Oil Companies* (New York, 1913), unpaginated pamphlet.

8. *Ibid.*

9. *Moody's Manual of Railroads and Corporation Securities, 1918,* Industrial Section, 1521.

10. F. S. Smithers & Co., *Standard Oil Companies* (1912), pamphlet.

11. *Oildom* (May 1914), 18.

12. FTC, *Pipe-Line Transportation of Petroleum, 1916,* 88.

13. *Ibid.,* 98.

14. 67 Cong., 2 and 4 Sess., Senate Subcommittee of the Committee on Manufactures (La Follette Committee), "High Cost of Gasoline and Other Petroleum Products," *Hearings,* 2 vols. (Washington, 1923), 233.

15. *Poor's Manual of Industrials, 1916,* 2192. By mid-1919 the last of these debentures had been retired. *Oildom* (March 1919), 60.

16. FTC, *Pipe-Line Transportation of Petroleum, 1916,* 88.

17. *Ibid.,* 90–91.

18. *Oildom* (April 1914), 32–33.

19. FTC, *Pipe-Line Transportation of Petroleum, 1916,* 91.

20. *Ibid.,* 35.

21. 67 Cong., 2 and 4 Sess., La Follette Committee, *Hearings,* O'Neil testimony, 234.

22. 70 Cong., 1 Sess., S. Doc. 61, *Petroleum Industry: Prices, Profits, and Competition,* Letter from Vice Chairman of the Federal Trade Commission Transmitting . . . a Report (Washington, 1928), 74.

23. Humphrey, "The Ohio Oil Company," 83.

24. *Ibid.,* 105.

25. F. S. Smithers & Co., *Standard Oil Companies* (1912).

26. *Oildom* (May 1914), 49. For the Wyoming story, see Hartzell Spence, *Portrait in Oil* (New York, 1962), 70–86.

27. Spence, *Portrait in Oil,* 214–215.

28. Gibb and Knowlton, *Resurgent Years,* 167.

29. Hidy and Hidy, *Pioneering,* 408.

30. Gibb and Knowlton, *Resurgent Years,* 166.

31. Loos, *Oil on Stream,* 77.

32. Gibb and Knowlton, *Resurgent Years,* 168.

33. Loos, *Oil on Stream,* 77.

34. *Ibid.,* 87.

35. *Ibid.,* 83.

36. Gibb and Knowlton, *Resurgent Years,* 171; *Oildom* (August 1915), 40; 72 Cong., 2 Sess., W. M. W. Splawn, *Report on Pipelines,* I, 379.

37. Quoted in Gibb and Knowlton, *Resurgent Years,* 172.

38. *Ibid.*

39. See *ibid.,* 153–165.

40. *Oildom* (April 1915), 49.

41. *Ibid.* (November 1914), 5, 28.

42. FTC, *Pipe-Line Transportation of Petroleum, 1916,* 20.

43. *Oildom* (April 1915), 28.

44. *Ibid.* (November 1914), 6.

45. Gibb and Knowlton, *Resurgent Years,* 174.

46. Loos, *Oil on Stream,* 77.

47. *Oildom* (November 1914), 5–6.

CHAPTER 7: State Regulation in the Southwest

1. Quoted in Gibb and Knowlton, *Resurgent Years,* 170.

2. U.S. Geological Survey, *Mineral Resources of the United States* (Washington, 1906), 833.

3. *Ibid.* (1907), pt. II, 353.

4. *Ibid.* (1911), pt. II, 397; *ibid.* (1915), pt. II, 648.
5. American Petroleum Institute, *Petroleum Facts and Figures,* 1959, p. 44.
6. *Ibid.*
7. U.S. Geological Survey, *Mineral Resources* (1914), pt. II, 993.
8. Clinton O. Bunn, ed., *Revised Laws of Oklahoma, 1910,* 2 vols. (St. Paul, Minn., 1912), I, Art. II, sec. 4309 .
9. *Ibid.,* sec. 4307.
10. *Ibid.,* sec. 4308.
11. *Pierce Oil Corporation v. Phoenix Refining Co.,* 259 U.S. 125 (1922), 127–129; Wolbert, *American Pipe Lines,* 116–117.
12. Rister, *Oil,* 128.
13. FTC, *Pipe-Line Transportation of Petroleum, 1916,* 344.
14. Rister, *Oil,* 129.
15. *Ibid.,* 128–129; FTC, *Pipe-Line Transportation of Petroleum, 1916,* 382–383.
16. FTC, *Pipe-Line Transportation of Petroleum, 1916,* 382–383, 393–394. Reportedly, Healdton crude with existing refining methods produced only 9–11 per cent gasoline, compared with 24–27 per cent for crude from other fields. See letter from H. G. James, Kansas City, Mo., in *Oil and Gas Journal* (April 13, 1916), 26.
17. Rister, *Oil,* 130; *Oil and Gas Journal* (March 5, March 12, 1914).
18. *Oil and Gas Journal* (March 12, 1918), 2.
19. *Ibid.,* 131.
20. *Ibid.* (June 24, 1915), 27.
21. See W. P. Z. German, "Legal History of Conservation of Oil and Gas in Oklahoma," in *Legal History of Conservation of Oil and Gas, A Symposium* (Chicago, 1938), 117–118.
22. Rister, *Oil,* 132; *Oildom* (May 1914), 89; U.S. Bureau of Corporations, *Conditions in the Healdton Oil Field* (Washington, 1915), 6.
23. See German, in *Legal History of Conservation of Oil and Gas,* 118.
24. 50 *Cong. Rec.* 1988 (June 13, 1913).
25. 63 Cong., 1 Sess., S. Res. 109.
26. 63 Cong., 2 Sess., S. 5550.
27. *Oildom* (June 1914), 11.
28. 63 Cong., 2 Sess., S. 5559.
29. 63 Cong., 2 Sess., H.R. 16581, A Bill to Regulate the Transportation of Oil by Means of Pipe Lines.
30. Rister, *Oil,* 132.
31. Franklin to *Oklahoma Oil and Gas News,* April 27, 1914, in 63 Cong., 2 Sess., House Committee on Interstate and Foreign Commerce, "Transportation of Oil by Pipe Lines," *Hearings,* Part I (Washington, 1914), 5.
32. West testimony, *ibid.,* 7.
33. *Ibid.*
34. J. J. Moroney testimony, *ibid.,* 34.
35. Moroney and W. B. Johnson testimony, *ibid.,* 37–50.
36. Wrightsman testimony, *ibid.,* pt. II, 51–52.
37. FTC, *Pipe-Line Transportation of Petroleum, 1916,* 347.
38. Wrightsman testimony, 63 Cong., 2 Sess., "Transportation of Oil by Pipe Lines," *Hearings,* pt. II, 56.
39. *Ibid.,* 57.
40. *Ibid.,* 66.
41. *Ibid.,* 57.
42. *Oildom* (June 1914), 11.
43. C. D. Chamberlin, "Declaration on Behalf of Independent Oil Men Advocating the Government Ownership and Operation of Pipe Lines for the Transportation of Petroleum in Interstate Commerce," in 51 *Cong. Rec.* 9867–9876 (June 5, 1914).
44. F. B. Dow and D. C. O'Hara, *The National Petroleum Association, 1902–1952* (Washington, 1952), 36, 39.

45. 51 *Cong. Rec.*, 9867–9876 (June 5, 1914). On the proposal for a pipeline to supply the Navy's needs, see *Oildom* (April 1914), 9.

46. Quoted in *Oildom* (June 1914), 11. Cato Sells, Commissioner of Indian Affairs, was in charge of preparing a report to Congress on the problems of insuring a fuel oil supply for the Navy. *Ibid.* (July 1914), 5.

47. *Ibid.* (June 1914), 53.

48. Oklahoma Corporation Commission, Order 829, July 1, 1914. See *Oildom* (July 1914), 3–4.

49. *Oildom* (September 1914), 9.

50. *Ibid.*

51. Oklahoma Corporation Commission, Order 846, September 22, 1914. See German, in *Legal History of Conservation of Oil and Gas*, 120–124.

52. *Oildom* (October 1914), 14.

53. Quoted by German, in *Legal History of Conservation of Oil and Gas*, 121.

54. *Oildom* (June 1914), 10.

55. *Ibid.* (July 1914), 14.

56. Quoting W. S. Fitzpatrick to Attorney General West of Oklahoma. *Ibid.* (October 1914), 4.

57. *In Re Conditions Affecting the Production, Transportation, and Marketing of Crude Petroleum*, 36 ICC 429 (1915), 445–446.

58. U.S. Bureau of Corporations, *Conditions in the Healdton Oil Field*, 19; German, in *Legal History of Conservation of Oil and Gas*, 126.

59. *Oildom* (October 1914), 3.

60. German, in *Legal History of Conservation of Oil and Gas*, 126.

61. *Ibid.*, 126–127.

62. *General Laws of Texas*, 26th Legislature, Regular Session, Ch. 117 (Austin, 1899).

63. *Ibid.*, 34th Legislature, Regular Session, Ch. 41 (Austin 1915).

64. R. L. Batts, *Batts' Annotated Revised Civil Statutes of Texas, 1895*, 2 vols. (Austin, 1897–1899), I, Title XXI, Ch. 2.

65. *Ramsey et al. v.* Tod, 69 S.W. 133 (1902). For an analysis, see Ira P. Hildebrand, *The Law of Texas Corporations* (Kansas City, Mo., 1942), I, 100 ff.

66. The Guffey Company, for example, endeavored in 1905 to obtain passage of the Myrick bill, authorizing the complete integration of functions under one charter. R. E. Ferris, "Texas Corporation and Anti-Trust Law, 1895–1917, and Their Effect on the Oil Industry, Particularly the Humble Oil and Refining Co. and Standard Oil (N.J.)," paper presented at the Business History Foundation Conference, Saybrook, Connecticut, September 18, 1948.

67. *Ibid.* The producers retaliated by promoting passage of the O'Brien-John bill and the Bryan bill to regulate pipelines.

68. *Ibid.* The Senate passed a resolution requesting the Attorney General to take action against oil corporations exercising illegal powers.

69. Henrietta M. Larson and Kenneth W. Porter, *History of Humble Oil & Refining Company: A Study in Industrial Growth* (New York, 1959), 42–43; *General Laws of Texas*, 34th Legislature, Regular Session, Ch. 41 (1915).

70. Larson and Porter, *History of Humble Oil & Refining Company*, 43–45.

71. See W. J. Farish letters to ICC, January 11, January 25, 1925, in ICC Docket 4199, vol. 5.

72. *General Laws of Texas*, 35th Legislature, Regular Session, Ch. 31 (1917).

73. *Ibid.*, Ch. 30.

74. *Oildom* (June 1917), 284.

CHAPTER 8: The Role of Pipelines in Integrated Oil Operations

1. For a summary of major events in Shell's history in the United States, see Kendall Beaton, *Enterprise Oil: A History of Shell in the United States* (New York,

1957), 751–760. For Deterding's strategy with respect to Standard Oil, see Gibb and Knowlton, *Resurgent Years*, 79.

2. *Ibid.*, 125.

3. *Ibid.*, 132; 72 Cong., 2 Sess., W. M. W. Splawn, *Report on Pipe Lines*, I, 149.

4. *Ibid.*, 139–140.

5. *Ibid.*, 140.

6. Ruth S. Knowles, *The Greatest Gamblers: The Epic of American Oil Exploration* (New York, 1959), 135–136.

7. U.S. Department of the Interior, *Oil Lands in Indian Territory and Territory of Oklahoma*, Hearings before the Secretary of the Interior on Leasing of Oil Lands and Natural-Gas Wells in Indian Territory and Territory of Oklahoma (Washington, 1906), 12.

8. Testimony of Ethan A. Hitchcock, Secretary of the Interior, *ibid.*, 25.

9. Knowles, *The Greatest Gamblers*, 136.

10. See *Oil and Gas Journal* (January 13, 1916), 43.

11. Beaton, *Enterprise in Oil*, 140–147.

12. Sanderson & Porter to Roxana Petroleum Company, February 29, 1916, "Cost Estimate on Proposed Pipe Line Healdton Oil Fields to Cushing Storage Station Oklahoma."

13. *Ibid.* Cost of the line without duplicate pumping units was placed at $875,000, exclusive of land.

14. Sanderson & Porter, "Oil Pipe Lines of the Yarhola Pipe Line Company, Oklahoma Oil Fields to East St. Louis, Illinois."

15. *Ibid.*

16. *Ibid.* Allis-Chalmers provided diesel engines and 12,000-barrel pumps; National Transit supplied the 8,000-barrel pumps.

17. Beaton, *Enterprise in Oil*, 146.

18. Testimony of R. B. High, Manager, Shell Pipe Line Corporation, in connection with ICC Docket 26570.

19. Beaton, *Enterprise in Oil*, 169. Ozark Pipe Line Corporation, ICC Form "P," 1920–1923.

20. Beaton, *Enterprise in Oil*, 211.

21. High testimony, ICC Docket 26570.

22. Rister, *Oil*, 205.

23. *Ibid.*

24. Memorandum of talk by President W. H. Allen, Shell Union Oil Corporation, May 6, 1922.

25. Beaton, *Enterprise in Oil*, 216. See John J. Mathews, *Life and Death of an Oilman: The Career of E. W. Marland* (Norman, Okla., 1951), 142–147. The Marland properties were eventually merged into the Continental Oil Company in 1928.

26. High testimony, ICC Docket 26570.

27. *Ibid.*; Beaton, *Enterprise in Oil*, 339–340.

28. High testimony, ICC Docket 26570.

29. *Ibid.*

30. Beaton, *Enterprise in Oil*, 336; 72 Cong., 2 Sess., W. M. W. Splawn, *Report on Pipe Lines*, I, 151, 155.

31. 72 Cong., 2 Sess., W. M. W. Splawn, *Report on Pipe Lines*, I, 151, 155; Ozark Pipe Line Corporation, ICC Form "P," 1919, p. 19.

32. 72 Cong., 2 Sess., W. M. W. Splawn, *Report on Pipe Lines*, I, 159.

33. Outside business is reported in a letter from R. B. High, Shell Pipe Line, to R. D. Parker, July 14, 1938.

34. Patrick J. White was a native of Warren, Pennsylvania. He went to the Mid-Continent field in 1903 as a representative of the Oil Well Supply Company and opened their Tulsa store in 1905. He and Sinclair joined forces in the Glenn Pool. Later, White brought in the second well in the Cushing field. White and Sinclair production in this

field was reportedly exceeded only by that of the McMan Oil Company. *Oil and Gas Journal* (January 27, 1916), 4, 25.

35. W. L. Connelly, *The Oil Business As I Saw It: Half a Century with Sinclair* (Norman, Okla., 1954), 56.

36. According to the *Oil and Gas Journal* (February 10, 1916), 31, producing territory, a pipeline system between tank farm and field, and 25 tanks of 55,000-barrel capacity were sold to Oklahoma Oil Company for $5,500,000.

37. This property embraced a reported 20,000 acres. *Ibid.*

38. Quoted *ibid.* (May 11, 1916), 38.

39. Sinclair Oil & Refining Corporation, Application to the New York Stock Exchange, March 12, 1917, Corporation Records, Baker Library, Harvard University Graduate School of Business Administration, Boston, Mass.

40. *Ibid.*

41. *Magnolia Pipe Line Company*, 48 ICC *Valuation Reports* 775 (1939), 789.

42. "Stanolind Pipe Line Company Corporate History," n.d., Service Pipe Line Company files, Tulsa, Okla.

43. Investors Public Service, Inc., "Sinclair Oil and Refining Corporation" (June 25, 1917), Corporation Records, Baker Library.

44. *Ibid.*; "Diary of Inspection Trip, Sinclair Oil & Refining Corporation," November 10–16, 1917, p. 1, Corporation Records, Baker Library.

45. Application to the New York Stock Exchange, March 12, 1917.

46. "Diary of Inspection Trip," 2.

47. Connelly, *The Oil Business As I Saw It*, 68. Connelly was a vice-president of the pipeline at this time.

48. "Diary of Inspection Trip," 2.

49. *Stanolind Pipeline Company*, 48 ICC *Valuation Reports.* 678 (1939), 710–711.

50. *Oil and Gas Journal* (October 7, 1926), C-103.

51. Lyman D. Smith & Co., "The Sinclair Consolidated Oil Corporation of New York: Its Present and Potential Position in the Oil World" (September 1919), Corporation Records, Baker Library.

52. G. F. Redmond & Co., Boston, "Sinclair vs. Cosden" (ca. 1921), Corporation Records, Baker Library.

53. See, for example, *National Petroleum News* (May 5, 1920), 111.

54. Giddens, *Standard Oil Company (Indiana)*, 224. See also Stewart testimony, 67 Cong., 2 and 4 Sess., La Follette Committee, *Hearings*, I, 802.

55. Chandler Bros. & Co., New York, Report on Sinclair Consolidated Oil Corporation, October 1920. Corporation Records, Baker Library.

56. *Ibid.*

57. See Kountz testimony, 67 Cong., 2 and 4 Sess., La Follette Committee, *Hearings*, I, 408–409.

58. U.S. Temporary National Economic Committee, *Verbatim Record of the Proceedings of the Temporary National Economic Committee* (Washington, 1939), VI, 433. Hereinafter cited as *TNEC Hearings*.

59. Giddens, *Standard Oil Company (Indiana)*, 224.

60. *Ibid.*

61. *Ibid.*, 224–225.

62. See Harry F. Sinclair testimony, 67 Cong., 2 and 4 Sess., La Follette Committee, *Hearings*, I, 646.

63. *Oil and Gas Journal* (May 5, 1920), C-104.

64. Expansion was partially financed by a public bond issue of $25,000,000 in 1922. "Stanolind Pipe Line Company Corporate History" n.d., Service Pipe Line Company files.

65. Giddens, *Standard Oil Company (Indiana)*, 235–237.

66. *Ibid.*, 445–446.

67. 48 ICC *Valuation Reports*, 678, 681.

68. Giddens, *Standard Oil Company (Indiana)*, 561.

69. See *ibid.*, 444.

70. "Stanolind Pipe Line Company Corporate History" n.d., Service Pipe Line Company files.

71. Giddens, *Standard Oil Company (Indiana)*, 444.

72. *Ibid.*, 446.

73. 72 Cong., 2 Sess., W. M. W. Splawn, *Report on Pipe Lines*, I, 200–201.

74. *Ibid.*

75. John G. McLean and Robert W. Haigh, *The Growth of Integrated Oil Companies* (Boston, 1954), 381.

76. 72 Cong., 2 Sess., W. M. W. Splawn, *Report on Pipe Lines*, I, 152.

77. *Ibid.*, 199.

78. *Ibid.*, 50.

79. Gibb and Knowlton, *Resurgent Years*, 73–74.

80. *Ibid.*, 462. Loos, *Oil on Stream*, 129–130.

81. Larson and Porter, *History of Humble Oil & Refining Company*, 74.

82. *Ibid.*, 64.

83. *Ibid.*, 22, 23, 28–30, 40.

84. *Ibid.*, 48–49, 55.

85. Quoted *ibid.*, 75.

86. *Ibid.*

87. *Ibid.*, 148.

88. The expansion of the Humble pipeline system is described *ibid.*, 148 ff.

89. *Ibid.*, 168–169.

90. *Ibid.*, 168.

91. *Ibid.*, 169.

92. Loos, *Oil on Stream*, 43.

93. *Ibid.*, 43–45.

94. *Ibid.*, 44, 82, 102–104.

95. Williamson, Andreano, et al., *Age of Energy*, 348.

96. *Texas-Empire Pipe Line Company et al.,* 48 ICC *Valuation Reports* 327 (1939), 345, 349–350, 359–360.

97. *Ibid.*, 353; 72 Cong., 2 Sess., W. M. W. Splawn, *Report on Pipe Lines*, I, 270–271.

98. *Ibid.*, 132–135.

99. *Ibid.*, 135, 137–138.

100. See Catherine C. Ellsworth, "Integration Into Crude Oil Transportation in the 1930's," *Business History Review* (Summer 1961), 188.

101. *Ibid.*, 186–187.

102. McLean and Haigh, *Growth of Integrated Oil Companies*, 240.

103. *Ibid.*

104. Ellsworth, "Integration into Crude Oil Transportation," 189, 191; 72 Cong., 2 Sess., W. M. W. Splawn, *Report on Pipe Lines*, I, 225.

105. 72 Cong., 2 Sess., W. M. W. Splawn, *Report on Pipe Lines*, I, 225; *Ajax Pipeline Company,* 48 ICC *Valuation Reports* 153 (1939), 172.

106. Ellsworth, "Integration into Crude Oil Transportation," 192; McLean and Haigh, *Growth of Integrated Oil Companies*, 244.

107. Ellsworth, "Integration into Crude Oil Transportation," 195.

108. Quoted in McLean and Haigh, *Growth of Integrated Oil Companies*, 244.

109. Quoted *ibid.*, 244.

110. Ellsworth, "Integration into Crude Oil Transportation," 205.

111. *Ibid.*, 206.

112. Williamson, Andreano, et al., *Age of Energy*, 349.

113. *Oil and Gas Journal* (June 19, 1930), 37.

114. *The Petroleum Almanac, 1946* (National Industrial Conference Board), 88.

115. *Ibid.*

CHAPTER 9: Adaptation to Dissolution: Three Former Standard Pipeline Companies

1. *Poor's Manual of Industrials: Manufacturing, Mining and Miscellaneous Companies, 1915*, p. 1572.

2. Kountz testimony, 67 Cong., 2 and 4 Sess., La Follette Committee, *Hearings*, I, 399.

3. *Poor's Manual of Industrials, 1915*, p. 1573.

4. Kountz testimony, 67 Cong., 2 and 4 Sess., La Follette Committee, *Hearings*, I, 394.

5. *The Petroleum Register* (New York, 1921), 448.

6. *Ibid.*

7. *The Petroleum and Natural Gas Register*, 1917–1918, p. 262.

8. In addition to deliveries to Standard at Whiting, Prairie delivered 35,000 barrels daily to Standard of Louisiana at Baton Rouge. *The Petroleum Register, 1921*, p. 448.

9. Questions asked by Mr. Plummer, Dept. of Justice, December 1923–January 1924; answered by William F. Gates, Prairie Pipe Line Company files.

10. *The Petroleum Register, 1921*, p. 448.

11. Questions asked by Mr. Plummer, Dept. of Justice, December 1923–January 1924; answered by William F. Gates, Prairie Pipe Line Company files.

12. Chart, Prairie Pipe Line Company files.

13. Graph showing monthly investment in trunk and gathering lines, 1915–1920, Prairie Pipe Line Company files.

14. "Comparative Statement of Trunk Line Investment," Prairie Pipe Line Company files.

15. Statement in answer to a questionnaire, Prairie Pipe Line Company to Cravath, de Gersdorff, Swaine, and Wood, lawyers, June 9, 1931, Prairie Pipe Line Company files.

16. A complete list of dividends 1915–1931 is given in 72 Cong., 2 Sess., W. M. W. Splawn, *Report on Pipe Lines*, II, 139–140.

17. Minutes of the Special Meeting of the Stockholders of the Prairie Pipe Line Company . . . December 20, 1922, *ibid.*, 229–231.

18. 70 Cong., 1 Sess., S. Doc. 61, p. 37.

19. Gibb and Knowlton, *Resurgent Years*, 462.

20. *Ibid.*, 465–466.

21. *Ibid.*, 467.

22. Questions asked by Mr. Plummer, Dept. of Justice, December 1923–January 1924; answered by William F. Gates, Prairie Pipe Line Company files.

23. 70 Cong., 1 Sess., S. Doc. 61, p. 37.

24. Gibb and Knowlton, *Resurgent Years*, 469; joint tariffs were settled as follows: 10 per cent was divided equally among the carriers, and 90 per cent was divided according to their respective mileages. Kountz testimony, 67 Cong., 2 and 4 Sess., La Follette Committee, *Hearings*, I, 417.

25. Gibb and Knowlton, *Resurgent Years*, 469.

26. *Ibid.*, 470.

27. *Ibid.*, 470, 472.

28. Because the Sinclair refinery was not finished and the government needed additional Mid-Continent crude at the seaboard, James O'Neil of Prairie Oil & Gas, a member of the Petroleum War Service Committee, secured permission for Prairie to ship over the line to Whiting and the seaboard. Thus Standard of Indiana, normally a Prairie customer, received the first oil run through the new Sinclair line. O'Neil testimony, 67 Cong., 2 and 4 Sess., La Follettee Committee, *Hearings*, I, 246; interview with C. M. Scott, retired chief engineer, Service Pipe Line Company, November 20, 1962.

29. Kountz testimony, 67 Cong., 2 and 4 Sess., La Follette Committee, *Hearings*, I, 407.

30. Giddens, *Standard Oil Company (Indiana)*, 226–234. For details of pipeline

extension into the field, see *Oil and Gas Journal,* October 21, November 25, and December 2, 1921.

31. Contracts between Pure Oil Co. and Prairie Pipe Line Company, dated November 12, 1925, and January 1, 1926, Prairie Pipe Line Company files.

32. Williamson, Andreano, et al., *Age of Energy,* 343.

33. T. J. Flannelly to E. J. Henry, Atlantic Refining Company, April 1926, Prairie Pipe Line Company files.

34. Prairie Pipe Line Company, Listing Statement, New York Stock Exchange, 1928, A8388. Corporation Records, Baker Library. See 72 Cong., 2 Sess., W. M. W. Splawn, *Report on Pipe Lines,* 11, 145–147, for principal shippers, consignees, and competitors, 1929–1931.

35. Analysis of surplus account prepared for the New York Stock Exchange, Prairie Pipe Line Company, December 1928; Prairie Pipe Line Company files; Listing Statement, New York Stock Exchange, 1928, A8388.

36. Minutes of a Special Meeting of the Board of Directors of the Prairie Pipe Line Company . . . November 28, 1928, in 72 Cong., 2 Sess., W. M. W. Splawn, *Report on Pipe Lines,* II, 231–233.

37. *Ibid.* Previously Prairie Pipe had been traded on the New York Curb Exchange.

38. Draft of Memorandum in Reference to Negotiations, Subject to Verification, December 11, 1933, p. 3, Prairie Pipe Line Company files.

39. Report on Producers and Refiners Corporation, "Position and Prospects," by Standard Corporation Reports, August 25, 1927. Corporation Records, Baker Library.

40. Giddens, *Standard Oil Company (Indiana),* 226–234.

41. *Ibid.,* 379.

42. *Ibid.*

43. G. Stanford to T. J. Flannelly, December 11, 1933, Prairie Pipe Line Company files. According to a Prairie memorandum, answering questions asked by the Prairie interests in regard to the merger, Bancamerica-Blair Corporation "initiated the proposal for the consolidation."

44. Prairie Oil & Gas, which acquired the Producers & Refiners Corporation in 1923, had also apparently considered acquiring an interest in the Cosden refining and marketing operations. See *Oil and Gas Journal* (November 29, 1923), 74.

45. Draft of Memorandum in Reference to Negotiations, Subject to Verification, December 11, 1933, Prairie Pipe Line Company files. Reliance was placed, in preparing this record, on the diary of Dana H. Kelsey, who had joined Prairie Pipe after serving as superintendent of the Five Civilized Tribes. See *Oil and Gas Journal* (October 7, 1921), 42.

46. Statement to L. R. Crawford, December 19, 1933, Prairie Pipe Line Company files. For changes in Prairie Pipe, see 72 Cong., 2 Sess., W. M. W. Splawn, *Report on Pipe Lines,* II, 134–135. In 1928 Blair & Co., bankers for Sinclair, bought from the Rockefeller trusts their holdings of stock in the Prairie Oil & Gas and Prairie Pipe Line companies. *New York Times,* July 17, 1930.

47. Draft of Memorandum in Reference to Negotiations, December 11, 1933, p. 5, Prairie Pipe Line Company files.

48. Sinclair Prairie Merger, Dates of Important Conferences, Statistics, Notices, 4, Prairie Pipe Line Company files.

49. The chronology of these events is in the Draft of Memorandum in Reference to Negotiations, December 11, 1933, Prairie Pipe Line Company files; see also 72 Cong., 2 Sess., W. M. W. Splawn, *Report on Pipe Lines,* II, 148–150.

50. The proposal was contained in H.R. 16695, 71 Cong., 3 Sess. (1931) to apply the commodities clause to pipelines.

51. Quoted in *National Petroleum News* (December 30, 1930), 35–37.

52. A. H. Lichty to C. H. Kountz, December 10, 1930, Prairie Pipe Line Company files.

53. 72 Cong., 2 Sess., W. M. W. Splawn, *Report on Pipe Lines,* II, 137. Although the company incurred an operating deficit for 1931, it still had no indebtedness, and

using surplus and income tax refunds for the years 1915–1928 paid dividends amounting to $6,075,000. Draft of memorandum to stockholders, dated February 8, 1932, Prairie Pipe Line Company files.

54. Answer prepared to possible questions relating to Prairie-Sinclair merger, Prairie Pipe Line Company files. (mimeo)

55. Draft of Memorandum in Reference to Negotiations, December 11, 1933, p. 5, Prairie files. Bancamerica-Blair had acquired Tide Water Associated stock from Jersey Standard and reportedly had working control of Tide Water. *New York Times*, July 17, 1930. As of January 30, 1932, the largest single interest in Prairie Pipe, 14.73 per cent, was held by the Rockefeller family. 72 Cong., 2 Sess., W. M. W. Splawn, *Report on Pipe Lines*, I, 48.

56. Letter to the Stockholders of the Prairie Oil & Gas Company from W. S. Fitzpatrick, January 14, 1932, in Sinclair Prairie Merger, Dates of Important Conferences, Statistics, Notices, 25, Prairie Pipe Line Company files.

57. *Moody's Investment Survey*, XXIV (January 25, 1932), 956.

58. 72 Cong., 2 Sess., W. M. W. Splawn, *Report on Pipe Lines*, II, 184.

59. *Sinclair Prairie Pipeline Company et al.*, 47 ICC *Valuation Reports* 613 (1937), 638.

60. 72 Cong., 2 Sess., W. M. W. Splawn, *Report on Pipe Lines*, I, 51, 54; *Standard Corporation Records* (New York, 1932), Vol. 10, C7-2.

61. 72 Cong., 2 Sess., W. M. W. Splawn, *Report on Pipe Lines*, I, 40, 42.

62. *Ibid.*, 50, 56.

63. Interview, November 28, 1962, with J. H. Contino, president of National Transit, 1942–1952.

64. *Standard Corporation Records* (New York, 1932), vol. 10, N55.

65. 72 Cong., 2 Sess., W. M. W. Splawn, *Report on Pipe Lines*, I, 379. For balance sheets for 1918 and 1931, investment in facilities, operating income, net income, and dividends, 1918–1931, see *ibid.*, 385–387.

66. National Transit Company, *Annual Report* (1915–1916).

67. For statistics for 1918–1931, see 72 Cong., 2 Sess., W. M. W. Splawn, *Report on Pipe Lines*, I, 383. For information for 1925, see National Transit Company, *Annual Report* (1925).

68. 72 Cong., 2 Sess., W. M. W. Splawn, *Report on Pipe Lines*, I, 385.

69. National Transit Company, *Annual Report* (1925).

70. S. Messer, Oil City, to N. H. Weber, vice-president of Pure Oil Co., January 18, 1927; J. A. Fawcett, Crystal Oil Works, to Weber, May 19, 1927; National Transit Company files, Oil City, Pa.

71. Protest Before the Public Service Commission of the Commonwealth of Pennsylvania, Application Docket No. 17525, 1927, National Transit Company files.

72. Petition and Protest to the Public Service Commission of the Commonwealth of Pennsylvania, Application Docket No. 17524 (1927), 11, National Transit Company files.

73. Transcript of Hearings, October 27, 1927, before the Public Service Commission of the Commonwealth of Pennsylvania, Application Docket No. 17524, pp. 31–40, 94–102, National Transit Company files.

74. Drafts of the agreement are in National Transit Company files.

75. National Transit Company, *Annual Report* (1927).

76. *Ibid.*

77. *Ibid.* (1928).

78. See 72 Cong., 2 Sess., W. M. W. Splawn, *Report on Pipe Lines*, I, 383.

79. *Ibid.*, 379–382.

80. National Transit Company, *Annual Report* (1931).

81. *Poor's Manual of Industrials, 1918*, 2205.

82. 72 Cong., 2 Sess., W. M. W. Splawn, *Report on Pipe Lines*, I, 396–397.

83. Bushnell to Kountz, March 24, 1921; Kountz to Bushnell, March 31, 1921, both in Buckeye Pipe Line Company files, New York, N.Y.

84. Buckeye Pipe Line Company, *Annual Report* (1927).

85. 72 Cong., 2 Sess., W. M. W. Splawn, *Report on Pipe Lines*, I, 397.

86. Based on author's analysis of revenues, January–June 1930, as shown in company records.

87. 72 Cong., 2 Sess., W. M. W. Splawn, *Report on Pipe Lines*, I, 395.

88. *Ibid.*, 388.

89. *Ibid.*, 425.

90. Joseph L. Massie, *Blazer and Ashland Oil, A Study in Management* (Lexington, Ky., 1960), 35, 63–64.

91. *Ibid.*, 64–65.

92. *Ibid.*, 65.

93. *Standard Corporation Records* (New York, 1919), C79; *Poor's Manual of Industrials, 1925*, II, 1032.

94. *National Petroleum News* (October 21, 1925), 29.

CHAPTER 10: Federal Investigations

1. 63 Cong., 1 Sess., S. Res. 109.

2. FTC, *Report on Pipe-Line Transportation of Petroleum, 1916*, xxvi, 4.

3. *Ibid.*, xxxi–xxxii.

4. *Ibid.*, 4.

5. *Oil and Gas Journal* (April 20, 1916), 25.

6. "The Pipe Line Industry," *New York Times* (February 28, 1916), 8.

7. Federal Trade Commission, *Report on the Price of Gasoline in 1915* (Washington, 1917), 159–162.

8. *Ibid.*, 160–164.

9. *Ibid.*, 164.

10. The headline employed by the *National Petroleum News* (December 19, 1917), 12, in connection with this report, screamed: "Standard Oil Company Still A Monopoly!"

11. Gibb and Knowlton, *Resurgent Years*, 191–193.

12. Quoted *ibid.*, 193.

13. Quoted in *National Petroleum News* (December 19, 1917), 12.

14. Federal Trade Commission, *Petroleum Trade in Wyoming and Montana* (Washington, 1922), 3.

15. FTC, *Prices, Profits, and Competition*, xviii.

16. *Ibid.*, xix. For Kansas–Oklahoma–North Texas, Prairie Oil & Gas was the price leader in most instances. For analysis of crude-oil price leadership, see *ibid.*, 196–201.

17. *Ibid.*, xxi.

18. *Ibid.*, 42.

19. *In re Magnolia*, FTC Docket 92, April 15, 1918. Dismissed 2 FTC 465 (1920). *In re Humble*, 10 FTC 426 (FTC Docket No. 964, January 26, 1926).

20. Giddens, *Standard Oil Company (Indiana)*, 314–315.

21. Belle Case and Fola La Follette, *Robert M. La Follette, June 14, 1855–June 18, 1925*, 2 vols. (New York, 1953), 771, 776, 911.

22. Warren C. Platt, "Oil Business Too Big For Probers To Grasp," *National Petroleum News* (January 24, 1923), 23.

23. 67 Cong., 2 and 4 Sess., La Follette Committee, *Hearings*, I, 591–592.

24. *Ibid.*, 588.

25. *Ibid.*, 589.

26. *Ibid.*

27. *Ibid.*, 595.

28. *Ibid.*, 1145, 1149.

29. *Ibid.*, 1146–1147.

30. *Ibid.*, 977.

31. *Ibid.*, 1148.

32. *Ibid.*, 1150.

33. *Ibid.*, 1149. Almost identical testimony was given the U.S. Industrial Commission at the turn of the century by another independent refiner and thorn in the side of Standard Oil, Lewis Emery, Jr.

34. *Ibid.*, 1168–1170.

35. *Ibid.*, 1144.

36. *Ibid.*, 1145.

37. *Ibid.*, 1174.

38. *National Petroleum News* (February 21, 1923), 94.

39. 67 Cong., 2 Sess., La Follette Committee, *Hearings*, I, 413.

40. *Ibid.*, 415–416.

41. *Ibid.*, 403–404.

42. *Ibid.*, 407–409.

43. *Ibid.*, 861.

44. *Ibid.*, 860.

45. *Ibid.*, 862–864.

46. *Ibid.*, 646–647.

47. *Ibid.*, 781.

48. See *ibid.*, 782–785.

49. *Ibid.*, 802.

50. *Ibid.*, 788.

51. *National Petroleum News* (February 7, 1923), 21.

52. 67 Cong., 4 Sess., Senate Subcommittee of the Committee on Manufactures, "High Cost of Gasoline and Other Petroleum Products," *Report* (Washington, 1923), 3.

53. *Ibid.*

54. *Ibid.*, 49.

55. *Ibid.*

56. *Ibid.*, 68.

57. *Ibid.*, 67–68.

58. *Ibid.*, 66.

59. *National Petroleum News* (March 21, 1923), 18.

60. *Ibid.* (April 4, 1923), 45.

61. *Oildom* (November 1923), 40.

CHAPTER 11: State and Federal Regulation

1. William Beard, *Regulation of Pipe Lines as Common Carriers* (New York, 1941), 68–70, 85, 105.

2. *Ibid.*, 87–88.

3. The states were Arizona, Arkansas, California, Colorado, Kansas, Kentucky, Louisiana, Michigan, Montana, Nebraska, Nevada, New Mexico, New York, Ohio, Oklahoma, Pennsylvania, South Dakota, Tennessee, Texas, West Virginia, and Wyoming. See Beard, *Regulation of Pipe Lines as Common Carriers*, 46–47.

4. *Associated Pipe Line Company v. Railroad Commission of California*, 176 Cal. 518 (1917); 169 Pac. Rep. 62.

5. *Producers' Transportation Company v. Railroad Commission of California*, 251 U.S. 228 (1920).

6. *In re Champlin Refining Company*, 129 Okla. 166, 264 Pac. Rep. 160 (1927).

7. Act No. 36, Louisiana Legislature, 1906.

8. Act No. 39, Louisiana Legislature, 1906.

9. Loos, *Oil on Stream*, 83–84.

10. A summary of complaints is in Louisiana Public Service Commission Order No. 118, Louisiana Public Service Commission *v.* Standard Oil Company of Louisiana, et al., April 14, 1923.

11. *Oil and Gas Journal* (June 10, 1915).

12. *Ibid.*

13. Act No. 76, Louisiana Legislature, 1920. As originally proposed, the bill would have been directed specifically against Louisiana Standard and some of the large oil companies, which thereby would have been effectively deprived of appeal to the courts. New Orleans *Times-Picayune* (July 6, 1920), 3.

14. *Oil and Gas Journal* (January 16, 1920), 83; New Orleans *Times-Picayune* (July 6, 1920), 23.

15. La. Pub. Serv. Com., Order No. 118.

16. Loos, *Oil on Stream*, 86–87.

17. *Ibid.*, 87–88.

18. The chronology of developments is reviewed in La. Pub. Serv. Com. Order No. 123; Louisiana Public Service Commission *v.* Standard Oil Company, et al., May 5, 1923.

19. New Orleans *Times-Picayune* (May 1, 1923), 1, 3.

20. La. Pub. Serv. Com., Order 123.

21. Loos, *Oil on Stream*, 98.

22. 67 Cong., 2 and 4 Sess., La Follette Committee, *Hearings*, I, testimony of W. H. Gray, President, National Association of Independent Oil Producers, 586.

23. Deductions of 1 per cent for each 25° change from 60°F. were also allowed.

24. George C. Butte, Chief Supervisor, Oil & Gas Dept., Railroad Commission of Texas, to ICC, December 4, 1919; Allison Mayfield, Chairman, Railroad Commission of Texas, to ICC, July 19, 1920, both in ICC files.

25. Beard, *Regulation of Pipe Lines as Common Carriers*, 64.

26. Mr. J. H. Contino, former president of National Transit, told the author in November 1962 that he helped to formulate destruction schedules adopted by the ICC.

27. George F. Getty to ICC, February 25, 1915, ICC Docket 4199, vol. 5.

28. Secretary, ICC, to W. D. Humphrey, Commissioner, Corporation Commission of Oklahoma, June 28, 1915, ICC Docket 4199, vol. 5.

29. W. S. Farish to ICC, January 11, 1917, January 25, 1917, ICC Docket 4199, vol. 5.

30. ICC to W. S. Farish, January 31, 1917, ICC Docket 4199, vol. 5.

31. *Midcontinent Oil Rates*, 36 ICC 109 (1915); *Crude Petroleum Oil from Kansas and Oklahoma*, 59 ICC 483 (1920); *Winona Oil Company v. Director General, Atchison, Topeka & Santa Fe Railway Co.*, 57 ICC 152 (1920).

32. *National Petroleum News* (January 31, 1923), 43.

33. *Depreciation Charges of Telephone Companies; Depreciation Charges of Steam Railroad Companies*, 118 ICC 295 (1926).

34. Hearings before the ICC, "Depreciation Charges of Carriers by Pipe Lines," Docket 19200 (April 12, 1927), 15–16.

35. *Ibid.*, 63–64.

36. *Ibid.*, 66.

37. 67 Cong., 2 and 4 Sess., La Follette Committee, *Hearings*, II, 1152.

38. Prairie Pipe Line Company Tariff, ICC No. 50, copy in Prairie Pipe Line files. The same stipulation was repeated in ICC No. 114, which superceded ICC No. 50 on July 3, 1919, copy in Prairie Pipe Line files.

39. Chronology is in records of Brundred Brothers case, Prairie Pipe Line files.

40. From a copy of petition filed with ICC against Prairie Pipe Line Company by Brundred Brothers, Prairie Pipe Line files.

41. *National Petroleum News* (June 16, 1920), 42.

42. 67 Cong., 2 and 4 Sess., La Follette Committee, *Hearings*, II, 1153.

43. T. J. Flannelly to C. H. Kountz, June 21, 1920, Prairie Pipe Line files.

44. C. H. Kountz to Forrest M. Towl, July 16, 1920; C. H. Kountz to D. S. Bushnell July 3, 1920, both in Prairie Pipe Line files.

45. D. S. Bushnell to C. H. Kountz, July 8, 1920, Prairie Pipe Line files.

46. Forrest M. Towl to C. H. Kountz, July 20, 1920, Prairie Pipe Line files.

47. Memorandum, September 24, 1920, Prairie Pipe Line files.
48. *Ibid.*; 67 Cong., 2 and 4 Sess., La Follette Committee, *Hearings*, II, Brundred testimony, 1158.
49. *Brundred Brothers v. Prairie Pipe Line Company et al.*, 68 ICC 458 (1922), 462–466.
50. Southern Pipe Line, to prevent contamination, operated two separate systems, one devoted exclusively to Pennsylvania-grade crude. Tax case testimony, National Transit files.
51. Allison Mayfield, Chairman, Railroad Commission of Texas to Interstate Commerce Commission, July 19, 1920, ICC files.
52. FTC, *Pipe-Line Transportation of Petroleum, 1916*, xxx.
53. *Oil and Gas Journal* (October 1920).
54. 68 ICC 458 (1922), 458–459. W. J. Brundred intimated that the producers' organization took merely a formal role in the proceedings for fear of reprisals. 67 Cong., 2 and 4 Sess., La Follette Committee, *Hearings*, II, 1157.
55. 68 ICC 458 (1922), 466.
56. 67 Cong., 2 and 4 Sess., La Follette Committee, *Hearings*, II, W. J. Brundred testimony, 1156.
57. W. J. Brundred to ICC, June 2, 1922; ICC to Brundred Brothers, June 6, 1922; W. J. Brundred to ICC, July 5, 1922; ICC to C. H. Kountz, July 8, 1922; ICC to W. J. Brundred, July 18, 1922, all in ICC Docket 11512, Miscellaneous letters and documents file.
58. Frank Lyon to T. J. Flannelly, May 15, 1922, Prairie Pipe Line files.
59. *Ibid.*
60. Telegram, T. J. Flannelly to D. S. Bushnell, May 24, 1922, Prairie Pipe Line files.
61. D. S. Bushnell to C. H. Kountz, May 19, 1920, Prairie Pipe Line files.
62. Kountz memo to F.A.L., May 23, 1922, Prairie Pipe Line files.
63. Rates based on Buckeye Pipe Line analysis of rates, in possession of author.
64. F. D. Williams, National Transit Company, to C. H. Kountz, Prairie Pipe Line Company, March 19, 1920, Prairie Pipe Line files.
65. 72 Cong., 2 Sess., W. M. W. Splawn, *Report on Pipe Lines*, II, 144.
66. *Ibid.*, 243–244, gives the full details of each of these tenders.
67. 67 Cong., 2 and 4 Sess., La Follette Committee, *Hearings*, II, 1162.
68. 72 Cong., 2 Sess., W. M. W. Splawn, *Report on Pipe Lines*, II, 144.

CHAPTER 12: The Changing Environment of Managerial Decision-Making

1. The text is reproduced in Robert E. Hardwicke, *Antitrust Laws, et al. v. Unit Operation of Oil or Gas Pools* (New York, 1948), 179–190.
2. Rister, *Oil*, 233–247; Gibb and Knowlton, *The Resurgent Years*, 445–453.
3. Larson and Porter, *Humble Oil & Refining Company*, 317.
4. Erich W. Zimmermann, *Conservation in the Production of Petroleum: A Study in Industrial Control* (New Haven, 1957), 145.
5. *General Laws of the State of Texas, 41st Texas Legislature, Acts of the Fifth Called Session*, Ch. 36 (Austin, 1930), 171.
6. As to legislative power of states to change unilaterally the status of pipeline companies after their incorporation, see *Producers' Transportation Company v. Railroad Commission of California et al.*, 176 Cal. 499; 169 Pac. 59 (1917); 251 U.S. 228 (1910); *Associated Pipe Line Co. v. Railroad Commission of California et al.*, 176 Cal. 518; 169 Pac. 62 (1917). These California cases indicated that private carriers could not be converted into common carriers by legislative or regulatory action without violating the 14th amendment. See Beard, *Regulation of Pipe Lines as Common Carriers*, 28–33.
7. See *State v. Humble Oil and Refining Company*, 263 S.W. 319 (Texas Civ. App.,

1924); a distinction was drawn between Jersey Standard and Humble despite the fact that the former owned the controlling shares of the latter.

8. *TNEC, Hearings,* VI, 191.

9. *Danciger Oil and Refining Company v. Railroad Commission of Texas et al.,* 49 S.W. 2d 837 (Texas Civ. App., 1932), 843.

10. *Ibid.*

11. *Alfred MacMillan et al. v. Railroad Commission of Texas,* 51 F 2d 400 (1931), 402–405.

12. *General Laws of the State of Texas, 42nd Texas Legislature, First Called Session,* Ch. 26 (Austin, 1931), 46.

13. *Oil and Gas Journal* (August 13, 1931), 101–102.

14. *Ibid.,* 98, 101.

15. *Supplement to the 1928 Complete Texas Statutes . . .* (41st–42nd Legislatures, 1929–1931) (Kansas City, 1931), 175.

16. *Oil and Gas Journal* (April 16, 1931), 58.

17. *General Laws of the State of Texas, 42nd Texas Legislature, 1st Called Session,* Ch. 28, sec. 6a (Austin, 1931), 60–61.

18. Railroad Commission of Texas, Oil and Gas Docket No. 122, Consolidated Docket 119, Notice of Hearings, September 8, 1931.

19. *Oil and Gas Journal* (October 1, 1931), 28.

20. *Pipe Line News* (January, 1933), 31.

21. *Oil and Gas Journal* (May 21, 1931), 62.

22. *Ibid.* (February 9, 1933), 121.

23. Railroad Commission of Texas, Oil and Gas Docket No. 139, Order Fixing and Establishing Rates of Charges for Gathering, Transporting, Loading, and Delivering Crude Petroleum by Common Carrier Pipe Lines in this State, August 31, 1933.

24. Railroad Commission of Texas, Oil and Gas Docket No. 138, Order Amending Rule Number Nine, Oil and Gas Circular Number Ten, August 31, 1933.

25. *Oil and Gas Journal* (December 31, 1931), 98.

26. N. K. Moody, President, Prairie Oil & Gas Company, to Prairie Pipe Line Company, December 31, 1930, Prairie Pipe Line files.

27. W. F. Gates, General Manager, Prairie Pipe Line Company, to all Superintendents and District Foremen, December 24, 1930, Prairie Pipe Line files.

28. *Oil and Gas Journal* (December 11, 1930), 135.

29. See, for example, *ibid.* (December 25, 1930), 40.

30. Quoted *ibid.* (December 4, 1930), 36, 152.

31. *Ibid.* (December 18, 1930), 105, 175.

32. *Ibid.* (February 5, 1931), 116.

33. 71 Cong., 3 Sess., House Committee on Interstate and Foreign Commerce, "Pipe Lines," *Hearings* (Washington, 1931), 25, 28, 30–31.

34. *Ibid.,* 18.

35. *Ibid.,* 34–35. At one point, Bowles was quite specific: "It seems to me the purpose of this bill is to make it possible for the producing end of the oil business to earn money where it is not able to earn money to-day." *Ibid.,* 67.

36. *Ibid.,* 46.

37. Joseph B. Eastman to James S. Parker, February 12, 1931, *ibid.,* 5–6.

38. H.R. 420, 72 Cong., 1 Sess.

39. 72 Cong., 2 Sess., W. M. W. Splawn, *Report on Pipe Lines,* I, lxxviii.

40. *Ibid.,* lxxvi.

41. *Ibid.,* xliii.

42. *Ibid.,* xlv.

43. *Ibid.,* xlviii.

44. *Ibid.*

45. *Ibid.,* xlii–xliii.

46. *Ibid.,* xlix.

47. *Ibid.,* xlii, 40.

48. *Ibid.*, lxiii–lxiv.
49. *Ibid., lxxii.* See also *ibid.*, 487–493, for a comparison of pipeline and rail rates.
50. *Ibid.*, lxxvii.
51. *Ibid.*
52. *Ibid.*, lxvi.
53. *Ibid.*, lxviii.
54. *Ibid.*, lxxiii.
55. *Ibid.*
56. *Ibid.*, lxxviii.
57. *Ibid.*
58. *The Secret Diary of Harold L. Ickes: The First Thousand Days, 1933–1936* (New York, 1953), 10.
59. Quoted in *The Texaco Star* (March–April 1933), 32.
60. Ickes, *The First Thousand Days*, 14.
61. Full text is in S. I. Rosenman, ed., *The Public Papers and Addresses of Franklin D. Roosevelt*, 13 vols. (New York, 1938–1950), II, 103–104.
62. H.R. 4681 (Disney, Oklahoma); S. 1579 (McAdoo, California); H.R. 5530 (Ford, California), H.R. 5044 (Marland, Oklahoma); S. 1712 (Wagner, New York), all in 73 Cong., 1 Sess.
63. *New York Times*, April 6, 1933, p. 33.
64. *Pipe Line News* (October, 1933), 3.
65. Blakely M. Murphy, ed., *Conservation of Oil and Gas: A Legal History, 1948* (Chicago, 1949), 695–696.
66. *Panama Refining Co. v. Ryan*, 293 U.S. 388 (1935), 415.
67. Mathews, *Life and Death of an Oilman*, 225–228.
68. *Pipe Line News* (November, 1933), 3.
69. *Ibid.*
70. Ickes to Beaty, April 10, 1934, in Planning and Coordination Committee for the Petroleum Industry, "Report upon Pipe Line Practices, Rates and Related Subjects," 1934, p. 2. (mimeo)
71. *Ibid.*, 4.
72. *Ibid.*, 87.
73. *Ibid.*, 86.
74. *Ibid.*, 87.
75. *TNEC Hearings*, VII, 425.
76. *Ibid.*, 454.
77. *United States Statutes at Large*, XL (Washington, 1919), 314–315.
78. Shell Petroleum Corporation, Tax Section, to Shell Pipe Line, November 26, 1935.
79. In one instance Internal Revenue insisted that the tax should be based on a flat rate that existed in the field for combined gathering and transporting, though the taxpayer in question was engaged only in gathering, and the flat rate would have returned 150 per cent on the taxpayer's investment. *National Pipe Line Co. v. United States,* 48 F. Supp. 655 (1943), 658–660.
80. See 78 *Cong. Rec.* 6555–6560, 6574 (April 13, 1934).
81. Interstate Commerce Commission, Bureau of Transport Economics and Statistics, *Selected Financial and Operating Statistics from Annual Reports of Pipe Line Companies* (Washington, 1921–1959).
82. Pew testimony in 73 Cong., Recess, House Subcommittee of the Committee on Interstate and Foreign Commerce, "Petroleum Investigation," *Hearings* (Washington, 1934), 2049–2053.
83. Weiner testimony, *ibid.*, 1651.
84. *Ibid.*
85. *Ibid.*
86. Danciger testimony, *ibid.*, 2200–2201, 2207–2208.
87. *Ibid.*, 2200.

88. *Ibid.*
89. Jones testimony, *ibid.*, 781.
90. Pratt testimony, *ibid.*, 2390.
91. *Ibid.*, 2821.
92. Sinclair testimony, *ibid.*, 2553.
93. *Ibid.*, 1806–1807.
94. Thompson testimony, *ibid.*, 1811.
95. *Ibid.*, 1808.
96. *Ibid.*, 1811.
97. Hamon testimony, *ibid.*, 1523.
98. Gore testimony, *ibid.*, 1439.
99. Marland testimony, *ibid.*, 1439–1440.

CHAPTER 13: Managerial Adaptation to Change: Crude-Oil Pipelines

1. Larson and Porter, *History of Humble Oil & Refining Company*, 520–521.
2. *Ibid.*, 521.
3. *Ibid.*
4. ICC Docket 26570, "Comparative Data in Connection With Gathering and Trunk Line Rate Charges," January 1, 1925 to July 12, 1938. (mimeo)
5. ICC Docket 26570, "Reduced Pipe Line Rates and Gathering Charges," Summary of Returns to Question VIII of Questionnaire, p. 196. (mimeo)
6. *Ibid.*, 194–195.
7. V. McC. to T. E. Swigart, January 11, 1933.
8. *Ibid.*, November 14, 1936.
9. Loos, *Oil on Stream*, 322.
10. *Ibid.*, 122.
11. Annual Report of the Sinclair Refining Company to the ICC for the Year ended December 31, 1937.
12. 85 Cong., 1 Sess., House Committee on the Judiciary, "Consent Decree Program of the Department of Justice," *Hearings before the Antitrust Subcommittee* (Subcommittee No. 5), Part I, *Oil Pipelines*, 2 vols. (Washington 1957–1958), 525.
13. "American Petroleum Institute meeting and plans for cooperating with Interstate Commerce Commission in valuation of pipelines," *ibid.*, 893–895.
14. *Pipe Line News* (December 1936), 3.
15. 85 Cong., 1 Sess., House Committee on the Judiciary, Consent Decree *Hearings*, 476.
16. "Method of Establishing Final Value of Common Carrier Oil Pipelines," *ibid.*, 476–477.
17. Testimony of ICC Chairman Clarke, *ibid.*, 449.
18. *Ibid.*, 446.
19. ICC Docket 26570, "Proposed Reductions by Pipe Lines of Trunk Line Rates and Gathering Charges on Crude Petroleum: Protest and Prayer for Suspension," June 11, 1934. (mimeo)
20. ICC Docket 26570, "Reduced Pipe Line Rates and Gathering Charges," Report Proposed by J. Paul Kelley, Examiner, April 1936. (mimeo)
21. Telegram, Stanolind Pipe Line to George B. McGinty, Secretary, ICC, June 18, 1934.
22. ICC, Office of the Secretary, Memorandum for the Press, June 20, 1934. Within the industry, Petroleum Administrator Ickes was credited with spurring the ICC to take action.
23. ICC Docket 26570, Report Proposed by J. Paul Kelley, 2–3.
24. Hearing before the Interstate Commerce Commission, "In Re: Reduced Pipeline Rates and Gathering Charges," Docket 26570, July 23, 1935, p. 23. (mimeo)
25. *Ibid.*, 19.
26. *Ibid.*, 21.

27. *Ibid.*, 8–9.

28. R. F. Smith to R. G. A. van der Woude, Shell Union Oil Corporation, June 12, 1936.

29. *Pipe Line News* (July 1936), 5.

30. ICC Docket 26570, *Reduced Pipe Line Rates and Gathering Charges. Reply of the Standard Oil Company (Ohio) and National Refining Company to Pipe Line Briefs of Exceptions* (Cleveland, July 2, 1936), 15.

31. *Ibid.*, 8.

32. Thompson, Mitchell, Thompson & Young to R. F. Smith, Shell Pipe Line Corporation, March 31, 1937.

33. Report on Pipe Line Rate Conference, Drake Hotel, Chicago, August 8, 1938.

34. Memo, R. B. High to Alexander Fraser, September 30, 1938, "Proposed Pipe Line Rate Reduction."

35. *Pipe Line News* (December 1938), 3.

36. *Reduced Pipe Line Rates and Gathering Charges*, 243 ICC 115 (1940).

37. *Ibid.*, 141.

38. *Ibid.*, 132.

39. *Ibid.*, 140–141.

40. *Ibid.*, 128.

41. *Ibid.*, 135.

42. *Ibid.*, 136–137.

43. *Ibid.*, 138–142.

44. *Ibid.*, 142.

45. *Ibid.*, 145.

CHAPTER 14: Innovation and its Repercussions: Gasoline Pipelines

1. API, *Petroleum Facts and Figures, 1959*, pp. 40–41; *Midcontinent Oil Rates*, 36 ICC 109 (1915), 112.

2. Joseph E. Pogue, *The Economics of Petroleum* (New York, 1921), 85.

3. *Midcontinent Oil Rates*, 36 ICC 109 (1915).

4. *Ibid.*, 110.

5. *Ibid.*, 111.

6. *Ibid.*, 112.

7. *Petroleum Rail Shippers' Association v. Alton & Southern Railroad et al.*, 243 ICC 589 (1941), 605.

8. See U.S. Bureau of Mines, *United States Government Specification For Lubricants and Liquid Fuels and Methods for Testing*, Technical Paper 323A (Washington, 1924).

9. C. P. Bowie, *Transportation of Gasoline by Pipe Line*, U.S. Bureau of Mines Technical Paper 517 (Washington, 1932), 17.

10. Dow testimony, *TNEC Hearings*, VI, 497; Pew testimony, *ibid.*, 62.

11. *Pipe Line News* (October, 1931), 30.

12. 72 Cong., 2 Sess., W. M. W. Splawn, *Report on Pipe Lines*, I, 244–246.

13. McLean and Haigh, *Growth of Integrated Oil Companies*, 208–209.

14. *Oil and Gas Journal* (February 27, 1920), 76; *ibid.* (March 12, 1920), 56.

15. Phillips Petroleum Company, *Annual Report* (1931), 4. For a detailed description of the Phillips system, see *Oil and Gas Journal* (September 10, 1931), 14.

16. *Pipe Line News* (August, 1931), 16.

17. 72 Cong., 2 Sess., W. M. W. Splawn, *Report on Pipe Lines*, I, 75.

18. *Pipe Line News* (June, 1933), 4; *ibid.* (August, 1933), 19.

19. 72 Cong., 2 Sess., W. M. W. Splawn, *Report on Pipe Lines*, I, 75–76.

20. *Pipe Line News* (December, 1932), 36.

21. *Oil and Gas Journal* (February 5, 1931), 25.

22. *TNEC Hearings*, VI, 91. Sixteen reporting companies showed that crude oil barrel-miles increased between January 1, 1929, and January 1, 1939, from

136,000,000,000 to 238,000,000,000. Mileage of eighteen major companies increased from 57,800 to 75,887 in the same period.

23. *Ibid.*, 92.

24. Interstate Commerce Commission, *A Review of Statistics of Oil Pipe Lines, 1921–1941* (Washington, 1942), 15.

25. *Ibid.*

26. *Ibid.*, 21.

27. *TNEC Hearings*, VI, 97.

28. *Ibid.*

29. *Pipe Line News* (March 1935), 1; *Champlin Refining Company v. United States et al.*, 329 U.S. 29 (1946).

30. Beaton, *Enterprise in Oil*, 430.

31. *Ibid.*, 435.

32. *Ibid.*

33. "A Confidential Report, Descriptive of the Construction and Operation of the Gasoline and Products Pipe Line," Shell Oil Co., Inc., St. Louis (August 1939). This study was also used by Beaton and is correctly described in n. 11, p. 736 of *Enterprise in Oil* as "lucid and attractive."

34. *Ibid.*

35. Beaton, *Enterprise in Oil*, 438.

36. *Ibid.*, 440–441. See also *Pipe Line News* (May 1948), 30.

37. "A Confidential Report . . ." Shell Oil Co. (August 1939).

38. *Ibid.*

39. Beaton, *Enterprise in Oil*, 442–445.

40. *Ibid.*, 447.

41. *Ibid.*, 494.

42. Quoted *ibid.*, 447.

43. ICC, *A Review of Statistics of Oil Pipe Lines, 1921–1941*, pp. 37–38.

44. *Petroleum Rail Shippers' Association v. Alton & Southern Railroad et al.*, 243 ICC 589 (1941).

45. *Ibid.*, 618.

46. *Ibid.*

47. *Ibid.*, 631.

48. *Ibid.*, 635.

49. *Ibid.*, 639.

50. *Ibid.*, 657.

51. *Ibid.*, 658.

52. *Ibid.*

53. *Ibid.*, 659.

54. *Ibid.*, 658.

55. *Ibid.*, 662.

56. *Ibid.*, 661.

57. *Ibid.*, 673.

58. *Ibid.*, 665.

CHAPTER 15: The Revival of Antitrust Interest in Integrated Oil Operations

1. 78 *Cong. Rec.* 3958–3959.

2. 73 Cong., 2 Sess., S. 2995.

3. 74 Cong., 1 Sess., S. 573.

4. 75 Cong., 1 Sess., S. 1398.

5. 76 Cong., 1 Sess., S. 2181.

6. *Ibid.*

7. 73 Cong., 2 Sess., H.R. 8572, H.R. 9676; 75 Cong., 1 Sess., H.R. 6794 and 76 Cong., 1 Sess., H.R. 2304 all dealt with pipelines; 75 Cong., 1 Sess., H.R. 7800,

75 Cong., 3 Sess., H.R. 10089 and 76 Cong., 1 Sess., H.R. 2318 all dealt with marketing. Only the latter reached the stage of committee hearings.

8. 76 Cong., 1 Sess., H.R. 7136.

9. 76 Cong., 1 Sess., Senate Committee on Interstate Commerce, "Transportation Act of 1939," *Hearings* (Washington, 1939), 427.

10. Telegram, Ellison to Peake, June 8, 1939.

11. 298 U.S. 492 (1936), 501. This decision was reaffirmed in *United States v. South Buffalo Ry. Co.*, 333 U.S. 771 (1948), which involved a railroad owned by Bethlehem Steel Corporation.

12. *United States v. Socony-Vacuum Oil Co.*, 310 U.S. 150 (1940).

13. *TNEC Hearings*, VI, 409, 413.

14. *Ibid.*, 413.

15. *Ibid.*, 434.

16. *Ibid.*, 438.

17. *Ibid.*, 411–412, 440.

18. *Ibid.*, 412.

19. *Ibid.*, 429.

20. *Ibid.*, 413, 429.

21. *Ibid.*, 429.

22. *Ibid.*, 414–415.

23. *Ibid.*

24. *Ibid.*, 415.

25. *Ibid.*, 414.

26. *Ibid.*, 431.

27. *Ibid.*

28. *Ibid.*, 412.

29. *Ibid.*, 431.

30. *Ibid.*, 209.

31. *Ibid.*

32. *Ibid.*, 212.

33. *Ibid.*, 195.

34. *Ibid.*, 495–496.

35. *Ibid.*, 258, 263–264.

36. *Ibid.*, 257–258, 263.

37. American Petroleum Institute, *Petroleum-Industry Hearings Before the Temporary National Economic Committee* (New York, 1942), 91.

38. *Ibid.*, 90–91.

39. *TNEC Hearings*, VI, 127.

40. *Ibid.*, 65.

41. *Ibid.*, 65, 128.

42. *Ibid.*, 64.

43. *Ibid.*, 127.

44. *Ibid.*, 195.

45. *Ibid.*, VII, 452.

46. *Ibid.*, 425.

47. *Ibid.*, 453.

48. *Ibid.*, 436.

49. *Ibid.*

50. *Ibid.*, 437.

51. *Ibid.*, VI, 581.

52. *Ibid.*, VII, 5.

53. *Ibid.*, 453.

54. *Ibid.*, VI, 454.

55. *Ibid.*, VII, 6.

56. *Ibid.*, 7.

57. *Ibid.*

58. *Ibid.,* VI, 485.
59. *Ibid.,* 494.
60. *Ibid.,* 495.
61. *Ibid.,* 497.
62. *Ibid.,* 503.
63. American Petroleum Institute, *Petroleum-Industry Hearings,* 52.
64. *Ibid.,* 54–55.
65. *Ibid.,* 56.
66. Roy C. Cook, *Control of the Petroleum Industry by Major Oil Companies,* TNEC Monograph 39 (Washington, 1941), 19–28.
67. W. S. Farish and J. Howard Pew, *Review and Criticism on Behalf of Standard Oil Co. (New Jersey) and Sun Oil Co. of Monograph No. 39 with Rejoinder by Monograph Author,* TNEC Monograph 39-A (Washington, 1941), 34.
68. *Ibid.,* 32.
69. John Scoville and Noel Sargent, comps., *Fact and Fancy in the T.N.E.C. Monographs* (New York, 1942), 705–717.

CHAPTER 16: Antitrust Conflict and Compromise

1. Henry D. Ralph, "Investigations Reflect Policy of Department of Justice," *Oil and Gas Journal* (May 25, 1939), 20.
2. Justice Department lawyers had the benefit of access to prepared statements of industry representatives prior to their presentation, and their cross-examination was aided by this fact. *Ibid.* (September 28, 1939), 15.
3. See Gillette's remarks in 86 *Cong. Rec.* (October 3, 1940), 13067–13069.
4. The Report of the Advisory Commission is in 85 Cong., 1 Sess., House Committee on the Judiciary, Consent Decree *Hearings,* 1278–1282.
5. Jackson to Gillette, September 28, 1940, reproduced *ibid.,* 1283.
6. *Ibid.,* 121–125, 141. The complaints of the Department of Justice in the Mother Hubbard and the Elkins Act cases are reproduced in full *ibid.,* 121–180.
7. *Ibid.,* 1323–1324.
8. *Ibid.,* 1327.
9. *Ibid.,* 158, par. 10.
10. *Ibid.,* 27. See also *ibid.,* 1320.
11. *U.S. v. Phillips Petroleum Company and Phillips Pipeline Company,* Civil Action No. 182 (D. C., Delaware, September 30, 1940), *ibid.,* 156–161.
12. *U.S. v. Standard Oil Company (Indiana),* Civil Action No. 201 (D. C., Northern District of Indiana, Hammond Division, September 30, 1940), *ibid.,* 166–169.
13. *U.S. v. Great Lakes Pipe Line Co.,* Civil Action No. 183 (D. C., Delaware, September 30, 1940), *ibid.,* 161–166.
14. 85 Cong., 1 Sess., House Committee on the Judiciary, Consent Decree *Hearings,* 158.
15. *Ibid.,* 164.
16. *Ibid.,* 168.
17. Interviews of George Harmon with Mac Asbill and Paul Hadlick, January 24, 1962.
18. Forrest R. Black, "Oil Pipe Line Divorcement," *Cornell Law Quarterly* (June 1940), 521.
19. See Sharfman, *The Interstate Commerce Commission,* I, 1–21.
20. Act of February 19, 1903, 32 Stat. 847.
21. 49 U.S. Code 41 (3).
22. See 85 Cong., 1 Sess., House Committee on the Judiciary, Consent Decree *Hearings,* 1381.
23. Thompson testimony, *ibid.,* 1285.
24. *Ibid.,* 1323.

25. Report read to counsel in antitrust case by Schofield Andrews of Ballard, Spahr, Andrews & Ingersoll, January 8, 1941, *ibid.*, 1323.

26. *Ibid.*, 1324.

27. *Ibid.*

28. See Giddens, *Standard Oil Company (Indiana)*, 101–121.

29. See Gillette's remarks in 86 *Cong. Rec.* (October 3, 1940), 13067–13073.

30. 85 Cong., 1 Sess., House Committee on the Judiciary, Consent Decree *Hearings*, 1326–1327.

31. *Ibid.*, 1328.

32. *Ibid.*, 1369.

33. *Ibid.*, 1371.

34. *Ibid.*, 1370.

35. *Ibid.*, 1372.

36. *Ibid.*, 1396.

37. *Ibid.*, 1395.

38. Thompson to Klein, March 21, 1941, *ibid.*, 1397.

39. *Ibid.*

40. *Ibid.*, 1412.

41. *Petroleum Rail Shippers Association v. Alton & Southern Railroad et al.*, 243 ICC 589 (1941), 663, 665.

42. 85 Cong., 1 Sess., House Committee on the Judiciary, Consent Decree *Hearings*, 1416.

43. *Ibid.*, 1436–1437.

44. *Ibid.*, 1439.

45. *Ibid.*, 1423.

46. U.S. Petroleum Administration for War, *A History of the Petroleum Administration for War, 1941–1945* (Washington, 1946), 14.

47. 85 Cong., 1 Sess., House Committee on the Judiciary, Consent Decree *Hearings*, 1537.

48. Jackson to Ickes, June 3, 1941, reproduced in *A History of the Petroleum Administration for War*, 382.

49. Ickes to Jackson, June 16, 1941, *ibid.*

50. Act of July 30, 1941, C. 333, 55 Stat. 610, amended by Acts of June 30, 1942 (C. 180, 57 Stat. 270); June 8, 1945 (C. 177, 59 Stat. 233); July 25, 1947 (C. 327, 61 Stat. 449).

51. 85 Cong., 1 Sess., House Committee on the Judiciary, Consent Decree *Hearings*, 1539.

52. *Ibid.*, 1597.

53. *Ibid.*, 1541.

54. U.S. Petroleum Administration for War, Supply and Transportation Division, Pipeline Engineering Section, "History Petroleum Pipeline Transportation" (Washington, 1945), 28. (mimeo)

55. 85 Cong., 1 Sess., House Committee on the Judiciary, Consent Decree *Hearings*, 1600, 1601.

56. *Ibid.*, 1619.

57. *Ibid.*

58. *Ibid.*, 1258–1259.

59. *Ibid.*, 1304. The agreement is published in full *ibid.*, 1304–1310.

60. *Ibid.*, 1303.

61. *Ibid.*, 1615.

62. 77 Cong., 1 Sess., S. Rpt. 676, p. 2.

63. 85 Cong., 1 Sess., House Committee on the Judiciary, Consent Decree *Hearings*, 1268.

64. *Ibid.*

65. *Ibid.*, 1620.

66. *Ibid.*, 1616.

67. *Ibid.*
68. *Ibid.*, 1648.
68. Arnold to Klein, December 11, 1941, *ibid.*, 1313.
70. *Ibid.*, 1261.
71. *Ibid.*, 1620.
72. 85 Cong., 1 Sess., House Committee on the Judiciary, *Report of the Antitrust Subcommittee (Subcommittee No. 5) on Consent Decree Program of the Department of Justice* (Washington, 1959), 170.
73. *Ibid.*
74. 77 Cong., 2 Sess., H.R. 472.
75. *United States v. Atlantic Refining Company et al.*, Civil Action No. 14060, Final Judgment (D.C., District of Columbia), December 23, 1941.
76. New York *Times*, December 24, 1941.

CHAPTER 17: Pipelines in the War Effort

1. Sam G. Spal, "War-Built Pipe Lines and the Post-War Transportation of Petroleum," ICC, Bureau of Economics and Statistics (August 1944), 34–35. (mimeo)
2. T. E. Swigart, "Oil's Wartime Achievement in Transportation," paper presented at Meeting of American Petroleum Institute, Southwestern District (April 29, 1943), p. 9.
3. ICC, *Review of Statistics of Oil Pipe Lines, 1921–1941*, p. 27.
4. *Ibid.*
5. Spal, *War-Built Pipe Lines*, 39, 41.
6. N. J. McGaw, Memorandum of Discussions Regarding Southern Pipe Line.
7. *Pipeline News* (February 1940), 2.
8. *Oil and Gas Journal* (April 18, 1940), 35.
9. 85 Cong., 1 Sess., House Committee on the Judiciary, *Consent Decree Hearings*, 1598–1599.
10. Act of July 30, 1941, c. 333, 55 Stat. 610 as later amended June 30, 1942, c. 180, 57 Stat. 270; June 8, 1945, c. 177, 59 Stat. 233; July 25, 1947, c. 327, 61 Stat. 499, cited in note preceding U.S. Code Title 15, Section 715.
11. Henry D. Ralph, "Petroleum Industry War Council at Work," *Oil and Gas Journal* (June 11, 1942), 16.
12. Report of Tulsa Pipe Line Conference by Temporary Joint Pipe Line Subcommittee, Districts 1, 2, and 3 (April 2, 1942), 15–16, (mimeo)
13. *Ibid.*, 41.
14. *Ibid.*, 44.
15. Bayou Pipe Line System, Plan and Agreement, August 28, 1942.
16. John W. Frey and H. Chandler Ide, eds., *A History of the Petroleum Administration for War, 1941–1945* (Washington, 1946), 419.
17. *Ibid.*, 87.
18. Petroleum Administration for War, "History, Pipeline Transportation during War Period, as of September 30, 1945" (Washington, October 1945), 29. (mimeo)
19. *Ibid.*, 30.
20. *Ibid.*
21. Wallace R. Finney and J. B. Adoue, "The 'Big Inch' Pipe Line," *Mining and Metallurgy* (October 1943), 442.
22. A complete chronology of events in the development of the Big Inch systems, 1940–1944, is in War Emergency Pipelines, Inc., *Fuel for the Fighting Fronts . . . via "Big Inch" and "Little Inch"* (New York, 1944), 4–8.
23. Frey and Ide, *History of the PAW*, 87.
24. WEP, *Fuel for the Fighting Fronts*, 8.
25. *Ibid.*, 11.
26. *Ibid.*, 8, 11.
27. See 79 Cong., 1 Sess., Senate Committee on Military Affairs, "War Emergency

Pipe-Line Systems and Other Petroleum Facilities," *Report to the Special Committee Investigating Petroleum Resources and to the Surplus Property Subcommittee of the Committee on Military Affairs* (Washington, 1945), 6–7.

28. John D. Goodloe, General Counsel, RFC, to Senator O'Mahoney, August 2, 1945, quoted *ibid.*, 6–7.

29. Frey and Ide, *History of the PAW*, 104.

30. *Ibid.*, 417.

31. Beaton, *Enterprise in Oil*, 610–615.

32. The Editors of *Look, Oil for Victory* (New York, 1946), 117.

CHAPTER 18: Pipeline Management Problems

1. PAW, *History, Pipeline Transportation as of September 30, 1945*, p. 5.

2. *Ibid.*

3. *Ibid.*, 68.

4. *Ibid.*, 15, PAW project 21.

5. *Ibid.*, PAW project 22.

6. *Ibid.*, 17, PAW project 27.

7. Geo. A. Wilson, Director of Supply and Transportation, PAW, to W. M. Averill, May 11, 1944.

8. Ickes to L. M. Glasco, June 3, 1944, in "Before the Petroleum Administrator for War, Application of Pacific War Emergency Pipelines, Inc., A Compendium" (pamphlet).

9. See 78 Cong., 1 Sess., House Select Committee to Conduct a Study and Investigation of the National Defense Program in its Relation to Small Business in the United States, "A Study and Investigation of the National Defense Program in Its Relation to Small Business," *Hearings* (Washington, 1943), esp. 2831.

10. Quoted in The Houston *Post*, August 10, 1945.

11. For criticism of this device, see Walter Adams and Horace M. Gray, *Monopoly in America: The Government as Promoter* (New York, 1955), 84–90.

12. Frey and Ide, *History of the PAW*, 371.

13. *Ibid.*, 383–384.

14. 85 Cong., 1 Sess., Senate Committee on the Judiciary, Subcommittee on Antitrust and Monopoly, "Petroleum, the Antitrust Laws and Government Policies," *Report . . . with Minority Views* (Washington, 1957), 14.

15. Frey and Ide, *History of the PAW*, 372.

16. See PAW, *History, Pipeline Transportation as of September 30, 1945*, pp. 6–20.

17. 85 Cong., 1 Sess., House Committee on the Judiciary, Consent Decree *Report*, 176.

18. 85 Cong., 1 Sess., House Committee on the Judiciary, Consent Decree *Hearings*, 1648.

19. *United States v. The Atlantic Refining Company et al.*, Civil Action No. 14060 in the District Court of the United States for the District of Columbia, Petition of Great Lakes Pipe Line Company filed August 3, 1942, and Orders Thereon Entered August 3, 1942.

20. Testimony of Fayette B. Dow, 85 Cong., 1 Sess., House Committee on the Judiciary, Consent Decree *Hearings*, 1010.

21. *Ibid.*, 896.

22. *Ibid.*, 897.

23. Shell Pipe Line Corporation, Estimated Fair Value of Owned and Used Property as of December 31, 1941.

24. The correspondence is reprinted in the 90 *Cong. Rec.* (March 28, 1944), 3202.

25. Justice Department representatives under questioning before the Celler Committee in 1957 were reluctant to go into details about FBI investigations of the industry.

26. 85 Cong., 1 Sess., House Committee on the Judiciary, Consent Decree *Report*, 185–186.

27. Memo, Paul Ryan to subcommittee members, September 20, 1943.

28. Robert E. Wilson, chairman of Committee on Petroleum Economics, PIWC, to T. E. Swigart, February 9, 1944.

29. *The Gasoline Retailer*, January 8, 1944.

30. *Platt's Oilgram*, December 11, 1945.

31. *Ibid.*, February 21, 1946.

32. Quoted in National Petroleum Council, *A Unique Experience in Government–Industry Cooperation: The First Seven Years, 1946–1953* (Washington?, 1961), 36.

33. Roeser to Davies, March 24, 1943.

34. T. E. Swigart, Shell Pipe Line, to Alexander Fraser, Shell Oil Company, June 12, 1943.

35. 79 Cong., 1 Sess., Senate Committee on Military Affairs, "War Emergency Pipe-Line Sysems and Other Petroleum Facilities," *Hearings before the Special Committee Investigating Petroleum Resources and the Surplus Property Subcommittee . . .* (Washington, 1945), 251.

36. *Ibid.*

37. *Ibid.*; T. E. Swigart, Shell Pipe Line, to Alexander Fraser, Shell Oil Company, June 20, 1945.

38. See *Platt's Oilgram*, September 11, 1945.

39. T. E. Swigart, "Postwar Uses of the War Emergency Pipe Lines for Petroleum Transportation," *Petroleum Technology* (September 1944), 28.

40. *Oil and Gas Journal* (November 18, 1944), 185–186. See 79 Cong., 1 Sess., Senate Committee on Military Affairs, "Pipe-Line Systems," *Hearings*, 28.

41. See Surplus Property Administration, *Government-Owned Pipe Lines: Report to the Congress* (Washington, 1946), 38, for comparison of cost estimates by various parties.

42. Finney and Adoue, "The 'Big Inch' Pipe Line," 444.

43. *Ibid.*, 445.

44. Testimony of Sidney A. Swensrud before 79 Cong., 1 Sess., House Select Committee to Investigate Disposition of Surplus Property, "Investigation, Disposition of Surplus Property," *Hearings*, 3 vols. (Washington, 1946), 2282.

45. 79 Cong., 1 Sess., Senate Committee on Military Affairs, "Pipe-Line Systems," *Hearings*, 263.

46. *Platt's Oilgram* (December 20, 1945).

47. 79 Cong., 1 Sess., Senate Committee on Military Affairs, "Pipe-Line Systems," *Report*, 2–3.

48. Surplus Property Administration, *Government-Owned Pipe Lines*, 26.

49. Swensrud testimony, 79 Cong., 1 Sess., House Select Committee to Investigate Disposition of Surplus Property, *Hearings*, 2281.

50. See 79 Cong., 2 Sess., Senate Committee on Military Affairs, "War-Plants Disposal: Bids for Big Inch and Little Inch Pipe Lines," *Report of the Surplus Property Subcommittee*. (Washington, 1946), especially 2, 36–37.

51. Statement of Ralph K. Davies, 79 Cong., 1 Sess., House Select Committee to Investigate Disposition of Surplus Property, *Hearings*, 2591.

52. *Pipe Line News* (November 1946), 11.

53. *Ibid.* (February 1947), 3.

CHAPTER 19: Postwar Pipeline Expansion: The First Round

1. *Oil and Gas Journal* (November 2, 1950), 32; API, *Petroleum Facts and Figures, 1959*, 156.

2. For an economic analysis of pipeline costs, see Leslie Cookenboo, Jr., *Crude Oil Pipe Lines and Competition in the Oil Industry* (Cambridge, Mass., 1955), chap. i.

3. Loren F. Kahle, "Continued Increased Petroleum Demands," *Oil and Gas Journal* (October 13, 1952), 198.

4. *Oil and Gas Journal* (September 20, 1947), 170.

5. *Pipe Line News* (June 1948), 6.

6. *Oil and Gas Journal* (March 1, 1947), 51. Agreement, Jal-Cushing Pipe Line System (Basin Pipeline System), 17 Sept. 1947.

7. *Pipe Line News* (October 1950), 55.

8. *Oil and Gas Journal* (July 19, 1947), 113.

9. *Pipe Line News* (June 1948), 4.

10. *Oil and Gas Journal* (July 20, 1950), 52.

11. *Ibid.* (January 5, 1950), 86.

12. See Beaton, *Enterprise in Oil*, 607n.

13. *Oil and Gas Journal* (June 29, 1950), 58.

14. *Ibid.* (September 21, 1950), 244; McLean and Haigh, *Growth of Integrated Oil Companies*, 198.

15. *Oil and Gas Journal* (July 26, 1951), 226–228; Sinclair Oil Corporation, *Annual Report* (1952), 9.

16. *Ibid.* (June 21, 1951), 350; The Ohio Oil Company, *Annual Report* (1952), 12.

17. *World Oil* (May 1953), 256–258.

18. Neill C. Wilson and Frank J. Taylor, *The Building of Trans Mountain: Canada's First Oil Pipeline Across the Rockies* (Vancouver, B.C., 1954), 15.

19. *Ibid.*, 24.

20. *Ibid.*, 87–88; Trans Mountain Oil Pipe Line Company, *Annual Report* (1954), unpaginated.

21. *Oil and Gas Journal* (October 12, 1950), 66; (November 10, 1949), 387.

22. Great Lakes *Annual Report* (1946).

23. *Ibid.* (1947).

24. *Ibid.*

25. *Oil and Gas Journal* (April 13, 1950), 127; *ibid.* (May 25, 1950), 88–90.

26. *Pipe Line News* (November 1946), 3.

27. Larson and Porter, *History of Humble Oil & Refining Company*, 628.

28. *The Sinclair Pipeliner* (November 1954), 7, 9.

29. *Ibid.*, 9.

30. *Oil and Gas Journal* (July 6, 1950), 77.

31. *Ibid.* (July 27, 1950), 343.

32. *Ibid.* (November 2, 1950), 29–30 and map.

33. *Ibid.* (February 22, 1951), 209; *ibid.* (July 26, 1951), 226.

34. Loos, *Oil on Stream*, 226–227.

35. API, *Petroleum Facts and Figures, 1959*, 153.

36. New York Transit Company, *Annual Report* (1941).

37. Plan of Unification of the Buckeye Pipe Line Company, Indiana Pipe Line Company, Northern Pipe Line Company, New York Transit Company, November 10, 1942, p. 2.

38. PAW, *History, Pipeline Transportation as of September 30, 1945*, p. 16. PAW project 25.

39. McLean and Haigh, *Growth of Integrated Companies*, 423.

40. Buckeye Pipe Line Company, *The Flow of Oil: The Story of the Buckeye Pipe Line Company and Its 75 Years of Service to the Petroleum Industry* (New York, 1961), 17.

41. *Oil City Weekly Derrick*, January 8, 1948.

42. *Ibid.*

43. See API *Daily Oil News* (November 10, 1948).

44. *Oil and Gas Journal* January 25, 1951), 173.

45. John E. Boice, special assistant to Director, Supply and Transportation Division, PAD, "Keeping Oil Flowing for National Defense," remarks before API Conference on Products Pipeline Technology, Fort Worth, Texas, April 21, 1952. (mimeo)

46. *Oil and Gas Journal* (March 10, 1952), 66–67; *ibid.* (September 15, 1952), 69.

47. *Ibid.* (November 17, 1952), 249.

48. *Ibid.* (December 8, 1952), 74.

49. *Ibid.* (January 12, 1953), 68.
50. API, *Petroleum Facts and Figures, 1959*, pp. 153, 157.

CHAPTER 20: Postwar Pipeline Expansion: The Second Round

1. *Oil and Gas Journal* (February 4, 1957), 88.
2. This account is based on the statement of the Shell Oil Company to the Senate Judiciary Subcommittee on Antitrust and Monopoly Relating to Complaint by Standard Pipe Line Company (typescript); *Petroleum Week* (December 2, 1955), 16.
3. U.S. Bureau of Mines, *Information Circular 7769* (1956), 1.
4. *Oil and Gas Journal* (January 28, 1957), 125.
5. *Ibid.* (February 11, 1957), 74.
6. *Ibid.* (December 9, 1957), 66.
7. *Petroleum Week* (December 2, 1955), 11–12.
8. *Ibid.*
9. *Oil and Gas Journal* (July 7, 1958), 84.
10. *Ibid.* (January 26, 1959), 150.
11. Arthur M. Johnson, *Government–Business Relations: A Pragmatic Approach to the American Experience* (Columbus, O., 1965), 66.
12. Trans Mountain Oil Pipe Line Company, *Annual Report* (1953), 3.
13. Interprovincial Pipe Line Company, *Annual Report* (1954), 4.
14. *Oil and Gas Journal* (September 16, 1957), 103.
15. This account was adapted from a mimeographed company report.
16. *Oil and Gas Journal* (January 27, 1958), 185.
17. R. P. Lennart, Service Pipe Line, "Pipelining Crude Oil," paper at 15th Joint Technical Meeting, April 20, 1957, p. 10.
18. U.S. Department of the Interior, *An Appraisal of the Petroleum Industry* (Washington, 1965), table 61.
19. Butte Pipe Line Company joint tariff from Poplar and Cabin Creek, Montana, to North Tonawanda, New York, ICC no. 65.
20. API, *Petroleum Facts and Figures, 1959*, p. 153.
21. U.S. Department of the Interior, *An Appraisal of the Petroleum Industry,* table 61.
22. U.S. Bureau of Mines, *Information Circular 7769* (1956), 2.
23. *Oil and Gas Journal* (September 20, 1954), 274.
24. *Ibid.* (October 26, 1953), 61.
25. *Oil and Gas Journal* (February 14, 1955), 94; Beaton, *Enterprise in Oil*, 657.
26. Loos, *Oil on Stream*, 300–308.
27. *Oil and Gas Journal* (February 17, 1958), 70.
28. API Division of Transportation, "Design Features of the Laurel Pipe Line System," *Report on the Annual Pipe Line Conference* (May 1959), D-1.
29. Texas Eastern Transmission Company, *Annual Report* (1956), 10; *Texas Eastern Transmission Corporation et al.*, 17 FPC 843 (1957).
30. Texas Eastern Transmission Company, *Annual Report* (1958), 2.
31. U.S. Department of the Interior, *An Appraisal of the Petroleum Industry,* tables 8 and 9.
32. *Oil and Gas Journal* (October 14, 1957), 110.
33. Phillips Petroleum Company, *Annual Report* (1954), 18.
34. *Oil and Gas Journal* (October 14, 1957), 110.
35. National Petroleum Council, *Report of the Committee on Oil and Gas Transportation Facilities* (Washington, 1962), 110.
36. API, *Petroleum Facts and Figures 1959*, p. 418.

CHAPTER 21: The ICC and Petroleum Pipelines

1. ICC, *Annual Report* (1940), 133–134.
2. *Ibid.*, 134.

3. Clarke testimony, 85 Cong., 1 Sess., House Committee on the Judiciary, Consent Decree *Hearings*, 445. See also ICC, *Annual Report* (1949), 128.

4. For the method revealed by the ICC in 1957, see 85 Cong., 1 Sess., House Committee on the Judiciary, Consent Decree *Hearings*, 476–478.

5. *Reduced Pipe Line Rates and Gathering Charges*, 272 ICC 375 (1948), 383.

6. ICC, *Annual Report* (1949), 128.

7. Reed to Mahaffie, February 18, 1948, in 85 Cong., 1 Sess., House Committee on the Judiciary, Consent Decree *Hearings*, 462.

8. Mahaffie to Reed, February 24, 1948, *ibid.*, 462–463.

9. *Increased Freight Rates, 1947*, 270 ICC 403 (1948).

10. Clarke testimony, 85 Cong., 1 Sess., House Committee on the Judiciary, Consent Decree *Hearings*, 448.

11. Interstate Commerce Commission, *ICC Activities, 1937–1962: Supplement to the 75th Annual Report* (Washington, 1962), 89.

12. *Petroleum Rail Shippers' Association v. Alton & Southern Railroad et al.*, 243 ICC 589 (1941).

13. *Minnelusa Oil Corporation et al. v. Continental Pipe Line Company et al.*, 258 ICC 41 (1944), 51.

14. *Ibid.*, 52.

15. *Ibid.*, 62.

16. *Ibid.*, 60.

17. *Ibid.*, 57.

18. *Ibid.*, 59.

19. *Reduced Pipe Line Rates and Gathering Charges*, 272 ICC 375 (1948), 380.

20. *Ibid.*, 380–381.

21. *Ibid.*, 381–382.

22. *Ibid.*, 384.

23. *Petition of the Valvoline Oil Company in the Matter of the Valuation of Its Pipe Lines*, 48 ICC *Valuation Reports* 10 (1938).

24. *Ibid.*, 14–15.

25. *Valvoline Oil Co. v. United States*, 308 U.S. 141 (1939).

26. Wolbert, *American Pipe Lines*, 124 n. 85.

27. *Ibid.*, 124.

28. *Champlin Refining Company, Valuation of Pipe Line*, 49 ICC *Valuation Reports* 463 (1942).

29. *Champlin Refining Company, Valuation of Pipe Line*, 49 ICC *Valuation Reports* 542 (1944). 548.

30. *Ibid.*, 545.

31. *Ibid.*, 543, 548.

32. *Champlin Refining Co. v. United States et al.*, 329 U.S. 29 (1946), 34–35.

33. *Ibid.*, 38.

34. ICC Docket No. 29912, "Champlin Refining Company Accounts and Reports," Report Proposed by J. Paul Kelley, Examiner, 3. (mimeo)

35. *Champlin Refining Company Accounts and Reports*, 274 ICC 409 (1949), 413.

36. *United States et al. v. Champlin Refining Co.*, 341 U.S. 290 (1951).

37. *Ibid.*, 298.

38. *Ibid.*, 306.

39. *Petroleum From Los Angeles and El Paso to Arizona and New Mexico*, 287 ICC 731 (1953), 737.

40. *Ibid.*, 738–739.

41. Southern Pacific Company, *Annual Reports* (1955–1957).

42. ICC Order No. 31544, "Augusta Pipe Line Company et al. — agreement — Transportation of Refined Petroleum Products," (1954).

CHAPTER 22: The Public Policy Process and Pipeline Management: Key Issues

1. 85 Cong., 1 Sess., House Committee on the Judiciary, Consent Decree *Hearings*, 77.

2. Eugene V. Rostow, *A National Policy for the Oil Industry* (New Haven, 1948), 57.

3. *Ibid.*, 65.

4. *Ibid.*, 62.

5. *Ibid.*, 63.

6. *Ibid.*, 145.

7. *Ibid.*, 60.

8. *Federal Power Commission v. Hope Natural Gas Company*, 320 U.S. 591 (1944).

9. Rostow, *A National Policy for the Oil Industry*, 61–62.

10. Cookenboo, *Crude Oil Pipe Lines*, 100, 111.

11. *Ibid.*, 111.

12. ICC Bureau of Transport Economics and Statistics, *Statistics of Oil Pipe Line Companies . . . December 31, 1950* (Washington, 1951), 4; Cookenboo, *Crude Oil Pipe Lines*, 98, 101.

13. Wolbert, *American Pipe Lines*, 43–45.

14. *Ibid.*, 161.

15. *Ibid.*, 103–104.

16. *Ibid.*, 163.

17. Cookenboo, *Crude Oil Pipe Lines*, 107.

18. *Ibid.*, 107–108.

19. *Ibid.*, 106.

20. Eugene V. Rostow and Arthur S. Sachs, "Entry into the Oil Refining Business: Vertical Integration Re-Examined," *Yale Law Journal* (June–July 1952), 856–914.

21. *Ibid.*, 912.

22. *Ibid.*, 902–903.

23. *Ibid.*, 883–885, 899.

24. *Ibid.*, 896.

25. *Ibid.*, 890.

26. John G. McLean and Robert W. Haigh, *The Growth of Integrated Oil Companies* (Boston, 1954).

27. *Ibid.*, 585.

28. Cookenboo, *Crude Oil Pipe Lines*, 125.

29. Rostow, *A National Policy for the Oil Industry*, 66.

30. Cookenboo, *Crude Oil Pipe Lines*, 119.

31. *Ibid.*, 128–133.

32. U.S. Office of Federal Co-ordinator of Transportation, *Public Aids to Transportation*, 2 parts, 4 vols. (Washington, 1940), I, 33–34, 51.

33. *Railway Age* (July 15, 1944), 118.

34. 77 Cong., 2 Sess., Senate Committee on Finance, "Revenue Act of 1942," *Hearings* (Washington, 1942), 7.

35. 81 Cong., 2 Sess., House Committee on Ways and Means, "Revenue Revision of 1950," *Hearings* (Washington, 1950), 15.

36. Gordon C. Locke to all members of the Committee for Oil Pipe Lines, April 7, 1958. (mimeo)

37. 84 Cong., 2 Sess., House Committee on Ways and Means, "Excise Taxes," *Hearings* (Washington, 1957), 559–560.

38. Press release issued by Gordon C. Locke, General Counsel, Committee for Oil Pipe Lines, August 28, 1958.

CHAPTER 23: The Continuing Attack on Integrated Operations

1. 76 Cong., 3 Sess., S. 3753.

2. Association of American Railroads, Railroad Committee for the Study of Transportation, "Report by Subcommittee on Pipe Line Transportation" (Washington, 1944), 2. (mimeo)

3. 78 Cong., 1 Sess., H.R. 1516.

4. 90 *Cong. Rec.* 3163–3164 (March 28, 1944).

5. 79 Cong., 1 Sess., H.R. 55.

6. 79 Cong., 2 Sess., H.R. 6972.

7. 81 Cong., 1 Sess., S. 571, S. 572, S. 573.

8. 83 Cong., 2 Sess., S. 3075.

9. 84 Cong., 1 Sess., S. 1853.

10. Aitchison testimony in 81 Cong., 2 Sess., House Committee on the Judiciary, Subcommittee on Study of Monopoly Power, "Study of Monopoly Power," *Hearings*, Part 4A "Steel" (Washington, 1950), 888.

11. 79 Cong., 1 Sess., Senate Special Committee Investigating Petroleum Resources, "Investigation of Petroleum Resources," *Hearings*, June 1945 (Washington, 1946); 79 Cong., 2 Sess., Senate Special Committee Investigating Petroleum Resources, "The Independent Petroleum Company," *Hearings*, March 1946 (Washington, 1946).

12. 79 Cong., 2 Sess., Senate Special Committee Investigating Petroleum Resources, "The Independent Petroleum Company," *Hearings*, March 1946, pp. 51–65. See also *Oil and Gas Journal* (March 30, 1946), 120–121.

13. 81 Cong., 1 Sess., Senate Special Committee to Study Problems of American Small Business (The Wherry Committee), "Oil Supply and Distribution Problems," *Final Report* (Washington, 1949).

14. *Ibid.*, 10.

15. *Ibid.*, 10–11.

16. *Ibid.*, 11.

17. *Ibid.*

18. *Ibid.*, 20.

19. *Ibid.*

20. *Ibid.*, 21.

21. *Ibid.*

22. *Ibid.*

23. *Ibid.*

24. *Ibid.*, 22–23.

25. *United States v. Standard Oil Company of California*, Civil No. 11584-C, Southern District of California, May 12, 1950.

26. *United States v. Standard Oil Company of New Jersey*, Civil No. 86-27, Southern District of New York, June 8, 1953.

27. 82 Cong., 1 Sess., House Committee on Interstate and Foreign Commerce, *Report . . . Consenting to Extension of the Interstate Compact to Conserve Oil and Gas* (Washington, 1951), 3.

28. 69 Stat. 385, 391.

29. *First Report of the Attorney General Pursuant to Section 2 of the Joint Resolution of July 28, 1955, Consenting to an Interstate Compact to Conserve Oil and Gas, September 1, 1956* (Washington, 1956), 7.

30. *Ibid.*, 24.

31. *Ibid.*, 25.

32. *Oil and Gas Journal* (December 10, 1956), 80.

33. *Ibid.* (February 4, 1957), 80.

34. *Ibid.*, 81.

35. *Ibid.* (January 7, 1957), 75.

36. *Ibid.* (February 25, 1957), 78.

37. *Ibid.* (March 25, 1957), 78.

38. *Vernon's Annotated Revised Civil Statutes of the State of Texas* (Kansas City, Mo., 1962), 16B, Article 6014.

39. *Attorney General's Report on the Interstate Compact to Conserve Oil and Gas, September 1, 1957*, p. 115.

40. *Ibid.*, 116.

41. *Ibid.*, 118.

42. Railroad Commission of Texas, "The Statewide Hearing," December 19, 1956, Transcript of Testimony, 54. (mimeo)

43. *Ibid.*, 24.

44. *Ibid.*, 5–13.

45. "Oil Regulation Report," *Texas State House Reporter* (April 3, 1957), 5–6.

46. *Ibid.*, 6.

47. *Ibid.*, 4.

48. See *Before the Railroad Commission of Texas, In re: In the Matter of the General Inquiry into the Status, Facilities, Extension, Capabilities, and Practices of Common Carriers of Crude Oil in Texas and Related Matters, Brief for Petitioners* (1957).

49. *Ibid.*, 13–14.

50. *Ibid.*, 37–38.

51. *Vernon's Revised Civil Statutes of the State of Texas*, Article 6049a, sections 7, 8, 11.

52. *Atchison, Topeka & Santa Fe Railroad v. Railroad Commission of California*, 173 Calif. 577 (1916); *Missouri Pacific v. Nebraska*, 164 U.S. 403, 17 Sup. Ct. 130 (1896); *State of Washington ex rel. Oregon Railroad and Navigation Company v. Fairchild et al.*, 224 U.S. 510, 32 Sup. Ct. 535 (1912); *Northern Pacific Railroad v. North Dakota*, 236 U.S. 585, 35 Sup. Ct. 429 (1915); *ICC v. United States ex rel. Los Angeles*, 280 U.S. 52, 74 L. Ed. 163 (1929).

53. *Before the Railroad Commission of Texas . . . Practices of Common Carriers . . . Brief for Petitioners* (1957), 45–47.

54. Railroad Commission of Texas, Oil and Gas Division, *Special Order Pertaining to the General Inquiry into the Status, Facilities, Extensions, Capacities, and Practices of Pipe Line Common Carriers of Crude Oil in the State of Texas, June 4, 1958* (Austin, 1958).

55. *Ibid.*, 3–4.

56. *Ibid.*, 4.

57. 85 Cong., 1 Sess., Senate Subcommittees of the Committee on the Judiciary and Committee on Interior and Insular Affairs, "Emergency Oil Lift Program and Related Oil Problems," *Joint Hearings* (Washington, 1957).

58. *Ibid.*, 2–8.

59. Minority views of Senator Dirksen in 85 Cong., 1 Sess., Senate Committee on the Judiciary, Subcommittee on Antitrust and Monopoly, "Petroleum, the Antitrust Laws and Government Policies," *Report . . . with Minority Views* (Washington, 1957), 88. This report is on the hearings entitled "Emergency Oil Lift Program and Related Oil Problems."

60. Majority report *ibid.*, 29.

61. *Ibid.*, 30.

62. *Ibid.*

63. Clark testimony in 85 Cong., 1 Sess., Senate Subcommittees, "Emergency Oil Lift Program," *Joint Hearings* (1957), 948.

64. *Ibid.*, 949–950.

65. *Ibid.*, 959–960, 973–974.

66. Senator Carroll *ibid.*, 975.

67. Clark testimony, *ibid.*

68. Delaney testimony, *ibid.*, 886.

69. *Ibid.*, 895.

70. *Ibid.*, 902.

71. Glasco testimony, *ibid.*, 1544–1545; Morison testimony, *ibid.*, 1561.
72. Glasco testimony, *ibid.*, 1543.
73. Oscar John Dorwin, The Texas Co., to Joseph C. O'Mahoney, April 24, 1957, *ibid.*, 1590–1591.
74. Morison testimony, *ibid.*, 1565.
75. *Ibid.*, 1566.
76. *Ibid.*, 1567–1572.
77. *Ibid.*, 1576.
78. W. A. Delaney, Jr., to Donald P. McHugh, Counsel, Senate Subcommittee on Antitrust and Monopoly, March 14, 1957, *ibid.*, 907.
79. Majority report in 85 Cong., 1 Sess., Senate Committee on the Judiciary, Subcommittee on Antitrust and Monopoly, "Petroleum," *Report* (1957), 7.
80. *Ibid.*, 8.
81. Minority views of Senator Dirksen *ibid.*, 128.
82. *Ibid.*, 128–129.
83. *Ibid.*, 131.
84. *Ibid.*, 132.
85. *Ibid.*, 133.
86. Gordon Gray to Joseph C. O'Mahoney, June 12, 1957, *ibid.*, 134–136.
87. Minority views of Senator Wiley *ibid.*, 161–162.
88. 85 Cong., 1 Sess., House Committee on Interstate and Foreign Commerce, "Petroleum Survey, 1957 Outlook, Oil Lift to Europe, Price Increases," *Preliminary Report* (Washington, 1957), 42.

CHAPTER 24: From Congressional Investigation to Judicial Decision

1. 85 Cong., 1 Sess., House Committee on the Judiciary, Consent Decree *Hearings*, 1.
2. Motion for order for carrying out final judgment, filed October 11, 1957, in Transcript of Record, pp. 23–28, *United States v. Atlantic Refining Co. et al.*, 360 U.S. 19 (1959).
3. Motion for order carrying out the final judgment entered in the above cause on December 23, 1941, filed October 11, 1957, *ibid.*, 183–187.
4. Motion for order for carrying out the final judgment entered in the above cause on December 23, 1941, filed October 11, 1957, *ibid.*, 203–211.
5. 85 Cong., 1 Sess., House Committe on the Judiciary, Consent Decree *Hearings*, 31–32.
6. *Ibid.*, 35.
7. *Ibid.*
8. *Ibid.*, 76–77.
9. *Ibid.*, 77.
10. Robert A. Bicks, Acting Assistant Attorney General, Antitrust Division to Emanuel Celler, July 31, 1957, *ibid.*, 105–106.
11. *Ibid.*, 78–80.
12. *Ibid.*, 80.
13. *Ibid.*, 81.
14. *Ibid.*, 82–83.
15. *Ibid.*, 378.
16. *Ibid.*, 447–448.
17. *Ibid.*, 449.
18. *Ibid.*, 456.
19. *Ibid.*, 456–457, 485.
20. *Ibid.*, 459–460.
21. *Ibid.*, 475.
22. *Ibid.*
23. *Ibid.*, 1015.

24. See Fayette B. Dow to J. L. Shoemaker, April 23, 1955, *ibid.*, 1028.
25. *Ibid.*, 1133.
26. *Ibid.*, 1134.
27. *Ibid.*, 1135–1136.
28. *Ibid.*, 1138–1142.
30. *Ibid.*, 1140. For a summary of the reports filed by Service for the years 1942–1956, showing valuation base and dividends, see *ibid.*, 241–243.
31. *Ibid.*, 1140–1141.
32. The Bergson letter is in *ibid.*, 212–213.
33. *Ibid.*, 1190–1191.
34. *Ibid.*, 1193, 1196.
35. *Ibid.*, 1192.
36. *Ibid.*, 1193.
37. *Ibid.*, 1141–1142.
38. *Ibid.*, 1147.
39. *Ibid.*, 1147–1150.
40. *Ibid.*, 1158–1162.
41. *Ibid.*, 1163–1167.
42. *Ibid.*, 1178–1179.
43. 85 Cong., 1 Sess., House Committee on the Judiciary, Consent Decree *Report*, introduction, xi.
44. *Ibid.*, 175.
45. *Ibid.*, 176.
46. *Ibid.*, 180.
47. *Ibid.*, 182–186.
48. *Ibid.*, 186.
49. *Ibid.*, 192.
50. *Ibid.*, 192–193.
51. *Ibid.*, 196.
52. *Ibid.*, 195–196, 298.
53. *Ibid.*, 243–244.
54. *Ibid.*, 245–246.
55. *Ibid.*, 248–249.
56. *Ibid.*, 249–262, 299–300.
57. *Ibid.*, 265.
58. *Ibid.*, 288–289.
59. *Ibid.*, 289, 301.
60. *Ibid.*, 301.
61. *Ibid.*, 296.
62. *Ibid.*, 304.
63. *Ibid.*, 327.
64. *Ibid.*, 306–307.
65. *Ibid.*, 306.
66. *Ibid.*, 324.
67. *Ibid.*, 328.
68. *Ibid.*
69. *Oil and Gas Journal* (March 31, 1958), 55.
70. *United States v. The Atlantic Refining Co. et al.*, U.S. District Court for the District of Columbia, Civil Action No. 14060, Official Transcript, March 25, 1958, p. 207.
71. *Ibid.*, 204.
72. *Ibid.*, 217–218.
73. *Ibid.*, 202–203.
74. *Ibid.*, 240–241.
75. *Ibid.*, 242.
76. *Ibid.*, 243–244.

77. *Ibid.*, 245.
78. *Ibid.*
79. *Ibid.*, 246.
80. *Ibid.*, 247.
81. *Ibid.*, 247–248.
82. *Ibid.*, 221–222, 229.
83. *Ibid.*, 213–214.
84. *Ibid.*, 249.
85. *Ibid.*, 250.
86. *Ibid.*, 251–252.
87. *Ibid.*, "Motion for Order for Carrying out Final Judgment," filed October 11, 1957, p. 4.
88. *Ibid.*, 5.
89. *Ibid.*, 6.
90. *Ibid.*
91. Affidavit of Arthur H. Dean, quoting transcript of hearing on January 27, 1958, *ibid.*, 14.
92. *Ibid.*, 5.
93. *Ibid.*, 6–7. "Motion to Dismiss Government's Motion and for Further Relief," filed by Interstate Oil Pipe Line Company and Tuscarora Pipe Line Company, Ltd., February 5, 1958.
94. Memorandum of Government in Support of Post Judgment Motions Filed October 11, 1957 against Arapahoe Pipe Line, in Civil Action No. 14060, Official Transcript, March 25, 1958.
95. *Ibid.*, 8–9.
96. *Ibid.*, 12.
97. *Ibid.*, 13.
98. *Ibid.*, 14.
99. *Ibid.*, 32.
100. *Ibid.*
101. *Ibid.*, 19.
102. *Ibid.*, 19–20.
103. *Ibid.*, 20.
104. *Ibid.*, 22.
105. *Ibid.*, 24.
106. *Ibid.*
107. *Ibid.*
108. *Ibid.*, 29.
109. *Ibid.*, 25.
110. *Ibid.*
111. *Ibid.*, 26–28.
112. *Ibid.*, 29.
113. *Oil and Gas Journal* (March 31, 1958), 55.
114. *Ibid.*
115. *United States v. The Atlantic Refining Co. et al.*, U.S. District Court for D.C. Civil Action No. 14060, "Order," 2.
116. 360 U.S. 19 (1959), 23–24.

INDEX

A. C. Bedford Pipe Line, 94
Act to Regulate Interstate Commerce, 23.
    See also Interstate Commerce Act
Adoue, J. B., 344
Aitchison, Clyde B., 243–244, 398, 422, 424
Ajax Pipe Line Company, 140–142, 143, 143n, 156, 158, 247, 248, 256, 267, 281, 315, 382–383
American Liberty Oil Company, 320
American Oil Pipe Line Company, 373
American Oil Works, 163
American Petroleum Institute, 158–159, 197, 210, 218, 240, 271, 279, 280, 282, 284, 287–288, 312, 336, 394, 419n, 444, 450, 477
American Pipe Line Company, 375, 377
Andreano, Ralph, 7
Andrews, Schofield, 294
Antitrust action: and Elkins Act pipeline cases, 288–290, 291, 295, 296, 302, 303, 334, 347; evaluation of, 471–475; and integrated oil companies, 284–285, 286–291, 424–425; and international oil companies, 424–425; and "Mother Hubbard" case, 290–293, 295, 297–303 passim, 425; and Standard Oil, 58–64, 115; wartime immunity from, 297, 318, 332. *See also* Consent decree; Madison case; Northern Securities case
Applegate, P. R., 366
Arapahoe Pipe Line Company, 373, 375, 441, 452, 454–457
Archbold, John D., 17, 27, 90, 103n
Ardmore Producers' Association, 107
Arnold, Thurman, 268, 271, 283, 286–288, 290–294, 296–299, 301–303, 425, 472, 474
Asbill, Mac, 292, 293, 294, 295, 298, 299, 302, 443
Ashland Refining Company, 168
Association of American Railroads, 345, 421
Association of Oil Pipe Lines, 340–341. *See also* Committee for Pipe Line Companies
Association of Railway Executives, 218
Associated Oil Company, 190
Atlantic Oil Producing Company, 206

Atlantic Pipe Line, 240–241, 322n, 329
Atlantic Refining Company, 85, 125n, 143n, 152, 164, 220, 255–256, 290, 292, 296

Badger Pipe Line, 382
Bailey, Senator Joseph W., 29
Ballinger, R. A., 40
Ballinger, Willis, 273, 276
Barnsdall Oil Corp., 211, 256
Basin Pipe Line System, 355, 355n, 356
Bayou Pipe Line System, 318–320
Beaty, Amos L., 182, 184, 225
Beck, James M., 67
Bedford, A. C., 176
Berge, Wendell, 276, 337
Bergson, Herbert A., 446–447
Berquist, Frederick E., 271, 276, 281, 293
Biddle, Francis, 290, 294, 296, 299, 337
Big Inch pipelines, *see* World War II
Black, Forrest, 289
Blackmer, Henry M., 151
Blair & Company, 153
Blazer, Paul G., 168
Borah, Senator William, 228, 228n, 268–269, 271, 287, 467
Bowles, Charles E., 218
Boyd, William R., Jr., 312
Brewster, Benjamin, 12
British American Oil Co., Ltd., 357
Brown, George R., 347
Brownell, Herbert, Jr., 426
Bruce, Andrew A., 67
Brundred, Benjamin F., 181, 199
Brundred, William J., 199, 204, 206, 222
Buckeye Pipe Line Company, 12–14, 35, 39, 43, 45–47, 59, 65n, 71, 82–83, 85, 86–88, 97, 141, 150n, 166–168, 169, 171–172, 329, 357, 365–367, 378n, 382, 437
Buffalo Pipe Line Corporation, 255–256
Bunje, C., 314n
Bunten, A. M., 197
Bureau of Corporations, U.S., 23, 43, 45, 47, 54–59, 71–72, 110, 173–174, 177, 191
Burke, J. L., 445–447, 448
Burton, William, 252
Bushnell, D. S., 86–87, 166, 168, 201, 204–205

Butte Pipe Line, 373, 374, 436

California, 19; common-carrier statute, 190
Campbell, Congressman Philip P., 23
Carmalt, Hagerty & Wheeler, 200
Carroll, Senator John A., 434–435
Carter Oil Company, 137, 141, 211, 364
Celler, Congressman Emanuel, 422, 440–445 passim. *See also* Antitrust action
Chaffetz, Hammond, 447–448, 452–453
Chamberlain, C. E., 74–75
Chamberlin, C. D., 110
Champlin Refining Company, 190–191, 258
Chanute Refining Company, 129
Cherokee Pipe Line, 383
Chicago & Atlantic Railroad, 12
Cities Service Oil Company, 139–140, 210, 312, 322n, 330, 355, 357, 382, 383
Clack, H. Earl Company, 364
Clark, Lester, 434–435, 436
Clarke, Owen, 444–445, 450
Clayton Antitrust Act, 67, 173, 177, 287
Coates & Burchard, 156
Coffee, Congressman John M., 294, 299
Cole Act, 297, 300, 310, 311, 312, 341
Cole, Congressman William P., 229, 295, 310
Colley, Robert H., 296
Colorado Public Utilities Commission, 189
Comar Oil Company, 123
Committee for Pipe Line Companies, 408, 418–419, 437, 439, 465
Commodities clause of Interstate Commerce Act, 27–29, 422; proposed extension to pipelines, 30, 217, 228n, 269. *See also* Divorcement
Common carriers, pipeline: and Department of Interior, 40, 121; effectiveness of statutory requirements, 21, 52, 58–59, 107, 115, 173, 175, 181, 185–186, 194–195, 206, 221, 226, 272–274, 279, 298, 413, 464–466, 473; elements affecting legal status of, 21, 75–76, 102–103, 191, 405; judicial view of, 77–80, 102–103, 399–405; legislation on, federal, 24–32; legislation on, state, 20–22, 37, 101–103, 113–115, 188–195, 210–216, 431–432; problems of regulating, 29, 30, 49, 55–57, 59, 63, 107, 127–128, 189, 474
Common purchaser laws, *see* Oklahoma; Texas
Connecting Pipe Line Company, 13, 87

Connolly, Dave F., 49
Consent decree, pipeline: negotiated, 290–301; provisions, 300–301; evaluated, 301–304; investigated, 440–452; interpreted, 332–338, 408–412, 449, 472–475; judicial decision on, 452–457
Conservation, oil, 210–216, 221, 226
Consolidated Oil Corporation, 160
Consolidated Pipe Line Company, 160
Continental Oil Company, 225, 238, 256, 279, 292, 358, 364, 365
Continental Pipe Line, 374, 395
Continental Refining Company, 163
Continental Trading Company, 153, 155
Cook, Roy C., 283
Cookenboo, Leslie, Jr., 414, 416–418
Corsicana Refining Company, 15, 65, 103–104. *See also* Navarro Refining Company
Cosgrove, James J., 292, 334
Cox, Hugh B., 271
Crawford, L. R., 155–156
Crescent Pipe Line Company, 59n, 63, 65n, 82, 88–89, 150n, 168–171
Crowley, Karl A., 274, 275
Crown Central Pipe Line and Transportation Company, 319
Crude-oil purchasing, 12, 50, 58, 64, 100, 109, 135, 225, 341, 428, 430–432, 437, 469
Crystal Oil Works, 163
Cudahy Refining Company, 129
Culberson, Olin, 330–331, 370
Cullinan, Joseph S., 15, 48–49, 52
Cullom, Senator Shelby M., 28
Cumberland Pipe Line Company, 9, 59n, 65n, 82, 83, 85, 86, 88–89, 150n, 168, 169, 198
Curran, Edward M., 299
Cygnet Pipe Line Company, 14, 87

Danciger, Joseph, 230–231
Danciger Oil & Refining Company, 213, 214, 230
Darrow, Clarence, 276n
Davenport, Congressman James S., 107
Davies, Ralph K., 294, 311, 342
Davison, George S., 48
Dawes, Henry M., 218
Defense Pipe Line, 294–298
Defense Plant Corporation, 322, 323, 324
Defense Supplies Corporation, 320, 322
Delaney, W. A., 435, 436, 437
Denison, Winfred T., 77
Department of Justice, *see* Antitrust action; Consent decree

Department of the Interior, 40, 121, 224, 340, 346, 375
Dirksen, Senator Everett, 434, 437–438, 439
Disney, Congressman Wesley E., 223
Divorcement of pipelines from integrated operations, 52–53, 55, 107–108, 110, 157, 171, 176, 185–186, 210, 217–219, 222–226, 230, 233–235, 268–269, 275, 279–280, 282, 287, 412–418, 421–422, 467, 468
Doherty, Henry L., 210
Donnell, James C., 35, 87n, 90, 93
Dow, Fayette B., 271, 275, 280–281, 445
Dundee Petroleum Company (N.Y.), 123

Eastern States Petroleum Company, 277
Eastman, Joseph B., 218, 310
Eckert, Samuel B., 339n
Elgin case, 269-270
Elkins Act, 23, 58, 284, 288, 289, 291, 295, 296, 302, 303, 447, 448, 450, 451, 455
Elkins Act Pipeline Cases, *see* Antitrust action
Elkins Amendment to Interstate Commerce Act (1906), *see* Commodities clause of Interstate Commerce Act
Elkins, Senator Stephen B., 28
Emergency Pipelines, Inc., 322
Emery, Don, 292
Eminent domain, right of, 20, 21, 24, 29, 70, 72, 76, 102, 113, 188, 190, 191, 295, 310. *See also* Common carriers; Cole Act
Empire Gas and Fuel Company, 139, 143
Empire Oil Works, 163
Empire Pipe Line, 140, 143n, 170
Esch, John J., 202
Esso Standard Oil, 363
Eureka Pipe Line Company, 59n, 65n, 82, 83, 86, 88, 97, 150n, 162, 169, 368
Evangeline Products System, 382
Exchange Oil Company, 129

Farish, W. S., 114, 137, 138, 196, 211, 226, 271, 275–277, 279, 283–284, 312
FBI, 337, 442, 443
Federal investigations of pipelines by: Bureau of Corporations (1905), 23–26 (1907), 56–58; Congress, 177–187, 217–221, 229–235, 422–424, 425–427, 433–439, 440–452, 467–468; Federal Trade Commission (1916), 173–177; Interstate Commerce Commission (1907), 54–56 (1911), 51–53; Tem-

porary National Economic Committee, 271–284
Federal Trade Commission, 67–68, 95, 108, 110, 173–177, 185, 187, 191, 198, 203, 273, 276, 283, 424
Fertig, John H., 17
Finney, Wallace R., 246, 296, 312, 314n, 344–345
Fitzpatrick, W. S., 74, 78–79, 89, 99, 151, 155, 157–159
Flagler, Henry M., 17
Flannelly, T. J., 89, 152, 155, 201, 202, 203, 204
Florida Emergency Pipe Line, 320, 347n
Folger, H. C., Jr., 15, 103n
Foraker, Senator Joseph B., 26, 30
Ford, Bacon & Davis, 156, 345
Ford, Peyton, 425n
Forest Oil Company, 17, 18
Four Corners Pipe Line, 374, 375n, 378–379
Franklin Pipe Company, Ltd., 85
Franklin, Wirt, 107, 224
Fraser, Alexander, 262

Galey, John H., 17
Garfield investigation of oil transportation (1905), 23–25, 28, 31, 70
Garfield, James A., 23
Gasoline pipelines: case study of, 259–262; common-carrier status of, 258, 262–263, 405; impact of, 258–259; integration of, 278–281; introduction and growth of, 254–258; minimum tenders of, 265, 267; ownership of, 258; rates of, 264–265. *See also* Great Lakes Pipe Line; Keystone Pipe Line; Phillips Petroleum Company; Pipelines; Susquehanna Pipe Line
Gates, William F., 147, 149, 152n, 153, 200
Getty, George F., 195–196
Gidney, H. A., 198
Gilbert, H. A., 311
Gillette, Senator Guy M., 269, 286–287, 289, 291, 294, 296, 297, 303, 337, 421–422, 425n
Glasco, Lowell M., 435
Globe Oil & Refining Company, 273
Golden, A. W., 181
Gore, Senator Thomas P., 107, 234
Government-industry cooperation, 339–341. *See also* World War II
Graham, Benjamin, 162
Graves, B. I., 345
Gray, William H., 179–180, 201

Great Lakes Pipe Line Co., 256, 258, 260, 264–267, 278–279, 281, 334–335, 360–361, 455–456
Green, John E., Jr., 292
Guffey, James M., 17
Guffey Petroleum Company, 15, 17, 36, 37
Gulf Coast Oil Producers Association, 114, 194, 196
Gulf Oil Corporation (and subsidiaries), 34, 36–39, 47, 50, 72, 113, 120–121, 136, 143, 175, 185, 211, 214, 292, 295, 297, 301, 308, 357, 366, 374
Gulf Pipe Line Company(ies), 37, 48, 74, 99, 109, 114, 125n, 143n, 156, 158, 170, 192, 196, 198
Gulf Refining Company, 37, 315, 322n, 330, 384

Hadlick, Paul, 279, 294
Haigh, Robert W., 416–417, 426–427
Hall, Edwin, 292, 294
Hall, Luther E., 191
Hamon, Jake, 234
Hanks, B. J., 314n
Hansen, Victor R., 440, 442, 443, 444, 457
Harbor Pipe Line System, 366, 382
Hare, Ralph G., 197–198
Harlan, James S., 252
Harrington, Congressman Vincent F., 421
Harris, Congressman Oren, 438
Hemphill, J. J., 74
Hepburn Amendment to Interstate Commerce Act (1906), 24–32, 38, 43, 45, 54, 62, 69, 70, 71, 72, 74, 77, 82, 273, 274, 289, 302, 395, 399, 404, 413; commodities clause of, 27–31, 56 (see also Commodities clause); interpretation of, 76–81, 399–405; Lodge (pipeline) Amendment to, 24–26, 28, 31, 32; managerial reaction to, 26–27, 32–33, 69–81
Hepburn, Congressman William P., 23
Higgins Oil and Fuel Company, 51
Hilton, J. C., 239
Hitchcock, E. A., 40
Hoch, Congressman Homer, 217, 219
Holmes, Justice O. W., 78–79, 80
Hull, Bert E., 314n, 322
Humble Oil & Refining Company, 114, 137, 138, 143, 146, 177, 211, 212, 213, 229, 231–232, 236, 237, 238, 297, 301, 314, 367n, 427
Humble Pipe Line Company, 125n, 138, 142, 143n, 170, 214, 236, 237, 238,

248–249, 315, 319, 322, 329, 357, 361, 384n
Humphrey, W. D., 196
Humphreys, Colonel A. E., 151

Ickes, Harold L., 222, 223, 225, 226, 239, 240, 242, 294, 295, 296, 303, 309, 322, 330, 331, 342
Illinois Pipe Line Company, 93, 125n, 146–147, 150, 169, 180, 315, 329, 357n
Illinois Pipe Line Company of Texas, 143, 357n
Imperial Oil Company, 87n, 367n
Independent Oil Producers Association, 111, 437
Independent Petroleum Association of America, 212, 218, 282
Independent Refiners Association of America, 419
Independent Refining Company, 163
Indiana Pipe Line Company, 13, 35, 43, 59n, 65n, 82, 86, 89, 90, 150n, 166, 169, 365
Indiana Refining Company, 181
Ingersoll, Sturgis, 290
Innovation, 251, 254–256, 266, 335, 381. See also Pipelines, technology
Integrated oil operations, 28, 29, 30, 34, 55–56, 57, 100–101, 110, 113, 115, 119, 127–130, 135–136, 142–143, 171, 408, 410, 412–413, 415–416, 420, 457, 465–466, 469–471, 474, 475; attack on, 286–288, 421–429; backward integration, 136, 141, 142, 145, 171; defense of, 39, 49, 101, 229–230, 278, 280, 282, 413; examples of, 120–130; pattern of, 119, 124, 176; role of pipelines in, 9, 30, 63, 119, 142–143, 145, 232–233, 242, 266–267, 281, 412, 414, 436, 457, 474
Internal Revenue Bureau (Service), 198, 227–228, 331, 394
Interocean Oil Company, 204
Interstate Commerce Act as amended by Hepburn Act: application to pipelines, 32, 75–79; commodities clause of, 27–31; common carrier requirements, 32, 248
Interstate Commerce Commission: arbiter between competing carriers, 196–197, 263, 272, 279–280, 405–406; attitude toward pipeline regulation, 55–56, 73, 195, 249, 474; cases on: minimum tender requirements, 199–204, pipeline jurisdiction, 75–76, 399–401, 401–405, pipeline rates, 241–250, 263–267, 395–

399; cooperation with pipeline companies, 197–199, 240–241, 391–395, 444, 450–451; criticism of, 272–273, 274, 279, 413–414, 436–437, 450–452, 473–474; effectiveness of pipeline regulation by, 229, 464–467 (*see also* Common carriers); "fair return on fair value" regulation, 188, 392, 414; investigations of pipelines (*see* Federal investigations); and pipeline consent decree, 410, 440, 446; and pipeline pooling, 406–407; reporting requirements of, 195, 240, 241; valuation of pipelines by, 240–241, 335–336, 391–395, 410, 446, 451

Interstate Oil Compact, 224, 426, 429, 442

Interstate Oil Pipe Line Company, 365, 454

Izac, Congressman Edouard V. M., 269, 421, 422

Jackson, Attorney General Robert H., 287, 294, 332

Jenks, Jeremiah, 66

Johnson, Senator Edwin C., 421

Joiner, C. M. "Dad," 213

Jones, Buell F., 292

Jones, J. Edward, 231

Jones, James K., 200

Jones, W. Alton, 312, 314, 322, 339–340, 344

Kansas, oil legislation, 22–23

Kansas Pipe Line and Gas Company, 133

Karsted, Alfred, 452, 453, 454–455

Keating, Congressman Kenneth, 442, 443, 444

Keech, Judge Richmond B., 453, 454

Kefauver, Senator Estes, 433

Kelley, J., 201, 244, 245, 246, 247, 248, 250

Kellogg, Frank B., 178

Kern Oil and Trading Company, 190

Keystone Pipe Line Company, 255, 256, 266, 316, 347n

Kilgore, W. D., Jr., 443

Kinsolving, W. C., 311

Klein, Colonel Harry, 240, 292, 296, 297, 298

Knox, Frank, 309

Korean Emergency, and pipelines, 368–371

Kountz, Clark, 151, 152n, 155, 158, 166, 168, 181–182, 197, 200, 201, 292, 204–205, 240, 314n

Krug, J. A., 340

La Follette, Senator Robert, investigation of oil industry, 177–187, 197, 201, 205–206

Lakehead Pipe Line Company, 358, 375

Landis, Judge Kenesaw M., 58, 291

Landon, Alfred M., 222

Lane, Franklin, 74

Langer, Senator William, 422

Laurel Pipe Line, 383

Lea, Congressman Clarence F., 340

Lee, Higginson & Company, 125

Leovy, F. A., 47–48

Locke, Gordon C., 419

Lodge, C. R., 196n

Lodge, Senator Henry Cabot, 24, 26, 30

Loevinger, Lee, 473–474

Long, Huey P., 192, 193, 194

Long, Senator Chester I., 29, 30

Lorenz, M. O., 196n

Louisiana-Arkansas Refiners' Association, 241

Louisiana: pipeline statute, 191, 192; Public Service Commission, 193, 194; Railroad Commission, 190, 191, 192

Lubrite Refining Company, 156–157

Lyon, Frank, 202, 204

Macksburg Pipe Line Company, 87

Madison case, 270, 339n, 347

Magnolia Petroleum Company, 15, 49, 103–106, 108–109, 146, 170, 177

Magnolia Pipe Line Company, 104–106, 108–109, 112, 125n, 135, 143n, 181, 211, 214, 330, 355, 363, 384

Mahaffie, Charles D., 250, 393

Mammoth Oil Company, 133, 155

Managerial adaptation to: changing conditions in Texas, 236–239; changing environment, 171–172; federal pipeline legislation, 239–240

Managerial reactions to: change, 464–465, 476–478; Lodge pipeline amendment, 26–27, 69–72

Mann-Elkins Act, 73, 76

Mapes, Congressman Carl, 231

Marland, Ernest W., 123, 225, 234

Marland Oil Company, 225

Maryland Pipe Line Company, 95, 161–162, 164

McColl-Frontenac Oil Co., Ltd., 357

McLaughlin, Ralph B., 240, 311

McLean, John G., 416–417, 426–427

Mellon family, 63, 168; and Gulf Oil, 36–38

Miami Valley Corporation, 363, 364

Mid-American Pipe Line, 384

Middle East Emergency Committee, 427, 429
Mid-Valley Pipe Line, 356–357
Midwest Refining Company, 151
Milliken Refining Company, 111, 129
Minimum tenders, see Pipelines
Minnelusa case, 395–397
Minnesota Pipe Line Company, 378
Montreal Pipe Line Co., Ltd., 357
Moody, Dan, 215
Morgenthau, Henry, 418
Morison, H. Graham, 435, 436–437
Murphy Corporation, 373
Murphy, Frank, 286
Murray, William H., 214

National Association of Independent Oil Producers, 179
National Defense Pipelines, Inc., 297, 317, 322
National Industrial Recovery Act and pipelines, 221–227, 467
National Oil and Development Company, 74
National Oil and Pipe Line Company, 15, 17
National Oil Marketers Association, 279
National Petroleum Association, 11, 110
National Petroleum Council, 340, 369
National Pipe Line Company, 10, 39, 72, 74n
National Refining Company, 36, 38–39, 59, 74n, 158, 245, 339
National Transit Company, 9, 11, 14, 15, 59n, 65n, 70–71, 72n, 76, 82–86, 88–89, 95, 96, 98, 150n, 161–165, 169, 170–171, 172, 199, 205, 206n, 365, 367–368
National Transit Pump and Machine Company, 86, 161, 164–165, 367
National Tube Company, 323, 356
Navarro Refining Company, 49. See also Corsicana Refining Company
Needham, Charles W., 78
Nelson, Senator Knute, 30–31, 56
New Domain Oil and Gas Company, 85
New York Stock Exchange, 153
New York Transit Company, 43, 45, 59n, 65n, 70–71, 76, 82, 83, 86, 88, 89, 95, 150, 168, 169, 365, 366
North Central Gas Company, 133
North Penn Oil Company, 9
North Texas Producers Association, 194
Northern Group of pipelines, 86–88, 90, 95, 150, 166, 170, 199, 201, 204–205, 275, 315, 366
Northern Pipe Line Company, 14, 59n, 65n, 71, 82, 83, 85, 86, 89, 150n, 166, 329, 365
Northern Securities case, 54, 77
Nye, Senator Gerald, 218

O'Brian, John Lord, 332
Office of Defense Mobilization, 365n, 375, 377, 438
O'Day, Daniel, 9, 22
Ohio Emergency Pipe Line, 320, 347n
Ohio Oil Company, 12–13, 21, 29, 34–36, 43, 59, 65n, 74n, 75, 78, 82, 83, 88, 89, 90, 93, 94, 97–98, 143, 323, 357, 358, 366, 382
Oil conservation, effect on pipelines, 226–227
Oil fields: Appalachian, 4–12; Caddo, 50n, 192; Conroe, 238; De Soto, 193; East Texas, 213; Four Corners, 374–375; Greater Seminole, 210–211; Gulf, 14–17, 36–39; Healdton, 103–109; Homer, La., 197; Illinois, 35–36, 281, 316, 354; Lima-Indiana, 12–14; Mid-Continent, 17–19, 36–39, 99–100, 190, 191, 199, 202, 315, 241, 245, 247, 251, 252, 253, 256; West Texas, 124–125, 211, 329–330, 355, 357; Williston Basin, 372–373, 375, 381; Yates, 211, 212
Oil industry, 4–5, 9, 14–15, 17, 19, 21, 23, 28, 29, 33, 54–55, 57–58, 67–68, 81, 82, 110, 115, 119, 143, 175, 185–187. See also Integrated oil operations
Oil storage policy, 211, 213, 215, 221, 230
Oklahoma: common carrier law, 37, 41, 101–102; Corporation Commission, 101, 102, 103, 106, 107, 108, 109n, 110, 111, 112, 196, 211; oil conservation, 111–112; common purchaser law, 212
Oklahoma Pipe Line Company, 41, 50, 74n, 94, 95, 97, 137, 141, 143n, 239, 246, 247, 315
O'Mahoney, Senator Joseph C., 271, 277, 280–281, 283, 344–345, 422, 434, 437, 439, 467
O'Neil, James E., 40, 41, 50, 89, 110, 155
Owen, Senator Robert L., 107, 110, 174
Ozark Pipe Line Corporation, 123, 124, 125, 127n, 170
Ozark Pipe Line System, 356

Pacific War Emergency Pipe Line, 330–331, 368, 370
Pan American Petroleum and Transport Company, 277, 322n
Pan American Pipe Line Company, 319
Panama Refining Company, 224

Paragon Refining Company, 151, 156
Parker, James S., 218
Parks, T. B., 217n
Parten, J. R., 311
Pasotex Pipe Line Company, 125n
Patterson, George S., 366
Patterson, William J., 250
Paulding, Charles C., 218
Payne, Calvin N., 15, 63
Peake, A. W., 157
Peper, J. H., 366
Petroleum Administration for Defense, 369–370
Petroleum Administration for War, 299, 311, 318, 324, 326, 329, 330–331, 332, 339, 341–342
Petroleum Industry War Council, 312, 314, 332, 339–340, 342
Petroleum Rail Shippers' case, 263–267, 273, 279n, 293, 396
Pew, J. Edgar, 38, 229–230
Pew, J. Howard, 224, 271, 275, 276, 277, 283
Phillips Petroleum Company, 256, 265–267, 293, 298, 301, 382
Phillips Pipe Line Company, 256, 258, 267, 288, 289, 301, 303, 384
Phillips-Shamrock Pipe Line, 361
Phoenix Refining Company, 102–103
Pierce-Fordyce Oil Association, 108n
Pierce Oil Corporation, 102–103, 160
Pioneer Pipe Line, 365
Pipe Line Cases, The, 78–81, 82, 86, 89, 90, 93, 95, 96, 97–98, 106, 111, 145–146, 190, 195, 240
Pipelines: academic critics of, 412–418; antitrust and (*see* Antitrust action); attacks on (*see* Antitrust action; Federal investigations; Producers' complaints; Refiners' complaints), strategy of attacks on, 20, 21–22, 58, 101, 106, 109, 110, 122, 186n, 198, 434, subsidy theory of attacks, 231–233, 276–278; capitalization, 221, 392 (*see individual companies*); characteristics, as plant facility, 219, 221, 274, 445, as common carrier (*see* Common carriers); competition with other carriers, 96, 149, 185, 264, 266, 267, 273, 277, 279n (*see also* Railroads); Congress and (*see* Federal investigations; Hepburn Amendment); construction, cost of, 55, 146, 148, 175 (*see also individual companies*), postwar crude-oil, 354–360, 372–375, 481–485, postwar products, 360–365, 381–384, 486–494, World War II, govern-

ment-financed, 320–326, World War II, privately financed, 328–330; costs, operating, 3n, 245, 248–249, 323, 343–344, 352, 409, 415; diameters of, 3, 316–317, 323, 327, 352, 374n; financing of, 125, 220, 320, 322, 328, 331–339, 411n, 472, 476; growth of, 99, 119, 214, 258, 351–352, 353, 371, 380–381, 410, 461, 462, 475–476; investment in (*see individual companies*); LPG, 384; minimum tender requirements of, 46–47, 59–62, 179, 181–182, 193, 194, 196, 199–205, 220, 232, 239, 243–244, 249, 255, 265, 267, 279, 283–284, 293, 387, 445, 463, 470, 476; misconceptions about, 232, 468–471; monopoly, relation to, 30, 77–79, 99, 109, 190, 193, 222–223, 268–269; operating income of, 169–170; organization of, corporate form joint-venture, 139, 267, 417–418, 476, as corporate entities, 97–98, as Departments, 95, 239, 288, in integrated structure, 220, 269–270, as undivided interests, 318–319; ownership of, 3, 119, 220, 258, proposals for government ownership of, 52, 107, 110, 185; post World War II, changes in, 386–388; productivity of employees, 353, 380; public market, relation to, 24, 79–80; prorationing, 212, 233, 434, 437–438, 469; and public policy alternatives, 29, 52, 101, 185, 412–418 (*see also* Antitrust actions; Common carriers; Divorcement); rates, 44–51, 60–61, 96–97, 130–131, 175n, 182–184, 188, 189, 193–194, 196, 203, 205–206, 215–216, 223, 236–239, 242, 245–247, 250, 258, 264–267, 273, 275–277, 409–410, 412, 413, 414, 416, 423, 424, 430, 463, 470, 476; regulation of (*see* Common carriers; Interstate Commerce Act; Interstate Commerce Commission); and refinery locations, 262, 273, 381–382; return on investment, 215, 216, 221, 237, 245, 248, 275, 281, 454, 455; return on valuation, 249, 276 (*see also* Consent decree; Interstate Commerce Commission); tanker competition with, 96, 149, 185, 255; taxation of, 198, 225, 227–228, 239, 331–332, 394, 418–419; technology of, 254, 261n, 351–354, 378–380; transportation for nonowners by, 52, 123, 127, 193, 220, 238–239, 273, 445, 476 (*see also* Common carriers); and World War II (*see* World War II)

Plantation Pipe Line, 295, 308–311, 319, 320, 347n, 364
Platt, Warren C., 178
Platte Pipe Line, 358, 362, 372–373, 375
Portland Pipe Line Corporation, 357
Powell, Frank, 191
Prairie Oil & Gas Company, 18, 19, 22, 36, 37, 39–41, 43, 47–48, 50, 51, 59, 65n, 74–78, 82, 85, 89–90, 93, 96, 106, 110, 111–112, 121, 128, 130, 135, 141, 145–147, 151, 152–153, 155, 156–160, 179, 185, 203, 205, 211, 217; customers, 91–92, 154, 157; sale to Sinclair, 155–161
Prairie Pipe Line Company, 90, 97, 109, 130, 133, 135, 136, 137, 139, 140, 141, 142, 143, 145–161, 169, 171–172, 179–182, 184, 199–200, 203, 204, 205, 217
Pratt, Charles, 7, 9, 27
Pratt, Wallace E., 231
Prior, Frank O., 133
Proctor, F. C., 48–49, 74
Producers': attitude toward public policy, 19, 20, 51–53, 106, 115; complaints against pipelines: Kansas (1905), 22–23, to ICC (1911), 51–53, general (1911–1914), 100–101, Oklahoma (1914), 103–110, Texas (1956–1957), 427–433, relation to governmental action, 466–467
Producers' and Refiners' Oil Company, 71–72, 74n, 85, 153, 155
Producers' Oil Company, 51, 106n, 113–114
Producers' Transportation Company, 190
Public Utility Act of 1935, 228
Pure Oil, 7, 26, 57, 59, 71–72, 74n, 140, 151–152, 156, 162–163, 168, 218, 256, 295, 308, 357, 358, 363
Pure Oil Pipe Line Company, 72
Pure Oil Pipe Line Company of Texas, 152, 196n
Pure Transportation Company, 249, 319
Pure-Van Pipe Line, 143n, 156, 158

Railroads: competition with pipelines, 129n, 174n, 179–180, 196–197, 242, 251–254, 255, 258, 263–267, 272, 289, 295, 308–309, 405–406; differences from pipelines, 30, 198, 218, 290, 424, 444; hostility toward pipelines, 21, 217n, 218, 309, 421; and oil traffic, 5, 24–25, 217–218, 251–253, 258
Rancho System, 357–358, 373
Rayburn, Congressman Sam, 219
Rebates, pipeline, see Consent decree

Reconstruction Finance Corporation, 320, 322, 324, 326, 345
Reduced Pipe Line Rates and Gathering Charges case, see Interstate Commerce Commission cases
Reeser, E. B., 218
Refiners' complaints against pipelines, 241–243, 251–254, 265
Regulation of pipelines, see Common carriers; Interstate Commerce Commission
Rhinock, Joseph L., 24, 30
Ritchfield Oil Company, 374, 425n
Ritchie, A. S., 218
Rockefeller Foundation, 83, 164
Rockefeller, John D., 5, 9, 12, 58, 83, 156
Rocky Mountain Pipe Line Company, 395
Roe, Gilbert E., 180, 181–182, 184
Roeser, Charles F., 341
Rogers, Henry H., 27
Roosevelt, President Franklin D., 222–223, 268, 271, 294, 309–310
Roosevelt, President Theodore, 24–25, 28, 54, 58, 67, 110, 178, 187, 464, 471
Rostow, Eugene V., 412–415, 416, 417, 418, 423, 427
Roxana Petroleum Company, 120–122, 123, 127n
Royal-Dutch Petroleum Company (The Hague), 123
Ryan, Paul, 339

Sachs, Arthur S., 416, 417
Salt Lake Pipe Line, 365
Sanderson and Porter, 122
Schwartz, Stephen, 181
Security Oil Company, 15, 17, 64, 103
Seep, Joseph, 12
Seep Purchasing Agency, 12
Service Pipe Line Company, 372–373, 375, 380, 410, 441, 443–444, 445, 446–454, 456
Seubert, E. C., 314
Sharp, Walter B., 51
Shatford, John E., 241, 243–244, 272–274, 279, 280
Shell Oil Company, 120–128, 135–136, 143n, 261, 262, 263, 264n, 266, 295, 309, 315, 322n, 355, 364, 374, 382, 436
Shell Oil Company of Canada, Ltd., 357, 358
Shell Petroleum Company, 259, 260, 261, 262
Shell Pipe Line Corporation, 125, 127, 185, 220, 221, 241, 244, 247, 250n,

260–261, 262, 263, 274, 319–320, 329, 355, 356, 373, 374, 384

Shell Transport and Trading Company (London), 123

Shell Union Oil Corporation, 125, 127

Sherman Antitrust Act, 54, 58, 65, 67, 77, 176, 270, 287, 370

Sinclair Consolidated Oil Corporation, 131, 160, 220

Sinclair Crude Oil Purchasing Company, 131, 133, 136, 151, 153, 185

Sinclair-Cudahy Pipe Line, 129, 130, 151

Sinclair Gulf Pipe Line, 130

Sinclair, Harry, 121, 128, 130, 131, 135, 155, 184, 232

Sinclair Oil and Refining Corporation (and successors and subsidiaries), 128–130, 140, 143, 155, 180, 202, 211, 220, 229, 250, 256, 315, 322n, 330, 355, 357, 358, 361–363, 366; expansion of, 131–133; and Indiana Standard, 130–136

Sinclair Pipe Line Company, 130, 131, 133, 135, 136, 143, 157, 158, 159, 170, 184–185, 250n, 441, 454

Sinclair Prairie Pipe Line Company, 237; (of Texas), 160, 239

Sinclair Refining Company, 160, 220, 239, 324, 346

Sinclair-Texas Pipe Line, 160, 220

Skelly Oil Company, 256

Smith, Commissioner of Corporations Herbert K., 56

Smith, Sidney S., 326

Snyder, John W., 418

Snyder, W. B. Watson, 271, 281, 293, 299, 422, 443

Socony-Vacuum Oil Company, 322n, 361

Solar Refining Company, 12

Southeastern Pipe Line, 308–311

South Penn Oil Company, 9, 206

South-West Pennsylvania Pipe Lines, 59n, 65n, 82, 85, 86, 89, 150n, 162, 169, 368

Southern Group of pipelines, 86–88, 90, 163, 168, 170, 201, 275, 315

Southern Pacific Company, 190, 384, 386, 462

Southern Pipe Line Company (Penn.), 59n, 62, 65n, 82, 85, 86, 88, 89, 150n, 309, 329, 368; (Texas), 137–138

Southwest Emergency Pipe Line, 320, 321–322, 347n

South Western Oil Company, 17

Spindletop oil discovery, 15, 36, 38, 113, 137

Splawn pipeline investigation, 219–221

Splawn, Walter M. W., 219, 220, 221, 233, 267, 274–275

Standard Oil, group of companies, 3–19, 20–31, 39–42, 54, 58, 69, 78, 99, 103, 115; affiliated pipelines, 5–14, 25, 35, 43–47, 50–51, 70, 85, common-carrier status of, 59, 63, impact of public policy on, 82–98, rates and practices of, 43–47, 56–58, 63–64; disaffiliated pipeline companies, 65n, 82–93; dissolution of (1911): 64–65, public reaction to, 66–68, results of, 464, 471–472; investigations of (*see* Federal investigations); position in oil industry, 3, 7, 11, 36; transportation strategy of, 4–7, 14, 18–19, 35–36, 56–58, 63, 185, 463; oil production of, 7–9, 12–14, 35; pipeline legacy of, 462–464. *See also* Standard Oil Company (New Jersey)

Standard Oil Company (California), 59, 65n, 374, 425n

Standard Oil Company (Indiana), 13, 18, 35, 58, 89–90, 130–136, 140, 147, 151, 153, 155, 156, 157, 158, 178, 180, 184–185, 263, 264n, 266, 277, 288, 291, 301, 361, 365, 410, 441, 447–448, 453

Standard Oil Company (Iowa), 65

Standard Oil Company (Kansas), 18, 158

Standard Oil Company (Kentucky), 295, 309, 364

Standard Oil Company of Louisiana, 40, 41, 50, 74, 78, 94, 95, 136, 138–139, 143n, 149, 150n, 191, 192–193, 194, 211, 309, 315

Standard Oil Company (New Jersey), 3–4, 7, 39, 43, 54, 58, 59, 64–66, 70–71, 74, 75–76, 78, 82–93, 94–98, 115, 122, 136–139, 140, 141, 145, 147, 150, 176–177, 180, 185, 187, 193, 206, 210, 236, 239, 251, 275, 285, 295, 297, 301, 309, 311, 322n, 329, 357, 363n, 364, 365, 382, 408, 412, 437, 464

Standard Oil Company of New York, 15, 156, 177

Standard Oil Company (Ohio), 140–142, 166, 245, 253, 261, 262, 316, 320, 347n, 356, 357, 363

Standard Pipe Line Company, 139, 193, 239

Stanolind Crude Oil Purchasing Company, 133, 135

Stanolind Oil and Gas Company, 133, 135

Stanolind Pipe Line Company, 133, 134, 135, 143n, 157, 190n, 220, 237–238, 241, 242, 244, 250n, 263, 289, 315, 329–330, 395, 396, 397

Sterling, Ross S., 114, 137, 138, 213–214
Stewart, Colonel Robert, 131, 155, 184–185
Stewart, D. C., 50, 104
Stocking, Dr. George, 293
Stoll, B. V., 180, 181
Stoll Oil Refining Company, 180
Strain-Yeager Law (Okla.), 37, 41, 101–102
Suez crisis, 427, 429, 433–434, 438–439, 440
Sun Oil Company, 36, 38, 121, 229, 255, 261, 266, 276, 316, 356, 357
Sun Pipe Line Company, 17, 114, 168, 196, 214, 255; of Texas, 322n, 329
Sun-Yount Lee Pipe Line, 143n
Susquehanna Pipe Line, 255, 266, 316, 320
Swigart, T. E., 314n, 343, 344–345

Taft, President William H., 40, 67, 99
Tarbell, Ida M., 25–26, 412, 471
Taxes, *see* Pipelines, taxation
Teagle, Walter, 138, 147, 149, 150, 186n
Teapot Dome, 133, 178, 187
Temporary National Economic Committee, *see* Federal investigations
Tennessee Gas Transmission Company, 347
Texas Company, 17, 34, 36, 37–38, 39, 47, 48, 49, 50, 72, 99, 106, 109, 113, 114, 121, 125n, 136, 143, 182, 184, 185, 221, 223, 229, 238, 256, 315, 356
Texas Company bill (Texas), 114
Texas Corporation, 139–140
Texas Eastern Transmission Corporation, 347, 375, 383
Texas-Empire Pipe Line, 139–140, 141, 143n, 156, 158, 221, 230, 241, 250, 256, 356
Texas Fuel Company, 15
Texas-Gulf Pipe Line, 357
Texas-New Mexico Pipe Line, 330, 374–375
Texas Oil Producers and Landowners Association, 114, 191
Texas Pipe Line Company, 273, 319, 329, 355, 356, 441–442, 452, 454
Texas, state of: antitrust laws, 15, 103; common carrier law, 115, 194; common purchaser law, 212, 213, 215, 216–217, 429, 430; conservation of oil, 211–215; corporation law, 113, 115; Railroad Commission, 113, 114, 115, 138, 189, 190, 194, 212, 213, 214, 215–216, 224, 230, 237, 238, 239, 330, 370, 427–433,

434; unconnected wells controversy, 427–433, 434, 440, 477
Texas Western Oil Lines, Inc., 368
Thompson, Charles I., 290, 292, 293, 294, 296, 297, 298, 299, 301
Thompson, Ernest O., 216, 233
Tidal Pipe Line Company, 322n, 441–442, 452, 454, 456
Tide Water Oil Company, 39, 128, 143n, 202, 330, 441
Tide Water Pipe Line, 7, 21, 71–72, 74, 76, 78, 94, 158–159, 180, 181, 329
Tillman, Senator Benjamin, 29
Titusville Oil Works, 163
Towl, Forrest M., 62, 86, 168, 198, 201
Transit and Storage Pipe Line, 367n
Trans Mountain Pipe Line Company, 358, 369, 378
Transportation Act of 1920, 179, 180, 188, 189, 195, 197, 253
Tuscarora Oil Company, Ltd., 94, 95, 150, 363
Tuscarora Pipe Line, 150, 255, 315, 329, 367n, 454

Uncle Sam case, 78–80, 399–404
Uncle Sam Oil Company, 72, 74n, 78–79, 81, 399–401
Union Oil Company, 124
United States Commerce Court, 76–77, 78, 81
United States Pipe Line Company, 71, 72n, 74n, 85, 370
United States Supreme Court, 78–81, 82, 86, 95, 102, 106, 109, 111, 176, 190, 214, 224, 240, 269, 270, 399–405, 414, 424, 456–457, 461, 464, 473
Utah Oil Refining Co., 396, 397

Valvoline Oil Company, 399–401

Wabash Pipe Line, 382
Wallis, C. L., 51–52
Walsh, Louis J., 277
War Emergency Pipe Lines, Inc., 322–323, 324, 329, 341
War Pipe Line Company, 130
Warren Petroleum Company, 384
Wasatch Oil Refining Company, 395, 396, 397
Waters-Pierce Company, 15
Watts, A. E., 226, 346
Waverly Oil Works, 185
Weaver, H. Douglas, 299
Weber, Norton H., 163
Weiner, Carl, 230

Weiss, H. C., 314
West Central Texas Oil and Gas Association, 429
West, Charles J., 41, 106, 107–108
West Coast Pipe Line Company, 369, 370, 377, 435–436, 438
Wheeler, Senator Burton K., 269
Wherry, Senator Kenneth, 422, 423
White, Chief Justice Edward D., 65, 79, 81
White, Patrick, 121, 128
White Star Refining Company, 156–157
Wiley, Senator Alexander, 438
Williams, F. D., 163
Williams, Robert L., 112
Williamson, Harold F., 7
Willock, Harry H., 185
Wilson, Albert L., 78
Wilson, G. A., 311
Wilson, President Woodrow, 67, 107, 178
Wilson, Robert E., 277

Wolbert, George S., Jr., 415, 416
Wolverine Pipe Line, 382
Wolverton, Congressman Charles A., 230, 233
World War II, pipelines in: contributions of, 326–327; government-financed pipeline projects, 320–326, and disposal of, 341–348; planning for emergency projects, 312–318; private wartime construction, 328–330; tax relief for, 331–332; results of, 475
Wrightsman, Charles J., 108–109, 181
Wyco Pipe Line, 361

Yarhola Pipe Line, 123
Yellowstone Pipe Line Company, 364–365
Young, Dewey, 215
Yount Lee Pipe Line, 214
Younts, C. R., 364

HARVARD STUDIES IN BUSINESS HISTORY

1. JOHN JACOB ASTOR, BUSINESS MAN, by Kenneth Wiggins Porter
2. JAY COOKE, PRIVATE BANKER, by Henrietta M. Larson
3. THE JACKSONS AND THE LEES: TWO GENERATIONS OF MASSACHUSETTS MERCHANTS, 1765–1844, by Kenneth Wiggins Porter
4. THE MASSACHUSETTS—FIRST NATIONAL BANK OF BOSTON, 1784–1934, by N. S. B. Gras
5. THE HISTORY OF AN ADVERTISING AGENCY: N. W. AYER & SON AT WORK, 1869–1949, revised edition, by Ralph M. Hower
6. MARKETING LIFE INSURANCE: ITS HISTORY IN AMERICA, by J. Owen Stalson
7. HISTORY OF MACY'S OF NEW YORK, 1858–1919: CHAPTERS IN THE EVOLUTION OF THE DEPARTMENT STORE, by Ralph M. Hower
8. THE WHITESMITHS OF TAUNTON: A HISTORY OF REED & BARTON, 1824–1943, by George Sweet Gibb
9. DEVELOPMENT OF TWO BANK GROUPS IN THE CENTRAL NORTHWEST: A STUDY IN BANK POLICY AND ORGANIZATION, by Charles Sterling Popple
10. THE HOUSE OF HANCOCK: BUSINESS IN BOSTON, 1724–1775, by W. T. Baxter
11. TIMING A CENTURY: HISTORY OF THE WALTHAM WATCH COMPANY, by C. W. Moore
12. GUIDE TO BUSINESS HISTORY: MATERIALS FOR THE STUDY OF AMERICAN BUSINESS AND SUGGESTIONS FOR THEIR USE, by Henrietta M. Larson
13. PEPPERELL'S PROGRESS: HISTORY OF A COTTON TEXTILE COMPANY, 1844–1945, by Evelyn H. Knowlton
14. THE HOUSE OF BARING IN AMERICAN TRADE AND FINANCE: ENGLISH MERCHANT BANKERS AT WORK, 1763–1861, by Ralph W. Hidy
15. THE WHITIN MACHINE WORKS SINCE 1831: A TEXTILE MACHINERY COMPANY IN AN INDUSTRIAL VILLAGE, by Thomas R. Navin
16. THE SACO—LOWELL SHOPS: TEXTILE MACHINERY BUILDING IN NEW ENGLAND, 1813–1949, by George Sweet Gibb
17. BROADLOOMS AND BUSINESSMEN: A HISTORY OF THE BIGELOW—SANFORD CARPET COMPANY, 1825–1953, by John S. Ewing and Nancy P. Norton
18. NATHAN TROTTER: PHILADELPHIA MERCHANT, 1787–1853, by Elva Tooker
19. A HISTORY OF THE MASSACHUSETTS HOSPITAL LIFE INSURANCE COMPANY, by Gerald T. White
20. THE CHARLES ILFELD COMPANY: A STUDY OF THE RISE AND DECLINE OF MERCANTILE CAPITALISM IN NEW MEXICO, by William J. Parish
21. THE RISE AND DECLINE OF THE

MEDICI BANK, 1397–1494, by Raymond de Roover

22. ISAAC HICKS: NEW YORK MERCHANT AND QUAKER, 1767–1820, by Robert A. Davison

23. BOSTON CAPITALISTS AND WESTERN RAILROADS: A STUDY IN THE NINETEENTH-CENTURY RAILROAD INVESTMENT PROCESS, by Arthur M. Johnson and Barry E. Supple

24. PETROLEUM PIPELINES AND PUBLIC POLICY, 1906–1959, by Arthur M. Johnson